CLEFT LIP AND PALATE
Perspectives in Management

VOLUME I

CLEFT LIP AND PALATE
Perspectives in Management
VOLUME I

Samuel Berkowitz, D.D.S., M.S., F.I.C.D.
Research Director, South Florida Cleft Palate Clinic
Clinical Professor of Pediatrics and Surgery
University of Miami School of Medicine and
Consultant to Plastic Surgery Department
Miami Children's Hospital
Miami, Florida

SINGULAR PUBLISHING GROUP, INC.
SAN DIEGO • LONDON

Singular Publishing Group, Inc.
401 West "A" Street, Suite 325
San Diego, California 92101-7904

19 Compton Terrace
London, N1, 2UN, UK

© 1996 by Singular Publishing Group, Inc.

Typeset in 10/12 Century by So Cal Graphics
Printed in Hong Kong by Paramount Printing Company

All rights, including that of translation, reserved. No part of this publication may be reproduced, stored in a retrieval system or transmitted in any form or by any means, electronic, mechanical, recording, or otherwise, without the prior written permission of the publisher.

Library of Congress Cataloging-in-Publication Data

Cleft lip and palate : perspectives in management / [edited] by Samuel Berkowitz
    p.   cm.
    Includes bibliographical references and index.
    ISBN 1-56593-588-8)v. 1). — ISBN (invalid) 1-56593-589-8 (v. 2)
    1. Cleft lip. 2. Cleft palate. 3. Cleft lip—Surgery. 4. Cleft palate—Surgery.
I. Berkowitz, Samuel, 1928–,
    [DNLM: 1. Cleft Lip. 2. Cleft Lip surgery. 3. Cleft Palate.
4. Cleft Palate—surgery. WV 440 C62154 1995]
RD524.C528   1995
617.5'.22—dc20
DNLM/DLC
for Library of Congress   95-20378
                                                                                 CIP

Samuel Berkowitz, D.D.S., M.S., F.I.C.D.

Dr. Berkowitz, the author of Volume I and the editor of Volume II of *Cleft Lip and Palate*, is Clinical Professor of Pediatrics and Surgery and a past Co-Director of the Craniofacial Anomalies Program at the University of Miami School of Medicine. He is a past President of the Florida Cleft Palate Association and current President of the Miami Cranoifacial Anomalies Association. Dr. Berkowitz has been active in study groups on cleft palate issues in many professional associations, including the American Cleft Palate Association and the American Association of Orthodontics.

He has published widely in the dental, medical, and cleft palate literature; co-authored a textbook with S. A. Wolfe, M.D., *Plastic Surgery of the Facial Skeleton* (Little, Brown, 1989); and published a book for parents of children with cleft palate. Dr. Berkowitz also is a popular speaker on cleft palate issues and has presented many workshops and seminars in the United States and abroad.

His research interests center on improving treatment planning for cleft lip and palate and craniofacial anomalies. Currently, Dr. Berkowitz is the Project Director for a multicenter research effort directed toward that end in which a consortium of centers in the United States and Europe has been created to study the long-term effects of various treatment procedures on palatal and facial development.

Contents

Foreword by T. M. Graber, D.M.D., M.S.D., Ph.D., Odont. Dr., D.Sc.		xi
Preface		xiii
Acknowledgments		xv
Introduction		xvii

CHAPTER 1   **TEAM MANAGEMENT: CONCERN FOR THE WHOLE CHILD**   1
Team Composition   2
Family-Centered Approach to Health Care   2
Team Coordinator   2
Support Groups   3
Team Responsibilities   4
References   5

CHAPTER 2   **THE VALUE OF LONGITUDINAL FACIAL AND PALATAL RECORDS IN CLINICAL RESEARCH**   7
Cephalometrics and Serial Dental Casts of the Maxillary and Mandibular Dentition   7
The Beginning of Longitudinal Cleft Palate Research Studies   9
Research Methods   10
References   12

CHAPTER 3   **FACIAL GROWTH**   13
Maxillary Growth Concepts   13
Mandibular Development in Cleft Palate   19
Patterns of Postnatal Growth   19
    Pierre Robin Sequence   20
    Hemifacial Microsomia   25
    Crouzon's Disease   26
References   26

CHAPTER 4 — THE EFFECT OF CLEFTING OF THE LIP AND PALATE ON THE PALATAL ARCH FORM — 29

Varieties of Cleft Lip and Cleft Palate **29**
Categories of Clefts **30**
   1. Clefts of the Lip **31**
   2. Cleft Lip and Cleft Palate **32**
   3. Isolated Cleft Palate **35**
   4. Submucous Cleft Palate **38**
Congenital Palatal Insufficiency (CPI) **39**
References **39**

CHAPTER 5 — LIP PITS, DENTITION, AND ASSOCIATED SKELETAL STRUCTURES — 41

Pits of the Lower Lip in Cleft Lip and/or Palate **41**
Dentition and Hygiene **44**
The Relationship Between the Clefting Process and Contiguous Skeletal Structures **46**
The Position of the Cleft Maxilla within the Cranium and the Mandible **46**
References **48**

CHAPTER 6 — THE NEONATAL CLEFT PALATE — 51

Palatal Embryopathology **51**
Effects of Reversing the Facial Force Diagram **55**
   Lip Surgery or Elastic Traction **55**
   Variations in the Palate's Arch Form **56**
References **64**

CHAPTER 7 — LIP AND PALATAL SURGERY — 65

The Influence of Surgery on Growth **65**
Surgical Closure of the Cleft Lip and Palate **66**
Lip Surgery **67**
Palatal Cleft Surgery: Type, Timing, and Sequence **68**
The Effect of Surgery on Maxillary Growth **76**
Surgical-Orthodontic Procedures and Sequences **79**
The Fourth Dimension of Time: Catch-up Growth **90**
References **99**

CHAPTER 8 — SECONDARY ALVEOLAR BONE GRAFTING: AFTER LIP AND PALATE CLOSURE — 103

The Demise of Primary Bone Grafting **103**
Secondary Alveolar Bone Grafting: A Better Way **103**
Current Approach to Bone Grafting of the Alveolar Crest **105**
Summary **113**
References **113**

CHAPTER 9	**NEONATAL MAXILLARY ORTHOPEDICS**	**115**

The Beginning 115
Closing the Alveolar Cleft Space: Primary Bone Grafting 116
The Zurich Concept 119
The Netherlands' Approach 119
Periosteoplasty 126
Millard-Latham Procedure: Presurgical Orthopedics Based on Fixed Mechanical Palatal Manipulation Followed by Alveoperiosteoplasty 127
The 9-Year Effects of Mechanical Presurgical Orthopedic Forces on the Dental Occlusion 139
Case Reports 145
Conclusions 161
References 161

CHAPTER 10	**MAXILLARY ADVANCEMENT**	**165**

Protraction of the Maxilla Using Orthopedics 165
Surgical Maxillary Advancement—Le Fort I Osteotomy 172
Stability of Maxillary Advancement 180
Total Maxillary Advancement and Its Possible Effect on Speech 186
References 186

CHAPTER 11	**DIAGNOSTIC PROCEDURES AND INSTRUMENTS USED IN THE ASSESSMENT AND TREATMENT OF SPEECH**	**189**

Articulation Tests 189
Rating Scales of Speech Intelligibility and Acceptability 189
Cephalometrics 189
Cine- and Videofluoroscopy 190
Multi-view Videofluoroscopy 190
Ultrasound 191
Video Nasopharyngoscopy 191
The Nasometer 192
Aeromechanical Measurement 193
Summary 193
References 193

CHAPTER 12	**MORPHOLOGIC CONSIDERATIONS OF THE NASOPHARYNGEAL PORT**	**195**

Muscles 195
Nasopharyngeal Growth 196
Functions 197
   Swallowing 197
   Speech 197
The Role of the Nasal Cavity 200

The Use of Lateral Roentgencephalometrics in Evaluating
    Skeletal Pharyngeal Architecture and Velar Elevation **201**
Cervical Spine Anomalies **201**
Velopharyngeal Closure **204**
Improving Velopharyngeal Closure **207**
References **216**

CHAPTER 13   CLEFTS OF THE LIP AND ALVEOLUS, ISOLATED CLEFT PALATE, THE COMPLETE UNILATERAL CLEFT OF THE LIP AND PALATE   209

Isolated Cleft Palate **219**
Clefts of the Lip and Alveolus **219**
Clefts of the Uvulae and Soft Palate **219**
Complete Unilateral Cleft Lip and Palate **219**
Facial Characteristics **223**
Case Reports **225**
References **225**

CHAPTER 14   COMPLETE BILATERAL CLEFT LIP AND PALATE   257

Premaxillary Protrusion: Real or Apparent? **257**
The Premaxillary Vomerine Suture **257**
Long-Term Results **261**
The Vomer Flap: Good or Bad? **265**
Management of the Protruding Premaxilla **266**
Profile Changes **272**
Conservative Surgical-Orthodontic Treatment Sequence **273**
Case Reports **274**
Conclusion **337**
Case Reports **338**
References **354**

CHAPTER 15   SUMMARY OF TREATMENT CONCEPTS   357

CHAPTER 16   A NEW DIRECTION FOR CLEFT PALATE RESEARCH   361

Clinical Research **361**
Palatal Embryopathology **363**
The Neonatal Palatal Form in Complete Clefts of the Lip
    and Palate **363**
The Need for Three-Dimensional Measuring Techniques **364**
Studies Using Three-Dimensional Techniques **365**
References **376**

Index   379

Foreword

It is most gratifying to be able to write a Foreword to this latest and most valuable addition to our compendium of knowledge about craniofacial anomalies in general and cleft lip and palate in particular The field has been close to my heart for over 45 years, even before I became Director of Research at Northwestern University's Cleft Lip and Palate Institute in 1948. It has been my good fortune to be associated with some of the outstanding pioneers in the Team Effort approach—Herbert Cooper, Wayne Slaughter, Sam Pruzansky, J. Daniel Subtelny, Howard Aduss, Jack Thompson, Alan Brodie, Herbert Koepp-Baker, Harold Westlake, Fred Merrifield, Wilton Marion Krogman, Sam Berkowitz, Robert Ricketts, Margaret Hotz, Rudi Hotz, Arnold Huddart, Sheldon Rosenstein, Bengt Johansson, Hans Friede, Mohammed Mazaheri, Karin Vargervik, Samir Bishara, Donald Warren, Hughlett Morris, Morten Rosen, Charles Kremenak, and many others in the United States and Europe. These dedicated and knowledgeable leaders in the field built a strong foundation of total service for patients unfortunate enough to develop this congenital defect.

My own research in the growth and developmental aspects and the influence of therapeutic ministrations has been replicated and serves to remind us of the complexities of the biologic continuum and their interrelationships. My maxim always has been, "From the abnormal, we learn much about the normal."

This exciting two-volume effort has drawn on an international array of scholars and practitioners—researchers, surgeons, orthodontists, speech therapists, pediatricians, psychologists, prosthodontists, pediatric dentists, radiologists, otolaryngologists, audiologists, and others. Dr. Berkowitz has carefully crafted and integrated the important contributions from each field, welding these diverse fields into an interdisciplinary team. These are described in the Preface. There is no doubt in my mind that this work will become the standard reference for all who work in the field of Craniofacial Anomalies, as we move into the 21st Century.

T. M. Graber, D.M.D., M.S.D., Ph.D., Odont. Dr., D.Sc.
Editor of the *American Journal of Orthodontics and Dentofacial Orthopedics*
Evanston, Illinois

Preface

In the first page of this volume, I quote Samuel Pruzansky[1] who, when participating in the Second International Symposium held at the Cleft Lip and Palate Institute, held at Northwestern University Dental School on April 19–20, 1969, and reflecting on what he heard at that meeting stated, "The same tired questions have been asked as at every similar clinical meeting. And I despair at the general unfamiliarity with the pertinent literature." As you can imagine, many of the participants were very upset by his comments.

Fortunately, since the 1950s, many clinical investigators in the field of cleft palate have performed excellent clinical studies in the management of cleft lip and palate, which have contributed to the intellectual ferment over the last 40 years. To these studies, I am indebted.

When selecting significant references for this text, every attempt was made to carry out an exhaustive literature search to include all of the excellent articles on each subject covered. That, however, has been an insurmountable task. To investigators whose research articles were not included, I apologize and advise readers to conduct their own literature search which must include papers on the opposing schools of thought. There is no doubt in my mind that their final conclusions would be the same as mine when they consider the results of long-term palatal and facial growth studies.

To familiarize clinicians with the appropriate literature and its importance to the treatment of cleft lip and cleft palate, the chapters in this book are structured to improve clinicians' understanding of the natural history of the cleft defect, the face in which it exists, the influence of surgery on palate growth and development, and equally importantly in developing an appreciation for the the heterogeneity that exists even within a single cleft type.

These chapters will show that chronologic age is not the parameter that really matters in determining the age at which to close the cleft space. What is important is morphologic age and physiologic fitness, that is, whether the tissues are adequate in quantity and quality and whether the geometric relationship of cleft parts is favorable or unfavorable for reconstruction. Some questions incident to growth, which date back 25 years, concern the relationship of the malformed palatal segments to the contiguous anatomy which, in turn, may be anomalous. These questions are also addressed. Are the palatal segments static in their deficiency or does the deficiency diminish in time, that is, is "catch-up-growth" a predictable phenomenon? And if so, what surgical procedures (as to age and type) make it possible?

Many of Pruzanky's thoughts, written so many years ago, still hold true today and are worth repeating. He stated that whoever sees things from their beginning will have the most advantageous view of them.[2(p116)] To that end, most of the serial cases presented in this volume start soon after birth when plaster casts and photographs of the palatal and facial defect are taken. Serial lateral cephaloradiographs are added as soon as the child is manageable and again periodically through adolescence.

It is hoped that clinicians who are just beginning their involvement in cleft palate will learn the pathology and its natural history of cleft palate from the cases presented in this book and appreciate the need to keep the careful records (casts, cephalometric, photographs, and panorexes) which are of vital importance to both the processing of knowledge and self-criticism.

One last note of great importance. It is rare that two members of a team, such as I, an orthodontist, and Ralph Millard, a plastic surgeon, can successfully work together when they have many differences in treatment philosophy. We succeeded because we were professionally compatible and because we shared an obsessive need to determine why some procedures are successful and others fail. Failures, we discovered, occur principally because of misinterpretation of physiological principles and/or a lack of technical proficiency.

Millard understands the value of serial objective records dating from birth as the essential starting point in determining the long-term utility of any surgical cleft treatment program. Although I was always free to voice a contrary opinion as to what surgery should be performed, and when, our working relationship was based on recognizing the right of the surgeon to reject recommendations and follow his own dictates. And it was my right, as a member of a team involved in growth studies, to document the anatomical changes to the face and palate for future analysis. Respecting our mutual rights and responsibilities was no simple task. Strong emotional and conceptual barriers had to be overcome in the process of communicating with each other.

Our 30-year search for better understanding of the natural history of cleft lip/palate growth and development and the effects of various surgical-orthodontic treatment procedures led Millard from utilizing a conservative approach of staged surgical treatment without the intercession of maxillary orthopedics to the use of neonatal maxillary orthopedics designed by Latham and the completion of all lip and palatal surgery by 2 years of age. With Latham performing the palatal manipulation soon after birth, my current role is limited to documenting the serial palatal and facial changes that occur. This is the fairest way to test the procedure's utility because I am known to have a strong bias against the need for any neonatal maxillary orthopedics. The only exception to my reluctance is the short-term use of extraoral forces in some cases of complete bilateral cleft lip and palate to ventroflex the protruding premaxilla prior to lip surgery.

Although the final conclusion as to which treatment concept is superior cannot be written at this time, a preliminary 15-year report of the results of using neonatal maxillary orthopedics is included. It may yield some insight into which procedures are physiologically sound and which leaders are to be followed.

REFERENCES

1. Pruzansky S. Early treatment of cleft lip and palate. In Cole RM, ed. *Proceedings of the Second International Symposium.* Chicago, Ill: Cleft Lip and Cleft Palate Institute, Northwestern University School of Dentistry; 1969:116.
2. Pruzansky S. Cleft lip and palate. *JADA 87* (Special Issue): 1048-1054; 1911.

Acknowledgments

I extend copious thanks to my office staff including Claudia Roberts, Lourdes Figueroa, Leslie Phipps, Gillian Kelley, and Maryland Jacobson, all of whom shared in typing the manuscript; also to Arnold Kanov for his organizational and computer skills; to Anna Belmonte and Francis Fink for their excellent cast photography; to Dr. Lin Hu who performed many of the lateral cephalometric tracings; and to Bradley Zacharin for carrying out many of the three-dimensional cast analyses. My appreciation also goes to Bruce Henderson for his editorial suggestions.

Special appreciation is extended to Little, Brown and Company for giving permission to use many photographs previously published in *Plastic Surgery of the Facial Skeleton* by S. A. Wolfe and Samuel Berkowitz in 1989.

Immeasurable thanks are likewise due to my many colleagues in the American Cleft Palate-Craniofacial Association and in various cleft palate clinics in Europe and Asia for contributing to my understanding of cleft lip and palate management. To them, too many to recognize by name, I shall be forever grateful for their professional knowledge and personal friendship.

My professional growth has been nurtured by my understanding wife, Lynn, who made it possible for me to spend endless uninterrupted evenings at my desk while at the same time encouraging me to "stay with it." And warm hugs also to my two daughters, Beth and Debra, for their endless expressions of support and love.

Last, but by no means least, I cannot say enough for the countless children with various palatal and facial clefts whom I have treated over the past three decades and for their parents. This book is dedicated to all of them as a token of my appreciation. In their enduring perseverance and fortitude, my young patients and their fathers and mothers have taught me much about the human spirit and the joy that can spring from surmounting nature's adversities.

Introduction

The general aim of this two volume set is to present recognized experts from the clinical sciences of dentistry, medicine, speech, audiology, psychology, genetics, ethics, and nursing so that all aspects of the treatment of cleft palate and other craniofacial anomalies can be scrutinized from a definite point of view: long-term clinical experience.

For the sake of brevity, many variations in cleft type and their treatment alluded to in this book were not presented. Because of the multiplicity of variables, no simple verbal description or classification and treatment plan could possibly satisfy everyone concerned with this problem.

Pruzansky[1(p590)] was once asked, "When should the orthodontist's speech pathologist's, or prosthothodontist's interest in the cleft palate child begin? He answered: "The answer is quite clear. Everyone who seeks to serve the needs of the child with a cleft should begin at the beginning. An interest in all events affecting these children is essential to the training and educational experience that each member of the team must obtain. Each specialist emerges not only better informed in his own field, but with an increased perspective regarding the means available for providing an integrated program of care for the handicapped child."

The material presented in Volume I examines the face with a cleft in all aspects as a biologic continuum from birth through post-natal growth and development to maturity at various stages of treatment. In the past several decades, many advances have taken place in cleft habilitation procedures. Unfortunately, many of these changes have not fulfilled all of their stated objectives, and in some instances, these procedures were found to be either injurious or at best unnecessary. These errors will be discussed in detail.

Volume II brings together clinicians and biological scientists from the United States and Europe, each of whom in his or her own ways has been seeking answers to the multifaceted problem of cleft palate, its embryopathogenesis, craniofacial growth, surgery, protraction of the maxilla, dental speech prostheses, secondary alveolar bone grafting, speech, hearing, genetics, psychosocial development, and craniofacial surgery.

Each contributor presents pertinent concepts so that a broad perspective of the entire habilitative process can be obtained. The conclusions the reader will reach will be the result of well-documented literature of selected well-controlled clinical research that has withstood the test of review and re-examination.

Because space limitations prevent thorough penetration of all aspects of each subject, a large bibliography is included for additional source material. In no way could these chapters be expected to cover all aspects of this complex subject.

It is my hope that, through a better understanding of the cleft palate defect and face, all clinicians will be better able to evaluate present day treatment practices and concepts to better plan their own treatment procedures.

Investigation and treatment of major craniofacial anomalies, other than clefts are in their beginnings. Although this volume has not been organized to consider all of the problems of persons with these anomalies, concern for them is so intertwined with issues related to clefting and so much a part of the future of the investigators working in the general area that mention of them was made here.

We fully acknowledge the important contributions made by the authors and research programs from the institutions which have strongly influenced much of what has been written in these volumes

All lip and palate surgery was performed by Dr. Ralph Millard, Jr., except where otherwise indicated.

S. A. Wolfe performed all skeletal surgery and secondary alveolar bone grafting.

They both performed superior based pharyngeal flaps.

No presurgical orthopedics were used unless specifically indicated.

Samuel Berkowitz, D.D.S., F.I.C.D.
Editor

REFERENCES

1. Pruzansky S. Description, classification, and analysis of unoperated clefts of the lip and palate. *Am J Orthod 1953;39:590.*

"The same tired questions have been asked at every clinical meeting. And I despair at the general unfamiliarity with pertinent literature."
Samuel Pruzansky, 1969

Team Management: Concern for the Whole Child

A cleft of the lip and/or palate is a structural defect—but a correctable one—that usually affects other functional areas (e.g., speech, hearing, and chewing) depending on the extent of the cleft defect. Complex problems may arise having to do with the child's feeding, facial appearance, speech, hearing, dental functioning, and psychosocial development. All of these problems can be managed best by bringing together many specialists from diverse disciplines to review the physical and psychological changes caused by the defect and to coordinate all treatment to the best advantage of the patient and his or her parents.

Clinical research into cleft lip/palate treatment as we now know it did not begin until the advent of multidisciplinary treatment for children with cleft lip or palate. In 1938, at Lancaster, Pennsylvania, Cooper established the first recognized cleft palate clinic in the United States. This was made possible by the passage of the Social Security Act in 1935 which gave impetus to a nationwide interest in the care of children with clefts. Through Part 2 of Title V of this act, Crippled Children's Programs, which encompassed children with clefts, were set up in all states and territories. As a result, The American Academy of Cleft Palate Prosthesis was established at Harrisburg, Pennsylvania, on April 4, 1943, under the auspices of the dental section of the Pennsylvania Department of Health, to help speech pathologists and dentists who, as part of their practices, were involved in the care of children with clefts.

This organization is now The American Cleft Palate-Craniofacial Association and has a much broader membership base which includes orthodontists; pediatric dentists; audiologists; otolaryngologists; ear, nose, and throat specialists; speech-language pathologists; psychologists; nurses; pediatricians; geneticists; dysmorphologists; oral surgeons; plastic surgeons; and social workers.

Before the advent of multidisiplinary teams, speech pathologists, dentists, and surgeons all contributed to the care of patients with clefts, but at separate and isolated points in the habilitative process. Inadvertently, they often worked at cross-purposes to each other. With the institution of the team approach, the level of care improved as specialists in each area, having gained a better understanding of the problems and communication terms used by the other team members, became less professionally parochial and more prepared to pool their efforts to solve habilitative problems that lend themselves to a multidisciplinary approach.

In the last 50 years, excellent progress has been achieved toward a better understanding of all aspects of the cleft defect and its habilitation. Not only has the outlook for a newborn child with a facial cleft been substantially improved, but the cost of treatment in dollars, time, and heartache also has been reduced.

The American Cleft Palate-Craniofacial Association and cleft palate associations worldwide agree that management of patients with craniofacial anomalies is best provided by a multidisciplinary team of specialists. For the individual born with a cleft, the optimum time for the first team evaluation is within the first few days or weeks of life. However, referral for team evaluation and management is appropriate for patients at any age. Teams give parents information about recommended treatment procedures, options, risk factors, benefits, and costs to assist them in making decisions on the child's behalf and preparing the child and themselves for all recommended procedures. Team members should be sensitive to linguistic, cultural, ethnic, and physical factors, which will improve their ability to communicate with patients and their families.

Care should be coordinated by the team, which may be in an adjacent city, but care should be provided at the local level whenever possible; however, complex diagnostic and surgical procedures should be restricted to major centers with the appropriate facilities and experienced care providers. Each team should monitor both short- and long-term outcomes. Follow-up of patients, using appropriate documentation and record-keeping, is essential.

Following the birth of a child with a cleft lip and/or palate, the attending obstetrician, pediatrician, nurse, or social worker may—if he or she is involved with a cleft palate team—be sufficiently well-informed to outline the general problems to the parents and to provide guidance. Often the family is referred initially to a plastic surgeon, who generally will recommend that the infant be examined by other cleft palate team specialists. The team then meets periodically for a cross-specialty discussion of the child's case to exchange knowledge and decide on the appropriate treatment plan. The parents are given an opportunity to ask questions and to discuss the child's proposed treatment with all of the specialists.

TEAM COMPOSITION

The American Cleft Palate-Craniofacial Association[1] states that at the minimum a cleft palate team should consist of a plastic surgeon, a speech-language pathologist, and an orthodontist. However, the team should also include a clinic coordinator prosthodontist, pediatric dentist, oral and maxillo-facial surgeon, general dentist, psychiatrist, audiologist, geneticist, radiologist, neurologist, neurosurgeon, psychologist, otorhinolaryngologist, social worker, public health nurse, and pediatrician. The team leader can be any of these professionals.

Team members should possess appropriate credentials and experience in the evaluation and treatment of patients with cleft palate and other craniofacial anomalies. Each specialist has a very important function to perform in assisting the child and the parents. For example, the psychologist will evaluate the child, the parents, and their relationships with each other as well as with other members of the family, such as brothers and sisters of the cleft child, and with friends. In this way, the psychological effects of having a cleft palate on the youngster and on the family can be assessed and the necessary help and support given to the parents during the emotionally difficult period immediately following the birth, to the entire family as the child matures, and to the child.

THE FAMILY-CENTERED APPROACH TO HEALTH CARE

This approach to health care enhances involvement of the family and invokes participation of the family who are given opportunities for choice and decision making.

Figure 1–1, created by Linda Linneweh, clinic coordinator for Central Washington Cleft Palate Programs, portrays the inter-relationship of the Family Centered Health Care Program with the various health care providers which enables parents and their children to achieve their maximum health potential.

TEAM COORDINATOR

In this system the role of the team coordinator is to provide case management for children with cleft palate and their families, facilitate cleft palate team meetings, and work with public health nurses (Fig 1–1).

The team coordinator's involvement is ongoing and involves the four critical stages of care:

1. Birth;
2. Beginning of formal speech (cleft palate team's first meeting);
3. Starting elementary school;
4. Preadolescence and adolescent years.

The initial meeting with the parents can include the clinic coordinator and another professional who can be any of the cleft palate team members but is usually the plastic surgeon. Linneweh writes that they must visit the family in the hospital as soon as possible (see Linneweh, Vol. 2), which is the most important opportunity for early education and emotional support. This early visit lays the foundation for the development of a relationship with the team and helps to alleviate the family's anxiety about financial concerns and fear of the unknown.

There are few choices for families of children with cleft lip/palate. The timetable for intervention—surgical, dental, speech—is fairly well delineated; however, there are occasions when families can be provided choices. An atmosphere of collaboration allows an opportunity for parents to ask questions and voice concerns. Linneweh[2] states that health care providers' biggest challenge as they work toward family-

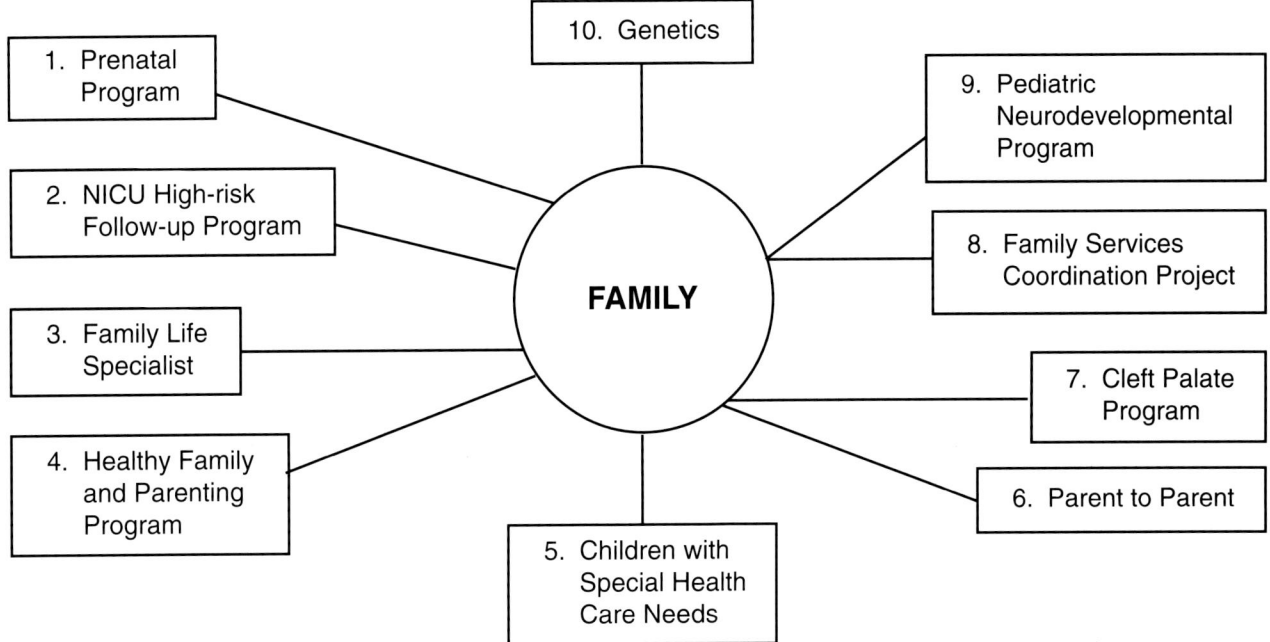

Fig 1–1. The constellation of services available to families through the center for Child Health Services, Yakima Valley Memorial Hospital. The Center for Child Health services provides routine outpatient, family-focused services from pregnancy through a child's 18th birthday. **1. Perinatal program:** Continuing medical education to professionals and paraprofessionals in the region served. **2. NICU High-risk Follow-up Program:** A developmental screening for NICU graduates conducted at 4, 9, and 18 months. **3. Family Life Specialist:** Ongoing child-parent education from birth to 1 year of age; ongoing parent classes developed in response to community needs. **4. Healthy Pregnancy and Parenting Program:** Program provides preventive health services to pregnant and post-partum women promoting positive birth and parenting outcomes. **5. Children with Special Health Care Needs (CSHCN):** Case management services to provide family-centered, community-based, culturally competent, coordinated care for children with special health care needs. **6. Parent-Parent Support:** Provides emotional support and information in English and Spanish to parents of children with special needs. **7. Cleft Palate Program:** One of five interdisciplinary teams in the State of Washington serving children born with cleft lip and/or palate. **8. Family Services Coordination Project:** An early intervention infant/toddler program funded by Part H funds. **9. Pediatric Neurodevelopmental Program:** Evaluation and Treatment of neuromuscular disorders and developmental delay for children from birth to 3 years. **10. Genetics Program:** Genetic counseling and monthly genetics clinics staffed by a geneticist.

centered services is to appreciate the differences and the range of social needs of their patient and their families.

For more information about the "Critical States" of Involvement the reader should write to: Ms. Linda Linneweh, Child Health Services, Memorial Hospital, Yakima Valley Memorial Hospital-2811, Yakima, WA 98902 (Tel: 509 575-8000).

SUPPORT GROUPS

The first months of life of a baby born with a cleft can be the most difficult time for parents. During the child's infancy, parents will want information about how others care for their babies with clefts. In addition to the counseling of a cleft palate team and talking with other parents who have a child with a cleft, many parents have joined together at a community level to exchange information and provide mutual emotional support. Most parents find it helpful simply to know how others cope with the problems of raising a child with a cleft.

Support groups enable parents to:

Talk with adult patients and parents who have a child with a cleft lip and/or palate,

Get practical help from others who share common problems,

Share information about treatment and community resources,

Provide special support for parents of newborns with cleft lip and/or palate,

Educate the public about cleft lip and cleft palate,

Accomplish more than any individual could do alone, such as lobbying for funds from government officials, or undertaking specific fund-raising projects.

Most support groups are interested in contacting other parents of newborns with clefts who are not yet enrolled in a group. The initial contact person should be trained by appropriate professionals, and should have coped with the actual experience of having a child with a cleft. Equally important in terms of support services is the development of programs for teenagers with clefts and their siblings and friends. At group sessions, professionals are invited to present information dealing not only with cleft treatment, but also with the best methods of rearing the cleft child and protecting the relationship of the parents to each other.

Another excellent source of information is About Face, a group whose members include both parents of children with clefts and patients with clefts. This parent-patient group meets annually in conjunction with the American Cleft Palate-Craniofacial Association's annual meeting, which is held in various regions of the United States. Still another information resource is a newsletter published by the American Cleft Palate Educational Foundation's Parent-Patient Liaison Committee, which reports on activities of parent groups and includes a calender of events.

Parents interested in receiving the newsletter should write to:
Parent-Patient Liaison Committee, American Cleft Palate Educational Foundation, 1218 Grandview Avenue, Pittsburgh, PA 15261 (Tel: 412-481-1376)

TEAM RESPONSIBILITIES

The following list was an outgrowth of a special conference, "Development of Standards for Health Care of Infants, Children and Adolescents with Craniofacial Anomalies" in 1991 sponsored by the Maternal and Child Health Bureau. The results of this conference were published as a supplement to the *Cleft Palate Craniofacial Journal*, March 1993, Volume 30, entitled "Parameters for Evaluation and Treatment of Patients with Cleft Lip/Palate or Other Craniofacial Anomalies."

This publication should be the guide for operation of all interdisciplinary teams. Individual copies may be obtained by contacting: American Cleft Palate-Craniofacial Association. 1218 Grandview Avenue, Pittsburgh, PA 15211 (Tel: 412-481-1376, Fax: 412-481-0847).

The principal role of the interdisciplinary team is to provide integrated case management to ensure quality and continuity of patient care and longitudinal follow-up. Each patient seen by the team requires comprehensive, interdisciplinary treatment planning to achieve maximum habilitation with efficient use of parent and patient time and resources.

Each interdisciplinary team should do the following:

- Maintain an office with a secretary and/or coordinator and a listed telephone number.
- Maintain centralized and comprehensive records on each patient, including histories, diagnoses, reports of evaluations, treatment plans, reports of treatment, and supporting documentation such as photographs, radiographs, dental models, and audiotaped speech recordings.
- Designate a coordinator who facilitates the function and efficiency of the team, ensures the provision of coordinated care for patients and families, and assists patients and families in understanding, coordinating, and implementing treatment plans.
- Designate a member(s) to make initial contact with the patient and/or family and also with direct care providers, as appropriate.
- Evaluate patients at regularly scheduled intervals, the frequency and specific content of the evaluations being determined by the condition and needs of the patient and family.
- Hold regularly scheduled face-to-face meetings for discussion of findings, treatment planning, and recommendations for each patient.
- Develop a longitudinal treatment plan for each patient and modify it as necessitated by craniofacial growth and development, treatment outcomes, and therapeutic advances.
- Weigh all treatment decisions against the expected outcomes and related factors such as facial growth, hearing, speech, dentition, and psychosocial impact on patient and family.

- Communicate the treatment recommendations to each patient and family in written form as well as in face-to-face discussion.
- Provide updated information to families as the treatment plan unfolds, and repeat information frequently enough to ensure its assimilation.
- Demonstrate sensitivity and flexibility in provision of care to accommodate linguistic, cultural, and ethnic diversity among patients and their families, ensuring that appropriate interpreters are available to assist in both verbal and written communication.
- Assist families in locating resources for financial assistance necessary to meet the needs of each patient.
- Communicate on a routine and ongoing basis with direct care providers in the home community and invite these care providers to participate in team meetings involving their patients.
- Perform regular, formal assessments of the quality of patient care with participation by each member of the team and, when appropriate, utilize external peer review. Teams should also conduct periodic surveys of patient satisfaction.
- Maintain a list of reliable sources for any services that are either not provided by the team itself or are better provided at the community level.
- Assist families in planning for treatment in a new geographic location by referring them to a interdisciplinary team in that area and facilitate contact with the new team.
- Provide assistance to adolescents and their families in planning for the termination of active treatment and offer information regarding services that, if needed, will be available to them as adults.
- Attempt to inform adult patients, who many have completed treatment, of new developments in diagnosis and treatment as they become available.
- Promote early identification of children with craniofacial anomalies through programs designed to inform delivery room personnel, neonatal care personnel, and primary care providers in the community about these birth defects.
- Provide education programs for hospital personnel and primary care providers addressing feeding and other critical aspects of early health care for children with craniofacial anomalies.
- Promote understanding of, and sensitivity to, the needs of patients by providing educational information about craniofacial anomalies and related disorders to parents and patients, other professionals, and the general public.
- Promote understanding of, and sensitivity to, the concerns of both parents, recognizing that each parent may have separate concerns.
- Aid in the formation and encouragement of parent-run support groups and encourage cooperation with hospital visitation programs by trained volunteers.

REFERENCES

1. American Cleft Palate-Craniofacial Assn. Parameters for evaluation and treatment of patients with cleft lip/palate. *Cleft Palate-Craniofac J.* 1993; 20:7.
2. Linneweh L. Cleft palate teams. In: Berkowitz, S, ed. *Cleft Lip and Palate, II: Introduction to Craniofacial Anomalies.* San Diego, Ca: Singular Publishing Group; in press.

The Value of Longitudinal Facial and Palatal Records in Clinical Research

After 30 years of treating children with various types of clefts, this author has concluded that the success or failure of a surgical procedure depends on the degree of palatal deformity at the time of surgery and the resulting facial growth pattern, as well as the surgical skills and the surgical procedure utilized. This conclusion will not be new to the experienced orthodontist, who in all probability recognizes that the progress recorded in treatment depends, for the most part, on the skeletal and facial growth patterns inherent in the patient, and the interaction of surgery with facial growth.

CEPHALORADIOGRAPHS AND SERIAL CASTS OF THE MAXILLARY AND MANDIBULAR DENTITION

To properly assess the results of treatment, there is a fundamental need for serial casts, lateral cephalometric films, and photographs in individual case reports.

Pruzansky[1,2] often stated that it is unfortunate that plastic surgeons' training in the realm of clefts and their variations tends to be totally inadequate, because their first encounters with patients usually occur in the clinic or operating room. Furthermore, there is seldom recourse to anatomical specimens to better appreciate the nature of the cleft deformity. The trainee is dependent on the empirical experience of his preceptor for knowledge of the natural history of the defect and long-term response to therapy. In most cases, other than before and after facial photographs, there are no objective records to determine why the outcome was a success or failure.

The collected serial data to be shown in this text will provide the clinician in training with an overview of the variations that can be encountered in each cleft type, the significance of genotype differences that influence growth and response to surgery, and the natural history of each cleft entity.

Over the years, certain cephalometric measurements have become standardized and have been applied to selected population samples to develop statistical means or averages. In the treatment of cleft lip and/or palate, this approach has provided useful data in studying morphologic growth changes in the head, evaluating dentofacial abnormalities, and assessing responses to surgical and orthodontic treatment. The data have been particularly useful in determining the timing and type of procedure selected to treat individual problems. The measurements and analyses utilized are primarily profile-oriented and reveal both anteroposterior and vertical relationships of the various parts of the dentofacial complex.

To assess changes during the course of general growth and treatment, head radiographs of the same individual taken at separate times are traced, and the tracings superimposed to ascertain the changes that have occurred. A common method is to register the two tracings at the point sella with the sella-nasion lines superimposed (Fig 2–2 a, b, c). This method provides a gross overview of changes in the dentofacial complex and in soft tissue, but is useful only in evaluating what has already occurred. In this text we also use The Coben[3] superimposition procedure (Basion Horizontal) because it more accurately reflects actual craniofacial growth direction (Figs 2–1d and 2–2d).

The use of "landmark," or baseline, images associated with the basicranium to show the composite results of facial growth can provide meaningful information, because it is the enlargement of the face relative to the cranial base that is being evaluated. In

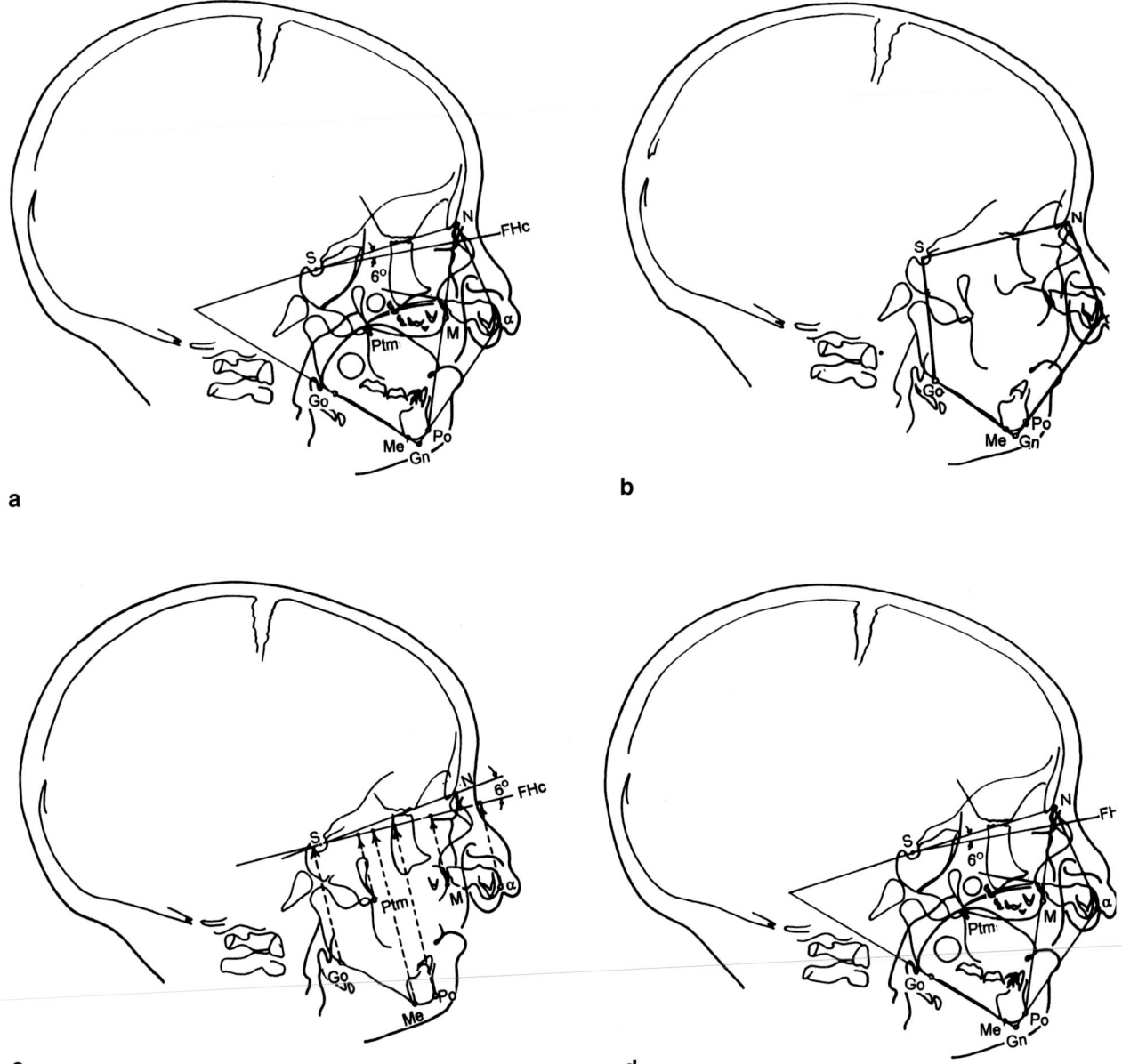

Fig 2-1. Various methods used to demonstrate facial changes using lateral cephalometrics.

a. Facial angles—These are just a few of the angles which describe changes in the skeletal profile. There are many more angles and linear measurements which can be used to relate the maxilla to the mandible and both jaws to the cranial base.

b. Facial polygon—This is a graphic method used to describe the boundaries of the skeletal face. (Pogonion constructed, Po', is the same point as Gnathion.) Facial growth changes can be shown by superimposing each succeeding polygon on the anterior cranial base (SN) and registering on Sella turcica (S).

c. Projecting facial landmarks to a constructed Frankfurt horizontal line which is arbitrarily drawn 6 degrees off the SN line. This angle can vary with steepness of the anterior cranial base. This graphic method will show the relative contribution of various structures within the maxilla and the mandible to the profile.

d. Basion horizontal created facial polygon (S.E. Coben). This method of superimposing tracings graphically reflects his overall concept of fixed growth. A plane at the level of the anterior border of foramen magnum (Basion) parallel to Frankfort horizontal where Basion is the point of reference for the analyses of craniofacial growth.

the child, further growth changes in the anterior part of the cranial base slow considerably at about 5 to 6 years of age, whereas facial growth continues actively through adolescence or beyond. Comparing the relative growth between these two regions, rather than simply focusing on a single fixed point, provides clinically useful information when cephalometrically evaluated.

THE BEGINNING OF LONGITUDINAL CLEFT PALATE RESEARCH STUDIES

Two major research problems were common in cleft palate surgical studies prior to the 1950s. Pruzansky[1,2] commented on the surgeon's tendency to group all types of clefts together in research and clinical treatment. He also stated that surgeons were limited in their study of pathologic anatomy of clefts due to the unavailability of serial dental casts, cephaloradiographs, and photographic records. The need for clinical records was apparent to many researchers, and within a decade, many retrospective clinical data sets were developed. These data sets spawned many investigators to determine the long-term influences of surgical and neonatal maxillary orthopedic procedures on palatal and facial growth and development. As a result of these early studies, useful diagnostic and prognostic information was obtained that provided a rationale for the management of individual cleft cases. These clinical records offered an accurate means for measuring and recording individual variation and for plotting the progress of each case in terms of growth and response to various treatments. As a result of these findings, the quality of care improved, resulting in more aesthetic and functional outcomes. Proper documentation, using objective records and individual treatment outcomes, has extended to many more modifications where it is possible to perform multicenter retrospective studies.

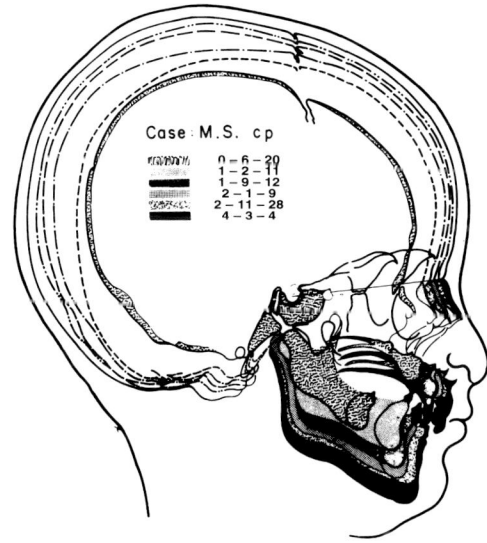

a

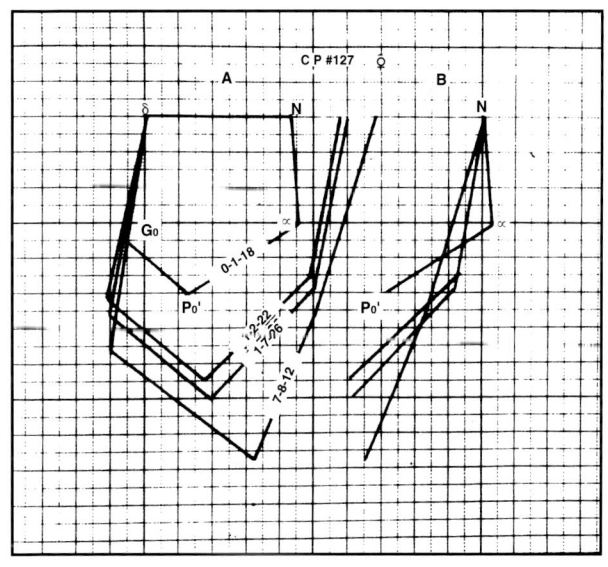

b

Fig 2–2.
a. Facial growth changes in a child with a complete bilateral cleft of the lip and palate superimposed on the anterior cranial base and registered at sella turcica (Courtesy of T. Graber). This method shows: (1) The basal portion of the occipital bone grows downward and backward while the anterior cranial grows upward and forward when the face is oriented in the Frankfort horizontal. (2) The palatal plane and the mandible descend in a parallel fashion. (3) The forward growth increments for the mandible exceed that of the maxilla resulting in the flattening of the facial profile. **b.** Case CP #127 (CPCLP). Superimposed facial polygons from 1 month, 18 days of age to 7 years, 8 months and 12 days of age. As a result of the mandible's downward growth increments exceeding its horizontal growth increments, this is an example of "poor" facial growth in that the profile fails to flatten as the mandible remains retrognathic. Note that in this and the following illustration the forward projection of the premaxilla does not increase after 1 year, 2 months and 22 days. *(continued)*

Fig 2-2. *(continued)*

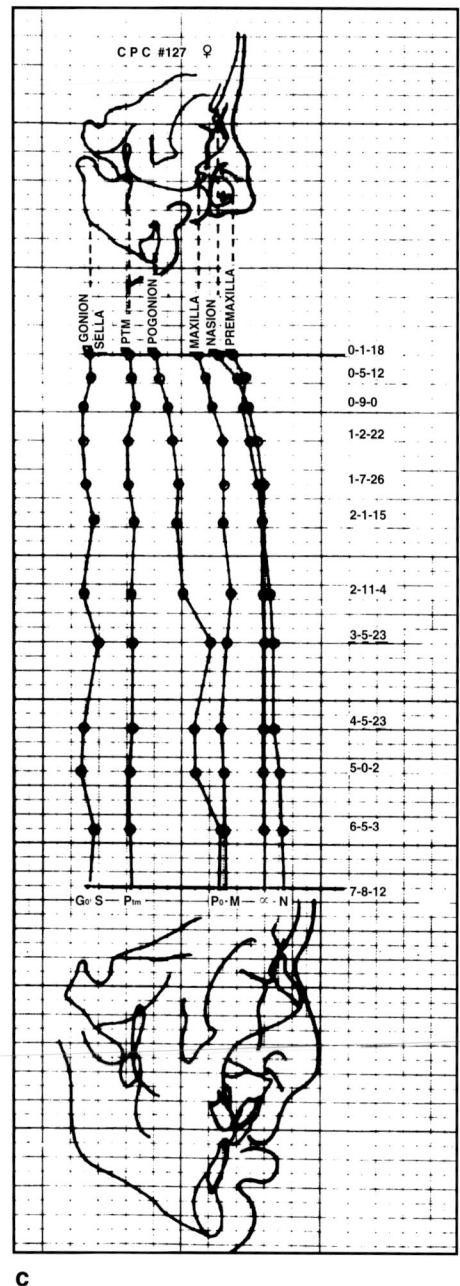

c

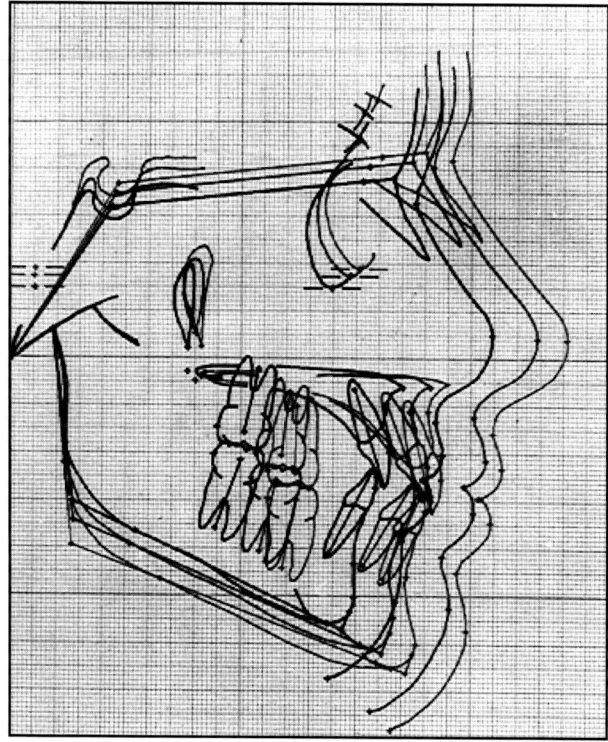

d

Fig 2-2. *(continued)*
c. Case CP #127. Projecting facial landmarks to a constructed Frankfort horizontal 6 degrees off the SN line. Although each of the skeletal structures except for the mandible has increased in size, the relative position of midfacial structures to the anterior cranial base has remained relatively stable. **d.** Basion Horizontal coordinate computer craniofacial serial tracings at ages 8, 13, and 18 years. Tracings are registered at Basion and oriented in Frankfort horizontal. Serial tracings maintain constant S-N/FH relationship. S-N and FH planes parallel. Tracings depict Coben's growth philosophy which states that craniofacial growth is reflected away from the foramen magnum (Basion) and the vertebral column (Reprinted from Coben, SE, *Basion Horizontal—An Integrated Concept of Craniofacial Growth and Cephalometric Analysis*. Jenkintown, Pa: Computer Cephalometrics Associated, The Benson; 1986.)

RESEARCH METHODS[4,5]

Retrospective Studies

In a retrospective study, the nature of the study group must be delineated precisely. Definite criteria should be established so that there is no ambiguity about types of cases and stages of growth development to be include in, or excluded from, the study. The choice of the case and control groups should be guided by concerns of validity. The advantages of retrospective studies are that they can be conducted relatively rapidly because the records of patients whose treatment is already complete can be used.

The investigator is protected against the circumstance of "subject drop-out" during the course of treatment, and they are relatively economical.

Prospective Studies

The advantages and disadvantages of prospective studies are in essence the inverse of those of retrospective studies. Provided that ethically and logistically satisfactory plans for random assignment to treatment can be developed, prospective trials afford an opportunity to control selection bias and to define and control the records acquisition process.

The main disadvantages of prospective trials are that they are expensive and a great deal of time must inevitably elapse between project initiation and the point at which data on most of the main outcome variables become available for analysis.

Multicenter comparisons of surgical-orthodontic treatment outcomes are an efficient way of testing the effectiveness of various treatment philosophies and surgical techniques. Differences among surgeons, variances in performance by the same surgeon over the years, and differences in techniques are difficult to identify and compare in isolation. However, in multicenter clinical studies, differences in clinical procedures among operators can, within defined limits, be compared and evaluated successfully without arousing criticism.

Clinical Trials

A clinical trial may be defined as a carefully designed, prospective study that attempts to answer a precisely defined set of questions with respect to the effects of a particular treatment. A clinical trial is a major undertaking which requires considerable money, personnel, facilities, time, and effort.

The simplest design for a clinical trial involves randomization between two different surgical treatment regimens to answer one specific question, for example, which of two surgical procedures is the most beneficial. To add a larger number of surgical procedures makes the trials more difficult to manage.

There are two reasons for not using a randomized clinical trial (RCT) method for surgical evaluation of cleft closure procedures whether done as a multicenter or single center trial. The first is the need for the surgeon to disregard the unique nature of the individual cleft defect and perform a standard surgical treatment being tested, the presumption being that clefts of all sizes and shapes will react the same way to the same surgical procedure. The second reason concerns the ethical questions involving the sequencing of surgical procedures and the use of the surgeon's skills.

Randomization of Surgical Procedures

In proposed multicenter RCT, it is expected that each surgeon will randomly utilize various surgical procedures sequentially for each type of cleft to determine the relative differences in outcome between procedures.

With the present restraints on certain types of human research, Human Subject Research Review Committees in most settings would be reluctant to permit the use of various elective surgical procedures in a research setting if there is a possibility that a surgical procedure might lead to facial disfigurement. Most surgeons would reject participating in a study employing a particular procedure they already have used and found to be inadequate. Many surgeons see the choice and timing of cleft surgical procedures as varying with the geometric characteristics of the palatal defect; therefore, the concept of randomization cannot be considered as an alternative to what they are already doing. The factor of surgical skill in a randomized trial must be considered as a variable in determining the effectiveness of a procedure. Can all participating surgeons be equally skilled in all procedures?

The Ethics of Surgical RCTs (Gifford,[6] Hellman & Hellman,[7] Israel,[8] Kakafka[9])

It is impossible to disassociate scientific from ethical considerations when dealing with cleft palate research. Different research protocols and evaluation methods carry different ethical problems the more so when life or death issues are not being considered.

Informed Consent

When a patient is deemed appropriate for a particular clinical trial, a first step is often to obtain informed consent. This is a legal requirement in the United States, although not in all countries. In some European countries each participating hospital decides on whether and how to handle informed consent.

Informed consent is a social construct based on ethical guidelines and supported by legal precedents.

In order for consent to be legally valid, it must be obtained voluntarily from a mentally competent person of legal age.

The greater the seriousness of the potential injury, even if the risk is minimal, the greater the obligation to inform the patient (or parent). The greater the chance of a risk occurring, even if the injury would be minimal, the greater the obligation to inform the patient (parent). The more elective the proposed treatment, the more serious injury will be perceived.

Sheldon Baumrind,[10(p236)] summarizing the role of clinical research in orthodontics which is also applicable to cleft palate research states:

> Cogent arguments can be made concerning the ethics of conducting structured clinical experiments in the kinds of long-term therapeutic situations which interest orthodontists. One telling argument is that since therapists have an absolute and transcendent obligation as professionals to deliver for each patient the treatment which they believe best for that patient, no subject can ethically be randomized to one of two possible treatments unless there is true uncertainty as to which of the two treatments is in the patient's best interest. For the same reason any experimental design that asks a clinician to treat a patient against the clinician's own professional bias is inappropriate at best. And even if ethical reservations could be overcome, it would clearly be of only minimal scientific value to accumulate data on how patients fare under treatments not considered optimal at the time they are delivered.

Baumrind[11(p239)] concludes:

> Except in special and very limited circumstances, clinical studies in orthodontics cannot and should not be expected to reveal categorically which of two or more treatments is better in a global sense. They can and should be expected to supply valid and reliable information about the mean effects of different treatments. But more important, they should supply information about the usual individual variability of human growth, development and response to therapeutic intervention.

Retrospective studies have permitted clinical investigators to evaluate the palatal and facial growth and development responses within a particular cleft type according to the type and timing of the surgical procedures employed. Such studies have shown that the degree of palatal scarring is directly related to the areas of denuded bone resulting from the displacement of the palates mucoperiosteum during cleft closure.

Roentgencephalometry has aided in the elucidation of the nature of the craniofacial malformation associated with facial clefts as it affects the mandible, maxilla, orbits, nasopharyngeal area, and the base of the skull and cervical vertebrae. Moreover, current studies on the variable growth and involution of tonsils and adenoids have raised a number of questions of interest to immunologists.

REFERENCES

1. Pruzansky S. Description, classification, and analysis of unoperated clefts of the lip and palate. *Am J Orthod.* 1953;39:590.
2. Pruzansky S. Factors determining arch form in clefts of the lip and palate. *Am J Ortho.* 1955;41:827.
3. Coben SE. *Basion Horizontal—An Integrated Concept of Craniofacial Growth and Cephalometric Analyses.* Jenkintown, Pa: Computor A Cephalometrics Associated, The Benson. 1986.
4. Atkins H. Conduct of a controlled clinical trial. *Br Med J.* ii, 1966:377.
5. Byse ME, Stagust MJ, Syvlester RJ, eds. *Cancel Clinical Trials—Methods and Practice.* London, England: Oxford University Press; 1983.
6. Gifford F. The conflict between randomized clinical trials and the therapeutic obligation. *J Med and Phil.* 1986;11:347–366.
7. Hellman S, Hellman DS. Of mice but not men: problems of the randomized clinical trial. *New Engl J Med.* 1991;324:1585–1589.
8. Israel L. Practical and conceptual limitations of best conceived randomized trials. *Biomedicine.* 1978;28 (special issue):36–39.
9. Kukafka AL. Informed consent in law and medicine: autonomy vs. paternalism. *J Law Ethics in Dent.* 1989;2:132–142.
10. Chiccone MV. Informed consent: in perspective. *Rental Rx.* 1990;3(2). (Publication of Mid-Atlantic Medical Insurance, Newark, NJ)
11. Baumrind S. The role of clinical research in orthodontics. *Angle Orthod.* 1993;63:235–240.

3

Facial Growth

MAXILLARY GROWTH CONCEPTS

It is not the author's intent to write a definitive treatise on facial growth and its control processes because there are better sources for such information. However, because the history of cleft palate treatment has been influenced by what clinicians think is the correct facial growth process, it behooves the author to support or refute the various facial-palatal growth concepts based on his own clinical findings.

Genetic Control Theory: Cranialfacial Growth Is Entirely Predeterminded

Enlow[1] writes that, in the past, it was thought that all bones having cartilage growth plates were regulated entirely and directly by the intrinsic genetic programming within the cartilage cells. Intramembranous bone (maxillary) growth, however, was believed to have a different source of control. This type of osteogenic process is particularly sensitive to biomechanical stresses and strains, and it responds to tensions and pressure by either bone deposition or resorption.

Tension, as traditionally believed, specifically induces bone formation. According to the traditional wisdom, when tension is placed on a bone, the bone grows locally in response. Pressure, on the other hand, if it exceeds a relatively sensitive threshold limit, specifically triggers resorption. According to this theory when muscle and overall body growth are complete, the bone attains biomechanical equilibrium, that is, the forces of the muscles are then in balance with the physical properties of the bone. This turns off osteoblastic activity, and skeletal growth ceases.

Unfortunately for traditional schools of thought, growth control in the human body is more complex than this. Moreover, it is now known that there is not a direct, one-to-one correlation between tension-deposition and pressure-resorption.

Functional Matrix Theory (Melvin Moss[2,3]) (Figs 3–1, 3–2)

Enlow[1] goes on to explain that, with the development of the Functional Matrix Principle, a number of important hypotheses began to receive attention. One of these is that the "bone" does not regulate its own growth. The genetic and epigenetic determinants of skeletal developments are in the functional tissue matrix, that is, muscle, nerve, glands, teeth, neurocranial fossa, and nasal, orbital, oral, and pharyngeal cavities. This is primary while the growth of the skeletal unit is secondary. However, although the Functional Matrix Principle describes what happens during growth, it does not account for how it happens. Experiments have shown that mechanical forces are not the principal factor controlling bone growth.

Most researchers agree that a notable advance was made with the development of the Functional Matrix Principle introduced by Moss. It deals with what determines bone and cartilage growth in general. The concept states, in brief, that any given bone grows in response to functional relationships established by the sum of all the soft tissues operating in association with that bone. This means that the bone itself does not regulate the rate and direction of its own growth; the functional soft tissue matrix is the actual governing determinant of the skeletal growth process.

The course and extent of bone growth are secondarily dependent on the growth of pace-making soft tissues. Of course, the bone and any cartilage present are also involved in the operation of the functional matrix, because they give essential feedback information to the soft tissues. This causes the soft tissues to inhibit or accelerate the rate and amount

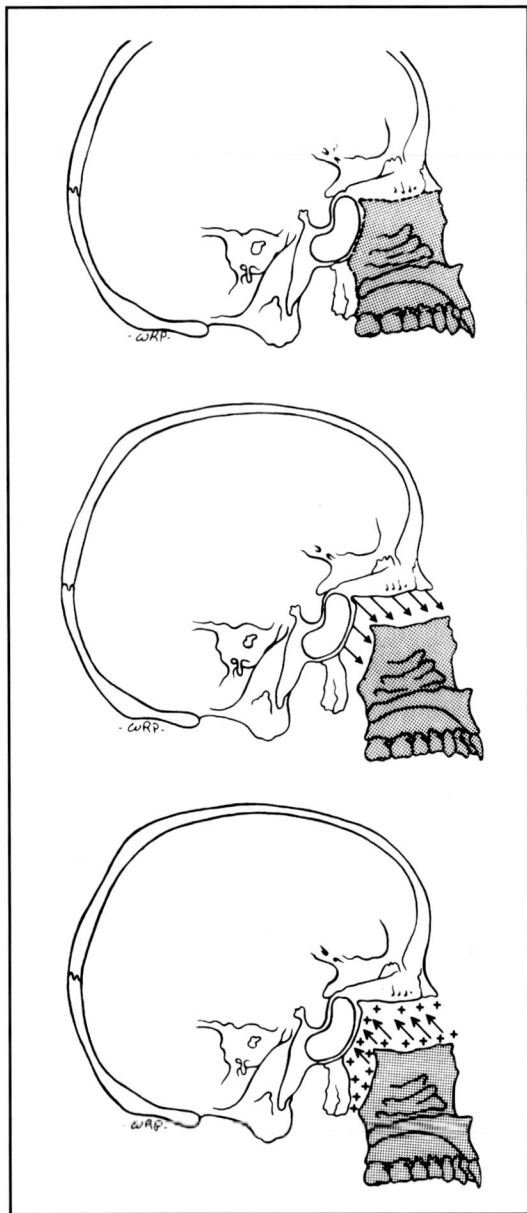

Fig 3-1. The process of new bone deposition does not cause displacement by pushing against the articular contact surface of another bone. Rather, the bone is carried away by the expansive force of all the growing soft tissues surrounding it. As this takes place, new bone is added immediately onto the contact surface, and the two separate bones thereby remain in constant articular junction. The nasomaxillary complex, for example, is in contact with floor of the cranium (*top*). The whole maxillary region, in toto, is displaced downward and forward away from the cranium by the expansive growth of the soft tissues in the midfacial region (*center*). This then triggers new bone growth at the various sutural contact surfaces between the nasomaxillary composite and the cranial floor (*bottom*). Displacement thus proceeds downward and forward as growth by bone deposition simultaneously takes place in an opposite upward and backward direction (i.e., toward its contact with the cranial floor). (From Enlow DH. *Handbook of Facial Growth*, 2ed. Copyright 1980 WB Saunders. Philadelphia: WB Saunders; 1980:30.)

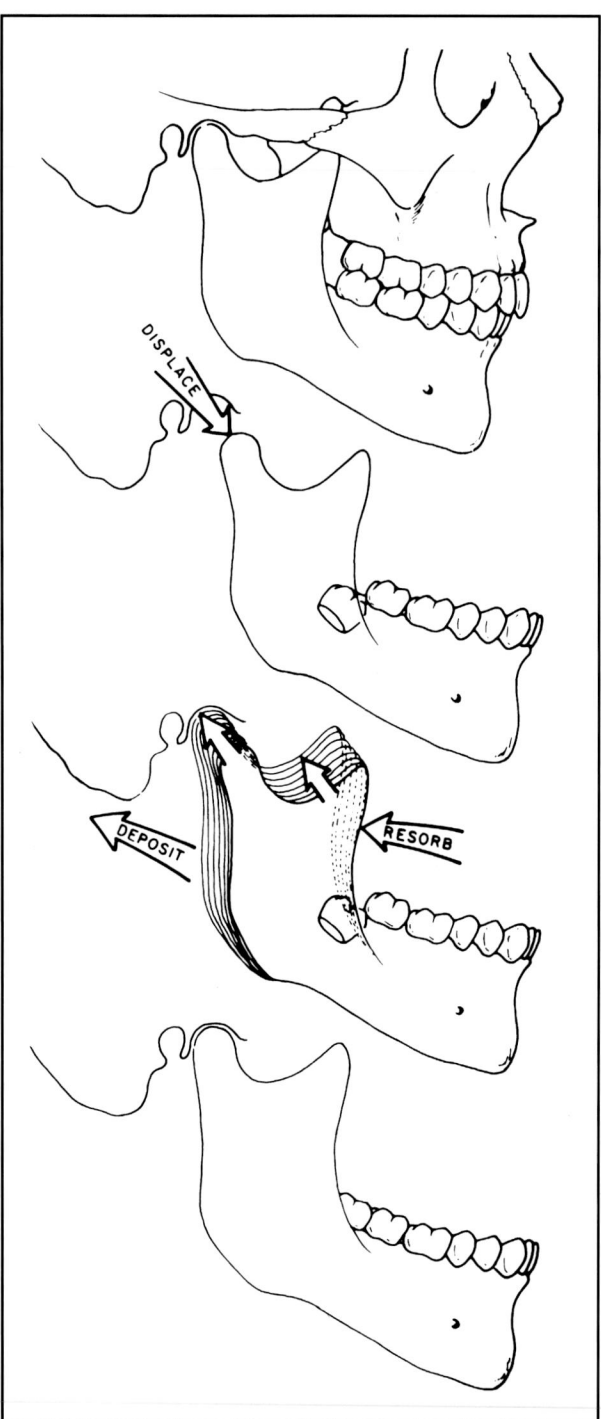

Fig 3-2. Similarly, the whole mandible is displaced "away" from its articulation in each glenoid fossa by the growth enlargement of the composite of soft tissues in the growing face. As this occurs, the condyle and ramus grow upward and backward into the "space" created by the displacement process. Note that the ramus "remodels" as it relocates posterosuperiorly. It also becomes longer and wider to accommodate (1) the increasing mass of masticatory muscles inserted onto it, (2) the enlarged breadth of the pharyngeal space, and (3) the vertical lengthening of the nasomaxillary part of the growing face. (Reprinted with permission from Enlow DH. *Handbook of Facial Growth*, Philadelphia: WB Saunders Co; 1980:30)

units to such separative movements (i.e., the alterations of size and shape in bones and cartilages are responses to matrix growth, not the cause of it).

The nasal skeleton is characterized by a relatively great normal variation in form. The nasal capsule (and septum), from its inception, serves to protect and support the functional spaces for respiration and olfaction. In man, the olfactory spaces are fully formed at birth. Postnatal cavity growth exclusively increases the respiratory functioning space.

The growth of the upper face is, in part, a response to the functional demands for increased respiratory volume. The nasal cavity is not a space haphazardly left over after the upper facial structures complete their growth. On the contrary, the expansion of the nasal cavity is the primary morphogenetic event; and nasal capsular growth, both osseous and cartilaginous, is secondary. The application of the theory of functional cranial analysis to nasal and mid-facial skeletal growth demonstrates that the growth of each of these two areas is independent of the other and that the nasal septal cartilage plays a secondary compensatory role, rather than a primary morphogenetic one.

At present, the nasal septum theory is somewhat accepted as a reasonable explanation by a number of clinicians who favor presurgical orthopedic treatment, although it is universally realized that much more needs to be understood about facial growth processes.[19] The use of presurgical orthopedic treatment is covered in greater detail in Chapter 9.

Clinically, there seems to be more support for the functional matrix theory than the nasal septum theory. Unfortunately, McNeil in espousing Scott's theory to explain the "retropositioned maxillary complex relative to the mandible and osteogenically deficient palatal processes" in complete clefts of the lip and palate did not have access to serial palatal and facial growth records to support such a view. However, Berkowitz's[20] serial casts study of CUCLP and CBCLP cases using the Angle occlusal classification system, which is the most reliable means of judging the geometric relationship of the maxillary to the mandibular arches within the face, showed that at 3 to 6 years of age, the teeth in the lateral palatal segments were in either Class 1 or Class 2 relationship but were never in a Class 3 relationship.

On this basis, one can conclude that it is not the lack of a growth impetus from the nasal septum that explains the presence of a small cleft palatal segment at birth. If palatal osteogenic deficiency does exist, it can more accurately be explained in relationship to the embryopathogenesis of facial development: the failure of migrating undifferentiated mesenchymal cells from the neural crest to reach the facial processes (Millard,[21] Ross and Johnston[43]) (see Chapter 4).

Basion Horizontal Concept: The Direction of Facial Growth (Coben[43])

No discussion on craniofacial growth is complete without including Coben's Basion Horizontal Concept of the direction of facial growth. Basion Horizontal is a concept based on a plane at the level of the anterior border of foramen magnum parallel to Frankfort horizontal where Basion is the point of reference for the analysis of craniofacial growth. Coben states that the growth concept which Basion Horizontal represents is that craniofacial growth is reflected away from the foramen magnum (Basion) and the vertebral column. The cranio-maxillary complex housing the maxillary dentition is translated upward and forward from Basion by growth of the cranial base. Growth of the mandible is reflected away from Basion, carrying the mandibular dentition downward and forward. The divergence of the two general vectors develops space for vertical facial growth and the eruption of the dentition.

Normal maxillo-mandibular development requires synchronization of the amount, timing, and direction of growth of the cranio-maxillary complex and of the mandible. The cranial base vector represents the upward and forward translation of the upper face by growth of the spheno-occipital synchondrosis, while growth of the spheno ethmoidal/circummaxillary suture system and the nasal septum increases the depth and height of the upper face.

The Basion-Articulare dimension is essentially stable post-natally, indicating that the mandible maintains a constant sagittal spatial relation to the foramen magnum as the reflection of mandibular growth carries the lower teeth downward and forward, away from the cranial base.

There are two distinct phases of craniofacial growth because of a change in the system of upper facial development after the approximate age of seven. Before age seven, growth of the upper face is dominated by the nasal septum, the eyeballs, and the spheno-ethmoidal/circummaxillary suture system (Fig 3-3). At these age, the growth in this suture system produces space for the eruption of the maxillary first molars. Longitudinal cephalometric findings of a continuous increase in the Sella-Frontale dimension with little increase in the thickness of the frontal bone before age seven support the concept that bone apposition and remodeling resorption are minor factors in these early years.

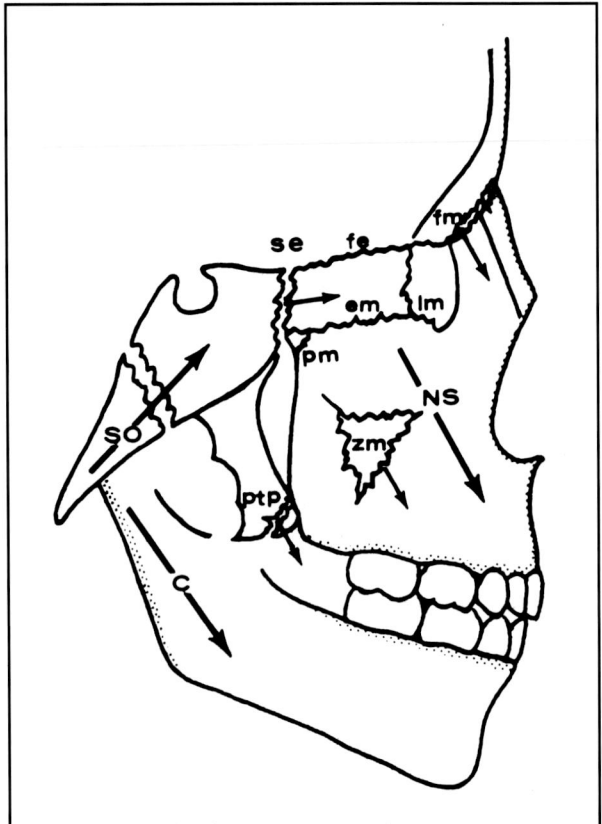

Fig 3–3. Postnatal craniofacial growth systems to the age of 7 years (first decade). Cartilaginous growth: **SO**, Spheno-occipital synchondrosis; **C**, reflection of condylar mandibular growth; **NS**, nasal septum. Spheno-ethmoidal circummaxillary suture system: **se**, Spheno-ethmoidal; **ptp**, pterygopalatine; **pm**, palatomaxillary; **fe**, fronto-ethmoidal; **em**, ethmoidal-maxillary; **lm**, lacrymal-maxillary; **fm**, frontomaxillary; **zm**, zygomaticomaxillary; **zt**, zygomaticotemporal (*not shown*). Surface apposition-modeling resorption development (*stippled area*): minor contribution. (Reprinted from Coben SE. *Basion Horizontal*. Jenkintown, Pa: Computer Cephalometrics Associated, The Benson; 1986, Fig 2 with permission)

does not explain the dynamics that can make this possible. How can segments be collapsed if there are no inwardly directed forces from the cleft lip-cheek muscle complex, especially when the tongue fits within the cleft space and acts to move the palatal segments apart?

Enlow's[1] report on current thinking on palatal growth processes delivers McNeil's thesis a mortal blow. Enlow[1(p368)] writes that recent research has shown that pressure is detrimental to bone growth.

Bone is necessarily both a traction- and pressure-adapted kind of tissue. The periosteal membranes are constructed to function in a field of tension (as by the pull of a muscle). Covering membranes are quite sensitive to direct compression because any undue amount causes vascular occlusion and interference with osteoblastic formation of new bone. Osteoclasts, conversely, function to "relieve" the degree of pressure by removing bone. Bone is pressure sensitive and high-level pressure induces resorption.

Moss et al,[18] responding to the role of nasal septal cartilage in mid-facial growth as put forth by Scott,[4-12] states that Scott's hypothesis is based on the following assumptions: (1) that in the fetal skull, the original nasal capsule and its derivatives are cartilaginous; (2) that all cranial cartilaginous tissues (septal, condylar, or in synchondroses) are primary growth centers, by virtue of the undoubted ability of all cartilaginous tissues to undergo interstitial expansive growth; and (3) that following the prenatal appearance of the intramembranous vomer (and of the several edochondral ossification centers of the ethmoid sinuses and the turbinates) the remaining unossified portions of the cartilaginous nasal capsule continue to be capable of such interstitial expansion. Moss further suggests that the nasal septal cartilage grows as a secondary, compensatory response to the primary growth of related oro-facial matrices and that mid-facial skeletal growth is not dependent on any prior, or primary, growth "impetus" of the nasal septal cartilages.

In Scott's hypothesis, it is assumed that cartilaginous interstitial growth is the major source of the expansive force that "pushes" on the subjacent mid-facial skeletal structures, causing both vertical and anteroposterior growth. Moss believes that it has been demonstrated repeatedly that growth in size and shape, as well as the changes in spatial position, of all skeletal units is always secondary to primary changes in their functional matrices. This secondary skeletal unit growth comes about in the following manner. All cranial bones and cartilages originate and grow within soft tissue capsules. The splanchnocranial skeleton exists within an oro-facial capsule. The primary growth of the enclosed oro-facial matrices causes the oro-facial capsule to expand responsively. Because the splanchnocranial bones are within this capsule, they are passively translated in space within their expanding capsule. As a result of such spatial displacement, the individual bones will be distracted (or separated) passively from one another.

The increments of growth observed at the sutural edges of these bones, and at the mandibular condylar cartilages, are secondary, compensatory, and mechanically obligatory responses of the skeletal the growing nasal septum, do not receive their growth impetus and, therefore, are not only retruded within the cranium but are also deficient in osteogenic tissue. He goes still further and believes that the deficient palatal processes can be stimulated to increased size through the use of functional orthopedics.

Stimulation of Bone Growth

As McNeil saw it, pressure forces created by "functional" orthopedic appliances, which are within the limits of tolerance, will act to stimulate bone growth in an anterior direction. This force needs to be applied to particular regions and in particular directions so that it can intensify normal forces. The resulting narrowing of the cleft is due to growth of the underlying bone brought on by such stimulating appliances. Additional growth leads to a reduction in the soft palate cleft as well, thereby increasing the chance of having a long, flexible well-functioning soft palate after surgical closure.

McNeil[14] goes on to suggest that an obturator alone is unsatisfactory because it will reduce "valuable" tongue space and lead to harmful speech habits. McNeil was correct in stressing that surgery should be reduced to a minimum compatible with sound clinical reasoning and accepted surgical principles.

Whereas McNeil states that his procedure stimulates palatal growth, thereby narrowing the cleft space, Berkowitz's[15] three-dimensional palatal growth studies—using a sample of cases that have not had neonatal maxillary orthopedic treatment and a control sample of noncleft cases—show that growth occurs spontaneously. This is an expression of the palate's inherent growth potential which can vary among patients. Berkowitz concluded that "catch-up growth" can occur after palatal surgery (with minimum scarring) is performed (see Chapter 16).

The Need to Prevent Collapse

McNeil[13-15] further believes that the palatal segments should be manipulated to an ideal relationship prior to lip surgery to prevent them from moving too far medially and becoming collapsed with the buccal segments in crossbite. This, he suspects, will lead to abnormal movements of the tongue and give rise to faulty respiratory, sucking, and swallowing patterns, also causing abnormal growth and development of the palatal structures.

Mestre et al,[16] studying palatal size in a cleft population that had not been operated on, report that the development of the maxilla appears to be normal in unoperated cases. They do conclude that it is the type, quality, and extent of the surgery that determines the effect on maxillary growth and that osteogenic deficiency does exist to varying degrees. Our research on serial palatal growth changes supports this conclusion that palates with clefts are highly variable in size, shape, and osteogenic deficiency.

Unfortunately, McNeil's interpretation of the effects of clefting on the various vegetative functions, and in reducing palatal growth, has not been supported by controlled objective research. The inability of the manipulated arch to remain intact after lip surgery, and not move medially into a collapsed relationship, has led many clinicians to question the accuracy of McNeil's other stated benefits such as reduction of middle ear infections.

McNeil[13-15] made other faulty observations. Among them:

1. He mistakenly believed that the orthopedic appliance will stimulate the underdeveloped cleft segment in unilateral clefts of the lip and palate (UCLP) to move forward, to make contact with the premaxillary portion of the greater segment and both palatal segments in bilateral clefts of the lip and palate (BCLP), after the lip is united. Even as early as the 1960s, many orthodontists found the opposite to be true. In UCLP the premaxillary portion of the larger segment moves medially and backward to make contact with the lesser segment due to the action of compressive lip muscle forces. If McNeil had had the benefit of serial casts, his interpretation of clinical events would, I am confident, have been totally different.

2. McNeil's claim that the lesser segments in UCLP, and both segments in BCLP, can be stimulated to grow forward is totally erroneous. His conclusions were based on conjecture, not on objective data. The results of Berkowitz's three-dimensional palatal growth studies (Wolfe and Berkowitz[17]) show marked acceleration in palatal growth during the first 2 years without orthopedic treatment, with most of the growth changes occurring at the area of the maxillary tuberosity and not at the anterior portion of the palate except for alveolar growth associated with canine development (Fig 3–3). Movement of the cleft palatal segment anteriorly is only possible as a result of reactive mechanical forces being applied through the use of pinned maxillary orthopedic appliances or from a protraction facial mask.

One last but significant characterization of a newborn cleft of the lip and palate needs to be refuted. McNeil states that "in BCLP lateral segments are collapsed toward the midline before birth." However, he of subsequent bone growth, depending on the status of the functional and mechanical equilibrium between the bone and its soft tissue matrix. The genetic determinants of the growth process reside wholly in the soft tissues and not in the hard part of the bone itself.

The Functional Matrix Concept is fundamental to an understanding of the overall process of bone growth control. This concept has had a great impact in the field of facial biology. The concept also comes into play as a source for the mechanical force that carries out the process of displacement. According to this now widely accepted explanation, the facial bones grow in a subordinate relationship with all the surrounding soft tissues. As the tissues continue to grow, the bones are passively (i.e., not of their own doing) carried along (displaced) with the soft tissues attached to the bones by Sharpey's fibers. Thus, for the nasomaxillary complex, the expansion of the facial muscle, the subcutaneous and submucosal connective tissues, the oral and nasal epithelia lining the spaces, the vessels, and the nerves, all combine to move the facial bones passively along with them as they grow. This continuously places each bone and all of its parts in correct anatomic positions to carry out its functions. Indeed, the functional factors are the very agents that cause the bone to develop into its definite shape and size and to occupy the location it does.

Growth control is determined by genetic influences and biomechanical forces, but the nature of the balance between them is still, at best, uncertain. No single agent is directly responsible for the master control of growth; the control process encompasses many factors. It involves a chain of regulatory links. Moreover, not all of the individual links are involved in all types of growth changes.

Enlow[1] identifies the maxillary tuberosity as being a major site of maxillary growth. It does not, however, provide for the growth of the whole maxilla, but rather is responsible for the lengthening of the maxillary arches. The whole maxilla is displaced in an anterior direction as it grows and lengthens posteriorly. However, the nature of the force that produces this forward movement is a subject of great controversy. The idea that additions of new bone on the posterior surface of the elongating maxillary tuberosity "push" the maxilla against the adjacent pterygoid plates has been abandoned.

Bones do not by themselves have the physiological capacity to push away bones. Another theory held that bone growth at the various maxillary sutures produces a pushing apart of the bones, with a resulting thrust of the whole maxilla downward and forward. This theory has also been rejected because bone tissue is not capable of growth in a field that requires the amount of compression needed to produce a pushing type of displacement. The sutural connective tissue is not adapted to a pressure-related growth process. It is believed that the stimulus for sutural bone growth is the tension produced by the displacement of the bone. Thus, the deposition of new bone is a response to displacement rather than the force that causes it. Although the "sutural push theory" is not tenable, Enlow reports that some students of the facial growth control processes are looking anew at growth mechanizing sutures, but not in the old conceptual way.

Cartilage-Directed Growth: Nasal Septum Theory (James Scott[4-12])

Cartilages are the leading factor. Synchondrosis, nasal septum, and mandibular condyles are actual growth centers. Sutural growth is compensatory. This theory developed from criticisms of the "sutural theory." Scott[4-5] believes that cartilage is specifically adapted to certain pressure-related growth sites, because it is a special tissue uniquely structured to provide the capacity for growth as a result of compression. The basis for this theory is that the pressure-accommodating expansion of the cartilage in the nasal septum is the source of the physical force that displaces the maxilla anteriorly and inferiorly. This, accordingly to Scott's hypothesis, sets up fields of tension in all the maxillary sutures. The bones then, while they enlarge at their sutures in response to the tension created by the displacement process, move in relation to each other.

The nasal septum hypothesis was soon adopted by many investigators in cleft palate centers around the world and became more or less the standard explanation, replacing the "sutural theory." Clinicians involved in cleft palate treatment, such as McNeil[13-15] and Burston[14-19] and their followers,[20-34] accepted Scott's thesis that cartilage and periosteum carry an intrinsic genetic message that guides their growth. They believed that the cartilaginous centers, such as the chondrocranium, the associated synchondroses, and the nasal septum, should be viewed as the true centers of skull and facial growth. Scott[4,5] further suggests that the nasal septum plays more than a secondary role in the downward and forward vector of facial growth.

McNeil,[13,14] following Scott's thesis, describing the embryopathogenesis of complete clefts of the lip and palate and their treatment at the neonatal period, wrote that the palatal processes, being detached from

15. McNeil CK. Orthopedic principles in the treatment of lip and palate clefts. In: Hotz R ed. *Early Treatment of Cleft Lip and Palate, International Symposium.* Berne: Hans Huber; 1964:59–67.
16. Burston WR. The pre-surgical orthopaedic correction of the maxillary deformity in clefts of both primary and secondary palate. In Wallace: AB, ed. *Transactions of the International Society of Plastic Surgeons, Second Congress, London, 1959.* London. England: E&S Livingston Ltd; 1960:28–36.
17. Burston WR. The early orthodontic treatment of alveolar clefts. *Proc R Soc Med.* 1965;58:767–771.
18. Burston WR. Treatment of the cleft palate. *Ann R Coll Surg Engl.* 1967;25:225.
19. Burston WR. The early orthodontic treatment of cleft palate conditions. *Dent Pract.* 1985;9:41–56.
20. Crikelair GF, Bom AF, Luban J, Moss M. Early orthodontic movement of cleft maxillary segments prior to cleft lip repair. *Plastic Reconstr Surg.* 1962;30:426–440.
21. Cronin TD, Penoff JH. Bilateral clefts of the primary palate. *Cleft Palate J.* 1971;8:349–363.
22. Derichsweiler H. Some observations on the early treatment of harelip and cleft palate cases. *Trans Europ Orthod Soc* 1958;34:237–253.
23. Dreyer CJ. Primary orthodontic treatment for the cleft palate patient. *J Dent Assoc, S. Africa.* 1962;13–119.
24. Georgiade N. The management of premaxillary and maxillary segments in the newborn cleft patient. *Cleft Palate J.* 1970;7:411.
25. Georgiade NG, Latham RA. Intraoral traction for positioning the premaxilla in the bilateral cleft lip. In: Georgiade NG, Hagerty RF eds. *Symposium on Management of Cleft Lip and Palate and Associated Deformities.* St. Louis, Mo: Mosby Co; 1974:123–127.
26. Georgiade NG, Latham RA. Maxillary arch alignment in the bilateral cleft lip and palate infant, using the pinned coaxial screw appliance. *J Plast Reconstr Surg.* 1975;52:52–60.
27. Graf-Pinthus B, Bettex M. Long-term observation following presurgical orthopedic treatment in complete clefts of the lip and palate. *Cleft Palate J.* 1974;11:253–260.
28. Hellquist R. Early maxillary orthopedics in relation to maxillary cleft repair by periosteoplasty. *Cleft Palate J.* 1971;8:36–55.
29. Huddart AG. Presurgical changes in unilateral cleft palate subjects. *Cleft Palate J.* 1979;16:147–157.
30. Kernahan DA, Rosenstein SW eds. *Cleft Lip and Palate, A System of Management.* Baltimore, Md: Williams and Wilkins; 1990.
31. Krischer JP, O'Donnell JP, Shiere FR. Changing cleft widths: A problem revisited. *Am J Orthod.* 1975;67:647–659.
32. Latham R. A new concept of the early maxillary growth mechanism. *Trans Eur Orthod Soc.* 1968;53–63.
33. Robertson N. Recent trends in the early treatment of cleft lip and palate. *Dent Practit.* 1971;21:326–338.
34. Monroe CW, Rosenstein SW. Maxillary orthopedics and bone grafting in cleft palate. In: Grabb WC, Rosenstein SW, Bzoch KR eds. *Cleft Lip and Palate.* Boston, Ma: Little, Brown and Co; 1971:573–583.
35. Berkowitz S. Cleft Palate. In: Wolfe SA, Berkowitz S eds. *Plastic Surgery of the Facial Skeleton.* Boston, Ma: Little, Brown and Co; 1989:291.
36. Mestre J, Dejesus J, Subtelny JD. Unoperated oral clefts at maturation. *Angle Orthod.* 1960;30:78–85.
37. Wolfe SA, Berkowitz S. The use of cranial bone grafts in the closure of alveolar and anterior palatal clefts. *Plast and Reconstr Surg.* 1983;72:659–666.
38. Moss ML, Brombery BE, Song C, Eiseman X. Passive role of nasal septal cartilage in midfacial growth. 1968;41:536–542.
39. Moss ML. The primacy of functional matrices in orofacial growth. *Dent Pract.* 1968;19:65.
40. Berkowitz S. Timing cleft palate closure-age should not be the sole determinant. In Cohen MM Jr., Rollnick BR, eds. *J Craniofac Gen and Devel Biol.* 1985;1(suppl):69–83.
41. Millard DR, Jr. Alveolar and palatal deformities. In: *Cleft Craft—The Evolution of Its Surgery—III.* Boston, Ma: Little, Brown and Co.; 1980:284–298.
42. Ross RB, Johnston MC. *Cleft Lip and Palate.* Baltimore, Md: Williams and Wilkins; 1972.
43. Coben SE. *Basion Horizontal—An Integrated Concept of Craniofacial Growth and Cephalometric Analyses.* Jenkintown, Pa: Computor A Cephalometrics Associated, 1986.
44. Dahl E. Craniofacial morphology in congenital clefts of the lip and palate—An x-ray cephalometric study of young adult males. *Acta Odontol Scand.* 1970;28(suppl):57.
45. Chierici G, Harvold EP, Vargevik K. Morphogenetic experiments in cleft palate: Mandibular response. *Cleft Palate J.* 1973;10:51–61.
46. Mazaheri M, Harding RL, Cooper JA, Meier JA, Jones TS. Changes in arch form and dimensions of cleft patients. *Am J Orthod.* 1971;60:19–32.
47. Aduss H. Craniofacial growth in complete unilateral cleft lip and palate. *Cleft Palate J.* 1971;41:202–212.
48. Rosenstein S. Orthodontic and bone grafting procedures in a cleft lip and palate series: An interim cephalometric evaluation. *Angle Orthod.* 1975;45:227–237.
49. Bishara SE. Cephalometric evaluation of facial growth in operated and non-operated individuals with isolated clefts of the palate. *Cleft Palate J.* 1973;3:239–246.
50. Bishara SE, Sierk DL, Huang KS. A longitudunal cephalometric study on unilateral cleft lip and palate subjects. *Cleft Palate J.* 1979;16:59–71.
51. Krogman WM, Mazaheri M, Harding RL, Ishigura K, Bariana G, Meir J, Canter H, Ross P. A longitudinal study of the craniofacial growth pattern in children with clefts as compared to normal birth to six years. *Cleft Palate J.* 1975;12:59–84.
52. Robertson NRE, Fish J. Early dimensional changes in the arches of cleft palate children. *Am J Orthod.* 1975;67:290–303.
53. Pruzansky S, Richmond JB. Growth of the mandible in the infants with micrognathia. *Amer J Dis Child.* 1954;88:29–42.
54. Douglas B. The treatment of micrognathia associated with obstruction by obstruction by a plastic procedure. *Plast and Reconstr Surg.* 1946;1:300–308.

The Effect of Clefting of the Lip and Palate on the Palatal Arch Form

VARIETIES OF CLEFT LIP AND CLEFT PALATE

Action of Intact Muscular Forces on the Maxillary Arch

In a normal jaw with intact lips and palate, the muscles of the lip, cheek, and pharynx exert their normal sphincter-like actions against the developing maxillary and mandibular arches. The compressive external muscular forces neutralize the expansion forces of the tongue (Fig 4–1). The neonatal arch form changes as these forces change with growth and maturation; yet the opposing muscles always maintain a precise and dynamic balance with each other. When this muscular balance is upset, the arch form and teeth relationships change.

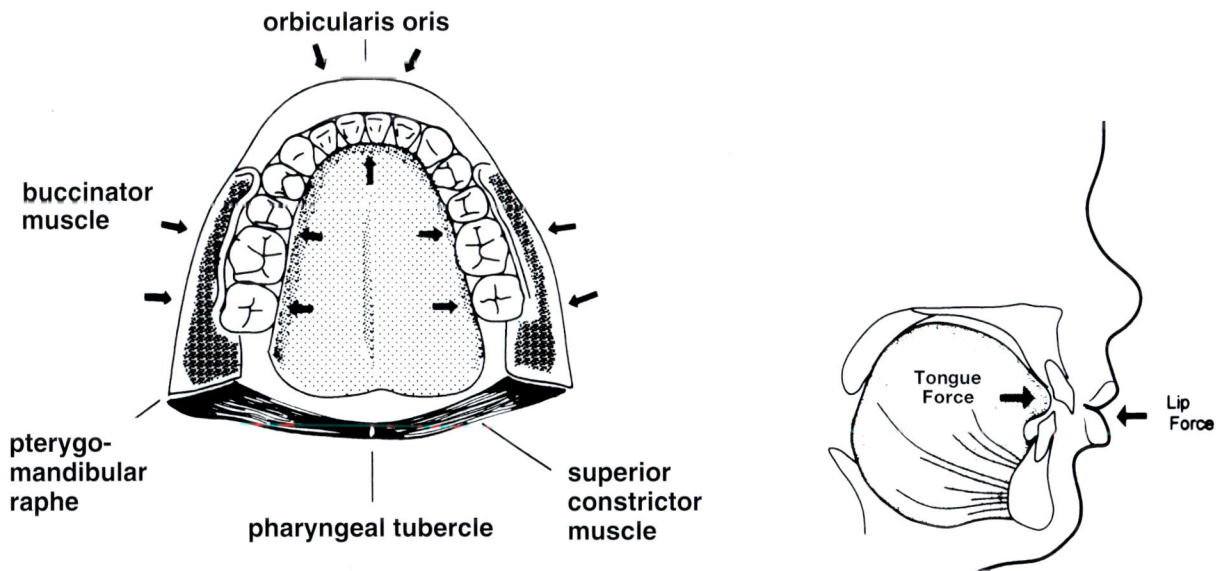

Fig 4–1. The balance between facial and tongue muscle forces. a. The outer muscles, the orbicularis oris, buccinator, and superior constrictor muscles, form a ring which acts to compress the palatal and mandibular arches with the teeth. b. The tongue force acts to expand the dental arches and teeth. Whether the teeth and arches align is determined by the resultant of these forces.

Aberrant Muscle Forces in Clefts of the Lip and Palate

A cleft of the lip and palate is the result of the failure of lip elements, and right and left palatal segments, to come together within the first 9 weeks of fetal life. The loss of muscular continuity of the orbicularis oris-buccinator-superior constrictor ring in complete unilateral and bilateral clefts changes the normal muscular force diagram. The aberrant muscular forces act to displace tissue masses. In complete clefts of the lip and palate, if the lateral palatal cleft segments are detached from the vomer, they will be pulled laterally by the external aberrant lip-cheek muscular forces, as well as spread apart by the tongue pushing into the cleft space (Fig 4–2). Because clefts differ in their location and extent, lip and palate clefts can vary in the degree of geometric distortion, as well as in the size and shape of the cleft palatal segments.

The muscular forces that act on the bony scaffolding of the palate and pharynx begin very early in intrauterine life; therefore, the palatal and facial configuration at birth has been molded and formed over the major portion of the infant's existence prior to birth.

In complete unilateral clefts of the lip and palate (CUCLP), the premaxillary portion of the noncleft segment is pulled antero-laterally. In addition to the lateral displacement of the lateral palatal segments, the premaxilla in the larger segment is carried forward in the facial skeleton. In complete bilateral cleft lip and palate (CBCLP), excessive growth in the premaxillary-vomerine suture is caused by increased tension at this site, precipitated by mechanical force stresses during periods of rapid growth (Berkowitz,[1] Pruzansky,[2,3] Friede[4,5]) (Fig 4–3). This growth is continuous during early postnatal years and provides a fourth dimension to the deformity, which can alter the cleft palatal segments and their associated parts and either simplify or complicate treatment.

If a soft tissue (mucous membrane, skin, and fibrous connective tissue), which collectively form Simonart's band, bridges the alveolar cleft, the attached palatal segments are limited in their degree of geometric displacement.

CATEGORIES OF CLEFTS

Depending on the elemental characteristics of the embryology, anatomy, and physiology of the cleft defect, the varieties of clefts of the lip and palate

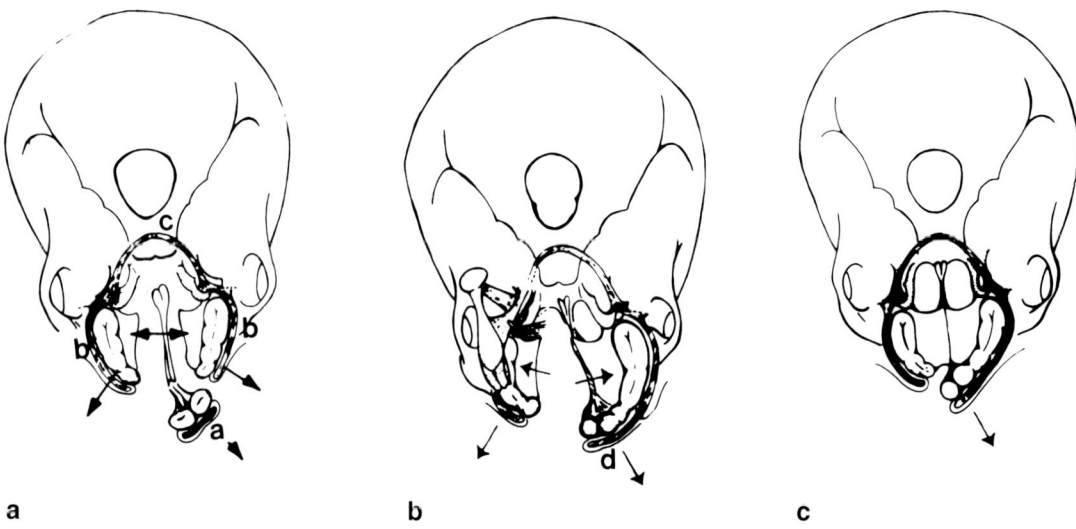

Fig 4–2. Effects of complete clefts of the lip and palate at birth. In complete cleft lip and palate, with a separation in the orbicularis oris (a) -buccinator (b) -superior constrictor (c) muscle ring, the aberrant muscle forces plus the plunger action of the tongue causes the palatal segments to be pulled and pushed apart. **a.** In bilateral clefts of the lip and palate, the premaxilla may be laterally or ventrally flexed with the fulcrum at the premaxillary vomerine suture. **b.** Complete unilateral clefts of the lip and palate at birth. The cleft's lesser segment and the premaxillary portion of the larger segment (d) are pulled outward. **c.** Cleft of the lip and alveolus. The bony distortion is determined by the extent of alveolar involvement. (Courtesy of J. D. Subtelny.)

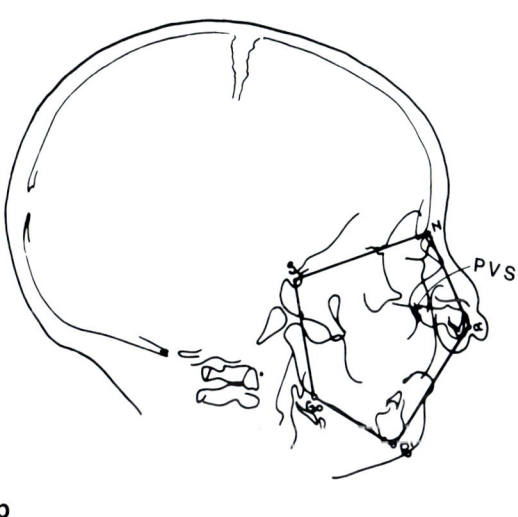

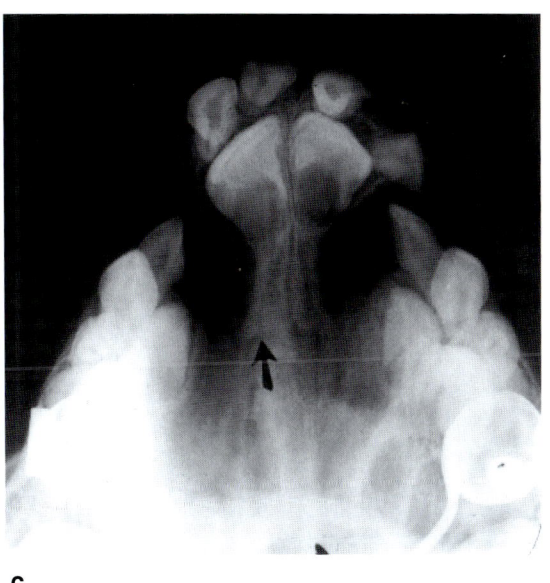

Fig 4–3. Skull with a bilateral cleft and palate. **a.** The palatal segments have been overexpanded and the premaxilla protruded by the resultant aberrant muscle forces. The premaxillary-vomerine suture separates the premaxilla and the vomer and is a growth site. **b.** Lateral cephalometric tracing at birth. Lines connecting various landmarks create a polygon depicting their geometric relationship. This tracing of a CBCLP at birth shows the degree of premaxillary protrusion. S = Sella Turcica, N = Nasion, ∝ = Alpha (the anterior extent of the premaxilla), Po = Pogonion, Gn = Gnathion, Go = Gonion, PVS = Premaxillary-vomerine suture. **c.** Occlusal radiograph of the premaxilla and vomer showing the premaxillary vomerine suture (arrow).

may be tabulated into four general categories: (1) those involving the lip and alveolus; (2) those involving the lip and palate; (3) those in which the palate alone is affected; and (4) congenital insufficiency of the palate. The term "palate" will include both the hard palate and the velum, or soft palate (Fig 4–4).

1. Clefts of the Lip (Figs 4–5 and 4–6)

A cleft of the lip may be complete, extending from the vermilion border to the floor of the nose, or it may be incomplete. There are various degrees of incomplete lip clefts. Minimal defects involving only the vermilion border are observed. In others, the defect may extend to the nose as a submucous cleft in the muscle band, bridged only by mucous membrane, skin, and fibrous connective tissue. The nasal alar cartilage on the side of the cleft is displaced and flattened to a greater or lesser degree, depending on the extent and width of the cleft. The tip of the nose is deviated toward the noncleft side.

The cleft in the lip may be unilateral or bilateral, occurring on one or both sides, respectively. If bilateral, it may be symmetrical or asymmetrical, that is, it may or may not involve the lip equally on both sides (Fig 4–5, b). It should be noted that, in bilateral clefts, a median portion of the lip is isolated in the

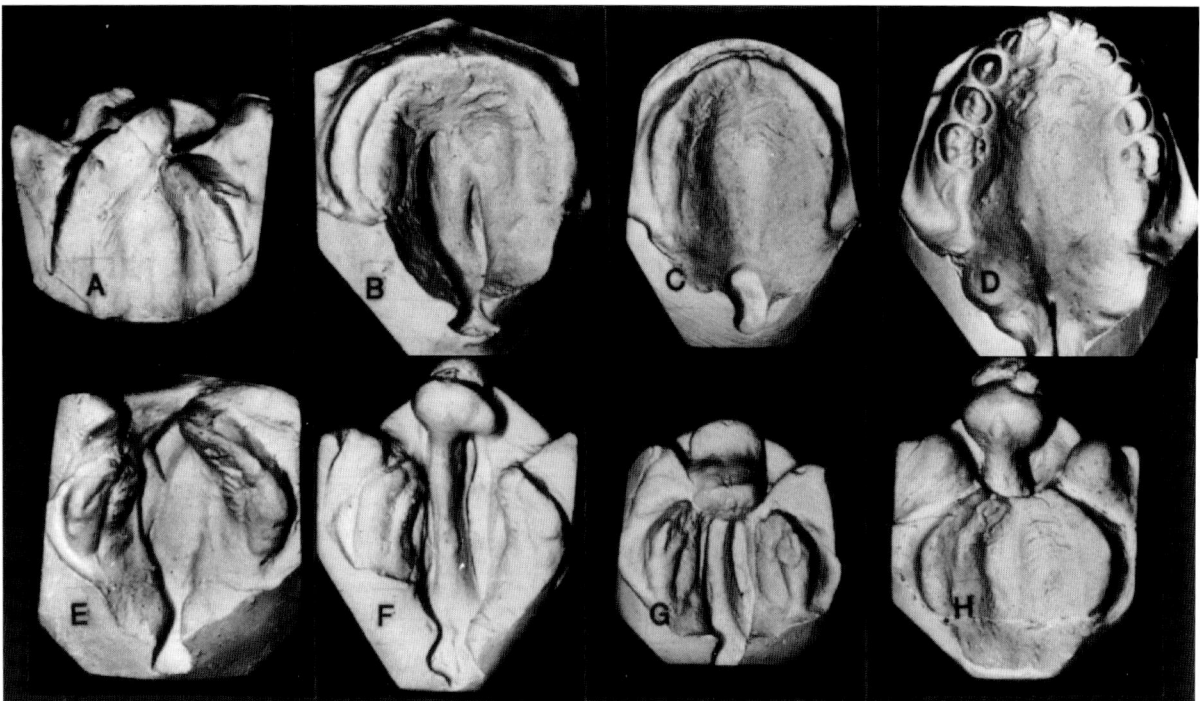

Fig 4–4. The anatomic classification system is based on the location, completeness, and extent of the cleft deformity. Because the lip, alveolus, and hard palate develop from different embryonic sources, any combination of clefting can exist. **A.** Cleft of the lip and alveolus. Normal palate. **B.** Isolated cleft of the hard and soft palate. Normal lip and alveolus. **C.** Cleft of the soft palate and uvulae. **D.** Cleft of the uvulae. **E.** Complete unilateral cleft lip and palate. **F.** Complete bilateral cleft of the lip and palate. **G.** Incomplete bilateral cleft of the lip and palate. **H.** Complete bilateral cleft of the lip and alveolus (Courtesy of Wolfe SA, Berkowitz S, eds. *Plastic Surgery of the Facial Skeleton.* Boston: Little, Brown and Co; 1989:292.)

midline and remains attached to the premaxilla and to the columella. This portion of the lip contains the philtrum. In complete bilateral clefts of the lip, the premaxilla protrudes considerably forward of the facial profile (Fig 4–5, b). It is attached to a stalk-like vomer and to the nasal septum. The columella appears to be deficient, and the alar cartilages are flattened on both sides. The effect on the facial profile is to accentuate further the protrusiveness of the premaxilla and the portion of the lip which is attached to the facial surface.

The more complete the defect in the lip, the greater the influence of the cleft on the alveolar process. Because of this constant relationship between the lip and alveolar process, it is not necessary to include the alveolar process as a separate entity in this description and classification. The maxillary alveolar processes arise from the mesoderm in the depths of a sulcus separating the lip and palate, while the tegmen oris gives rise only to the soft palate and the central part of the hard palate.

The relationship between the degree of the cleft's effect on the alveolar process and defects in the deciduous and permanent dentition is interesting. The dental defect may be assessed in terms of the number of teeth, their shape, and structure as well as the position of the teeth in the dental arch. Irregularities in the alveolar process range from small dimples in association with minor clefts in the lip to actual grooves in the alveolar process to, in extreme cases of total clefts in the alveolar ridge, displacement of the premaxillary segment toward the noncleft side. Small dimples or grooves in the alveolar ridge tend to fill in as the jaw grows. However, the deciduous lateral incisor that erupts in this area may be T-shaped, or otherwise misshapen, and malpositioned in the line of occlusion. Further documentation and analysis of serial records should provide detailed information concerning the eruption of teeth adjacent to the cleft in the alveolar process.

2. Cleft Lip and Cleft Palate (Fig 4–7)

Clefts of both the lip and palate may be unilateral or bilateral. They may be complete or incomplete. In a complete unilateral cleft of the lip and palate, a direct communication exists between the oral and nasal cavities on the side of the palate where the cleft is situated. The nasal septum is attached to the

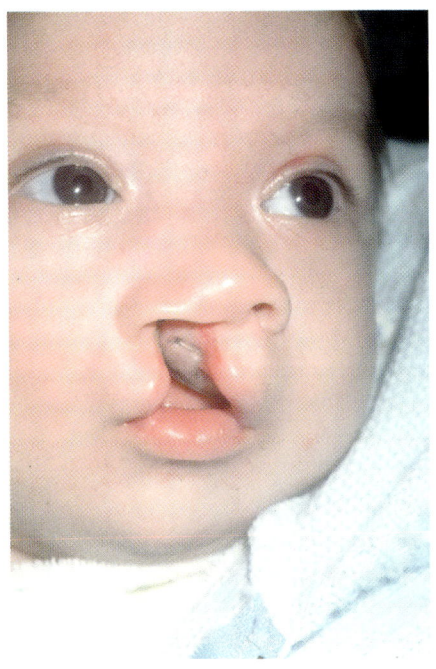

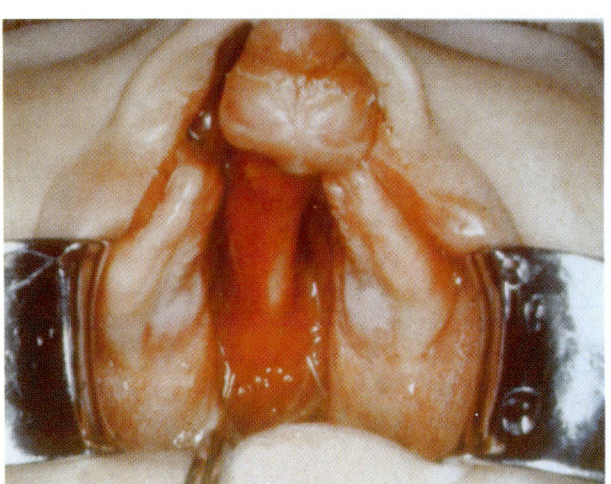

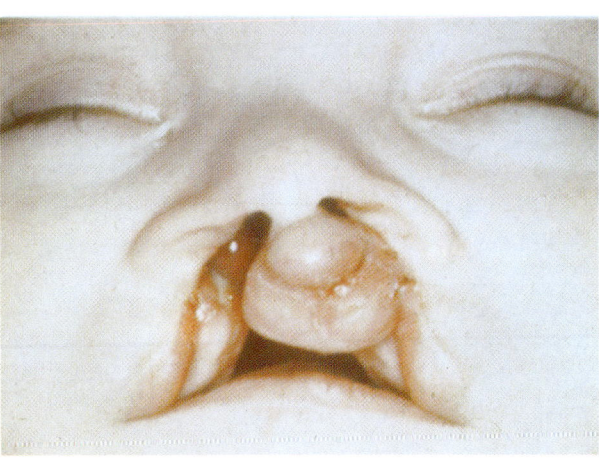

Fig 4–5. a. Complete unilateral cleft lip and palate. The distorted nostril is caused by the aberrant lip muscle forces. **b.** Complete bilateral cleft lip and palate with a widely separated lateral palatal segment. The protruding premaxilla extends forward of the lateral palatal segments and is attached to the vomer. The prolabium (central portion of the lip) overlies the premaxilla.

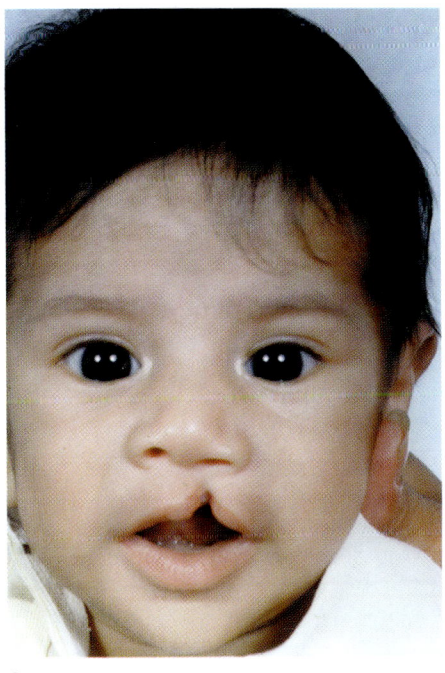

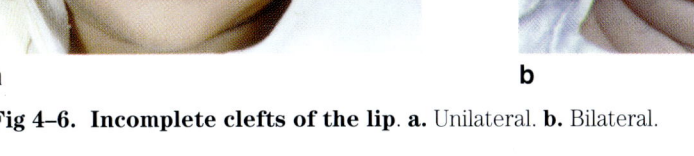

Fig 4–6. Incomplete clefts of the lip. a. Unilateral. **b.** Bilateral.

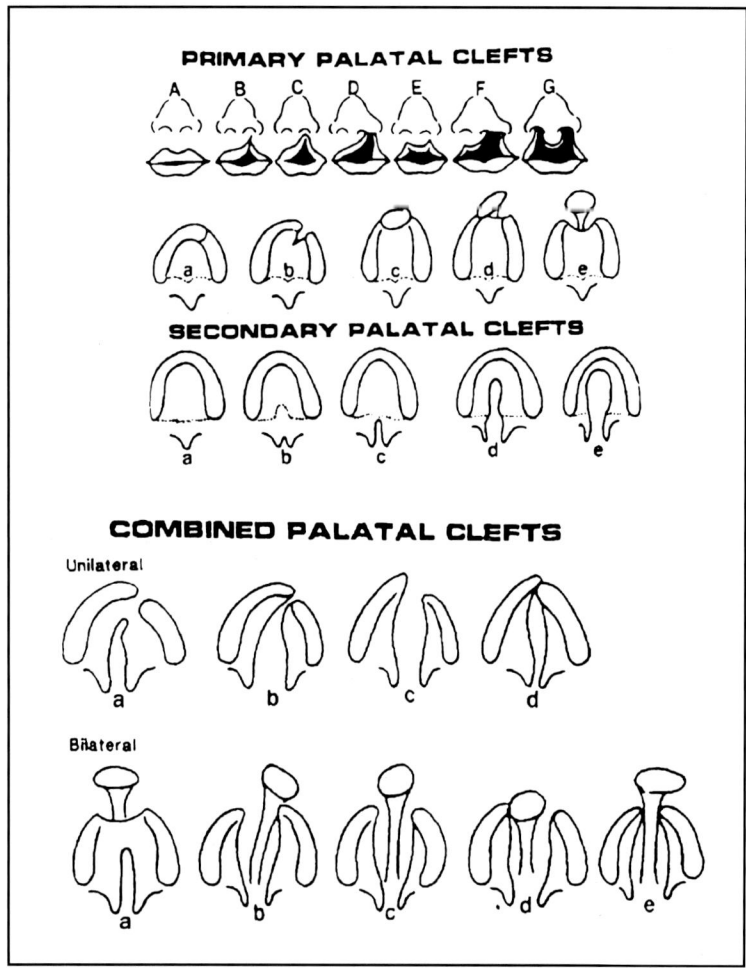

Fig 4–7. Variations in the form, size, and extent of clefting in primary, secondary, and combined palatal clefts. **Primary Palatal Clefts** (with normal hard palate): *Top row:* **a.** Normal lip; **b-g.** The clefts may involve the lip only or may include the alveolus (tooth-bearing area) as well. The cleft can extend toward the nostril on one or both sides. *Middle row*, the cleft of the alveolus can extend to the incisal papilla on one or both sides to any degree. Bilateral alveolar clefts: **c.** incomplete on both sides; **d.** incomplete on one side and complete on the opposite side; **e.** complete on both sides. **Secondary Palatal Clefts: a.** normal palate; **b.** bifid uvula; **c.** cleft of soft palate; **d.** isolated cleft palate (moderate); **e.** isolated cleft palate (extensive). **Combined Palatal Clefts:** Unilateral: **a.** Isolated CP with cleft lip and alveolus; **b.** Incomplete unilateral cleft lip and palate (IUCLP), cleft lip and alveolus are incomplete; **c.** Complete unilateral cleft lip and palate (CUCLP); **d.** Incomplete unilateral cleft lip and palate (IUCLP). *Bilateral:* **a.** Complete bilateral cleft of lip and alveolus; **b.** Bilateral-complete on one side, incomplete on the opposite with complete hard palate cleft; **c.** Complete bilateral cleft of the lip and palate; **d.** Bilateral incomplete alveolar cleft on one side, complete alveolar cleft on opposite side; **e.** Complete bilateral alveolar clefts with both palatal segments attached to the vomer.

palatal process on the opposite side, thus separating the nasal chamber from the oral cavity.

A remarkable range of variation exists in each category. Indeed, various degrees of incompleteness of the cleft in the lip and palate may exist in combinations too numerous to describe conveniently. Moreover, some unilateral clefts of lip and palate exhibit wide separation of the palatal shelves. Others exhibit less separation, and in some cases, the segments actually overlap (Fig 4–8). The palatal segment on the side of the cleft is often tilted medially and upward. The vomer is deviated from the midline at the line of attachment to the palatal process on the noncleft side. This deviation may be so extreme that the vomer assumes a nearly horizontal position at its inferior margin.

The bilateral cleft lip and palate also may be complete or incomplete (Fig 4–9). If incomplete, it may be symmetrical or asymmetrical, depending on the equality of involvement on both sides. In the complete bilateral cleft lip and palate, both nasal chambers are in direct communication with the oral cavity. The palatal processes are divided into two equal parts, and the turbinates are clearly visible within both nasal cavities. The nasal septum forms a midline structure that is firmly attached to the base of the skull, but is fairly mobile in front where it supports the premaxilla and the columella. Cephalometric roentgenograms reveal the existence of a suture line, the premaxillary vomerine suture, between the vomer and the premaxilla. This suture plays an important role in facial growth, and is also a point of flexion for the premaxilla upon the vomer (Fig 4–3, b and c).

The premaxilla may be small or large, symmetrical or asymmetrical. The number of incisor teeth contained in this segment is directly related to its size and shape. When the cleft of the lip is complete on both sides, the premaxilla projects considerably forward from the facial aspect of the maxillae. This anterior protrusion is less evident if the lip is incompletely cleft on one or both sides.

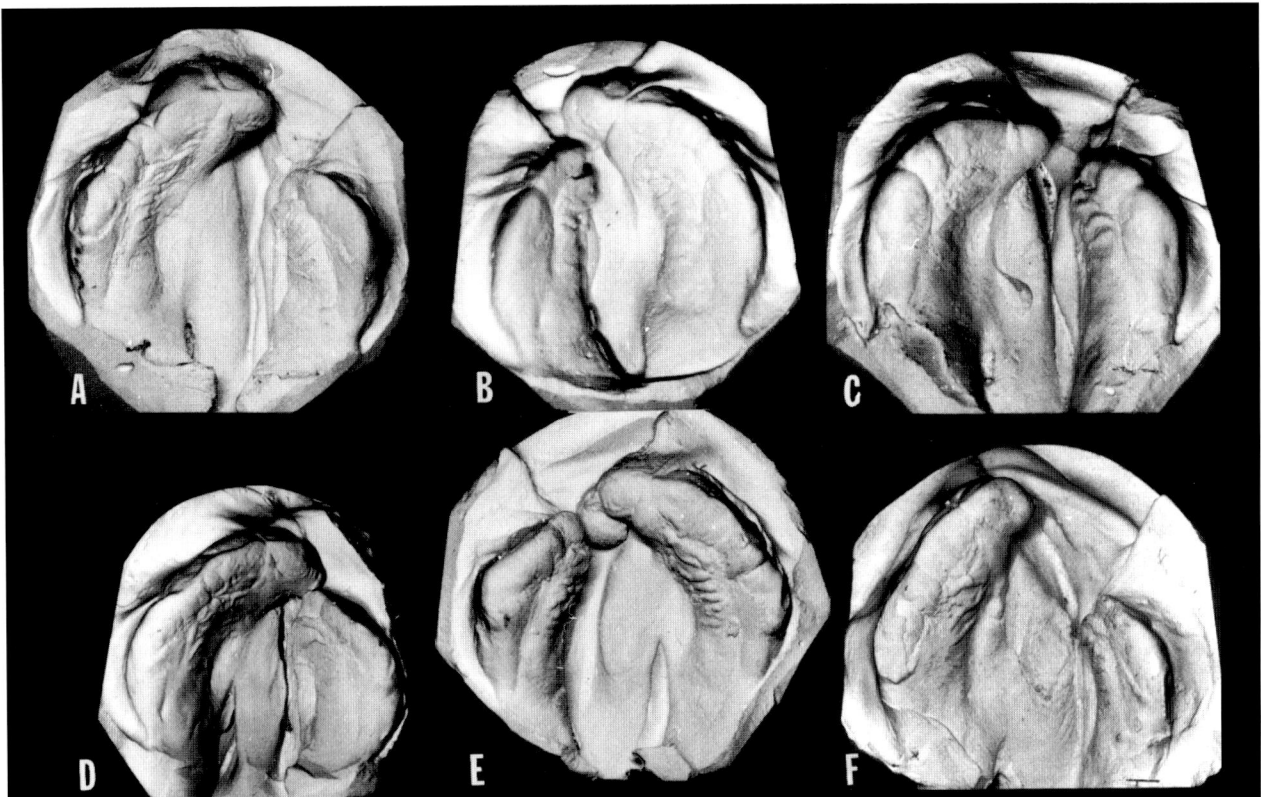

Fig 4–8. Variations in unilateral clefts of the lip and palate at birth. The palatal segments may be complete (**A, C, E** and **F**) or incomplete (**B** and **D**); the cleft segment may be almost of the same length or shorter. The cleft space may be relatively narrow (**B** and **D**) or wide (**A, C, E** and **F**).

3. Isolated Cleft Palate

In this defect, neither the lip nor the alveolar process is involved (Fig 4–10). The cleft may involve only the soft palate or both the soft and hard palates, but never the hard palate alone. This observation is in accordance with the finding that fusion of the hard and soft palates proceeds from front to back (Fig 4–11).

The cleft may extend forward from the uvula to varying degrees. In some cases, the cleft is limited to the uvula or to the uvula and soft palate. In others, it may extend into the hard palate. It is recommended that a digital examination of the posterior edge of the hard palate be performed. A midline notching will reveal the presence of a submucous cleft. The full extent of submucous clefts can be mapped by cephalometric laminagraphy or by transillumination through the nose.

In the extreme form, the cleft palate may extend anteriorly as far as the nasopalatine foramen, the incisal canal. When the cleft involves a considerable portion of the hard palate, the nasal chambers are in direct communication with the oral cavity. In most instances, the nasal septum is not attached to either palatal process throughout the extent of the cleft. However, occasional asymmetries may be noted in which the septum is attached to a portion of the palatal process on one side to a greater extent than to the palatal process on the opposite side.

The outline of the cleft may be wide or narrow, pyriform or V-shaped. Excessively wide dental arches often are associated with wide clefts that extend to a considerable degree into the hard palate. In such instances, the mandibular dental arch may be in complete lingual relation to the maxillary arch so that the cusps of the teeth do not interdigitate in occlusion.

Lateral cephalometric headplates reveal that the dorsum of the tongue, at rest, is elevated and postured within the nasal cavity. During deglutition the thrusting action of the tongue operates to separate the palatal processes. These abnormalities in the posture and movements of the tongue are supported by the observations of speech pathologists. In this type of cleft, the vomer is significantly different in

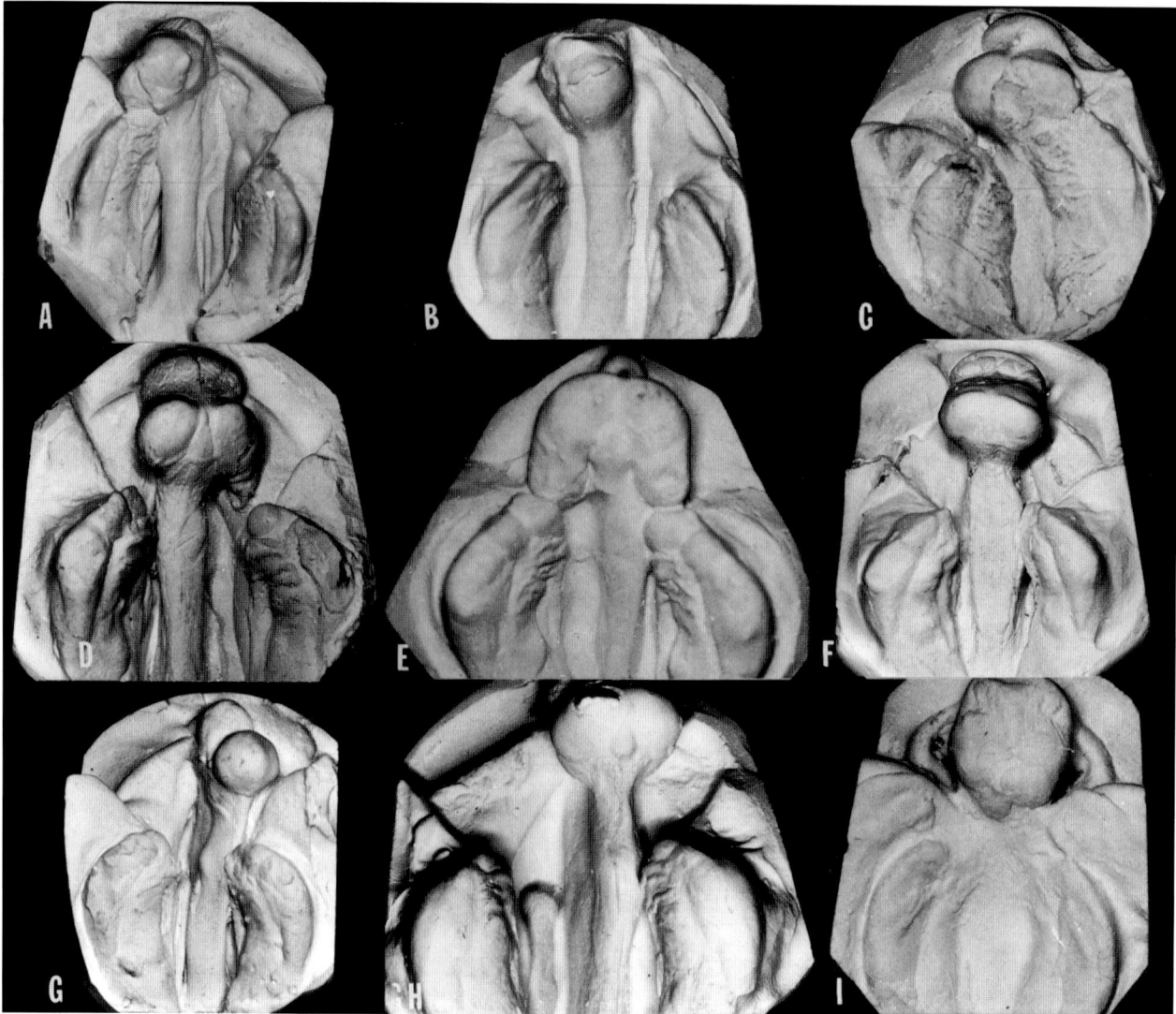

Fig 4–9. Variations in bilateral cleft lip and palate. The size of the premaxilla varies with the number of teeth it contains. Classification is dependent on the completeness of clefting of the lip and alveolus and whether there is a cleft of the hard and soft palate. Yet one or both sides of the hard palate may or may not be attached to the vomer. If it is attached to the vomer, it is classified as being incomplete. Even in complete clefts of the lip and alveolus the extent of premaxillary protrusion will vary. **A**. Incomplete bilateral cleft lip and palate. Complete cleft lip and palate—left side. Incomplete cleft lip and palate—right side. **B**. Complete bilateral cleft lip and palate. Complete cleft palate—both sides. **C**. Incomplete bilateral cleft lip and palate. Incomplete palatal clefts—both sides. **D**. Complete bilateral cleft lip and palate. Incomplete right and complete left palate. **E**. Incomplete bilateral cleft lip and palate. Incomplete left palate and complete right palate. **F**. Complete bilateral cleft of the lip and palate. incomplete right and left palatal segments. **G**. Complete bilateral cleft of lip and palate. Incomplete left palate and complete right palatal segment. **H**. Complete bilateral cleft lip and palate. incomplete left palate and complete right palate. **I**. Incomplete bilateral cleft lip and alveolus. Normal palate.

size and form from that observed in bilateral cleft lip and palate. In both types, the vomer is seen as a midline structure extending downward from the base of the skull. However, in bilateral cleft lip and palate, the inferior border of the vomer is thick and rounded, whereas in this category—cleft palate only—the vomer is thin and knife-edged. Serial observations reveal that the pattern of growth exhibited by the vomer is different in these two types of clefts.

Several other distinguishing characteristics apparent in some of the clefts in this category merit further comment. The high incidence of mandibular

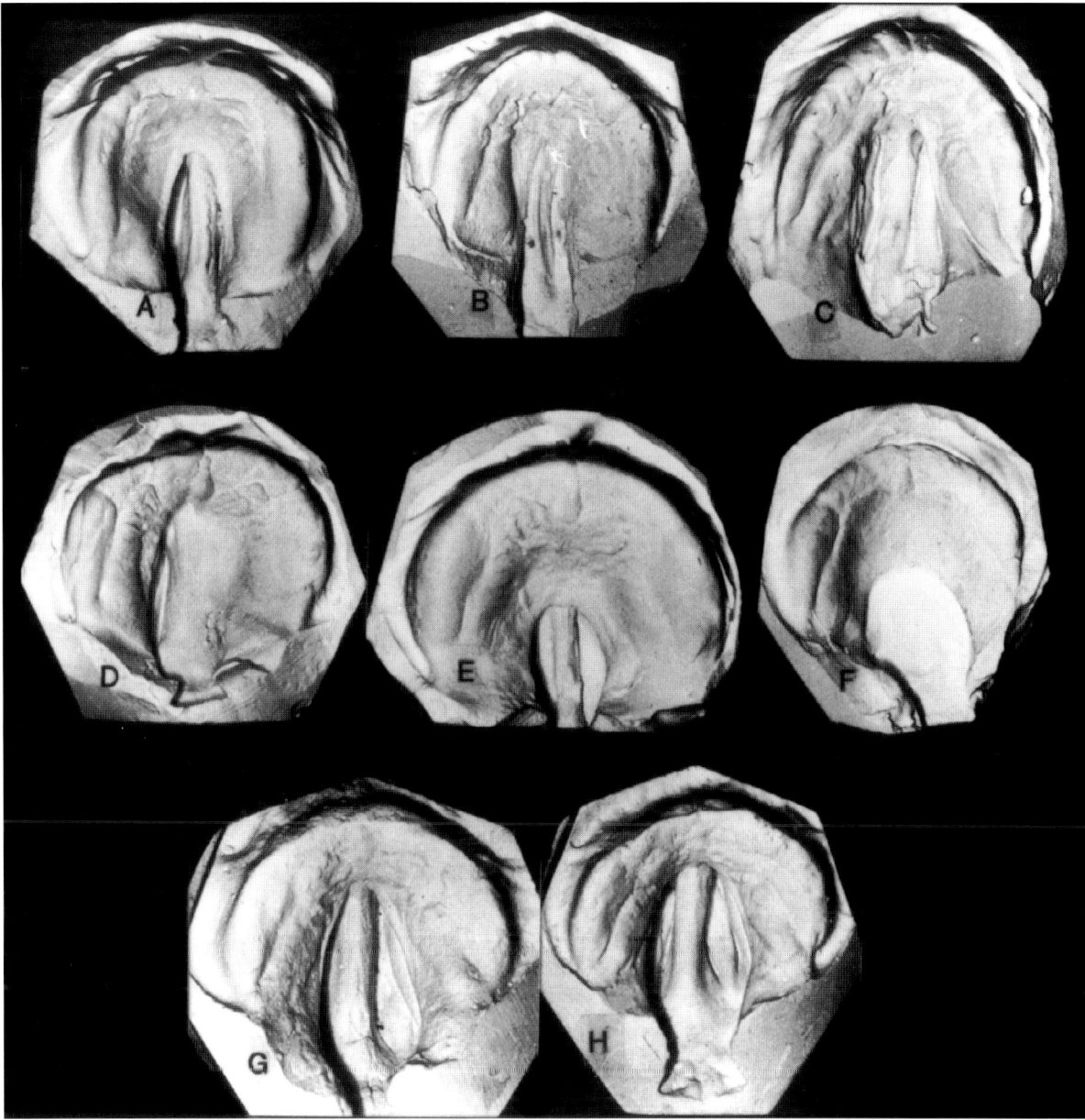

Fig 4–10. Variations in isolated cleft palate. The length and width of the cleft space is highly variable. The cleft extends anteriorly to various distances but not beyond the incisal canal.

micrognathia found in patients with cleft palate gives credence to the theory that during embryonic development the tongue did not sink below the palatal processes, and thereby prevented their fusion in the midline. This raises the question of whether more than one causal mechanism might exist to produce the various kinds of clefts of the lip and palate.

In an extensive study of the mode of inheritance of cleft lip and cleft palate, Fogh-Andersen[6,7] concluded that there are two malformations with no genetic connection. In one group are clefts that involve the lip and occur most frequently in male patients. The other group is limited to clefts of the palate, which are more frequent in female patients.

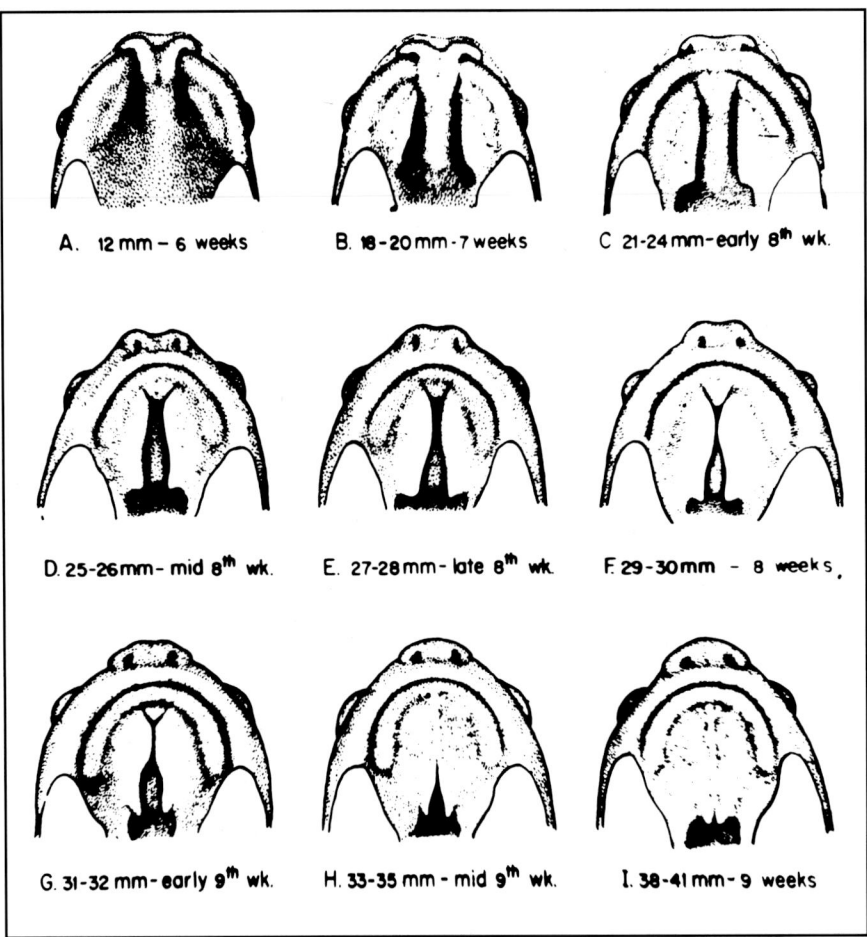

Fig 4–11. Graphic summary of palatal fusion. (Redrawn from illustration in Kraus, Kitamura, and Latham. *Atlas of Developmental Anatomy of the Face*. New York, N.Y.: Hoeber Medical Division of Harper and Row; 1966.) The measurements and estimated ages given should be regarded as averages.

According to Fogh-Andersen, the manner of inheritance differs for the two groups.

4. Submucous Cleft Palate (Fig 4–12)

The classic triad of diagnostic signs is the bifid uvula, partial muscle separation in the midline with an intact mucosal surface, and the midline notch in the posterior edge of the bony palate. Hypernasality may or may not exist. Caution needs to be exerted prior to performing tonsillectomies and adenoidectomies because the velum may be functionally too short without the presence of the adenoid mass.

Berkowitz's cephalometric and nasopharyngoscopic studies have shown wide and unpredictable variability in the pharyngeal skeletal architecture and velar size and shape in submucous cleft palate as well as in all other cleft types (see Chapter 11). In some cases, due to a shallow pharyngeal space with relatively good velar length and mass with good lateral pharyngeal wall movement, no hypernasality existed. However, in most cases, the velum is usually too short, as well as too thin, and it fails to obturate the pharyngeal space properly. The problem appears to be due to an inadequate velum rather than a deficiency in lateral wall movements.

The treatment of choice is a well-positioned and adequately wide superior-based pharyngeal flap. There is no apparent need to combine a palatoplasty with the pharyngeal flap. In patients with recurring infections of the adenoids, it is recommended that the adenoids be removed before the flap is placed. Speech therapy is an integral part of postoperative management.

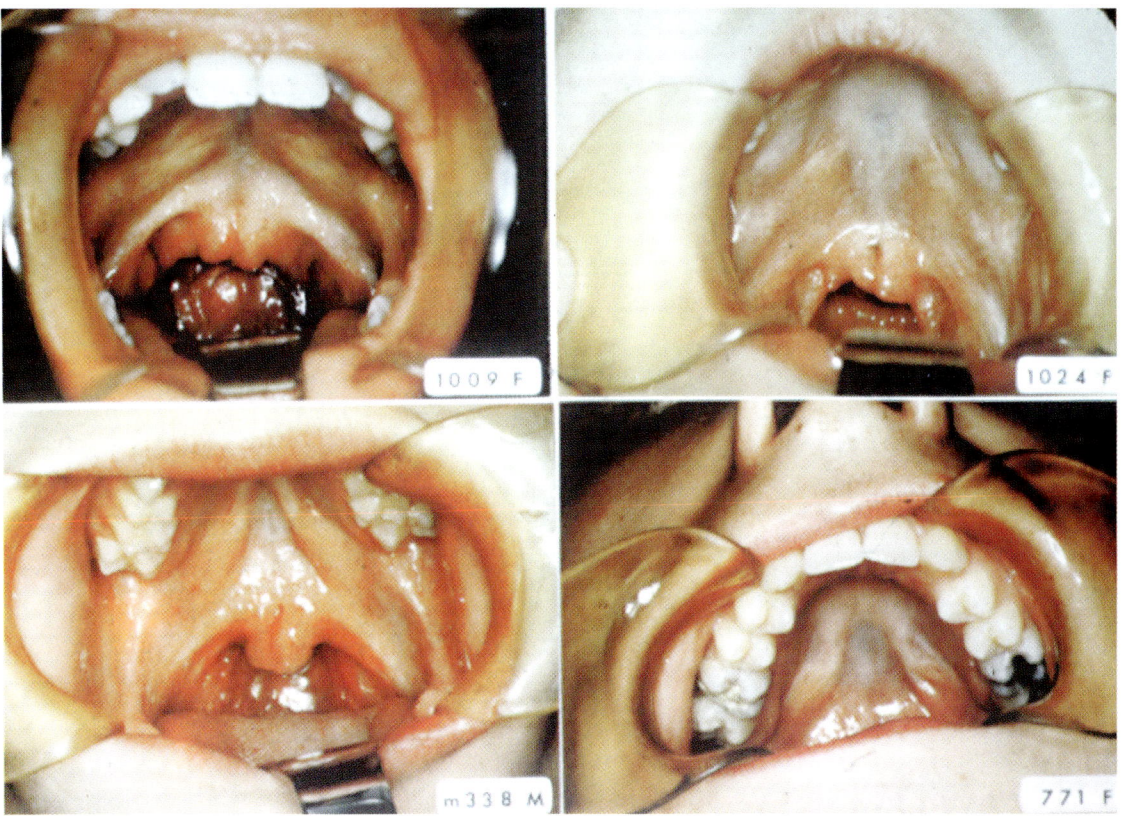

Fig 4–12. Submucous cleft palate. This cleft is characterized by a bifid uvula, lack of muscle continuity across the soft palate, and a pink zone of mucosa (zona pellucida) across the cleft in the hard palate. A palpable notch in the posterior border of the hard palate is always indicative of the presence of a cleft.

CONGENITAL PALATAL INSUFFICIENCY (CPI)

It has been said that cleft palate is a type of defect that can be "seen, felt, and heard." By contrast the defect known as congenital palatal insufficiency (CPI), until recently, has been more readily heard than seen or felt. This anomaly is seldom apparent at birth, and the first awareness of the defect occurs when the child develops the hypernasality characteristic of uncorrected cleft palate speech. The variety of factors producing this kind of speech defect can be examined by roentgenographic and nasopharyngoscopic methods (see Chapter 11).

Normally, during deglutition and during phonation, except for the sounds of "m," "n," and "ng," the soft palate elevates, making contact with the posterior and lateral walls of the pharynx. The complicated synergies that contribute to this multi-dimensional contraction serve to separate the nasopharynx from the oropharynx. If for any reason this velopharyngeal closure cannot be achieved, deglutition is compromised, and in phonation the air stream necessary to create speech is misdirected through the nose. Palatal insufficiency may be caused by the velum being too short and/or by a deficiency in the anteroposterior dimension of the hard palate.

REFERENCES

1. Berkowitz S. *Growth of the Face with Bilateral Cleft Lip from 1 Month to 8 Years of Age*. Chicago: University of Illinois Graduate School; 1959. Thesis.
2. Pruzansky S. Description, classification, and analysis of unoperated clefts of the lip and palate. *Am J Orthod*. 1953;39.590.
3. Pruzansky S. The growth of the premaxillary-vomerine complex in complete bilateral cleft lip and palate. *Tandlaegebladet*. 1971;75:1157–1169.
4. Friede H. Histology of the premaxillary-vomerine suture in bilateral cleft case. *Cleft Palate J*. 1973;10:14–22.

5. Friede H. *Studies on Facial Morphology and Growth in Bilateral Cleft Lip and Palate*. Göteborg, Sweden: University of Göteborg; 1977.
6. Fogh-Andersen P. Inheritance patterns for cleft lip and palate. In: Pruzansky S, ed. *Congenital Anomalies of the Face and Associated Structures*. Springfield, Ill: CC Thomas; 1961:123–133.
7. Fogh-Andersen P. *Inheritance of Harelip and Cleft Palate*. Copenhagen, Denmark: Nyt Nordisk Forlag, Arnold Busck; 1942.

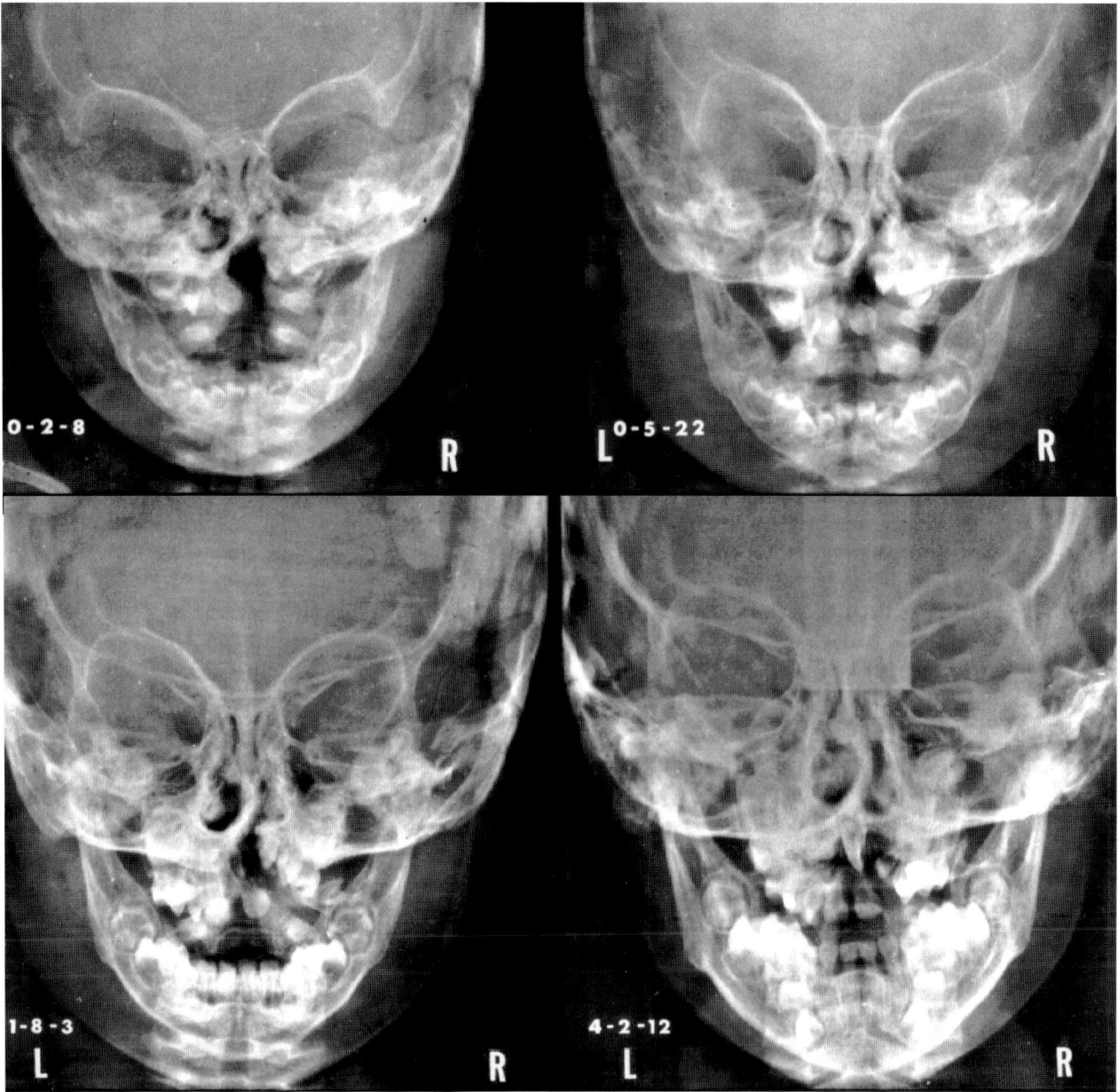

Fig 5–7. Serial frontal cephalometric radiographs illustrating geometric changes to the nasal chamber in a CUCLP from birth to 4 years of age before and after palatal expansion.
Top:
  0-2-8. At birth-a widened nasal chamber is evident.
  0-5-22. After lip surgery the nasal chamber has narrowed.
Bottom:
  1-8-3. The interior turbinate on the cleft side (R) makes contact with the vomer.
  4-2-12. After palatal expansion the nasal width and the septum to inferior turbinate distance has increased.

Because the roof of the mouth is also the floor of the nose, any disarrangement in the architecture of the roof of the mouth is reflected in the nasal chamber. Prior to lip repair, the nasal septum is displaced to the noncleft side. After lip repair with the medial movement of the cleft segment, the septum bows toward the nasal chamber on the cleft side. After palate repair there is continual palatal movement with septal uprighting and decreased septal bowing. The turbinates on the cleft side are flatter, and the buccal teeth on the cleft side may be in crossbite. The nasal chamber on that side is narrowed. (Reprinted from Aduss H, Pruzansky S. Nasal cavity in complete unilateral cleft lip and palate. *Arch Otolaryngol.* 1967;85:53–58)

In conditions of facial clefting, dental development is, except for the third molars, delayed for all teeth, both maxillary and mandibular.[26,27] Asymmetrical development of tooth pairs, with delayed development on the cleft side, was recorded in approximately half of a group of children with congenital lip and/or palate clefts.[28] This supports other observations that eruption is delayed in both dentitions.[29-48]

Zilbermam,[49] from a study on clefts of the lip and alveolar structures, and Mirsa and colleagues,[50] after investigating clefts of the lip and palate, reported that unilateral clefts are more frequent on the left side and are more common in males than in females.

The incidence of dental malocclusion reported in patients with cleft lip and/or palate varied widely in studies by Huddart and Bodenham,[51] Hellquist et al,[52] Dahl et al,[53] Norden and associates,[54] Bergland and Sidhu,[55] Nylen and co-workers,[56] Ranta and colleagues,[57] and Hellquist and Skoog.[58] This may be because the patients had varying types of clefts and their cases were recorded at different ages. Rehrman and co-authors[59] found the incidence of malocclusion in the mixed dentition to be twice that in the deciduous dentition.

In cases of cleft palate only, Ranta and colleagues[60] found only a slight increase in anterior cross-bite at the transition from the deciduous to the mixed dentition. A noticeable increase in the incidence of anterior cross-bite in the mixed dentition, in cases of complete unilateral clefts of the lip and/or palate, was reported by Bergland and Sidhu.[55] This was irrespective of the arch configuration in the deciduous dentition. They also reported that palatal segments stabilized early after lip repair and that further collapse was the exception. However, contrary to the findings just cited, Nylen and coworkers[56] found no increase in the frequency of anterior cross-bite in their mixed-dentition group.

Dahl et al[61] reported the incidence of caries, gingivitis, and dental abnormalities in preschool children with cleft lip and/or palate in Stockholm, Sweden. Oral health was studied in 49 children 5 to 6 years old with clefts of the lip and/or palate (CL/P) and 49 healthy children matched for sex and age. The results showed a statistically significant increase in the prevalence and activity of caries among the CL/P children. The average number of decayed and filled tooth surfaces in the cleft group was 7.0 compared with 3.9 in the control group ($p < 0.05$).

The most evident difference between the two groups was found in the number of decayed proximal surfaces. The mean number of decayed proximal surfaces in the CL/P group was 2.5, compared with 0.9 in the control group ($p < 0.001$). No significant differences were found in the prevalence and activity of caries among children with isolated clefts of the lip or palate.

The children with cleft lips/palates also exhibited a significant increase ($p > 0.01$) in the number of gingival units with gingivitis. Other dental abnormalities included increased enamel hypomineralization ($p < 0.05$), supernumerary teeth (p less than 0.001), unilateral crossbite ($p < 0.001$), and mesial terminal plane ($p < 0.01$). These results clearly show that children with CL/P as a group must be considered to have an increased risk of caries and gum disease, and should therefore have the benefit of additional preventive programs.

THE RELATIONSHIP BETWEEN THE CLEFTING PROCESS AND CONTIGUOUS SKELETAL STRUCTURES

Some studies have indicated that clefting is not an isolated defect but may be a syndrome phenomenon with ramifications in contiguous and often remote structures.

In a study of Danish males, Dahl[62] suggested that the presence of cleft palate, with or without cleft lip, may have ramifications for distant craniofacial structures and their development. Farkas and Lindsay[63] identified consistent variations in facial morphology in the cleft population and concluded that the cleft defect was not an isolated condition. They reported that what might otherwise be considered the normal side of the face in cases of unilateral clefts was not completely normal, and that the anomaly influenced the development of the face equally on both sides.

THE POSITION OF THE CLEFT MAXILLA WITHIN THE CRANIUM AND THE MANDIBLE

Berkowitz[64] undertook a mixed cross-sectional study of CUCLP and CBCLP cases to determine whether the maxillary complex is posteriorly positioned within the face by studying the dental occlusion. None of the cases had presurgical orthopedics, and the hard palate clefts were closed between 18 and 28 months of age using a modified von Langenbeck procedure with a vomer flap. This study was designed to test McNeil's thesis that the palatal segments, being detached from the nasal septum, are not only reduced in mass but also have not been brought forward with the developing nasal septum. This failure would lead to retrusive midface with a Class 3 malocclusion.

Berkowitz[64] found that the occlusal relationships at 6 years of age did show Class 1 and Class 2 occlusions, but none of the cases had a Class 3 occlusion, which would have been present if McNeil's[65,66] hypothesis had been valid. Of the 29 bilateral cases, 5 cases had a crossbite on one side, 1 case had a complete bilateral crossbite, and 6 cases had no crossbites at all. It is quite evident that a buccal crossbite is not, as stated by McNeil, a predictable outcome of the presence of a palatal cleft.

Semb's[67,68] and Ross's[69,70] studies and those already acknowledged elsewhere established that in the cleft population both the maxilla and mandible are repositioned within the face. However, if McNeil's beliefs were accurate, the bilateral cleft palatal segments would have been left behind in their growth, and a greater proportion of the cases would have shown a Class 3 malocclusion on one or both sides.

Chierici and associates[71] and Bishara[72,73] found a relative retrusion of the maxilla and mandible as well as increased steepness of the mandibular plane in various cleft types. Krogman and his colleagues[74] reported significant differences in the cleft population in the size of the cranial base, its configuration, and direction of growth. They concluded that the clefting process has growth and/or development implications for the contiguous cranial base and facial structures as well as for the maxilla.

Bishara[72] reported that the posterior positioning of the maxilla and mandible relative to the anterior cranial base may result from the cleft's influence on contiguous skeletal structures, and that clefting affects maxillary development and facial morphology.

The Cranial Base

Hayashi and colleagues[75] investigated cranial growth of a large sample of subjects from 4 to 18 years of age with complete unilateral clefts. The investigators found that the cranial base angle was flatter, the maxilla was more retruded, and underdevelopment in both the maxilla and the mandible was more pronounced in girls than in boys. They speculated that upper face height in patients of both genders was less than normal as a result of cleft interference with nasal septal and maxillary suture growth and changes in the configuration of the nasal floor. Bishara and co-workers[66] studied untreated adults in India who had clefts of the lip and alveolus only, unilateral cleft lip and palate, and bilateral cleft lip and palate. They observed that the maxilla and cranial base were not different from a matched normal population, but that the relation of the maxilla and mandible to the cranial base varied according to cleft type. Moss,[76,77] Blaine,[78] Dahl,[62] and Krogman et al[6] have stated that the cranial base in cleft palate patients differed in both size and shape from noncleft individuals.

Relationship of the Nasal Cavity to Arch Form
(Fig 5–8)

Aduss and Pruzansky[79] wrote that the anatomic distortions common to all of their patients with clefts included marked deviation of the nasal septum toward the noncleft side; flattening, particularly of the inferior turbinate on the cleft side; and an anterolateral displacement of the noncleft segment, with an outward and lateral rotation of the premaxillary area adjoining the cleft.

These distortions are the result of unbridled septal growth, deviant maxillary growth, and aberrant vectors of muscle pull. Establishing a continuous muscle band across the cleft, by lip repair, can bring the palatal shelves closer together and modify the configuration of the palatal segments, as well as the configuration of the internal nares.

Peyton and Ritchie,[80] measuring the displacement of the soft tissues of the nose in complete unilateral cleft lip and palate, have shown that deviation of the external part of the nose toward the noncleft side extends for the entire length of the nose, with the greatest displacement at the tip. They further demonstrated that growth of the nasal structures is the same in noncleft children and children with complete unilateral cleft and that the early cleft deformity decreases with time. The natural tendency for self-correction of the septal deviation was evident in the continual uprighting and medial movement of the end of the septum observed in all cases.

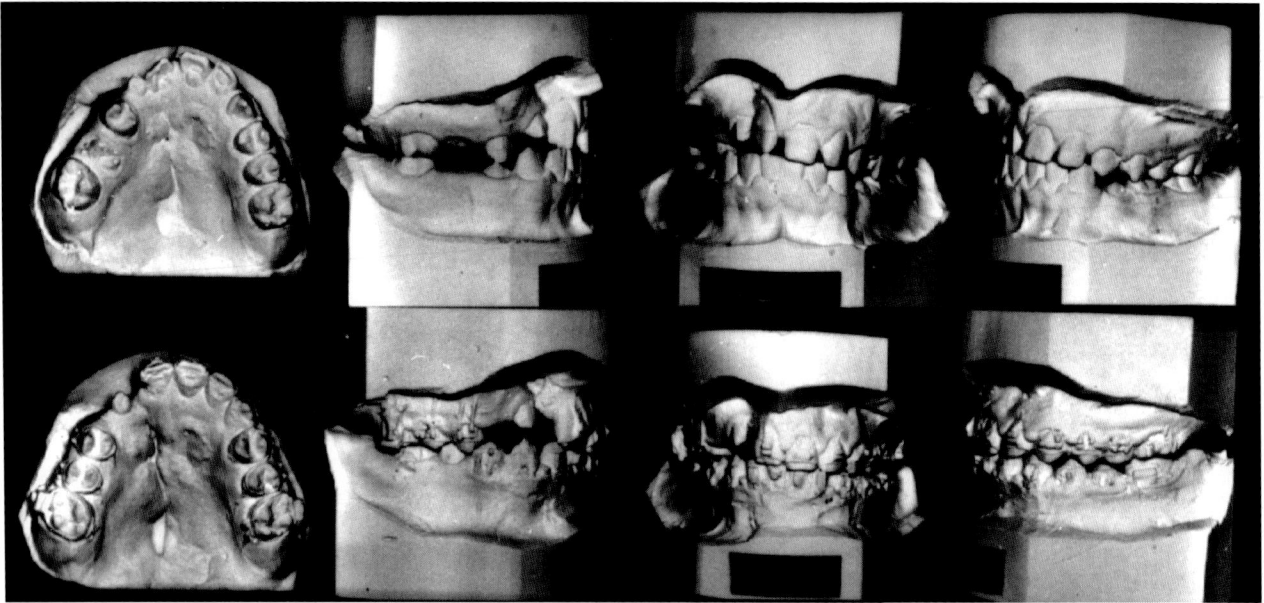

Fig 5–8. Palatal expansion increases nasal width. At 12 years of age buccal crossbite correction of the cleft segment was performed by palatal expansion. Crossbite correction is orthopedic in that the cleft bone segment is moved laterally, widening the nasal chamber on that side. **Top:** Right buccal segment is in crossbite. **Bottom:** After expansion: Palatal fistulae are exposed with the separation of the overlapped palatal segments.

REFERENCES

1. Demarquay JN. Quelques considerations sur le bee-de-lievre. *Gax Med Paris.* 1845;13:52–53.
2. Gorlin RJ, Pindborg JJ. *Syndromes of the Head and Neck.* New York, NY: McGraw-Hill; 1964:117–125.
3. Van der Woude A. Fistula labii inferioris congenita and its association with cleft lip and palate. *Amer J Hum Genet.* 1954;6:244–256.
4. Lannelongue. Observation de division transversale congenitale de la levre inferieure. *Bull Mem Soc Chir, Paris.* 1879;5:642.
5. Radcliff W. Rare congenital malformations of the upper lip. *Brit J Surg.* 1940;28:329–330.
6. Lemke G. Über Fisteln der Lippen inschliesslich der Mundwinkel. *Derm Wchnschr.* 1959;140:1085-1098.
7. Everett FG, Wescott WB. Commissural lip pits. *Oral Surg.* 1961;14:202–209.
8. Witkop CJ, ed. *Genetics and Dental Health.* New York, NY: McGraw-Hill, 1964:44.
9. Witkop CJ Jr, Barros I. Oral and genetic studies of Chileans 1960. I. Oral anomalies. *Amer J Phys Anthropol.* 1963;21:15–24.
10. Schuermann H, Greither A, Hornstein O. *Krankheiten der Mündschleimhaut und der Lippen.* Müchen: Urban & Schwarzenberg; 1966:23–25.
11. Bernauds. Discussion. *Bull Soc Chir Gaz Hop.* 1861. Cited by Stieda 1906;174.
12. Test AR, Falls HF. Dominant inheritance of cleft lip and palate in five generations. *J Oral Surg.* 1947; 5:292–297.
13. Sorricelli DA, Bell I, Alexander WA. Congenital fistulas of the lower lip. *Oral Surg.* 1966;21:511–516.
14. Baxter II. Congenital fistulas of the lower lip. *Amer J Orthod Oral Surg.* 1939;25:1002–1007.
15. Oberst. Über die angeborenen Unterlippenfisteln. *Beitrage z klin Chir.* 1910;68:795–801.
16. Neuman Z, Shulman J. Congenital sinuses of the lower lip. *Oral Surg.* 1961;14;1415–1420.
17. Gorlin RJ, Psaume J. Orodigitofacial dysostosis: a new syndrome. A study of 22 cases. *J Pediat.* 1962; 61:520–530.
18. Fogh-Andersen P. Inheritance patterns for cleft lip and palate. In: Pruzansky S, ed. *Congenital Anomalies of the Face and Associated Structures.* Springfield, Ill: CC Thomas; 1961;123–133.
19. Fogh-Andersen P. *Inheritance of Harelip and Cleft Palate.* Nyt Copenhagen, Denmark: Nordisk Forlag, Arnold Busck; 1942.
20. Cervenka J, Gorlin RJ, Anderson VE. The syndrome of pits of the lower lip and cleft lip and or palate, genetic considerations. *Amer J Hum Gen.* 1967;19:416–430.
21. Bailit HL, Doykos JD III, Swanson LT. Dental development in children with cleft palates. *J Dent Res.* 1968;47:664.
22. Bailit HL, Niswander JD, Maclean C. The relationship among several prenatal factors and variation in the

permanent dentition in Japanese children. *Growth.* 1968; 32:331–345.
23. Bailit HL, Sung B. Maternal effects on the developing dentition. *Arch Oral Biol.* 1968;13:155–161.
24. Bohn A. Dental anomalies in hare lip and cleft palate. *Acta Odontol Scand.* 1963;21(suppl):38.
25. Brook AH. A unifying aetiological explanation for anomalies of human tooth number and size. *Arch Oral Biol.* 1984;29:373–378.
26. Garn SM, Lewis AB, Polacheck DL. Variability of tooth formation. *J Dent Res.* 1959;38:135–148.
27. Brabant H. Comparison of the characteristcs and anomalies of the deciduous and permanent dentition. *J Dent Res.* 1967;46:897–902.
28. Garn SM, Lewis AB, Blizzard RM. Endocrine factors in dental development. *J Dent Res.* 1965;44(suppl to no. 1): 243–258.
29. Garn SM, Lewis AB, Polacheck DL. Interrelations in dental development. I. Interrelationships within the dentition. *J Dent Res.* 1960;39:1049–1055.
30. Garn SM, Burdi AR, Nagy JM. Distance gradient in prenatal dental development. *J Dent Res* I. 1971;40:785.
31. Ranta R. The development of the permanent teeth in children with complete cleft and palate. *Proc Finn Den Soc.* 1972;68(suppl.3).
32. Ranta R. Asymmetric tooth formation in a permanent dentition of cleft-affected children: an orthopantomographic study. *Scand J Plast Reconstr Surg.* 1973;7:59–63.
33. Ranta R. Development of asymmetric tooth pairs in the permanent dentition of cleft-affected children. *Proc Finn Dent Soc.* 1973;69:71–75.
34. Garn SM, Cole PE, Wainright RL. Dimensional communalities of the deciduous teeth. *J Dent Res.* 1977; 56:1208.
35. Ranta R. Eruption of the premolars and canines and factors affecting it in unilateral cleft lip and palate cases: an orthopantomographic study. *Suom Hammaslaak Toim.* 1971;67:350–355.
36. Fanning EA. A longitudinal study of tooth formation and root resorption. *NZ Dent J.* 1961;57:202–217.
37. Garn SM, Cole PE, Wainright RL. Dimensional correspondences between deciduous and permanent teeth. *J Dent Res.* 1977;56:1214.
38. Dixon DA. Defects of structure and formation of teeth in persons with cleft palate and the effect of reparative surgery on the dental tissues. *Oral Surg.* 1968; 25:435–446.
39. Falkner F. Deciduous tooth eruption. *Arch Dis Child.* 1957;32:386–391.
40. Delgado H, Habicht J-P, Yarbrough C, et al. Nutritional status and the timing of deciduous tooth eruption. *Am J Clin Nutr.* 1975;28:216–224.
41. Demirjian A. Dentition. In: Falkner F, Tanner JM, eds. *Human Growth—A Comprehensive Treatise.* vol 2, 2nd ed. New York, NY: Plenum Press; 1986:269–298.
42. Fishman LS. Factors related to tooth number, eruption time, and tooth position in cleft palate individuals. *J Dent Child.* 1970;37:31–34.
43. Foster TD, Lavelle CLB. The size of the dentition in complete cleft lip and palate. *Cleft Palate J.* 1971; 8:177–184.
44. Galili G, Rosenzweig KA, Klein H. Eruption of primary teeth and general pathologic conditions. *J Dent Child.* 1969;36:51–54.
45. Haring FN. Dental development in cleft and non-cleft subjects. *Angle Orthod.* 1976;46:47–50.
46. Hatton ME. A measure of the effects of heredity and environment on eruption on the deciduous teeth. *J Dent Res.* 1955;34:397–401.
47. Haavikko K. Development of the dentition. In Thilander B, Ronning O, eds. *Introduction to Orthodontics.* 5th ed. Stockholm, Sweden: Tandlakarforetaget; 1985: 45–62.
48. Haataja J, Rintala A, Ranta R. On asymmetric development of the first and second permanent molars in children with craniofacial anomalies. An orthopantomographic study. *Proc Finn Dent Soc.* 1972;68:15–19.
49. Zilberman Y. Observations on the dentition and face in clefts of the alveolar process. *Cleft Palate J.* 1973; 10:230–238.
50. Mirsa FM, Ray RK, Kapoor DN. Dental abnormalities in cases of cleft lip and palate. *J Indiana Dent Assoc.* 1972;44:1–9.
51. Huddart AG, Bodenham RS. The evaluation of arch form and occlusion in unilateral cleft palate subjects. *Cleft Palate J.* 1972;9:194–209.
52. Hellquist R, Linder-Aronson S, Norling M, Ponten B, Stenberg T. Dental abnormalities in patients with alveolar clefts, operated upon with or without primary periosteoplasty. *Eur J Orthod.* 1979;1:169–180.
53. Dahl E, Hanusardottir B, Bergland O. A comparison of occlusions in two groups of children whose clefts were repaired by three different surgical procedures. *Cleft Palate J.* 1981;18:122–127.
54. Norden E, Aronson SL, Stenberg T. The deciduous dentition after only primary surgical operations for clefts of the lip, jaw and palate. *Am J Orthod.* 1973;63:229–236.
55. Bergland O, Sidhu SS. Occlusal changes from the deciduous to the early mixed dentition in unilateral complete clefts. *Cleft Palate J.* 1974;11:317–326.
56. Nylen B, Korlor B, Arnander C, Leandersson R, Barr B, Nordin KK. Primary, early bone grafting in complete clefts of the lip and palate. *Scand J Plast Reconstr Surg.* 1974;8:79–87.
57. Ranta R, Oikari T, Haataja J. Prevalence of crossbite in deciduous and mixed dentition in Finnish children with operated cleft palate. *Proc Finn Dent Soc.* 1974; 70:20–24.
58. Hellquist R, Skoog T. The influence of primary periosteoplasty on maxillary growth and deciduous occlusion in cases of complete unilateral cleft lip and palate: a longitudinal study from infancy to the age of 5 yrs. *Scand J Plast Reconstr Surg.* 1976;10:197–208.
59. Rehrman A, Koberg W, Koch H. Die Auswirkungen der Osteoplastik auf das Wachstum des Oberkiefers-Erhebungen der Ergebnisse mit Hilfe der Elektronischen

Datenverarbeitung Fortschr, *Kiefer Gesichtschir*. 1973; 16/17:102–108.
60. Ranta R, Oikari T, Rintala A, Haataja J. Effect of the periosteal flap technique on cleft width and the formation of alveolar ridge in relation to the bite level in surgery for cleft lip and palate. *Scand J Plast Reconstr Surg*. 1974;8:62–66.
61. Dahl G, Ussisoo-Joandi R, Ideberg M, Modeer T. Caries, gingivitis, and dental abnormalties in preschool children with cleft lip and/or palate. *Cleft Palate J*. 1989;26: 238–238.
62. Dahl E. Craniofacial morphology in congenital clefts of the lip and palate—An x-ray cephalometric study of young adult males. *Acta Odontol Scand*. 1970;28(suppl):57.
63. Farkas LG, Lindsay WK. Morphology of adult face after repair of isolated cleft palate in childhood. *Cleft Palate J*. 1972;9:132–142.
64. Berkowitz S. Timing cleft palate closure—Age should not be the sole determinant. *J Craniofac Gen and Devel Biol*. 1985;1(suppl):69–83.
65. McNeil CK. Orthodontic procedures in the treatment of congenital cleft palate. *Dent Rec*. 1950;70:126–132.
66. McNeil CK. *Oral and Facial Deformity*. London, England: Sir Isaac Pitman and Sons; 1954.
67. Semb G. A study of facial growh in patients with unilateral cleft lip and palate treated by the Oslo CLP team. *Cleft Palate Craniofac J*. 1991:28:1–47.
68. Semb G. A study of facial growth in patients with bilateral cleft lip and palate treated by the Oslo team. *Cleft Palate Craniofac J*. 1991; 28:22–39.
69. Ross RB. Treatment variables affecting facial growth in complete unilateral cleft lip and palate. Parts I, V, VII. *Cleft Palate J*. 1987;24:5.
70. Ross RB. Treatment variables affecting facial growth in complete unilateral cleft lip and palate. Part VII: An overview of treatment and facial growth. *Cleft Palate J*. 1987;24:71–77.
71. Chierice G, Harvold EP, Vargevik K. Morphogenetic experiments in cleft palate: Mandibular response. *Cleft Palate J*. 1973;10:51–61.
72. Bishara SE, Iversen WW. Cephalometric comparisons on the cranial base and face in persons with isolated clefts of the palate. *Cleft Palate J*. 1974;11:162–175.
73. Bishara SE, de Arrendondo RSM, Vales HP, Jakobsen JR. Dentofacial relationships in persons with unoperated clefts: comparisons between three cleft types. *Am J Orthod*. 1985;88:481–507.
74. Krogman WM, Mazaheri M, Harding RL, et al. A longitudinal study of the craniofacial growth pattern in children with clefts as compared to normal birth to six years. *Cleft Palate J*. 1975;12:59–84.
75. Hayashi Il, Sakuda M, Takimoto K, Miyazaki T. Craniofacial growth in complete unilateral cleft lip and palate: a roentgenocephalmetric study. *Cleft Palate J*. 1976;13:215–237.
76. Moss ML. The primary role of functional matrices in facial growth. *Am J Orthod*. 1969;55:566.
77. Moss ML, Bromberg BE, Song IC, Eisenmann G. The passive role of nasal septal cartilage in midfacial growth. *Plast Reconstr Surg*. 1968;41:536–542.
78. Blaine HL. Differential analysis of cleft palate anomalies. *J Dent Res*. 1969;48:1042–1048.
79. Aduss H, Pruzansky S. The nasal cavity in complete unilateral cleft lip and palate. *Arch Otolaryngol*. 1967;85:53–61.
80. Peyton WT, Ritchie HP. Quantitative studies on congenital clefts of the lip. *Arch Surg*. 1936;33:1046–1053.

The Neonatal Cleft Palate

PALATAL EMBRYOPATHOLOGY

Studies of unoperated clefts have produced conflicting interpretations regarding deficiency in mass and/or displacement of the palatal segments in space. Information relating to the complexities of embryonic facial development is fundamental to an understanding of the growth potential of the primary and secondary palate. Studies (Slavkin,[1] Ross and Johnston[2]) have shown that the facial mesenchyme, which gives rise to the skeletal and connective tissues, originates from neural crest cells and undergoes extensive migration and interaction (Fig 6–1, 6–2, 6–3).

Coalescence of the facial processes results in the formation of the primary palate, which constitutes the initial separation between the oral and nasal cavities and eventually gives rise to portions of the upper lip and anterior maxilla. The exact mechanism of primary palate formation is not clear. However, most clefts of the primary palate appear to result from variable degrees of mesenchymal deficiency in the facial processes.

The suspected causes of clefts of the secondary palate are also varied. Slavkin[1] reports several possible mechanisms:

Tongue Resistance: The tongue, arched up between the shelves, delays palatal shelf movement.

Decreased Shelf Forces: Although there are no examples of mutant genes that can cause this, there are many teratogens for which this mechanism has been invoked.

Failure to Fuse: This possible cause may be associated with delayed shelf reorientation.

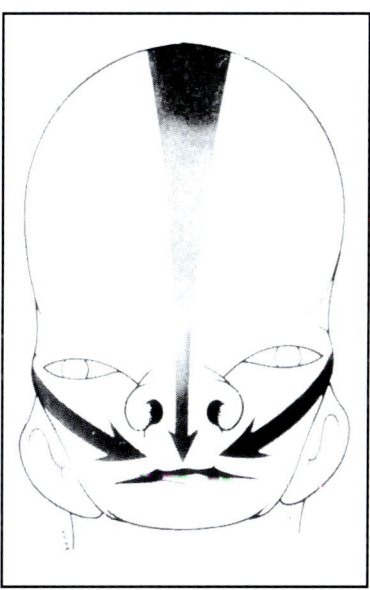

Fig 6–1. The theory of "Mesodermal Migration" suggests that the upper lip and jaws are formed by the penetration of mesoderm between the layers of a pre-existing epithelial membrane formed by the invagination of the oral pit. The mesenchyme may originate from neuroectoderm at the neural crest and migrate from the back of the head by two routes. The first route is over the top of the developing head and down into the central part of the face. The other routes are around the sides of the head into the areas of the developing cheeks. Theory of mesodermal reinforcement of epithelial membranes (Reprinted with permission from Stark, RB In: Converse JM, ed. *Reconstructive Plastic Surgery*, 2nd ed, Vol. 4. Copyright 1977 WB Saunders Co. page 1943.)

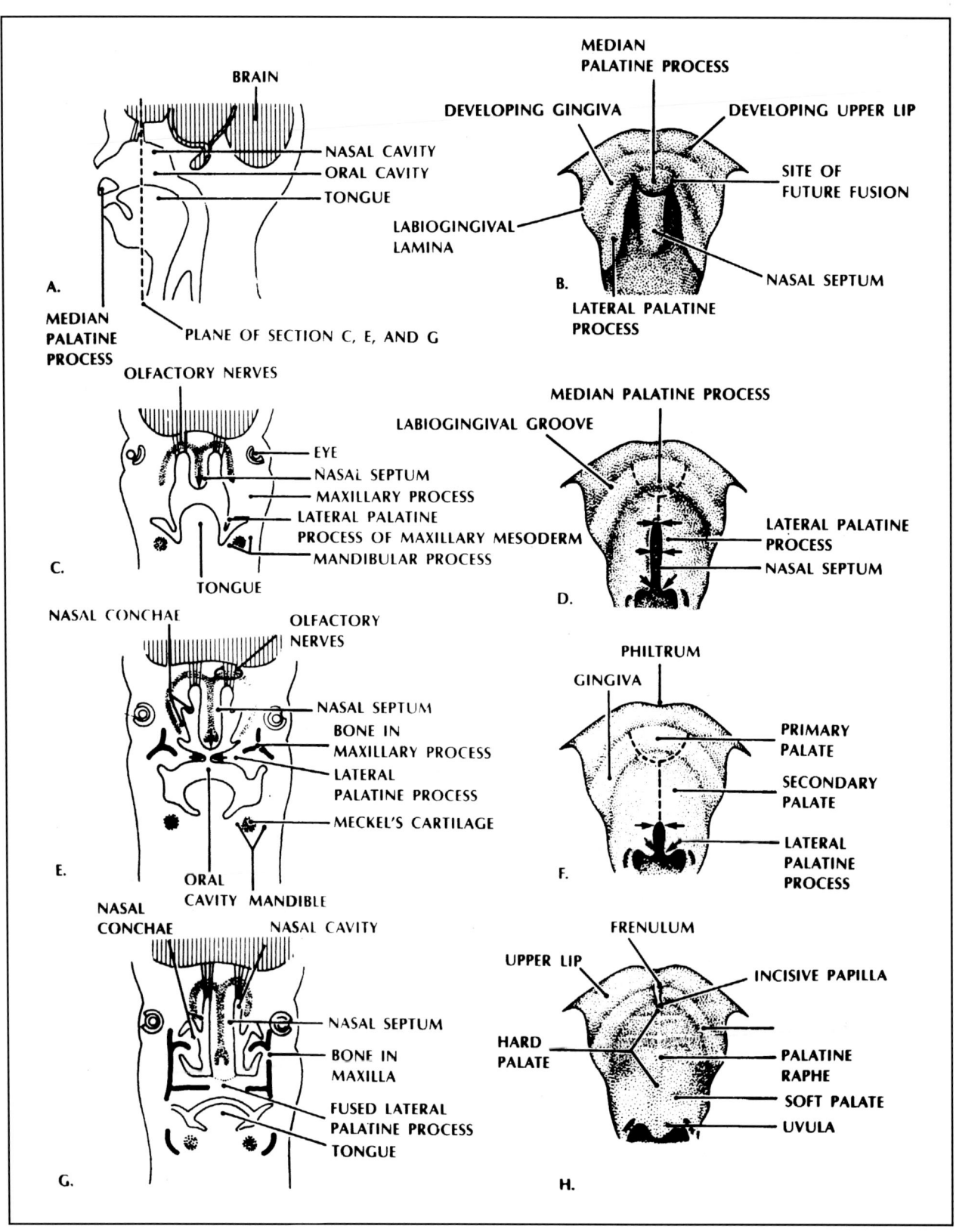

Fig 6-2. Primary and secondary palate morphogenesis. A. Sagittal section of a 6-week embryo showing the primary palate: **B, D, F,** and **H.** Roof of the mouth from 6 to 12 weeks. The broken lines in **D** and **F** demonstrate the sites of fusion of the palatine processes. **C, E,** and **G.** Frontal sections showing fusion of the lateral palatine processes with one another and with the nasal septum. This results in the separation between the oral cavity and the nasal chambers. (Reprinted from Slavkin HC In: *Developmental Craniofacial Biology*; 1979. Copyright 1979 Lea and Febiger.)

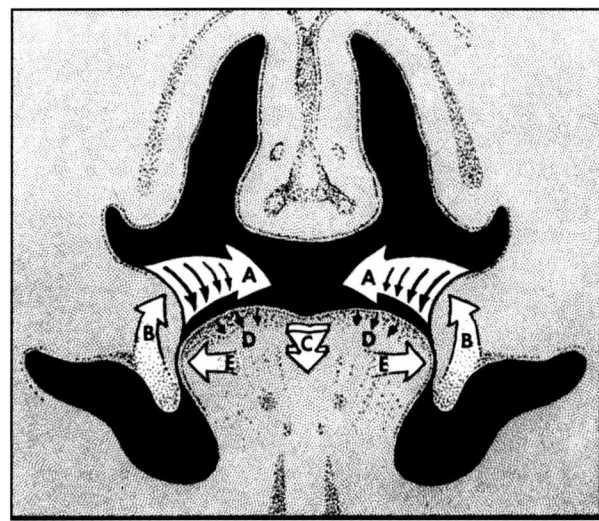

Fig 6–3. **Movements of palatal shelves and tongue during palatal closure.** Tongue moves anteriorly (C) depressing downward (D), and laterally (E), as palatal shelves slide from B to A over the tongue and below the nasal septum. (Reprinted with permission from Avery JK. Prenatal facial growth. In: Moyers, RE ed. *Handbook of Orthodontics*. 3rd. ed. Chicago, Ill: Year Book Medical Publishers; 1973).

Narrow Shelves: This theory suggests that the palatal shelves can move normally enough to reach the horizontal, yet still be too narrow to reach each other. This condition could be explained by a more generalized deficiency of facial mesenchyme reaching the palatal area, making the hard palatal shelves and soft palate inherently smaller.

The causative factor has important clinical implications, because it suggests that, in some unilateral clefts of the lip and palate, the size of the cleft space may be disproportionately very large and more variable in shape than found in other clefts of the secondary palate. Also, the velum in this cleft type may be deficient in muscular tissue and predispose the child to velopharyngeal incompetency. Thus, it would be helpful to be able to identify infants with skeleto-muscular deficiencies at an early age (within the first 2 years of life) in order to customize the cleft closure procedure to enhance proper speech production as well as normal palatal growth and development. Obviously, a child with a cleft due to palatal tissue deficiency will have a different set of problems than the patient with cleft palate with palatal tissue adequacy and a cleft caused by failure of proper shelf force or failure to fuse.

Is the Palate Deficient in Mass and/or Displaced in Space?

Adequacy of Parts

The first question that is apt to occur when the clinical professional sees a cleft in a newborn child is whether or not something is missing. But the real questions are more complex: Does the cleft represent a nonunion of parts that are intrinsically adequate or are the parts inadequate or overgrown? If the individual parts are inadequate in themselves, any attempt to bring the parts into direct apposition by surgical means will produce an inadequate total structure. Excessive developmental growth is sometimes apparent in the alveolar process and may be reflected by the presence of supranumerary teeth.

The maxillary arch in a repaired unilateral cleft of the palate may be asymmetrical in outline and narrow in its transverse diameter. The palatal process on the side of the cleft is observed to be inclined medially and superiorly. This spatial configuration of parts not only reduces the effective width of the total palate but, because the roof of the palate is also the floor of the nose, serves to narrow the nasal chamber and restrict ventilation on that side. Thus, a decrease in the width of the maxillary arch is not necessarily due to a deficiency in the size of the palatal processes, but rather to their spatial inter-relationship.

Distortion of Palatal Parts

Aside from the problem of the intrinsic adequacy of the palatal segments, it is important to know whether the segments are in any way distorted. Muscle tissue develops and begins to contract in the womb prior to the calcification of the hard structures. It is conceivable in complete clefts of the lip and palate that the perverted pull of a divided orbicularis oris or the soft palate muscles may deform the bony and cartilaginous structures during their active formative periods. The aberrant vectors of muscle pull, and possibly the misplaced insertions of muscle fibers, act in utero on bony and cartilaginous structures to modify the palatal segments geometric relationship (Fig 4–2). In addition, the action of the tongue, the orbicularis-buccinator-superior constrictor muscle ring, and the pharyngeal muscles on the unbuttressed bony segments at birth can contribute to spatial derangements. The flattened alar cartilage, devoid of a distinct medial and lateral crus, is an example of such deformation of an anatomic part (Fig 6–4).

Supporting Literature

One of the fundamental controversies in the past centered on whether a deficiency of tissue invariably

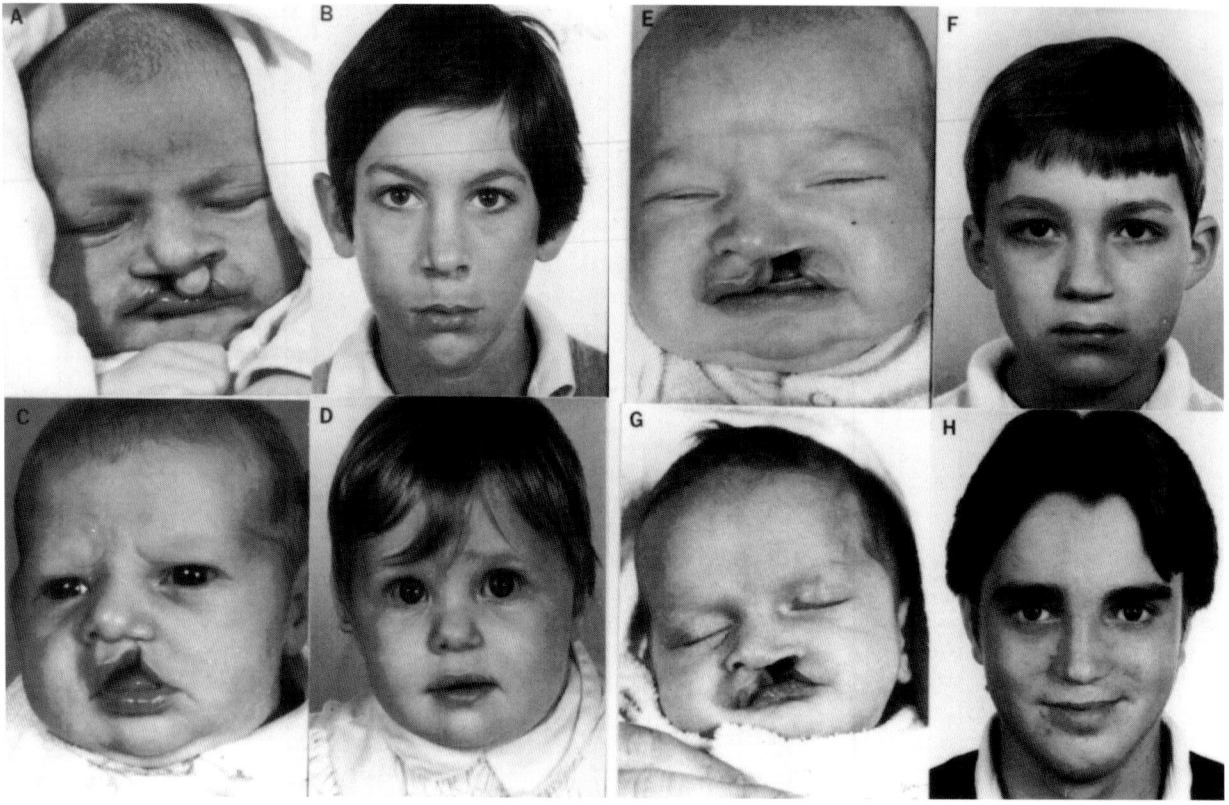

Fig 6–4. Pre- and postsurgical facial pictures. A. and B. Incomplete bilateral cleft of the lip and palate. **C. and D.** Incomplete cleft of the lip. **E. and F.** Complete unilateral cleft lip and palate. **G. and H.** Complete unilateral cleft of the lip and palate.

exists in cleft palate patients. Some researchers expressed the opinion that the cleft itself represents a deficiency of hard palate tissue (Coupe and Subtelny[3]). Others believed that the hard palate shelves bordering a cleft are not deficient in structure but are displaced from the normal position.

Coupe and Subtelny,[3] using cephalometric laminography, solved this controversy by comparing the hard palate dimensions of 127 cleft palate children under 3 years of age, who had not been operated on, with noncleft children of comparable age. Bony palatal shelves were measured to determine the quantity of tissue. Comparisons with measurements obtained from the noncleft children indicated the deficiency or adequacy of hard palate tissues in the cleft palate subjects. Distances between the right and left lateral walls of the nasal cavities of the subjects with clefts were measured to determine whether the maxillary bones bordering the cleft were medially or laterally displaced compared with the noncleft children.

Their measurements revealed that there was a definite tendency toward hard palate tissue deficiency in children with clefts involving the palate, although this did not apply in the cleft cases that involved only the lip and alveolar process. However, the deficiency of hard palate tissue varied considerably among individual patients and according to the type of cleft. Subjects with bilateral clefts of the palate were most likely to have a deficiency of tissue and to show the greatest degree of deficiency, followed by patients with posterior clefts, and then by those with unilateral clefts.

Coupe and Subtelny[3] also found that, in the lateral displacement of the maxillary bones in the oronasal area of all cleft palate types, the greatest displacement, as well as deficiency, was found in patients with bilateral clefts. Although more deficiency of tissue was found in bilateral clefts than unilateral clefts, a greater displacement of the maxillary bones was found in the subjects with unilateral clefts of the lip and palate. From all indications, therefore, both lateral displacement of the maxillary bones and a deficiency of hard palate tissue can exist in cleft palate subjects; it is not a matter of either deficiency or displacement. Both can be present, although neither may be readily evident (Fig 6–5).

Mars and Houston[3] studied the effects of surgery on facial growth and morphology in Sri Lankan males with unilateral cleft lip and palate who were over 13 years of age. The research was conducted with cephalometry and dental study models. Three separate subgroups were analyzed: those who had totally unrepaired cleft lip and palate; those who received lip repair in infancy but not palatal repair; and those who had lip and palate repair in infancy. For purposes of comparison, a control group was formed made up of 23 healthy Sir Lankan males over 13 years of age and from the same racial background. The results showed that subjects who had had no surgery exhibited a potential for normal maxillary growth. Subjects who had had lip repair in early infancy showed relatively normal maxillary growth, but maxillary hypoplasia was evident in most cases when the palate had been repaired early.

Ross and Coup,[5] Osborne,[6] Blaine,[7] Dahl,[8] Bishara and Iversen,[9] Krogman et al,[10] and Smahel[11] all reported that the cleft maxilla and mandible were positioned more posteriorly within the skull than in normal faces. Huddart's[12] findings indicated that palatal segments were displaced and deficient in palatal tissue in both unilateral and bilateral clefts of the lip and/or palate. Mazaheri and associates,[13] using xerographic techniques to study serial cases of cleft palate only and patients with both cleft lip and palate, demonstrated laterally expanded palatal segments in the latter cases.

From cephalometric observations Momma and colleagues[4] concluded that, in persons with complete clefts, the maxilla was smaller than noncleft palates in all dimensions. However, Bishara,[15,16] in a study of adults with clefts that had not been operated on, found that, although the palates were geometrically displaced, they had developed within normal limits. Peat[5] indicated that the neonatal cleft palate, when it involves the lip, can be displaced either laterally or medially and only rarely is deficient in mass. Wada and Miyazaki[18] agreed. Studying complete unilateral clefts of the lip and/or palate, they found that the neonatal palatal size was within normal limits in all three dimensions.

Ortiz-Monasterio and co-workers[19] demonstrated that adults with complete clefts that had not undergone surgery experienced good facial growth, although the palatal segments were displaced laterally.

Nakamura and co-authors[20] found a significant difference in maxillary and mandibular dimensions corresponding to sex. Berkowitz[21] measured various serial cleft palate casts three-dimensionally using a stereophotogrammetric technique. This study demonstrated that the cleft palate was geometrically distorted in all frames of space and that, in complete clefts of the lip and palate, the lateral segments at birth were laterally displaced.

Changes in the size and position of the mandible indicated an attempt by the body's own forces to achieve favorable dental occlusion. Orthodontic treatment in early mixed dentition enhanced a dentoalveolar compensatory mechanism to alleviate an anteroposterior discrepancy between the maxilla and mandible.

Smahel[11] found that individuals with clefts of the soft palate alone had shorter mandibles than persons with clefts of the hard and soft palate.

EFFECTS OF REVERSING THE FACIAL FORCE DIAGRAM

Lip Surgery or Elastic Traction

The influence of soft-tissue forces on palatal form and growth has been the topic of several studies. Ritsila and co-authors[22] reported that there was "slight shortening" of the maxilla, "marked shortening" of the body of the mandible, and alterations of several mandibular angles after closure of the lip.

As perhaps an interesting footnote (Bardach et al[23]), physical changes to the palate in clefts of the lip and palate in animals are very similar to the corresponding changes that are seen in humans. Bardach et al[23] studied lip pressure changes following lip repair in infants with unilateral clefts of the lip and palate. They confirmed the belief that lip repair significantly increases lip pressure when compared with a noncleft population.

Berkowitz's[24,25] data demonstrated that the force of the united lip against the protruding premaxilla in complete bilateral clefts of the lip and palate (CBCLP) acts first to bring about premaxillary ventroflexion. After 2 to 3 years there is some appearance of midfacial growth retardation to various degrees. There is strong evidence that uniting the lip does not "telescope" the premaxilla into the vomer, whereas mechanical premaxillary retraction "telescopes" the premaxilla in almost all instances (see Chapter 9). In very rare instances it may even cause a vomer fracture.

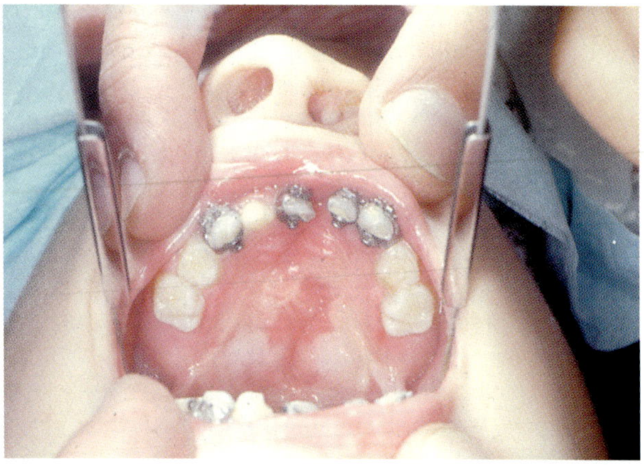

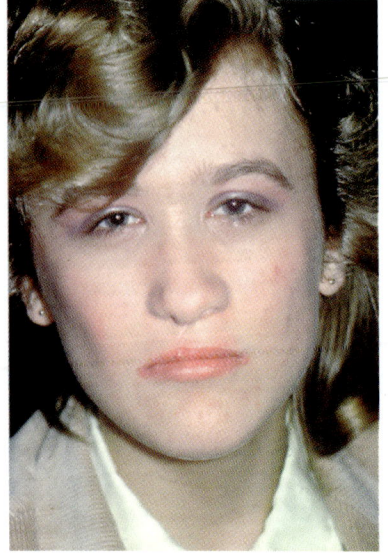

Fig 6–5 a and **b.** Premaxillary agenesis or Binder's syndrome. Before orthodontic treatment: Failure of the premaxilla to develop resulted in the medial-angular movement of both palatal segments closing off the anterior space and placing the cuspids into crossbite. **c.** Intraoral photograph after orthodontic expansion and maxillary protraction forces opened the promaxillary space and brought the maxilla forward placing the dentition into ideal occlusion. **d.** Removable dental prosthesis designed to replace missing teeth and to bumper the upper lip. **e.** Facial photograph wearing the dental prosthesis.

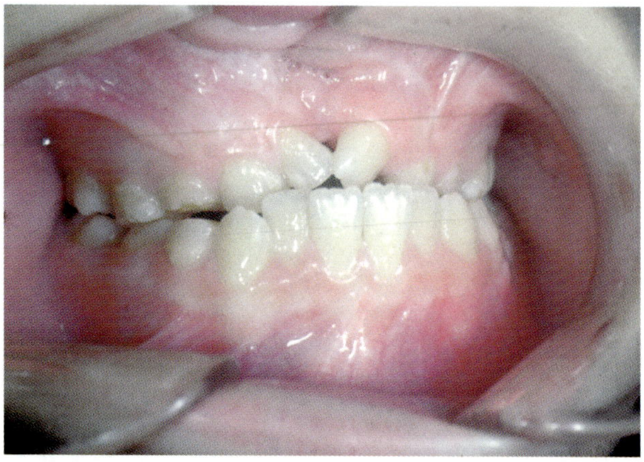

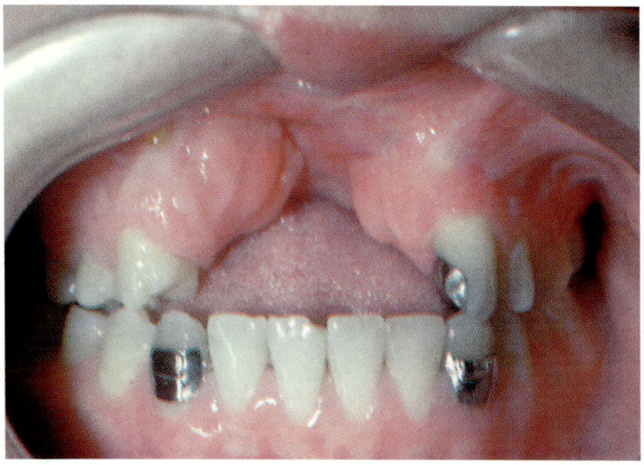

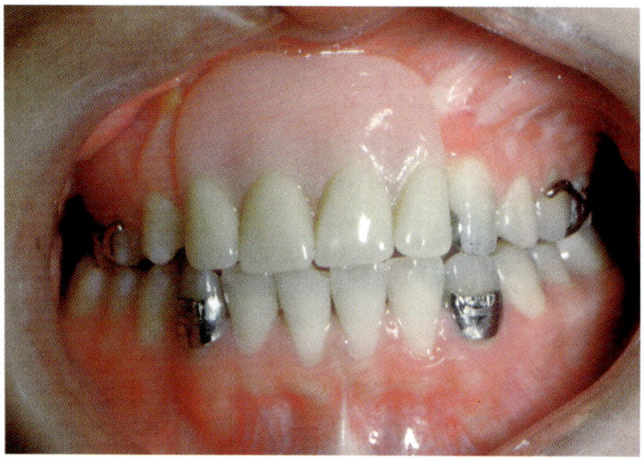

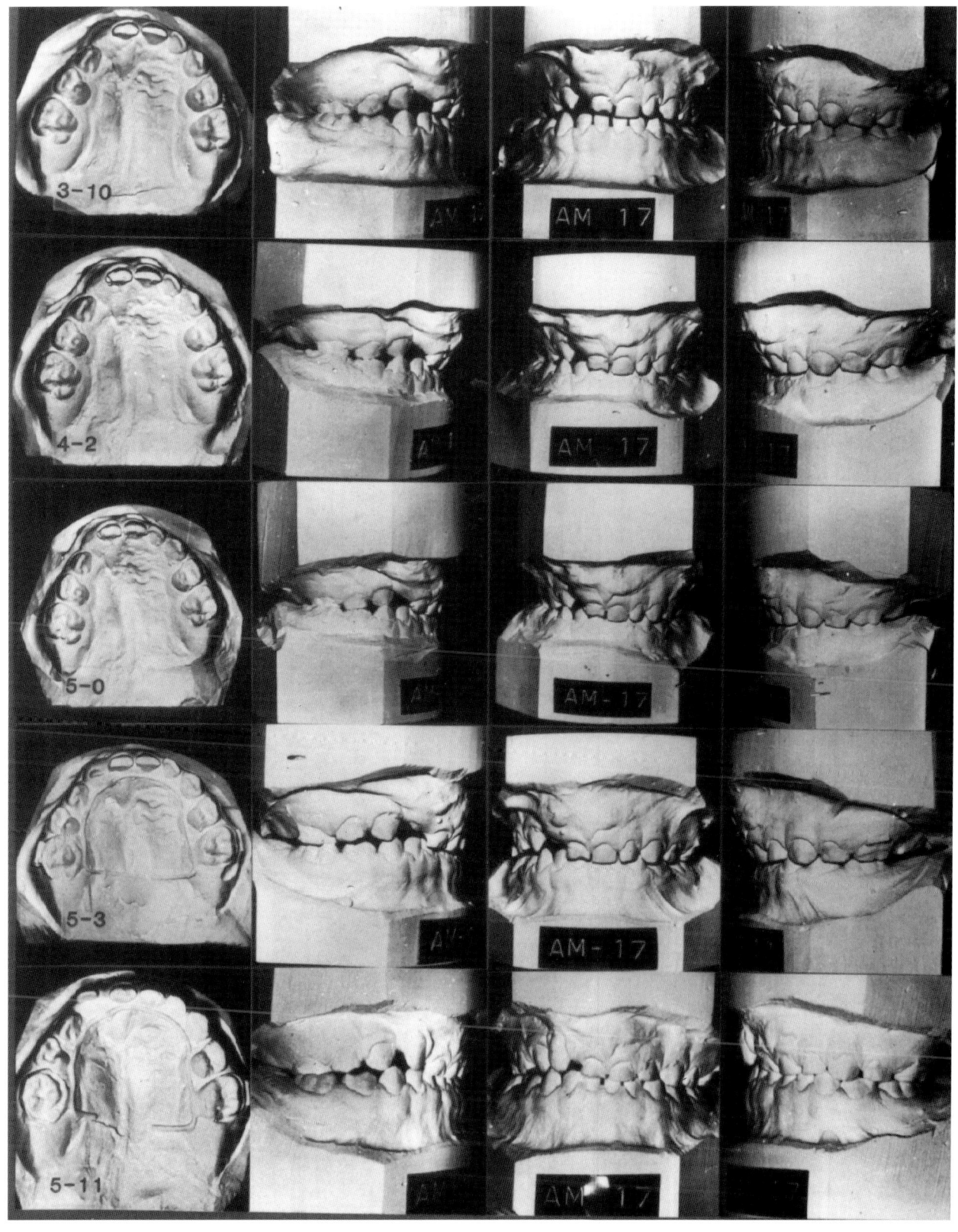

(continued)

Fig 6–9. *(continued)*

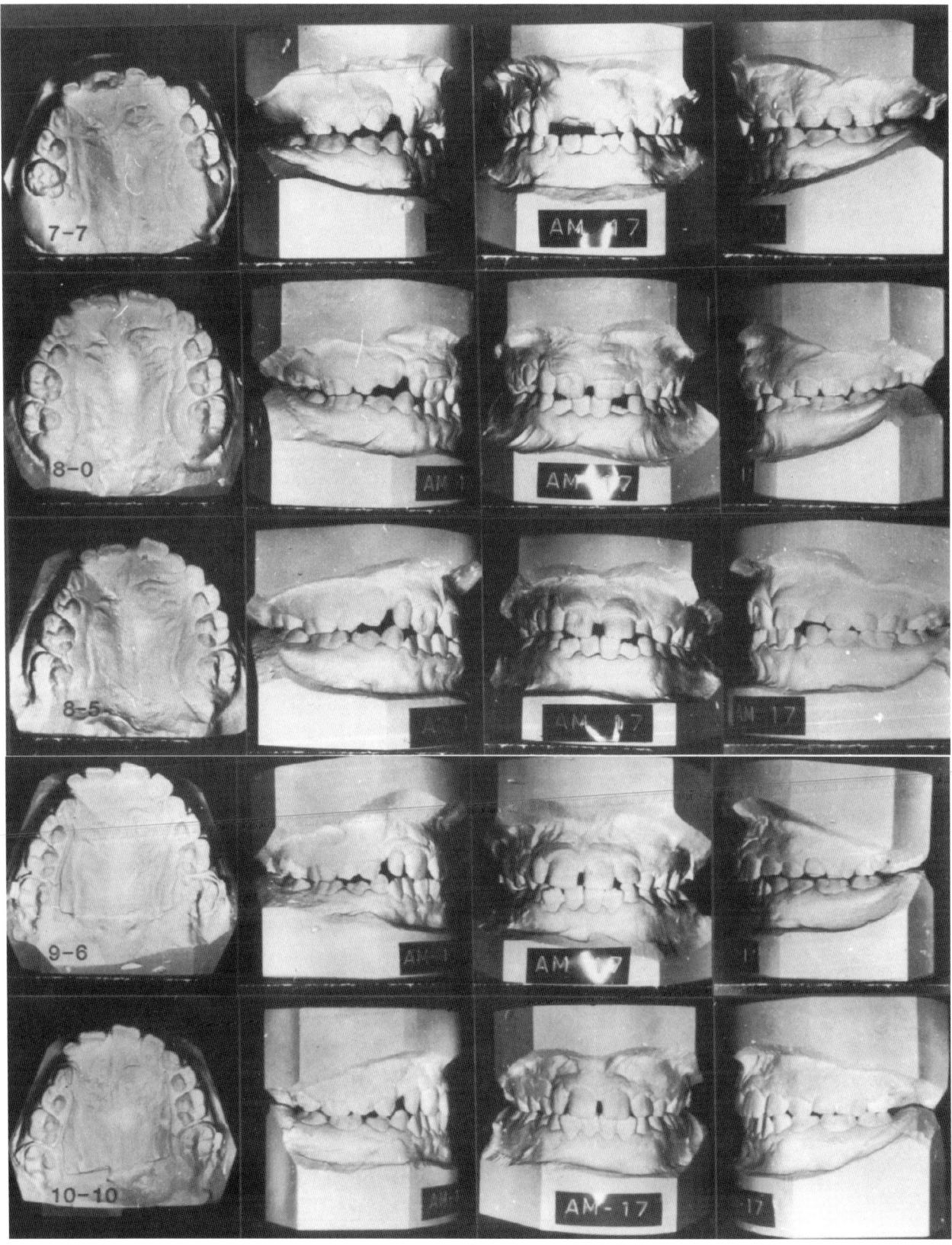

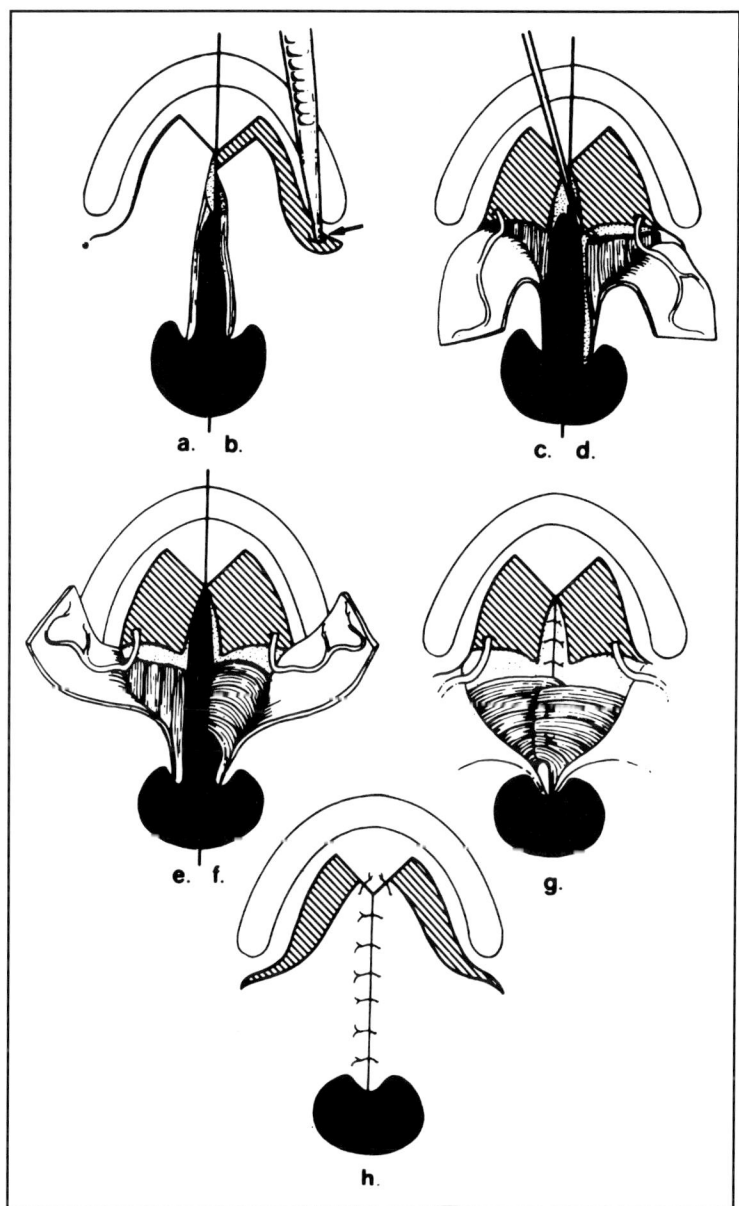

Fig 7–10. The three flap Wardell-Kilner push-back modified after Braithwaite. a. The margins of the soft palate cleft have been pared and the cleft of the hard palate incised along the junction of oral and nasal mucoperiosteum. The lateral incision has been made inside the alveolar ridge from opposite the canine anteriorly to a point just behind the hamulus posteriorly. An oblique incision joins the anterior end of the lateral incision to the cleft margin. **b.** The mucoperiosteal flap has been elevated from the hard palate. **c.** The oral mucoperiosteal flap has been turned back showing the greater palatine vessels passing from the greater palatine foramen to the flap. The mucosa has been elevated from the septum (the vomer) which is attached to the margin of the palate on this side. **d.** The muscles have been detached from the back of the hard palate. The soft palate is falling away from the hard and becoming elongated. This is the "push back." **e.** The muscle has been freed from the overlying mucosa. **f.** The muscle has been freed laterally and has been rotated medially. **g.** The two muscle bundles have been overlapped and sutured under slight tension to construct the muscle sling. The nasal mucosa has been sutured. **h.** Suturing of the oral layer is completed. The tips of the oral mucoperiosteal flaps are sutured to the apex of the anterior flap, indicating the degree of palatal lengthening (Reprinted from Edwards M., Watson ACH. Primary surgery. In: *Advances in the Management of Cleft Palate*. New York, NY: Churchill Livingstone; 1980:151 with permission).

speech development, many others began to think differently and emphasized the need for normal midfacial and palatal development. They recommended that cleft palate closure be postponed until either the deciduous or the permanent dentition had erupted. Advocates of delaying palatal closure were influenced by Graber,[19,20] and also by Slaughter and Brodie,[21] who were disturbed by the results of Brophy's[22] and other procedures in vogue at that time. They wanted to avoid secondary malformations to the palate and severe deformities of the maxilla caused by extensive mucoperiosteal undermining with wide lateral areas of denuded bone which led to severe scarring. Similar malformations were created in animals by Kremenak et al.[23-25]

THE EFFECT OF SURGERY ON MAXILLARY GROWTH

Kremenak and his colleagues[24,26,27] reported a series of follow-up studies on beagles, based on earlier work, showing that surgical denuding of palatal bone adjacent to deciduous teeth resulted in inhibiting maxillary growth. More recent efforts by this group have focused on the contraction phase of early healing of surgical wounds on the canine palate. Olin and associates[28] presented data based on measurements between tattoo points on wound margins on hard palates of young beagles. They noted that major interruptions in the increase of arch width coincided with the period of soft-tissue contraction. This led Olin et al[28] to suggest that the contraction of wounds following surgery could be the first link in a causal chain leading eventually to secondary skeletal deformities.

Kremenak and associates[23] reported related evidence that the contraction seen in palatal mucosa was analogous to that reported in the healing of skin wounds. Transplanting autogenous grafts from other oral mucosa into mucoperiosteal excision wounds of the hard palate resulted in a reduction in contraction and was followed by normal or "supranormal" increases in maxillary arch width. They concluded that more research in this area was warranted.

It is becoming apparent that the factor of contractility in some types of nonmuscular connective tissue cells may be a common denominator for research on surgical wound healing, as well as for research on normal and abnormal growth and function in the craniofacial complex. There is a large body of literature dealing with advances in the understanding of contractile phenomena. Much of it is collected in a bibliographic review by Morris and Kremenak.[29] The report by Madden and associates[30] also provides an excellent overview of this area of inquiry.

Is surgery for the repair of cleft lip and palate to be determined by the age of the patient or by the palate's morphological characteristics and the effects of surgery on the subsequent growth of the face? This was one of the driving questions being asked by surgeons in the 1940s. Slaughter and Brodie[21] and Graber[19,20] deserve historical credit for bringing this issue to the world's attention. Their condemnation of the results of cleft palate surgery, as mentioned, led to a new conservatism and forced a reexamination of surgical practice.

The beginning of serial facial growth studies, Graber's[19,20] cross-sectional study of 60 cases of mixed cleft palates of various types at various ages, had a profound effect on surgical planning. He compared jaw development of 46 operated cases with 14 cases that had no surgery, and found that the unoperated palates resembled normal palates more than they did the operated palates. He noted that the growth of the operated palates was retarded in all three dimensions. It should be understood that it was not unusual in those days to encounter patients with a history of 35 operations. A common operation of the day involved wiring compression of the cleft segments (Brophy[22]). As already noted, this procedure was notorious for its mutilating effects. Dental neglect was common, resulting in rampant caries, and the associated malocclusions were often so severe as to discourage orthodontic treatment.

Graber[19(p405)] concluded that, "to minimize interference with growth centers, it seemed advisable to postpone surgical correction at least until the end of the fourth year of life, when five-sixths of the total maxillary width has been accomplished." As a result, early surgical repair of the palate fell into disfavor, and prosthodontists came to dominate the rehabilitation of cleft palate.

Graber[19(p403)] suggested that the following questions should be asked:

1. How does the pattern of growth and development of a cleft palate individual compare with that of a noncleft person?
2. What is the effect of early and repeated surgical intervention on this pattern?
3. What happens to a tissue that has been manipulated and traumatized?
4. Does increased tension of soft tissue stimulate or depress cellular proliferation?
5. What is the growth potential of fibrous bands of scar tissue?

6. Can cicatricial (scar) bands influence the normal growth and development of the surrounding soft tissue structures and the bony skeleton?
7. How do cleft palate individuals with surgically closed clefts compare with those who have had no surgery?

Pruzansky, in 1969 at an international symposium on cleft palate held at Northwestern University Dental School, recognized the important contributions of Graber[19,20] and Slaughter and Brodie[21] for their condemnation of the deleterious effects of traumatic surgery on midfacial growth (Cole[31]) and recommended that surgery on the palate should be delayed until 5 or 6 years of age to minimize facial growth malformations. In questioning the validity of their conclusion on the timing of surgery, Pruzansky goes one step further, citing findings from his longitudinal palatal and facial growth studies (Cole[31(pp165,166)]).

> I saw patients whose palates had been repaired early and yet their faces developed well and their speech was free of the stigma associated with the stereotype. On the other hand, some children, for whom palatal surgery had been delayed, did not do well at all. Their midface did not develop normally and their speech was hypernasal and unintelligible. I saw all kinds of permutations and combinations.

He went on to explain that the faultless error was in not recognizing the heterogeneity that exists within a single cleft type. Pruzansky stressed that morphological and physiological variants in the individual child should provide the rational basis for therapeutic design, not age alone.[32–34]

In the early 1920s the cleft space was considered a "hole" that needed immediate closing either by orthopedics and surgery. Early surgical closure in the first 6 months led to disastrous results. As a reaction the timing pendulum was to swing to the opposite extreme to favor surgical closure at 5 to 9 years of age, when the hard palate's growth was 90% completed. To satisfy the speech-language pathologists obturators were worn until the cleft was closed. Based on theoretical and anecdotal evidence, many surgeons chose 18 to 24 months for closure without the use of obturators as a compromise between speech and growth requirements.

Many variations in surgical procedures arose. Gillies and Fry[35] and Slaughter and Pruzansky[36] believed it was important to delay hard palate closure to 2 or 3 years of age and chose to close the lip and soft palate first to aid speech development (Fig 7–11). Others (e.g., Robertson and Jolleys[37] and Hotz[38] and their associates) delayed midpalatal closure to the deciduous dentition, and Schweckendick[39] went to the extreme and delayed closure into adolescence, favoring the need to maximize palatal growth above all else. The Slaughter and Pruzansky[36] method was associated with good speech development; the Schweckendeck delayed palatal closure procedure, although producing satisfactory midfacial growth, left the patients with very poor speech.

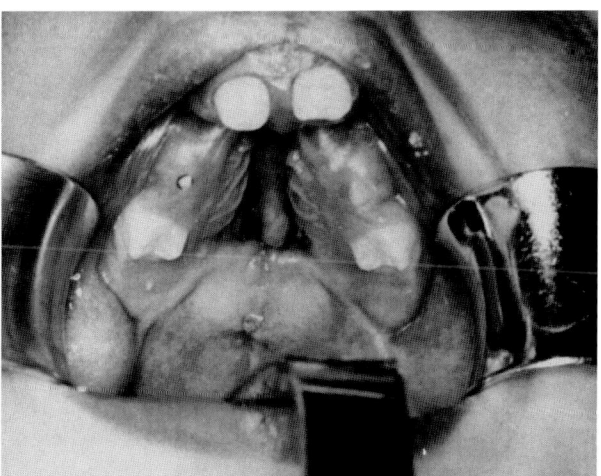

Fig. 7–11. Palatal view showing the lip and soft palate closure as a primary procedure. The hard palatal cleft is closed at a later date, usually between 18 to 30 months.

Some surgeons believe that good speech requires palatal cleft closure between 6 and 9 months, the child's stage of phonemic development of articulation, and are willing to accept the trade-off of creating some maxillary growth inhibition (Dorf and Curtin[40]). Other surgeons believe that good speech development is not related to the age of cleft closure but depends on the growth integrity of the entire midface: the palatal vault space, the size and shape of the pharyngeal space, and the size and neuromuscular action of the soft palate and pharyngeal muscles, along with hearing and the patient's phenotype (Bzoch[41]).

Blocksma et al,[42] and Lindsay,[43] Kaplan et al,[44] Krause et al,[45] and Musgrave et al[46] found good speech with the von Langenbeck procedure in most cases. This repair gave slightly better speech results than the lengthening procedures in soft palate clefts, but the V-Y push back was superior in the more extensive clefts. However, the authors do not discuss the effects of the procedures on palatal growth and dental occlusion. Dreyer and Trier[47] compared the speech results when three different palatal surgeries were performed: (1) V-Y or island pushback, (2) von Langenbeck method utilizing two bipedical mucoperiosteal flaps advanced to the midline, and (3) von Langenbeck procedure with the addition of levator reconstruction (intravelor veloplasty). The speech results after palatoplasty revealed no significant difference between children with simple von Langenbeck closure and those undergoing palatal lengthening procedures. Children with levator reconstruction demonstrated superior speech results.

As to maxillofacial development, Jolleys[48] found better speech results in his patients who had surgery prior to age 2 and found no difference in maxillofacial development. Koberg and Koblin[49] suggested that 2 to 3 years old is the best age for surgery without damaging maxillary development. Friede et al[50] and Berkowitz's[51] facial and palatal growth studies do not support Ross's[52] conclusion that early (before 18 months) palatal repair provides better facial growth than does delayed hard palate repair. The opposite appears to be true because deformed palates are more closely related to early (within the first year) surgery than delayed (4–9 years of age) surgery. For example, Graber[19(p405)] reported:

> In various studies of facial growth and development, it is seen that the lateral width of the maxilla is accomplished quite early in life, but the downward and forward growth is not complete until the second decade of life. Any growth disturbance induced by environmental interference would be possible in the sutural sites of proliferation for a number of years, but any appreciable withholding of the palate in width would require interference during the first 4 years of life.

Most orthodontists and surgeons agree that the skills of the surgeon need to be considered when evaluating all surgical procedures.

Attainment of normal speech, facial and palatal development, and dental occlusion is possible without compromising one objective for another. Although speech development may benefit from early palatal closure, there are instances when the cleft space is very wide and cleft closure should be postponed to a later age to permit additional palatal growth and allow for conservative palatal surgery. Berkowitz's palatal growth studies, presented in this text, show that an increase in palatal size with the spontaneous narrowing of the cleft space can occur early, late, or not at all; and, in rare instances, the cleft may even widen. Nonphysiological surgery causes facial and palatal deformation due to the destruction of blood supply with scar formation. To avoid these consequences, timing of palatal closure should be related to the anatomical and functional assets in the individual and not determined by age alone. Berkowitz's[51] serial studies of 36 unilateral (UCLP) and 29 bilateral (BCLP) cleft lip and palate cases with good speech demonstrated that conservative palatal surgery is conducive to good speech as well as good palate and facial development. Speech appliances, in very rare instances, may be necessary as an interim device to close off the cleft space after 2 years of age.

van Demark and Morris[53] found that early surgery (before 24 months of age—before the child begins to talk) to close the cleft space was associated with better articulation skills when the children were tested at 8 years of age, but after that age, differences were less often seen. They believed that other variables, for example, velopharyngeal competence and cleft type, were better predictors of eventual articulation skills than was age at surgery.

McWilliams et al,[54] in reviewing the literature, found better speech to be associated with earlier palatal repair (before 24 months of age). However, they noted that design flaws in the studies make it difficult to interpret results. Failure to define "normal," "perfect," or "acceptable" speech and the omission of information about cleft type and surgical techniques are significant shortcomings in comparing results.

Most speech-language pathologists still advocate closure of the palatal cleft before 1 year of age, believing that early closure prevents development of patterns of speech that would require prolonged and difficult therapy at a later age (McWilliams et al[54]). Most of their studies and conclusions are based on the use of only two variables: timing of surgery and speech outcome, omitting other significant variables; therefore, their conclusions must be questioned. The error in relating speech adequacy to the age that a palatal cleft was closed has only confused the issue of individualizing treatment planning based on differential diagnosis of the cleft defect.

Speech studies of individuals or a small sample of subjects are often sufficient, and sometimes essential, to finding solutions to a particular problem being investigated; however, the fact that a "correlation" exists between two variables (speech proficiency and age) does not indicate or prove causation. Although the age at which surgery is performed may be the sole relevant variable studied, sensory function, genotype, the geometrics of the original deformity, the facial growth pattern, and the surgical procedure performed are also factors that must be considered. It is difficult, and perhaps impossible, to demonstrate the effectiveness of a treatment philosophy in a clinical setting, where many variables cannot be identified, controlled, or manipulated. Therefore, conclusions drawn from such investigations should be considered with caution (Berkowitz[51]).

Some past surgical strategies also emphasized early palatal closure and velar lengthening with the goal of resolving immediate problems with cleft space and, hopefully, preventing future speech problems associated with hypernasality. In addition, velum lengthening procedures, originally advocated in the newborn period—often without evidence of incompetent air flow control—to avoid a possible second surgical procedure, were found to be ineffective even when performed at a later age (Millard[3]).

Surgery can either aid in directing the natural growth into proper channels by establishing muscle balance across the cleft defect, or it can grossly interfere with the normal developmental changes by hindering growth through interference with blood supply, introducing a scar, or destruction of growth centers. In view of the wide range of individual variations of the defect, the surgical procedure must be altered to fit the particular case, in terms of both time and technique.

Determining which surgical-orthodontic procedures are best utilized for different types of clefts is the goal of all clinicians. Unfortunately, palatal and facial growth patterns are not predictable at birth, and therefore one needs to wait to see the effects of initial treatment on the developing face before deciding what next needs to be done. When decisions to act are made under conditions of uncertainty, it is always appropriate to consider not only the probability of success but also the consequences of failure.

SURGICAL-ORTHODONTIC PROCEDURES AND SEQUENCES

It is impossible to review all of the surgical-orthodontic approaches to the closure of lip and hard and soft palatal clefts with or without the use of orthopedic plates. Some surgeons will first unite the lip, followed either by closure of the hard and soft palate in one stage, or first unite the soft palate and then the hard palate at a later age. Some even favor closing the soft palate before uniting the lip. There are as many different surgical procedures as there are differences in the timing and surgical sequence to be utilized. Some surgeons favor a vomer flap with or without a mucoperiosteal flap, others with/without a pushback, still others a mucosal tissue closure without involving the periosteum. Yet each clinical report tells of both good and bad results usually using the number of buccal and anterior crossbites in the deciduous dentition to designate whether the procedures have failed or succeeded. Unfortunately, most reports do not have final post-pubertal facial/palatal records, which are more meaningful in describing the final outcome.

Palate Cleft Closure Controversies Revisited

Present day corrective procedures involve surgery, the type and timing of the operation depending on whether the surgeon is a von Langenbeck soft tissue descendant, with or without presurgical maxillary orthopedics, or a Brophy "steel-clamp and silver wire" bony closure man. There is a basic philosophical conflict between the two major groups. Some surgeons employ staphylorrhaphy for closure of the cleft palate, a variation of the von Langenbeck, Furlow, or Veau-Wardell Kilner V-Y pushback procedure using mucoperiosteal flaps. They may or may not use vomer flaps to line the surface of the mucoperiosteal flap. The soft tissue is repositioned over what many surgeons consider a normal bony framework (with the exception of the cleft area) that had failed for some reason to unite in the midline. Today, most surgeons are convinced that aberrant embryonal and fetal influences force the lateral halves of the maxilla apart, making the intramaxillary width excessive. In the past, it was Brophy, today it is many McNeil disciples who utilize presurgical maxillary orthopedics, believing that the first step in habilitation is to restore what they believe to be a normal segmental relationship at a very early age. Each school of thought has intense convictions that there is only one correct approach—its own.

Four surgical approaches are commonly used to close the palatal cleft.

1. Early complete palate repair (3–9 months). *Rationale:* to achieve maximum speech results with a possible chance of inhibiting midfacial growth and creating severe dental occlusion. This approach favors speech above facial growth and development.
2. Delayed complete palate repair (12–24 months). *Rationale:* speech results are nearly as good as with earlier repair and the facial growth disturbance is less.
3. Late complete palate repair (2–5 years). *Rationale:* to prevent facial-palatal growth inhibition, accepting the poorer speech results. Use of a palatal obturator is needed in most cases.
4. Early lip and soft palate repair (2–9 months) and delayed hard palate repair. *Rationale:* to avoid facial and dental deformity but perhaps still achieve good speech with the aid of an obturator.

Scarring Inhibits Palatal Growth

Surgery to the hard and soft palate with temporary disruption with the blood supply does not, by itself, cause damages to the underlying bone. Most surgeons and orthodontists believe that the principal growth inhibitor seems to be the quantity and distribution of scar tissue that is created after surgery. When evaluating the effects of surgery on maxillary growth and development, it is necessary to consider that clefts of the palate can differ greatly in size and form at the same age due to the amount of osteogenic deficiency in the hard and soft palate and lip. The great individual variation in the relationship of the size and form of the cleft space relative to the size of the palatal segments is responsible for the differences in the amount of scar tissue formed even when the same surgical procedure is performed by the same surgeon.

A review of cleft palate surgical history clearly shows that a single mode of surgery for all cases invariably resulted in severe palatal and midfacial deformities, as well as poor speech development. Unfortunately, the same poor results still occur despite the timing of surgery and the skill and experience of the plastic surgeon. This is so because of failure to define the criteria for the timing of palatal surgery and failure to agree on which surgical procedures interfere with normal growth and development of the structures involved. Poor results were understandable when there were no standardized methods for estimating success or recording the effects of surgery on speech and facial growth and development; these shortcoming no longer exist. Nonetheless, some present-day surgical reports still do not adequately describe the original deformity; thus the efficacy of the surgical effort cannot be evaluated.

Mapes and co-authors,[55] Robertson and Fish,[56] and Berkowitz (unpublished data) all concluded that nontraumatic palatal surgery accelerated the growth rate of the maxilla, helping it reach more normal dimensions in the following years. Berkowitz and associates[57] demonstrated that, in the patient with complete bilateral cleft lip and palate, after conservative palatal surgery the palatal surface area doubled from birth to the age of 1½ years. Also, in an isolated cleft palate of a patient with Pierre Robin Sequence, there was a 50% increase in the palatal surface area from birth to 1 year of age. The acceleration in growth tapered off after palatal surgery in both instances. Palatal growth accelerates 6 to 12 months post-surgery in some cases.

Berkowitz found that cases with relatively small cleft spaces prior to using modified von Langenbeck surgery grew the best after surgery. This can be interpreted to mean that the smaller the laterally placed areas of denuded bone, the less scar tissue will result with a better chance of obtaining "catch-up-growth."

Bardach[58] questions the validity of claiming that palatoplasty is detrimental to maxillary growth. He believes there is no adequate substantiation of this concept from clinical or experimental studies. However, Berkowitz's[3] clinical report on Millard's Island Flap pushback procedure, which creates large areas of denuded bone, has conclusively shown that this procedure deforms the palate and causes major maxillofacial growth aberrations (Figs 7-12 through 7-19). However, this study does not find fault with palatoplasties that produce small areas of exposed palatal bone. The same palatoplasty can yield different long-term results because all clefts within the same cleft type are not the same. They may have different size of cleft spaces. Unfortunately, Bardach focuses only on the surgery performed and does not consider the geometric variations in the cleft deformity as critical factors in predicting the long-term outcome of surgery.

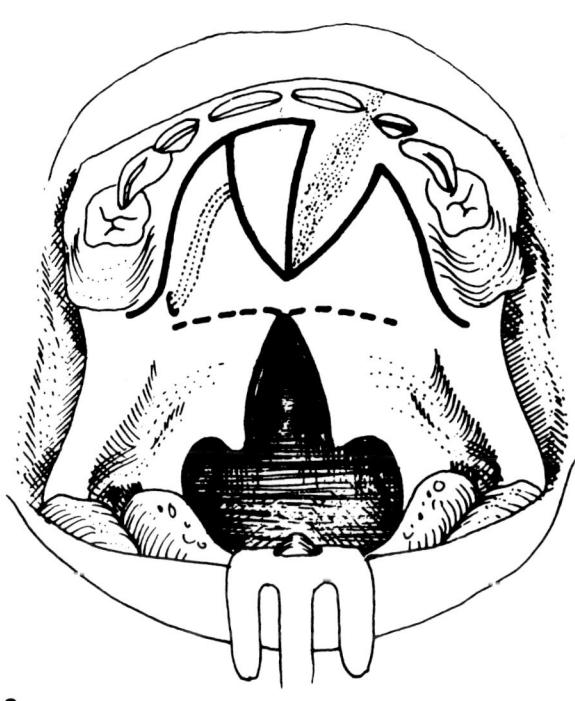 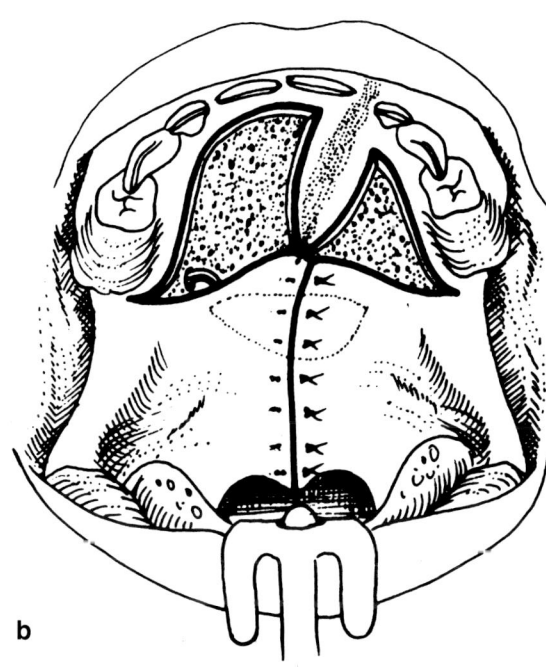

Fig 7–12. "Island flap" for a unilateral cleft lip and palate. a. Outline of incisions at 21 months. **b.** At 21 months a V-Y pushback of the palate was achieved, leaving the V over the anterior closure untouched, and taking a unilateral island flap for nasal lining. (Courtesy of D.R. Millard, Jr.)

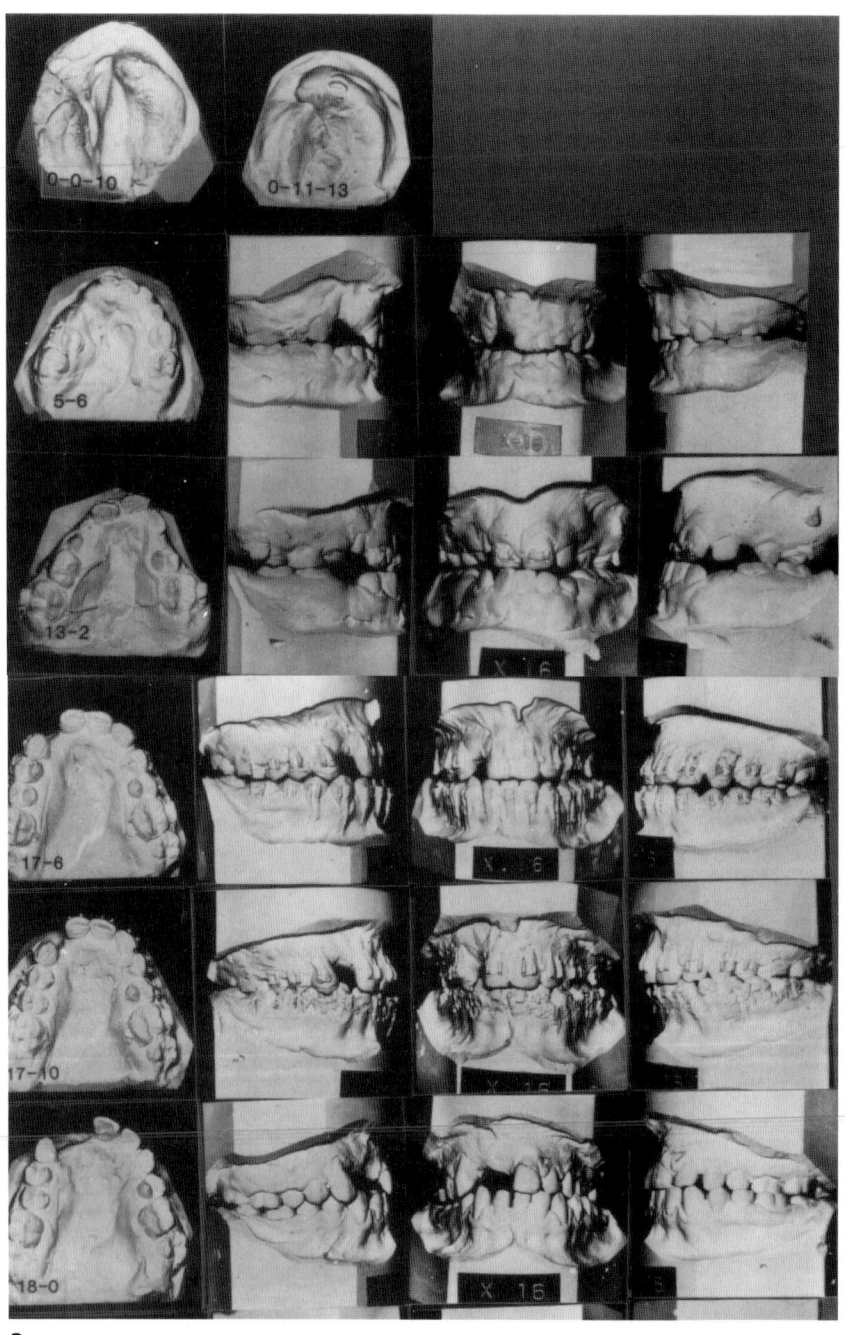

a

Fig 7–13. Case JB. No. X-16. Serial palatal changes after "Island flap" leading to LeFort I maxillary advancement. a. Serial casts. The Island flap V-Y procedure was performed at 5 months. **0-11-13**: The palate shows severe scarring and collapse. **5-6**: Even after a difficult attempt at palatal arch expansion, the buccal and anterior occlusion are still in a tip-to-tip relationship with the opposing teeth. **13-2**: The palatal arch collapsed again due to the strong medial pull of the transpalatal scar placing the buccal and anterior teeth in crossbite. Note that midfacial recessiveness increased as the face grew even with orthodontia and protraction mechanics and by 17-6 a class 3 malocclusion existed. **17-10**: After Lefort 1 maxillary advancement. **18-0**: The right maxillary incisor and alveolar labial plate exfoliated as a result of the severance of the blood supply to this area. **19-3**: A "round

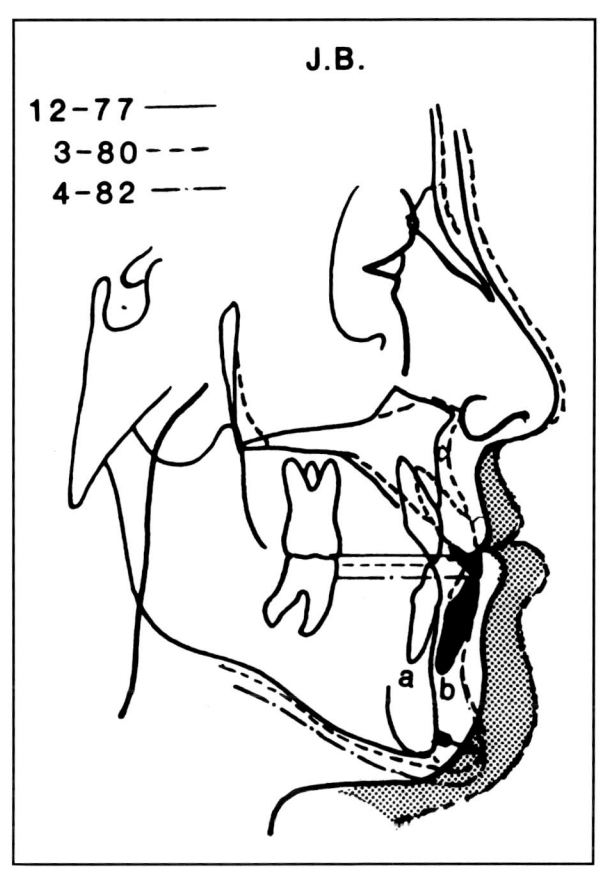

b

house" fixed bridge was utilized to replace the missing teeth and stabilize the arch form. A transpalatal removable metal strut helps to maintain the corrected arch by counteracting the medial pull of the severe scarring. **b. Superimposed cephalometric tracings pre- and post-maxillary advancement show changes to the skeletal and soft tissue profile.** The upper lip is more recessive than the lower lip due to the lack of maxillary basal bone coupled with additional mandibular growth.

Comment: Growth disturbance caused by severe palatal scarring is three-dimensional. Although palatal osteotomies can reposition the bony segments, the force of scar contracture will prevail, causing arch collapse if it is not counteracted. This can only occur with dental bridges of various types and/or transpalatal struts.

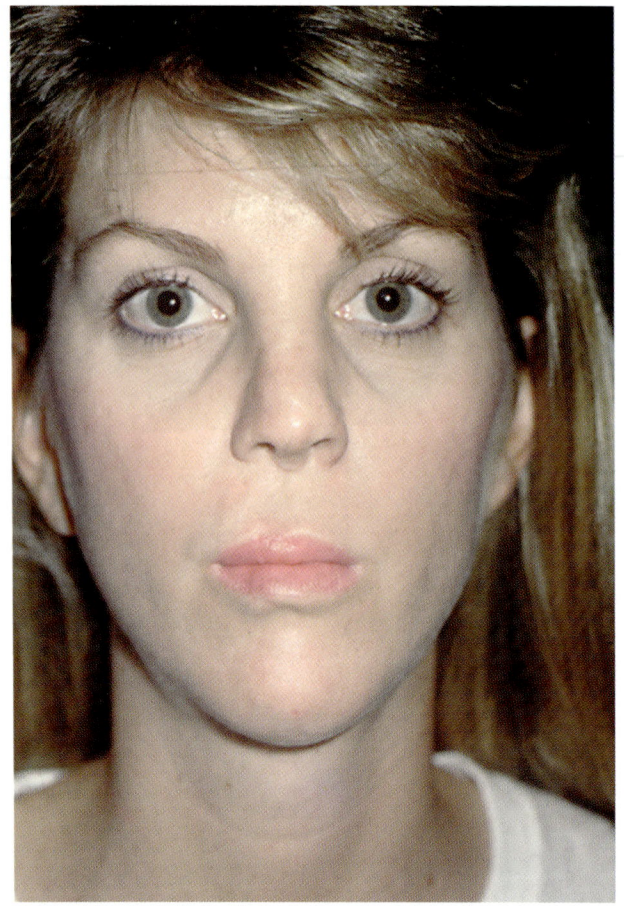
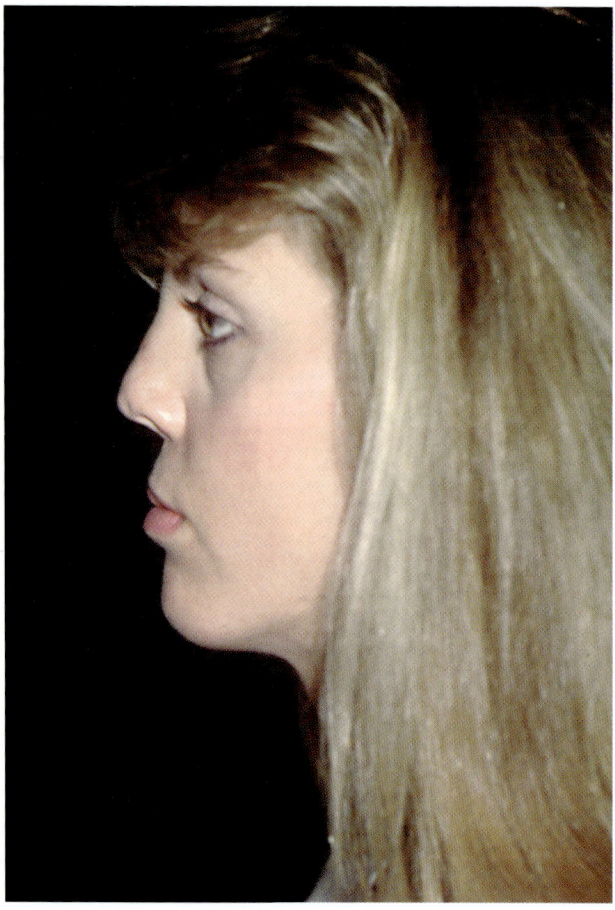
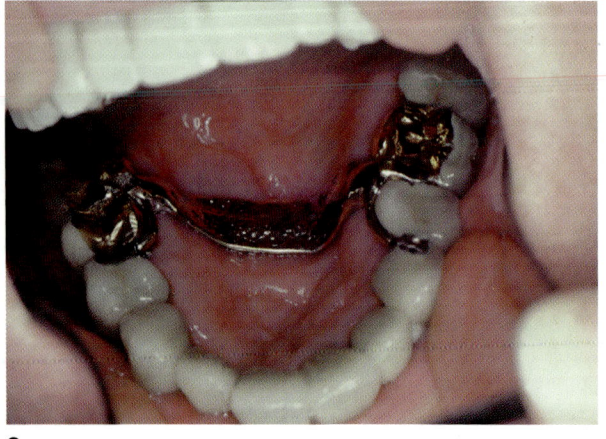
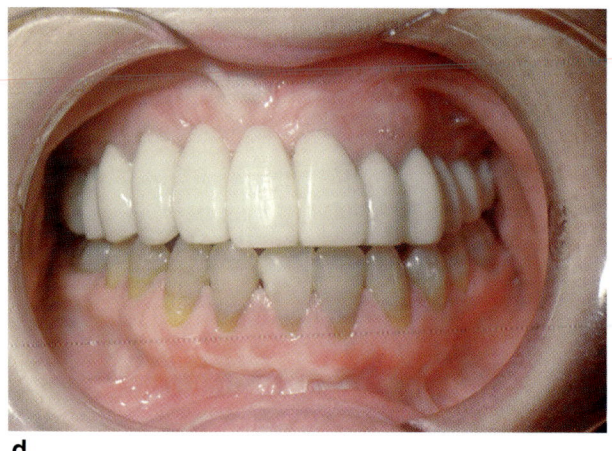

Fig 7–14. Post-surgery after LeFort I maxillary advancement to correct a retrusive midface. **a.** Frontal and **b.** lateral facial photographs. **c.** Transpalatal strut to help maintain maxillary arch size and form. **d.** "Round house" bridge.

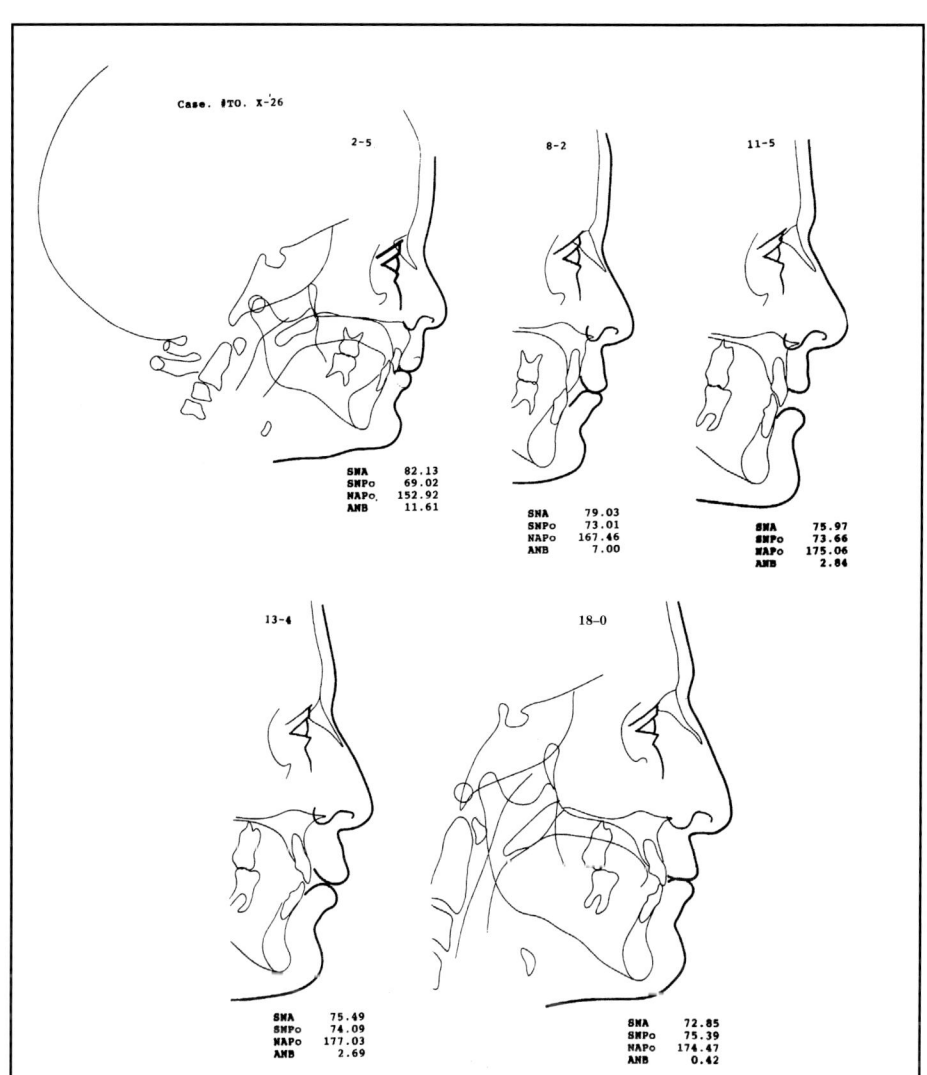

Fig 7–17. Lateral cephalometric tracings for Case TO (No. X-26) between 2-5 and 18-0. The mandibular prominence (SNP) increased from 69° to 75° while the midfacial protrusion (SNA) decreased from 82.13° to 72.85° during the same time period reflecting the effects of midfacial growth retardation.

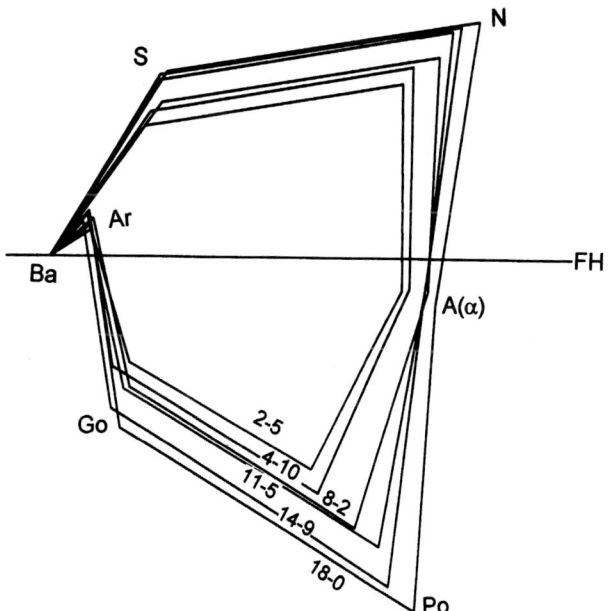

Fig 7–18. Superimposed polygon tracings for Case TO (No. X-26) using the Basion Horizontal method of Coben. Changes from 2-5 to 18-0 clearly show retarded midfacial growth when compared to normal growth of the upper and lower portions of the face. The soft tissue profile is able to mask the skeletal discrepancy in this instance.

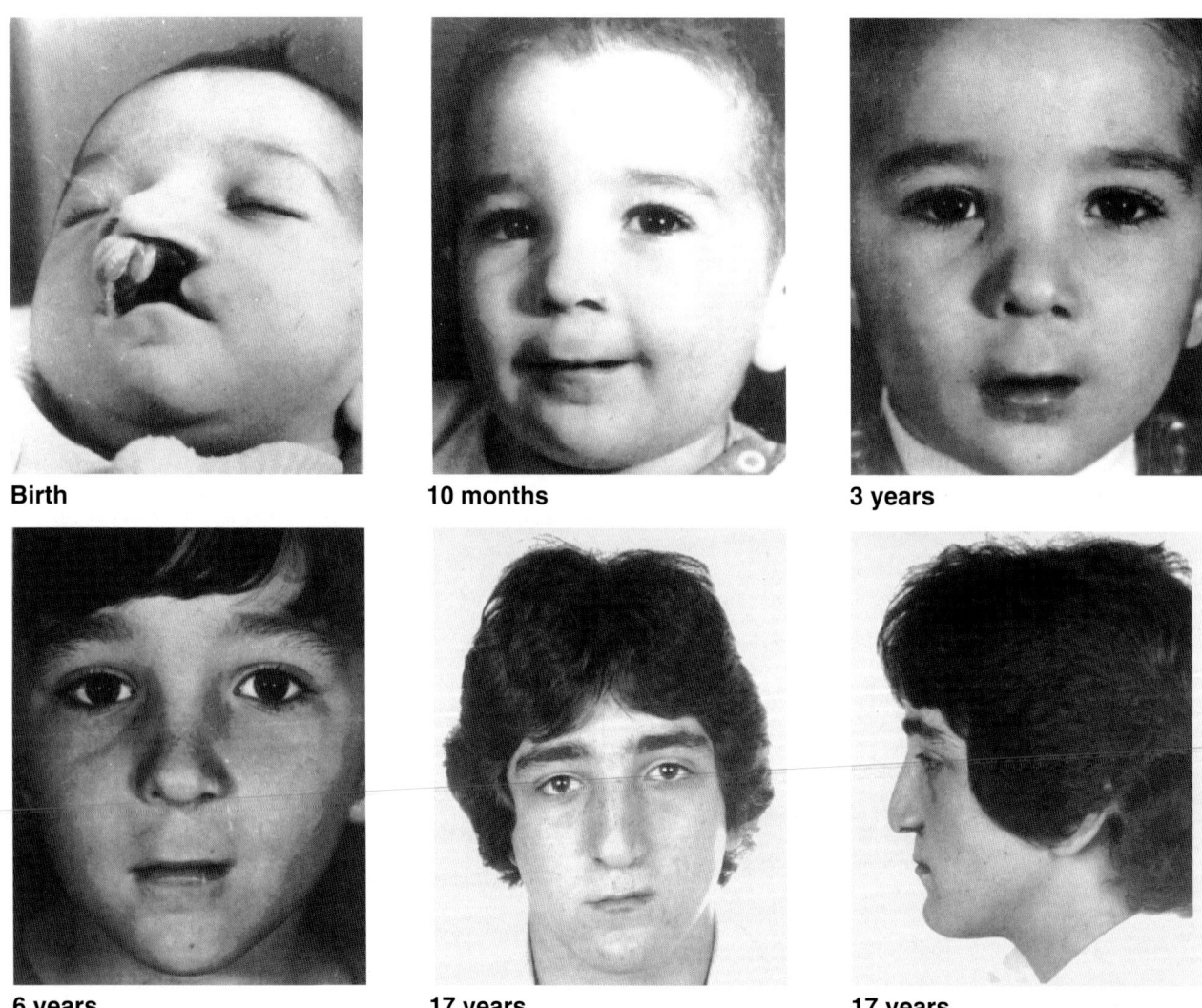

Fig 7-16. Facial changes from birth to the mixed dentition do not usually show the effect of midfacial growth retardation. The effects on facial growth becomes more evident after the post-pubertal facial growth period. At birth *(upper left)*, 10 months *(upper right)*, 3 years *(middle left)*, 6 years and 9 months *(lower right)*. Frontal and lateral views at 17 years *(bottom)*.

Fig. 7–15. (continued)

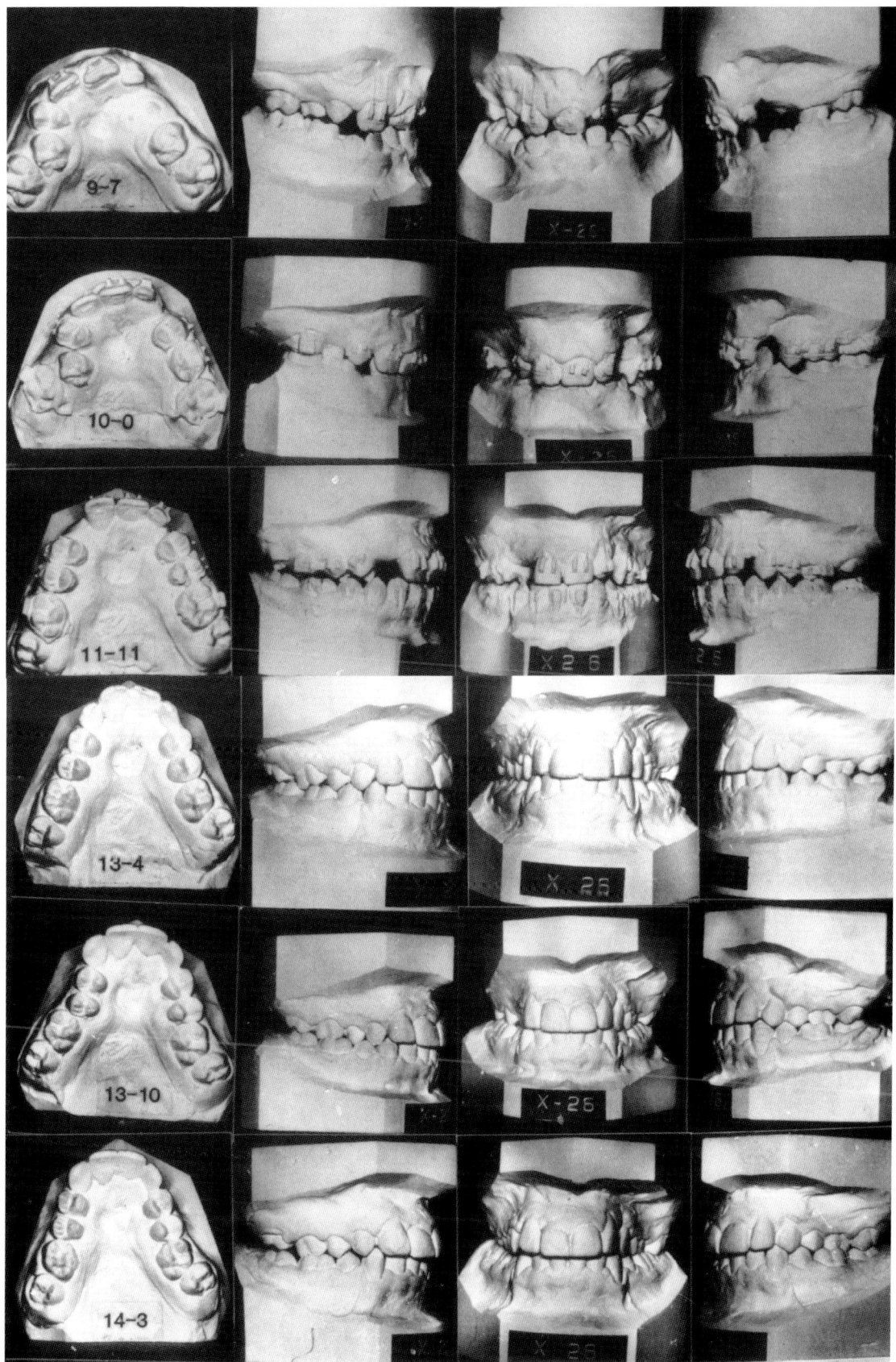

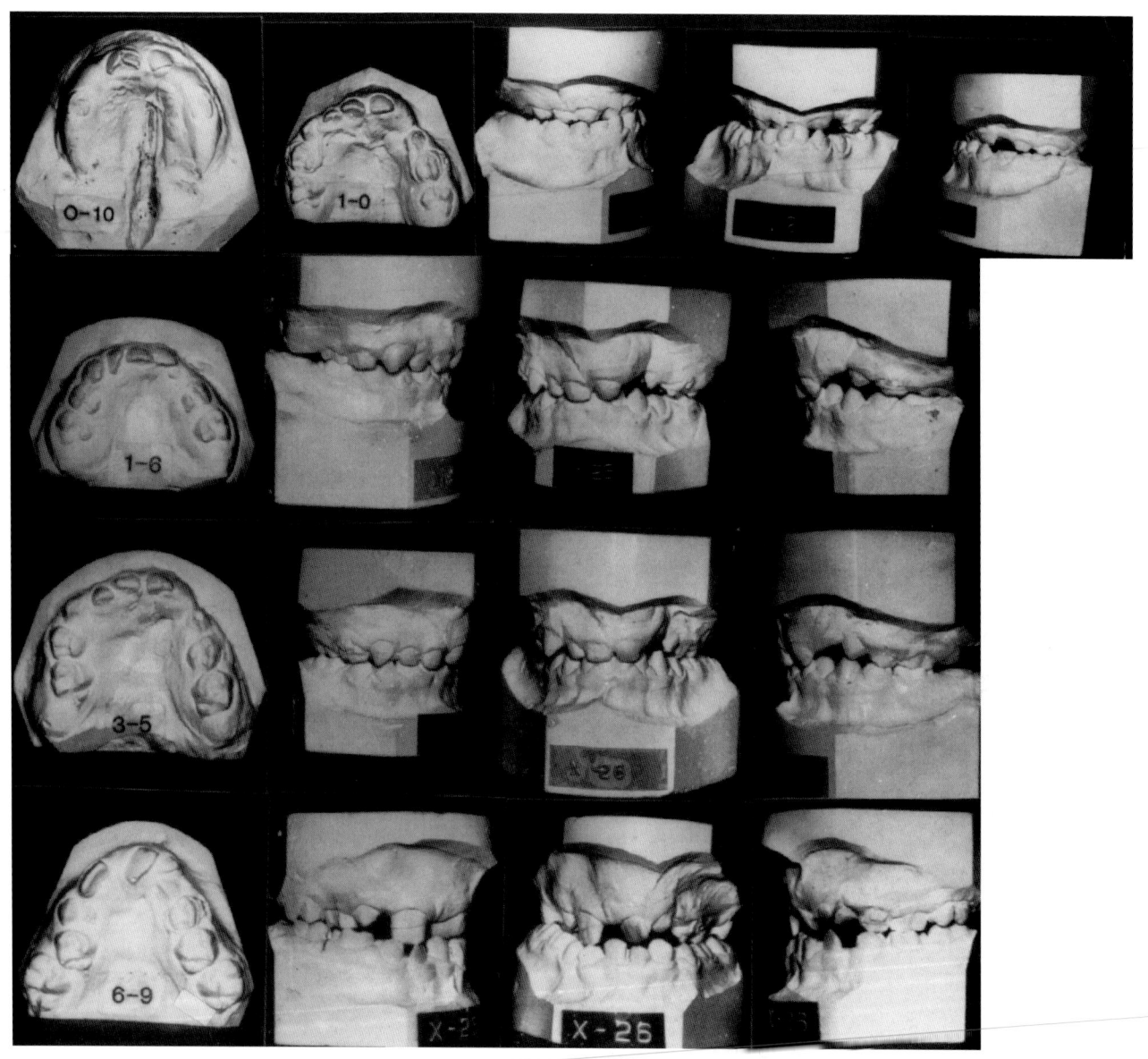

Fig 7–15. Case TO (No. X-26) demonstrates the deleterious effects of excessive scarring associated with an Island flap on palatal growth, and arch form in a CUCLP.
Palatal casts. 0-10: After lip surgery which brought the alveolar segment is good approximation. A small palatal cleft and good arch form before the Island Flap. **1-0:** After the Island Flap and resulting collapse of the palatal segments. The child had to protrude the lower jaw to obtain a comfortable posterior occlusion. **1-6:** Anterior and buccal occlusion. **3-5:** Palatal deformation becomes more apparent leading to left buccal crossbite. **6-9:** Marked palatal form changes reflecting growth retardation. Further palatal and occlusal changes between **9-3, 9-7,** and **10-0** are evident. The strong transpalatal scar contracture narrows the transverse palatal width and reduces palatal growth leading to severe dental crowding. **11-11:** Orthodontia was able to temporarily produce good palatal arch changes and improve the occlusion. **13-4:** Both maxillary cuspids were transposed to the lateral incisor spaces. **13-10:** Again the transpalatal scar tissue caused the arch form to narrow across the bicuspids and first molars. **14-3:** The narrowed palatal arch width stabilized with a good anterior overjet and overbite remaining.

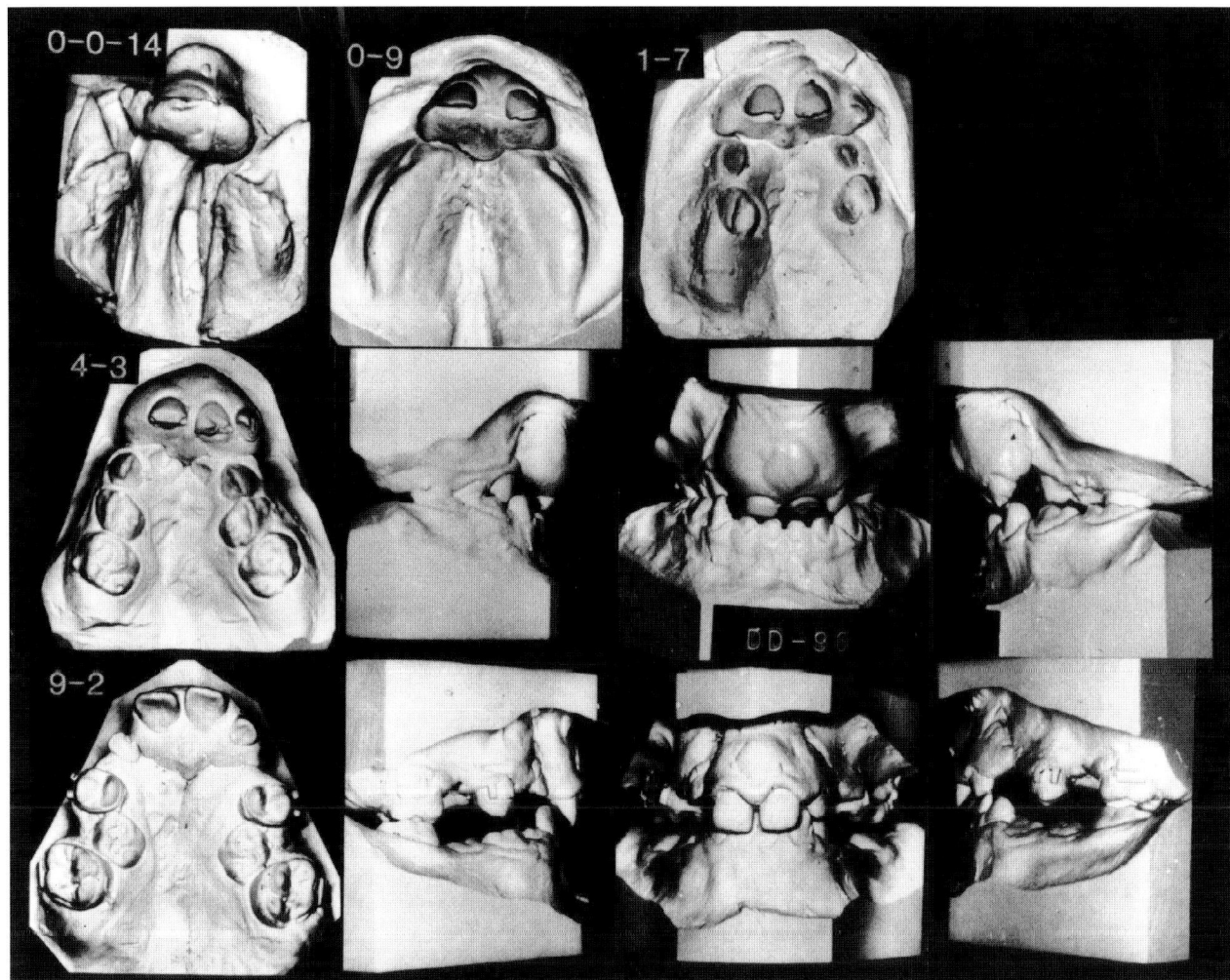

Fig 7–19. Case No. DD-96. Serial casts of bilateral cleft lip and palate show marked palatal scarring following early "Island flap" push back. **0-0-14:** At birth. **0-9:** Excellent palatal arch form after the lip was united. The premaxilla-lateral palatal segments are in good relationship. **1-7:** Narrow and distorted palatal arch due to Island Flap scarring performed earlier. **4-3:** Bilateral buccal crossbite with the anterior incisor overjet in a tip-to-tip relationship. **9-2:** The palatal arch width narrowed at the line of the Island flap.

Comments: The Island Flap is a variant of a V-Y pushback that is very similar to the Wardill-Kilner V-Y pushback procedure in that a large anterior area of denuded bone remains. In the "Island flap," the anterior palatal mucoperiosteum is transposed to nasal surface creating a mucoperiosteum sandwich. This is the area that creates the transpalatal scar. Because the denuded bone heals by epithelialization becoming scar tissue, the larger the denuded area, the more the resulting scar tissue will negatively affect maxillary growth in 3 dimensions. The maxillary deficiency usually becomes apparent in the late mixed or permanent dentition when facial appearance is affected. Lateral cephalometric studies have shown that this or other "pushback" procedures have not resulted in a net gain in soft palate length. We speculate that, in most cases, good velopharyngeal closure would have occurred even if a "pushback" had not been performed as a primary palatal cleft closure procedure. The singular lesson to learn from these longitudinal facial-palatal growth studies is the need to avoid creating large areas of denuded bone when performing palatal surgery.

Research is presently underway in Berkowitz's laboratory to determine why "catch-up-growth" occurs in some but not all cases even when surgery is performed by the same surgeon using the same surgical procedures.

In the course of a set of related experiments, Latham and Burston,[59] Latham,[60,61] and Calabrese and co-workers[62] suggested that new tissue could be induced to form in the growing face by applying appropriately controlled physical stress through neonatal maxillary orthopedics. However, no known supportive objective data have ever been presented. This subject was covered in depth in Chapter 6.

Viteporn et al,[63] utilizing longitudinal cephaloradiographs, showed that patients with extensive cleft palate who had a pushback procedure reached maximum growth spurt later than patients with less extensive surgery and that the surgery had an inhibitory effect on midfacial growth. They concluded that, because the sample was of the same ethnic group and received surgical treatment at the same age by the same surgeon, significant differences in mid-face development between the two groups should be attributed to the treatment itself. Scar tissue associated with the denuded bone left after the V-Y pushback technique, they claimed, played a major role in inhibiting forward displacement of the maxilla and in distorting dentoalveolar growth.

THE FOURTH DIMENSION OF TIME: CATCH-UP GROWTH

Substantial evidence from the many excellent facial and palatal growth studies (Figs 7–20 and 7–23, Table 7–1) has determined that a "catch-up" potential exists in children with cleft lip and/or palate, which allows for reasonably good growth of the maxillary complex and face. Inherent factors alone, however, do not determine this growth. Clinicians are cognizant of the very strong influence—which quite often is adverse—of extraneous factors (e.g., iatrogenic and functional). These factors are complex and varied. It becomes obvious that surgical skill, the type of surgery, the timing of surgery, and even the sequence and numbers of surgical procedures all complicate the overall end result of facial growth in any given situation. It would appear that just the primary surgical closure of the lip and palate produces a myriad of sequences and variables to be dealt with, and they in turn introduce more sequences and variables.

To take into account both the inherent insult and extraneous factors, and to recognize and quantify the extent to which each contributes to the overall severity of the problem, is a much needed step in the correct habilitative effort. The inherent problem, such as the anomalous cleft, should of necessity emphasize habilitative efforts with minimal adverse effects on growth. At present there is no consensus as to how this could be achieved, a fact attested to by the wide variety of successful treatment regimens employed throughout the world. A long-term assessment of the approach to this problem can be brought about only by the use of objective serial clinical records, such as serial roentgenocephalographs and serial dental casts, by research consortium members working together.

From Berkowitz's serial palatal growth studies, he has deduced that the intrinsic growth potential of the maxillary processes and basal bone in cleft palate patients on the whole is slightly less in all three dimensions than in noncleft children. Various cleft types have different degrees of osteogenic deficiency, with bilateral clefts potentially being the most deficient at birth and remaining that way even as the palatal processes grow and develop. It has conclusively been shown that surgical trauma with developing scar tissue at an early age can further inhibit palatal bone growth and its forward translation within the face (Ross[64]).

The structure and function of the physiological elements involved in cleft lip and/or palate, as previously explained, are not static. They exist not only within a framework of three-dimensional space, but also in a functional continuum of time. This fourth dimension of time involves the modifications induced by the processes of growth and development, which determine the ultimate nature of the congenital defect. To understand time-space relationships as they affect the individual cleft palate patient requires a longitudinal study of the patient by means of casts, photographs, and cephalometric roentgenograms.

Catch-up growth has been defined as growth with a velocity above the statistical limits of normality for age during a defined period of time. Such an increase in the rate of growth, before and after palatal surgery, with or without neonatal maxillary orthopedics, may allow the palate to attain normal adult size, or despite the increase in velocity, the palate may still fail to do so. In the latter case it is called "incomplete" catch-up growth. The duration and severity of the insult (the surgical procedure used to close the cleft space in the hard palate) may positively or negatively affect the ability of the palate to recover and undergo catch-up growth.

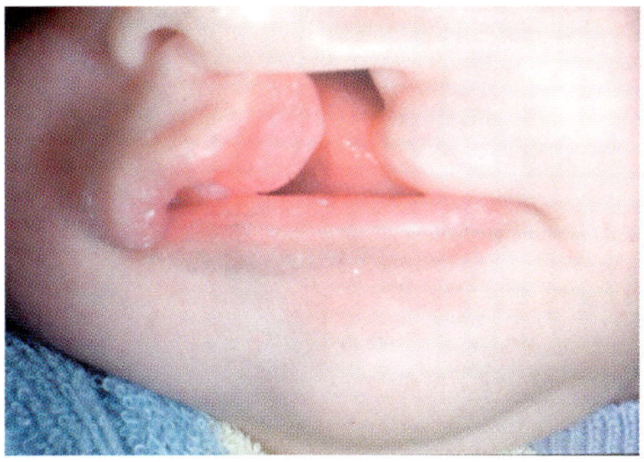

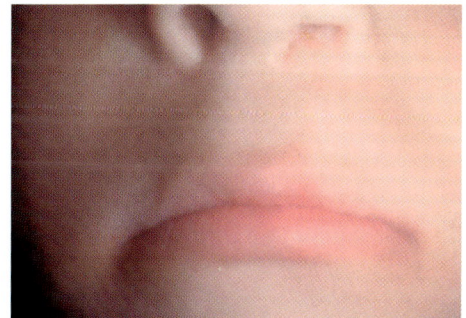

Fig 7–20. Case CM (AC-33) illustrates excellent palatal growth in a CUCLP treated conservatively without presurgical orthopedic treatment. Lip closed with a Millard Rotation Advancement at 7 months. Soft palate united at 16 months and the hard palatal cleft closed at 24 months of age using a modified von Langenbeck. **a.** Newborn: 24 days. **b.** After lip adhesion at 3 months. **c.** After definitive lip surgery at 7 months. **d.** 4 years, 10 months. **e** and **f.** 5 years. **g** and **h.** 8 years, 4 months. **i.** and **j.** Left cuspid crossbite. **k.** Palatal view showing mesioangular rotation of the left palatal segment. **l.** Palatal expander after expansion. **m.** 17 years. **n.** 18 years. **o, p, q,** and **r.** 17 years.
Comments: A mandibular central incisor was extracted to allow a proper overjet-overbite relationship.

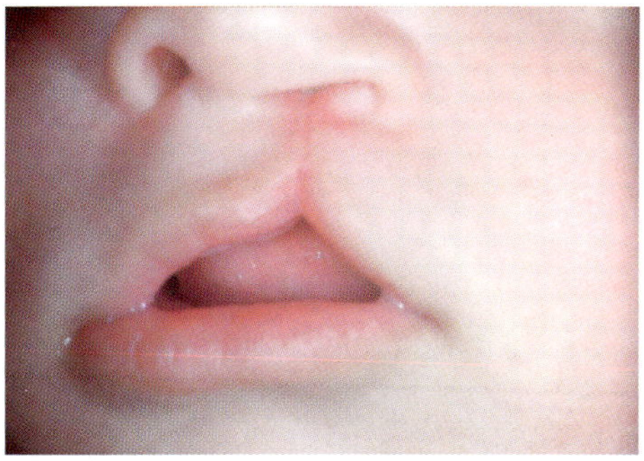

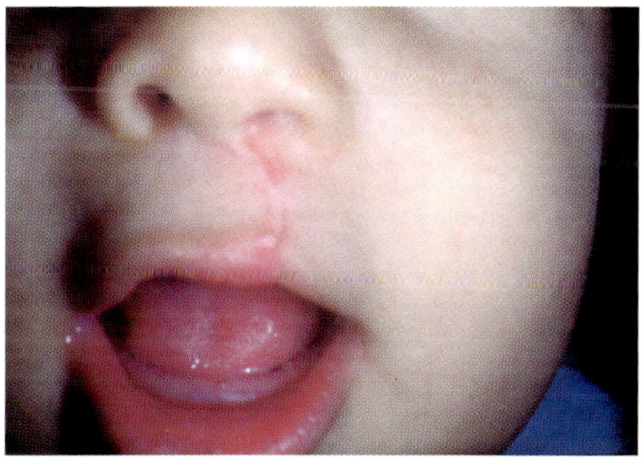

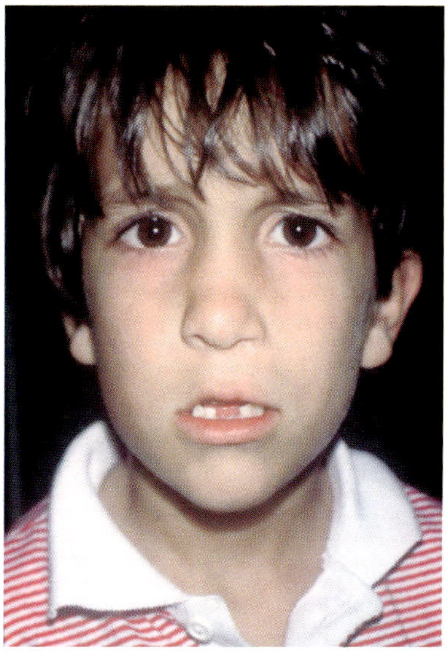

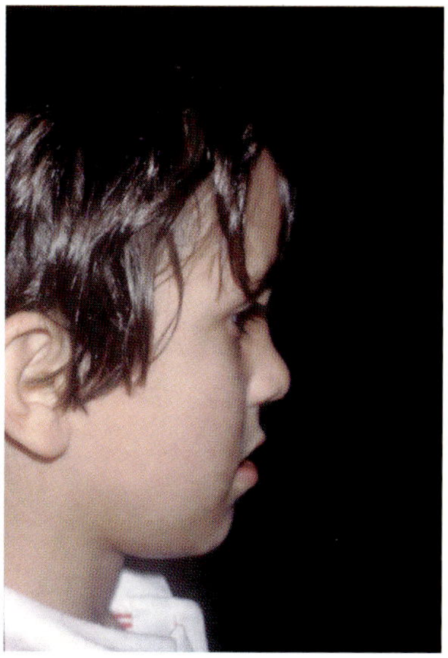

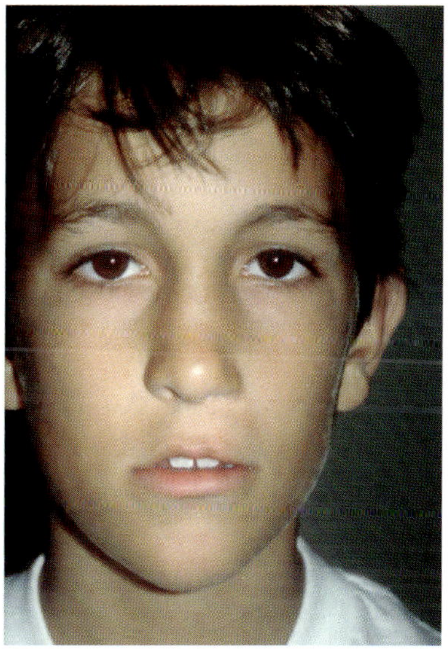

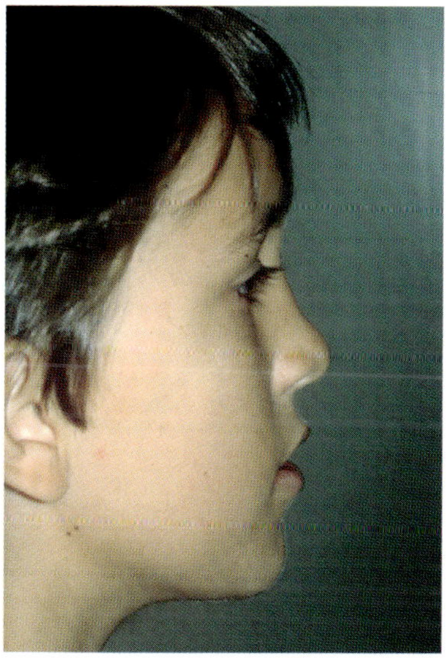

(continued)

Fig 7–20. *(continued) Comment:* Even with the extraction of a mandibular incisor it was difficult to create more of an incisor overbite relationship due to the relative palatal midfacial recessiveness. Note the short midfacial vertical dimension with a relatively long lower facial height.

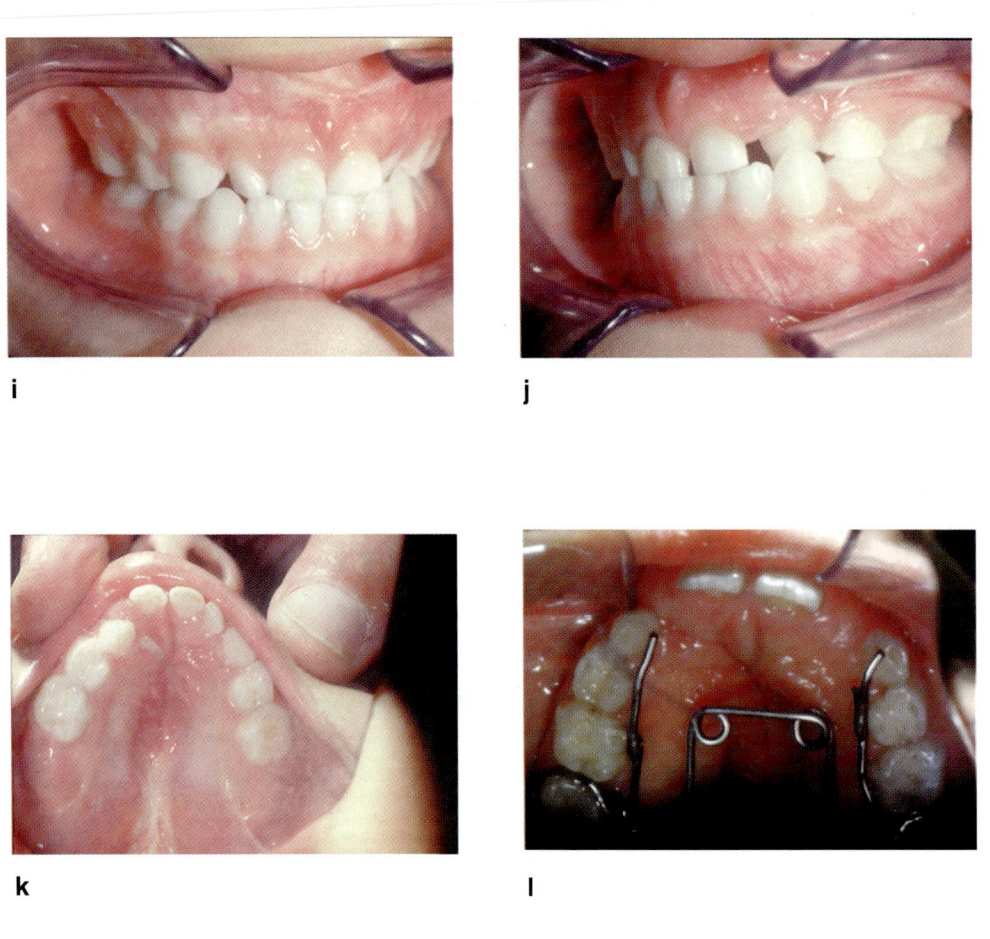

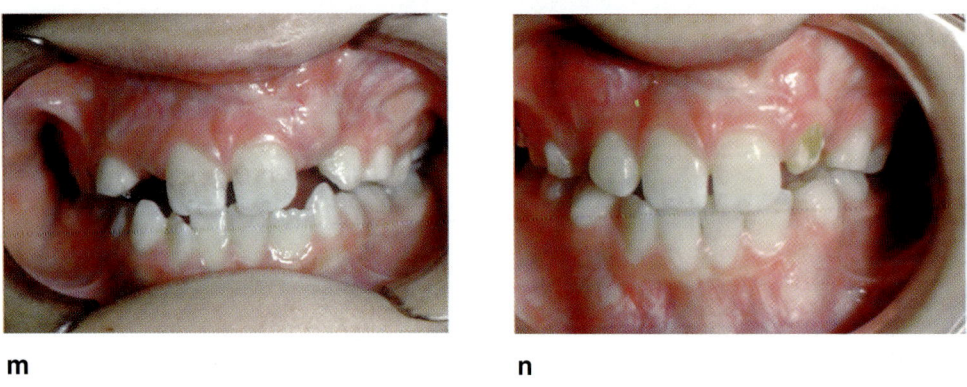

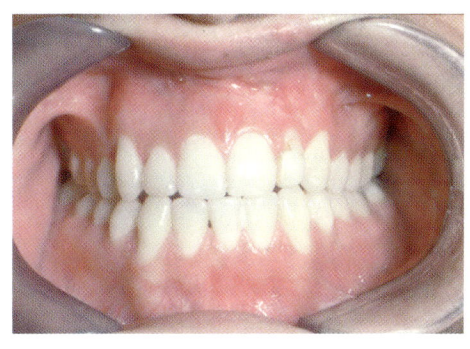
o

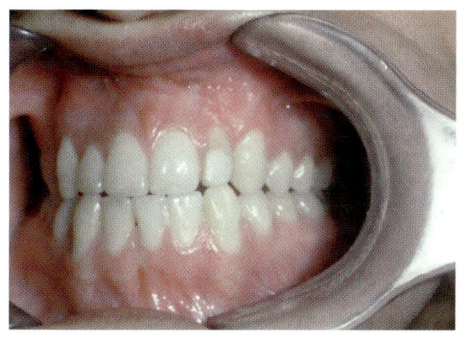
p

q

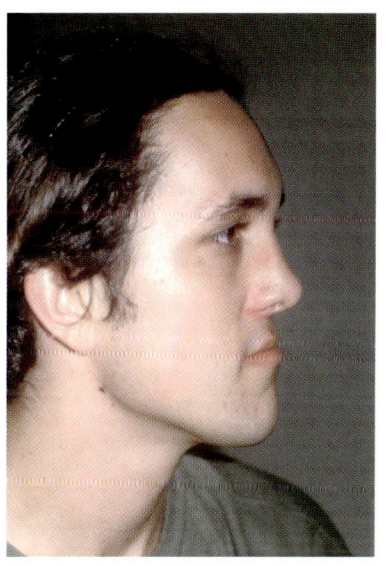
r

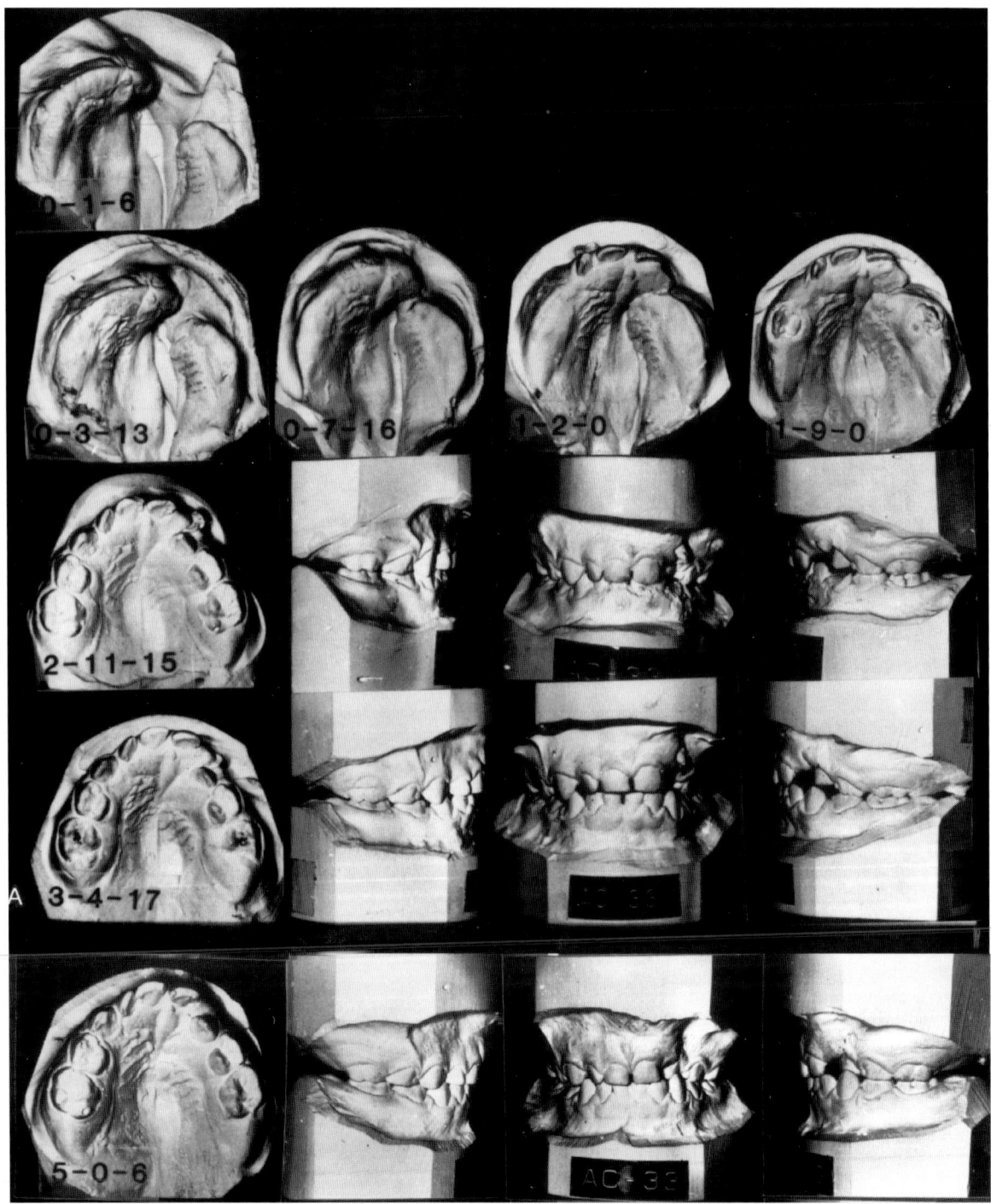

Fig 7–21. Case CM (AC-33) serial dental casts. 0-1-6 at birth, **0-3-13, 0-7-16, 1-2-0** and **1-9-0**. With lip closure the palatal segments moved together with a slight overlap of the smaller cleft segment by the noncleft segment. **3-4-17, 5-0-6,** and **5-7-0**. Only the left deciduous cuspid is in crossbite. **6-1-2**. Excellent vault space to accomodate the tongue, as attested by the good dental occlusion. The deciduous cuspid crossbite did not cause a functional problem nor did it inhibit palatal growth of the lesser segment. **13-5-0**. The left lateral incisor and cuspid erupted through the secondary alveolar bone cranial bone graft performed at 8 years and 5 months of age. Tip-to-tip anterior occlusion. A lower central incisor was extracted to permit a proper overjet overbite relationship to be established. **16-0** and **17-8-0**. Excellent anterior and buccal occlusion with ideal palatal vault space.

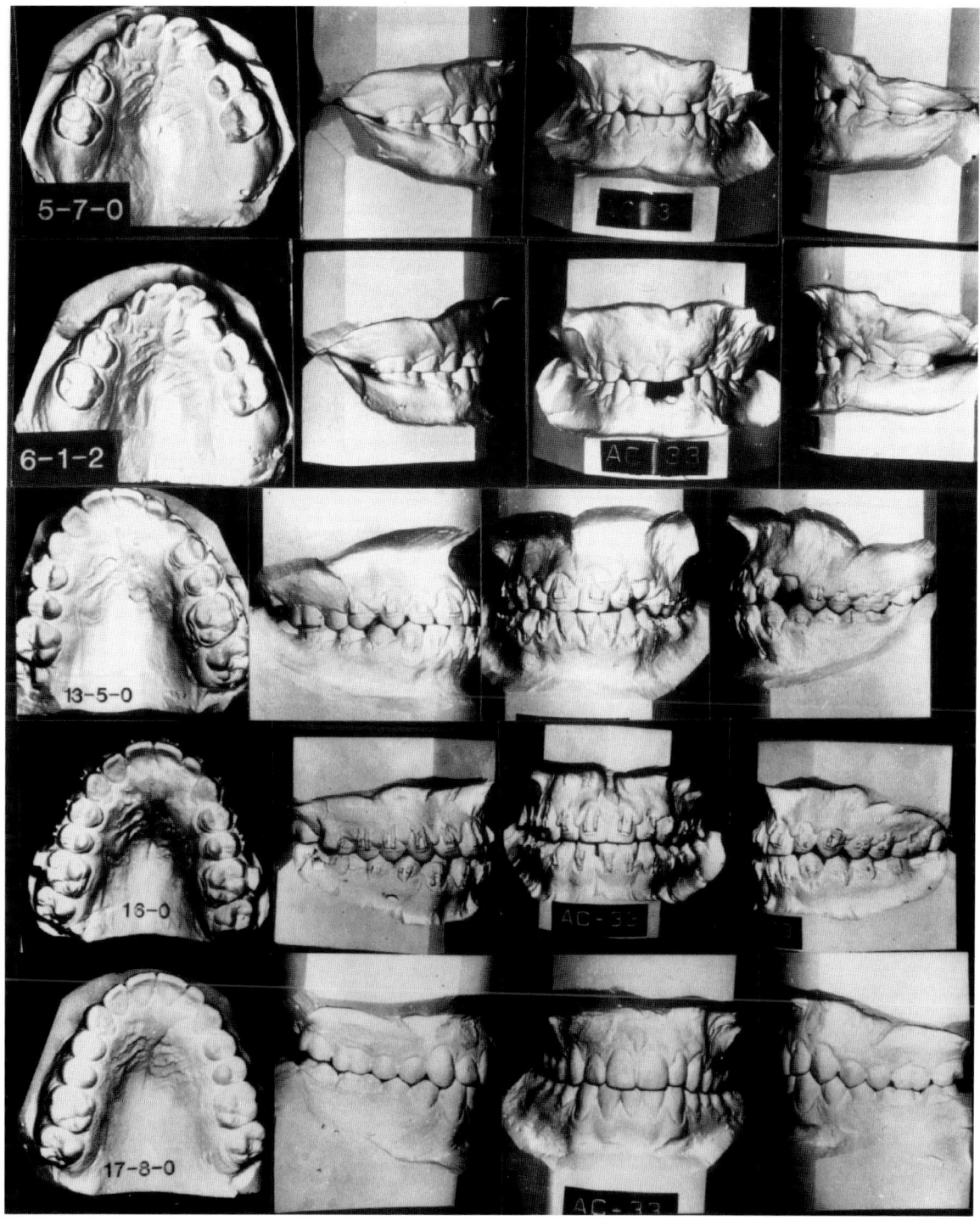

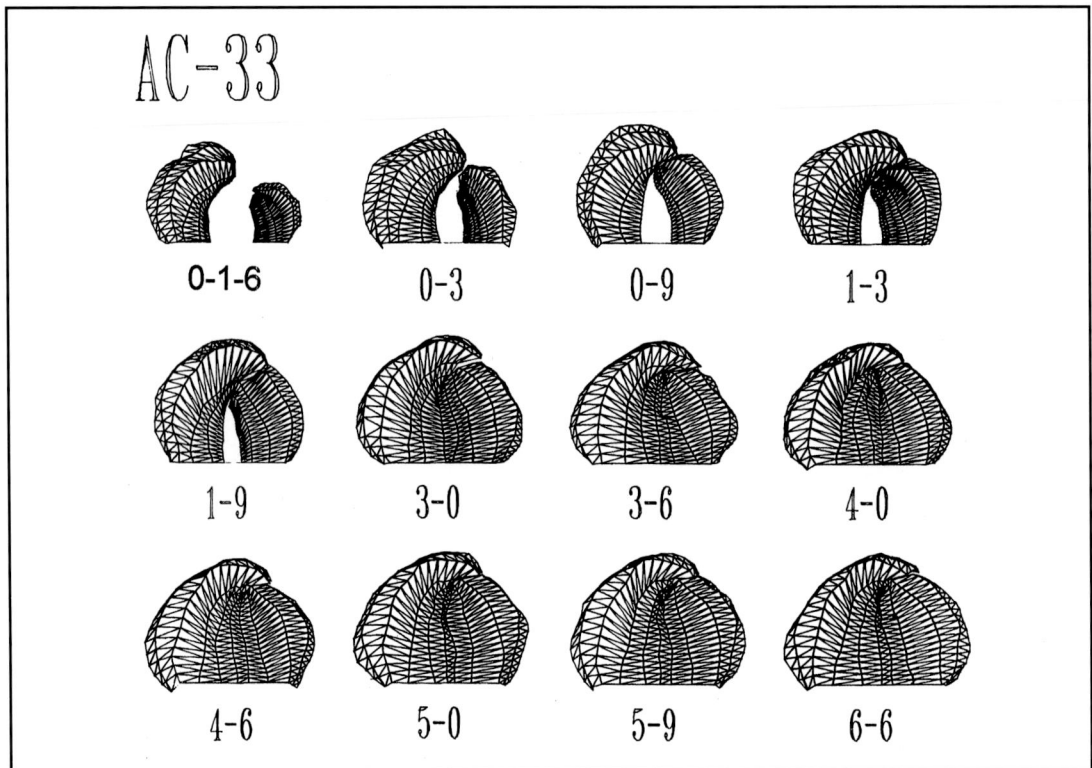

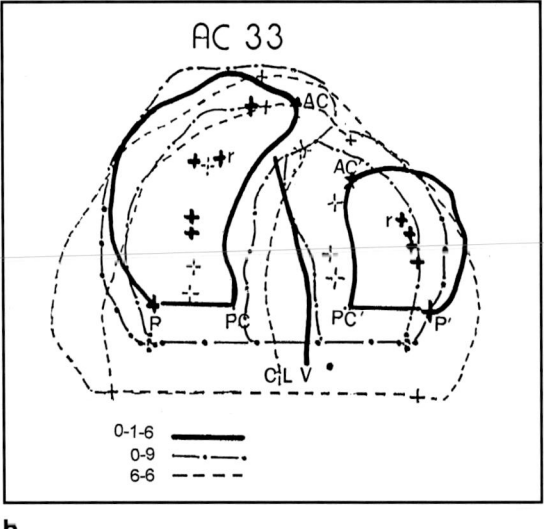

Fig 7–22. Case CM (AC-33) from 0-1-6 to 6-6. a. Computer-generated outlines of serial casts drawn to scale. Three-dimensional serial palatal growth representation using an electromechanical digitizer and cadcam software shows the degree and location of growth changes and the relative changes in cleft space size.

b. Superimposing computer-drawn cast tracings taken at 0-1, 0-9, and 6-6 on the palatal rugae and registered on the vomer point (V) as it crosses the P-P^1 (postgingivale point) line which is posterior limit of the hard palate. This graph demonstrates the great increase in palatal size and direction of palatal growth that occurs when physiological surgery is performed (see chapter 16). P and P': Postgingival. This landmark is comparable to point PTM (pterygomaxillary fissure) which is found between the maxillary tuberosity and the perpendicular plate of the sphenoid. **Pc** and **Pc'**—Landmark on line **PP'** at the cleft space. **Ac** and **Ac'**—Landmark at the anterior most point of the alveolar ridge of the cleft space. **V**—Point at which the vomer crosses the PP' line.

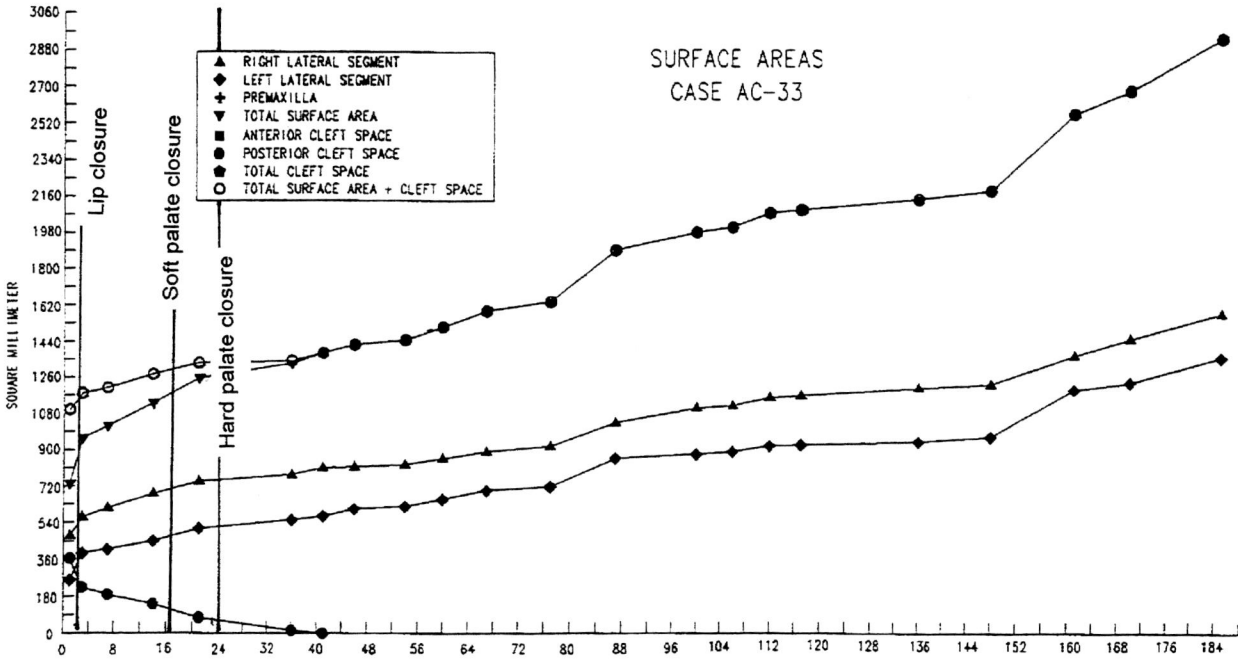

Fig 7-23. Case CM (AC-33). The palatal growth chart shows a very rapid period of acceleration occuring the first year. During the first 8 months the palatal surface area (bordered by the alveolar crests) increased by 45%. Growth gradually slowed down after 20 months.
Comment: Note that both lateral palatal segments grew at parallel growth rates. The growth acceleration curve after palatal surgery was the same as that before surgery. The cleft palatal segment shows two growth periods; at 80 and 152 months. Since rapid palatal growth occurs in all cleft palate children during the first year, caution should be exerted when closing the cleft spaces at this age period to avoid creating excessive scar tissue when its negative effect would be greatest.

TABLE 7-1. Surface Area of CUCLP. Case. #CM (AC-33)

	Skeletal Area			Cleft Space	Total
Age	RLS	LLS	Tot	Post	SA+CS
0-0-21	474.7	259.3	734.0	364.9	1098.9
0-3	567.6	389.6	957.2	223.1	1180.3
0-7	611.3	407.7	1019.0	187.5	1206.5
1-2	682.5	448.4	1130.9	141.7	1272.6
1-9	743.2	510.4	1253.6	75.6	1329.2
3-0	775.3	552.1	1327.4	13.9	1341.3
3-5	809.6	570.8	1380.4		1380.4
3-10	814.3	606.5	1420.8		1420.8
4-6	825.5	618.9	1444.4		1444.4
5-0	855.1	654.4	1509.5		1509.5
5-7	890.0	698.8	1588.8		1588.8
6-5	917.3	718.4	1635.7		1635.7
7-3	1033.5	857.7	1891.2		1891.2
8-4	1103.6	875.8	1979.4		1979.4
8-10	1116.6	888.7	2005.3		2005.3
9-4	1157.8	918.8	2076.6		2076.6
9-9	1168.0	924.4	2092.4		2092.4
11-4	1204.9	938.8	2143.7		2143.7
12-4	1223.3	962.6	2185.9		2185.9
13-5	1366.9	1197.5	2564.4		2564.4
14-2	1448.8	1231.7	2680.5		2680.5
15-5	1575.8	1357.7	2933.5		2933.5

Note: RLS = Right Lateral Segment; LLS = Left Lateral Segment; Tot = Total Surface Area; SA+CS = Bony Surface Area+Cleft Space Area

No studies have conclusively shown that palatal growth can be accelerated by orthopedic appliances as Weil[65] claims or that "physiological" surgery with the establishment of functional occlusion will accelerate bone growth. Yet, Berkowitz,[51] Krogman and associates,[66] and Cooper et al,[67] suspect that catch-up growth must happen in some clefts after surgery due to the amount of additional growth that occurs, as measured by changes in palatal surface area (the area between the alvolar ridges and limited posteriorly by the end of the hard palate).

Berkowitz's palatal growth charts have shown a marked increase in palatal surface area in the first 2 years before palatal surgery. After palatal cleft closure between 18 and 24 months, there appears to be a growth hiatus, creating a plateau in the growth graph; but 6 to 12 months post-surgery there is frequently a second period of growth acceleration which extends to 6 years of age. The palatal surface area continues to increase as the molars develop and erupt into the arch.

Dental Occlusion Associated with Early Palatoplasty Using a Vomer Flap

Dahl et al[68] reported on the prevalence of malocclusion as seen in early mixed dentition with complete unilateral clefts of the lip and palate. The frequency of posterior lingual crossbite they found was extremely high. This might be partly an effect of the two-layer palato-vomerplasty used for closing of the cleft in the hard palate at 12 months of age. It has been shown that bone formation in the palatal cleft is common subsequent to this procedure (Prydso et al[69]). It was supposed that the newly formed bone might act as a bony ankylosis, inhibiting the transverse growth of the maxilla. A longitudinal study, by the implant method, of patients operated on by this method substantiated this supposition. To reduce the adverse effects on transverse maxillary growth, Dahl recommended the surgical procedure be changed to a one-layer closure of the cleft in the hard palate by a vomer flap. There has not been a follow-up study to evaluate the effect of changing the procedure—whether it is the timing or the surgery that needs changing. Dahl's Danish group of treated patients were characterized by unilateral lingual crossbite, high frequencies of midline deviation, mesial molar occlusion, and mandibular overjet. There were very few cases with an anterior open bite. A tendency was seen for a difference in the sagittal molar relationship on the cleft side, as compared with the noncleft side, with distal molar occlusion being more frequent on the cleft side. This may be explained by a primary difference in the sagittal position of the two segments of the maxilla, and also as a result of secondary changes, such as lateral shifting of the mandible caused by lingual crossbite on the cleft side, medial rotation of the cleft segment subsequent to surgery, and tipping the teeth toward the cleft on the affected side.

Berkowitz's[51] serial occlusal study of complete unilateral clefts of the lip and palate, which involved the use of modified von Langenbeck procedure with a vomer flap between 18 and 24 months of age, lists an absence of distal molar occlusion with a minimal number of anterior crossbites and only a few complete buccal crossbites. By comparison with studies that do not use vomer flaps, one can conclude that the obvious cause for the deleterious occlusal results in the Dahl et al[68] study lies in the timing and not the surgical procedure utilized because Millard Jr.[3] also utilizes a similar vomer flap with success. This conclusion does not mean that all cleft closure procedures need to be delayed until 18 months of age since narrow clefts in the palate can exist before 12 months of age. A narrow cleft suggests that less scar tissue will be created. The age of surgery is a primary variable in determining the effect of surgery on palatal development only when the width of the cleft space is also placed into the equation.

Facial Changes in Successfully Treated Cases

Lateral Cephalometric Results from the Oslo Team

Semb's group[70-73] conducted a serial lateral and frontal cephalometric study of 90 cases from the Oslo archives with bilateral cleft lip and palate. Since 1962 the treatment procedure has involved uniting the lip and hard-palate cleft space closing in two stages. No presurgical orthodontics were utilized since the surgeons and Bergland, an orthodontist and director of the program, believe that any bilateral cleft lip can be closed without presurgical palatal manipulation.

In the period spanning 1950 to 1960, a von Langenbeck procedure was performed to close the hard-palate cleft between 3 and 4 years of age; after 1960 the timing of the closure was reduced to 18 months of age. Secondary alveolar bone grafting using cancellous iliac crest bone was performed prior to the eruption of the permanent canine teeth (Abyholm et al,[73] Vol. II, Chapter 15). Twenty-five percent of the

8

Secondary Alveolar Bone Grafting: After Lip and Palate Cleft Closure

THE DEMISE OF PRIMARY BONE GRAFTING

Primary bone grafting was introduced in the late 1950s in the hope that it would stimulate and stabilize the orthopedically aligned palatal segments prior to surgical repair. Its advocates speculated on an increased ability of the bone-grafted maxilla to utilize the thrust of the growing nasal septum. They also thought that the frequency of crossbite due to maxillary collapse would decrease if a bone graft bridged the cleft.

There is almost total condemnation of early or primary bone grafting by many authors (Johanson et al,[1] Pruzansky,[2] Robertson and Jolleys,[3] Koch,[4] Pickrell et al,[5] Rehrman et al,[6] Friede and Johansson[7]) because of an association with late disturbances in maxillary development. Nordin,[8] Schmid,[9] Jaworski,[10] and especially Rosenstein et al[11,12] still, however, continue to recommend it. Rosenstein emphasizes an operative technique not involving the vomero-premaxillary suture to be of paramount importance to the maxillary growth attenuation. Sadove (oral communication, 1990) is utilizing the Kirnaham-Rosenstein procedure to determine if Rosenstein's claimed good results can be duplicated, but as of this date he has no final report.

Reichert and Manzari[13] from Stuttgart, Germany reported on 25 years of experience with primary bone grafting. Supporting Edward Schmid's enthusiasm for the procedure in the 1950s to prevent collapse of the maxillary segments by filling the bony defect with autogenous bone graft, this procedure became routine in their clinic. Interestingly, in their report they state, as one of the advantages, that the use of dentures is frequently needed at a later age and that an intact hard palate aids prosthetic retention. Examination of the alveolar arch showed that bone grafting was effective in preventing maxillary collapse in all but two patients. However, in examining the occlusion, they found hypoplasia in the area of the cleft and an open bite in 25 of 43 patients. They further reported that orthopedic correction of the deformity was extremely difficult and time-consuming. These findings stimulated them to change their entire approach in 1982 to a more conservative technique by adopting the Zurich procedure of not performing primary bone grafts (Hotz and Gnoinski,[14] Hotz et al[15]).

SECONDARY ALVEOLAR BONE GRAFTS: A BETTER WAY

There is presently almost total agreement that the residual alveolar defect needs to be filled (Fig 8–1). The only questions remaining concern the timing of the procedure, the material to be used, and the source for autogenous bone.

Advantages cited generally include:

1. No need for permanent bridgework if erupting teeth can be brought into the new bone-grafted cleft space.
2. Better periodontal and bony support for teeth (lateral incisor and canine) located along the edges of the cleft that were inadequately embedded in alveolar bone.
3. An end to nasal irritation and crusting resulting from passage of food into the nose through the oronasal fistula.
4. Stabilization of the palatal segments.
5. Improvement in appearance with better support for the alar base and nasal platform.
6. Prevention of air escaping via the oronasal communication.

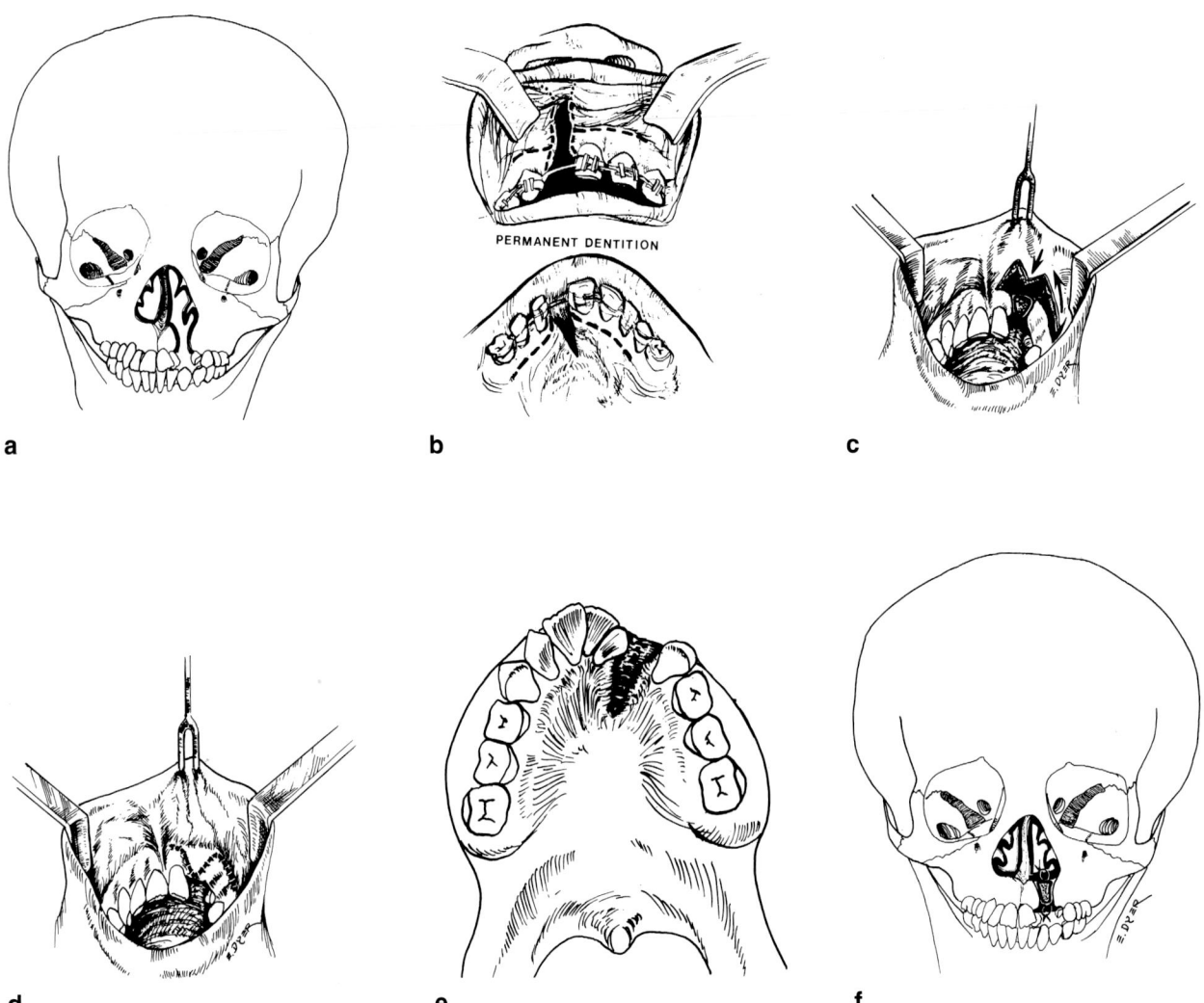

Fig 8–1. Kinds of bone grafts. Osteoplasties differ in three main regards: (1) whether performed at lip repair (primary) or later (secondary, after the palate cleft is closed); (2) whether pre- and/or postoperative orthodontic treatment is given or not; and (3) what kind of bone is employed (cranial, rib, chips, cancellous, osteochondral junction, boneless = periosteum). The use of epiphyseal cartilage is no longer being utilized. The following drawings demonstrate the surgery involved in performing a secondary alveolar bone graft (SABG). **a.** Frontal view showing the cleft extending from the alveolar crest into the nose. **b.** Incision lines in the soft tissue. **c.** Exposure of the cleft. The isolation of the graft from the nasal and oral cavities. The triangular flap is brought down for alveolar closure. Closure of the overlying soft tissue: **d.** Labile view, **e.** Palatal view, and **f.** Frontal view showing a separation of the graft site from the nasal and oral cavities. (From Wolfe SA, Berkowitz S. The use of cranial bone grafts in the closure of alveolar and anterior palatal clefts. *Plast and Reconst Surg.* 1983;72:659–666.)

7. Allowing for tooth movement across and adjoining the cleft.

Sources of Material to Fill the Alveolar Cleft

It is generally agreed that an autograft is superior to an allogenic graft or allioimplant for reconstruction and that autogenous particulate marrow and cancellous bone is the ideal bone to encourage tooth eruption (Abyholm et al,[16] Boyne and Sands,[17] Waite and Kersten,[18] El Deeb et al,[19] El Deeb,[20] Boyne and Sands,[21] Kalaaji et al[22]). If the demands require support, strength and obliteration of the defect, El Deeb[20] suggests a cortical or corticocancellous graft. Particulate marrow and cancellous bone revascularizes faster than corticocancellous bone, regardless of the origin.

Rib

Rib bone is less favored because it contains more cortical than cancellous bone and because spontaneous eruption of teeth and orthodontic movements of teeth through rib bone is extremely difficult.

Witsenburg[23] in his review of the literature lists the main arguments against the use of rib bone:

1. Teeth erupt only with great difficulty.
2. It does not have a tendency to grow with the maxilla.
3. In a small child there is only a small quantity to be obtained and especially very little cancellous bone available.
4. It does not respond to orthodontic movement of teeth and arch expansion and is to a large extent nonviable.

Ilium

These are extensive reports in the literature (Abyholm et al,[16] Boyne and Sands,[17,21] Waite and Kersten,[18] El Deeb et al,[19] Boyne[24]) advocating secondary bone grafting of alveolar clefts using iliac bone before the eruption of the permanent canine teeth, and no disturbances in the maxillary growth have been attributed to bone grafting at this age (9–12 years), when one quarter to one half of the canine root has formed.

The Oslo Clinic, in a classic report (Abyholm et al[16]), recommended that secondary alveolar bone grafts be performed prior to eruption of the permanent cuspids, preferably when the unerupted permanent cuspid root is approximately two-thirds to three-quarters formed and the central incisors and palatal arches have been properly aligned (see Abyholm in Volume II). Their techniques followed the principles laid down by Boyne and Sands[17] and Boyne.[24]

Boyne[24] recommends orthodontics after bone grafting because placing slight tension at the grafted area by palatal expansion may induce formation of additional alveolar bone.

If the alveolar bone grafting surgery is successfully performed at 8 to 10 years of age, it is possible that both an unerupted and displaced lateral incisor and/or cuspid can erupt into the cleft site with normal periodontal fibers. Incorporation of the bone graft was usually seen after 16 months (Turvey[25]).

Tibia

Very few reports are available on this source (Jaworski,[10] Johanson and Ohlsson,[26] Jackson et al,[27] Johnsson et al,[28] Friede and Johanson,[29] and Kalaaji[22]). These reports are very favorable.

Mandible

Symphysis bone grafts can be successful when treating small alveolar bone grafts (El Deeb[30]). Borstlap et al[32] and Freihofer et al,[32] on the other hand, believe enough bone is available in the chin to bridge most clefts and have found it superior to all other transplant material.

Cranium

The most frequently used system for harvesting cancellous bone involves taking bone from the iliac crest but, due to the postsurgical pain involved in using the iliac crest versus the ease of harvesting bone from the cranium, the latter procedure is becoming more popular (Wolfe and Berkowitz[32]). Although LaRossa et al[34] report that iliac bone grafts yield superior results when compared to cranial bone, Cohen et al[35] concluded that bone grafts from both sites were equally as good.

Advantages of cranial bone include:

1. Rapid time of harvesting cancellous diploic bone with assurance of as much bone as needed.
2. Donor area in same operative field.
3. Virtual absence of postoperative pain in the donor area and an invisible scar.
4. Shorter length of hospitalization (1–2 days) as a result of less pain in the donor area.

Berkowitz found that most patients treated in the 7- to 11-year-old age group had some orthodontic expansion just prior to grafting which left a 3 to 5 mm gap in the alveolar ridge at the time of the surgery, but this did not pose a problem in achieving a successful graft.

CURRRENT APPROACH TO BONE GRAFTING OF THE ALVEOLAR CLEFT

There are a number of reasons for our preference of calvarial bone[36]:

1. Hidden scar and minimal pain
2. Same operative field
3. Diploic cancellous bone is readily available in younger patients, and we are now bone grafting patients earlier between 7 to 9 years of age depending on alignment of the central incisors.

Our preference for cranial bone is not absolute, and when older patients say they would prefer iliac bone, we are happy to use it. Certainly, there is nothing wrong with iliac bone. The main thing is that the bone that is used is as purely cancellous as possible.

We generally use the right parietal region as a donor area. This is over the nondominant hemisphere, and the bone is thickest in the parietal occipital region.

Generally no hair need be shaved.

A zigzag incision is made to better hide the scar.

The outer table is scored with a oscillating saw, and then a modified Hendel osteotome is placed on the reciprocating saw and used as an impact osteotome to remove the outer table. This comes off as strips of bone about 1 cm wide and 1 to 3 cm in length. Once the outer table is removed, one is looking at a layer of pure diploic cancellous bone. This cancellous bone is then further removed using the Hendel osteotome and maintained separately. Generally, as much cancellous bone can be removed as is required. Bleeding from the bone is controlled by minimal amounts of bone wax, and the previously removed outer table segments are contoured and placed back over the donor area to prevent any subsequent weakness of the skull. A piece of gel foam is placed over the harvest areas and the incision is closed in layers, generally with a suction drain. Cost effectiveness is another reason for the use of calvarial bone. Patients enter the hospital the morning of surgery and in virtually all cases now leave the morning after surgery following removed of the drain.

The method we originally described, using a Hudson brace, has been changed because it gave an admixture of both cortical and cancellous bone in a fairly powdery form. There was probably also some damage to the bone by the inevitable heat generated by the brace.

We believe that, if there is a diploic space, the quality of the bone that is removed from the skull will be just as good as from the hip. Most patients do have a good cancellous space at this age. In an effort to identify which patients are not candidates for calvarial bone grafting, we have begun a research study at Miami Children's Hospital to see if ultrasound can be used preoperatively to estimate the thickness and location of the diploic space. Preliminary results are encouraging, and we feel that this will be a useful tool in deciding which donor area to use.

In our opinion, the donor site is irrelevant. The Scandinavians for many years have used the tibia, and the American literature generally dwells on the iliac region (where there is not much cancellous bone until the age of 7 or 8).

We continue to use the skull as a donor source and feel that the only important factor is that pure cancellous bone be used to fill alveolar defects. We have had little if any trouble with tooth eruption through this type of bone, whereas centers using other types of bone have reported difficulty with teeth erupting through the grafted bone.

Bilateral clefts are generally grafted in two stages, because dissection on both sides at once would leave the premaxilla with a precarious blood supply. The cranial bone is packed into the maxillary (nasal floor) cleft as far back as is possible, and bone is packed in at the anterior maxillary level to construct the missing piriform rim. Most important, bone is packed as far interiorly as possible into the alveolar cleft to bring bone between the teeth at the level of the alveolar ridge (Figs 8–2 through 8–7).

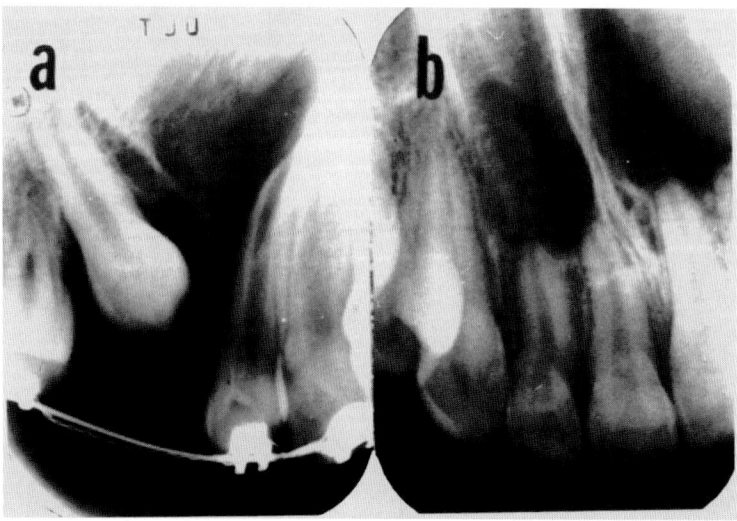

Fig 8–2. Cranial secondary alveolar bone graft (CSABG). Bone was placed at 9-2 after the lateral incisor was orthodontically aligned. The lateral incisor had undergone slight root changes. **a.** Before bone grafting. **b.** After bone grafting. Note that the cuspid and lateral incisor are aligned.

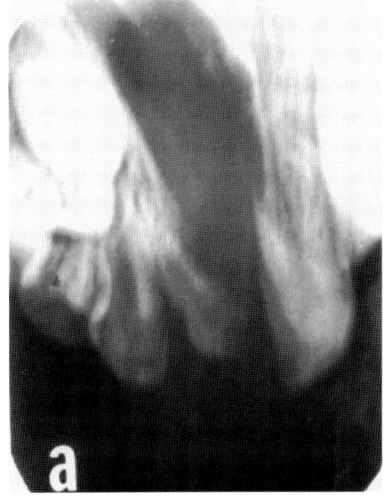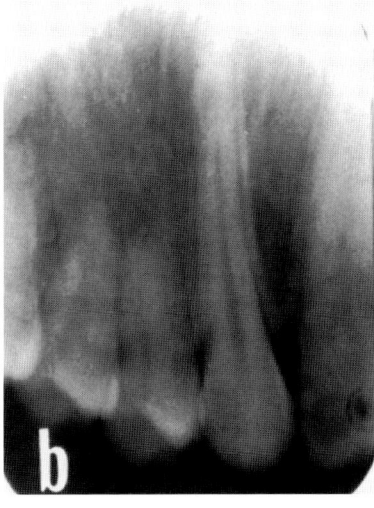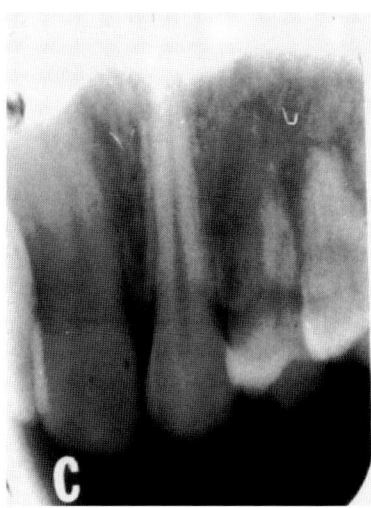

Fig 8–3. **Cranial secondary alveolar bone graft (CSABG) placed prior to the eruption of the permanent cuspid.** After the cuspid erupted through the graft, it was orthodontically aligned. **a.** Before graft. **b.** and **c.** 5 years after surgery.

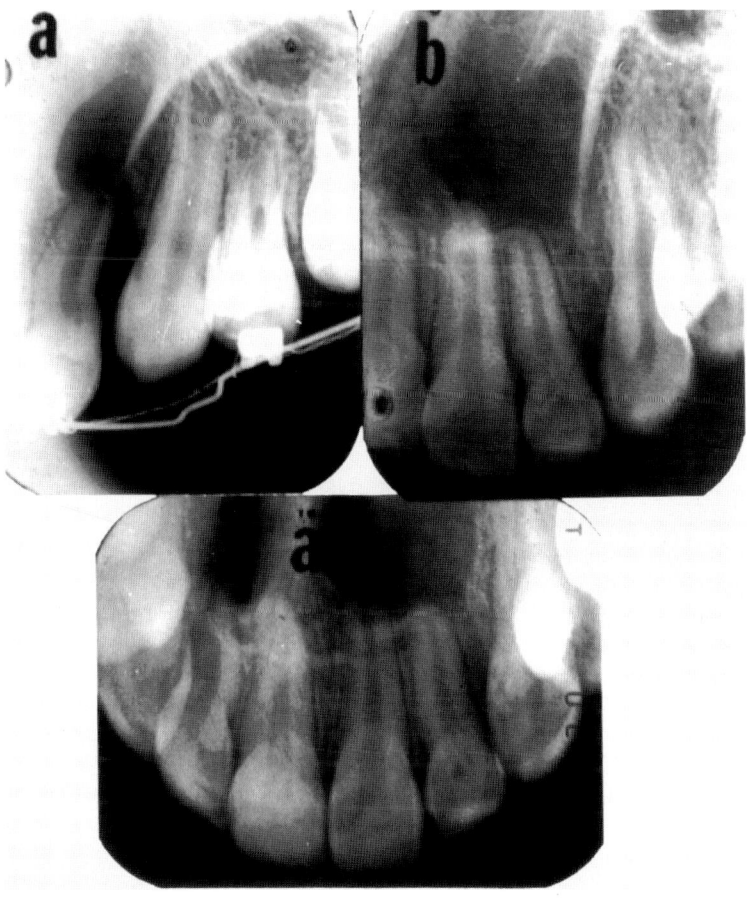

Fig 8–4. **Cranial secondary alveolar bone graft (CSABG) placed after the cuspid and lateral incisor were in position within the arch.** **a.** Before surgery. **b.** and **c.** 3 years after bone graft.

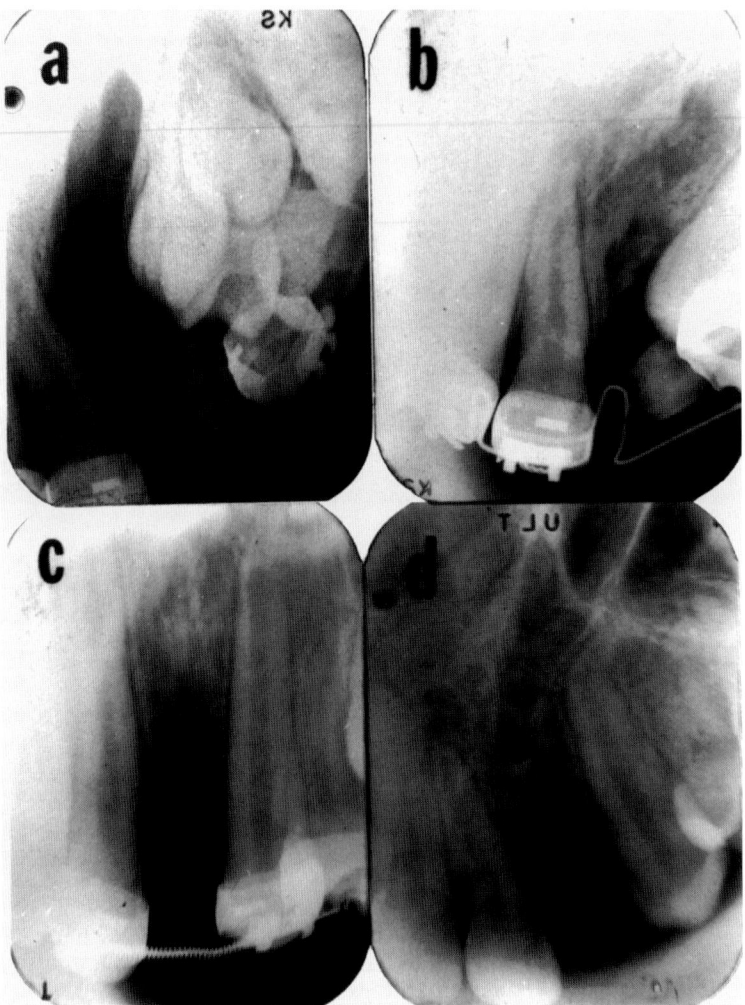

Fig 8–5. **Cranial secondary alveolar bone graft (CSABG) placed at 7½ years of age. a.** 7-6. **b.** 3 months after surgery. **c.** 16 months after surgery. **d.** 3 years after surgery

Long-term Effects

In his review of the literature, Witsenburg[23] noted that results are difficult to compare because one author still considers the operation successful if the oronasal fistula does not recur although the grafted bone disappeared, while another author would regard such a result as a failure. Hogeman et al[37] reported results from a 1-year follow-up of 145 patients treated from 1961 to 1969 with secondary bone grafting after preoperative orthodontic correction of the occlusion. Using their final operative technique (42 cases), the surgery was successful in 98% of the cases, and they concluded that the method was effective in stabilizing the occlusion and improving lip appearance.

Johanson et al[1] in an excellent follow-up study reported that, in addition to the fistula closure, the bony graft brought about normalization of the palatal arch.

Intraoral radiographic follow-up of the cranial bone grafts by Berkowitz showed that about three quarters of the patients had a bony structure in the graft region which corresponded well with the surrounding maxillary bone. The transformation of the bone graft was considered terminated 6 months after the operation in 90% of the patients. Delay in most cases could be laid to infection of the region. In a few instances, the transformed bone graft regressed to total resorption. This may have been due to infection or inadequate isolation of the graft.

In the youngest group of patients (soon after the eruption of central incisors), the bone graft facilitated the

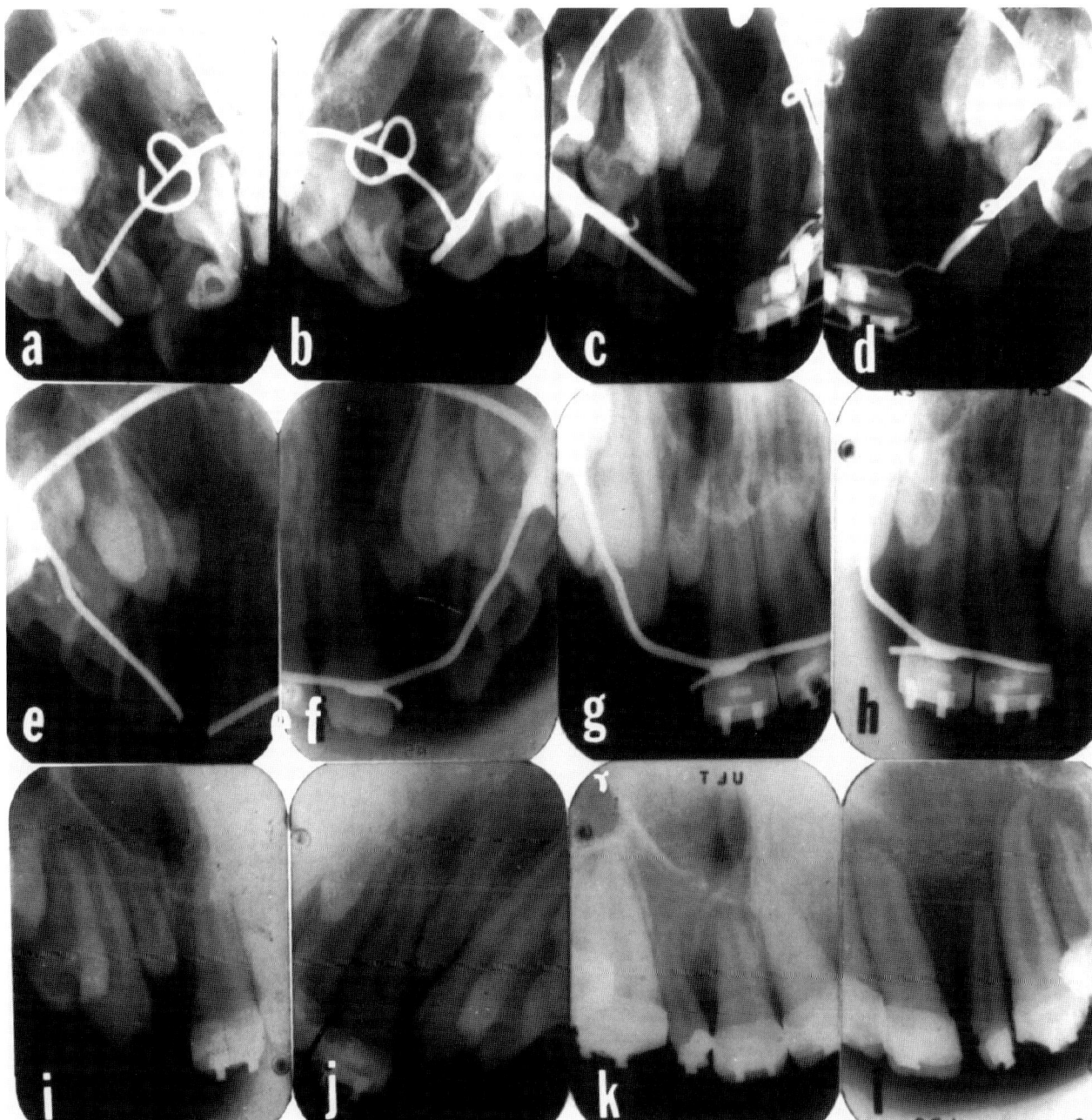

Fig 8-6. Cranial secondary alveolar bone graft (CSABG) in a bilateral cleft lip and palate. a. and b. At 6 years of age prior to CSABG. c. and d. Graft placed at 8 years of age after the central incisors were aligned. e. and f. At 9 years of age, the unerupted lateral incisors have moved into the graft. g. and h. At 11 years of age, the lateral incisors are well positioned and are undergoing normal root development. i. and j. At 11 years and 9 months. k. and l. The lateral incisors are in proper occlusion with good bone support.

eruption of lateral incisor and cuspid teeth near the cleft, which otherwise would have been lost in adulthood due to periodontal disease associated with insufficient bone support. A further advantage of performing this surgery between 8 and 9 years of age is that the eruption of teeth in the graft region seems to lead to an improved alveolar contour compared to that seen when bone grafting is performed after the cuspid is already in position.

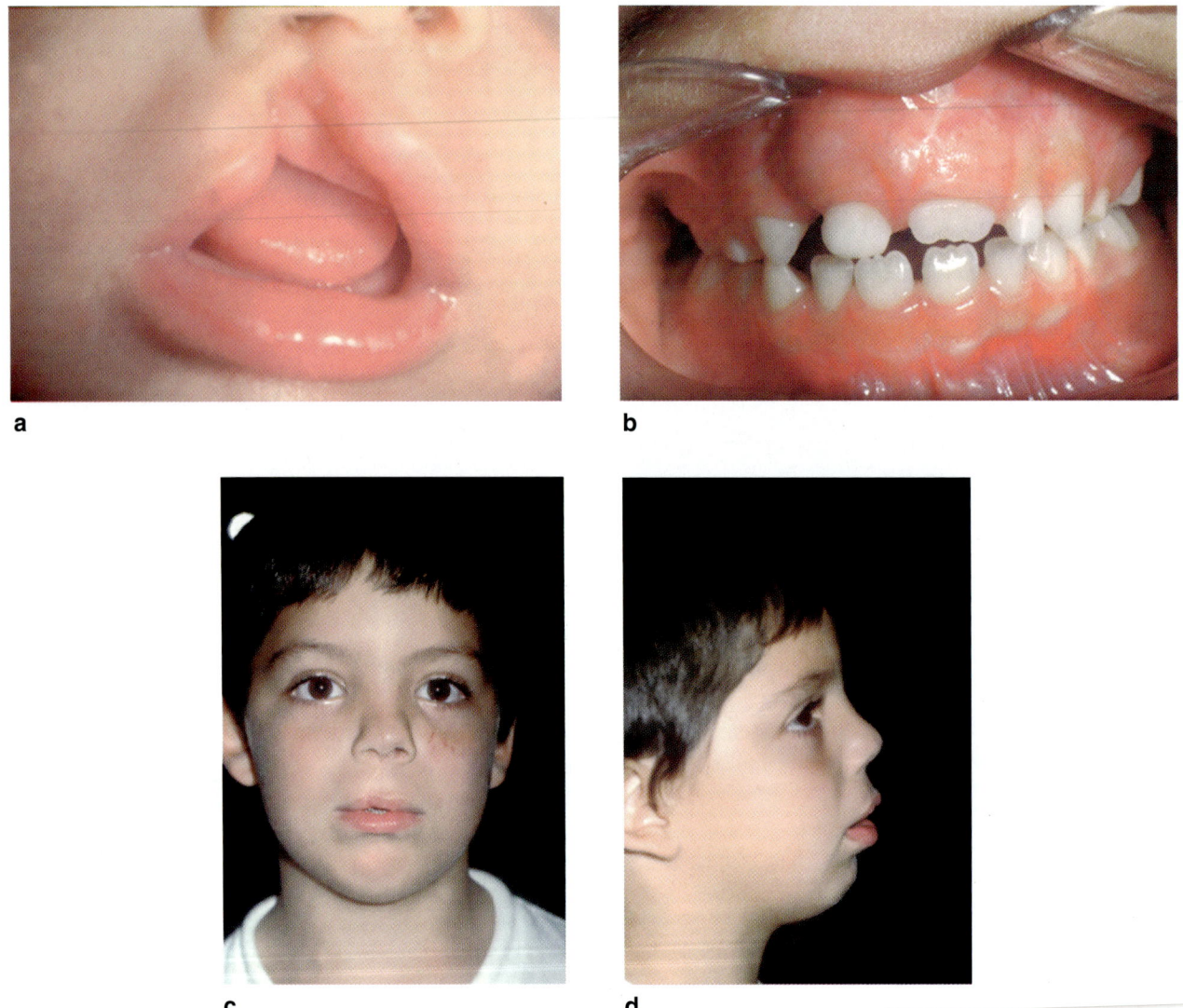

Fig 8–7. Case RL. An example of an unerupted cuspid erupting through the alveolar cranial bone graft into the lateral incisor space. a. Incomplete cleft of the lip. However, the cleft of the alveolus is complete and extends through the alveolar bone. **b.** No right deciduous lateral incisor is present. **c.** and **d.** Facial photographs. **e., f.,** and **g.** At 8 years, the central incisors were brought together to increase the cuspid space and allow the left lateral incisor to erupt spontaneously. **h.** The right cuspid is erupting into the lateral incisor space. **i.** At 14 years, the left lateral incisor is in place. **j.** and **k.** At 15 years, the cuspid is in the lateral incisor space. **l.** and **m.** Final facial photographs at age 15.

Comment: If a lateral incisor is presented but unerupted, a bone graft placed soon after the central incisors are aligned will aid in allowing the lateral incisor to erupt into place. In some instances, when much alveolar bone with its surrounding gingival tissue is absent, it will be better to perform the alveolar graft prior to opening the lateral incisor space by orthodontics in order to obtain a better soft tissue pocket. Increasing alveolar arch length prior to bone grafting, especially in bilateral clefts of the lip and palate, will frequently lead to soft tissue inadequacy for isolating the graft material from the oral and nasal cavities. In these cases, orthopedics or orthodontics to align the teeth should be instituted no later than 4 weeks after the graft is placed.

Europe in the mid-1950s in conjunction with presurgical maxillary orthopedics. The graft, usually of autogenous rib or bone from the iliac crest, was inserted into the alveolar area via a buccal approach. The graft created a bony bridge into which, theoretically, new bone and teeth would migrate. By the 1970s many of those who initially advocated the procedure had abandoned it because their experience showed a negative effect on the growth of the maxilla and midface. From a study of a series of bone grafts, Jolleys and Robertson[50] concluded that the procedure resulted in no positive effects. On the contrary, they found reduced anteroposterior maxillary development with an increased incidence of crossbites. Robinson and Wood,[51] Friede and Johanson,[52,53] and Matthews et al[54] also had strong doubts about the benefits of primary bone grafting. Peat[55] did not recommend bone grafting for stabilizing the maxillary palatal position after orthopedic treatment, but suggested that it might have a place as a secondary procedure after the age of 6 years.

The Kernahan-Rosenstein Procedure[56]

Today's foremost proponents of neonatal maxillary orthopedic procedures with primary bone grafting are Kernahan and Rosenstein,[56] who had been influenced by McNeil in 1954. In CBCLP children with a protruding premaxilla, Rosenstein uses a passive orthopedic appliance to cover the lateral palatal segments to permit the premaxilla to be molded back by an elastic extraoral facial strap (Fig 9–1, a). In a complete unilateral cleft of the lip and palate (CUCLP), the acrylic appliance covers only the back two thirds of the larger palatal segment up to the alveolar ridge. The action of the surgically repaired lip will move this segment to an end-to-end relationship with the lesser segment. If the palatal segments overlap, Rosenstein uses a small jackscrew to create a gradual expansion of the contracted arch, prior to uniting the lip (Fig 9–1, d).

Bone grafting to the alveolus, using autogenous bone taken from the patient's sixth rib, is not done until the alveolar ridge is in an "optimum position" and then is performed to stabilize the segment. The appliance is worn for 6 to 8 weeks and may be used until just before closure of the cleft palate at approximately 18 months of age. They claim that the arches are stabilized within 4 to 5 months.

Although most cleft palate centers in the United States and Europe have abandoned primary bone grafting, Kernahan and Rosenstein still defend its use, claiming that the surgical procedure they use in placing the autogenous bone is significantly different from the procedures used by others and is the essential reason for their greater success-to-failure ratio.

Sadove (oral communication, 1990), attempting to duplicate the Kernahan-Rosenstein procedure, advises that, since none of the cases have reached maturity, it is still too early to file a final report.

Critical Review

No discussion of presurgical orthopedics and primary bone grafting would be complete without the critical review of the neonatal orthopedic procedures published by Samuel Pruzansky[57] in 1964. In his article, the first paragraph sets the mood of Pruzansky's[57(p164)] dissent:

> It is not simple or a lightly assumed task to write a brief challenging the rationale for presurgical orthopedics and bone grafting for infants with cleft lip and palate. The advocates are numerous and international . . . Their battle cry is a cabalistic mumbo-jumbo invoking the mystic of embryology and growth and development. Their proposal to make things right and whole as early as possible seems sensible and has emotional appeal. Regrettably, and despite all this enthusiasm, what has been offered so far is a prolonged and costly manipulation and a surgery that is needless and sometimes barbaric.

Pruzansky strongly criticized the adoption of procedures whose results had not been adequately reviewed on the basis of objective diagnostic records of serial casts and cephaloradiographs to support their conclusions.

Long-term Results

Many of McNeil's original followers soon found the results of these procedures to be disappointing. Not only were additional orthodontics necessary, but it was suspected that presurgical orthopedics, as it was then practiced, might be causing more problems than had been anticipated, especially when the procedure incorporated primary bone grafting. Usually the autogenous bone graft is placed in the alveolar cleft space soon after the palatal segments are aligned at the time of closure of the cleft lip or shortly thereafter but before closure of the palate.

In 1978 Berkowitz[58] chaired a "State of the Art" report in cleft palate orofacial growth and dentistry. An international committee of 12 members reviewed the literature on the stated advantages of presurgical orthopedics. They found that most of the supposed benefits were not supported by the literature. As of this publication, the same conclusions hold because there is no new supporting literature.

A decade after Pruzansky's 1964 critique, many Europeans who had previously supported the procedure also changed their minds and condemned the results. Skoog[59] of Sweden, who had never favored the technique, wrote that presurgical neonatal orthopedics are both unnecessary and unhelpful, and suggested that well-performed lip repair would mold and reposition the maxillary segments into proper alignment.

Fara et al,[60] reporting on their long-term experience with neonatal maxillary orthopedics and primary bone grafting, concluded that it did not benefit maxillofacial growth, and indeed had a detrimental effect.

Huddart,[29,30,61] who knew McNeil personally, reports that McNeil put great emphasis on the use of stimulator plates as a means of reducing the hard palate defect, and stressed that they should be worn up to the time of palate repair at about 18 months of age. Huddart also observed that it was very difficult to get babies to wear these appliances consistently, especially beyond the age of 4 to 6 months.

Unfortunately, there are very few detailed reports of the results of presurgical treatment with active appliances that move palatal segments. In most cases, using passive appliances which control palatal molding action appears to be equally as ineffective on a long-term basis as employing active appliances which move palatal segments.

There are as many different types of passive plates as there are reasons for using them. Huddart's passive orthopedic appliance is a simple plastic plate that is inserted 24 to 48 hours after birth. It obturates the cleft space but does not extend into the nasal cavity; it still, however, protects the underside of the nasal septum during feeding.

Huddart uses two adjustable wire wings that extend laterally from the corner of the mouth and lie on the cheeks to prevent the baby from swallowing the appliance. In complete unilateral clefts of the lip and palate (CUCLP), the plate is utilized in conjunction with external elastic strappings to correct the anterior cleft defect by molding the premaxillary portion of the larger segment. Huddart reports a subsequent narrowing of the hard palatal cleft and believes that McNeil's type of treatment, which employ pressure pads, has an opposite effect, actually reducing the rate of tissue growth on the margins of the palatal cleft; however, this has not been proven. After years of using orthopedic appliances on cleft infants soon after birth, Huddart concluded that there appears to be no difference in occlusion between patients who receive presurgical orthopedic treatment and patients who do not.

Although many cleft palate treatment centers do not believe that orthopedic devices can stimulate palatal growth, they still advocate the use of neonatal maxillary orthopedics not only to aid in feeding but to bring the displaced palatal segments into proper position to facilitate the closing of the lip (Maisels,[62] Huddart and Crabb,[63] Perko,[64] Hotz,[65] Nordin et al,[66] Komposch,[67] and Trankmann[68]). Some claim that the procedure is also psychologically beneficial to the parents at a critical time (Robertson[69]).

Friede[70] (Goteberg, Sweden), having gone through many changes in treatment philosophy, now argues that normalizing the arch form and postponing all palatal surgery to 5 to 6 years of age, when 80% of palatal growth is completed, can be highly beneficial. He suggests using external elastic forces with passive orthopedic appliances to retrude the premaxilla in CBCL/P and the premaxillary portion of the larger segment in CUCL/P. The orthopedic appliance is utilized to maintain the arch form prior to the use of external elastic forces or lip repair. Although the Goteberg team claims excellent palate and facial development, superior to that achieved when the cleft space was closed at 1 to 2 years of age. They, nevertheless, are willing to accept the trade-off of increased management problems associated with a longer use of an obturator.

Even with all the ballyhooed but unsupported benefits a small core of orthodontists still spoke out strongly against presurgical orthopedics (Pruzansky, Aduss, Subtelny, Berkowitz, Olin, Ross, Mayo, Bishara, Mazahari, Tindlund, Shaw, Bergland, Semb, Figueroa, Friede and Collito).

A Critique of Primary Bone Grafts

Cronin[71] was a strong supporter of early presurgical orthopedics and primary bone grafts in the 1960s. The many glowing reports by various European authors[77] were instrumental in encouraging him to use neonatal orthopedics with a primary bone graft to close the anterior palate followed by a vomer flap at 18 months and pushback repair of the hard and soft palates at 24 months of age. He also used secondary alveolar bone grafts in older patients, after the arch and occlusion had been corrected by orthodontics.

At a second international symposium in 1969 held at the Cleft Palate Institute of the Northwestern University Dental School, Cronin[71] stated that the ideal of bridging the bony defect with a bone graft seemed logical. He listed the goals of the grafting procedure as: (1) to fix the alveolar segments together and equalize the growth; (2) to prevent collapse of the maxillary segments; (3) to stabilize the premaxilla in complete bilateral clefts; (4) to provide more bone for teeth adjacent to the cleft; and (5) to better support the ala and improve the contour of the cheek.

At this symposium, he reported that the bone grafting failed to prevent collapse but, to some degree, did stabilize the premaxilla in bilateral clefts. It also enabled teeth to erupt in the area of the lateral incisor and gave the ala support. At that time, he claimed that it was too early to judge the long-term effect on midfacial growth; however, he later reported that facial growth was retarded (personal communication, March 1982). Most significantly Cronin, as cited by Cole,[70(p30)] stated,

> In looking over these cases through the years, it seems to me that the orthodontist has accomplished just as much at age 4 or 5 years as we have working with the infant, and that he has done it more easily and in a shorter period of time. My own view is that I would be willing to wait until that period of time for this work to begin, after what I've seen.

A multicenter cephalometric study (Ross[73]) of orthopedic versus nonorthopedic treatment in complete unilateral cleft lip and palate cases between 10 and 11 years of age involving 13 cleft palate centers showed no differences in the effect of presurgical orthopedics on the maxilla in either anteroposterior dimensions or growth patterns.

Berkowitz's unpublished serial growth study of the use of the Latham-Millard pinned orthopedic appliance in complete unilateral cleft lip and palate case reported in 1995 at the American Cleft Palate-Craniofacial meeting in Tampa (Abstract 88) that, in the treated cases, a number of detrimental effects were related to use of anterior-directed forces on the cleft's lesser segment and the reactive posterior-medial-directed force against the premaxillary portion of the larger segment. The findings of this study showed that the cleft segment was usually displaced anteromedially, putting the buccal teeth in crossbite with the deciduous cuspid positioned in the lateral incisor space. The premaxillary portion of the larger palatal segment was displaced too far posteriorly and to the opposite side, causing the incisors to be positioned in an anterior crossbite relationship (Figs 9–1 to 9–11). Berkowitz's observation of serial casts of neonatal maxillary orthopedic treated cases reported at this meeting that the position of the cleft's smaller segments within the maxillary arch was not stable, and it often moved medially into crossbite, even in the presence of a bone bridge across the cleft.

THE ZURICH CONCEPT[74] (Fig 9–2)

This approach is presented to demonstrate the treatment philosophy at a clinic where the main goal is to maximize palatal growth, and team members do not believe they are sacrificing speech development. They also believe that their presurgical orthopedic treatment has long-term utility.

Passive plates used in conjunction with delayed surgical procedures were introduced in Zurich, Switzerland in the 1960s after clinicians there had tried McNeil-type orthopedic procedures and found them wanting. The Zurich appliance is a combination of both soft and hard acrylic (Fig 9–2). The plate penetrates into the nasal chamber to some extent, is worn continuously for about 16 to 18 months and is replaced every 6 months. Reduction of the gingival side of the plate every three to 8 weeks allows for palatal growth changes. A posterior extension to the top of the cleft uvula is a specific feature which Gnoinski[74] claims makes swallowing more normal. She stresses that the plate, while allowing for spontaneous development without the tongue or other mechanical interference in the cleft, does not stimulate growth as claimed by McNeil,[2-3] and Weil.[42] In connection with this sequence of treatment, the lip is united surgically at 6 months of age, the soft palate at 18 months, and the hard palate cleft is closed at between 4 and 5 years of age.

Gnoinski[74] lists the following benefits of the procedure: (1) It aids in feeding. (2) It maintains the width of the maxilla and lets the palate increase spontaneously in all three dimensions without impeding its growth potential. And (3) it permits the soft palate to grow to its maximum length prior to surgery.

THE NETHERLANDS APPROACH

Presurgical orthopedic treatment in cleft lip and palate is provided in three centers in the Netherlands: Nijmegen, Amsterdam, and Rotterdam.

Unilateral Cleft Lip and Palate (UCLP) (Fig 9–3)

A baby born with a cleft is referred to a Cleft Palate Centre, preferably within 2 weeks after birth. The plastic surgeon and the orthodontist decide on the first treatment stages. In cases where the cleft is wide, presurgical orthopedic treatment usually is

Fig 9–2. Presurgical orthopedic appliances used in complete unilateral (a-e) and bilateral (f-h) cleft lip and palate. The palatal acrylic extends posteriorly to the uvulae. (Courtesy Wanda Gnoinski, Zurich University Dental Clinic, Cleft Palate Institute.)

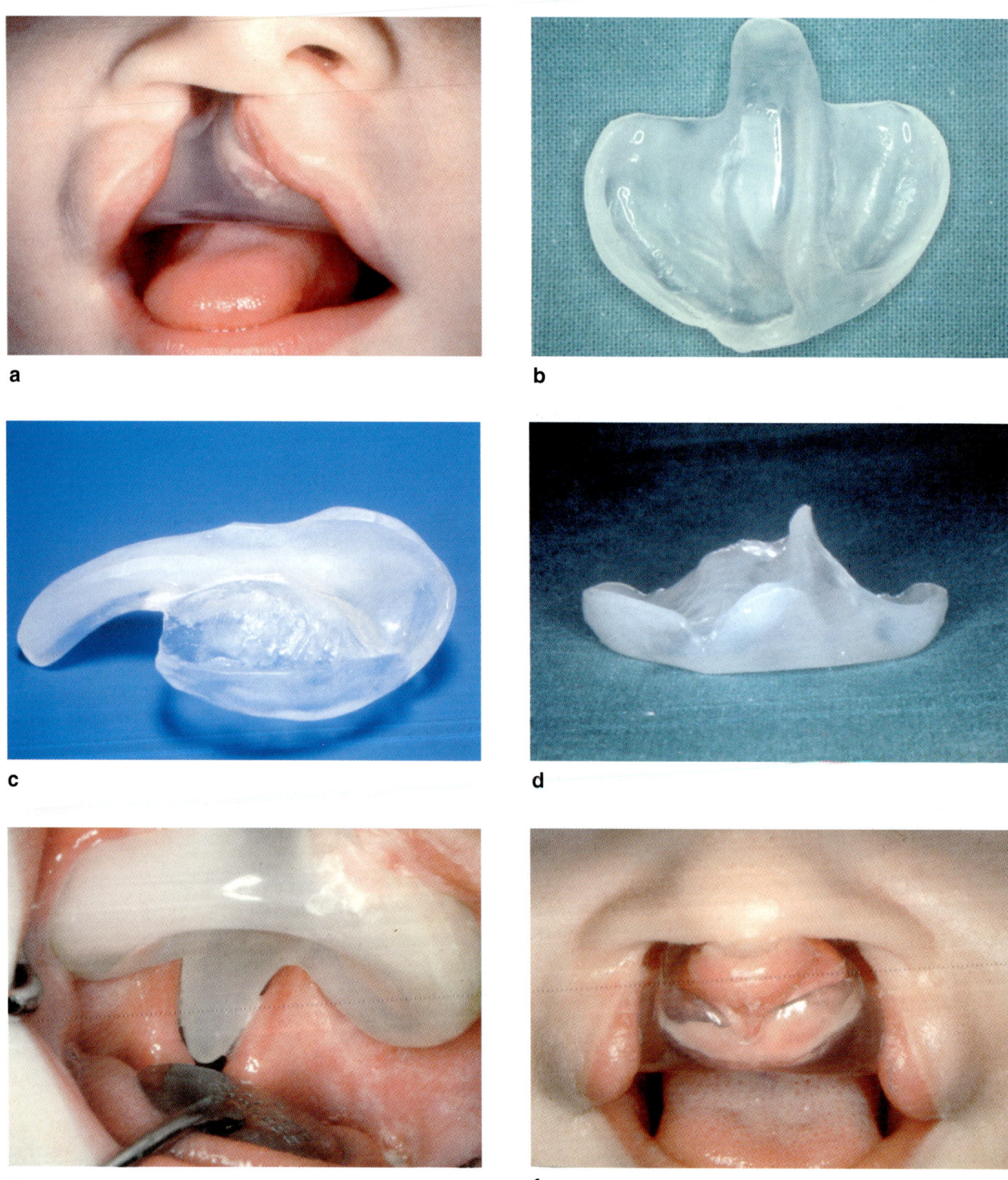

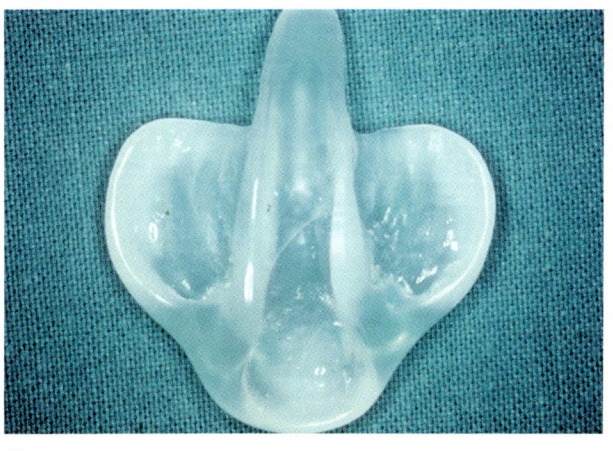
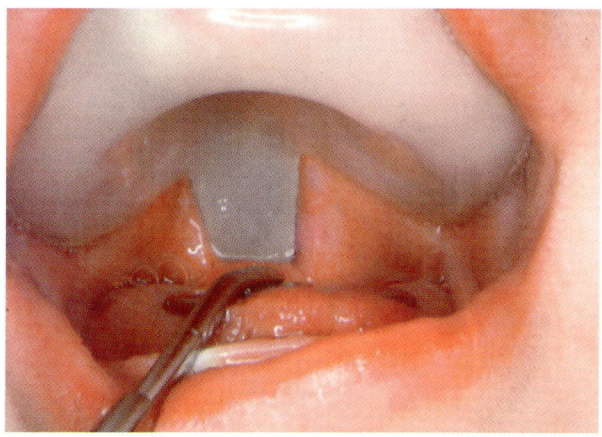

g   h

Fig. 9–2. *(continued)*

started immediately. The decision to start treatment is based purely on clinical experience.

To fabricate the appliance, an impression of the upper jaw is made with an elastomeric material. A plate, consisting of compound of soft and hard acrylic, is carefully designed and fabricated to obturate the whole cleft laterally from right buccal vestibulum to the left (soft palate and alveolar ridge included) and placed in situ within a few days. The plate keeps the tongue out of the cleft. The support offered by the artificial alveolar ridge is thought to be important for speech development. The oral and nasal cavities are separated and nasal breathing is restored (Hotz[75]). The plate is worn 24 hours a day and held by suction and adhesion only.

Every 3 weeks the patient returns to the clinic to have the plate adjusted. Adjustments are made by grinding the plate to guide the segments during growth. The direction and total amount of growth are used to indicate when a new plate is necessary. A new plate is made the week before lip closure, which is done at approximately 5 to 6 months of age, to ensure that a well-fitting plate can be placed immediately after lip surgery. At this time, the alveolar cleft has narrowed considerably, which possibly facilitates lip closure (Kuijpers-Jagtman[76]). In addition, because labial sounds appear in normal development at this age, a lip seal becomes essential.

After lip closure (Millard rotation advancement), the new plate is inserted the same day to prevent positional changes of the maxillary segments, which are undesirable side effects of the operation. Then a two-stage palatal closure (modified von Langenbeck) is performed (i.e., the soft palate is closed at about 12 to 18 months and hard palate closure is done at 6 to 9 years of age) together with bone grafting of the alveolar cleft. The plate is worn until soft palate closure is performed (about 12 to 18 months of age). In the interim, the patient visits the clinic every 3 weeks. Later, when the growth velocity slows, visits are every 6 weeks. The plate is continually adjusted, as mentioned previously, taking into account the emerging deciduous teeth. Depending on maxillary growth, the plate is remade as necessary.

Bilateral Cleft Lip and Palate (BCLP) (Fig 9–4)

The same procedures are performed, but extra-oral strapping is used. A one-stage lip closure (modified Manchester) is performed at about 6 to 9 months of age.

Most surgeons believe, quite frankly, that one benefit of these procedures is to help fulfill the psychological need of parents of children with clefts to feel that "something" is being done to help their child at birth, and feel that this is very important in maintaining harmonious family dynamics.

The Spread of Presurgical Orthopedic Treatment Clinics

Rudolph and Margaret Hotz have attracted a following of eminent orthodontists who are more constrained in stating the benefits of their orthopedic procedures and have influenced the creation of presurgical orthopedic treatment clinics throughout Europe and the United States.

For an in-depth review of their treatment philosophy, the reader is referred to Hotz,[20,21] Hotz and Gnoinski,[77] and Hotz Hotz et al.[78,79]

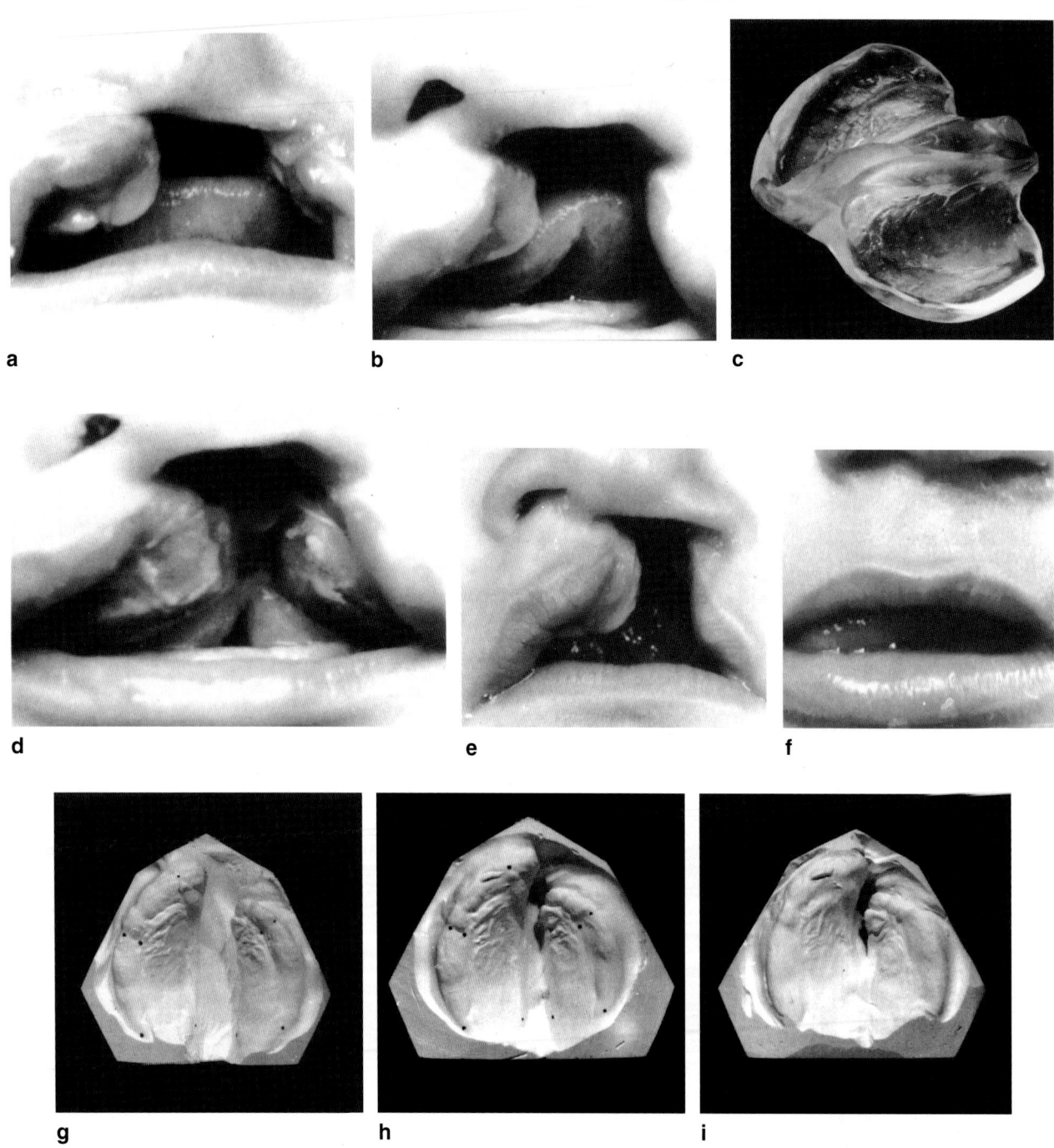

Fig 9–3. **Presurgical orthopedic treatment (PSOT) appliance for a CUCLP utilized from birth to 1½ at the University of Nijmegen** (Courtesy of AM Kuijpers-Jagtman). **a.** Lip and nose distortion at birth; **b.** Tongue posture within the cleft, **c.** Orthopedic appliance; **d.** Orthopedic plate prevents the tongue from entering the cleft; **e.** 15 weeks after PSOT and before lip closure; **f.** 6 weeks after palate closure; **g.** 17 months before soft palate closure; **h.** At 14 months of age, before soft palate closure; **i.** 8 weeks after lip closure.

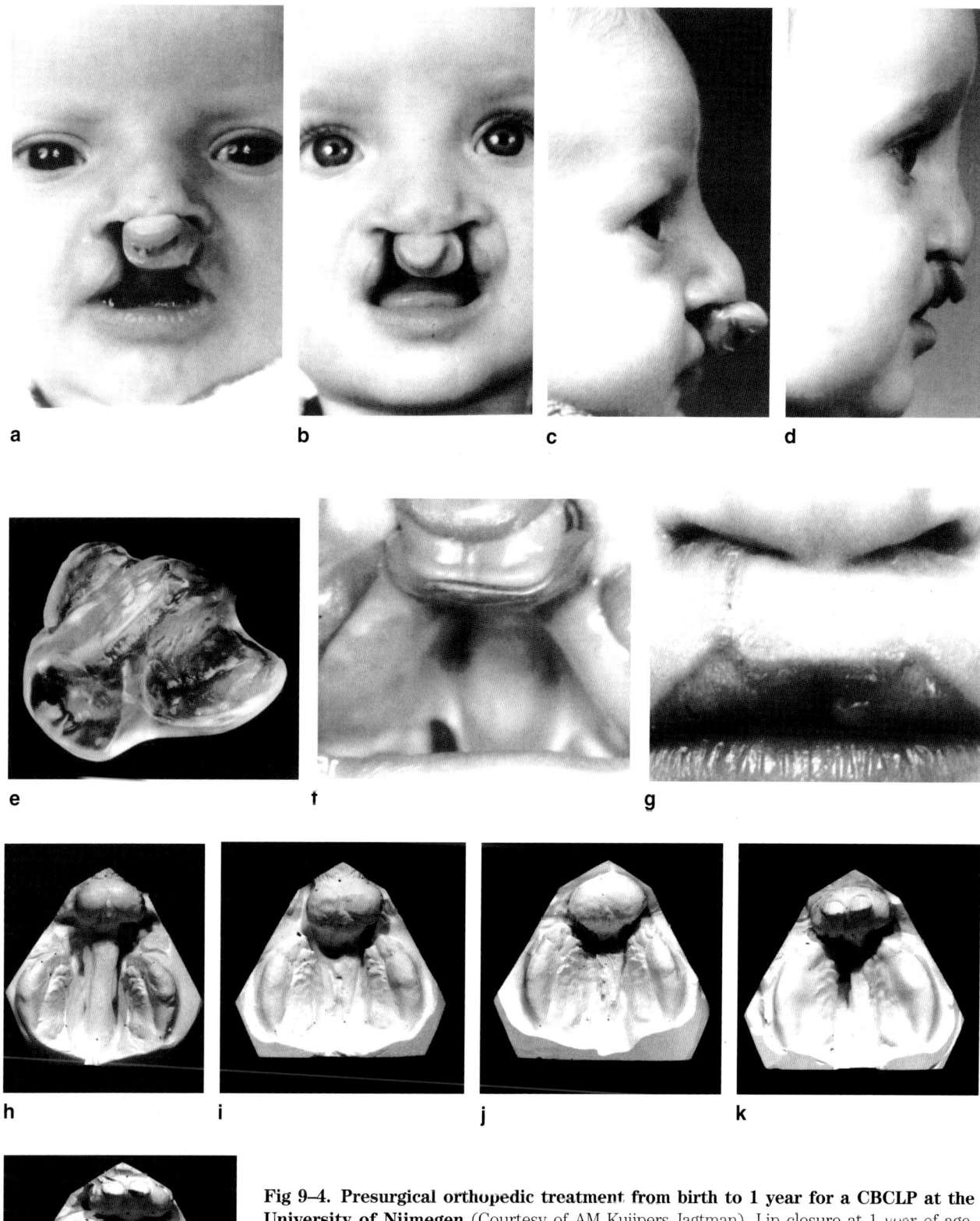

Fig 9–4. **Presurgical orthopedic treatment from birth to 1 year for a CBCLP at the University of Nijmegen** (Courtesy of AM Kuijpers-Jagtman). Lip closure at 1 year of age. Hard palatal cleft is closed between 6 and 9 years of age together with bone grafting of the alveolar cleft. **a**, **b**, and **c**. Facial photographs and palatal cast at birth; **d**. 6 months after wearing PSOT appliance; **e**. Presurgical orthopedic appliance, and when placed on the palate; **f.** wearing appliance. **g.** 8 weeks after lip closure. **h**. At birth. **i**. After 6 months of PSOT and before lip closure. **j**. 8 weeks after lip closure. **k**. 1 year and 6 months, before soft palate closure. **l**. 6 weeks after soft palate closure. *(continued)*

Fig 9-4. *(Continued)*

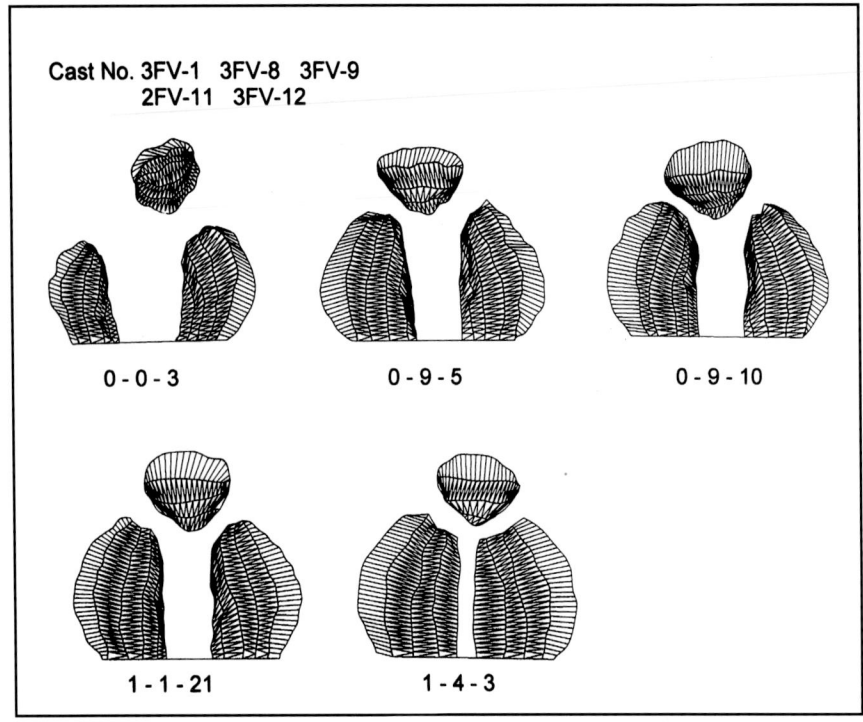

m. Computer drawn images of the serial BCLP casts—same scale. Only the surface area with triangles is measured.

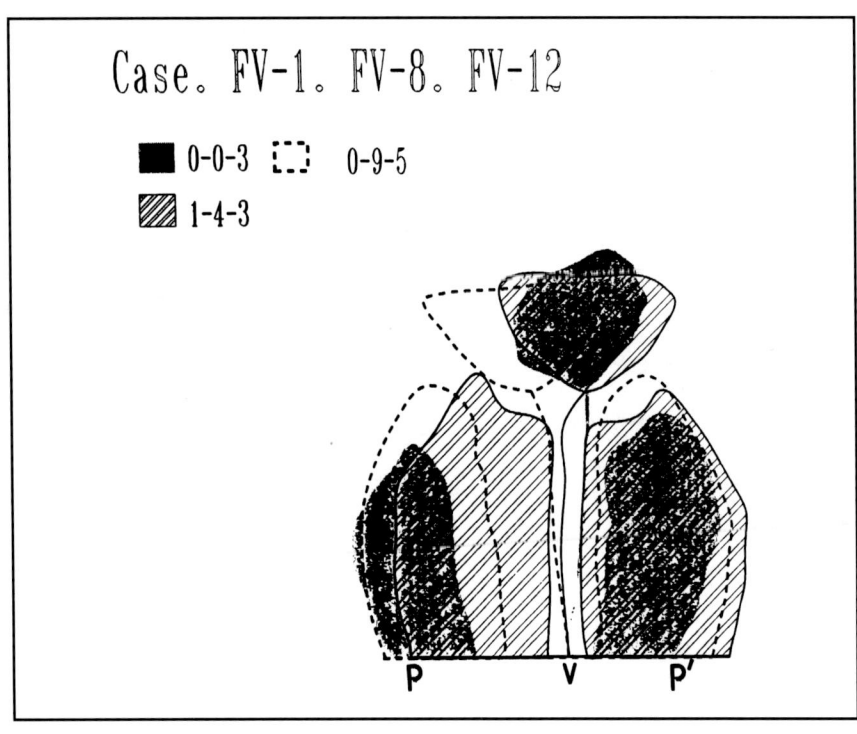

n. Casts at three age periods are superimposed on the baseline P-P' (the posterior limit of the hard palate drawn between postgingival points) and registered at V (vomer point on P-P' line). This shows the initial geometric changes in the alignment of the premaxilla to the vomer and the changes brought on by medial movement of the palatal segments, more on the right than the left side, and palatal growth increases with the reduction in the anterior and posterior cleft spaces.

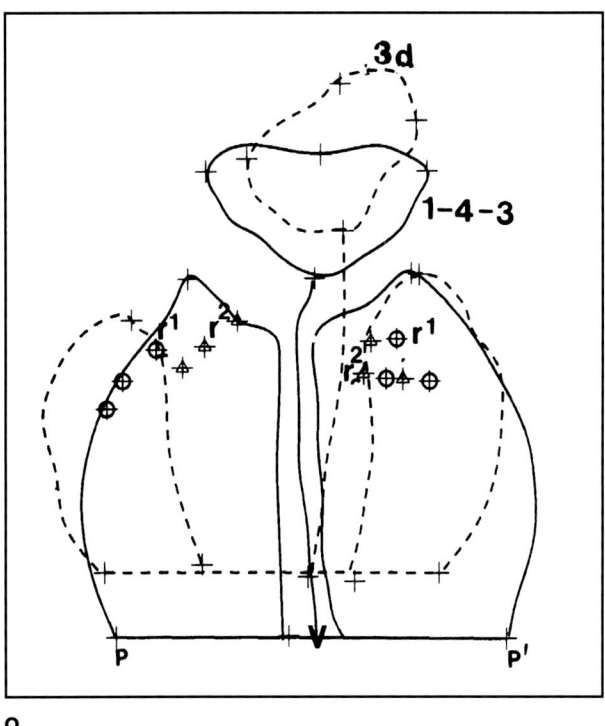

o. Superimposing the casts from ages 3 months and 1-4-3 on rugae points shows the location of growth and molding changes of the palate. The premaxilla's protrusion was slightly reduced. Most of the lateral palatal segment's. **p.** Changes in the palatal slopes. P-P' line is the baseline for angular measurements. AR = alveolar ridge, C = medial limit of palatal segment in the cleft space. The angle between the two lines represents the slope.

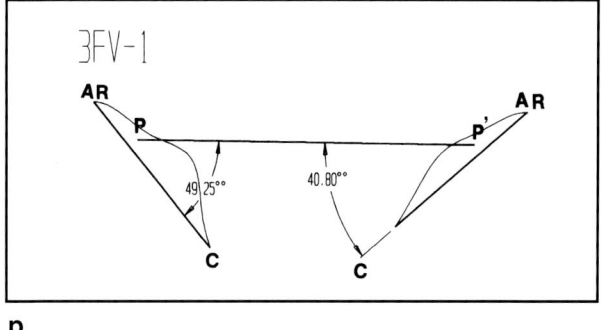

q. Serial changes of the palatal slopes and the cleft width between right and left segments. (MP = The slope at the middle of each palatal segment. P-P' line = The posterior limit of the hard palate. C = Medial limit of each palatal segment at the cleft.) This series shows the gradual reduction in width of the cleft space. Between 1-1-21 and 1-4-3, the palatal slopes (MP) flatten, further reducing the cleft width. **r.** Graph showing palatal surface area changes. The lines representing the surface area of the right and left palatal segments, starting at 300 mm are superimposed and represent the growth curves of each palatal segment. The total surface area includes the premaxilla. The posterior cleft space at 14 months reduces from 650 to 500 mm. It then is markedly reduced to 200 mm at 16 months as a result of the flattening of the palatal vault. In 1 year, the palatal surface area shows an almost 50% increase, and the acceleration curve slows down.

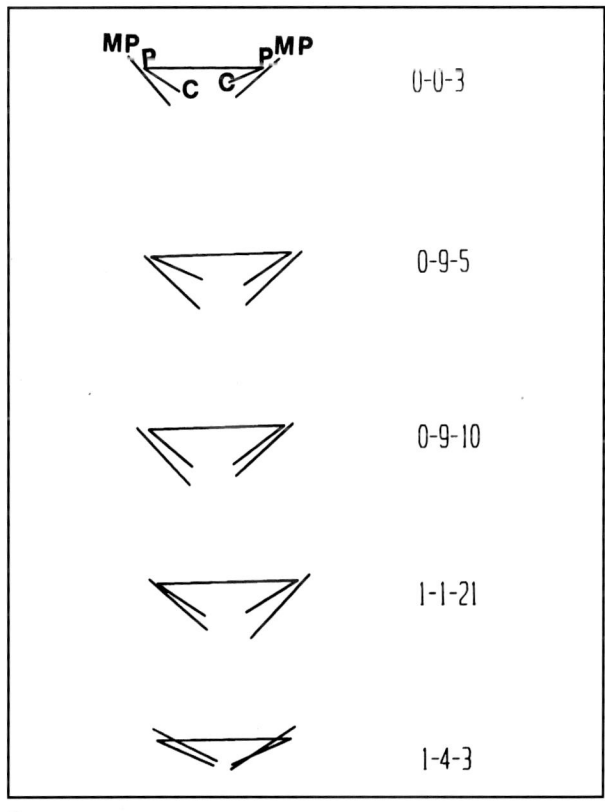

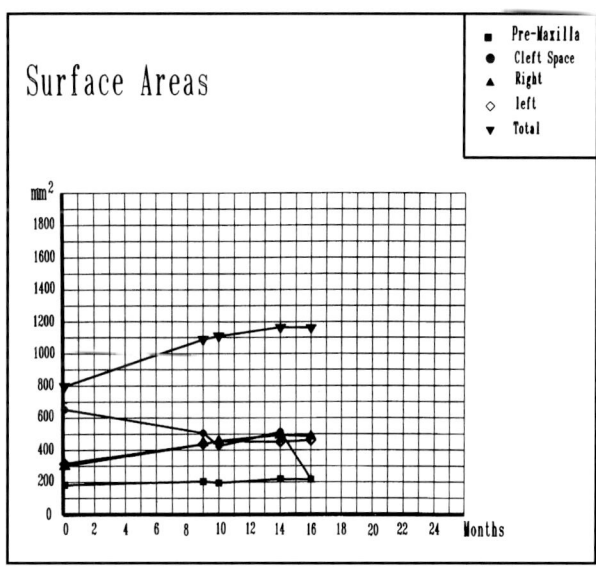

Although clinics in Zurich and other European cities have accumulated an extensive number of lateral cephalometric films, photographs, and serial patient casts, they have not as yet proven that the Zurich-style orthopedic procedures have produced better long-term orofacial growth results than clinicians who have not utilized neonatal maxillary orthopedics and have performed palatal closure between 1 and 3 years of age.

Long-term Utility of Presurgical Orthopedic Treatment (PSOT)

The hard fact is that, although many reasons have been offered to justify the use of orthopedic appliances in cleft treatment, no long-term utility has ever been established. An unpublished study, reported at one of the "Great Debates" that took place at the annual American Cleft Palate-Craniofacial Society meeting held in St. Louis in May 1990, "On the Thesis Presurgical Infant Orthopedics Is By and Large a Waste of Time," Ross and Cutting argued that one of the main reasons for utilizing the procedure is for parents to believe that something important is being done to help their child and that doing something is better than doing nothing. Bardach and Berkowitz, on the other hand, argued that parents do not need to be misled and should be properly instructed to accept the need for staged treatment over a long period of time. If the only use of the appliance is to make parents feel better, those who advocate its use should say so! After 30 years, it is time to settle this issue once and for all. Hopefully, a well-structured prospective clinical trial on the long-term utility of presurgical orthopedic treatment now underway in the Netherlands by Kuijpers-Jagtman and Prahl-Anderson will help resolve some of the questions.

The Long-term Effect of Primary Bone Grafting

There are still divergent opinions on the benefits of primary bone grafting. The reason for the differences in part reflects the different goals of the investigators. Most of the clinical reports since have shown that buccal crossbites can still occur. Not surprisingly, the negative effect of primary bone grafting on maxillary growth is best summarized by Ross's[73] multicenter study of cases with complete unilateral clefts of the lip and palate (CUCLP). It indicated that early surgical repair of the alveolus by means of infant and early childhood bone grafting or soft tissue repair of the alveolus resulted in a deficiency in the vertical growth of the anterior maxilla. When a bone graft or periosteoplasty was used, the vertical growth deficiency was found to be slightly worse and lower face height was greater, so that the vertical proportions of the resulting face were poor. Ross also reported observing a slight anteroposterior maxillary deficiency following bone graftings; however, this effect was not noted when bone grafting was delayed until 9 years of age. Surprisingly, he found that anterior maxillary vertical growth was inhibited following bone grafting, even as late as 9 to 13 years of age. Ross concluded that vertical growth effects can be avoided only if bone grafting is postponed until age 15 or later.

Berkowitz (unpublished data) has not found that growth problems result from bone grafting after 8 to 9 years of age; and the anterior vertical growth deficiency, as measured by the presence of an anterior open bite, was not commonly observed in his ongoing palatal growth study. He has, however, found anterior growth problems in cases treated with pinned appliances used soon after birth to retract the premaxilla in complete unilateral and bilateral cleft lip and palate.

Vertical maxillary growth leads to a more horizontal columellar plane and a reduced nasolabial angle. In individuals with unilateral clefts, this angle is almost 90° degrees instead of the approximately 110° degrees found in noncleft individuals. As Bergland et al[80] and Wolfe and Berkowitz[81] have suggested, because of the resulting midfacial growth interference, it is obviously best to delay alveolar repair at least until the mixed dentition when secondary alveolar bone grafting offers excellent clinical benefits of closing fistulae and allowing tooth migration into the lateral incisor space.

Smahel and Mullerova,[82] in a cephalometric study of males with UCLP at puberty, compared developmental changes in patients treated with primary periosteoplasty with those treated with primary bone grafting. At puberty, patients with primary bone grafts characteristically were found to have anterior crossbites and a posterior rotation of the mandible. Deterioration of growth of the maxilla was the same in both groups, leading to the flattening of the facial profile.

PERIOSTEOPLASTY

Skoog[83] developed a periosteoplasty procedure designed to encourage bone development across the alveolar cleft with no prior palatal manipulation. The technique is based on three major premises:

TABLE 9–7. CBCLP. Dental occlusion, 18 cases, 3 years ± 6 months from Millard-Latham Neonatal Maxillary Orthopedics.

Case No	Class I Right	Class I Left	Class II Right	Class II Left	Class III Right	Class III Left	Anterior Crossbite	Buccal Crossbite Right	Buccal Crossbite Left
AT-40			X	X					
AZ-51			X	X					
BA-24			X	X					
BA-64			X	X			X	EDC	CDE
BF-7			X	X			X	C	C
BH-47		X	X					C	
BJ-28	X	X					X		
BK-36	X	X					X	C	C
BL-28	X	X					X	EDC	CDE
AY-46		X	X						
BH-34	X	X							
BA-74		X	X				X	EDC	C
BC-87	X	X					X	C	
BM-50	X	X							
BQ-54	X	X							
BQ-76	X			X			X		C
BR-68		X	X					C	
BL-90[a]	X	X					X	DC	
BL-69[a]	X			X			X		
BG-12[a]	X	X					X	C	
BG-72[a]	X	X							
BP-18	X	X					X	C	

[a] IBCLP

TABLE 9–8. CBCLP. Dental occlusion, 15 cases, 6 years ± 6 months from Millard-Latham Neonatal Maxillary Orthopedics.

Case No	Class I Right	Class I Left	Class II Right	Class II Left	Class III Right	Class III Left	Anterior Crossbite	Buccal Crossbite Right	Buccal Crossbite Left
AT-40			X	X			X	C	C
AZ-51			X	X					
BA-24			X	X					
BA-64			X	X			X	DC	CDE6
BF-7	X	X					X	DC	C
BH-47		X	X					C	
BJ-28	X	X					X		
BK-36	X	X					X	DC	C
BL-28					X	X	X	E	
AY-46	X	X					X		
BG-72	X	X							
BH-34	X	X							
BA-74	X	X					X		CDE
BC 87	X	X					X		C
BM-91	X	X					X		C
BL-90[a]	X	X					X		CD
BG-12[a]	X	X					X	C	CE

[a] IBCLP

TABLE 9–9. CBCLP. Dental occlusion, 4 cases, 9 years ± 6 months from Millard-Latham Neonatal Maxillary Orthopedics.

Case No	Class I Right	Class I Left	Class II Right	Class II Left	Class III Right	Class III Left	Anterior Crossbite	Buccal Crossbite Right	Buccal Crossbite Left
BF-7	X	X					X	DC	C
AY-46		X	X				X		
BA-74	X	X					X	C	CDE
BC-87	X	X					X		C
BG-12[a]	X	X					X	C	

[a] IBCLP

TABLE 9–10. Complete unilateral cleft lip and palate crossbites.

Age	Cases	A,B (%)	Unilateral C	Unilateral CDE (%)	Bilateral C	Bilateral CDE	U+B CDE%	Side of Cleft CDE – C
3±6	41	17 (41.5)	19	14 (34.1)	5	0	34.1	13-14
6±6	31	24 (77.4)	10	12 (38.7)	3	2	45.2	9-8
9±6	13	8 (61.5)	2	3 (23)	3	2	38.0	3-4(D+6)

TABLE 9–11. Complete bilateral cleft lip and palate crossbites.

Age	Cases	A,B (%)	Unilateral C	Unilateral CDE	Bilateral C	Bilateral CDE	C-CD(E)
3±6	18	8 (44.4)	6	2	2	2	1
6±6	15	10 (66.7)	3	2	1	1	3
9±6	4	4 (100)	2		0	0	2
(IBCLP)	1	1			1		

> **Tables 9–10 and 9–11 identify and compare the number of teeth which are in crossbite at various ages.**
> *Deciduous Teeth:* A. Central incisor B. Lateral incisor C. Cuspids D. First molar E. Second molar
> *AB%:* The percentage of cases in anterior crossbites at the various ages.
> *Unilateral:* The number and percentage of crossbites on one side only.
> *Bilateral:* The number and percentage of crossbites on both sides.
> *U & B:* The total number and percentage of crossbites.
> *Side of cleft:* The number and percentage of crossbites of the cleft segment.

CASE REPORT: MECHANICAL PREMAXILLARY SETBACK (LATHAM-MILLARD PSOT) RESULTING IN MIDFACIAL RETRUSION NECESSITATING PROTRACTION TREATMENT AT AN EARLY AGE.

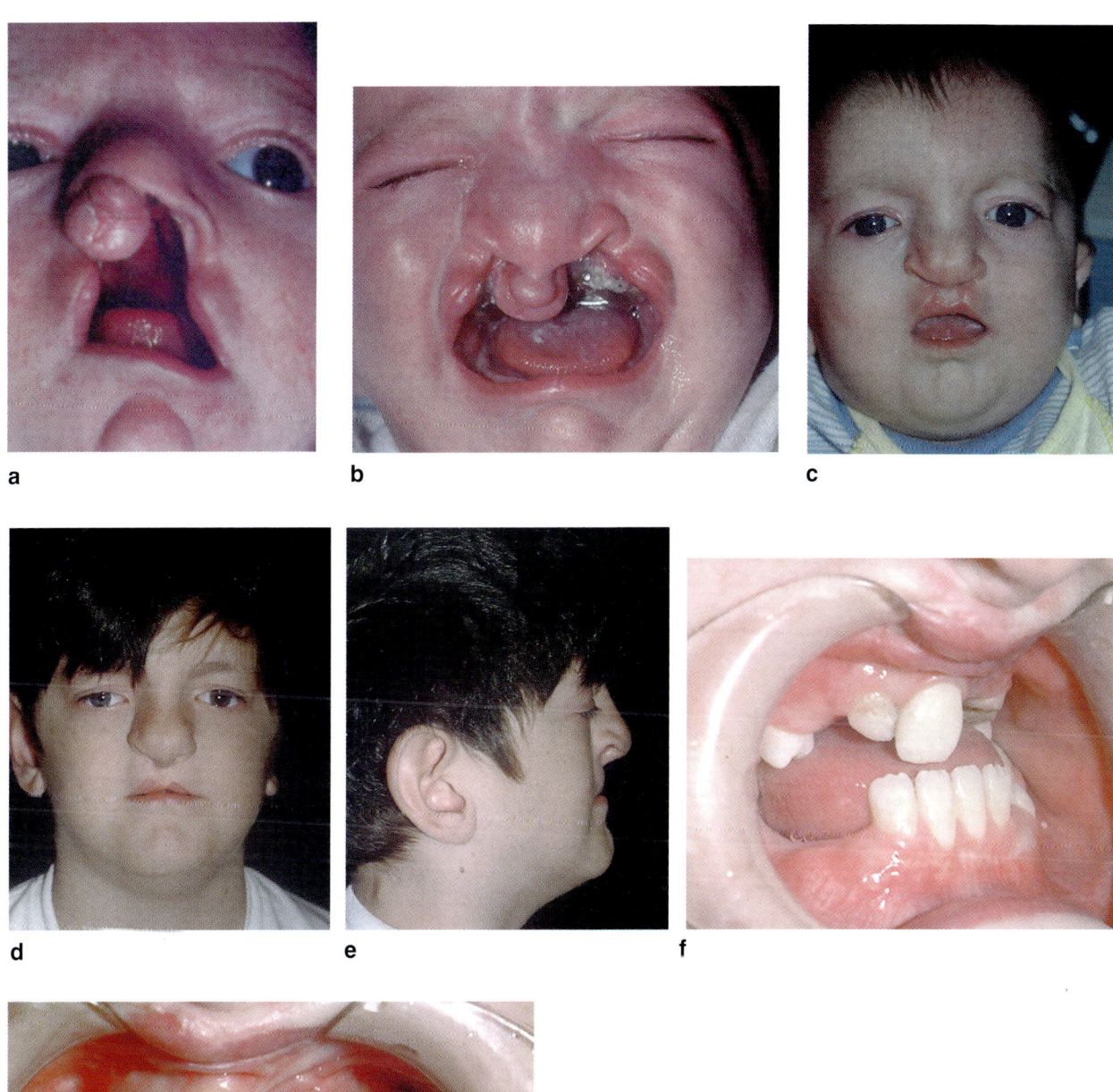

Fig 9–14. Case TR (BA-64) CBCLP. A retruded midface at 9 years of age. **a.** Facial photograph at birth. **b.** Wearing the Latham appliance to retract the premaxilla within the arch. **c.** Facial photograph at 5 months shows a depressed nasal tip with a short columella and upper lip. **d**, **e**, **f**, and **g**. Face and occulsion at 9 years showing a retruded midface with an anterior open bite and crossbite. The palatal cleft was closed at 13 months of age.

(continued)

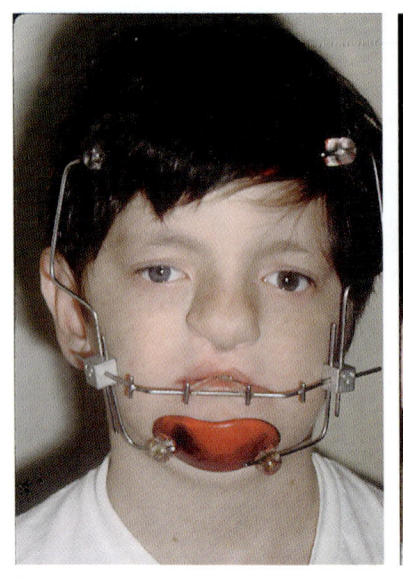
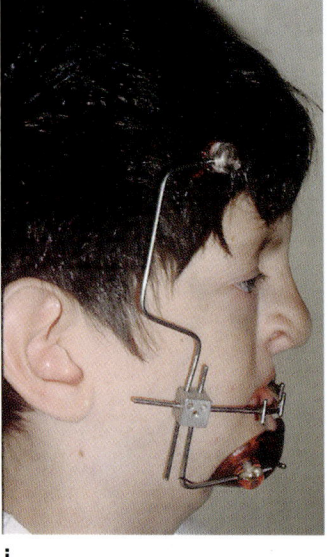
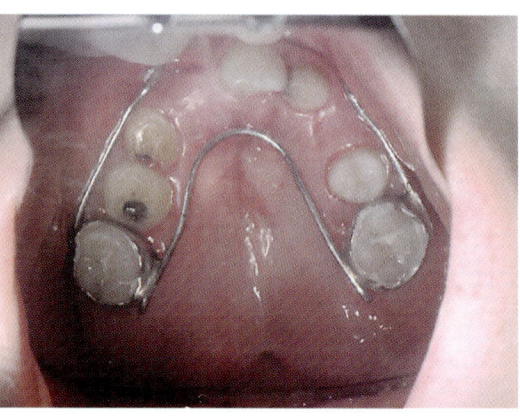

h i j

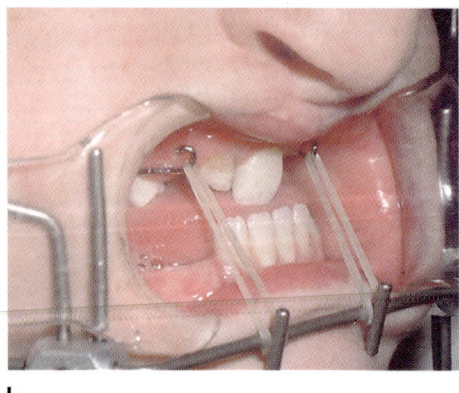

k l

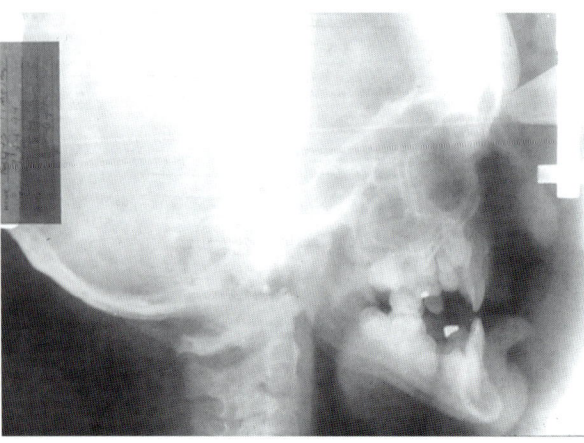

m

Fig 9–14. *(continued)*
h and **i**. Delaire style protraction facial mask being used to advance and extrude the maxillary complex; **j**, **k**, and **l**. Intraoral views showing a fixed labial-lingual palatal appliance with elastics exerting 400 grams of force per side. They are attached to hooks on the arch wire mesial to the cuspid and are directed downward and forward to the outer face bow; **m.** Lateral cephaloradiograph at 9 years and 5 months showing a retruded midface with an anterior open bite.

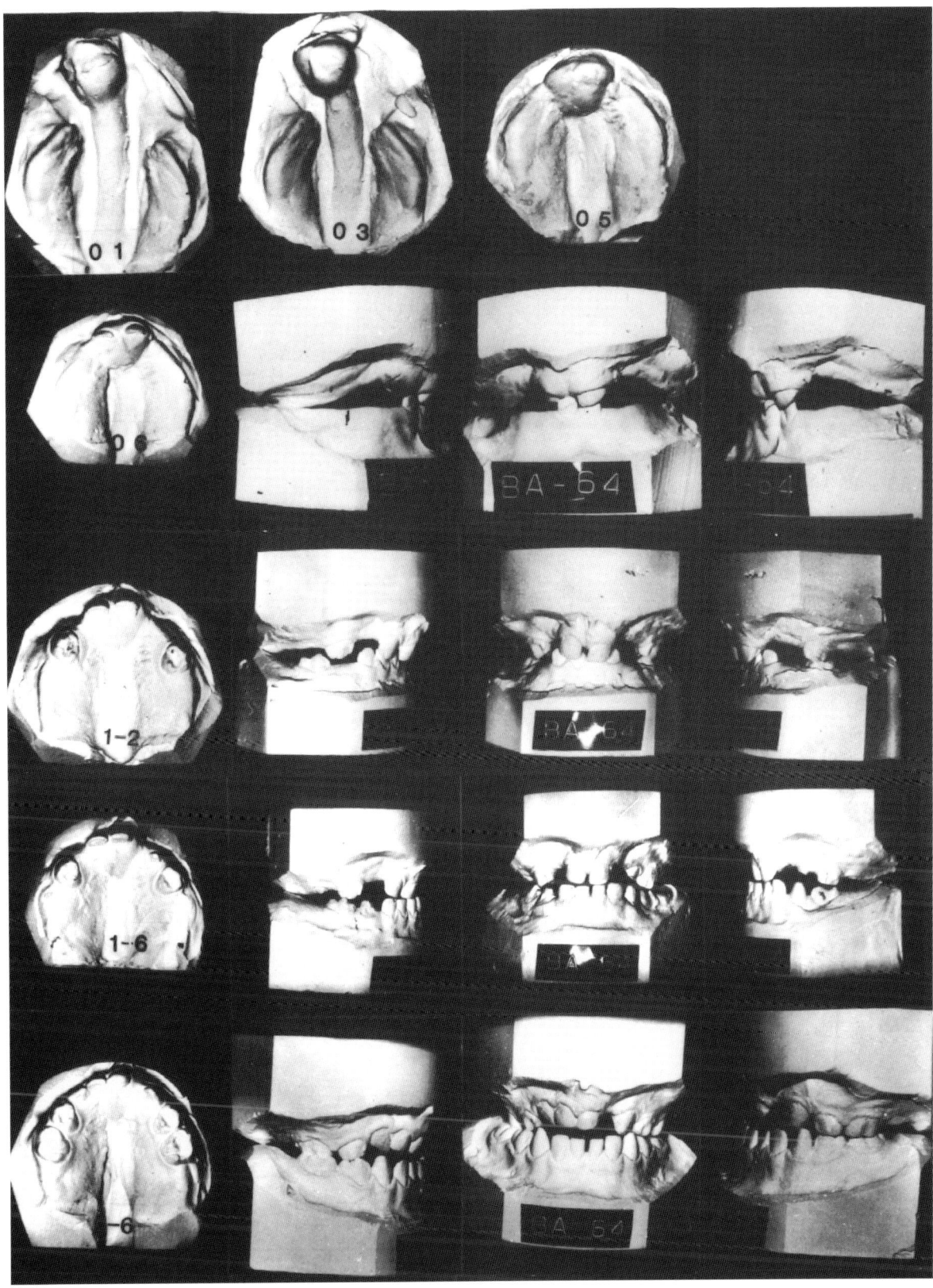

Fig 9–15. Serial casts of the case TR (BA-64) shown in Fig 9–14. 0-1 and **0-3**. Prior to PSOT; **0-5**. After the premaxilla has been repositioned between the lateral palatal segments; **1-2**. The palatal cleft was closed at 13 months. The incisors are in a good overbite and overjet relationship; **1-6**: The incisors are now in a tip-to-tip relationship. The casts **1-6** to **6-9** show the development of a buccal and anterior crossbite with an open bite due to the retardation of midfacial growth in three dimensions. *(continued)*

Fig 9–15. *(continued)*

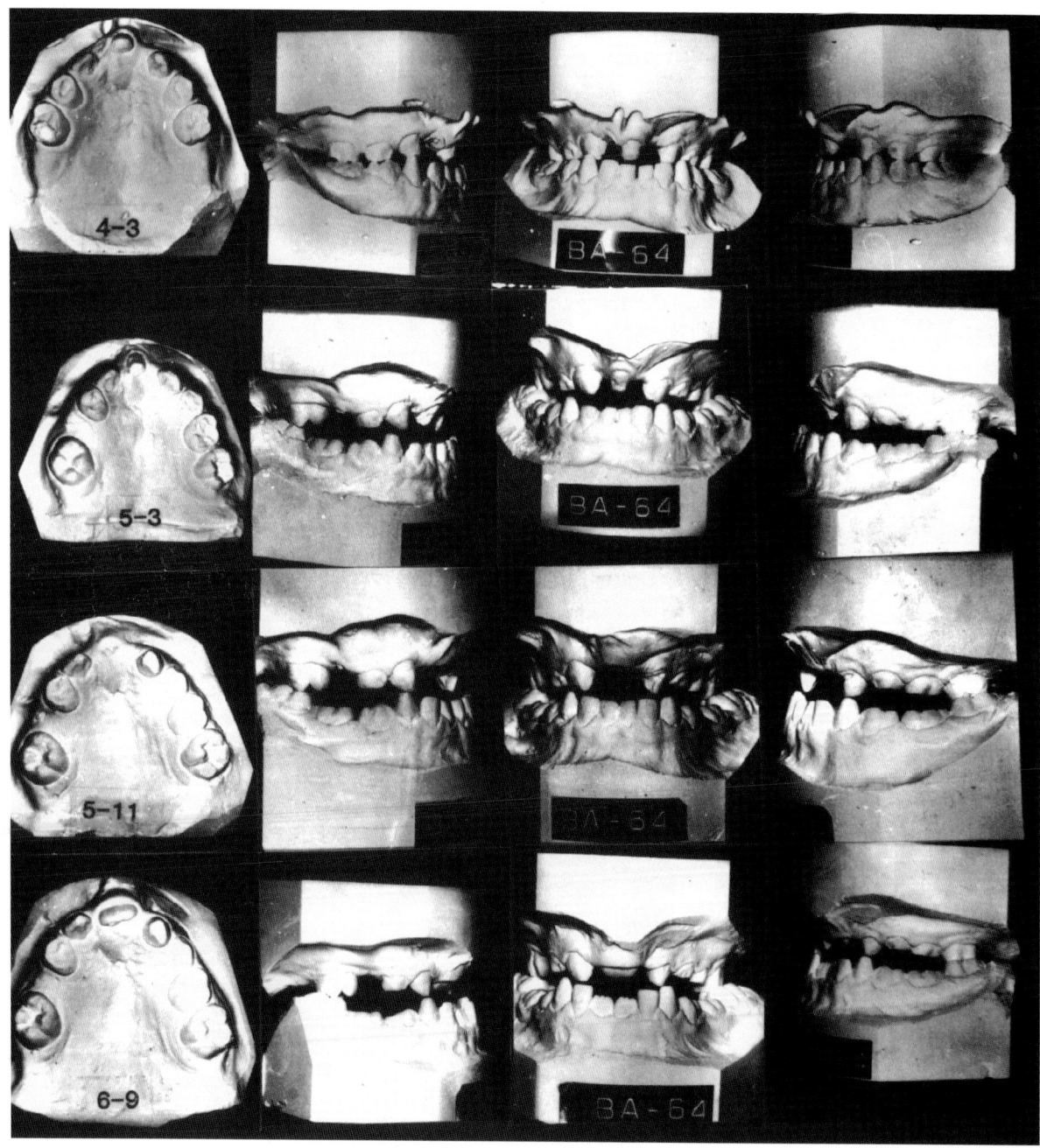

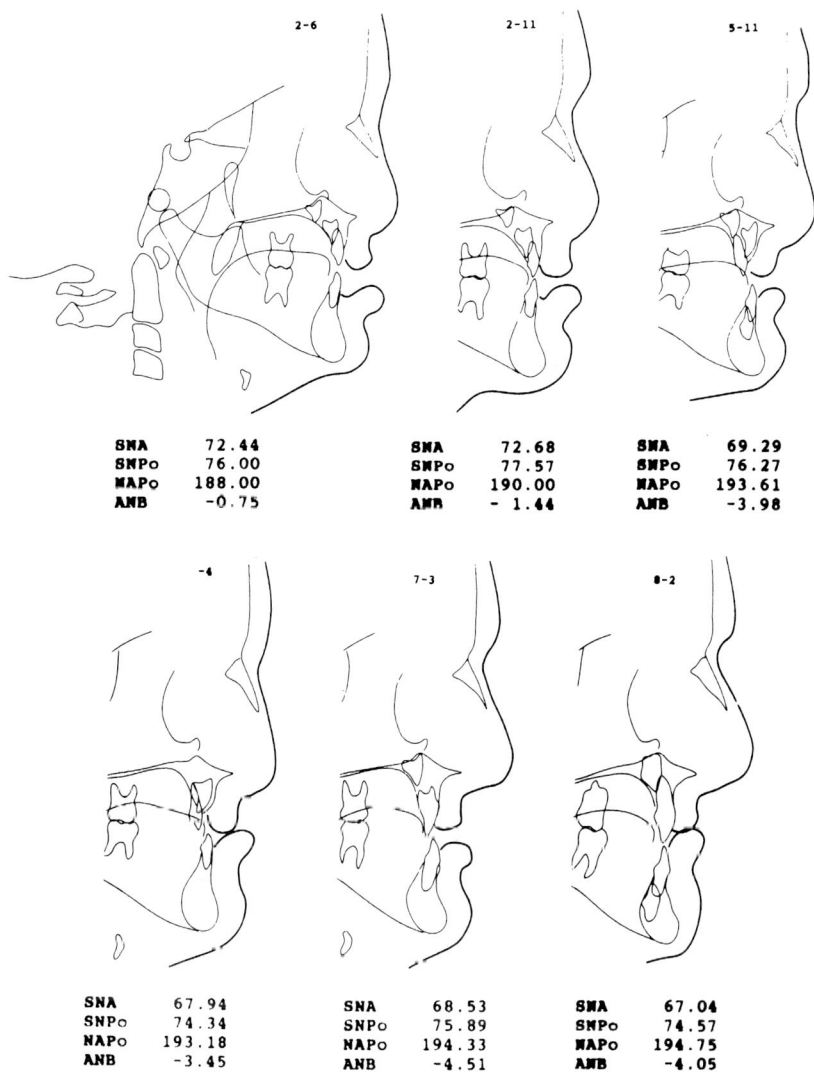

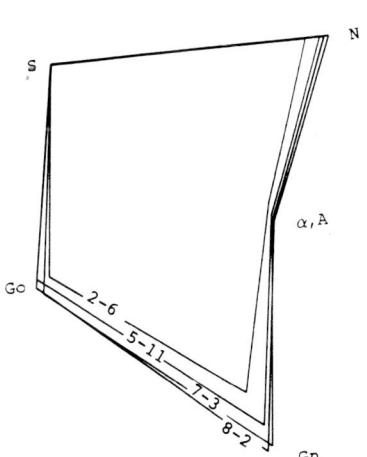

Fig 9–16. a. Serial lateral cephaloradiographs show a progressive reduction in midfacial protrusion with an increase in upper facial and mandibular growth. **b.** Superimposed facial polygons on the anterior cranial base, registered at Sella turcicar (S) demonstrate the increase in profile concavity brought on by the failure of midfacial growth to keep up with growth at the anterior cranial base and at the mandible.

Fig 9–17. Case. DR. CUCLP. Serial photograph using Millard-Latham PSOT demonstrates the loss of the cleft lateral incisor space. **a.** At birth. **b.** After PSOT and lip adhesion. **c.** 6 months after definitive lip surgery. **d** and **e.** 3 years. **f.** and **g.** 7 years of age. **h.** Bite at 3 years of age. **i.** 5 years. **j.** 6 years, anterior open bite has become more severe. There is less room for the deciduous lateral incisor. **k.** 7 years of age. **l.** 7 years and 9 months. Orthodontics reduced the open bite. The blocked out right lateral incisor has erupted labially to the deciduous cuspid through the bone that developed in the alveolar cleft. **m.** 8 years of age. The deciduous cuspid was extracted to provide space to align the displaced lateral incisor within the arch.

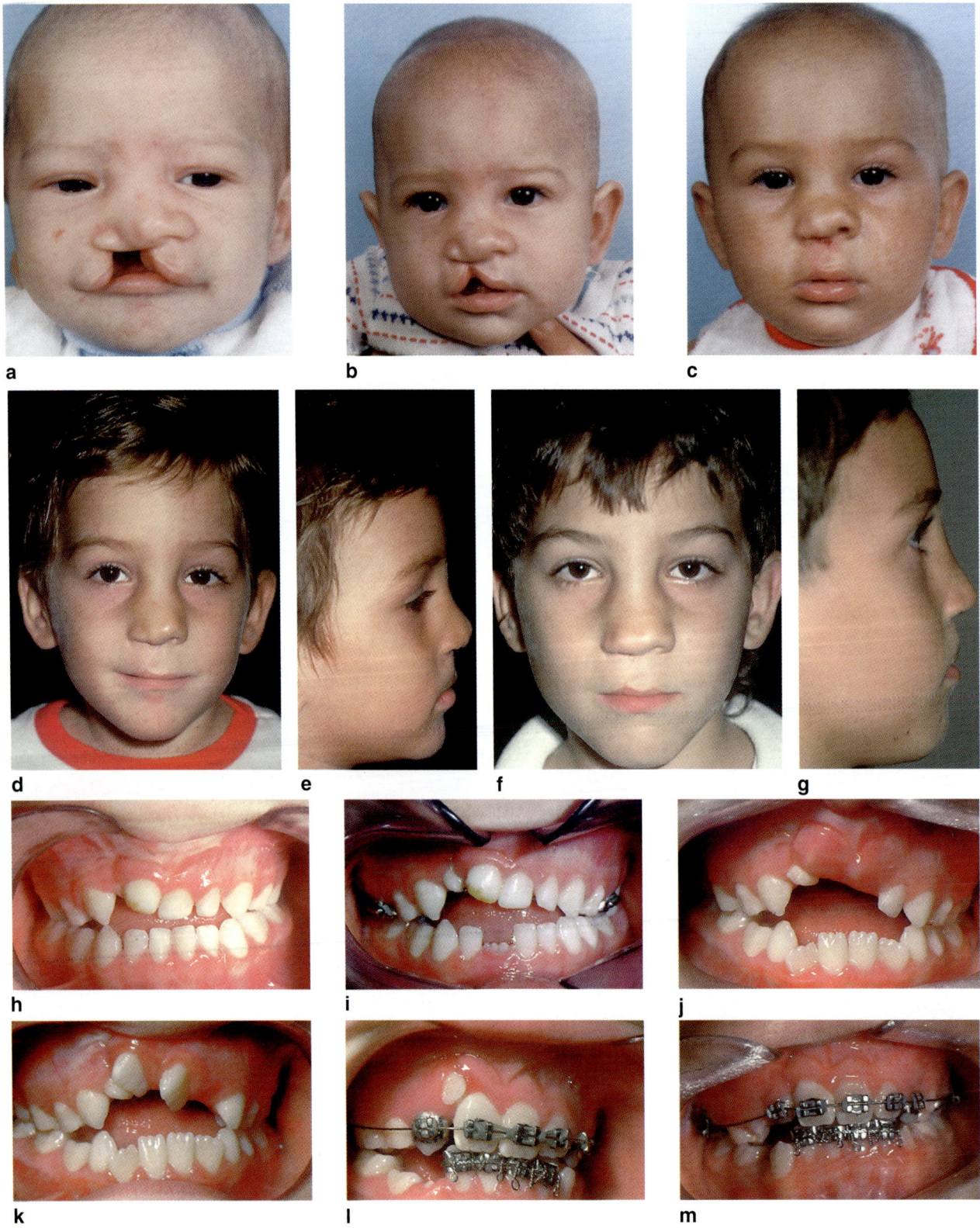

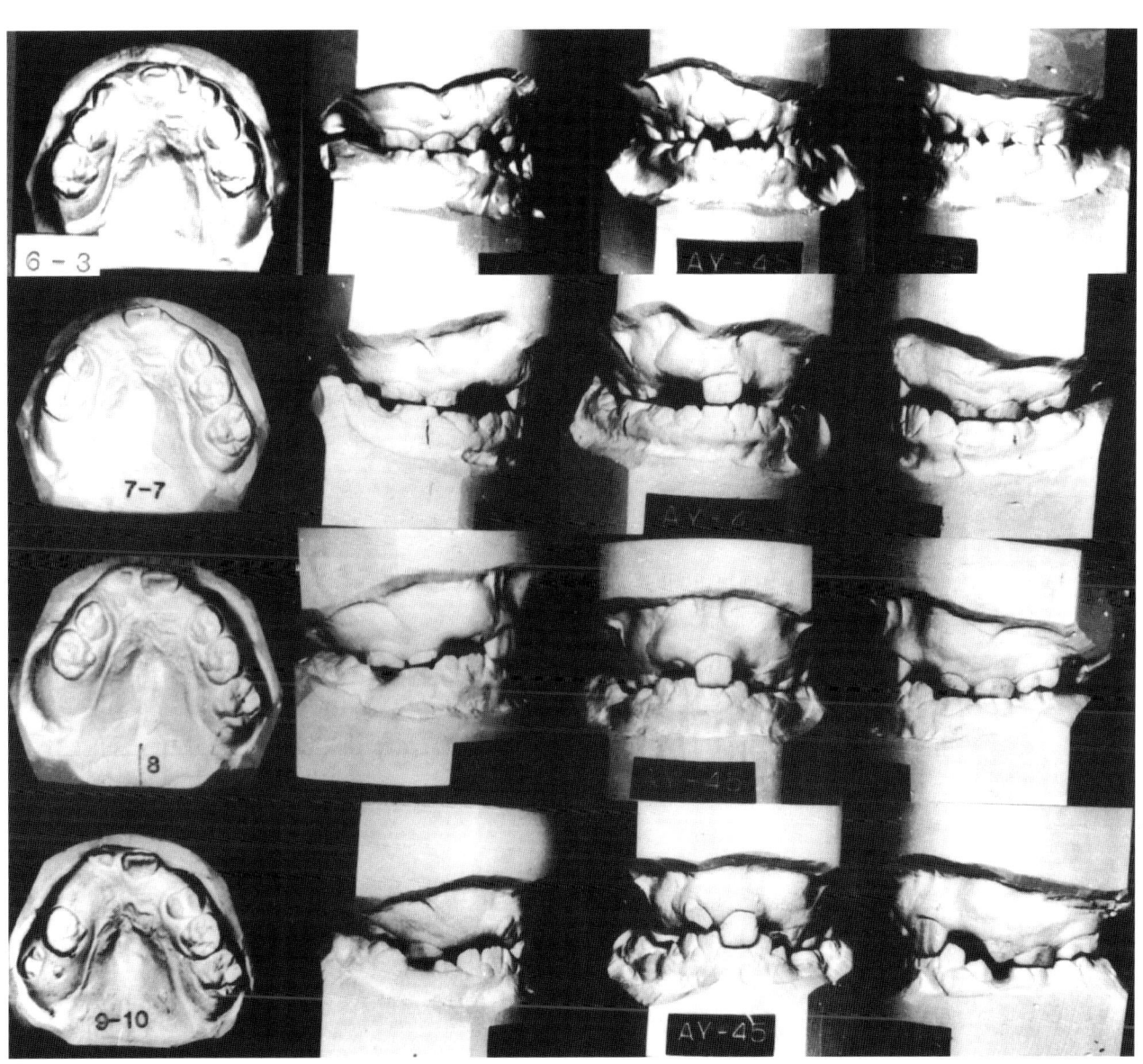

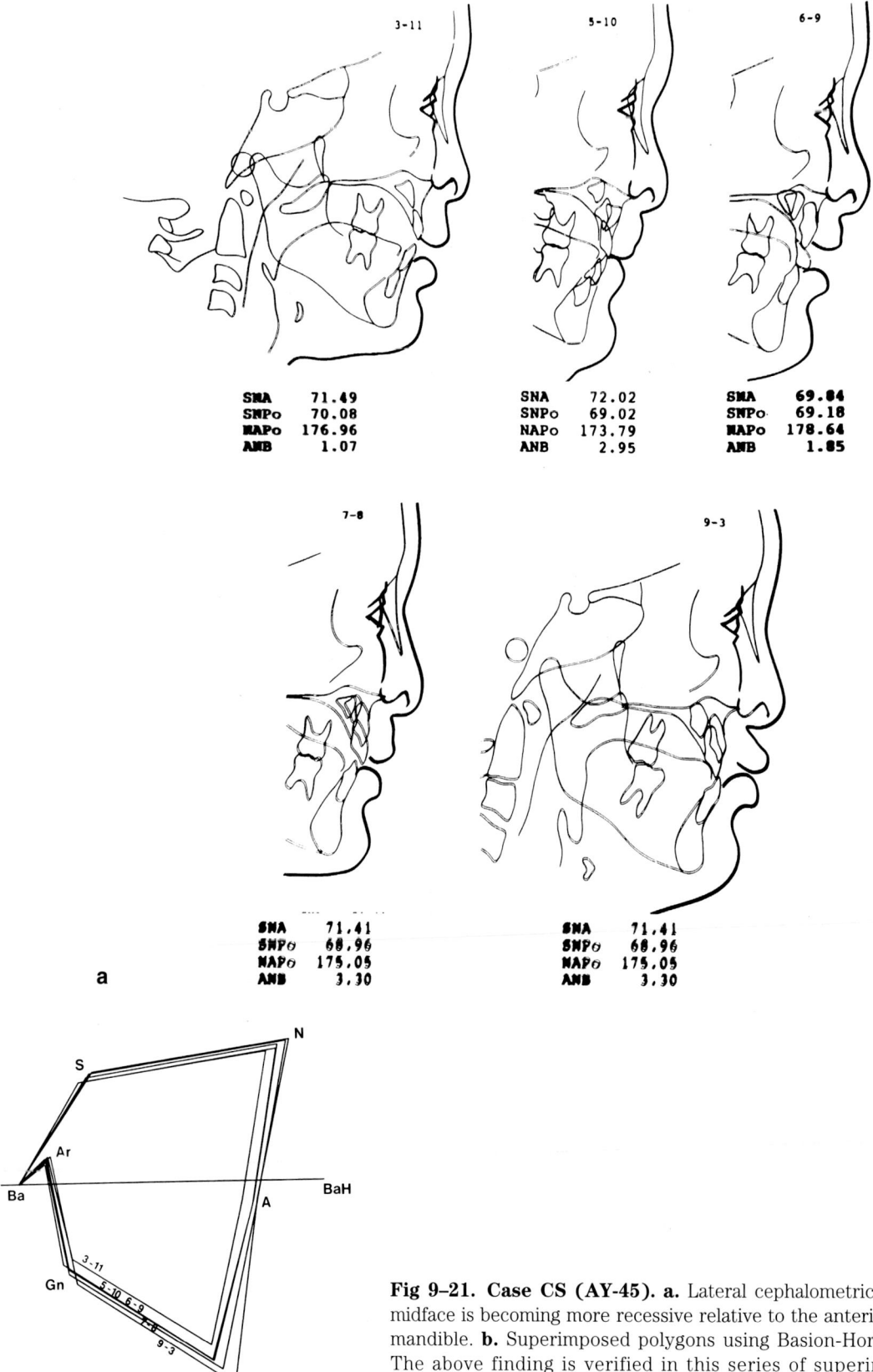

Fig 9–21. Case CS (AY-45). a. Lateral cephalometric tracings show the midface is becoming more recessive relative to the anterior cranial base and mandible. b. Superimposed polygons using Basion-Horizontal procedure. The above finding is verified in this series of superimposed polygons. Although slight forward growth of the midface is evident between 3-11 and 7-8, no further growth is seen between 7-8 and 9-3 years of age.

Fig 9–22. Case AS (AY-46). CBCLP with Millard-Latham PSOT. Retarded midfacial growth in the mixed dentition. **a** and **b**. Newborn. **c**. Latham's pinned appliance in place. **d**. At 6 months. Premaxilla is aligned within the arch. **e**. At 6 months. **f, g,** and **h**. 6 years and 6 months. Frontal and lateral face. **i**. Small columella with depressed nasal tip. **j**. Good arch alignment. Small palatal fistula. **k**. Good occlusion. **l, m,** and **n**. 9 years. Raised nasal tip. **o, p, q,** and **r**. Facial and dental occlusion. The left deciduous lateral incisor is in crossbite.

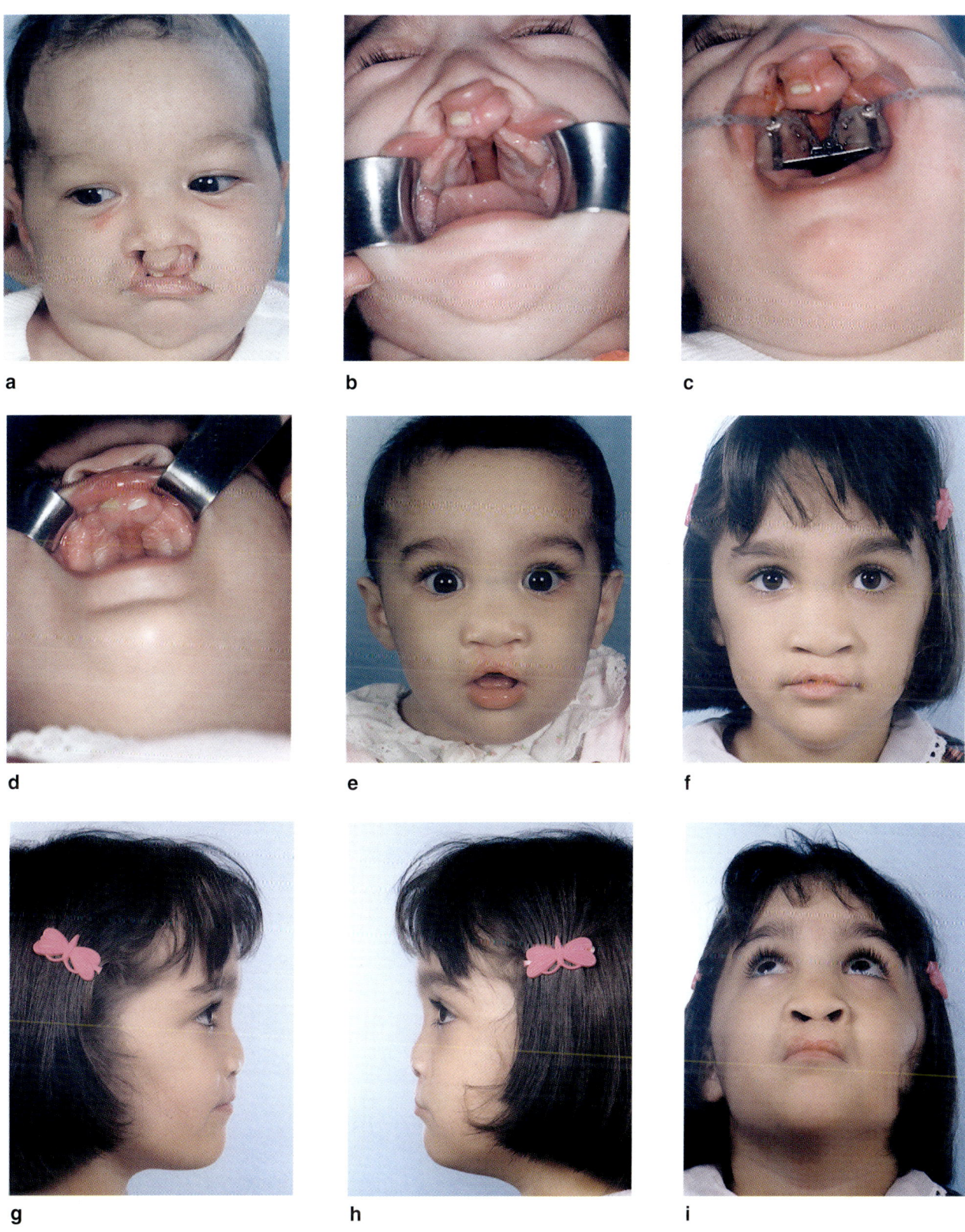

(continued)

Fig 9–22. *(continued)*

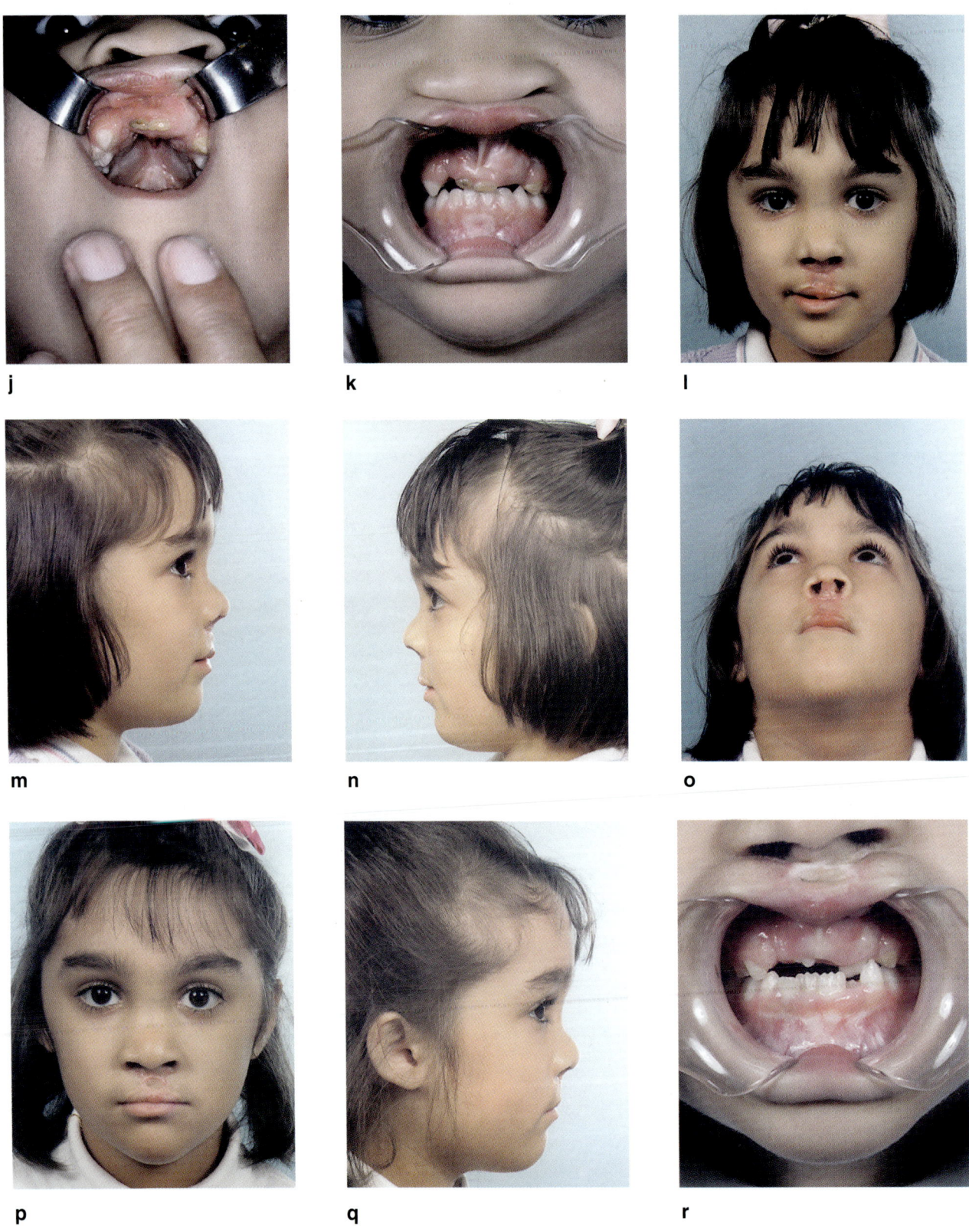

158

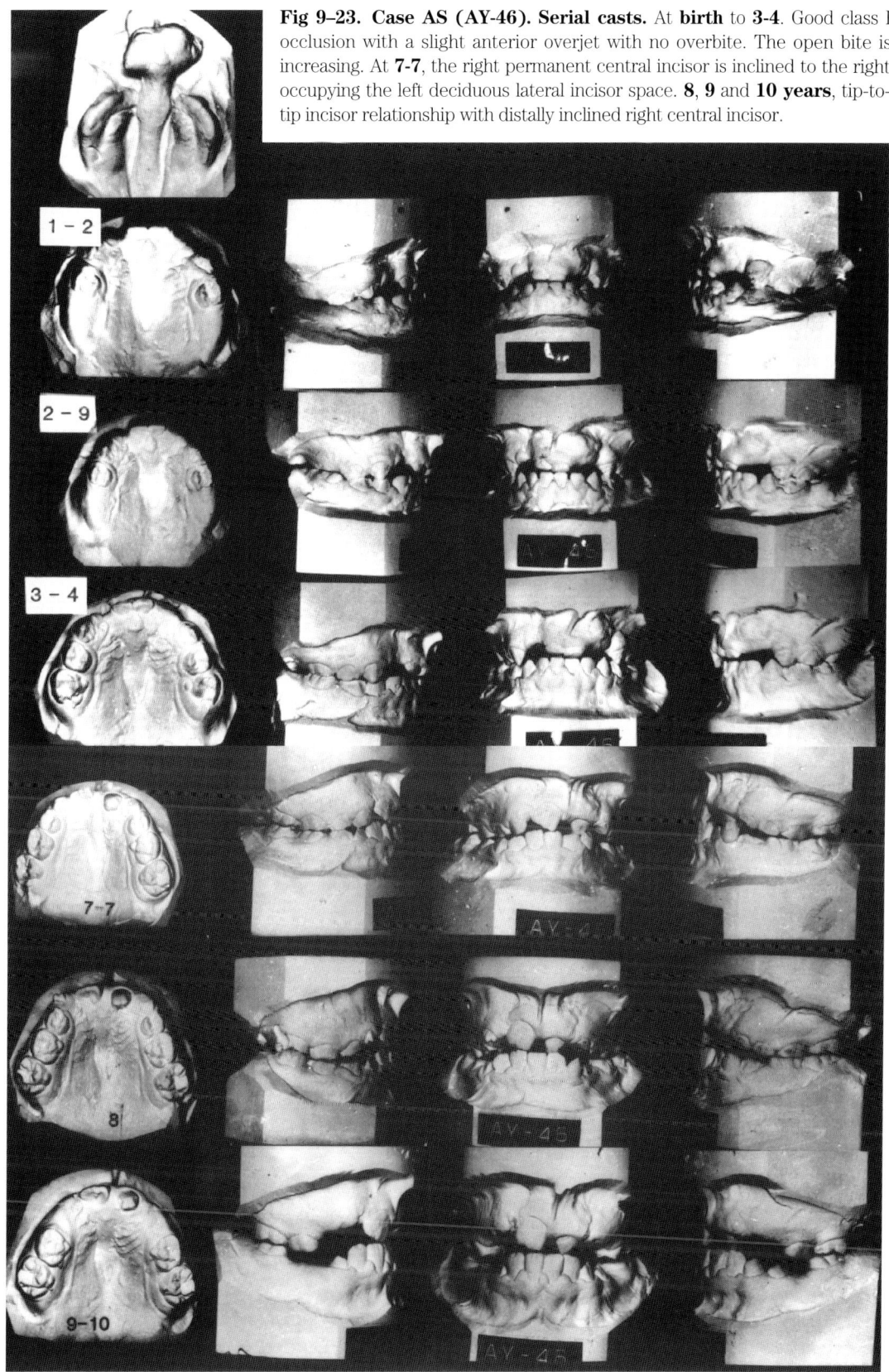

Fig 9–23. Case AS (AY-46). Serial casts. At **birth** to **3-4**. Good class I occlusion with a slight anterior overjet with no overbite. The open bite is increasing. At **7-7**, the right permanent central incisor is inclined to the right occupying the left deciduous lateral incisor space. **8, 9** and **10 years**, tip-to-tip incisor relationship with distally inclined right central incisor.

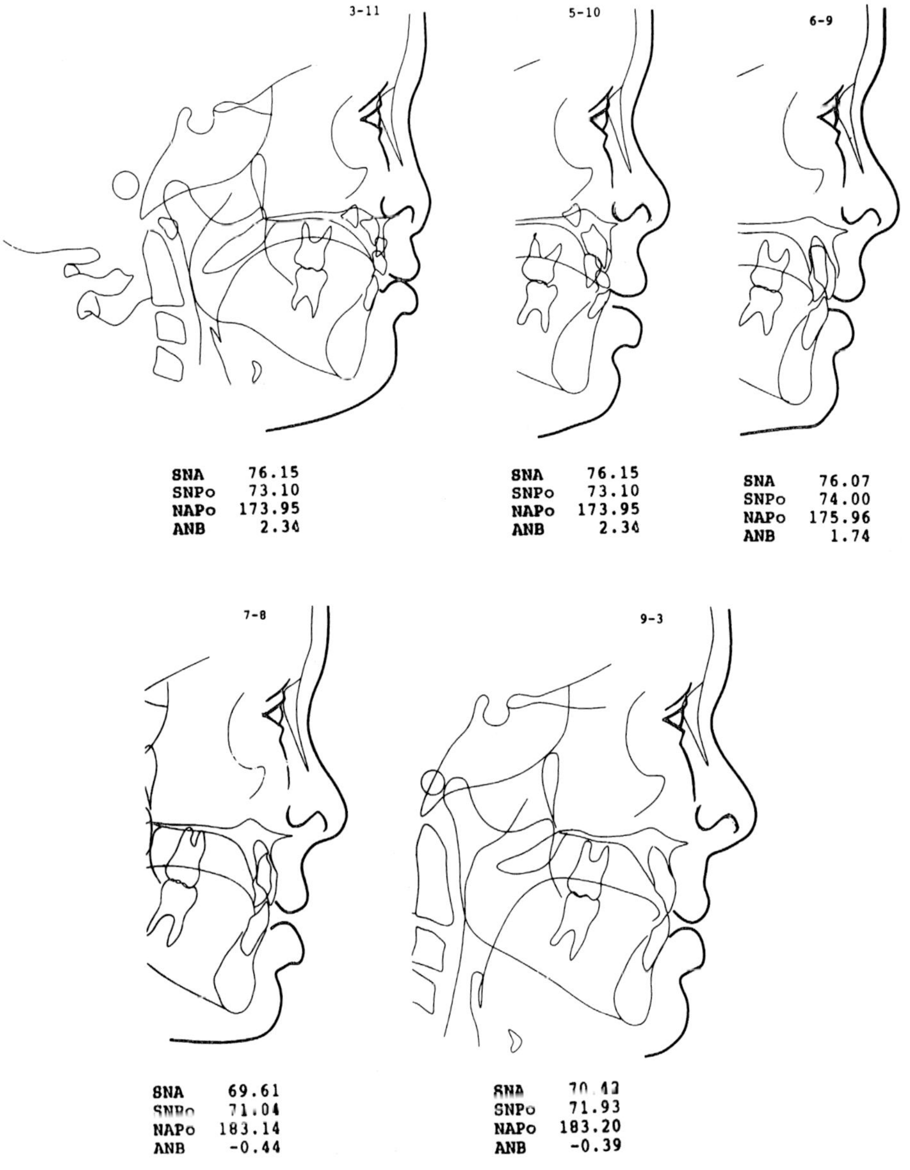

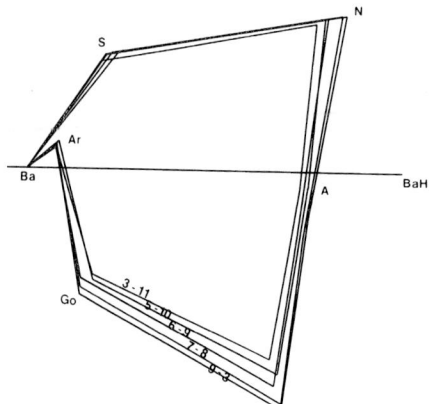

Fig 19–24. Case AS (AY-46). a. Serial lateral cephalometric tracings and **b.** Serial superimposed polygons (Basion Horizontal method) show retarded midfacial growth. Fortunately, the vertical mandibular growth pattern compliments a reduced midfacial growth preventing the creation of an anterior crossbite.

Comments: Protraction orthopedic forces will be initiated when more permanent teeth have erupted.

CONCLUSIONS

Based on the understanding of the facial growth processes and the importance of the premaxillary vomerine suture, some conclusions can be drawn as to this procedure's long-term utility even though none of the patients in this orthopedic series have as yet all of their permanent dentition nor have had a postpubertal growth spurt.

There seems to be a direct correlation of the amount of segmental manipulation and the involvement of the PVS with the degree of growth disturbance.

Wolfe (personal communication, 1995) suggests that premaxillary retropositioning in the newborn period is beneficial because it permits attainment of an excellent periosteoplasty with new alveolar bone spanning the cleft space, even at the risk of causing midfacial retrusion. He believes midfacial surgical advancement is preferable because it is an easier and frequently a more successful a procedure than closing the cleft alveolus and the anterior cleft space in some bilateral clefts of the lip and palate. Berkowitz does not share this point of view, especially when Wolfe suggests that all complete bilateral cleft lip and palate cases should be treated in one way even with the outside risk hypernasality may result from LeFort I advancement in some cases.

In complete unilateral clefts of the lip and palate, crossbite of the cleft buccal segments and the premaxillary portion of the larger segment with the loss of the cleft alveolar space is a predictable result in the deciduous dentition. The loss of the lateral incisor space is usually found in the permanent dentition as well.

In both cleft types, correction of the anterior crossbites needs to be postponed until the late mixed dentition stage when the permanent incisors have erupted and they can be orthodontically aligned, which usually requires extraoral protraction forces.

With the loss of the lateral incisor space on one or both sides, the permanent cuspid(s) must either remain in the lateral incisor space, necessitating the extraction of the lateral incisor, if present, or be repositioned to its ideal location, which requires the removal of the first bicuspid(s).

REFERENCES

1. McNeil CK. Orthodontic procedures in the treatment of congenital cleft palate. *Dental Record.* 1950; 70:126–132.
2. McNeil CK. *Oral and Facial Deformity.* London, England: Sir Isaac Pitman and Sons; 1954.
3. McNeil CK. Congenital oral deformities. *Brit Dent J.* 1956;101:191–198.
4. Scott JH. The cranial base. *Am J Phys Anthropol.* 1958; 16:319.
5. Scott JH. The analysis of facial growth, I: The anteroposterior and vertical dimensions. *Am J Orthod.* 1956;44:507.
6. Scott JH. The analysis of facial growth, II: The horizontal and vertical dimensions. *Am J Orthod.* 1958; 44:585.
7. Burston WR. The pre-surgical orthopaedic correction of the maxillary deformity in clefts of both primary and secondary palate. In: Wallace AB, ed. *Transactions of the International Society of Plastic Surgeons, Second Congress, London, 1959.* Edinburgh and London: E&S Livingston Ltd; 1960:28–36.
8. Burston WR. The early orthodontic treatment of alveolar clefts. *Proc R Soc Med.* 1965;58:767–771.
9. Burston WR. Treatment of the cleft palate. *Ann R Coll Surg Engl.* 1967;25:225.
10. Rosenstein S. A new concept in the early orthopedic treatment of cleft lip and palate. *Am J Orthod.* 1969;55:765–775.
11. Rosenstein S. Orthodontic and bone grafting procedures in a cleft lip and palate series: an interim cephalometric evaluation. *Angle Orthod.* 1975;45:227–237.
12. Rosenstein SW. Management of the maxillary segments in complete unilateral cleft lip and palate patients. Symposium on: *Management of Cleft Lip and Palate and Associated Deformities*, held at Duke University Medical Center, Durham, NC; 1973;7.
13. Georgiade N. The management of premaxillary and maxillary segments in the newborn cleft patient. *Cleft Palate J.* 1970;7:411.
14. Cronin TD. Management of the bilateral cleft lip with protruding premaxilla. *Am J Surg.* 1956;92:810.
15. Cronin TD. An overall plan of treatment for complete cleft lips and palate. In: Hotz R, ed. *Early Treatment of Cleft Lip and Palate. International Symposium*, 1964. Bern, Switzerland: Huber; 1964:174–178.
16. Brauer RO, Cronin TD, Reaves EL. Early maxillary orthopedics, orthodontia and alveolar bone grafting in complete clefts of the palate. *Plast Reconstr Surg.* 1962; 29:625–641.
17. Gruber H. Discussion. In: Cole RM, ed. *Early Treatment of Cleft Lip and Palate. Proceedings of Second International Symposium, 1969.* Chicago, Ill: Cleft Lip and Palate Institute, Northwestern University Dental School, 1969;31.
18. Manchester WM. Bilateral cleft lip and plate repairs. In: Bardach J, Morris HL, eds. *Multidisciplinary Management of Cleft Lip and Palate.* Philadelphia, Pa: WB Saunders Co; 1990:227.
19. Davies D. Early treatment of cleft lip and palate. In: Cole RM, ed. *Early Treatment of Cleft Lip and Palate. Proceedings of Second International Symposium, 1969.* Chicago, Ill: Cleft Lip and Palate Institute, Northwestern University Dental School; 1969;143–149.

20. Hotz R. The indications for preoperative and postoperavite orthopedic treatment of cleft lip and palate. In: Hotz R, ed. *Early Treatment of Cleft Lip and Palate.* International Symposium, University of Zurich, Dental Institute, 1964;78–82.
21. Hotz M. Aims and possibilities of pre- and post-surgical orthopedic treatment in uni- and bilateral clefts. *Trans Eur Orthod Soc.* 1973;553–558.
22. Hotz M. Pre- and early post-operative growth guidance in cleft lip and palate cases by maxillary orthopedics (an alternative procedure to primary bone grafting). *Cleft Palate J.* 1969;7:368–372.
23. Nordin KE, Johanson B. Freie Knochentransplantation bei Defekten in Alveolarkamm nach Kieferortopädischer Einstellung der Maxilla bei Lippen-Kiefer-Gaumenspalten. *Fortschr Kiefer Gesichtschir.* 1955;1:168.
24. Monroe CW. Use of bone grafts in clefts of the alveolar ridge. In: Georgiade NG, ed. *Symposium on Management of Cleft Lip and Palate and Associated Deformities.* St Louis, Mo: CV Mosby Co; 1974;8:242–247.
25. Graf-Pinthus B, Bettex M. Long-term observation following presurgical orthopedic treatment in complete clefts of the lip and palate. *Cleft Palate J.* 1974; 11:253–260.
26. Graf B, Bettex M. The narrowing of the palatal cleft following presurgical orthopedic treatment in unilateral cleft lip and palate subjects. In: Cole RM, ed. *Early Treatment of Cleft Lip and Palate. Proceedings of Second International Syumposium, 1969.* Chicago, Ill: Cleft Lip and Palate Institute, Northwestern University Dental School; 1969;20–25.
27. Huddart AG. Presurgical dental orthopaedics. *Trans Br Soc Orthod.* 1961;107–117.
28. Huddart AG. An evaluation of pre-surgical treatment. *Br J Orthod.* 1974;1:21–25.
29. Huddart AG. Presurgical changes in unilateral cleft palate subjects. *Cleft Palate J.* 1979;16:147–157.
30. Huddart AG. An analysis of the maxillary changes following presurgical dental orthopaedic treatment in unilateral cleft lip and palate cases. *Trans Eur Orthod Soc.* 1967;299–314.
31. Huddart AG. Presurgical orthopedic treatment in unilateral cleft lip and palate. In: Bardach J, Morris HL, eds. *Multidisciplinary Management of Cleft Lip and Palate.* Philadelphia, Pa: WB Saunders Co; 1990;574–578.
32. Robertson NRE. Early treatment—A critique. *Trans Eur Orthod Soc.* 1973:547–551.
33. Jolleys A. A review of the results of operations on cleft palate with reference to maxillary growth and speech function. *Br J Plast Surg.* 1984;7:229.
34. McComb H. Primary unilateral and bilateral cleft nose reconstruction. In Bardach J, Morris HL, eds. *Multidisciplinary Management of Cleft Lip and Palate.* Philadelphia, Pa: WB Saunders Co; 1990:197–203.
35. Salyer KE. Unilateral cleft lip nasal reconstruction. In Bardach J, Morris HL, eds. *Multidisciplinary Management of Cleft Lip and Cleft Palate.* Philadelphia, Pa: WB Saunders Co; 1990:173–184.
36. Heubener DV, Marsh JL. Alveolar molding appliance in the treatment of cleft lip and palate infants. In Bardach J, Morris HL, eds. *Multidisciplinary Management of Cleft Lip and Cleft Palate.* Philadelphia, Pa: WB Saunders Co; 1990:601–607.
37. Stal S, Netscher D, Spira M. Unilateral cleft lip repair. In Bardach J, Morris HL, eds. *Multidisciplinary Management of Cleft Lip and Cleft Palate.* Philadelphia, Pa: WB Saunders Co; 1990:212–217.
38. Nordhoff MS, Huang CS, Wu J. Multidisciplinary management of cleft lip and palate in Taiwan. In Bardach J, Morris HL, eds. *Multidisciplinary Management of Cleft Lip and Cleft Palate.* Philadelphia, Pa: WB Saunders Co; 1990:18–26.
39. Asher C, Shaw W. Multidisciplinary Management of Cleft Lip and Palate in The United Kingdom. In Bardach J, Morris HL, eds. *Multidisciplinary Management of Cleft Lip and Cleft Palate.* Philadelphia, Pa: WB Saunders Co; 1990:10–18.
40. Norden E, Aronson SL, Stenberg T. The deciduous dentition after only primary surgical operations for clefts of the lip, jaw and palate. *Am J Orthod.* 1973;63:229–236.
41. Schmid EW, Widmaier W, Reichert H, Stein K. The development of the cleft upper jaw following primary osteoplasty and orthodontic treatment. *J Maxillofac Surg.* 1974;2:92–95.
42. Weil J. Orthopaedic growth guidance and stimulation for patients with cleft lip and palate. *Scand J Plast Reconstr Surg.* 1987;21:57–63.
43. Rosenstein SW, Monroe CW, Kernahan DA, Jacobson BN, Griffith BH, Bauer BS. The case for early bone grafting in cleft lip and cleft palate. *Plast Reconstr Surg.* 1982;70:297–307.
44. Georgiade NG, Latham RA. Intraoral traction for positioning the premaxilla in the bilateral cleft lip. In: Georgiade NG, Hagerty RF, eds. *Symposium on Management of Cleft Lip and Palate and Associated Deformities.* St. Louis, Mo: CV Mosby Co; 1974:123–127.
45. Georgiade NG, Latham RA. Maxillary arch alignment in the bilateral cleft lip and palate infant, using the pinned coaxial screw appliance. *J Plast Reconstr Surg.* 1975;52:52–60.
46. Latham RA. The septopremaxillary ligament and maxillary development. *J Anat (Lond).* 1969;104:584.
47. Latham RA. Maxillary development and growth. The septomaxillary ligaments. *J Anat (Lond).* 1970;107:471.
48. Latham RA. Orthopaedic advancement of the cleft maxillary segment: a preliminary report. *Cleft Palate J.* 1980;17:227.
49. Latham RA. Development and structure of the premaxillary deformity in bilateral cleft lip and palate. *Br J Plast Surg.* 1973;26:1–11.
50. Jolleys A, Robertson NRE. A study of the effects of early bone grafting in complete clefts of the lip and palate— Five year study. *Br J Plast Surg.* 1972;25:229–237.
51. Robinson F, Wood B. Primary bone grafting in the treatment of cleft lip and palate with special reference to alveolar collapse. *Br J Plast Surg.* 1969;22:336–342.

52. Friede H, Johanson B. Adolescent facial morphology of early bone grafted cleft lip and palate patients. *Scand J Plast Reconstr Surg.* 1982;16:41–53.
53. Friede H, Johanson B. A follow-up study of cleft children treated with primary bone grafting. *Scand J Plast Reconstr Surg.* 1974;8:88–103.
54. Matthews D, Chir M, Broomhead I. Early and late bone grafting in cases of cleft lip and palate. *Br J Plast Surg.* 1970;23:115–129.
55. Peat JH. Early orthodontic treatment for complete clefts. *Am J Orthod.* 1974;65:28–28.
56. Kernahan DA, Rosenstein SW, eds. *Cleft Lip and Palate: A System of Management.* Baltimore, Md: Williams and Wilkins; 1990.
57. Pruzansky S. Pre-surgical orthopedics and bone grafting for infants with cleft lip and palate: a dissent. *Cleft Palate J.* 1964;1:154.
58. Berkowitz S. Section III: Orofacial growth and dentistry: a state of the art report on neonatal maxillary orthopedics. *Cleft Palate J.* 1977;14:288–301.
59. Skoog T. *Plastic Surgery: New Methods and Refinements.* Stockholm, Sweden: Almgvist-Wiksell International; 1974.
60. Fara M, Mullerova Z, Smahel Z. Presurgical orthopedic treatment in unilateral cleft lip and palate. In: Bardach J, Morris HL, eds. *Multidisciplinary Management of Cleft Lip and Palate.* Philadelphia, Pa: WB Saunders Co; 1990:586–600.
61. Huddart AG. The effect of form and dimension on the management of the maxillary arch in unilateral cleft lip and palate conditions. *Scand J Plast Reconstr Surg.* 1987;21:53–56.
62. Maisels DO. The influence of presurgical orthodontic treatment upon the surgery of the cleft lip and palate. *Br J Orthod.* 1974;1:15–20.
63. Huddart AG, Crabb JJ. The effect of presurgical treatment on palatal tissue area in unilateral cleft lip and palate subjects. *Br J Orthod.* 1977;4:181–185.
64. Perko M. Die Zusammenarbeit der Kieferorthopäden und Kieferchirurgen bei der Fruhbehandlung von Spaltpatienten. *Zähnarzl Prax.* 1977;28:71–72.
65. Hotz M. Multidisziplinare Betreuung von Patienten mit Lippen-Kiefer Gaumen-Spalten in Zürich. *Stomatol DDR.* 1979;29:944–954.
66. Nordin KE, Larson O, Nylen B, Eklund G. Early bone grafting in complete cleft lip and palate cases following maxillofacial orthopedics. I. The method and the skeletal development from seven to thirteen years of age. *Scand J Plast Reconstr Surg.* 1983;17:33–50.
67. Komposch G. Die prechirurgische kieferorthopädische Behandlung von Sauglingen mit Lippen-Kiefer-Gaumen-Spalte. *Fortschr Kieferorthop.* 1986;47:362–369.
68. Trankmann J. Postnatale pre- und postoperative kieferorthopädische Behandlung bei Lippen-Kiefer-Gaumen-Spalten. *Die Quintessenz.* 1986;1:69–78.
69. Robertson NRE. Facial form of patients with cleft lip and palate. *Br Dent J.* 1983;155:59–61.
70. Friede H. *Studies on Facial Morphology and Growth in Bilateral Cleft Lip and Palate.* Göteborg, Sweden: De-partment of Orthodontics, University of Göteborg; 1977.
71. Cronin TD, Brauer RO, Penoff JH. Maxillary Orthopedics, Orthodontia and Bone Grafting. In: Cole RM, ed. *Early Treatment of Cleft Lip and Palate. Proceedings of Second International Symposium, 1969.* Chicago, Ill: Cleft Palate Institute, Northwestern University Dental School; 1969:15–19.
72. Cole RM, ed. *Early Treatment of Cleft Lip and Palate. Proceedings of Second International Symposium, 1969.* Chicago, Ill: Cleft Lip and Palate Institute, Northwestern University Dental School; 1969:19–20.
73. Ross RB. Treatment variables affecting facial growth in unilateral cleft lip and palate. Part 2: Presurgical orthopedics. *Cleft Palate J.* 1987;24:24–30.
74. Gnoinski W. Infant orthopedics and later orthodontic monitoring for unilateral cleft lip and palate patients in Zurich. In: Bardach J, Morris HL, eds. *Multidisciplinary Management of Cleft Lip and Palate.* Philadelphia, Pa: WB Saunders Co; 1990:576–585.
75. Hotz M. Orofacial development under adverse conditions. *Eur J Orthod.* 1983:91–103.
76. Kuijpers-Jagtman AM. Changes in maxillary arch dimensions and occlusion in unilateral cleft lip and palate subjects. Noordwijkerhoot, Studieweek NVOS; 1985:9–21.
77. Hotz M, Gnoinski W. Comprehensive cure of cleft lip and palate children at Zurich University: a preliminary report. *Am J Orthod.* 1976;70:481–504.
78. Hotz MM, Gnoinski WM, Nussbaumer H. Early maxillary orthopedics in cleft lip and cleft palate cases: guidelines for surgery. *Cleft Palate J.* 1978;15:405.
79. Hotz M, Gnoinski W, Perko M, Nussbaumer H, Hof E, Haubensak R, eds. *Early Treatment of Cleft Lip and Palate. Proceedings of the Third International Symposium, 1984.* Toronto: Huber; 1986.
80. Bergland O, Semb G. Abydholm F, Borchgrevink H, Eskeland G. Secondary bone grafting and orthodontic treatment on patients with bilateral complete clefts of the lip and palate. *Ann Plast Surg.* 1986;17:460–471.
81. Wolfe SA, Berkowitz S. The use of cranial bone grafts in the closure of alveolar and anterior palatal clefts. *Plast and Reconstr Surg.* 1983;72:659–666.
82. Smahel Z, Mullerova Z. Facial growth and development in unilateral cleft lip and palate during the period of puberty: comparison of the development after periosteoplasty and after primary bone grafting. *Cleft Palate-Craniofac J.* 1994;31:105–115.
83. Skoog T. The use of periosteal flaps in the repair of clefts and of the primary palate. *Cleft Palate J.* 1965;2:332–339.
84. Hellquist R, Porter B. The influence of infant periosteoplasty on facial growth and dental occlusion from five to eight years of age in cases of complete unilateral cleft lip and palate. *Scand J Plast Reconstr Surg.* 1979;13:305.
85. Millard DR Jr. *Cleft Craft III: The Evolution of its Surgery, III: Alveolar and Palatal Deformities.* Boston, Mass: Little, Brown and Co; 1980:240.

86. Millard DR Jr. *Cleft Craft III. Alveolar and Palatal Deformities.* Boston, Mass: Little, Brown and Co; 1980;284–298.
87. Brophy TW. *Cleft Lip and Palate.* Philadelphia, Pa: Blakiston's Son and Co; 1923:131–132.
88. Georgiade NG, Miadick RA, Thorne FL. Positioning of the premaxilla in bilateral cleft lips by oral pinning and traction. *Plast Reconstr Surg.* 1968;41:240.
89. Graber TM. The congenital cleft palate deformity. *J Am Dent Assoc.* 1954;48:375.
90. Graber TM. Changing philosophies in cleft palate management. *J Pediat.* 1950;37:400–415.
91. Graber TM. Craniofacial morophology in cleft palate and cleft lip deformities. *Surg Gynecol Obstet.* 1949; 88:359.
92. Millard DR Jr, Latham RA. Improved surgical and dental treatment of clefts. *Plast Reconstr Surg.* 1990; 86:856–871.
93. Millard DR Jr. *Principlization of Plastic Surgery.* Boston: Little, Brown and Co; 1986;77.
94. Georgiade, NG, Mason, R, Riefkohl R, Georgiade G, Barwick W. Preoperative positioning of the protruding premaxilla bilateral cleft lip patient. *Plast Reconstr Surg.* 1989;83:32–38.
95. Ross RB. Discussion of: Georgiade NG, Mason R, Riefkohl R, Georgiade G, Barwick W. Preoperative positioning of the protruding remaxilla bilateral cleft lip patient. *Plast Reconstr Surg.* 1989;83:39–40.

Maxillary Advancement

PROTRACTION OF THE MAXILLA USING ORTHOPEDICS

Children with complete unilateral and bilateral cleft of the lip and palate are usually at risk for poor facial growth. They are prone to developing midfacial retrusion related to maxillary hypoplasia or growth retardation secondary to excessive palatal scarring. Usually, this results in an anterior dental crossbite or severely rotated maxillary incisors which may occlude in a tip-to-tip relationship with the mandibular incisors. Depending on the age of the patient and the extent of midfacial maldevelopment, some of these early problems can be corrected using midfacial orthopedic protraction forces which increase growth at the circummaxillary sutures as they are repositioned anteriorly (Fig 10–1). When all else fails midfacial surgery is available.

Some of the earlier work in this field, which encouraged a rethinking of the use of orthopedic forces for the correction of midfacial retrusion, includes Haas,[1] Delaire,[2] Delaire et al,[3-5] Irie and Nakamura,[6] Ritula,[7] Subtelny,[8] Delaire et al,[9] Friede and Lennartsson,[10] Sarnas and Rune,[11] Berkowitz,[12] Tindlund,[13] Nanda,[14] and Molstad and Dahl.[15] More recently this area has been influenced by the work of Tindlund et al[16-18] and Buschang et al.[19]

Earlier attempts by Kettle and Burnapp[20] in which anteriorly directed extraoral forces were derived from chin caps were relatively unsuccessful. Facial mask therapy seems to offer better control and a wider range of force application.

In many cases, in the mixed dentition, palatal expansion using fixed orthodontic appliances was applied simultaneously with protraction to correct a bilateral crossbite and create a more favorable condition for midfacial growth and development.

Prior to the use of orthopedic forces, many standard orthodontic treatments designed to move the dentition to correct a Class 3 malocclusion due to midfacial retrusion in the absence of mandibular prognathism failed. Orthodontic forces applied to the teeth by Class 3 elastics would not displace the maxilla; at best they would flare the maxillary incisors without creating an adequate incisor overbite and axial inclination. This treatment was found to be unsatisfactory and soon fell out of favor.

Since 1975 Berkowitz has been using a modified protraction facial mask originally popularized by Delaire et al[3] (Figs 10–2 and 10–3). It has been very successful in controlling the direction of protruding forces without causing severe sore spots on the chin or forehead. He has found that protraction forces do not modify the direction of mandibular growth as Delaire et al[3] claimed, but by increasing midfacial height, the mandible is repositioned downward and backward with growth to make the patient's maxillary retrusion appear less evident.

Protraction forces (350 to 450 grams per side) must be intermittent (the mask is worn only for 12 hours per day), and directed downward and forward from a hook located mesial to the maxillary cuspids. Pulling downward from the molars should be avoided because it will tilt the palatal plane downward in the back by extruding the molars and thus opening the bite. When the midfacial height is deficient, protraction forces need to be modified to increase vertical as well as anterior growth. This is done by using more vertically directed elastic forces.

Berkowitz has found 350–450 grams of force per side to be adequate in most instances, but there are rare instances when the elastic force needs to be reduced to prevent sore spots at the chin point. Friede and Lennartsson[10] have used protraction forces between 150 to 500 grams per side. Ire and Nakamura[6]

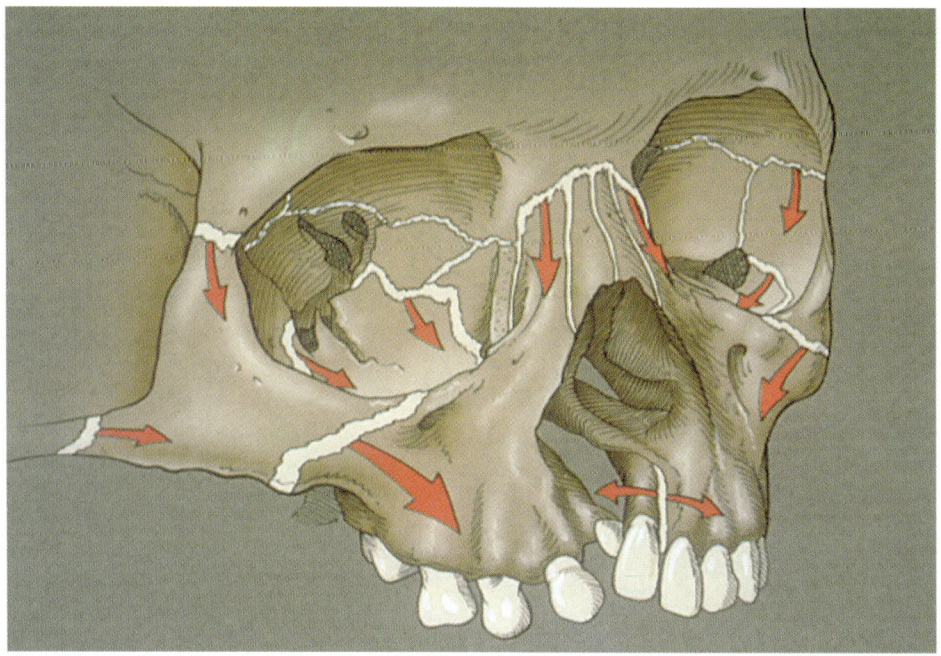

a

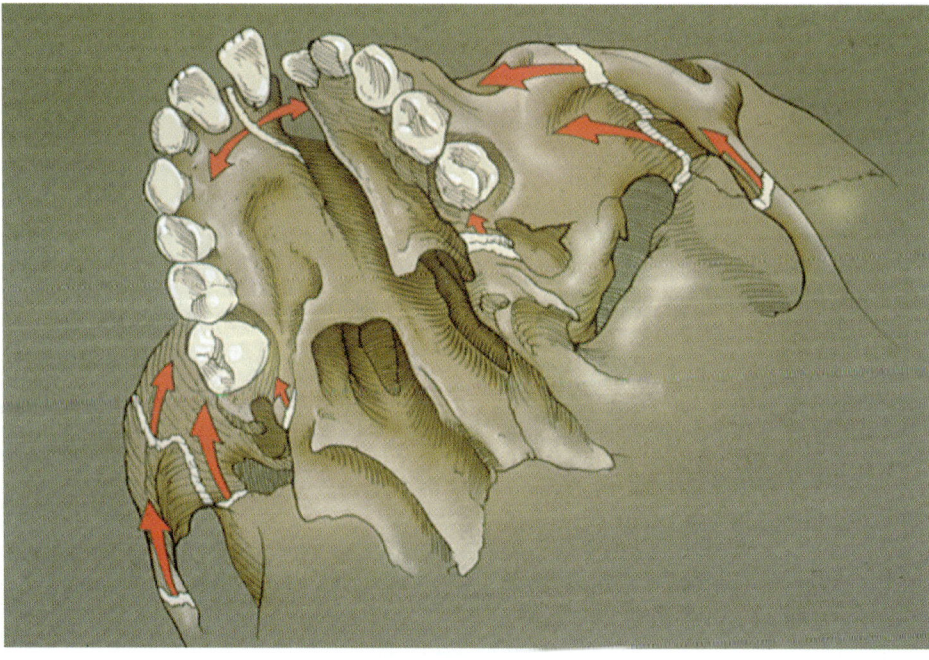

b

Fig 10-1. Protraction of the maxillary complex using orthopedic forces. The maxilla articulates with nine bones: two of the cranium, the frontal and ethomoid, and seven of the face, viz., the nasal zygomatic, lacrimal, inferior and nasal concha, palatine, vomer and its fellow of the opposite side. Sometimes it articulates with the orbital surface, and sometimes with the lateral pterygoid plate of the sphenoid. Illustration showing how protraction forces applied to the maxilla depend on the disarticulation and growth at all the dependent sutures. (Courtesy of Edward Genevoc.)

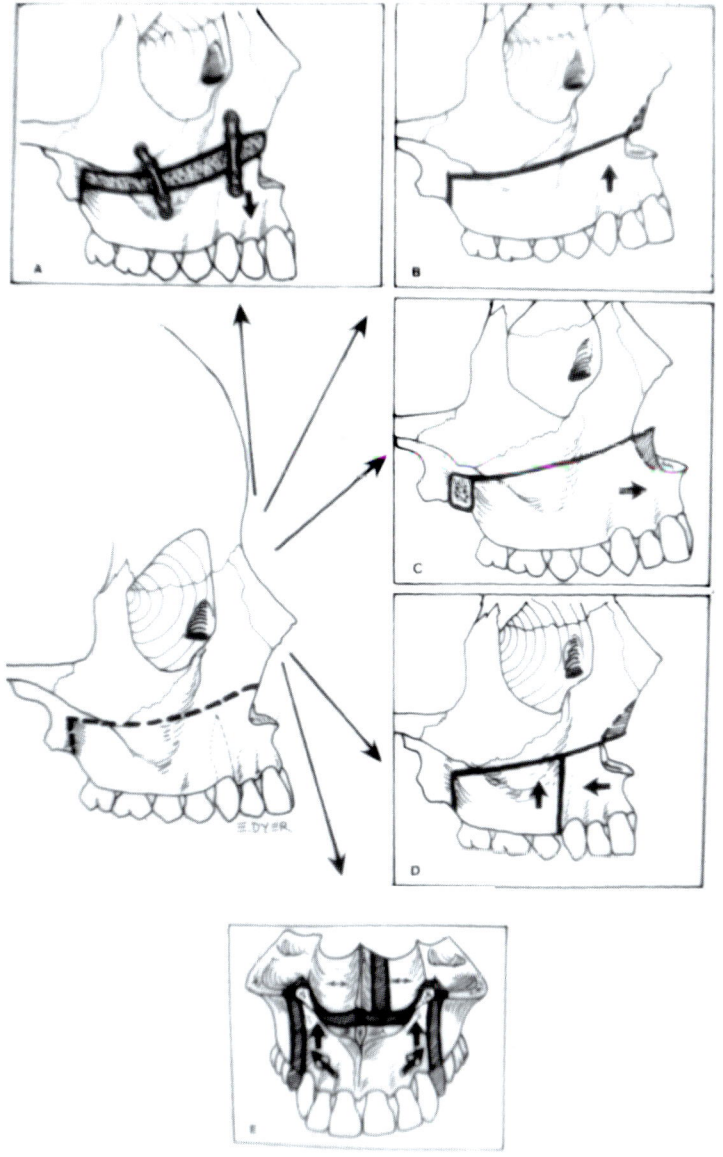

Fig 10–5. a. LeFort I surgical procedures: Various directions the maxilla can be moved. (Courtesy of SA Wolfe.) **A.** Inferiorly: requires bone grafts to maintain the new position. **B.** Superiorly: No grafts required. **C.** Forward: Requires a posteriorly supporting bone graft. **D.** The posterior segment is moved superiorly while the anterior segment is moved posteriorly. When the premaxilla is retruded it usually needs to be surgically widened through the midpalatal suture between the central incisors to maintain good cuspid interdigitation. **E.** The premaxilla is moved superiorly.

(continued)

Fig 10-5. *(continued)*

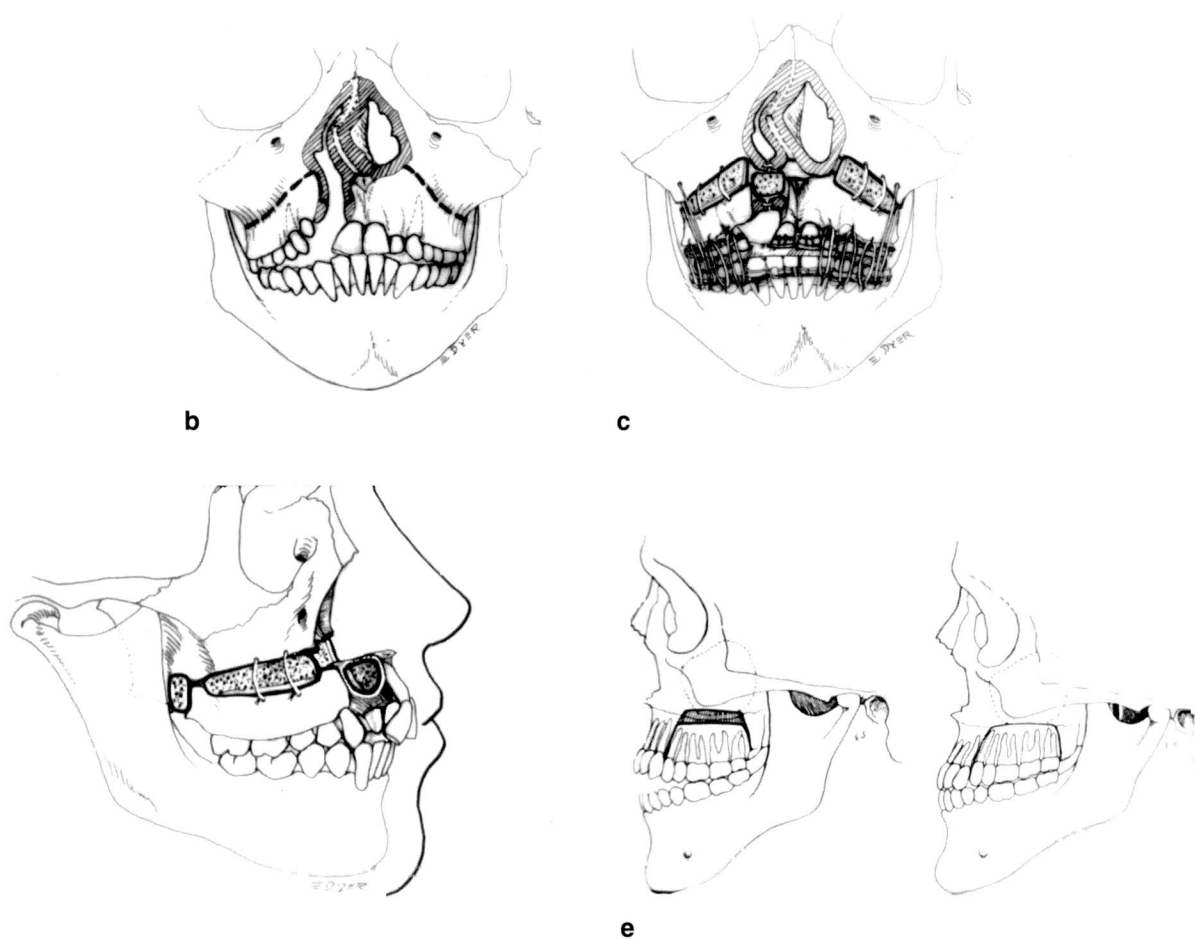

Fig 10-5. *(continued)*
b. Initial incisions for LeFort I surgery with a secondary alveolar bone grafting to be performed simultaneously. **c.** The maxilla is moved inferiorly with bone grafts placed at the surgical cite to support the lengthened maxilla. Alveolar bone graft placed from the nasal aperture to the alveolar crest. Prior to the use of metal plates (rigid fixation) steel sutures were used to stabilized the separated segments. An acrylic surgical wafer is used to position the bony segments according to prior mock surgery performed on plaster casts. Intermaxillary fixation of the maxilla to the mandible using intermaxillary rubber bands for 4 to 6 weeks is recommended in cases with severe palatal scarring in conjunction with the use of rigid fixation. **d.** Lateral view shows a bone block placed between the perpendicular plates of the sphenoid and the maxillary tuberosity with a bone graft to the premaxillary-maxillary junction. **e.** Buccal segments are superiorly positioned to permit mandibular auto-rotation and reduction of the anterior open bite.

Fig 10–6. Case JR (AT–94). LeFort I advancement in CBCLP. Surgical advancement to correct a slight midfacial retrusion when the patient refused to wear a protraction facial mask. **a**, **b**, **c**. and **d**. At 6 and 14 years of age, prior to orthodontic treatment, facial photographs show a midface recessiveness with an anterior crossbite. **e**. At 14 years after surgical-orthodontic treatment. **f**, **g**, **h**, and **i**. At 16 years after nose and lip revision.

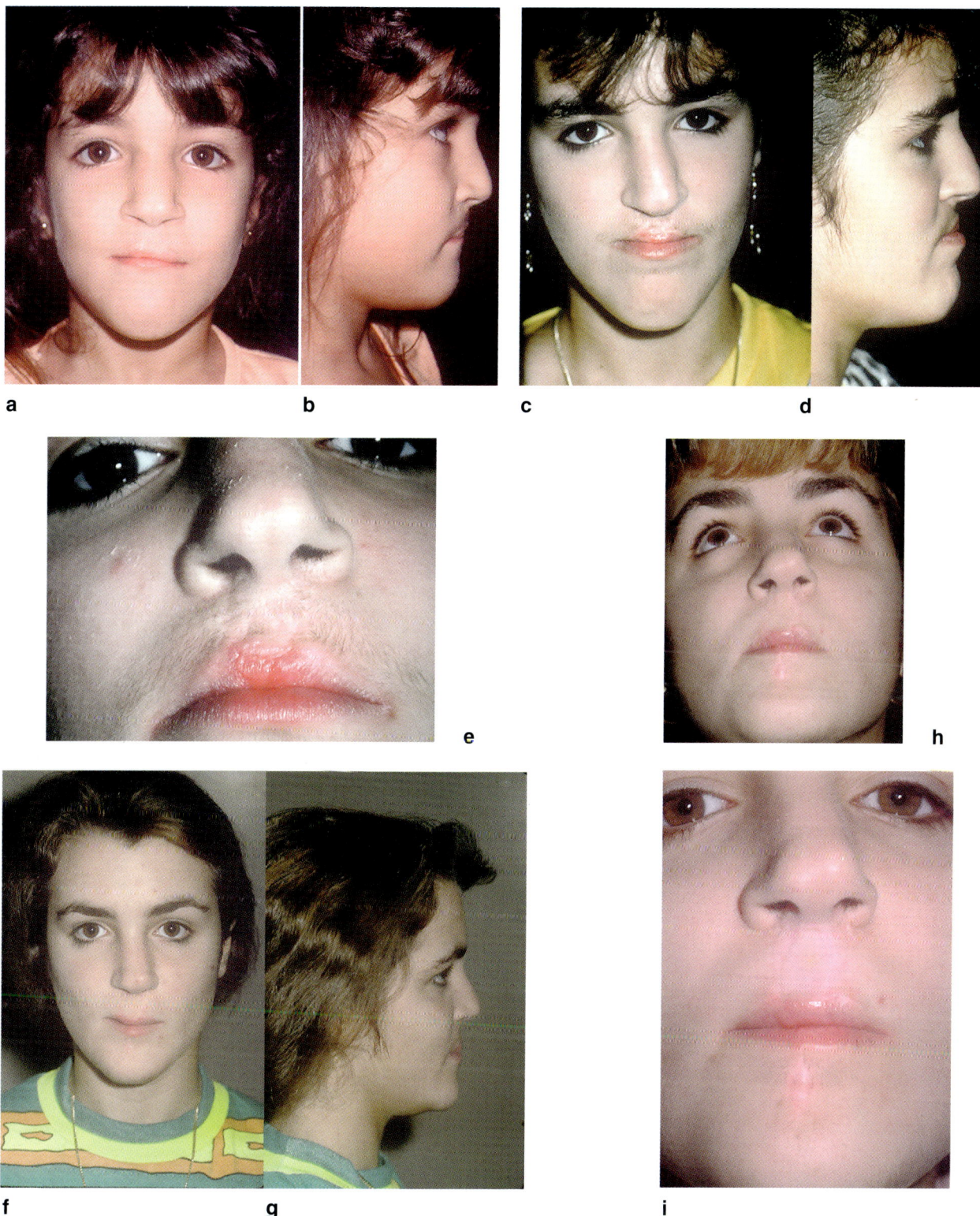

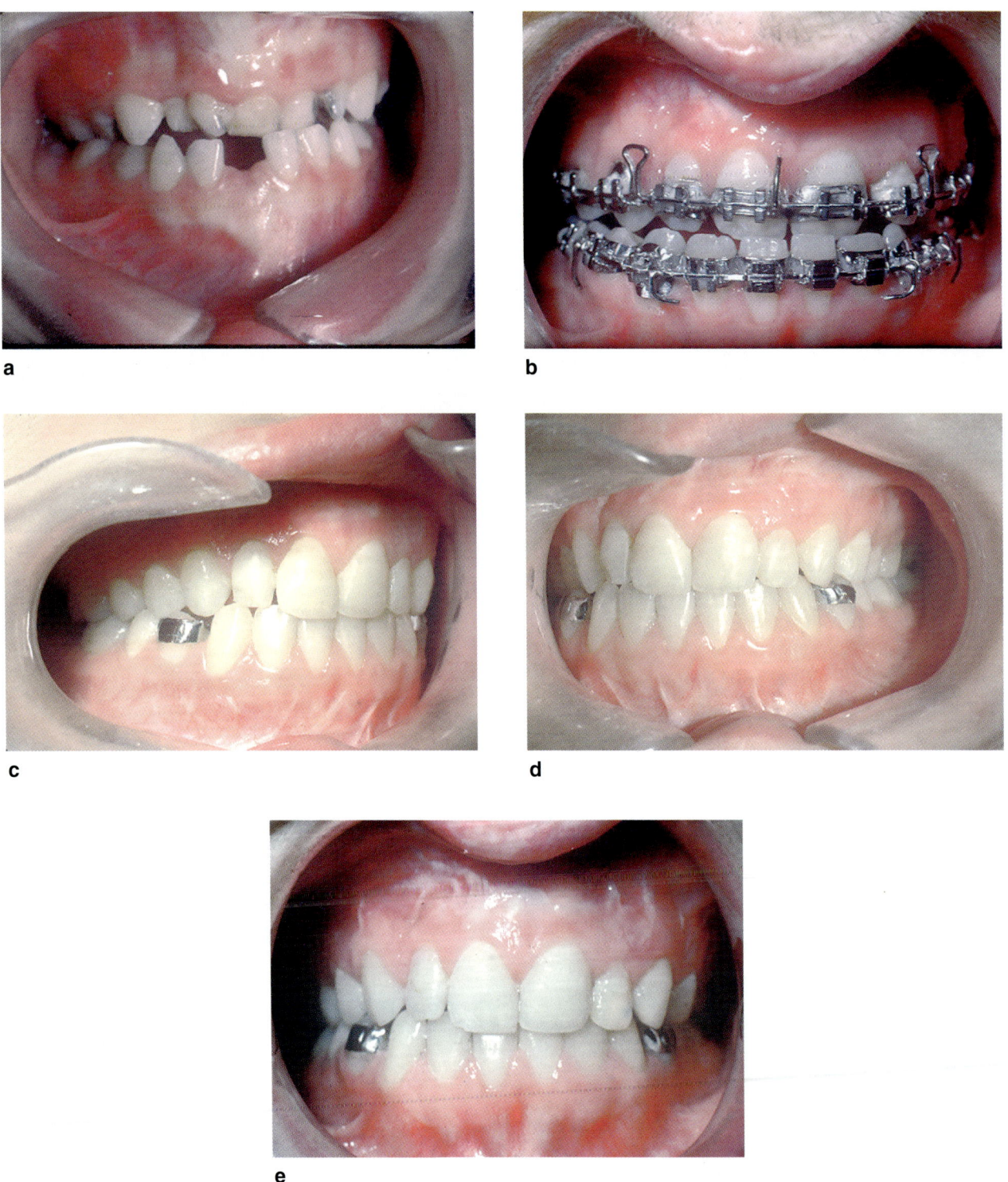

Fig 10–7. Case JR (AT-94). Occlusal changes after LeFont I surgical advancement and orthodontics. a. Occlusion at 6 years. **b.** Orthodontic preparation for surgical maxillary advancement. **c, d,** and **e.** After orthodontic treatment.

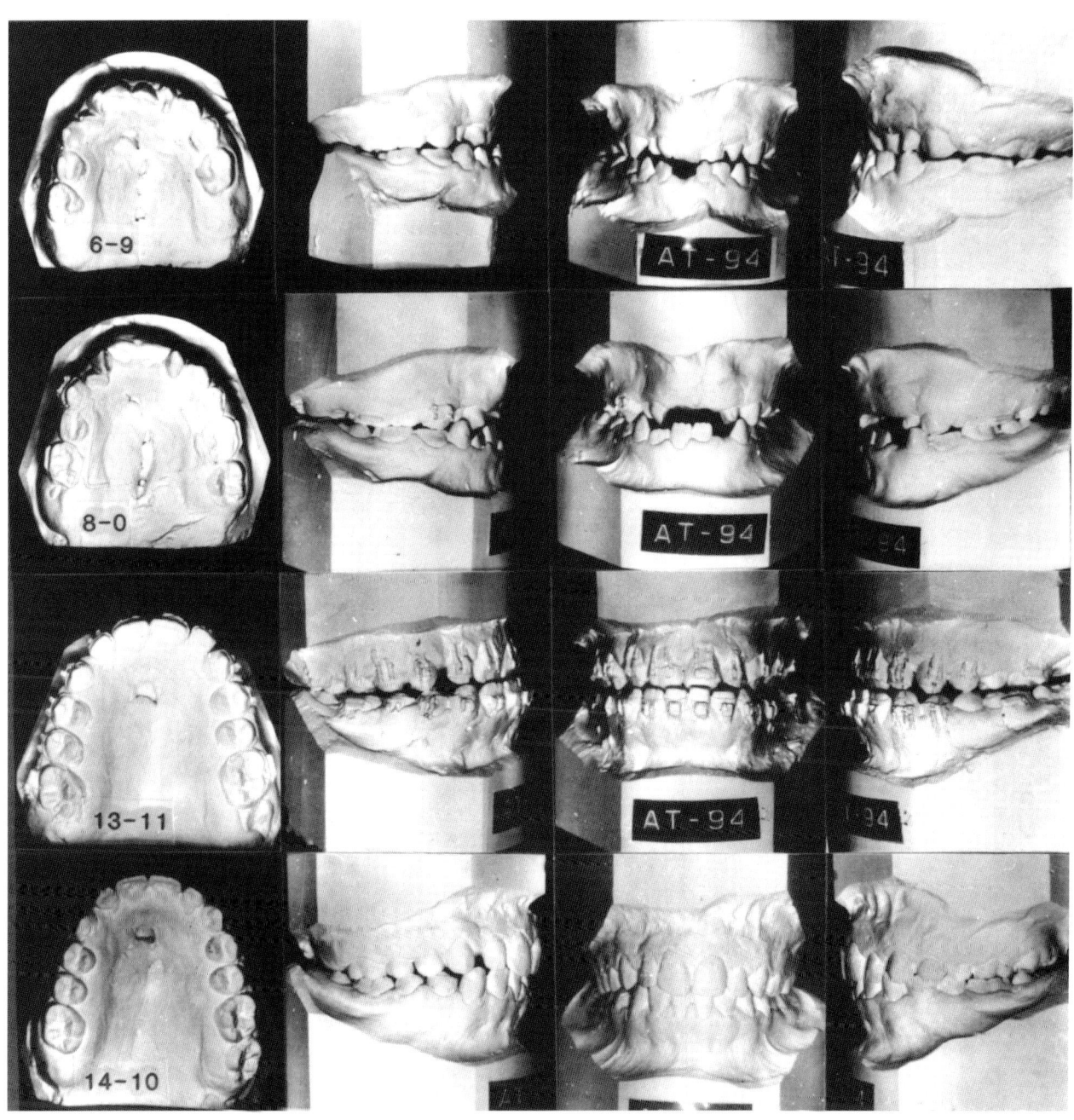

Fig 10-8. Case JR (AT-94). **Surgical maxillary advancement (LeFort I)**. Pre-and post maxillary advancement

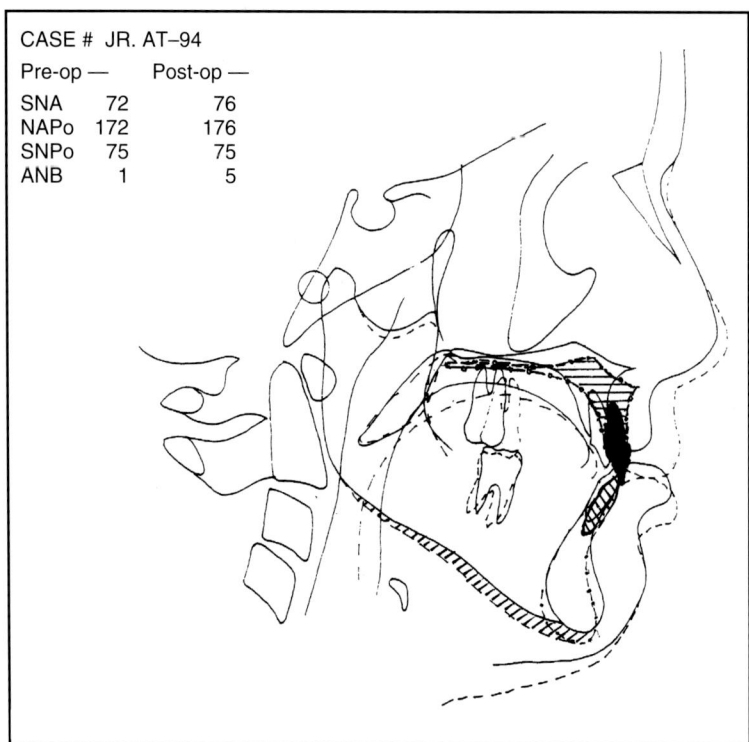

Fig 10-9. Case JR. Lateral cephalometic tracings before and after LeFort I maxillary advancement and inferior positioning. The mandible autorotated posteriorly reducing the mandibular prominence. Maxillary advancement moved the upper lip forward while the lower lip remained practically in the same position.

to the pterygomaxillary space. If the dissection is strictly subperiosteal, there is no bothersome exposure of the buccal fat. The piriform aperture is dissected, sometimes removing a portion of the nasal spine, and the nasal mucoperiosteum is dissected back to the hard palate-soft palate junction. The septum can either be separated bluntly from the vomer or a guarded osteotome can be used. The osteotomy is performed largely with the reciprocating saw, starting laterally in the thick bone beneath the buttress of the zygoma and proceeding medially through thinner bone. The osteotomy through the piriform aperture and medial wall of the antrum is done with the saw blade pointed laterally.

Sectioning of the palatine bone, the sole attachment of the maxillary tuberosity to the pterygoid plate of the sphenoid, follows. The lateral osteotomy can be taken a bit farther back by a few taps on a straight osteotome, and the medial antral wall can be further sectioned with a guarded nasal osteotome.

At this point, the only remaining attachment of the lower maxillary segment is the posterior wall of the antrum, and firm, downward finger pressure on the maxilla is usually enough to produce a down-fracture. If not, the forceps can be inserted underneath the nasal mucosa and the maxilla completely mobilized with a downward and side-to-side motion. It can be further mobilized with a blunt elevator used as a lever.

The maxilla is then placed in the desired occlusal relation with the mandible, and both jaws are placed in the desired relationship with the rest of the face. An autogenous iliac or cranial bone graft is used when the face is to be lengthened, when the degree of maxillary advancement is more than 5 mm, or when the patient has a cleft. If the maxilla is shortened, the resected bone is placed over the osteotomy lines.

Sometimes the alveolus is intact, but the maxilla needs to be expanded, as may occur in a cleft patient who has a buccal crossbite and an alveolar cleft. This procedure is easily performed from above the hard palate, and the palatal mucosa is kept intact if possible. The sectioning is performed with the reciprocating saw, and an elevator is inserted to gently pry the two segments apart. Expansion forceps can be used if required. If the palatal mucosa absolutely prevents expansion, it is divided, creating an alveolar and anterior palatal cleft.

If there is an alveolar cleft to begin with, the two maxillary segments are handled independently and brought into proper occlusion with the mandible. The palatal cleft-nasal floor defect is bone-grafted, and if necessary a transportation flap is developed from the buccal sulcus (Burian) to close the palatal defect. In rare instances, a tongue flap is required. The nasal lining, which will have been carefully dissected at the beginning, is closed before the palatal bone graft is inserted.

The procedure has now been refined to the stage that is the same regardless of whether the alveolus was initially intact. Miniplates are placed between the upper and lower portions of the maxilla for rigid fixation. If bone grafts are required, they are placed either between or over the bone cuts.

If the desired maxillary advancement measures more than 6 mm, bone grafts can be wedged into the pterygomaxillary gap. This step is facilitated by using a traction wire placed through the thick bone beneath the nasal spine. The wire is used to pull the maxilla to the opposite side, which opens the gap and allows impaction of the bone graft. Circumzygomatic wires are almost never used, because they pull the maxilla back, they are too long (long wires can "stretch" more than short wires), and they do not prevent the anterior maxilla from rocking downward.

Wolfe[24] uses an iliac or cranial bone graft on all cleft patients, as these patients are likely to have a maxillary relapse. Generally, the bone can also be used as an onlay to fill out a deficient maxilla. If the advancement is less than 5 mm, bone is placed only over the anterior osteotomies and in the alveolar and palatal cleft, if present.

The use of anything other than a fresh autogenous bone graft is unsafe. It takes about 15 minutes to harvest the needed amount of iliac or cranial bone. In the former, the patient will be comfortable as far as the hip is concerned within 1 to 2 weeks. By this time, the autogenous graft will have consolidated. Consolidation with cadaver or demineralized bone or with hydroxylapatite may require months.

Like the sagittal splitting procedure for the mandible, the Le Fort I osteotomy, once mastered, can provide a solution to a number of maxillary problems. After the horizontal osteotomy, down-fracture, and mobilization, the maxilla can be:

1. Advanced directly with or without a bone graft (in the noncleft class III patient).
2. Advanced, or advanced and expanded transversely, with a bone graft (in the cleft patient).
3. Moved superiorly after resection of a measured amount of maxilla above the horizontal osteotomy (in cases of "long face," resulting from vertical maxillary excess).
4. Moved inferiorly with a bone graft (in cases of "short face," or vertical maxillary deficiency).
5. Sectioned into multiple segments with teeth Wassmund or Schuchardt procedure which is done from above.
6. Moved directly backward, although this is difficult to do. (The resection should be of the maxillary tuberosity after extraction of the third molars rather than of the pterygoid plate.) The same result can generally be achieved by an associated segmental osteotomy performed more anteriorly.

With the maxilla in the down-fractured position, multiple osteotomies can be performed from above, which, coupled with or without dental extractions, permit the dental correction of complex malarrangements of the maxilla in one stage. The circulation of blood to the anterior segment comes entirely through the palatal mucoperiosteum, and one must be certain that there are no protrusive edges from the occlusal splint to impinge on the anterior palate. Any number of transverse sagittal osteotomies can be performed, depending on the requirements of the individual case.

Attempts to treat an anterior open bite by mandibular ramus osteotomies are often unsuccessful due to relapse caused by the predominance of the masticatory muscles. Anterior segmental osteotomies of the mandible are appropriate when there is dental crowding and a downward angulation of the mandibular occlusal plane.

The Schuchardt procedure can be used to shorten posterior maxillary height, but it is rarely used in the United States because it requires either an interdental osteotomy or a tooth extraction (Fig 10–9).

If the orthodontist can level the maxillary occlusal plane, even by accentuating the open bite, the simplest and most stable solution is the Le Fort I osteotomy. If the position of the maxillary central incisors relative to the lower vermilion border of the upper lip is satisfactory beforehand, this relationship is preserved. If desired, the maxillary incisors can be raised or lowered relative to the upper lip.

After the maxilla has been completely mobilized, intermaxillary fixation is established and the maxillomandibular complex seated with firm upward and posterior pressure to set the condyles. Appropriate resection of the posterior and, if necessary, the anterior maxilla is performed until the desired anterior maxillary height is obtained. Stabilization of the maxillary osteotomy is then performed with miniplates, and the intermaxillary fixation, if utilized, is temporarily discontinued to evaluate the occlusal relationship. This examination will reveal whether the condyles were inadvertently pulled out of the glenoid fossae. A Class 2 relationship indicates that the maxilla must be posteriorly repositioned, either by resecting a portion of pterygoid plates (which is difficult) or by extracting the maxillary third molars and resecting a portion of the maxillary tuberosity (which is easier) (Figs 10–10 to 10–11). The case reports in Figs 10–12 through 10–16 demonstrate two other types of midfacial surgery (see Volume II, Chapter 20).

STABILITY OF MAXILLARY ADVANCEMENT

A disappointing yet frequent sequel to orthognathic surgery to advance the maxilla is its partial or complete return to the original state (relapse). The maxillary advancement occurs within a limiting soft tissue envelope (the skin and muscles). Mandibular advancement surgery, especially when it involves the mandibular ligaments, has a great tendency to relapse. The degree of relapse is often judged by measuring occlusal or skeletal landmark changes.

Hochban et al,[25] in a review of the literature, reported that the use of miniplates (in rigid fixations) is superior to wire fixation in overcoming the tendency to relapse. Currently most reports favor the use of miniplates (Freihofer,[26] Ward-Booth et al,[27] Houston et al,[28] Champy,[29] Horster,[30] Luyk and Ward-Booth,[31] Rosen[32]). Proffit and Phillips[33] found a skeletal relapse at 32% after midface advancement using wire fixation compared with 25% after miniplate fixation.

Some investigators believe that the amount of relapse is directly related to the amount of advancement (Carpenter et al,[34] Houston et al,[28] Wolfe and Berkowitz[24]), whereas others think there is no correlation between displacement of the maxilla and relapse (Rosen,[32] Iannette et al,[35] Proffit and Phillips[33]). Proffit and Phillips also believe that it is important to achieve excellent occlusion following the operation to reduce the tendency to relapse. Epker[36] suggests that interpositioning of bone grafts increases stability by enhancing bony consolidation.

It is generally accepted that the tendency toward relapse starts immediately after surgery and continues for up to about 6 months after the operation. After about 1 year, the correction can be considered stable (Epker,[36] Teuscher and Sailer,[37] Persson et al,[38] Houston et al[28]). Hochban et al,[25] in an excellent review of the subject of postoperative maxillary relapse, reported cephalometric analyses of 31 patients preoperatively, postoperatively, and 1 year later. Fourteen patients had clefts of the lip and palate; the others were noncleft patients with maxillary deficiency. All had maxillary advancement by Le Fort I osteotomy and miniplate fixation. Hochban et al[25] found that the amount of relapse was between 20 and 25% in the cleft group and about 10% in the noncleft group. The degree of relapse was related to the amount of advancement, thus confirming the earlier work by Rosen[32] and Houston et al.[28] The authors recommended surgical overtreatment and a good overbite-overjet relationship after orthodontic treatment.

Berkowitz sometime uses very light Class III elastics for 6 months to improve bony consolidation when he notices a maxillary relapse occurring. He believes that the muscular drape to the midface changes very slowly in adapting to skeletal changes, and therefore, some over-treatment is necessary in all instances.

Posnick and Ewing[40] studied the outcomes in 30 adults and adolescents judged skeletally mature, who had unilateral cleft lip and palate and underwent Le Fort I advancement. This group was investigated to determine the amount and timing of relapse, the correlation between advancement and relapse, the effect of performing multiple jaw procedures, the effect of different types of bone grafts, the effect of pharyngoplasty in place at the time of osteotomy, and the effectiveness of various methods of internal fixation.

Tracings of preoperative and serial postoperative lateral cephalograms were digitized to calculate horizontal and vertical maxillary changes. No significant differences in outcomes were seen between patients who had maxillary surgery alone and those who had operations on both upper and lower jaws, nor did the outcomes vary significantly with the type of autogenous bone graft used or the segmentalization of the Le Fort I osteotomy. Average "effective" advancement was greater both immediately and 2 years after surgery in patients who did not have a pharyngoplasty in place before the operation.

Advancement also was more stable both immediately and 2 years after surgery in the patients with miniplate fixation than in patients with direct-wire fixation. Mean downward (vertical) displacement was 2.6 mm with a relapse of 1.4 mm after 2 years. The degrees of relapse and of advancement or displacement did not correlate significantly.

There is another obvious risk factor, the tonicity of the orbicularis oris muscle ring, which needs to be considered. Unfortunately, there are no pressure measurements that can be utilized to improve the success to failure ratio.

CASE REPORT: LeFORT I MIDFACIAL ADVANCEMENT

Fig 10–10. Case JS (AV–64) UCLP showing LeFort I advancement to correct midfacial retrusion. Treatment: Increase midfacial height, and widen the palatal arch. **a–g.** Pre– and postsurgical facial and intraoral photographs showing changes in the profile and occlusion. Chin augmentation is usually contraindicated with midfacial advancement since it may lead to a concave profile after some maxillary relapse. **h.** An illustration showing type of surgery performed.

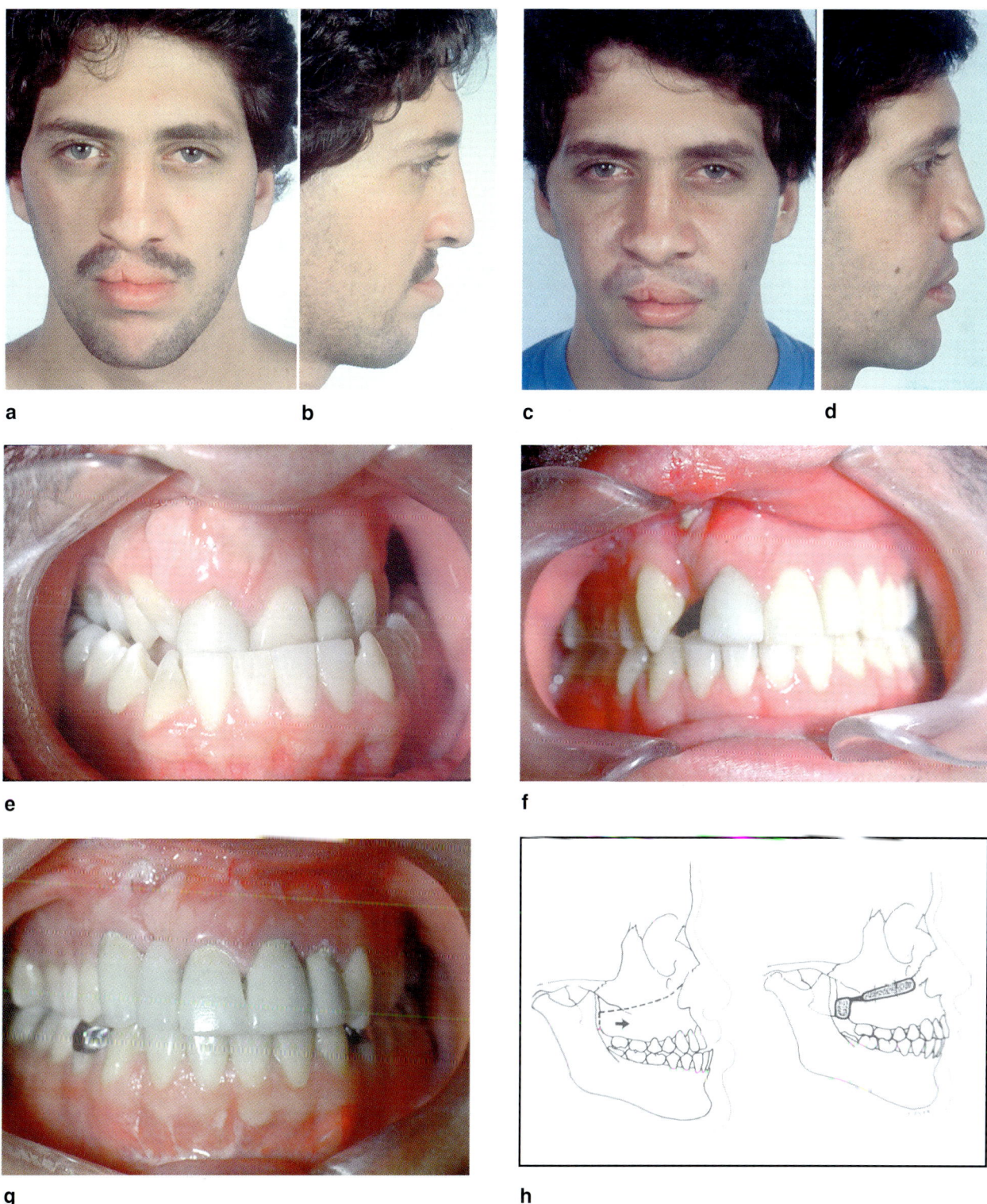

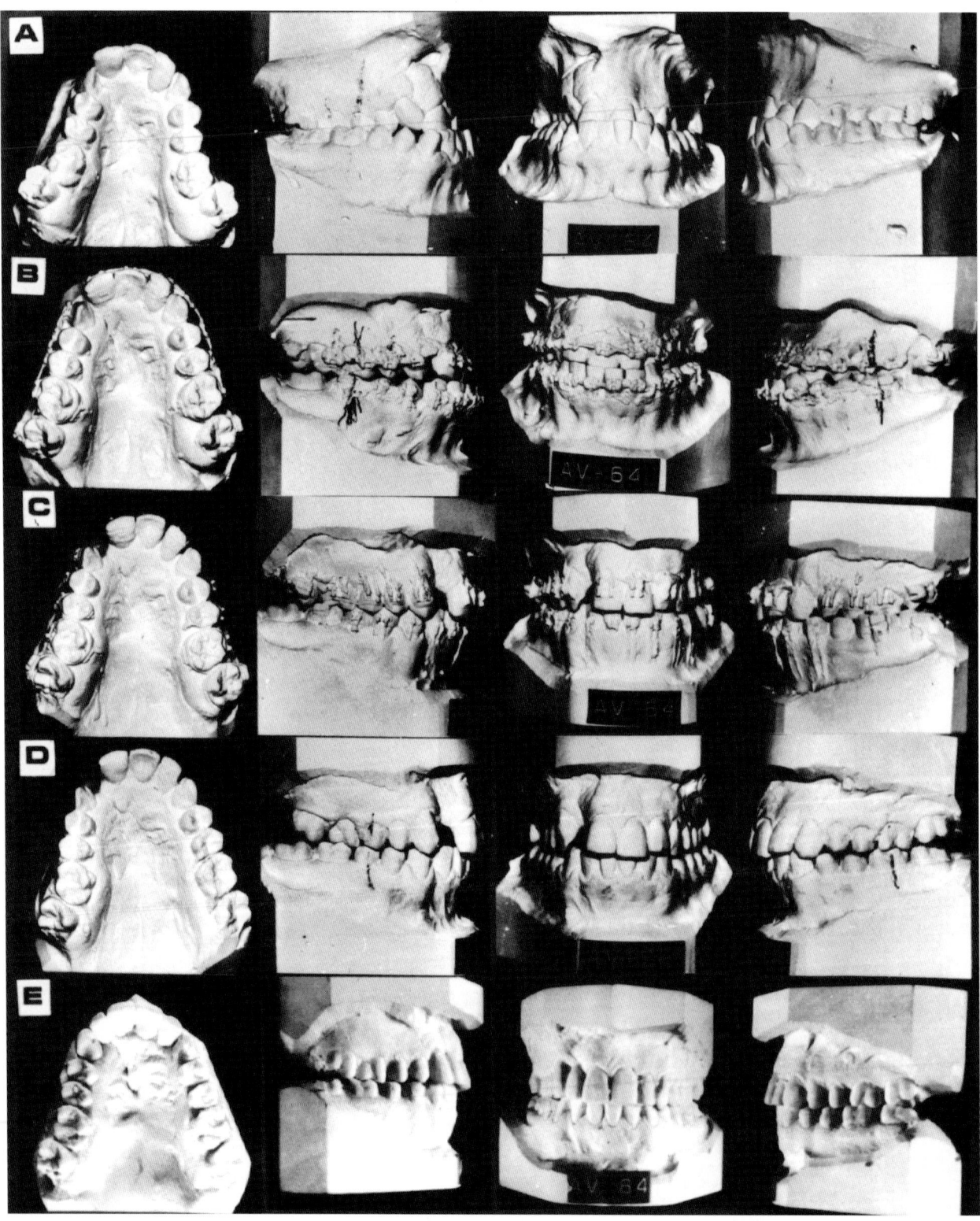

Fig 10–11. Case JS (AV–64). Serial dental casts. This case shows severe palatal collapse and scarring leading to buccal and anterior crossbite. Pre- and postsurgical orthodontics plus maxillary surgery reduced the anterior crossbite. The maxillary arch was orthodontically expanded to open the upper right lateral incisor space and to avoid additional surgery with more palatal scaring.

CASE REPORT: HEMIFACIAL MICROSOMIA

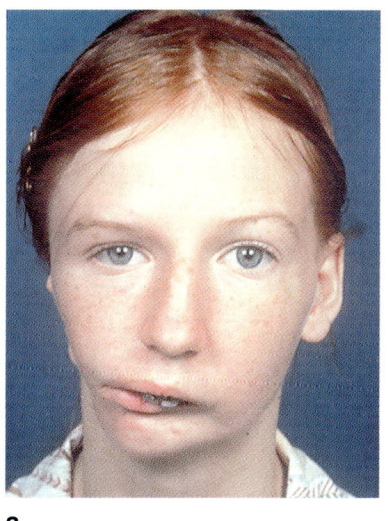
a

b

Fig 10–12. Facial photographs of a young woman with hemifacial microsomia. With maldevelopment of the condyle and ramus the mandible shifts to the affected side. The loss of ramal height prevents the maxillary buccal teeth on that side from erupting, thereby skewing the transverse occlusal plane. **a** and **b.** Before and after facial photographs of a patient who had surgery to correct facial asymmetry due to hemifacial microsomia.

Comments: Some bony relapse is to be expected since the involved soft tissue—ligaments, muscle, and overlying skin—have been stretched and put under tension. The amount of relapse is unpredictable. The rigid fixation plates cannot totally overcome this relapse tendency. Long-term retention is always prefered.

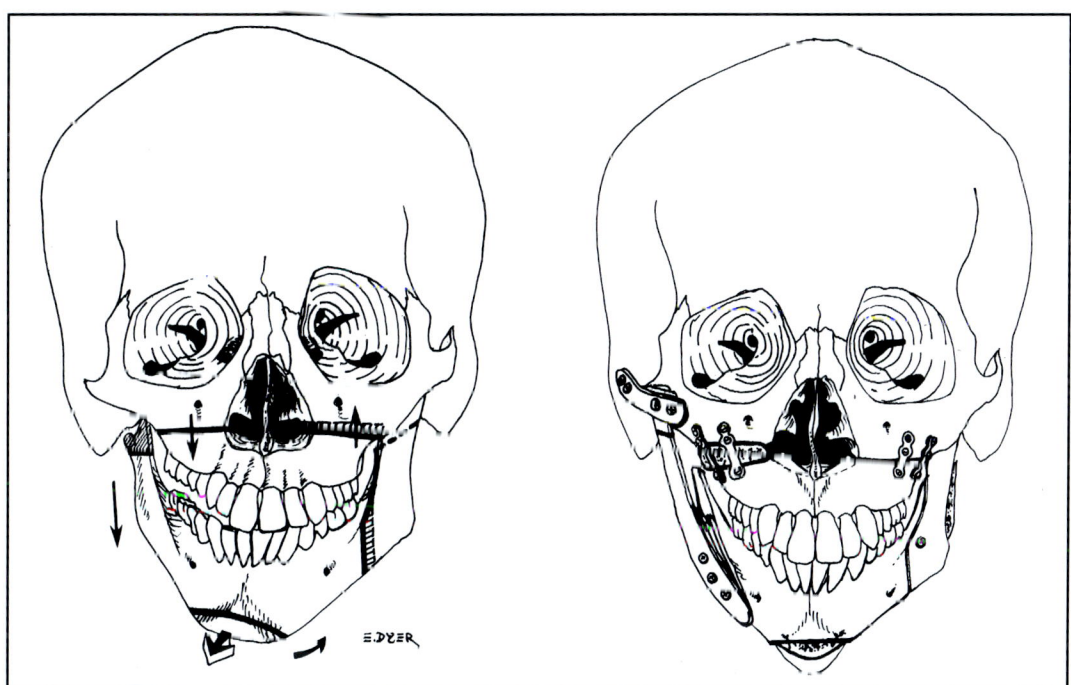

Fig 10–13. Illustration of skeletal surgery to correct facial asymmetry associated with hemifacial microsomia. All cuts and bone movements are stabilized with autogenous bone, bone screws, and metal fixation plates. A new glenoid fossa is reconstructed to house the "new condyle." (See Chapter 3, page 23, for the surgery performed in this case.) In some cases, distraction osteogenesis may be the treatment of choice for both jaws.

CASE REPORT: CROUZON'S DISEASE

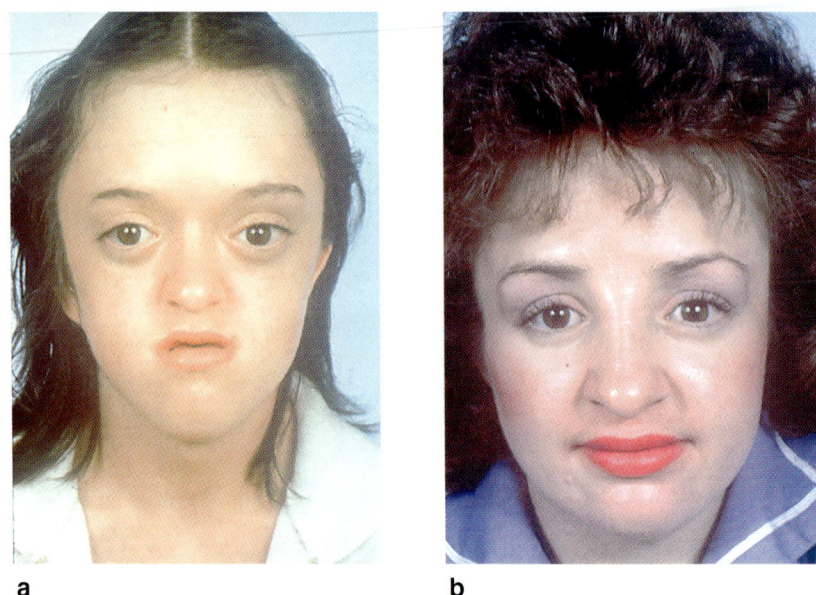

Fig 10–14. Crouzon's disease. Extracranial LeFort III osteotomy followed by a LeFort I 12 mm advancement at a later age. Onlay bone graft to the syperior orbital rim with zygomatic arch reconstruction.

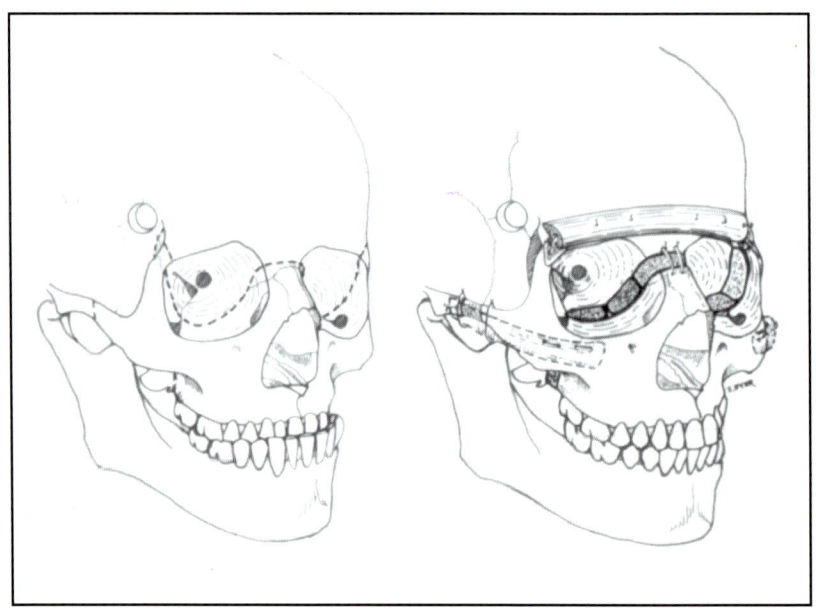

Fig 10–15. Illustration for case shown in Fig 10–14. **Left:** Before surgery. **Right:** After surgery.

Diagnostic Procedures and Instruments Used in the Assessment and Treatment of Speech

ARTICULATION TESTS

An articulation test is a paper and pencil test used by speech-language pathologists to systematically evaluate the formation and production of the sounds of speech in different contexts in word and sentences. It is used to record the sounds that are produced correctly as well as the errors in speech including omissions, distortions, and substitutions of normal or compensatory sound errors. Systematic evaluation of the articulation of speech is helpful in ensuring complete and consistent analysis of the problems so that effective and efficient treatment can be planned.

Many different types of tests are available, but the most useful tests for patients with cleft palate are those that assess both place and manner of production of speech sounds in the vocal tract. Individuals with cleft palate often produce sounds in a more anterior or more posterior (this is a more frequent error) location in the vocal tract than normal speakers. Careful notation of the types of errors and the probable causative factors sets the stage for determining the method and duration of treatment. These tests also provide a baseline measure or description of speech articulation against which progress, improvement, developmental changes, and treatment outcome can be evaluated. The examiner scores articulation of individual sounds or sound units by listening to and observing the production of these sounds. In some cases, traditional articulation testing alone cannot completely describe the manner or place of the error sounds and visualization techniques such as multiview videofluoroscopy and nasopharyngoscopy are useful in completing the description and diagnosis of the error(s).

RATING SCALES OF SPEECH INTELLIGIBILITY AND ACCEPTABILITY

Rating scales are often used by speech-language pathologists and other members of the cleft palate team to score the overall severity of an individual's communication impairment in several categories. Ratings of intelligibility describe how well an individual's speech can be understood by others, whereas ratings of acceptability describe the pleasingness of the sound and appearance of speech. These scales usually consist of 5 or 7 points, with 1 being normal and 5 or 7 indicating unintelligible or unacceptable speech. Effective use of these scales is related to rater reliability, and raters must establish and re-establish their reliability on a regular basis when using these scales for clinical or research purposes. These scales are useful as overall measures of severity and treatment outcome; however, they are descriptive in nature and are not useful in isolating causative factors.

CEPHALOMETRICS

Orthodontists and specialists in facial growth have developed the technique of cephalometrics. This is a still sagittal x-ray taken with the patient stabilized in a headholder which positions the head relative to a cranial landmark called the Frankfort horizontal plane. The head is secured by earposts, and the subject's midline is positioned at a constant distance from the x-ray source. The standard position and photon source relationship to the subject provide a means of comparing the measurements from the resulting x-rays. It should be understood that x-ray films provide an image that is a summation of the tissue through which the x-ray beam has passed. If a person had soft palatal closure on one side but not on the other, the midsagittal view would show velopharyngeal closure because the beam would pass through the tissue on the closed side, and the resulting image would not yield information about the opening. The velopharyngeal valve is three-dimensional, and its attributes cannot all be captured in the midsagittal view alone. This is a shortcoming of cephalometrics when used for speech purposes. Another problem with the technique is that it is capable of filming only a single point in speech production. Connected discourse cannot be studied by this means, nor is it possible to specify precisely what will be filmed in the course of production of a single sound.

Of particular interest to speech physiologists are the cephalometric studies that have defined structures and growth patterns of pharynx, velum, and lymphatic tissue.[1,2,3,4] Compositely, these cephalometric studies have provided objective data pertaining to normal skeletal and soft tissue structures and their postural relationships.

This information also has been stated within the complex and important reference of a specified stage of growth and development. The diagnostic value of such normative data becomes obvious in considering the oral examinations speech-language pathologists routinely perform to evaluate speech structures. In such examinations, skeletal, dental, and soft tissue components of the speech apparatus are evaluated.

In addition to the normative data provided, cephalometric analyses have also been undertaken to evaluate skeletal characteristics and growth disturbances in pathologic conditions. Especially valuable for speech-language pathologists are the studies which have defined the intra-oral, intra-nasal, and pharyngeal architecture of individuals with clefts of the lip and palate.[5,6,7,8,9] Speech-language pathologists have learned a great deal about morphologic variation in cleft palate patients, whose total rehabilitation, of necessity, includes multi-professional concerns, from these cephalometric studies.

The fact that cephalometric head plates can be reliably compared has made them attractive to speech-language pathologists intent on defining physiological differences that result in defective speech production.

There is probably universal agreement that a midsagittal cephalometric view, although useful, yields incomplete information about soft palate and lateral pharyngeal valving. It provides little insight into the location, configuration, or movement of structures off the midsagittal plane. In particular, it offers no information about movement of the lateral pharyngeal walls.

CINE- AND VIDEOFLUOROSCOPY[10]

Cinefluoroscopy (x-rays recorded on motion picture film) and videofluoroscopy (x-rays recorded on videotape) with simultaneous voice recordings are useful procedures in the evaluation of individuals with cleft palate. The key to development of motion x-rays was the advent of image intensification, which permitted greater contrast with reduced x-ray dosages. Video recording involves lower radiation dosage than does cinefluoroscopy. Videofluoroscopic recording can be done with less radiation than is required for a single still x-ray of the head.

To extract more information from videofluoroscopy, Skolnick[11] introduced multiview videofluoroscopy, a technique that adds a base view to the traditional lateral and frontal projections.

MULTI-VIEW VIDEOFLUOROSCOPY

This fluoroscopic x-ray technique allows visualization of the velopharyngeal port, or valve, during speech in several different planes (Skolnick[11,12]). This is important because the mechanism of velopharyngeal closure is three-dimensional and may involve movement not only of the soft palate, but also of the lateral and posterior pharyngeal walls. Descriptions of the technique include the lateral, base, Towne's, frontal, Waters', and oblique views (see Volume II, Chapter 11). Not all views are required for a complete examination. The view selected depends on the information needed, the anatomy of the skull, and the anatomy and function of the vocal tract. In most cases, a complete examination consists of three views, including the lateral view; the base, or Towne's view; and the frontal, Waters' or oblique view. The examinations are usually recorded and maintained on videotape with audio recording for purposes of interpretation and comparison. The procedure is conducted and interpreted jointly by a radiologist and speech-language pathologist. This contributes to a valid study which includes an adequate speech sample, appropriate visualization of the velopharyngeal valve, and interpretation of the findings which are consistent with the patient's speech. Radiation dosage is kept to a minimum by using videofluoroscopy, as opposed to cinefluoroscopy; coning the x-ray beam to the smallest area, ensuring that the equipment is emitting the minimum radiation necessary to produce the image; and using lead sheets to shield the patient except for the area of interests.

Technique

To enhance the velopharyngeal area, high density barium is instilled into each nostril using a syringe with a plastic tip. This results in barium coverage of the soft palate, lateral and posterior pharyngeal walls, and posterior aspect of the tongue. A standard speech sample is used during each view. The lateral view is obtained first, with the patient sitting upright. In this view, judgments can be made about the length and thickness of the soft palate, the depth of the pharynx, and the size and location of adenoid and tonsillar tissue. The anterior-posterior excursion of the soft palate and, in some cases, the anterior movement of the pharynx are observed and judgments of velopharyngeal contact during speech are made. This view alone is not sufficient to determine velopharyngeal closure because it does not confirm velopharyngeal contact along its width.

The lateral view permits excellent visualization of the function of the tongue during speech and is helpful in the differential diagnosis of compensatory articulation errors. In some cases, the tongue is observed to elevate the soft palate in an attempt to effect velopharyngeal closure, particularly for the velar stop sounds /k/ and /g/. Abnormal posterior movements of the epiglottis and elevation of the larynx during speech are also apparent in this view.

The frontal view is usually performed next to determine the degree and location of mesial movements of the lateral pharyngeal walls. Lateral pharyngeal wall movements may occur at a specific location in the vocal tract or along an extensive area. This information is thought to be useful in planning the approximate width of a pharyngeal flap or designing a prosthetic speech appliance in cases of velopharyngeal insufficiency. To obtain this view, the patient is seated upright facing the image intensifier with his or her head positioned in the Frankfurt horizontal plane. Complete coating of the nasopharynx with barium is essential to gather information for adequate interpretation. The standard speech sample is used.

In cases where the overlying bony structures obscure the lateral pharyngeal walls and their movements, the Waters' view is a helpful alternative. In this view, the head is tilted upward approximately 45° from the Frankfurt horizontal plane so that the bony structures do not impede the view of the lateral walls.

When asymmetric movement of the lateral pharyngeal walls is observed, Shprintzen et al[13] recommend rotation of the head to the right and left along the x-axis to more clearly identify the extent of movement.

The third view to be performed is either the base or Towne's view. These views outline the shape of the velopharyngeal valve; the pattern, symmetry, and consistency of velopharyngeal valving movements; and the size and location of velopharyngeal gaps during speech. The Towne's view is the more useful of the two views when the soft palate approximates adenoid tissue during valving creating an oblique axis of velopharyngeal closure or when patients have large tonsils or posterior compensatory tongue movements. These situations interfere with adequate visualization and interpretation of velopharyngeal movements in the base view.

To obtain the base view, the patient lies prone on the x-ray table in a sphinx-like position with the head hyperextended. To obtain the Towne's view with over-table tube fluoroscopy equipment, the patient is seated upright with his or her head in the horizontal plane. The camera is then rotated in relation to the face until the velopharyngeal valve is visualized. This view is similar to that used in nasopharyngoscopy. The standard speech sample is used for both the base and Towne's views.

Multi-view videofluoroscopy may be reliably performed in patients as young as 3 or 4 years old. Because this test involves radiation, it should be used judiciously. It is most reliable when the child is mature enough to cooperate for the examination and has sufficient speech development to allow visualization of the valve throughout all classes of speech sounds. The test should be used when the clinical speech assessment suggests velopharyngeal inadequacy, particularly when surgical or prosthetic management is being considered.

ULTRASOUND

Ultrasound is a device that has been employed in the evaluation of velopharyngeal function, particularly movements of the lateral pharyngeal walls. It is not suitable for displaying motion of the velum because of problems in transmitting ultrasound through bone overlying the palate (Hawkins and Swisher[14]).

VIDEO NASOPHARYNGOSCOPY

This technique involves inserting a flexible fiberoptic tube into the nose to obtain a direct superior view of the velopharyngeal valve and vocal tract during speech. In the hands of an experienced and patient examiner, the test provides information about the anatomy and function of the velopharyngeal valve during speech; the relative size, location, and consistency of velopharyngeal gaps; the function of the posterior aspect of the tongue during speech, which is helpful in the differential diagnosis of compensatory articulation errors; and the anatomy and function of the laryngeal structures. It is also useful in the identification of pulsations in the pharynx which may be indicative of abnormally placed carotid arteries that might preclude pharyngeal flap or sphincter pharyngoplasty surgery. Although the latter finding is rare, it occurs most often in patients with Velocardiofacial syndrome. This technique is useful not only for pretreatment diagnostic assessment of velopharyngeal function but also to evaluate the outcome of surgical, prosthetic, and/or speech therapy treatment. It may also be used for biofeedback therapy to enhance velopharyngeal movements during speech and correct some compensatory articulation errors. For ease of examination in young children, a flexible nasopharyngoscope with a distal tip diameter between 2 and 3.7 mm is recommended.

McWilliams et al[15] note that lateral wall movement is not reliably assessed by either measurements or judgments of nasendoscopic images. A major reason for using endoscopic procedure is to learn about the contribution of the lateral pharyngeal walls to velopharyngeal function. Some investigators have assumed symmetry of lateral wall movement in making their judgments, but this assumption is questionable. Further data relative to the realizability and validity of endoscopic measurements are needed. In the meantime, the technique is quite commonly used clinically and has much to offer in the hands of trained examiners.

Technique

A topical anesthetic such as 3% lidocaine or 2% tetracaine hydrochloride mixed in equal parts with .5% phenylephrine is applied through one side of the patient's nasal cavity to allow comfortable insertion of the scope and enhance cooperation. Some patients are able to tolerate the procedure without anesthesia, particularly when a smaller scope is used. The nasopharyngoscope is inserted through the middle meatus of the nasal passage to first visualize the velopharyngeal area to document anatomy and function and scan the pharynx for abnormal pulsations.

The scope is then passed down into the vocal tract to document the anatomy and function of the tongue and larynx. In patients with a pre-existing pharyngeal flap, the scope can be passed through one or both ports to visualize the lower vocal tract as long as the ports are not stenosed. A standard speech sample is used at each observation point in the vocal tract. Care must be taken when positioning the scope in the velopharynx. A false positive or false negative diagnosis of velopharyngeal closure will be obtained if the distal end of the scope is not positioned directly above the velopharyngeal port. The quality of the study and interpretation, treatment planning, and outcome analysis are enhanced by audio-video recording which allows playback of the study for repeated analysis, comparisons with previous examinations, and demonstration of the findings to the professionals involved in the treatment and the patient and/or parents.

THE NASOMETER

The nasometer is a computer-assisted instrument produced by Kay Elemetrics (Pinebrook, New Jersey) which is designed to measure the relative amount of nasal acoustic energy compared to oral acoustic energy during continuous speech production (Dalston et al[16]). This instrument uses a sound separator that rests on the patient's upper lip. Microphones on either side of the sound separator sense oral and nasal acoustic energy during speech, and this energy is filtered and digitized by custom electronic modules. The computer with Kay Elemetrics software (Version 1.7) processes the information and produces a "Nasalance Score." This score is a ratio of nasal to oral acoustic energy multiplied by 100. The nasal and oral acoustic energy is averaged during the production of vowels and consonants in test sentences to produce the nasalance score. The length of the speech sample used to calculate the nasalance score may be up to 100 seconds. This instrument is based on the Tonar II developed by Fletcher in 1976.[17] An abnormally high nasalance score during production of non-nasal consonants suggests velopharyngeal inadequacy and hypernasality, and an abnormally low nasalance score during production of nasal consonants is suggestive of hyponasality and/or nasal airway impairment (Dalston et al[16]). Dalston et al[16] studied the sensitivity and specificity of the Nasometer and found it to be an appropriate instrument for use in corroborating listener judgments of hypernasality. Sensitivity and specificity values for assessing hyponasality were in the expected range for patients without any indication of concurrent velopharyngeal inadequacy, but the scores did not identify hyponasality in patients who exhibited both hyponasality and excessive nasal air emission. Therefore, the instrument may be less useful as a diagnostic procedure in patients who exhibit both velopharyngeal inadequacy and nasal airway impairment (Dalston et al[16]). The Nasometer is not a substitute for listener judgments of hyper- and hyponasality but can be useful in providing baseline data to assist in the identification of velopharyngeal inadequacy, assessment of treatment outcome, fitting of a palatal prothesis, and providing visual biofeedback in speech therapy.

Technique

Care should be taken to ensure that the system is calibrated according to the specifications of the manufacturer. The headgear is then adjusted to fit the patient, and the patient is asked to read or repeat a standard speech sample. This procedure is usually used with patients age 3 and older because younger patients may have shorter attention spans and less well-developed speech and language skills. Once the speech sample is recorded on the computer terminal, the software cursors are used to mark the beginning and end of the speech display. The "calculate" function is then activated, and the mean and standard deviation of the nasalance score are determined.

AEROMECHANICAL MEASUREMENT

Warren and Dubois Technique[18]

Measurements of nasal airflow and of the difference in air pressure above and below the velopharyngeal port may be used to estimate both the area of the velopharyngeal orifice, if any, during the production of stop consonants and the resistance of the port to airflow. Pressure-flow measurements provide information about the coupling of the oral and the nasal cavities during speech and about resistance in the system. They do not describe the movement of particular structures, such as the velum and lateral pharyngeal walls, or the location and configuration of any opening that is present.

PERCI

Warren[19] introduced an instrument called the PERCI (Palatal Efficiency Rating Computed Instantaneously) for use in the evaluation of the velopharyngeal mechanism during speech. PERCI records and displays the difference in air pressures in the mouth and in the nose. From a study of 75 cleft palate patients, Warren reported that patients with differential pressure readings >3.0 on the PERCI had velopharyngeal orifice areas of 10 mm^2 or less, whereas those with PERCI readings of <1.0 had areas greater than 20 mm^2. PERCI readings of 1.0 through 2.9 were associated with velopharyngeal areas between 10 and 20 mm^2.

TONAR

Fletcher and Bishop[17] advanced the study of oral and nasal sound intensity measures as indices to hypernasality through the development of an instrument which they named TONAR (The Oral-Nasal Acoustic Ratio). The instrument prints out voltages associated with the nasal and oral signals and also a trace reflecting the ratio of the voltages from the sound detected in the oral and nasal chambers.

SUMMARY

Several instrumental procedures are available for assessing the velopharyngeal mechanism and its function. Each has advantages and disadvantages, and choosing among them depends on the specific purpose of the evaluation. The reliability of endoscopic procedures is not well documented.

Aerodynamic measures provide data about the area of the velopharyngeal opening, velopharyngeal resistance to air flow, and air pressure available for the production of obstruent sounds. These measures provide no information about the relative contributions of the velum and the pharyngeal walls to velopharyngeal function.

An important warning in the use of any instrumentation for the study of speech is that data taken during speech production must be interpreted within the context of the patient's repertoire of speech proficiency.

REFERENCES

1. King EW. A roentgenographic study of pharyngeal growth. *Angle Orthod.* 1952;22:23.
2. Rosenberger HC. Growth and development of the nasorespiratory area in childhood. *Ann Otol Rhinol & Laryngol.* 1934;43:495.
3. Subtelny JD. A cephalometric study of the growth of the soft palate. *Plast Reconstr Surg.* 1957;19:49.

4. Subtelny JD, Baker HK. The significance of adenoid tissue in velopharyngeal function. *Au Journal.* 1956;17:235.
5. Brader AA. A cephalometric appraisal of morphologic variations in cranial base and associated pharyngeal structures: implications in cleft palate therapy. *Angle Orthod.* 1957;27.179.
6. Prusansky S. Description, classification, and analysis of unoperated clefts of the lip and palate. *Am J Orthodont.* 1953; 39:590.
7. Ricketts RM. The cranial base and soft structures in cleft palate speech and breathing. *Plast Reconstr Surg.* 1954;14:74.
8. Slaughter WB, Prusansky S. The rationale for velar closure as a primary procedure in the repair of cleft palate defects. *Plast Reconstr Surg.* 1954;13:341
9. Subtelny JD. Width of the nasopharynx and related anatomic structures in normal and unoperated cleft palate children. *Am J Orthodont.* 1955;41:889.
10. McWillams BJ, Girdny B. The use of Televex in cleft palate research. *Cleft Palate J.* 1965;2:46.
11. Skolnick ML. Videofluoroscopic examination of the velopharyngeal portal during phonation in lateral and base projections—a new technique for studying the mechanics of closure. *Cleft Palate J.* 1970;7:803.
12. Skolnick ML, Azgzebski JA, Watkin KL. Two-dimensional ultrasonic demonstration of lateral pharyngeal wall movement in real time—a preliminary report. *Cleft Palate J.* 1975;12:299.
13. Shprintzen RJ, Rakoff SJ, Skolnick ML, Lavaroto AS. Incongruous movements of the velum and lateral walls. *Cleft Palate J.* 1977;14:148–157.
14. Hawkins CF, Swisher WE. Evaluation of real-time ultrasound scanner in assessing lateral pharyngeal wave motion during speech. *Cleft Palate J.* 1978;15:161.
15. McWilliams BJ, Morris HS, Shelton RL, eds. *Instruments for Assessing Velopharyngeal Mechanisms in Cleft Palate Speech.* St. Louis, Mo: CV Mosby; 1984.
16. Dalston RM, Warren DW, Dalston ET. The use of Nasometry as a diagnostic tool for identifying patients with velopharyngeal impairment. *Cleft Palate Craniofac J.* 1981;28:184–188.
17. Fletcher SG, Bishop ME. Measurement of nasality with TONAR. *Cleft Palate J.* 1970;7:610.
18. Warren DW, DuBois AB. A pressure-flow technique for measuring velopharyngeal orifice area during continuous speech. *Cleft Palate J.* 1964;1:52.
19. Warren DW. PERCI: A method for rating palatal efficiency. *Cleft Palate J.* 1979;16:279.

12

Morphologic Considerations of the Nasopharyngeal Port

MUSCLES

Pharynx and Velum (David and Wilma Dickson)[1]

The adult pharynx is the common pathway for food and air in human beings. It extends from the cranial base behind the nasal cavities to the upper end of the esophagus behind the larynx. The pharynx is widest at its upper portion and narrows as it descends to the esophagus. The pharynx lies immediately in front of the vertebral column, separated from it by prevertebral muscles and fascia. Anteriorly, the pharynx communicates with the nasal cavities, the oral cavity, and the aditus of the larynx. Inferiorly, the pharynx is continuous with the esophagus. The part of the pharynx that extends upward to the level of the velum (soft palate) is commonly called the nasopharynx (Fig 12–1).

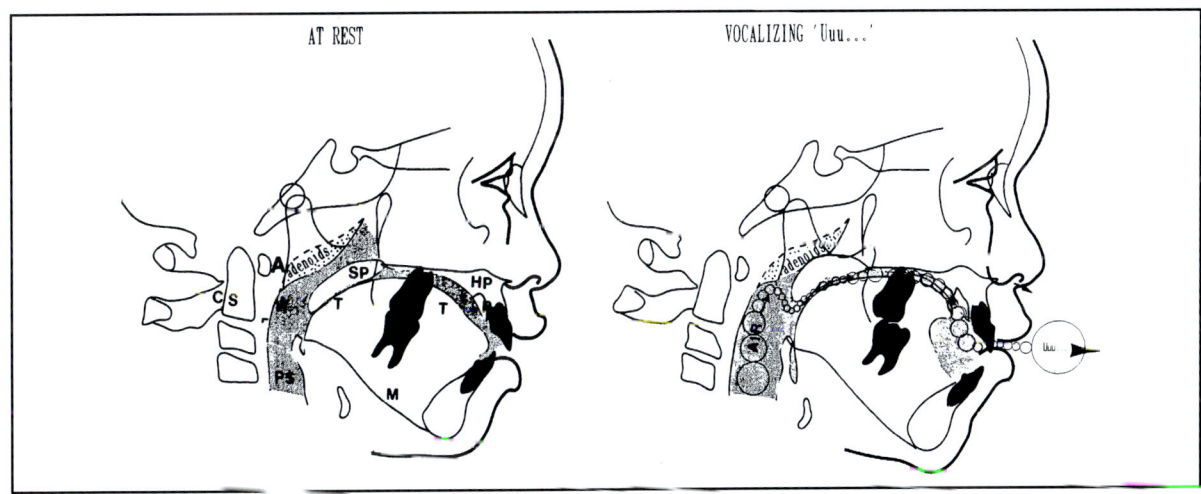

a

Fig 12–1. Lateral cephaloradiograph shows the skeletal structures surrounding the pharyngeal space and allows evaluation of the pharyngeal depth, **shape of cervical spine, soft palate size and length, and extent of soft palate elevation**. Because it is a two-dimensional representation of the velopharyngeal area and does not show lateral pharyngeal wall motion, this record cannot be used to diagnostically determine velopharyngeal functions. **a.** *Left:* Structures involved in controlling airflow as seen in a lateral cephalograph at 5 years of age (A = anterior tubercle of the atlas, CS = cervical spine, S = odontoid process, W = posterior pharyngeal wall, PS = pharyngeal space, SP = soft palate (velum), HP =

(continued)

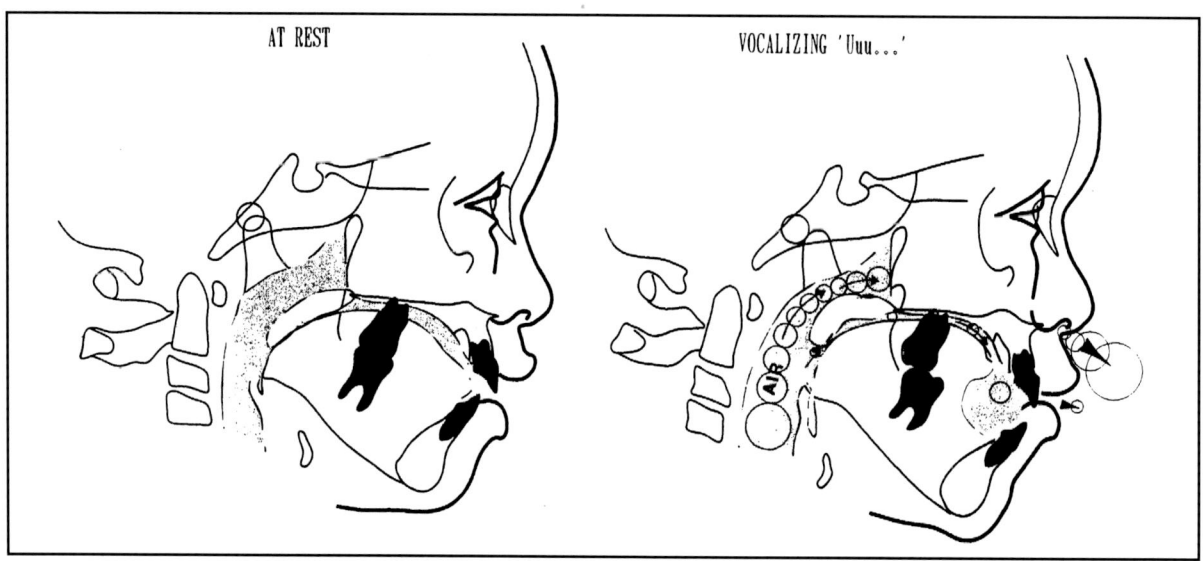

Fig 12–1. *(continued)*
hard palate, T = tongue, M = mandible). *Right:* Air flow when vocalizing "Uuu" during normal speech. The soft palate elevates and makes contact with the adenoids (if present) or the posterior pharyngeal wall during normal speech and swallowing. When the lateral pharyngeal muscles operate in coordination with a competent (adequate length, width, and timing of action) soft palate in a normal skeletal environment most of the air is channeled through the mouth while some enters the nose. This is designated as velopharyngeal competency (VPC). **b.** Velopharyngeal Incompetency (VPI). There are usually many reasons for inadequate air flow control. Some are: (1) a relatively deep pharynx when related to velar length; (2) inadequate velar elevation and/or pharyngeal wall motion (neuromuscular function); and (3) poor timing of speech with pharyngeal and velar muscle (sensory-motor) function.

The pharyngeal orifices of the auditory tubes open into the lateral walls of the nasopharynx. The auditory tube connects the pharynx with the middle ear and serves to maintain an equilibrium of air pressure between the middle ear and the external atmosphere. The superoposterior part of the pharynx contains the pharyngeal tonsil (also called the adenoid).

The velum (soft palate) forms the boundary separating the nasopharynx from the oropharynx. Because the velum is mobile, this boundary is arbitrary. The velum is a muscular body that attaches to the posterior rim of the hard palate and the lateral walls of the posterior part of the oral cavity. The posterior free border of the velum hangs into the oropharynx and ends in a small midline projection, the uvula.

The oropharynx extends inferiorly to the level of the hyoid bone. The anterior wall of the oropharynx, inferior to the opening into the oral cavity, is formed by the posterior surface of the root of the tongue.

The palatopharyngeal fold (posterior faucial arch) extends from the sides of the velum into the lateral walls of the pharynx. This muscular fold forms the greatest lateral constriction between the oropharynx and oral cavity. The superior end of the epiglottis extends superiorly from the larynx into the oropharynx immediately posterior to the root of the tongue.

The nasopharynx and auditory tube are lined by ciliated, pseudostratified columnar epithelium rich in goblet cells and glands that secrete mucus. The pharynx is lined with stratified squamous epithelium where contact between the pharynx and velum takes place and in the portion that serves as a food channel.

NASOPHARYNGEAL GROWTH

Variations in the height and depth of the nasopharynx are apparent from birth through the early years of growth and development. Rosenberger[2] made a longitudinal study of naso-respiratory areas in children from 3 months to 5 years of age. It was his opinion that an enlargement of the naso-respiratory area lungs. They serve to filter the air as it enters the airway and to control air temperature and humidity. They also serve as resonators for nasal sounds that are produced with the velopharyngeal valve open. The two nasal cavities are separated from each other by the nasal septum in the midsagittal plane. The nasal septum is composed of three parts. The superior part is the perpendicular plate of the ethmoid bone. The inferior and posterior parts are composed of the vomer bone. The anterior part is composed of the cartilage of the nasal septum.

The roof of the nasal cavities is formed by the cribriform plate of the ethmoid bone, which is penetrated by the olfactory nerves. Immediately posterior to the perpendicular plate of the ethmoid is the body of the sphenoid, which contains the sphenoid sinus. The floor of the nasal cavities is formed by the hard palate. Anteriorly, the nasal cavities are bounded by the external nose. The framework of the external nose includes the nasal bones and the nasal cartilages. The bridge of the nose is formed by the nasal bones. Inferiorly, the nasal bones articulate with the lateral nasal cartilages. The tip of the nose is supported by the greater alar cartilages. Small lesser alar cartilages support the lateral walls of the anterior nasal openings.

The lateral wall of each nasal cavity is convoluted owing to the presence of the superior, middle, and inferior nasal conchae. The conchae have an extremely rich blood supply and provide a large surface area for humidity and temperature control of the air passing over them.

Although the terms VP "incompetence," "inadequacy," and "insufficiency" historically have been used interchangeably, they do not necessarily mean the same thing. For this reason, standardization of nomenclature has been recommended. Trost-Cardamone[16(p68)] has proposed a taxonomy for VP disorders, based on causative factors in which "velopharyngeal inadequacy is the generic term used to denote any type of abnormal velopharyngeal function." In the broad group of inadequacies, there are subgroups of structural (VPI), neurogenic (VP incompetence), and mislearning (VP mislearning) or functional origins. VPI includes any structural defects of the velum or pharyngeal walls at the level of nasopharynx with insufficient tissue to accomplish closure or some kind of mechanical interference with closure. The all-encompassing term "velopharyngeal dysfunction (VPD)" does not assume or exclude any possible cause of the perceived speech symptoms or management approach. It applies to speech disorders that may be the result of structural deficits, neurologic disorders, faulty learning, or a combination of sources (Witt and D'Antonio[17]).

THE USE OF LATERAL ROENTGENCEPHALOMETRICS IN EVALUATING SKELETAL PHARYNGEAL ARCHITECTURE AND VELAR ELEVATION

Velopharyngeal valving is dependent not only on the sensorimotor adequacy of the velum and its synergistic musculature, but also on the morphologic skeletal dimensions of the nasopharyngeal port. The size and shape of the nasopharynx are determined, in part, by the contiguous osseous anatomy of the maxilla (Subtelny[18]), cranial base, and vertebral column (Fig 12–4, b).

The mechanism of velopharyngeal closure can be studied to some degree by cephalometric roentgenography, but it must be stressed that this is not a functional test for velopharyngeal competency (Fig 12–5). The vowel /u/, as in "boom," is generally employed to achieve maximal elevation of the soft palate during vowel production. After careful rehearsal, the subject is instructed to maintain the sound at a constant pitch and intensity for a time sufficient to cover the roentgenographic exposure period. This procedure ensures that the soft palate will remain in a reasonably stable position during the recording interval.

In a noncleft individual, as seen in the lateral headplate, the soft palate elevates to contact the posterior pharyngeal wall. In doing so, the longitudinal axis of the soft palate becomes continuous with that of the total palatal plane, while the uvula projects downward and nearly at right angles to the rest of the velum. If for any reason this velopharyngeal closure cannot be achieved, deglutition is impaired, and in phonation the air stream is misdirected through the nose. However, it is possible to have good swallowing activity but poor velopharyngeal closure during speech. The term "palatal insufficiency" is more descriptive of a physiologic deficiency than of an anatomic defect.

CERVICAL SPINE ANOMALIES (Fig 12–6)

Osborne et al[19] wrote that fusion of the posterior spines at C^2–C^3 does not appear to influence the osseous antero-posterior diameter of the nasopharyngeal port. On the other hand, occipitalization of the atlas, a smaller than normal anterior arch of the atlas, or atlanto-axial dislocation will have a direct effect on the antero-posterior dimension of the pharynx. It is clear that the population of congenital palatopharyngeal incompetence (CPI) patients with cervical anomalies, of whatever kind, present greater

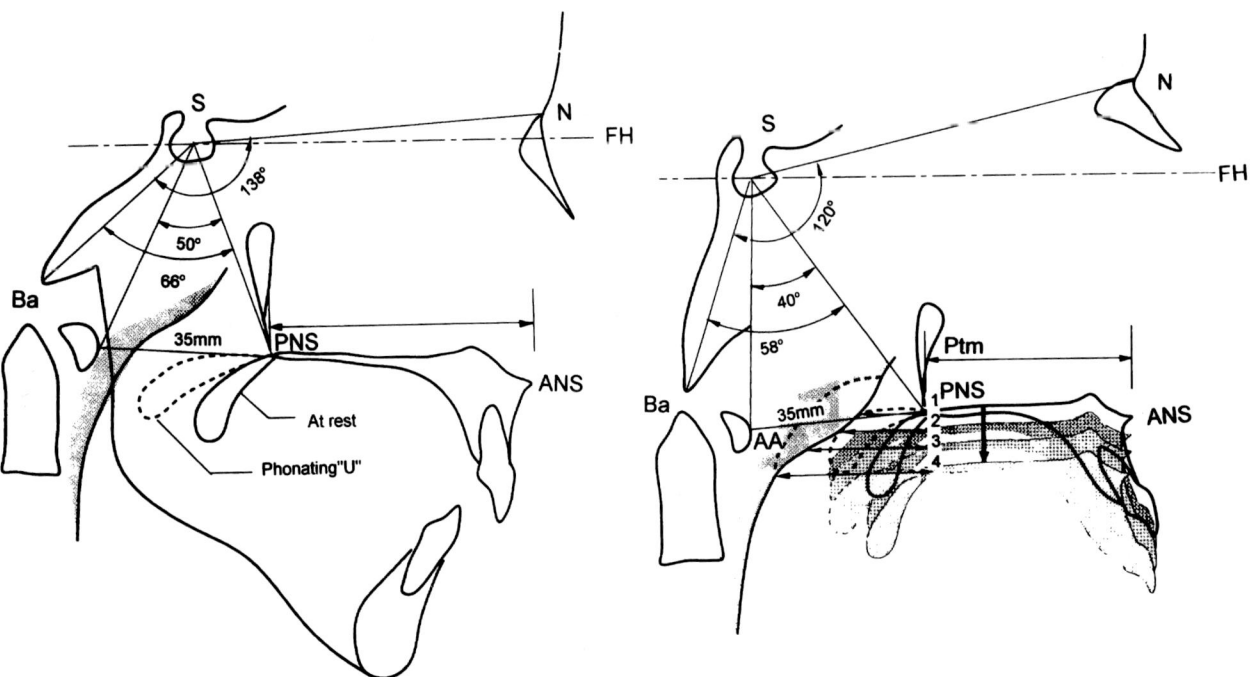

Fig 12–5. The influence of the skeletal architecture on the pharyngeal form and size. The pharyngeal space is bounded superiorly by the cranial base and laterally by the cervical spine on one side and the tongue/hard palate complex on the opposite side. The odontoid process (axis) of the cervical spine points to the posterior extent (Basion-Ba) of the basilar portion of the occipital bone. It is the median point of the anterior margin of the foramen magnum. The hard palate of the maxillary complex is anatomically associated with the anterior cranial base and can vary in its anteroposterior dimension. The importance of cranial base angle (Ba-S-N) *Left:* Obtuse cranial base angle. In cases with a severe obtuse cranial base angle, the pharyngeal space is usually deeper than normal even in the presence of a long hard palate. An obtuse cranial base positions the cervical spine more posteriorly since it must be associated with the basilar portion of the occipital bone. This condition is usually seen when hypernasality exists in the absence of an overt palatal cleft and is called congenital palatal insufficiency (CPI). *Right:* With an acute cranial base angle, the cervical spine is positioned close to the hard palate creating a shallow pharyngeal depth.

Comment: These relationships change with growth. The palate descends from the anterior cranial base in a parallel fashion. Due to changing slope of the posterior pharyngeal wall, the pharyngeal depth increases with age. The influence of adenoids: The adenoid is attached to the posterior pharyngeal wall above the level of the hard palate. Its size is highly variable according to age. It usually increases until 13 years of age and then retrogresses, but many variations in this growth pattern have been observed. The influence of cleft size: The severity of the cleft size in complete clefts of the lip and palate at birth does influence the nasopharyngeal width before lip and/or palatal surgery but not after the lip is united. The degree of mesodermal deficiency of the hard and soft palate can determine not only the size of the cleft space by influencing palatal size but also the length and width of the soft palate and, therefore, its functional ability to affect velopharyngeal closure (VPC). A short anteroposterior maxillary dimension, as is usually found with submucous clefts, does not by itself signify that VPC will be inadequate. Short anteroposterior hard palate dimension can be associated with a shallow pharyngeal depth.

osseous nasopharyngeal depth (the distance between the hard palate and retropharyngeal wall) than do CPI patients without cervical anomalies.

The importance of the anterior tubercle of the atlas and the upper cervical vertebrae in achieving adequate velopharyngeal closure and speech is well-established. One need know only that the musculofascial layer covering the upper cervical vertebrae, and forming the posterior pharyngeal wall, is only 2 to 5 mm thick to realize the morphologic importance of these vertebrae to velopharyngeal closure.

The influence of anomalies of the upper cervical vertebrae on the size and shape of the nasopharynx, with resulting effects on velopharyngeal valving, was first reported by McCarthy,[20] and shortly thereafter reemphasized by Schuller.[21] Epidemiologic studies have shown that patients with craniofacial birth defects, many of which are accompanied by velopha-

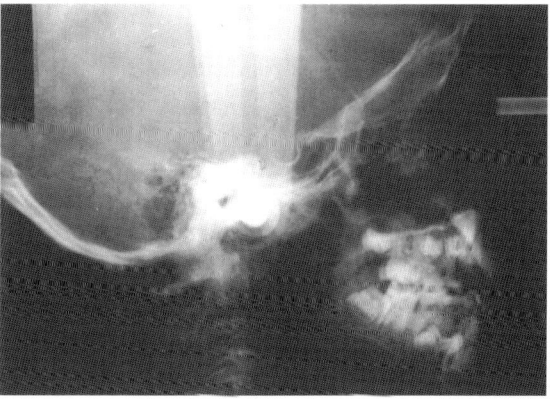

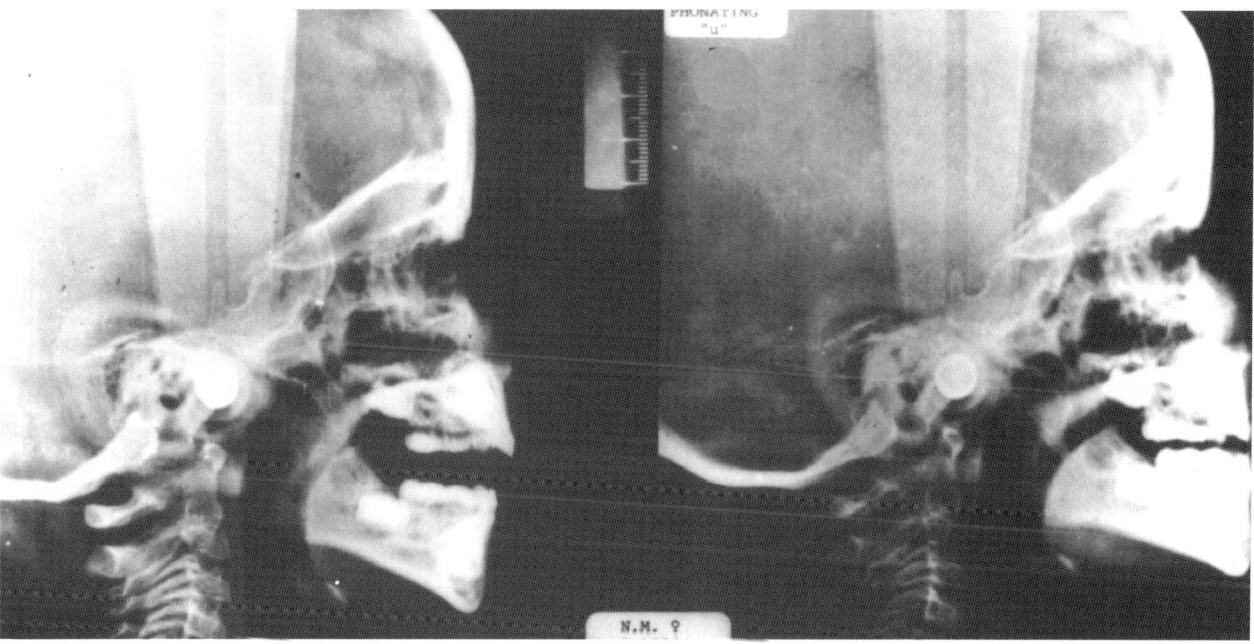

Fig 12–6. Cervical spine anomalies and their effects on the pharyngeal space configuration. a. The absence and **b.** malformation or dislocation of the anterior tubercle of the atlas result in the lack of support to the posterior pharyngeal wall, thus increasing the depth of the pharyngeal space. These anomalies coupled with a small velum will compound the problem. *Left:* Velum at rest. *Right:* Velum in function. No contact with the posterior pharyngeal wall. Other cervical spine anomalies include:

(continued)

ryngeal incompetence, have a higher prevalence of upper cervical spine anomalies than the general population (Osborne et al[22]). This survey also found that a surprisingly large number (18.8%) of patients with CPI demonstrated anomalies of the upper cervical vertebrae, as discerned in lateral cephalometric head film.

Simply stated, congenital palatopharyngeal incompetence (CPI) can be defined as the presence of hypernasality (rhinolalia aperta) in the absence of an overt cleft palate. Based on detailed studies of 110 subjects, Pruzansky and Mason[23] found that CPI may be caused by one or more of the following variables:

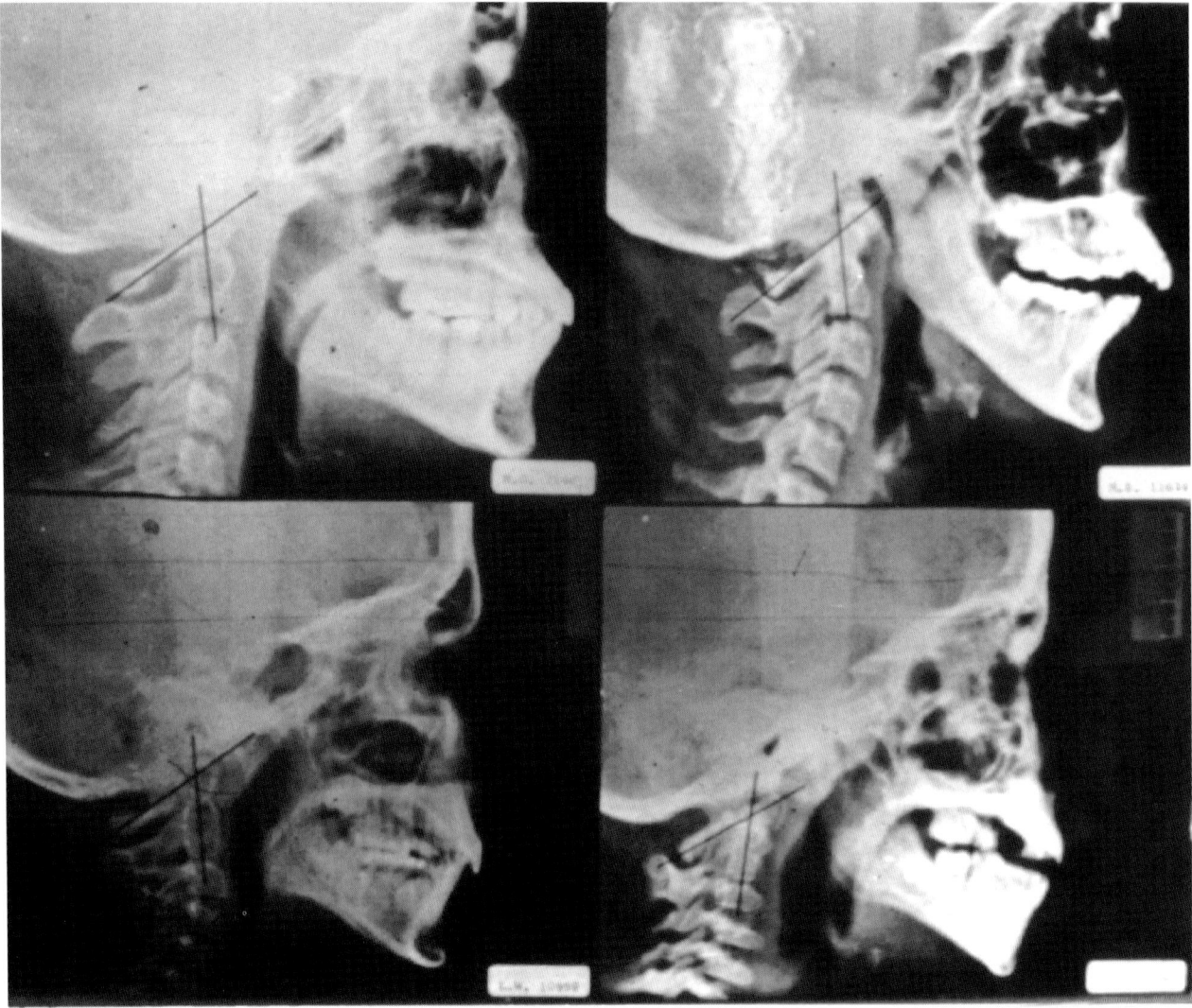

Fig 12-6. *(continued)* **c.** Abnormal Atlanto-dental angulation.

a bifid uvula; a short or thin soft palate, with or without a pink translucent area ("zona pellucida") usually seen in submucous cleft palate; anomalies of the upper cervical vertebrae and cranial base; and scanty adenoid development or early involution or excision of the adenoid.

As we shall point out in more detail later, our own concept of the defect in congenital palatal insufficiency has been extended to include a broader view of the pharynx and its contiguous structures.

VELAR CLOSURE

During the clefting process, the muscular forces that act in the region of the pterygoid plates account for the divergence of the pterygoid plates and the consequent increased lateral width of the nasopharynx, the separation of the tuberosities of the maxillae, and the width of the cleft itself. The failure of the hard d

e

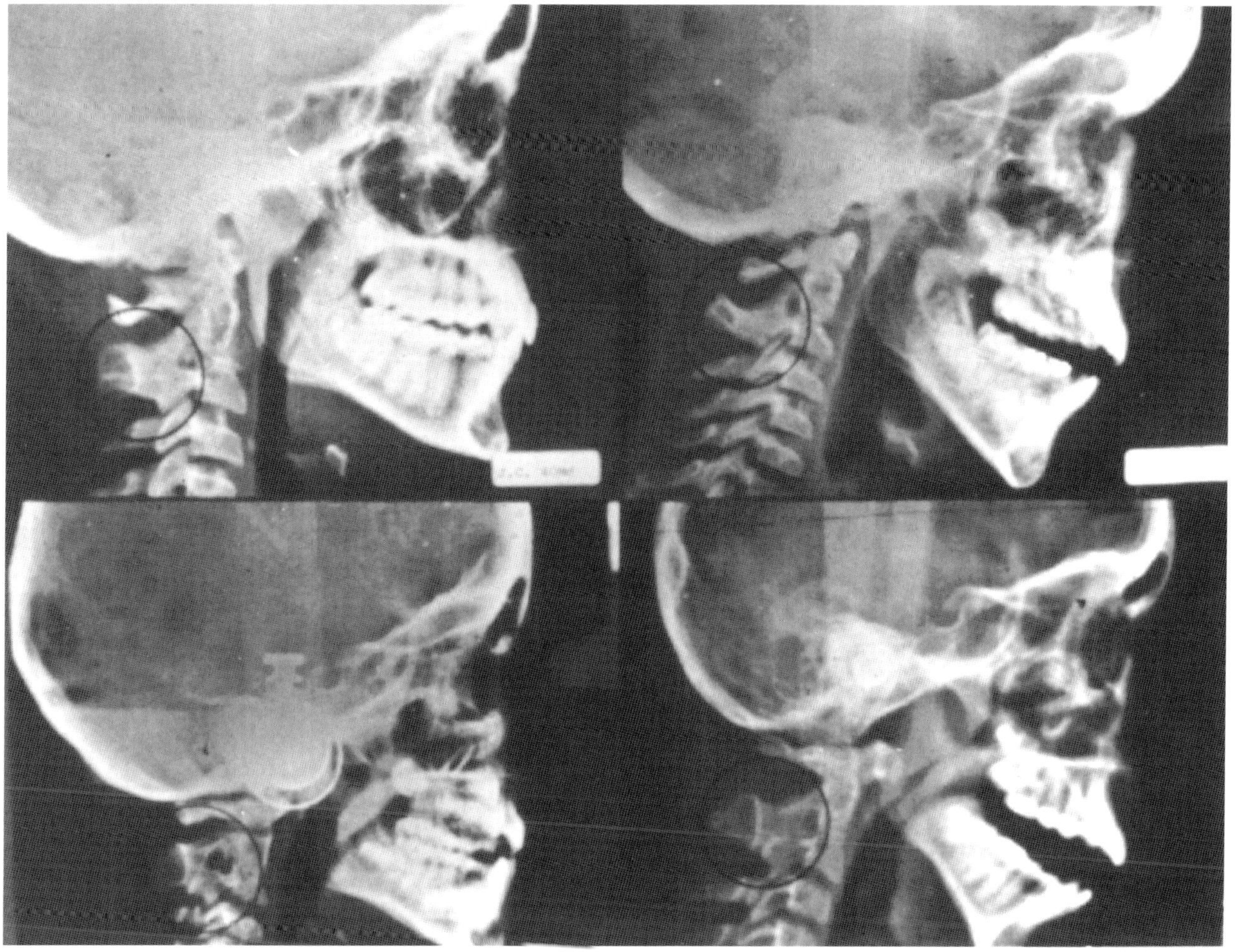

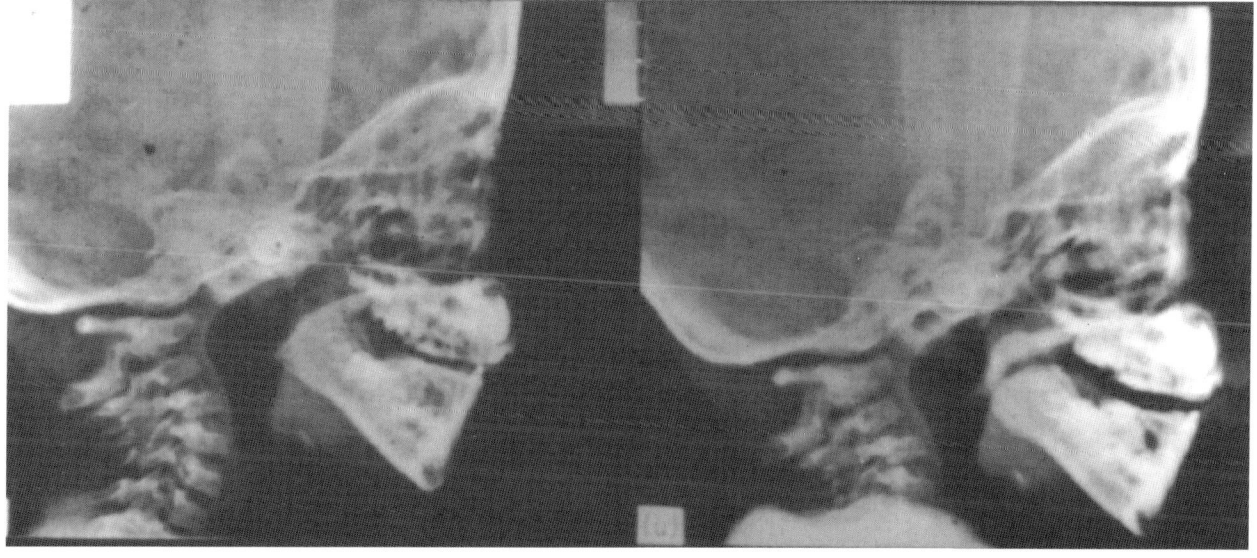

d. Fusion of posterior arches C_2-C_3. **e.** Abnormalities to the axis and atlas. (Courtesy of S. Pruzansky.)

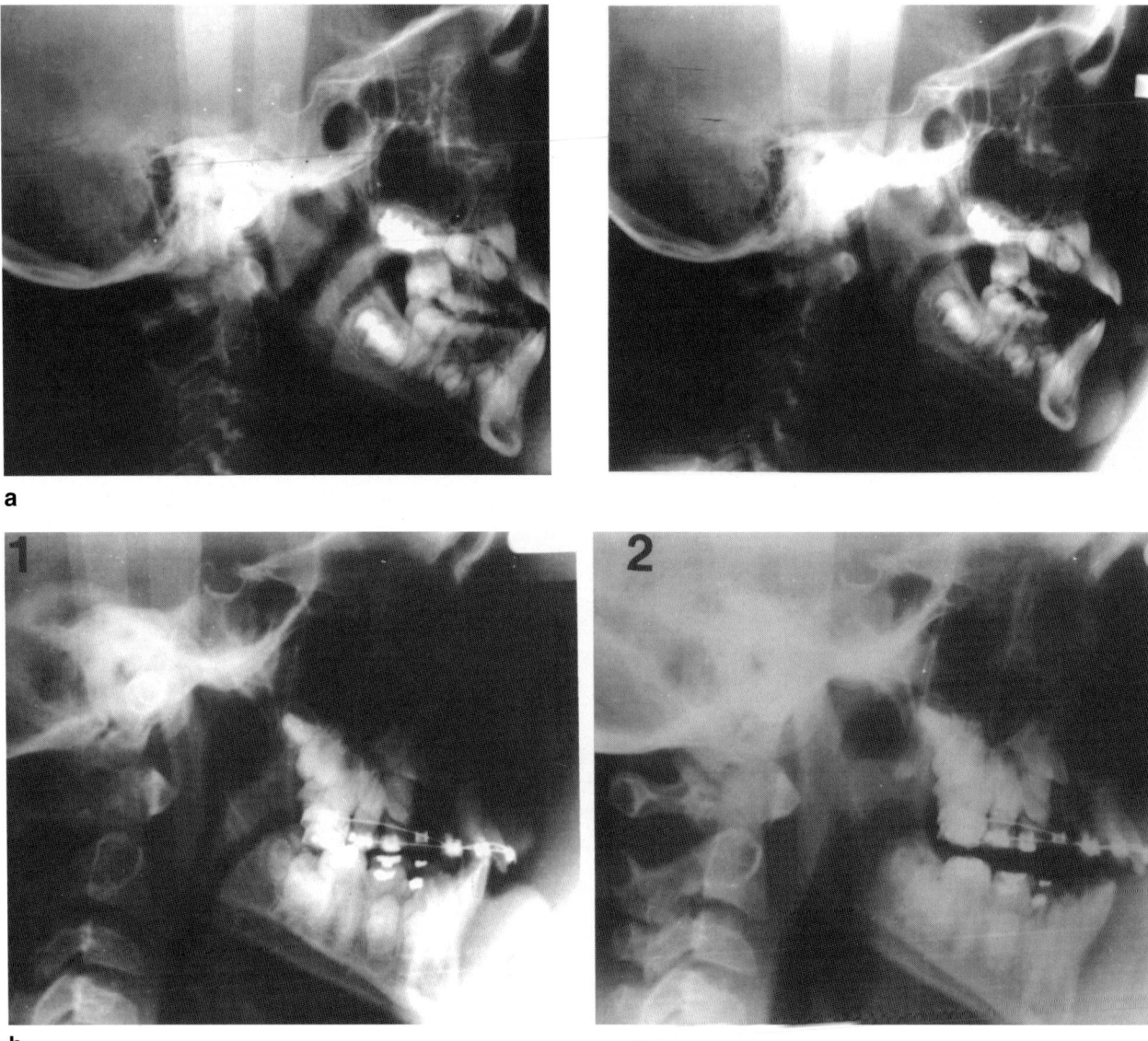

and soft palate to unite in the midline produces a profound disturbance in the interplay and balance among the involved muscle groups. The tongue, pterygoid muscles, levators, and tensors of the velum tend to aggravate the malformation that has resulted from the failure of union in the midline of the palate.

A more favorable alignment of the osseous segments of the palate will follow reestablishment of balanced muscle forces. Slaughter and Pruzansky[24] concluded that, since repairing the lip altered the spatial configuration of the skeletal framework so profoundly in the anterior segment of cleft, repairing the velum might achieve comparably beneficial results in the region of the nasopharynx.

In reviewing the morphologic variants that might contribute to inadequate velopharyngeal function, a number of factors must be considered. For example, the velum might be too short, the hard palate could be deficient in its anteroposterior dimension, or there may be unilateral or bilateral and posterior pharyngeal wall dysfunction. In other cases, both the hard and soft palates might be shorter than normal (Fig 12–7, a–e). In rare instances the soft palate may be paralyzed and incapable of movement (Fig 12–7, f). The cases presented in Figs 12–8 and 12–9 show variations in adenoid size and pharyngeal architecture which influence velar pharyngeal closure.

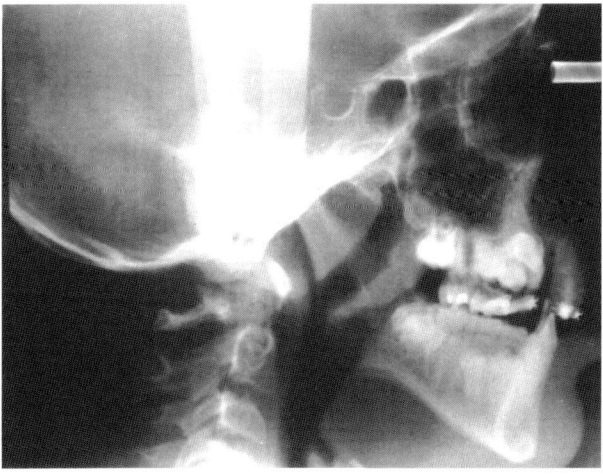 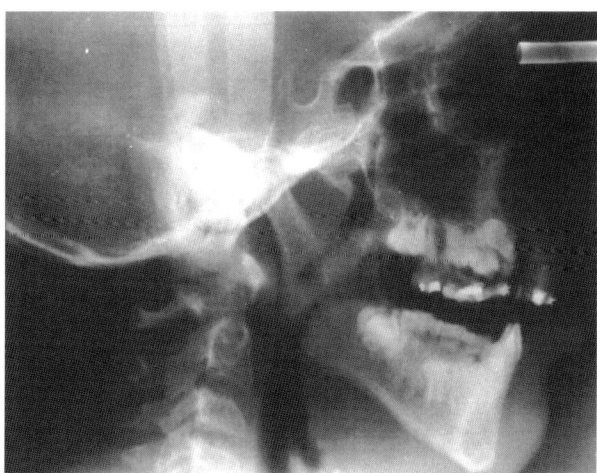

Fig 12–11. Inferior based pharyngeal flap in the presence of a small adenoid. Even with good velar length and elevation, a pharyngeal flap was necessary because of poor lateral pharyngeal wall muscular movement. *Left:* At rest. *Right:* While vocalizing "Uuuu." Inferiorly based flaps and/or flaps placed below the anterior tubercle of the atlas usually do not function adequately because that may not be the position for maximum lateral pharyngeal muscle action.

of the procedure's success, and patients still need to undergo extensive speech therapy.

Occasionally, a patient will remain hypernasal and continue to produce articulation errors in spite of a seemingly good surgical result. This can occur even when there seems to be a good speech mechanism, good muscular motion, and a good family environment.

An excessively wide flap can block off too much air flow into the nose, leading to mouth breathing and denasalized nasal consonants, and patients may suffer other side effects ranging from severe snoring to sleep apnea. As in normal speech, the opening and closing functions of the nasopharynx necessary for speech must be achieved by lateral wall movements in the nasopharynx. The lateral walls need to move medially to make contact with the flap during speech to prevent nasal escape of air.

A pharyngeal flap was also used in conjunction with push-back procedures at the time of palatoplasty, thinking that when combined the retropositioned velum would be better maintained in its posterior position. Experience has shown that this should never be performed as a primary procedure because there is no evidence that velopharyngeal incompetency can be detected with certainty prior to speech production. Scar contracture resulting from push-back procedures not only inhibits palatal growth but causes any velar length increase to relapse. It does not seem wise to tether the push-back tissue with the pharyngeal flap because negative changes occurring to the palatal tissue can distort the flap.

In the treatment of cleft palate, the superiorly posterior based pharyngeal flap is almost universally favored. Some clinicians are also using inferiorly based flaps in some cases (Millard[30,31]). It is still debated whether the superior or inferiorly based procedures is better. However, Trier[32] points out there are compelling reasons why the superiorly based flap is employed more frequently. The inferiorly based flap not only has severe length limitations but also has the disadvantage of tethering the flap in an inferior direction, away from the palatal plane and motion for affecting VP closure.

Most speech-language pathologists tend to favor performing a pharyngeal flap at 4 years of age to avoid the problems of prolonged training. Early pharyngeal flap surgery carries no systemic risk of interference with facial growth, but can cause some reduction in forward maxillary growth. It also can cause hyponasality and sleep apnea if it significantly obstructs air flow through the nose (Subtelny and Nieto[33]). The ability of patients to achieve proper velopharyngeal closure after pharyngeal flap surgery is unpredictable. Retrospective studies have shown that, when performed prior to 3 years of age, there are no significant morphological differences in the velopharyngeal area among the various cleft groups. Harding and his colleagues[34] advocated a superiorly based pharyngeal flap at a mean age of 6.5 years. Randall et al[35] advocated performing the procedure even earlier, between 2 and 3 years of age, especially when associated with a short, scarred, immobile palate with severe hypernasality and virtually no anterior articulation.

Failed pharyngeal flaps are generally due to the inability of the lateral pharyngeal walls to gain firm contact with the sides of the pharyngeal flap. This can result if the flap is too narrow and/or the lateral pharyngeal walls do not move far enough medially to reach it. In some instances, the flap may be set below the point of maximum medial movement, which is usually at the level of the hard palate. He also states that, under no circumstances, should a pharyngeal flap operation be performed simultaneously with other procedures.

Speech Aid Appliances

Wolfaardt et al[36] noted that the functional integrity of the palatopharyngeal valve can be compromised by a number of factors, including neurologic disorders such as stroke or head trauma; degenerative diseases such as multiple sclerosis, Parkinsonism, or bulbar polio; craniofacial birth defects, such as overt and covert clefts of the palate; and some behavioral disorders (e.g., functional articulation disorders).

In addition, in the absence of a palatopharyngeal control problem, resonance balance in speech also may be rendered aberrant by hearing loss or faulty sensorimotor learning patterns. These include impairments associated with congenital neurologic disorders (e.g., cerebral palsy) that impair a speaker's ability to regulate the articulatory dimensions of speech that influence the acoustical expression of nasality.

Prosthetic dental appliances are used for the replacement of missing or malformed teeth in the line of the cleft and, when indicated, in the design of speech appliances.

In the event that surgery is contraindicated, delayed, or performed unsuccessfully, a dental speech appliance may provide a satisfactory substitute. Such appliances are usually made of acrylic plastic and retained by clasps about the teeth. Metallic castings of nonprecious and precious metals also may be used in the design of speech appliances.

For purposes of description, the appliance consists of three parts: the (a) palatal, (b) velar, and (c) pharyngeal sections (Fig 12–11). The palatal section may consist of little more than a covering for the hard palate and carry the clasps for attachment to the teeth. This section may also supply replacements for missing teeth. In cases in which vertical dimension must be increased because of arrest of vertical growth of the middle face, the palatal section may cover the natural teeth. In these circumstances, the teeth should be crowned to protect them from dental caries. By forward extension, the palatal section may also plump the upper lip and improve the facial profile.

The velar section is in the shape of a bar connecting the palatal section to the pharyngeal portion of the appliance. The pharyngeal portion extends into the nasopharynx and assists in palatopharyngeal closure (Figs 12-12 through 12-14). The skill of prosthodontists in designing these devices has added a fortunate dimension to speech habilitation of cleft palate whenever surgery is unable to provide good results.

This treatment technique is logically combined with auditory training. The patient needs to learn to rely on auditory and intraoral somesthetic perceptions of resonance balance and palatopharyngeal control. Articulation training is likewise conducted to normalize consonant distortion or substitution patterns that patients may have developed as compensatory maneuvers in the face of palatopharyngeal incompetence.

Some speech-language pathologists and dentists utilize a palatal lift appliance (PLA) which is designed to hold the soft palate up and backward and to ultimately improve its function by acting as an isometric training appliance (Fig 12–15) (Wolfaardt et al,[36] Mazaheri and Mazaheri[37]). D'Antonio (personal communication, 1995) suggests that the PLA be used for patients in whom there is adequate tissue but poor control of coordination and timing of VP movements. It is hoped that the degree of lift can be reduced gradually until the appliance can be discarded. Unfortunately, in many instances the prosthesis must be worn indefinitely. The use of a palatal lift appliance (PLA) is still controversial. Some believe that, at best, its use produces inconsistent results even with speech therapy. The palatal lift appliance (PLA) has also proved useful in reducing drooling and improving mastication and tongue movement. Speech therapy associated with use of a PLA may include any one or a number of techniques, many of which are practiced by the patient with and without the appliance in place (Wolfaardt et al[36]).

Auditory training should be used to enhance the patient's auditory awareness of normal and deviant resonance balance. Articulation training is used to develop a patient's palatopharyngeal control to regulate nasal resonance.

Push-back Procedures (Velar Lengthening)

These are surgical procedures designed to lengthen the soft palate done either in conjunction with primary palatoplasty or as a secondary procedure after

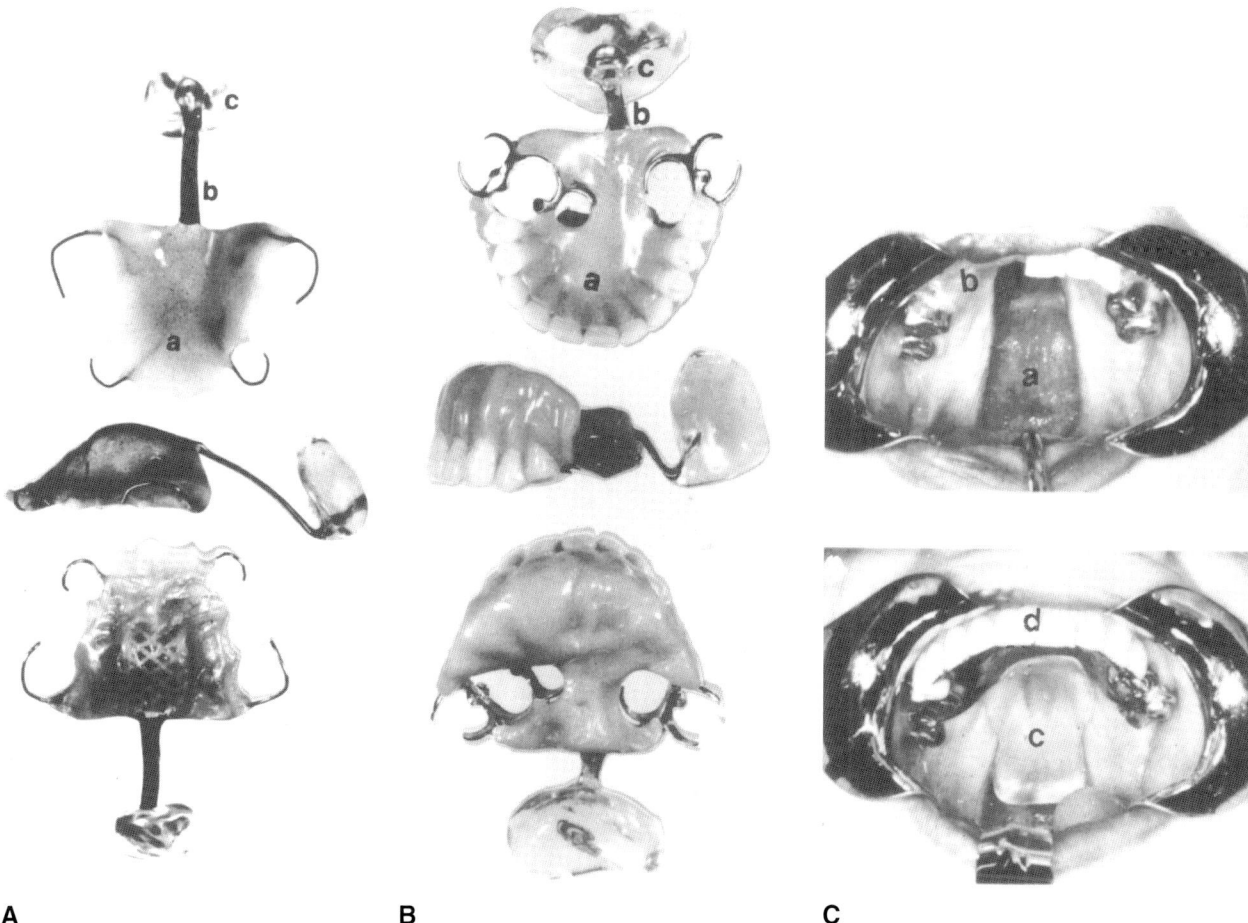

Fig 12–12. Speech aid appliances. In the event that surgery is contraindicated or delayed or, if performed, does not produce proper palatopharyngeal closure, a dental speech appliance may be substituted. Such appliances may be made of acrylic plastic retained by clasps about the teeth. Metallic castings of nonprecious and precious metals may also be used. **A.** The appliance consists of three parts: (a) the palatal, (b) the velar, and (c) the pharyngeal sections. The palatal section (a) covers the palate and carries the clasps for attachment to the teeth. **B.** The palatal section supports placement for the missing teeth and may also plump the upper lip to improve the facial profile. The velar section (b) is in the shape of a bar connecting the palatal section to (c) the pharyngeal portion of the appliance which extends into the nasopharynx and assists in palatopharyngeal closure and reducing nasal resonance. **C.** When midfacial vertical dimension is lost (top photo) and must be increased the palatal section will need to replace missing teeth and cover the natural teeth (bottom photo, wearing appliance). In such cases the teeth need to be crowned in gold to protect them from dental caries. The unoperated cleft space (a) is covered with a posterior extended acrylic section (c) to help control air flow, and permit proper feeding. (d) Replacement teeth. The pharyngeal section needs to extend into the nasopharynx and make contact with the posterior pharyngeal wall. (Courtesy S. Pruzansky.)

the palatal cleft has been closed and velopharyngeal incompetence has been detected (see chaps 7–10). The most common surgical procedure is the V-Y pushback, commonly called the Wardill-Killner,[38,39] or Veau-Wardill-Killner procedure. There are a number of variations of this basic design. This procedure involves the use of two unipedicle or single-base flaps of palatal mucoperiosteum, the soft tissue on both sides of the cleft space. The flaps are elevated from the bony palate and retropositioned so that the cleft space is covered and the length of the soft palate increased. Push-back palatoplasty procedures performed at an early age require an extensive amount of mucoperiosteal undermining and soft tissue displacement leaving large areas of denuded bone. These areas are later covered over by scar tissue which inhibits palatal bone growth and causes palatal deformation. This problem exists even when the push-back procedure is performed as a secondary procedure after the palatal cleft has already been closed.

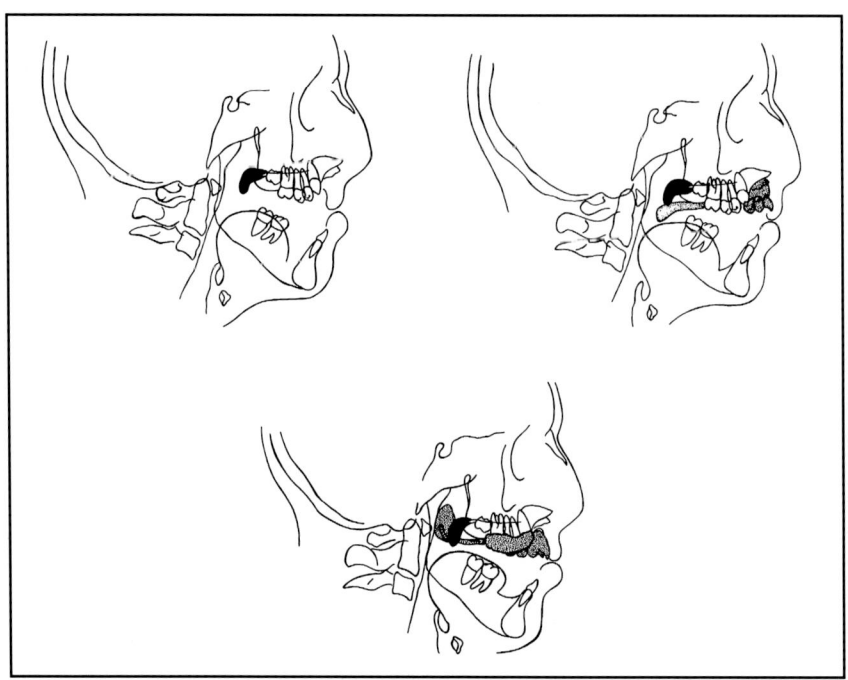

Fig 12–13. **The pharyngeal bulb in a speech appliance is viewed in cross-section in place in the nasopharynx. a.** Incompetent velopharyngeal closure. **b.** Inadequate nasopharyngeal bulb. **c.** Pharyngeal bulb (pharyngeal extension) is well positioned within the nasal chamber. (Courtesy J.D. Subtelny.)

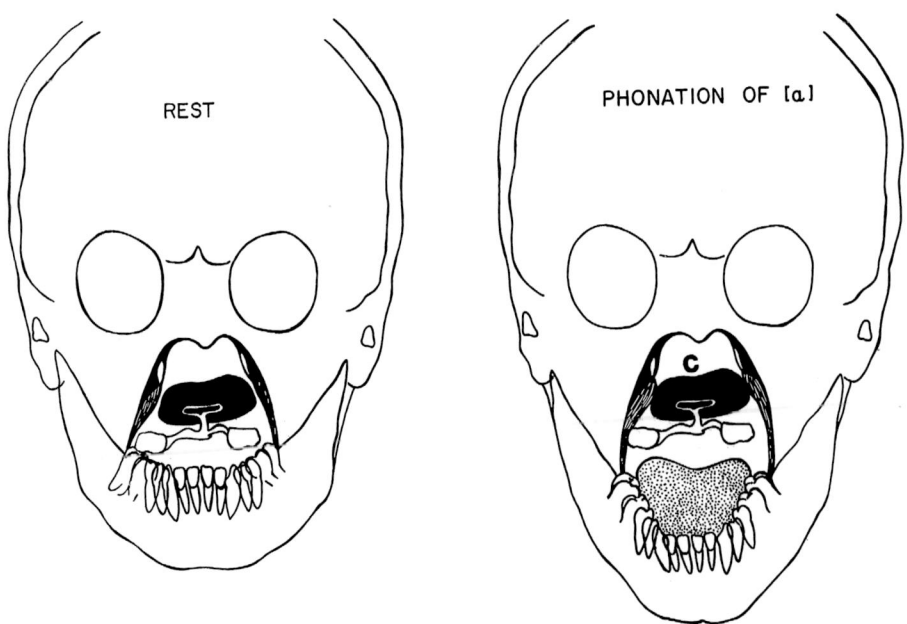

Fig 12–14. **The pharyngeal bulb on a speech aid appliance is viewed in the nasopharynx.** At rest (left), a lateral space on either side of the bulb allows for normal nasal drippings to enter the mouth. When phonating /a/, the lateral pharyngeal walls make contact with the speech bulb, reducing nasal air flow. (Courtesy of J.D. Subtelny.)

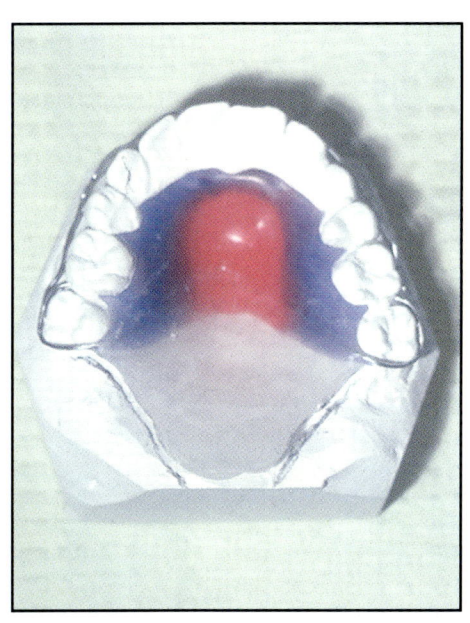
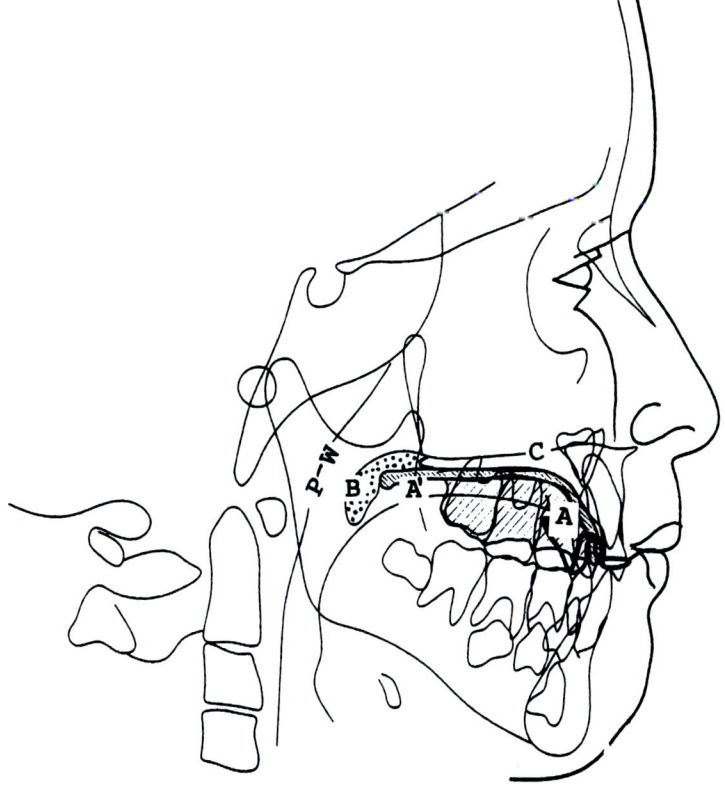

Fig 12–15. A palatal lift appliance. It is used to improve velopharyngeal function by improving velar muscle action. **a.** The appliance on a dental model. The velar extension extends posteriorly to the uvulae. **b.** Lateral cephalometric tracing showing the appliance (A-A') velar section making contact up to the uvulae (B). The appliance can be well stabilized by using orthodontic bands with soldered buccal shelves to establish undercuts for the clasps.

Lateral cephalometric evaluation of this and other push-back techniques has shown that the net gain in soft palatal length is not as great as the amount of mucoperiosteum brought posteriorly because of contraction of scar tissue. Yet, some speech-language pathologists believe this technique yields a higher success rate, as measured by speech results, than any other surgical technique. Harding et al[40] criticized this procedure because large surfaces of denuded bone are left in the anterior palate which result in excessive scarring and midfacial growth retardation. Other palatal lengthening procedures, such as Millard's Island Flap, have not been successful, because the extensive mucoperiosteal shifting leaving large areas of denuded bone has been shown to have a deleterious effect on palatal development.

Witt and D'Antonio[17] recommend Furlow's double-opposing Z-plasty for patients with a small central VP gap seen in submucous cleft palate or in patients with previously repaired cleft palate who demonstrate a midline "trough" or muscular diastasis.

Sphincteric Pharyngoplasty (SP) of Orticochea[41,42]

No discussion of pharyngeal surgery could be complete without mentioning the Orticochea operation. Jackson[43] described the procedure most commonly used today. This surgical procedure was designed to occlude the lateral ports by changing the lower insertion of the posterior pillars from the lateral walls to the posterior wall of the pharynx. Orticochea believed that this created a dynamic muscle sphincter of the pharynx, which could open and close dozens of times a minute. Furthermore, this sphincter has the same cerebrocortical role as the nasopharyngeal sphincter described by Passavant because the palatopharyngeus and superior constrictor muscles that are part of the Passavant nasopharyngeal sphincter are used in its constriction.

In patients with very short palates in whom there is a greater risk of dehiscence, only one of the palatopharyngeus muscles is transplanted. Three months later, in a second operation, the sphincter is completed by transplanting the second palatopharyngeus muscle.

The sphincter is created by transposing the posterior tonsillar pillars with the enclosed palatopharyngeus muscles from the lateral pharyngeal walls to the midsection of the posterior pharyngeal wall. Three openings conduct air between the oral and nasal pharynges. The central opening's shape and width remain unchanged postoperatively, with no reduction of the lumen. The two lateral openings completely disappear (see Vol. II, chap. 11, p. 107).

This sphincter tends to close off the nasopharynx. Some surgeons use it as a secondary corrective procedure.

Sphincter palatoplasty's cited advantages include: (1) dynamic sphincteric closure as a result of retained neuromuscular innervation, (2) technical ease of execution, (3) a low complication rate, (4) nonobstruction of the nasal airway, and (5) no violation of the velum. Unfortunately, the question of whether it attains superior speech results is still open. It also must be emphasized that many surgeons have developed variants of the original procedure. The SP procedure has theoretic advantages and is an effective means of management of VPI for some patients. More studies need to be performed to determine when this or the pharyngeal flap should be the treatment of choice (Witt and D'Antonio[17]).

Posterior Pharyngeal Wall Augmentation

Teflon® and other materials have been implanted in the posterior pharyngeal wall with no reported long-term success. Potential problems include tissue incompatibility and migration of the implant. Injectable forms of these substances also can create problems with respect to embolism or transport of the prosthetic matter to regional lymph nodes.

Although pharyngeal flap surgery is the treatment of choice in most cleft palate patients, Denny et al[44] believe that a posterior pharyngeal wall implant of costal cartilage should be used in cases of extremely shallow pharyngeal spaces with inadequate lateral pharyngeal wall motion and when the side effects of a pharyngeal flap should be avoided. Shprintzen et al[45] and Sher et al[46] believe that pharyngeal flaps should be avoided in patients with primary neuromuscular disease or pharyngeal hypotonia.

Pharyngeal implants have been carried out with a variety of materials by a number of surgeons over the years (e.g., Teflon®, by Smith and McCabe[47]; Silastic by Blocksma[48]; Silicone Gel by Brauer[49]; Proplast by Wolford et al[50]; and Homologous Cartilage by Trigas et al[51]).

Surgical procedures as well as injection techniques have been used. Furlow et al[52] reported one instance of obstructive sleep apnea (OSA) 6 years post-Teflon® injection due to the downward displacement of the Teflon® particles resulting in a narrowing of the patient's airway. In a series of studies, Vinas and Jager[53] obtained the best results with surgically inserted cartilage implants.

REFERENCES

1. Dickson DR, Dickson WM. *Anatomical and Physiological Basis of Speech*. Boston: Mass: Little, Brown and Co; 1982.
2. Rosenberger HC. Growth and development of the naso respiratory area in childhood. *Ann Otol Rhinol Laryngol.* 1934;43:495–522.
3. Brodie AG. On the growth pattern of the human head from the third month to the eighth year of life. *Am J Anat.* 1941;68:209–262.
4. King EW. A roentgenographic study of pharyngeal growth. *Angle Orthod.* 1952;22:23–37.
5. Scott JH. The cartilage of the nasal septum. *Br Dent J.* 1953;95:37–43.
6. Scott JH. The growth in width of the facial skeleton. *Am J Orthod.* 1957;43:366.
7. Scott JH. The analysis of facial growth, Part II: the horizontal and vertical dimensions. *Am J Orthod.* 1958;44:585.
8. Todd TW, Tracy B. Racial features in the American Negro cranium. *Am J Phys Anthropol.* 1930;15:53–110.
9. Subtelny JD. Width of the nasopharynx and related anatomic structures in normal and unoperated cleft palate children. *Am J Orthod.* 1955;41:889–909.
10. Subtelny JD, Baker HK. The significance of adenoid tissue in velopharyngeal function. *Plast Reconstr Surg.* 1956;17:235.
11. Berkowitz S. Cleft Lip and Palate. In Wolfe SA, Berkowitz S, eds. *Plastic Surgery of the Facial Skeleton.* Boston: Mass: Little, Brown and Co; 1989:366–371.
12. Ricketts RM. The cranial base and soft structures in cleft palate speech and breathing. *Plast Reconstr Surg.* 1954;14:47–16.
13. Brader AC. A cephalometric x-ray appraisal of morphological variations in cranial base and associated pharyngeal structures: implications in cleft palate therapy. *Angle Orthod.* 1957;27:179–195.
14. Moss ML. Malformation of the skull base associated with cleft palate deformity. *Plast Reconstr Surg.* 1965;17:226–234.
15. Coccaro PJ, Subtelny JD, Pruzansky S. Growth of soft palate in cleft palate children. *Plast Reconstr Surg.* 1962;30:43–55.

16. Trost-Cardamone JE: Come to terms with VPI: a response to Loney and Bloem. *Cleft Palate J.* 1989;26:68
17. Witt PD, LL D'Antonio: Velopharyngeal insufficiency and secondary palatal management. A new look at an old problem. *Clin I Plast Surg.* 1993;20:707–721
18. Subtelny JD. Width of the nasopharynx and related anatomic structures in normal and unopoerated cleft palate children. *Am J Orthod.* 1955;41:889–909.
19. Osborne GS. The prevalence of anomalies of the upper cervical vertebrae in patients with craniofacial malformations, and their effects on osseous nasopharyngeal depth. Unpublished doctoral dissertation, Southern Illinois University, Carbondale. 1968.
20. McCarthy MF. Preliminary report of studies on the nasopharynx. *Ann Otol Rhinol Laryng.* 1925;34:800–813.
21. Schuller A. X-ray examination of deformities of the nasopharynx. *Ann Otol Rhinol Laryng.* 1929;38:108–129.
22. Osborne GS, Pruzansky S, Koepp-Baker H. Upper cervical spine anomalies and osseous nasopharyngeal depth. *J Speech Hear Res.* 1971;4:14–22.
23. Pruzansky S, Mason R. Morphologic signs of congenital palatopharyngeal incompetence. Paper presented at the annual convention of the American Speech and Hearing Association; November, 1966; Washington, DC.
24. Slaughter WB, Pruzansky S. The rationale for velar closure as a primary procedure in the repair of cleft palate defects. *Plast and Reconstr Surg.* 1954;13:341.
25. Warren DW. Velopharyngeal orifice size and upper pharyngeal pressure flow patterns in normal speech. *Plast Reconstr Surg.* 1904;33:148.
26. Warren DW. Velopharyngeal orifice size and upper pharyngeal pressure flow patterns in cleft palate speech, a preliminary study. *Plast Reconstr Surg.* 1964;34–15.
27. Bjork L. Velopharyngeal function in connected speech. *Acta Radiol.* 1961;(Suppl):202.
28. Bjork L, Nylan BO. Ceveradiography with synchronized sound spectrum analysis: a study of velopharyngeal function during connected speech in normals and cleft palate cases. *Plast Reconstr Surg.* 1961;27:397.
29. Shprintzen RJ, Lewin ML, Craft CB, et al. A comprehensive study of pharyngeal flap surgery. *Cleft Palate J.* 1979;16:46.
30. Millard DR, Jr. *Cleft Craft, III: The Evolution of Its Surgery: Alveolar and Palatal Deformities.* Boston, Mass: Little, Brown and Co; 1980:240.
31. Millard DR Jr. The island flap in cleft palate surgery. *Surg Gynecol and Obstet.* 1963;116:297–300.
32. Trier WC: The pharyngeal flap operation. *Clin Plast Surg.* 1985;12:697
33. Subtelny JD, Nieto RP. A longitudinal study of maxilary growth following pharyngeal-flap surgery. *Cleft Palate J.* 1978;15:118.
34. Harding RL. Surgery. In Copper RL, Harding RL, Krogman WM, Mazahiri M, Millard RT, eds, *Cleft Palate and Cleft Lip: A Team Approach to Clinical Management and Rehabilitation of the Patient.* Philadelphia, Pa: WB Saunders; 1975:5.
35. Randall P, Whitaker LA, Noone RB, Jones WDF, III. The case for the inferiorly based posterior pharyngeal flap. *Cleft Palate J.* 1978;15:262–265.
36. Wolfaardt JF, Wilson FB, Rochet A, McPhee L. An appliance based approach to the management of palatopharyngeal incompetency: a clinical pilot project. *J Prosthet Dent.* 1993;609:186–195.
37. Mazaheri M, Mazaheri EH. Prosthodontic aspects of velar elevation and velopharyngeal stimulation, presented at the 22nd annual meeting of the American Academy of Maxillofacial Prosthodontics. 1974; Williamsburg, Va.
38. Wardill WEM. Cleft palate. *Br J Surg.* 1933;21:347.
39. Wardill WEM. The technique of operation for cleft palate. *Br J Surg.* 1937;25:117–130.
40. Harding RL, Mazaheri M, Krogman W. Timing of the Pharyngeal Flap: A Retrospective Study. Presented at the meeting of the American Association of Plastic Surgeons. 1977; Chicago, Ill.
41. Orticochea M. Results of the dynamic muscle sphincter operation in cleft palates. *Br J Plast Surg.* 1970;23:108–114.
42. Orticochea M. The dynamic muscle sphincter. In Bardach J, Morris HL, eds. *Multidisciplinary Management of Cleft Lip and Palate.* Philadelphia, Pa: WB Saunders Co; 1990:378.
43. Jackson IT: Sphincter pharyngoplasty. *Clin Plast Surg.* 1985;12:711
44. Denny AD, Marks SM, Oliff-Carneol S. Correction of velopharyngeal insufficiency, by pharyngeal augmentation using autologous cartilage: a preliminary report. *Cleft Palate Craniofacial J.* 1993;30:46–54.
45. Shprintzen RJ, Siegel-Sadewitz VL, Amato J, Goldberg RB. Anomalies associated with cleft lip, cleft palate, or both. *Am J Med Genet.* 1985;20:585–595.
46. Sher AE, Shprintzen RJ, Thorpy MJ. Endoscopic observations of obstructive sleep apnea in children with anomalous upper airways: predictive and therapeutic value. *Int J Pediatr Otorhinolaryngol.* 1986; 11:135–146.
47. Smith JK, McCabe BF. Teflon injection in the nasopharynx to improve velopharyngeal closure. *Ann Otolaryngol.* 1977;86:559–563.
48. Blocksma R. Correction of velopharyngeal insufficiency by Silastic pharyngeal implant. *Plast Reconstr Surg.* 1963;31:268–274.
49. Brauer RO. Retropharyngeal implantation of silicone gel pillows for velopharyngeal incompetence. *Plast Reconstr Surg.* 1973;51:254–262.
50. Wolford LM, Oelschlaeger M, Deal R. Proplast as a pharyngeal wall implant to correct velopharyngeal insufficiency. *Cleft Palate J.* 1989;26:119–128.
51. Trigas I, Ysunza A, Gonzales A, Vasquez MD. Surgical treatment of borderline velopharyngeal insufficiency using homologous cartilage implantation with videona-

sopharyngoscopic monitoring. *Cleft Palate J.* 1988;25: 167–170.

52. Furlow LT, Block AJ, Williams WN. Obstructive sleep apnea following treatment of velopharyngeal incompetence by Teflon injection. *Cleft Palate J.* 1986;23: 153–158.

53. Vinas JC, Jager E. The push-forward in velopharyngeal incompetency. In Hueston JT, ed. *Transactions of the 5th International Congress of Plastic and Reconstructive Surgery.* Sydney, Australia: Butterworth, 1971:252–259.

13

Clefts of the Lip and Alveolus, Isolated Cleft Palate, the Complete Unilateral Cleft of the Lip and Palate

ISOLATED CLEFT PALATE (Fig 13–1)

In this cleft type, neither the lip nor the alveolar process is involved. The cleft may extend only through the soft palate or through the soft and hard palates, but it cannot exist in the hard palate alone because the fusion of the hard and soft palates proceeds from front to back.

The cleft may extend anteriorly as far forward as the nasopalative foraman. The outline of the cleft space may be wide or narrow, long or short; any variation in geometric form can exist (see Chapter 4).

Timing of surgical closure depends on the width and not the length of the cleft space. Hard palate clefts are frequently closed simultaneously with the soft palate cleft. In some instances, surgical closure of very wide hard palate clefts may need to be postponed until there is additional palatal growth, which may be as late as 5 or 6 years of age. An obturator with a pharyngeal extension (speech aid apliance) can be worn until the palate is closed (see Chapter 11).

CLEFTS OF THE LIP AND ALVEOLUS (Fig 13–2)

The alveolar portion is usually distorted outward in complete lip clefts. When the lip is united, the newly created lip force molds the alveolar section into proper alignment. A secondary alveolar bone graft is performed at the same age as in other cleft types.

CLEFTS OF THE UVULAE AND SOFT PALATE

When the health of the child permits, soft tissue clefts can be sutured within the first 3 months.

COMPLETE UNILATERAL CLEFT LIP AND PALATE

As previously described,[1] in complete unilateral and bilateral clefts of the lip and palate, after the lip is united, the overexpanded palatal segments move together, reducing the cleft width along its entire posterior length. Subtelny,[2] using laminographs, has shown that newborns with complete clefts of the lip and palate have wider than normal pharyngeal widths, and the perpendicular plates of the sphenoids are distorted in their relationship. Aduss and Pruzansky[3] have demonstrated that, in complete unilateral cleft lip and palate, any one of three arch forms can result after the lip is repaired (Fig 13–3):

1. The alveolar segments can move into end-to-end contact, producing a symmetrical arch form.
2. The alveolar segments can overlap, producing what is known as a "collapsed" arch form.
3. The alveolar segments can move closer together but without contact. This occurs because of an inhibiting factor of the inferior turbinate on the cleft side making contact with the distorted bulge of the nasal septum.

In a series of 58 patients who had no presurgical orthopedics or primary bone grafting, Aduss and Pruzansky[3] found that approximately 43% had overlap of the alveolar processes (collapsed arch). Among these patients, crossbites of the canine and first deciduous molar were the most common finding at 5 years of age. There were no anterior crossbites. Other investigators have reported similar results (Bergland,[4] Bergland and Sidhu[5]). Berkowitz,[6] in a serial study of

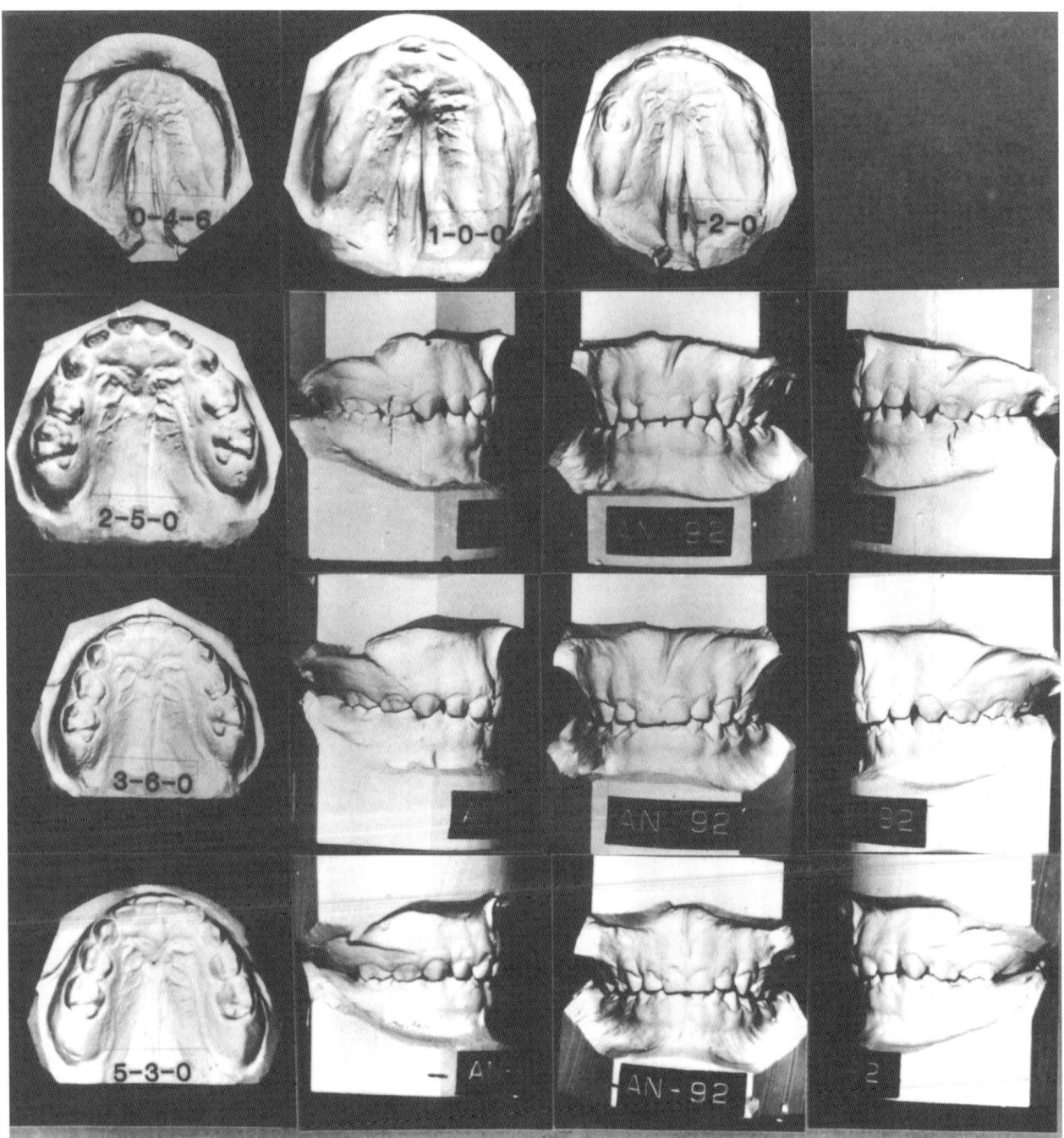

Fig 13-1. Isolated cleft palate. Serial casts demonstrate that, in some cases, good Class I occlusion can occur when closing the cleft space at 18 months of age, or even later, using a modified von Langenbeck surgical procedure. This occlusal result supports Berkowitz's contention that the "critical threshold level" for good palatal growth is determined by the size of the cleft space relative to the amount of available mucoperiosteal tissue. This threshold, which still needs to be determined, is critical to the development of good arch form and occlusion. The threshold ratio, if exceeded by early palatal closure when the palatal size is relatively small compared to cleft size, will cause excessive palatal scar tissue resulting in midfacial growth inhibition.

CASE REPORT: INCOMPLETE CLEFT OF LIP AND ALVEOLUS

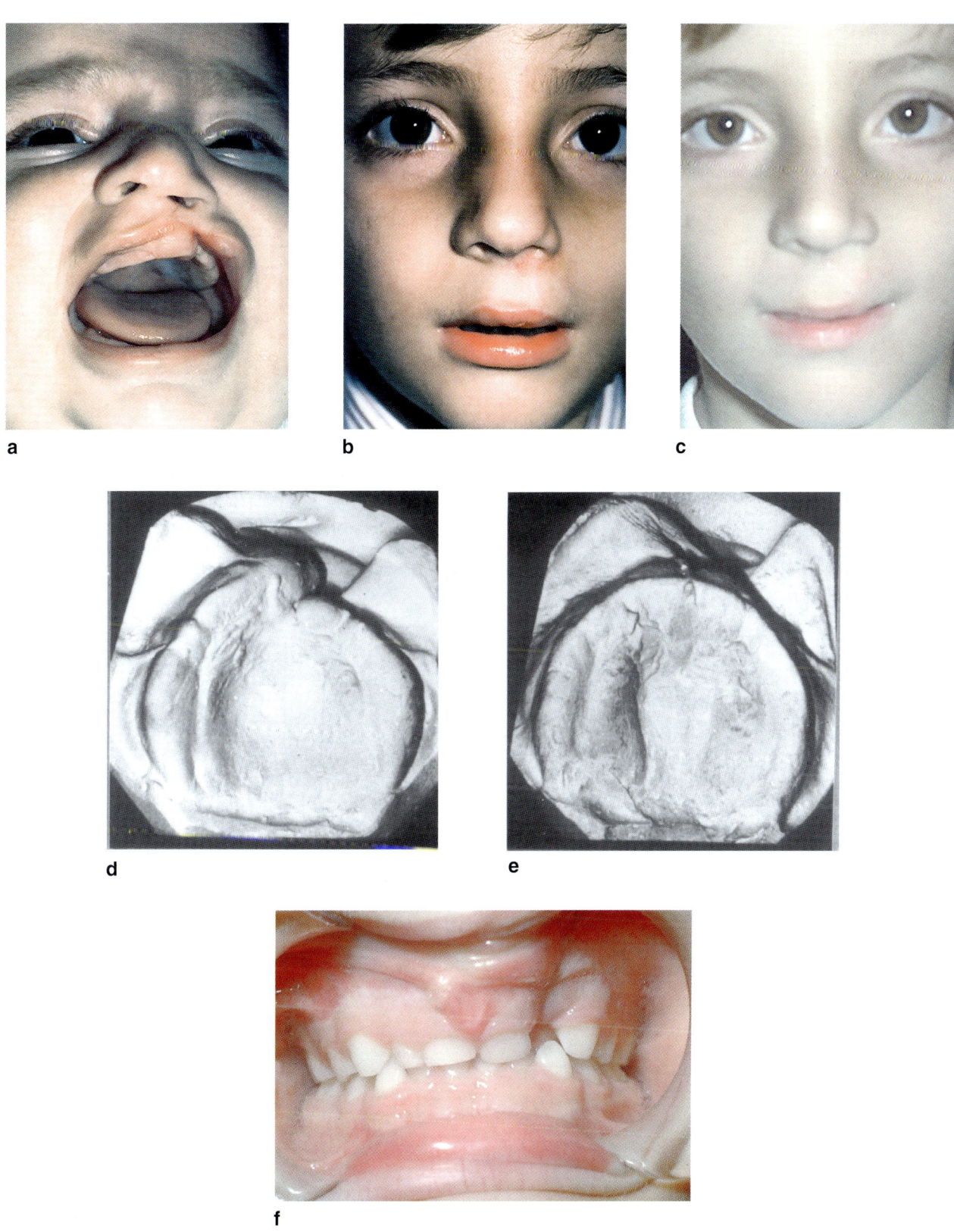

Fig 13-2. Cleft of the lip and alveolus. Facial photographs **a.** before and **b.** after surgery. **c.** 4 years later showing good lip/nose aesthetics. Palatal casts **d.** before and **e.** after surgery showing the molding of the cleft alveolar segment into alignment. **f.** Ideal anterior and buccal occlusion.

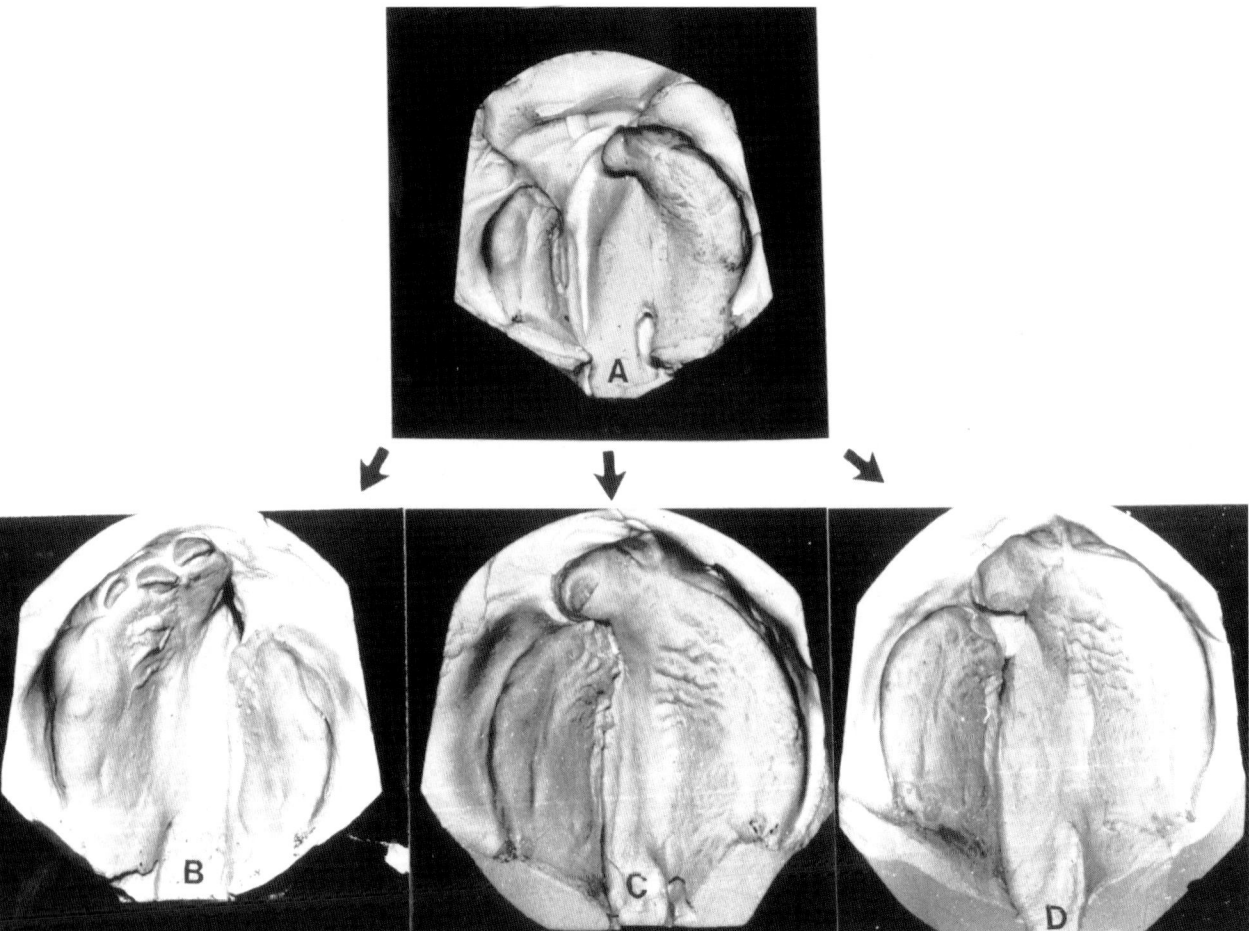

Fig 13-3. Complete unilateral cleft lip and palate (CUCLP) before (A) and after (B) lip surgery. With the establishment of muscle continuity, the lesser segment moves medially while the premaxillary portion of the larger segment moves medioinferiorly, both acting to reduce the cleft width. Any of the following segmental relationships can result: **B.** No contact between segments. The inferior turbinate on the cleft side makes premature contact with the bowed nasal septum. **C.** The premaxillary portion of the larger segment overlaps the smaller segment. **D.** The segments form a butt joint showing good approximation. Pruzansky and Aduss have shown that there is no correlation between the original cleft width and the resultant arch form. Wider clefts seemed to demonstrate less of a tendency toward collapse than did the narrower clefts. (Pruzansky S, Aduss H. Prevalence of arch collapse and malocclusion in complete unilateral cleft lip and palate. *Trans Europ Orthod Soc.* 1967:1–17)

36 cases with complete unilateral clefts of the lip and palate in which the lip had been united between the ages of 3 and 5 months and the palatal cleft closed between 18 and 24 months without neonatal maxillary orthopedics, showed that 5 of the 36 cases had a complete buccal crossbite which was corrected within 6 to 10 months with fixed palatal expanders. Cuspid crossbite was the most frequent occurrence and was due to angular palatal rotation as well as to ectopic eruption of the deciduous cuspids. The cleft and noncleft segments were in either a Class 1 or Class 2 occlusal relationship. In no instance were any of the segments in a Class 3 relationship.

This confirms Berkowitz's belief that the cleft palatal segment is not retropositioned within the skull relative to the mandible and that the maxillary-mandibular relationship is similar to that seen in the noncleft population. Therefore, the palatal segments do not need to be brought forward by the use of neonatal protraction forces as Latham[7] and his mentor McNeil[8] have suggested. There are, however, some cases when, because of an unfavorable facial growth pattern coupled with a retruded maxilla relative to the anterior cranial bases, orthopedic protraction forces will be beneficial in the mixed (transitional) and permanent dentition.

According to Aduss and Pruzansky,[3] four factors govern arch form:

1. *The size and shape of the alveolar process adjacent to the cleft.* A bulbous and fully toothed alveolar process acts as an impediment to the collapse of the arch, whereas a thinly formed and dentally impoverished alveolar process leads to the overlapping of segments.

2. *The size and shape of the inferior turbinate on the side of the cleft.* A thick, rounded, well-modeled inferior turbinate can block excessive medial movement of the palatal segments.

3. *The size and geometrical inclination of the nasal septum.* A highly inclined septum with a contiguous bulbous turbinate will affect the movement of the palate and its final position.

4. *The size and shape of the palatal shelves.* Shelves of disproportionate size are more prone to overlap. One can certainly visualize that a long noncleft segment coupled with a short cleft segment will end up with the premaxillary portion overlapping the short cleft palate segment.

FACIAL CHARACTERISTICS

The Oslo Study

Because of the stable and long history of meticulous record keeping and protocols that characterizes the data acquisition of the Oslow team, the following studies on unilateral cleft lip and palate are presented to provide a unique perspective on treatment strategies and facial growth standards based on longitudinal data. The author does not follow the same surgical strategies as those of the Oslow team, but recognizes that the differences are not significant enough to interfere with obtaining a successful long-term outcome.

Semb's[9] 20-year serial cephalometric study taken from the Oslow Archives gathered during Bergland's leadership involved 76 males and 81 females (157 individuals) who did not have neonatal maxillary orthopedics. All of the children in the study had lip closure in infancy using a modified Le Mesurier or, after 1969, a Millard procedure. During the same operation, the nasal floor was closed using a one-layer vomer flap. The remaining posterior palatal cleft was closed between 4 and 5 years of age using a von Langenbeck palatoplasty. Secondary alveolar bone grafts from the iliac crest were placed at between 8 and 11 years of age. By 1974 all palate repairs were completed by 18 months of age. Superior-based pharyngeal flap surgery for velopharyngeal insufficiency was performed in about 20% of the cases.

Compared with normal males and females, the pooled sample with unilateral cleft lip and palate showed: (1) skeletal and soft tissue maxillary retrusion; (2) elongation of the anterior face (even though the upper face height was shorter); (3) a retrusive mandible; (4) reduction in posterior face height; and (5) a slight increase in the angle of the cranial base.

The pattern of growth also was different from that of noncleft individuals. Between 5 and 18 years of age there was almost no increase in the length of the maxilla. There was a marked reduction in maxillary and mandibular prominence. Vertically, the excessive lower face angulation changed slightly.

Multicenter CUCLP Study (Ross[10])

Ross's multicenter study involved data from 15 cleft palate centers around the world collected for the purpose of determining the effects of manipulative and surgical treatment on facial growth. A sample of 1,600 cephalometric radiographs of males with complete unilateral cleft lip and palate were traced, digitized, and analyzed in the Craniofacial Center of The Hospital for Sick Children. The seven series of studies considered virtually every aspect of treatment that might influence facial growth.

Ross concluded that the type of surgical repair used does not make an appreciable difference to facial growth. It appears, however, that there are differences that can only be explained on the assumption that some surgeons induce less growth inhibition than others. Variation of the timing of hard and soft palate repair within the first decade does not influence facial growth in the anteroposterior or vertical dimension. Ross admits that very early soft palate repair was not well represented in this study, and there is some suspicion that there might be untoward results.

Berkowitz's clinical findings suggest that, in most cases, early surgery (before 12 months) will have a negative effect on palatal growth in all three dimensions.

Ross's study also reported that the resulting face is flat in profile and decreased in depth, with a vertical deficiency in the midface and vertical excess in the lower face. The mandibles in these faces characteristically are slightly shorter in total length so that the chin is retruded. The occlusion is more of a molar and incisor mesioocclusion in clefts with less overbite and overjet. The soft palate in this sample is appreciably more posterior. The mandibular plane angle is greater, possible due to the need for more interincisal space.

Ross further stated that the bony pharynx was unaffected by treatment and that the variation in midface development can be attributed to maxillary length rather than to maxillary position. He also noted that the mandible is not directly affected by treatment. Facial growth is intrinsically compromised by an underlying deficit, and surgery acts to further interfere with growth of the midface by inhibiting forward translation.

The best results appear to follow lip repair at 4–5 months with no repair of the alveolus. Early alveolar repair restricts its vertical growth and should be avoided in individuals with poor growth potential.

This leads to deficient midfacial height and poor vertical height proportions, with more acute nasolabial angles. There is no evidence that periosteoplasty will cause similar results.

The maxilla in the UCLP is not more posteriorly positioned to any appreciable extent, but it is much shorter in length. The repaired lip affects the basal maxilla more than the alveolar process. Vertical development of the posterior maxilla is more deficient than the anterior part. The mandible is shorter with a steeper mandibular plane angle.

Hard and soft palate surgical repair procedures provide the greatest potential for inhibiting the maxilla in length, forward translation, and posterior height.

Reflection on Ross' Multicenter Study[30]

In the Foreword of the multicenter study, Treatment Variables Affecting Facial Growth in Complete Unilateral Cleft Lip and Palate, Bruce Ross discussed the difficulty of performing this type of study due to the variability in sample size, age, sex, precise cleft type, and ethnic origin. He then mentioned the problems associated with doing cephalometric measurements and suggested using one center to control measurement errors. This was an excellent solution. According to Ross,[10(pp3–4)]

> The study considered virtually every aspect of treatment that might influence facial growth. An attempt was made to control many variables that influence growth research, so that a clear picture of the effects of each procedure would be available. Two major assumptions about the study are necessary if any conclusion can be drawn from these studies. The first is that all groups of infants with complete unilateral cleft lip and palate have exactly the same facial morphology at birth in spite of enormous individual variation within the group. The second assumption is that one group of infants will respond on the average in exactly the same way as any other group to a particular treatment. The intent was to assemble relatively pure samples of individuals who had received the given management techniques used consistently on all subjects from a particular center.

Berkowitz believes the study was a noble attempt by excellent clinican/researchers to pool their sample cases to investigate treatment results. Unfortunately, it was limited to cephalometric records. By lumping all CUCLP cases together, regardless of the degree of palatal deformity at birth, much potential prognostic information for the treatment of individual cases is unavailable. Ross discounts Slavkin's[6] and Ross and Johnston's[7] statements that palatal defects may be caused by either the failure of the separated palatal segments to fuse or, possibly, palatal osteogenic deficiency, a variable that needs to be considered in treatment planning. This statement on the embryo-pathogenesis of cleft palate explains why all clefts within a cleft type are not alike. It is not hard to reason that, as the extent of the cleft palatal defect varies, so will the resulting quantity of palatal surface area and the resulting quantity of post-surgical scar tissue. Because excessive scarring inhibits palatal growth and development, the palatal surface area at the time of closure needs to be considered in treatment planning. Berkowitz believes that the variability of palatal surface area within a particular cleft type weakens the value of Ross's[10(p3)] conclusions, which are based on the second assumption that "one group of infants will respond on the average in exactly the same way as any other group to a particular treatment." Berkowitz concludes that the next level of treatment evaluation studies designed to improve differential diagnosis requires the establishment of specific criteria based on quantitative and qualitative characteristics of the palatal defect when related to treatment outcome.

CASE REPORTS

In this section, treatment outcomes of selected cases are presented with photographs starting at birth and continuing through adolescence to show the natural history of palatal and facial growth and development when conservative surgery was performed without the use of presurgical orthopedics.

In some cases, the lip was united after the use of a Logan's Bow (Fig 13–4), in others after lip adhesion at approximately 3 months of age. In some cases the cleft of the soft palate was united at the same time. Definite lip surgery was performed at 6 months and hard palate closure using a modified von Langenbeck procedure with a vomer flap was performed between 12 and 24 months of age.

Selected cases are presented in Figures 13–5 through 13–20 to show various treatment solutions to complex problems.

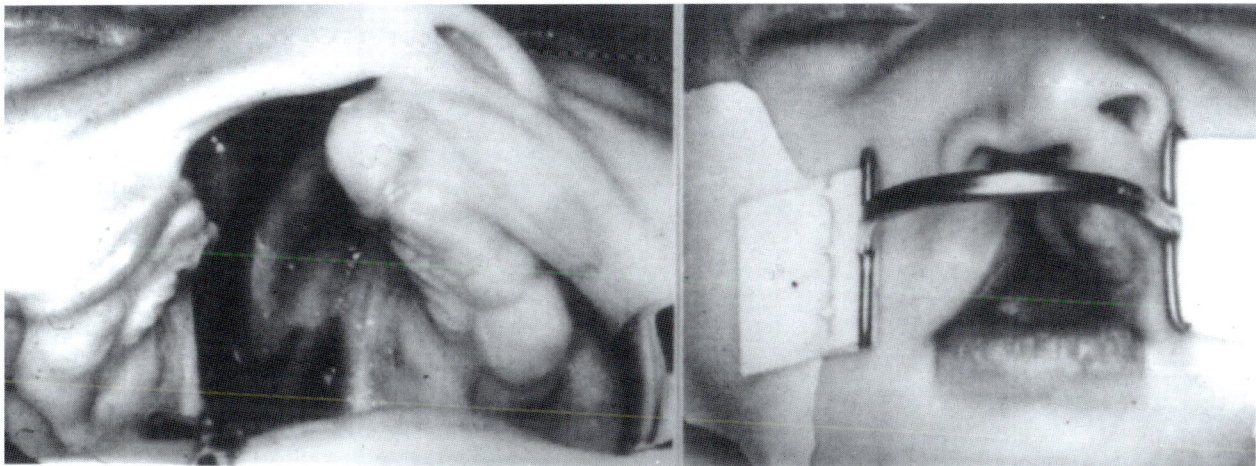

Fig 13–4. Logan's bow. Pressure is placed on the cheeks to bring the lips together prior to surgery. The bow helps to reduce tension at the suture line.

CASE REPORT: CUCLP WITH EXCELLENT FACIAL AND PALATAL DEVELOPMENT

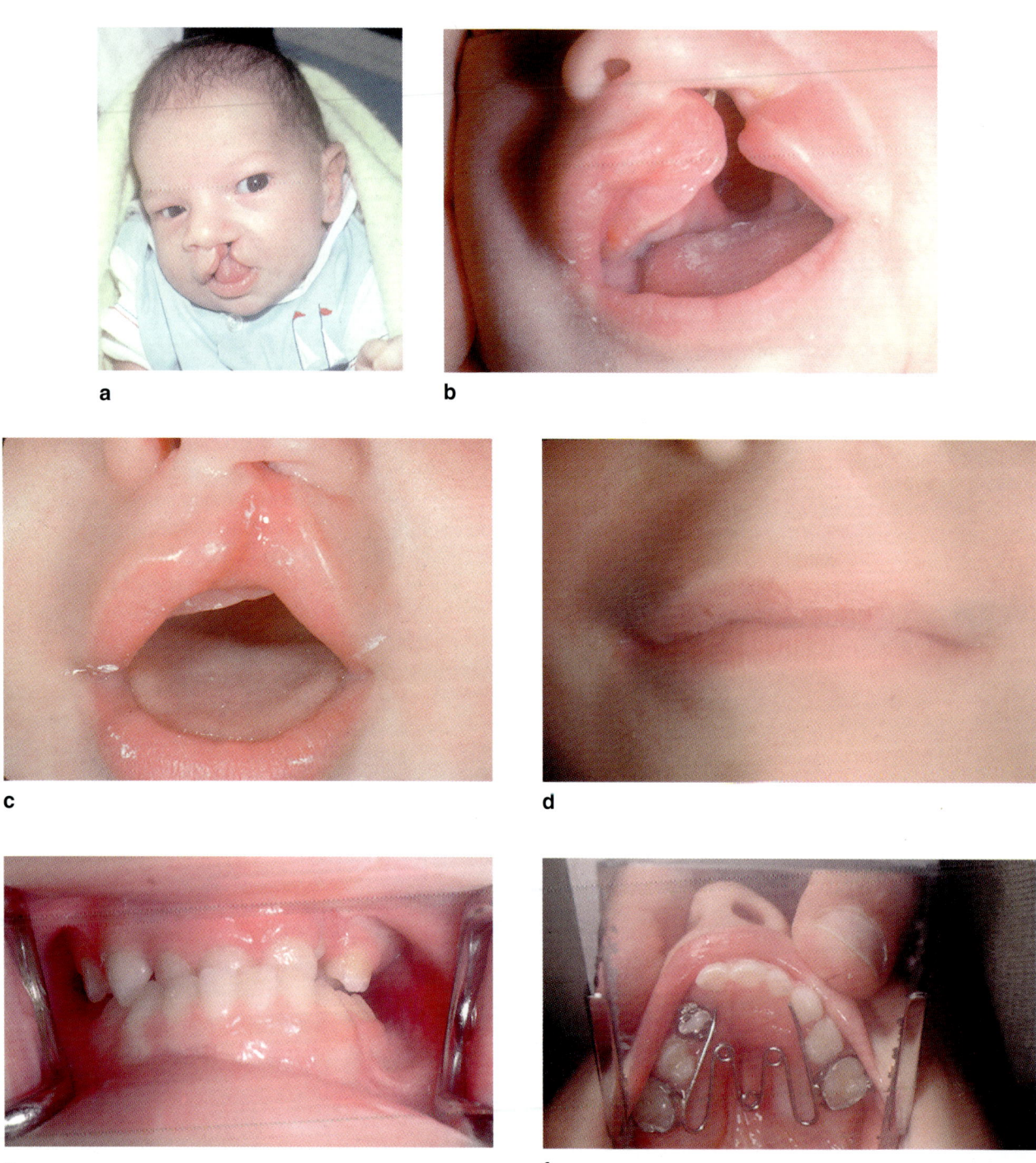

Fig 13-5. Case: KC (ZZ-1) demonstrates good palatal and facial growth in CUCLP. A very small cleft space at 5 months of age allowed for easy closure without much scar formation. *Surgical treatment:* No presurgical orthopedics. Lip adhesion followed by Millard's Rotation Advancement. Soft palatal closure at 2 months. Palatal cleft closure at 15 months using modified von Langenbeck procedure. Secondary alveolar cranial bone graft at 6 years and 8 months. Photographs showing various treatment stages from birth to 17 years of age. **a** and **b.** Newborn. **c.** Lip adhesion at 4 months **d.** Lip at 2 years of age. *Orthodontics during the deciduous dentition:* **e.** 2 years, showing anterior crossbite. **f.** 2 years, 7 months: Palatal view showing fixed buccal expander.

(continued)

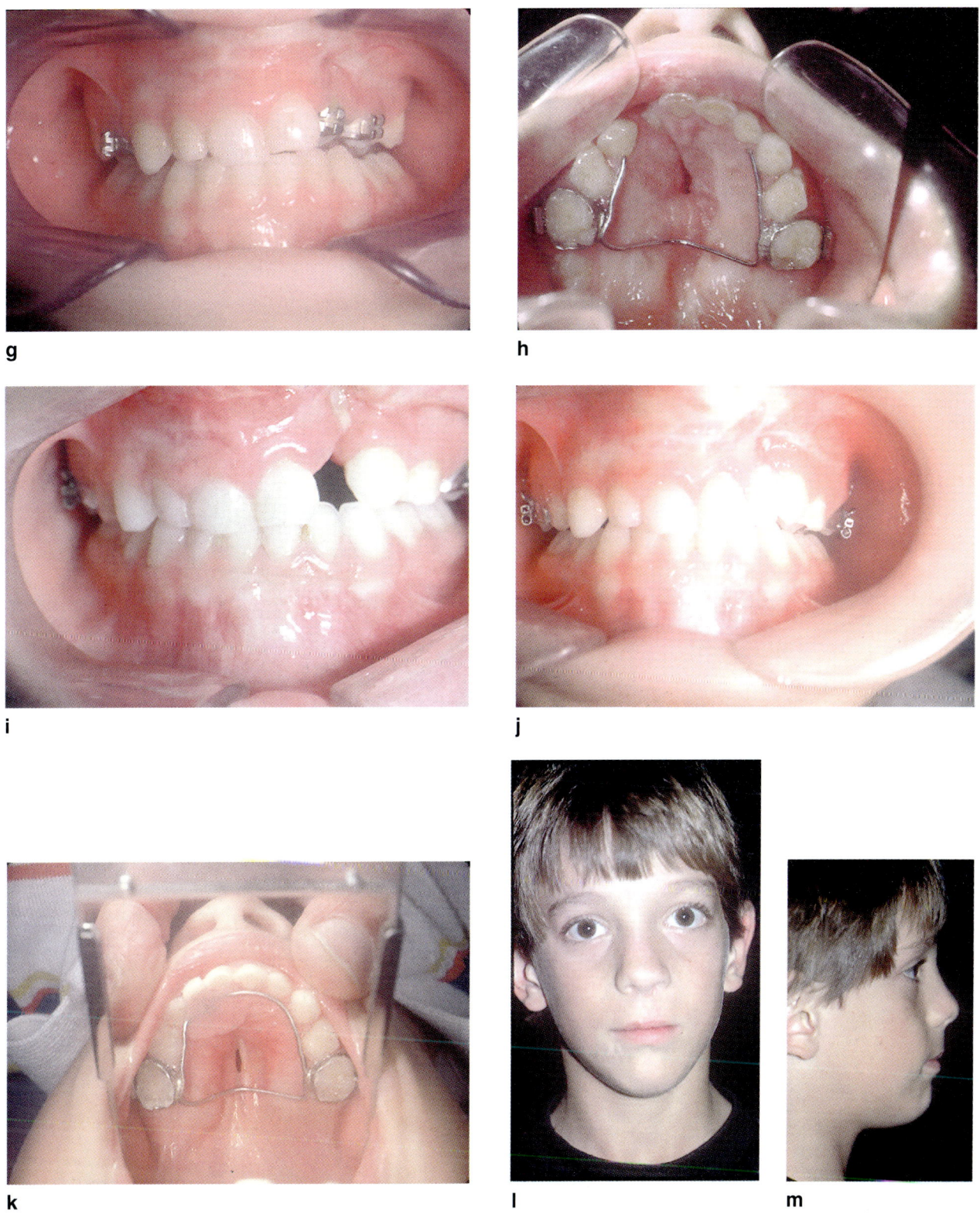

Fig 13–5. *(continued)*

g. Anterior teeth were advanced and the cleft buccal segment expanded. **h.** 5 years. Fixed palatal retainer. **i**, **j**, and **k.** Fixed palatal retainer with lateral incisor pontic (tooth). **l** and **m.** Facial photographs at 6 years.

(continued)

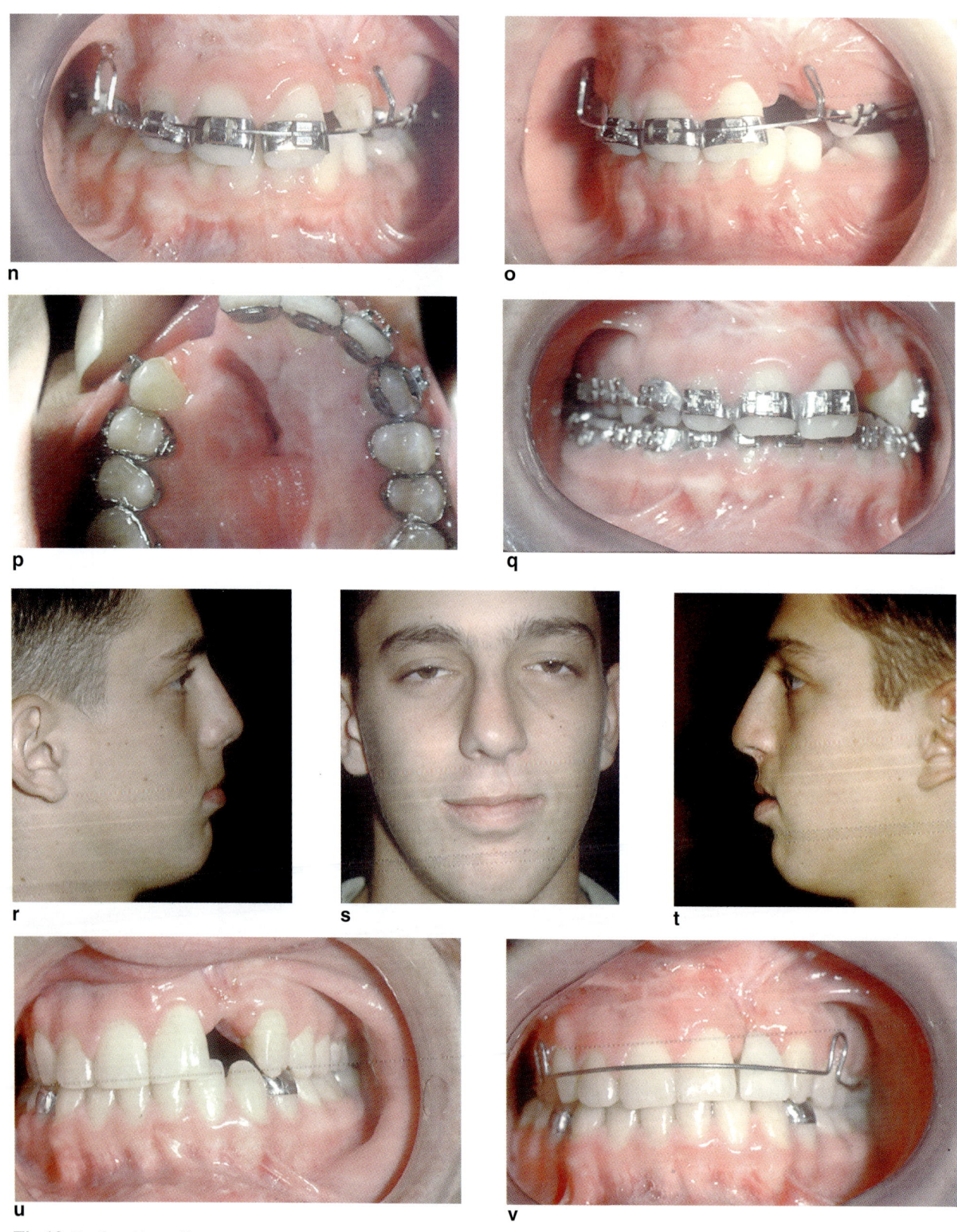

Fig 13–5. *(continued)*

n and **o**. 7 years, 3 months: Lateral incisor is erupting through cranial bone graft. Orthodontics in the adult dentition: **o**. Lateral incisor is extracted due to poor root development. **p**, and **q**. Conventional orthodontics. Surgery to close the palatal fistula was unsuccessful. **r**, **s**, and **t**. Facial photographs at 17 years. **u**, and **v**. Intraoral photographs. Hawley orthodontic retainer with lateral incisor pontic.

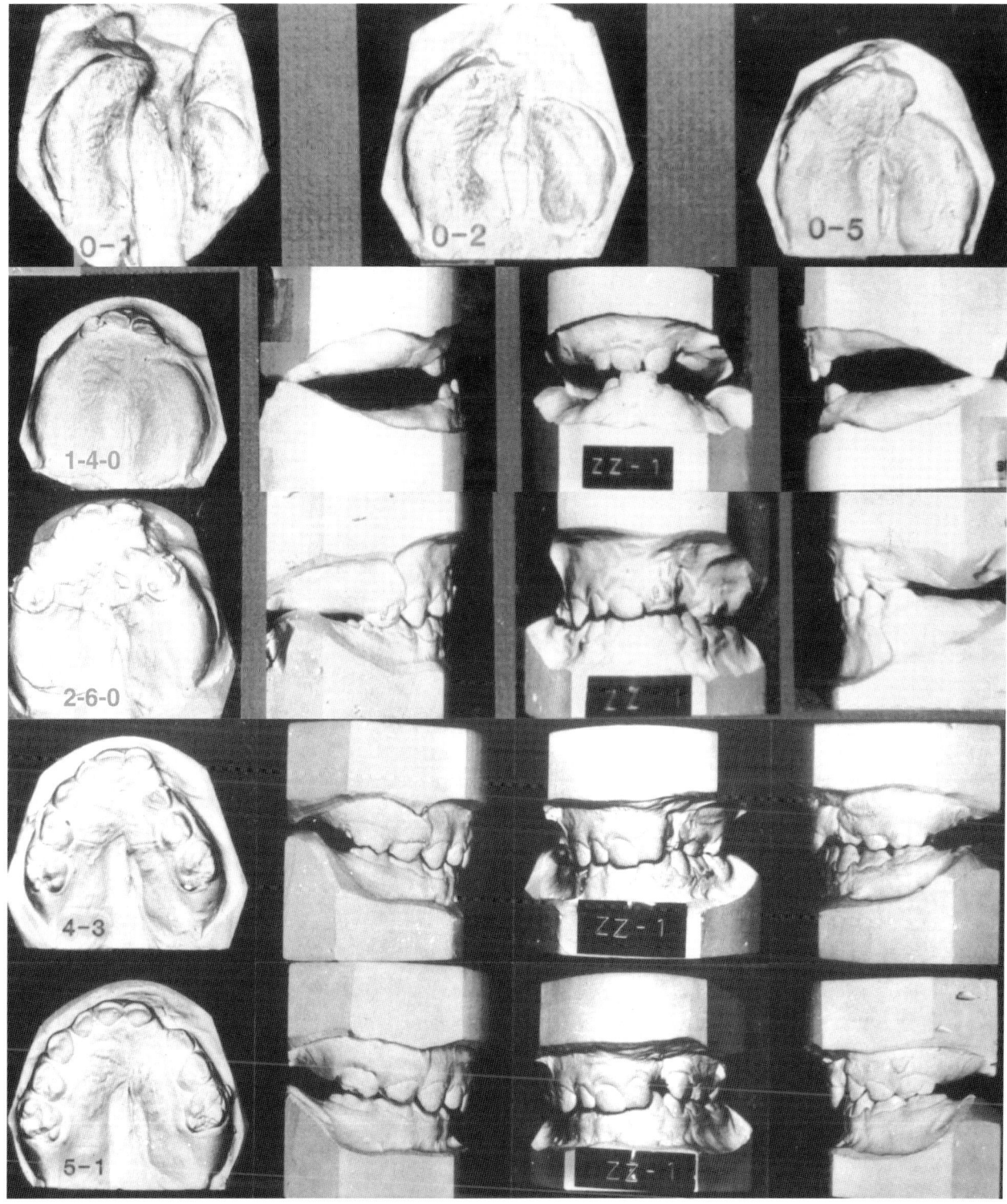

Fig 13–6. Case KC (ZZ-1). Serial casts from **0-1** to **0-5** shows medial movement and growth changes to the palatal segments. **0-5.** The cleft space is extremely small with the palatal segments making contact anterior to the cleft space. **2-6-0** and **4-3.** Mesioangular rotation of the lesser segment placed the deciduous cuspid in crossbite. **5-1.** A fixed palatal expander rotated the segment outward, placing the teeth in ideal occlusion. *(continued)*

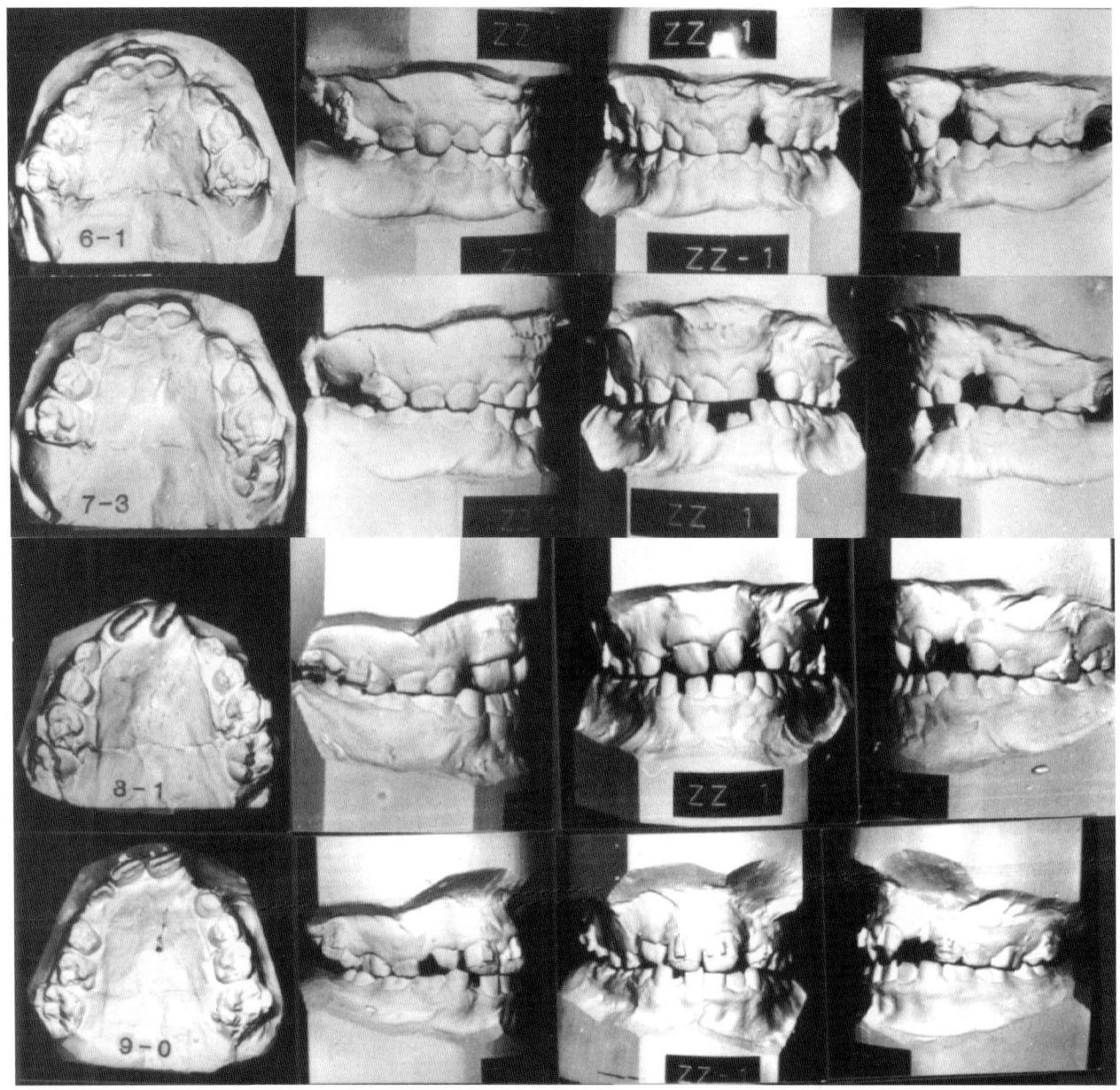

Fig 13–6. *(continued)*
6-1. Fixed retainer maintained the correction. Secondary alveolar bone graft was performed at 7 years, 3 months of age.

9-0. The maxillary anterior teeth were rotated for aesthetic reasons.

(continued)

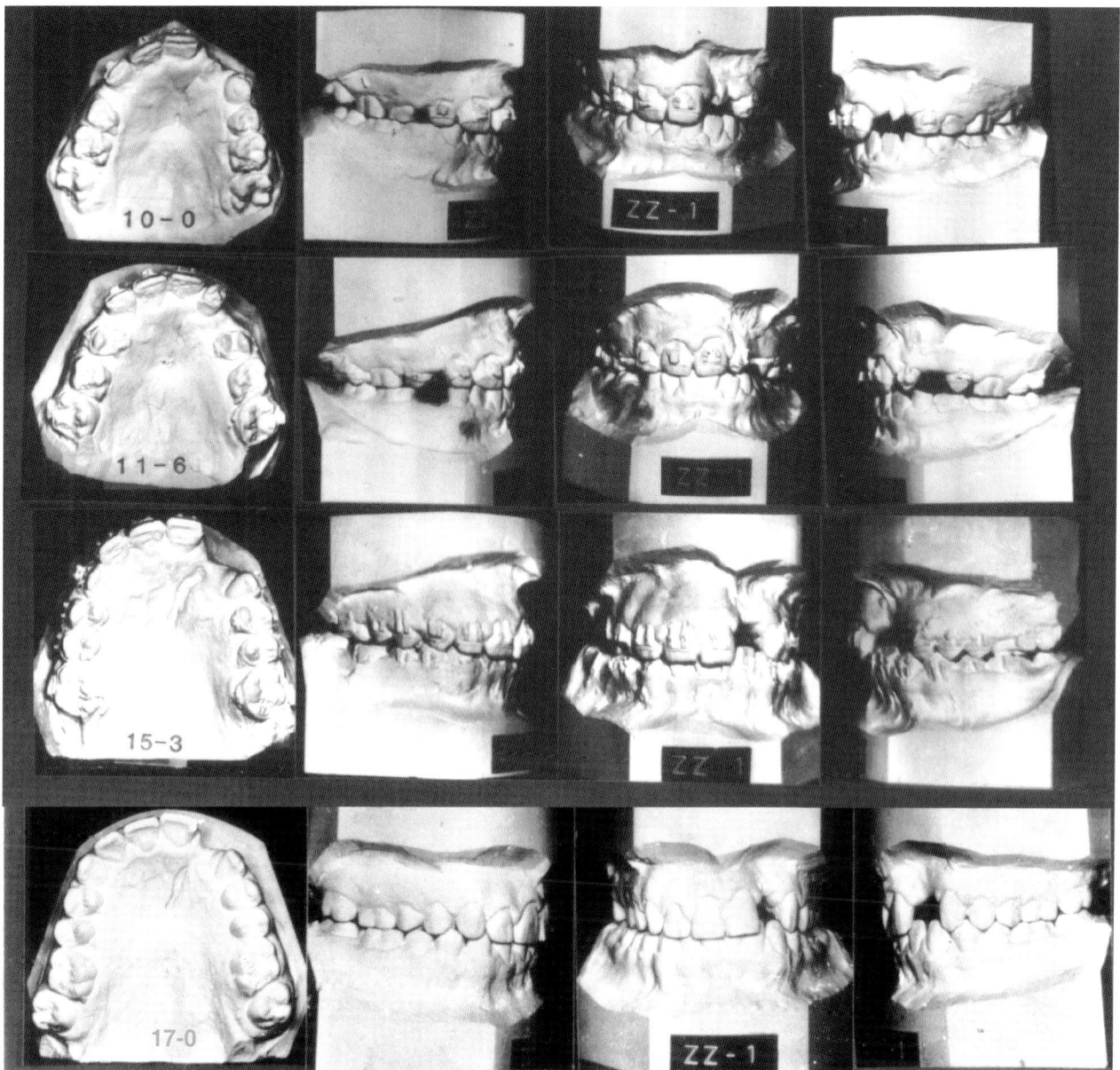

Fig 13–6. *(continued)*
11-6. The left lateral incisor is now in place within the arch. As a result of poor root development, it had to be extracted.
11-6. Conventional orthodontics was instituted and completed by **15-3**. Maxillary fistula was surgically closed at 16-3, and the arch form maintained with a removable Hawley retainer with a lateral incisor pontic. **17-0.** Final occlusion.

Comment: Because most cleft palatal arches have some degree of osteogenic deficiency, when all bicuspids are retained, it is usual for the second molars to be blocked out and be impossible to position within the arch. This then necessitates their removal with possible replacement by the still unerupted third molars. In some instances, a small palatal fistula may not pose a speech problem or be a source of nasal drainage

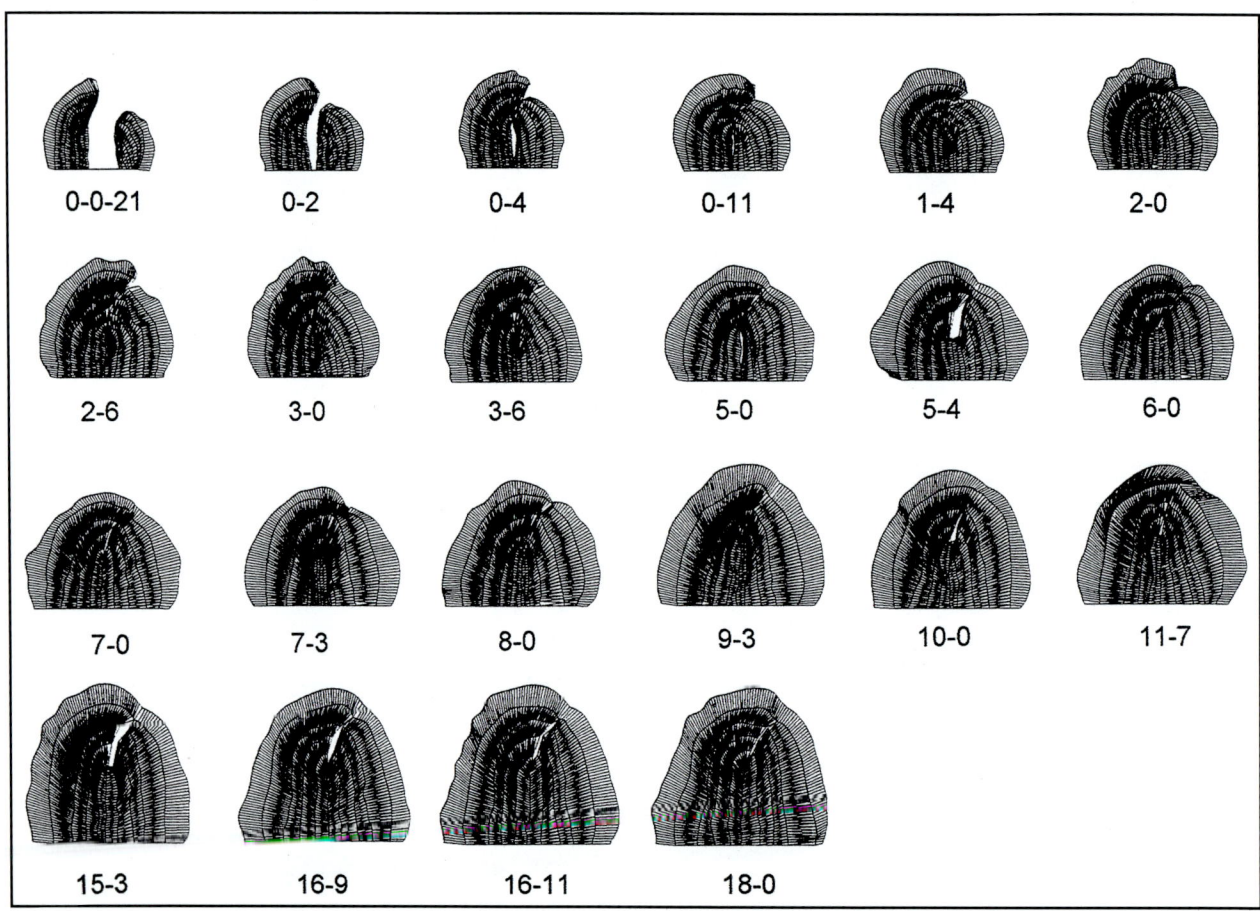

Fig 13–7. Case KC (ZZ-1). Computer-generated drawings of serial casts which are in the same scale. The soft palate was united at 2 months and the hard palate closed at 15 months. This series demonstrates a rapid reduction in palatal cleft size with molding action and palatal growth. A palatal "fistula" was exposed when the cleft buccal segment was expanded to correct the crossbite. It was closed but reappeared when final orthopedic treatment moved the palatal segments slightly apart. The "fistula" did not penetrate into the nasal chamber. Therefore, it did not pose a speech or feeding problem.

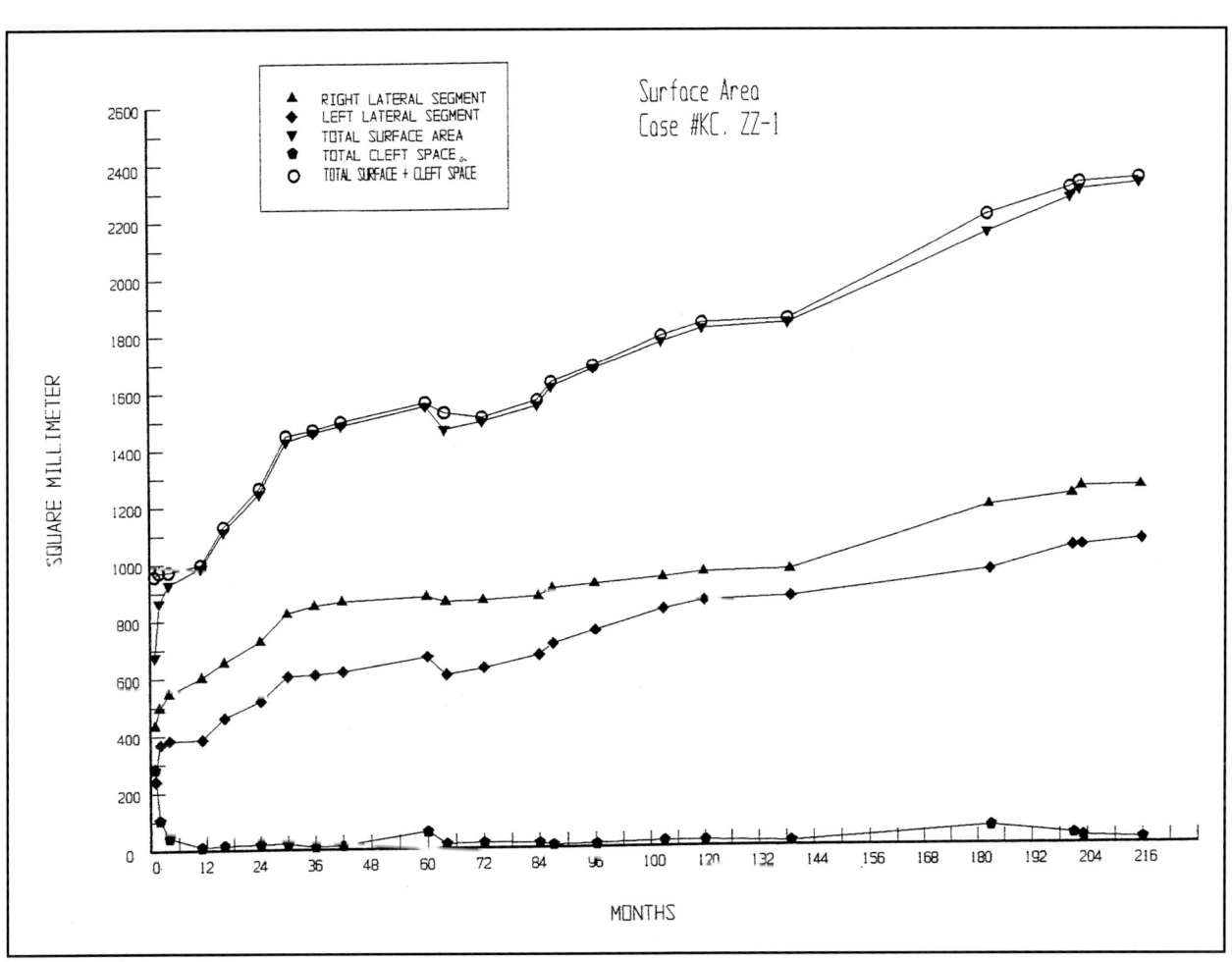

Fig 13-8. Case KC (ZZ-1). The palatal growth chart shows: (1) rapid growth acceleration in the first year which continues only slightly decreased until 36 months; (2) the palatal growth rate did not diminish after palatal surgery at 15 months; palatal growth slowed between 60 and 84 months, and then steadily increased; between 60 and 120 months, the growth of the lesser cleft segment increased more rapidly than the noncleft segment; and (5) the palatal growth rate accelerated after 136 months.

Comment: Based on palatal growth acceleration rates and the developing occlusion, one can safely conclude that palatal surgery did not interfere with its growth and development.

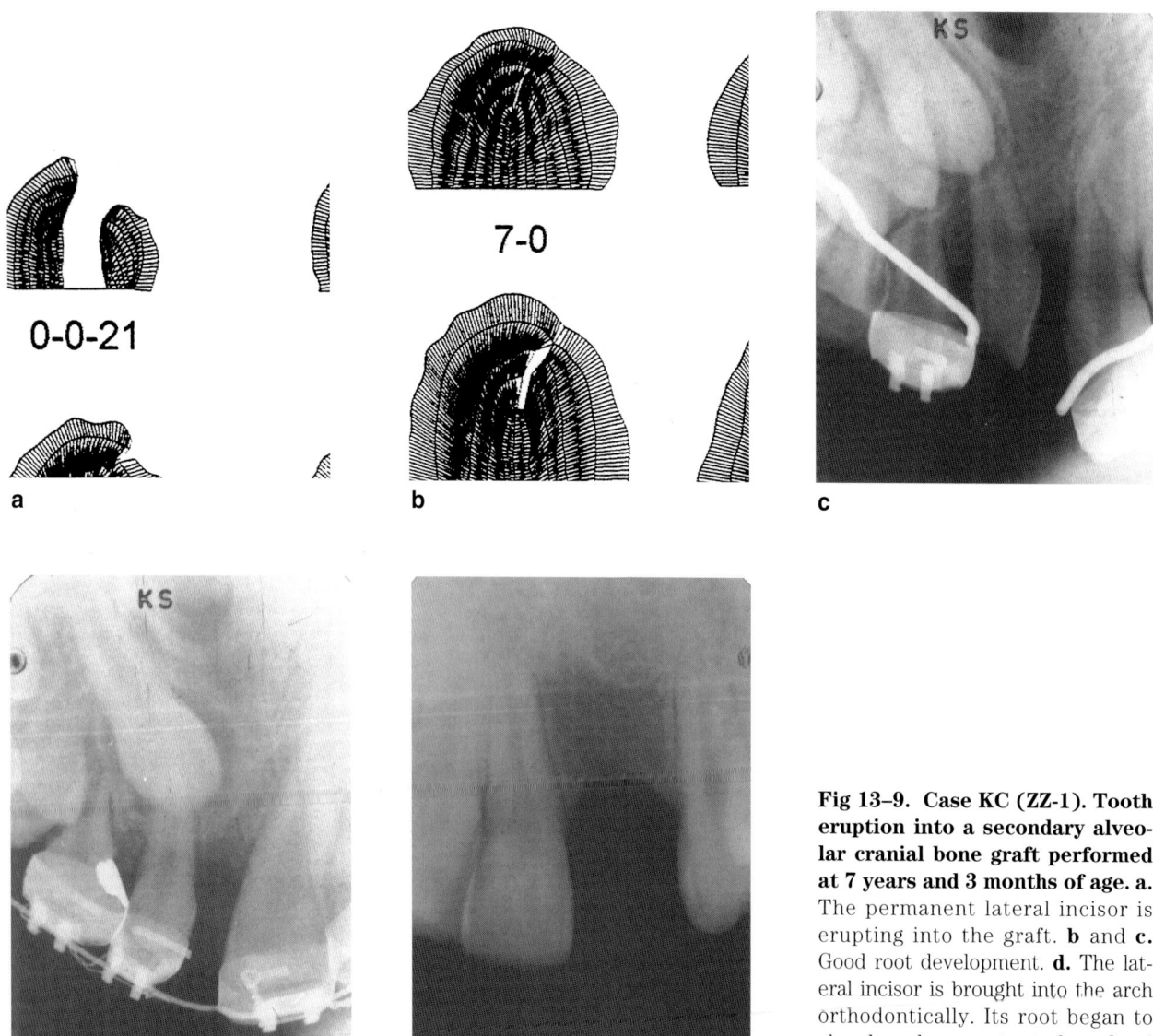

Fig 13–9. Case KC (ZZ-1). Tooth eruption into a secondary alveolar cranial bone graft performed at 7 years and 3 months of age. **a.** The permanent lateral incisor is erupting into the graft. **b** and **c.** Good root development. **d.** The lateral incisor is brought into the arch orthodontically. Its root began to absorb and was extracted. **e.** Good alveolar bone in the cleft space.

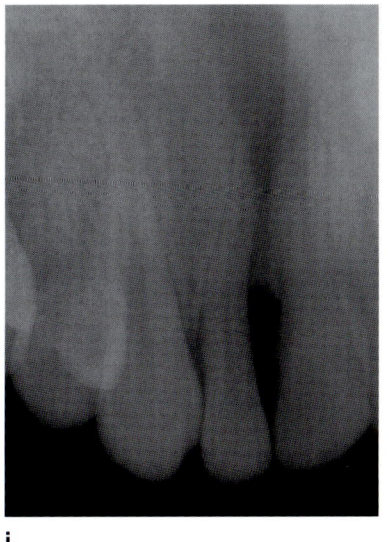
j

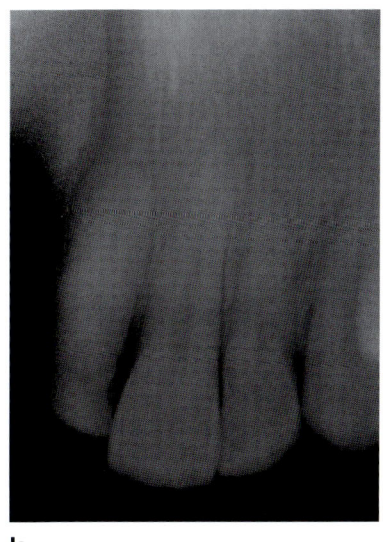
k

SERIAL CASTS

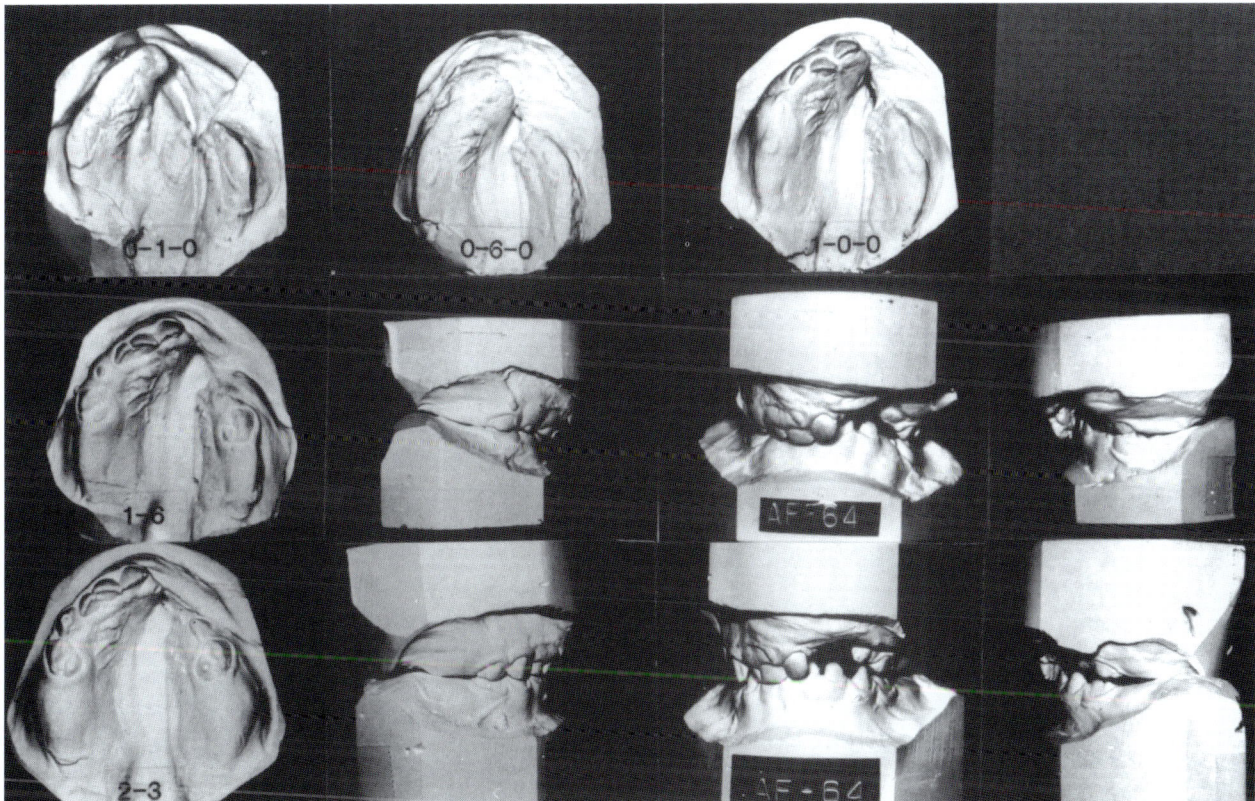

Fig 13–13. Serial casts of Case JK. Newborn: The nasal septum bows toward the cleft segment creating a very small cleft space. The great distance between alveolar segments is due to the upward tilt of the larger segment coupled with a small cleft segment. **0-6-0.** After the lip is united, both palatal segments move toward the midline narrowing the cleft space, more on the right than the left side. However, the alveolar segments still do not meet due to the inferior turbinate on the lesser segment making premature contact with the septum preventing the lesser palatal segment from further medial movement. Note that the premaxillary portion of the larger segment has not moved medioposteriorly. **1-0-0**, **1-6**, **2-3**, and **3-2.** The palatal segments are still apart. **5-3.** After removal of the inferior turbinate and

239

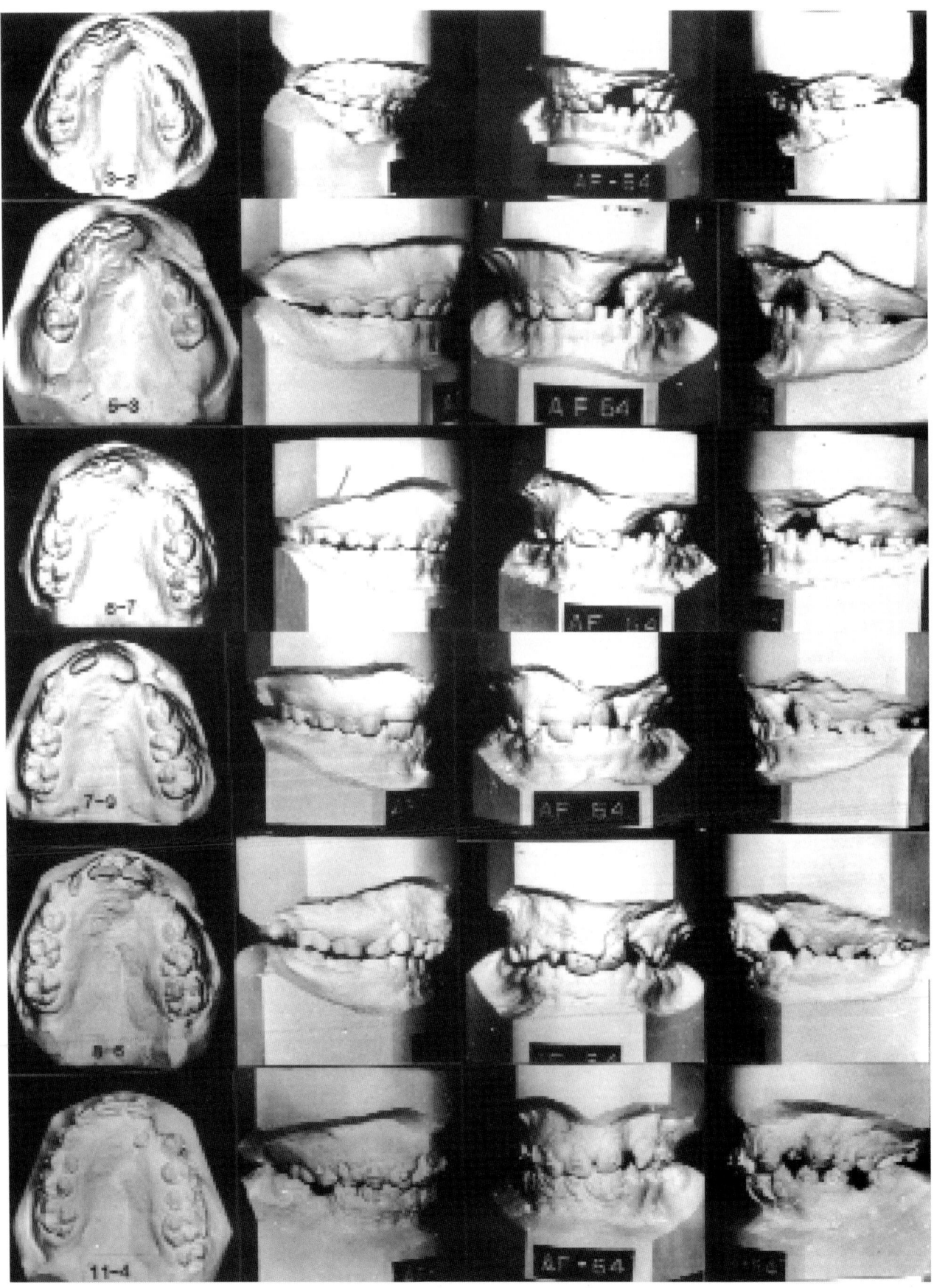

Fig 13-13. (continued)

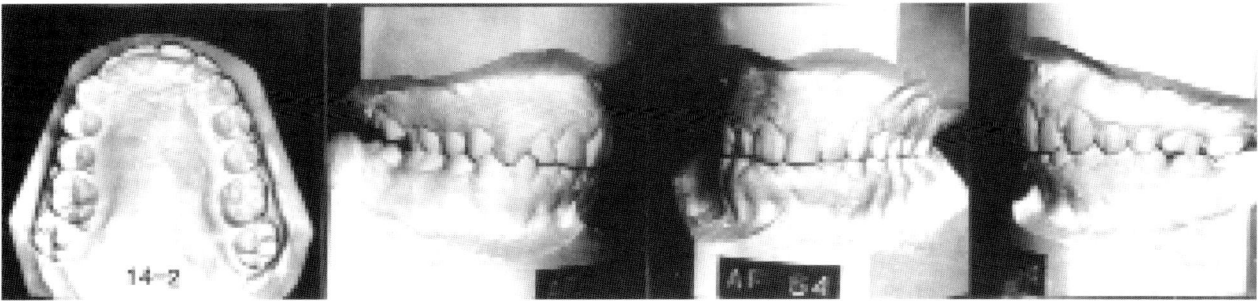

Fig 13–13. *(continued)*
with palatal closure, the tissue contracture created by the modified von Langenbeck procedure pulls the palatal segments together, placing the buccal teeth in the cleft segment in crossbite. **6-7.** The palatal segments have been expanded. **7-9.** Without palatal arch retention the crossbite returned. The ectopically erupted left central incisor is in crossbite. **8-6.** Arch expansion mechanics was reinstituted and the left central incisor advanced into proper overjet. **11-4** and **14-2.** Final orthodontic treatment was instituted and completed when 14 years of age. The impacted left lateral incisor was brought into alignment through the secondary alveolar cranial bone graft.

Comment: After secondary alveolar bone grafting, arch expansion in most cases is stable. However, in cases where new bone does not extend to the nasal aperture, we believe the buccal crossbite has a good chance of returning. The left side was in Class 2 occlusion, because it was not certain that the left lateral incisor could be properly aligned. If it was to be extracted, the cuspid would be positioned in the lateral incisor space.

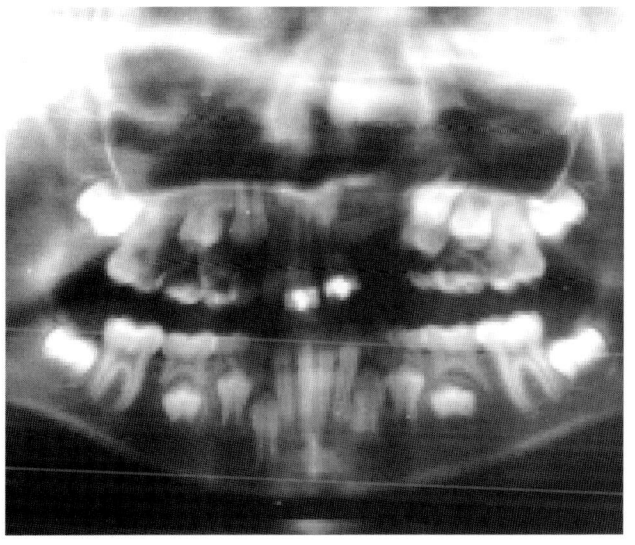

a

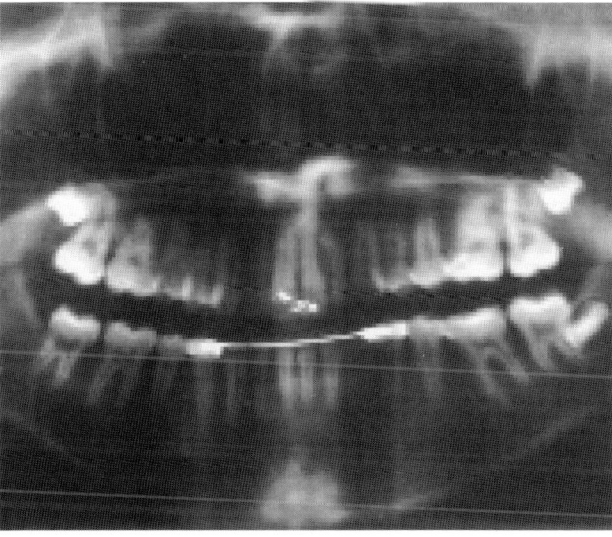

b

Fig 13–14. Case JK (AF-64). a. Panorex: The left lateral incisor is palatally and horizontally impacted. **b.** After treatment, the lateral incisor is well-aligned within the arch. Note that the curvature to the root possibly occurred before it was fully formed and during orthodontic movement.

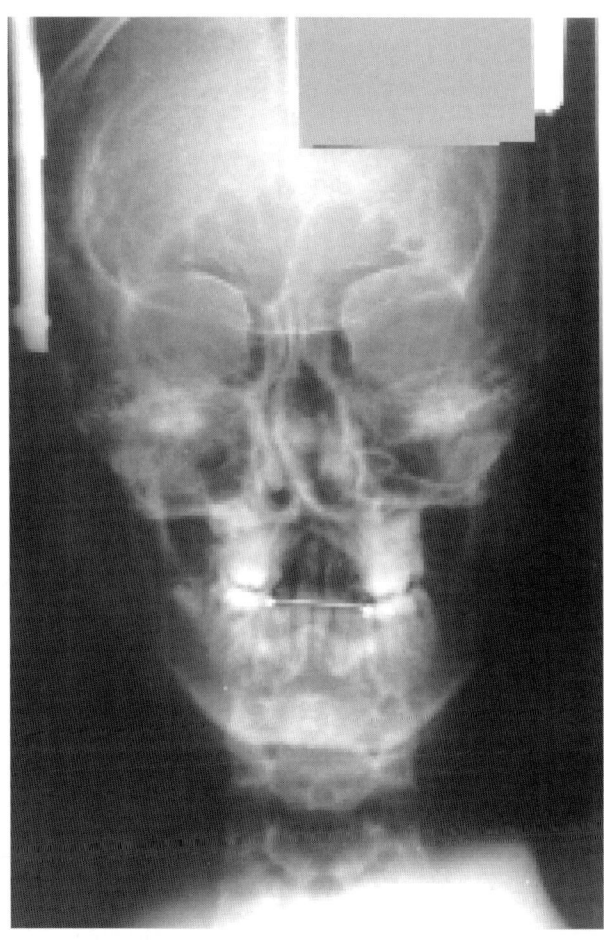

Fig 13–15. Case JK (AF-64). **Frontal cephaloradiograph shows that the nasal chamber on the cleft side is very narrow with a very flattened inferior conchae.** The nasal septum is extremely bowed toward the cleft side. A lower cuspid to cuspid retainer is being worn

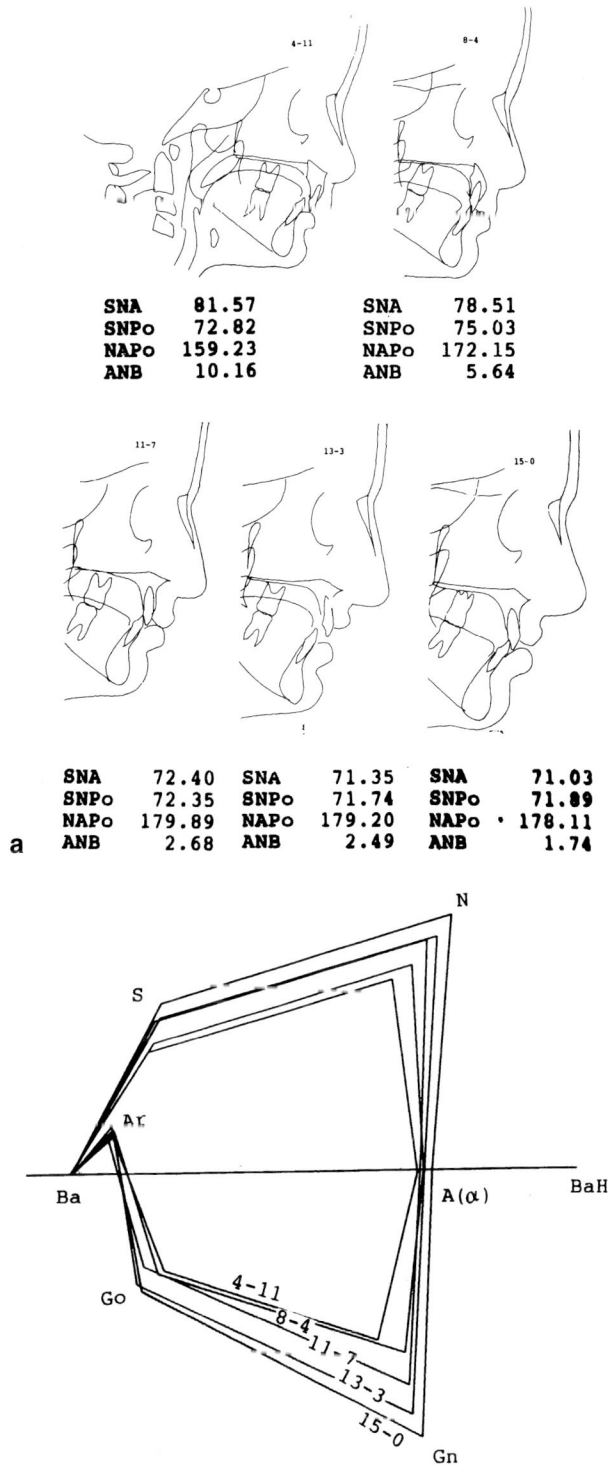

Fig 13–16. Case JK (AF-64). a. Skeletal and soft tissue profile changes shown by lateral cephalometrics. The anterior projection of the midface and mandible relative to the anterior cranial base decreases with time as the profile flattens. The decreasing ANB angle reflects this change. **b.** Superimposed polygons using the Basion-Horizontal method. This series clearly shows that the flattening of the skeletal facial profile occurred around 8 years of age and was brought about by the growth at the anterior cranial base and the mandible whose plane angle increased with time. There was almost no forward growth of the midface between 4-11 and 13-3 years with only a small postpubertal growth increment between 13-3 and 15-0 years of age.

CASE REPORT: EXCELLENT PALATAL AND FACIAL GROWTH IN CUCLP

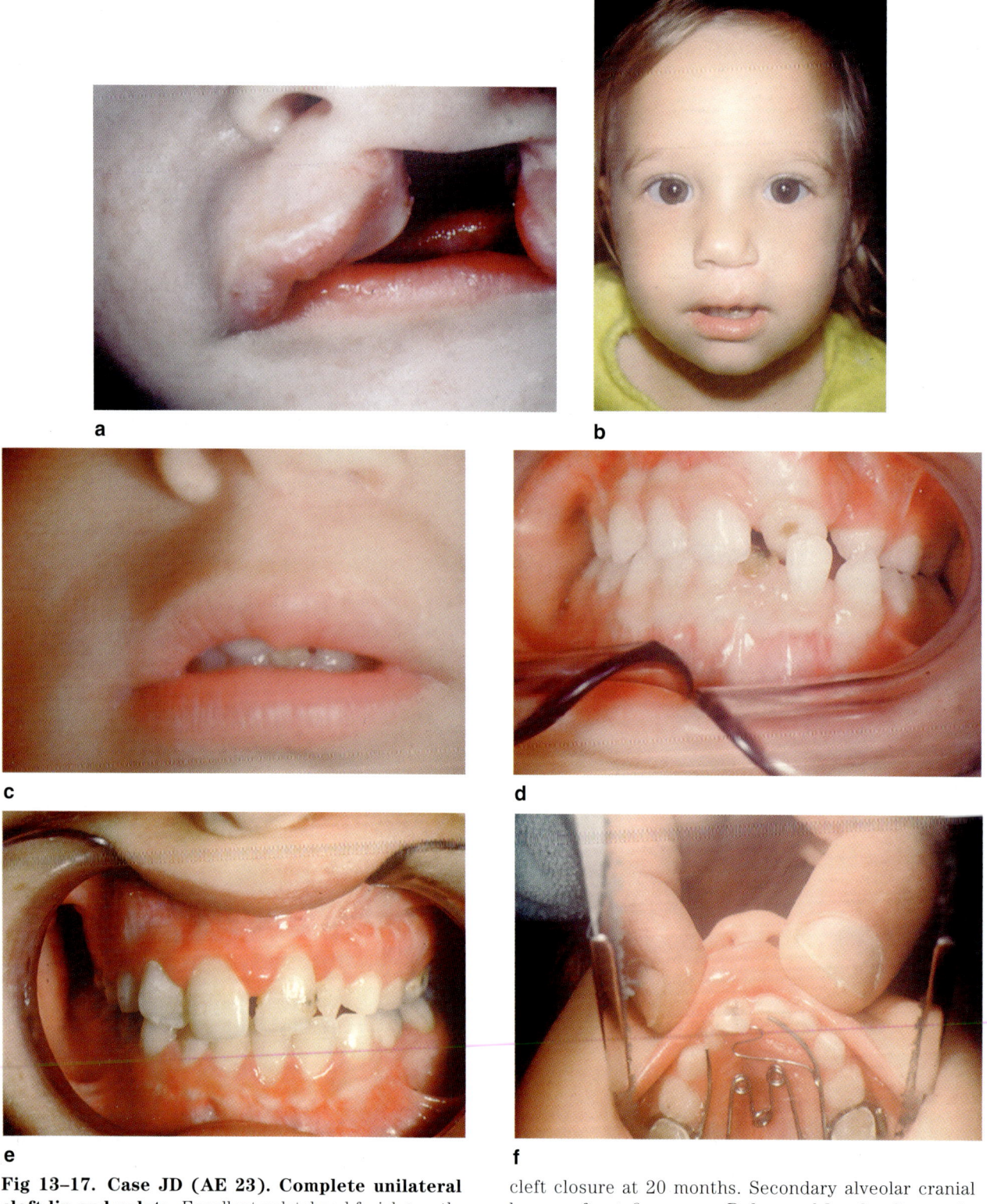

Fig 13–17. Case JD (AE 23). Complete unilateral cleft lip and palate. Excellent palatal and facial growth. A relatively large cleft space necessitated postponement of palatal closure until 20 months. Early secondary alveolar bone graft. *Surgical history:* Lip adhesion at 3 months followed by Rotation Advancement definitive lip repair at 6 months. Modified von Langenbeck palatal cleft closure at 20 months. Secondary alveolar cranial bone grafts at 6 years. **a.** Before and **b.** after lip repair. **c.** 2 years, 5 months. Anterior and buccal crossbite. **e** and **f.** 3 years, 4 months. Anterior and buccal crossbite correction with fixed palatal expander.

(continued)

CASE REPORT: CUCLP-PROTRACTION MAXILLARY ORTHOPEDICS TO CORRECT MIDFACIAL RECESSIVENESS

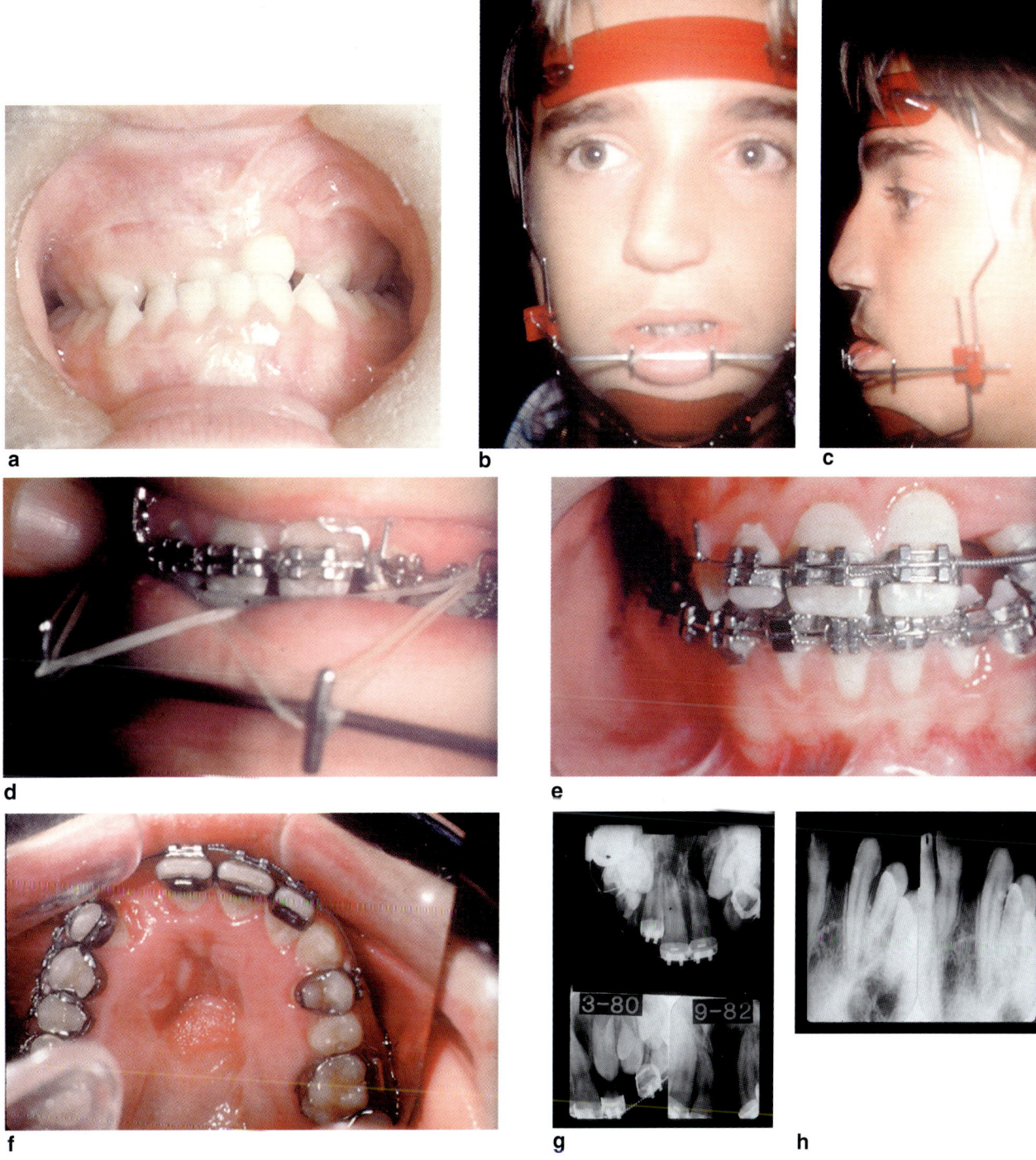

Fig 13–20. Case AB (EE-49). UCLP illustrating use of protraction maxillary orthopedics to correct midfacial retrussiveness secondary to growth-inhibiting scar tissue and/or maxillary osteogenic deficiency. *Surgical history:* Lip closure at 6 months. Hard and soft palate cleft closure at 16 months using an Island flap pushback. Secondary alveolar cranial bone graft at 10 years of age. **a.** 2½ years of age. Anterior and bilateral buccal crossbite could not be corrected in the deciduous or mixed dentition. **b**, **c**, and **d.** Orthodontic-orthopedic forces to correct an anterior crossbite were initiated at 12 years of age using a Delaire-style protraction facial mask. **e** and **f.** Ideal Class I (neutroclusion) with an ideal overjet and overbite. Palatal view shows thick transpalatal scar tissue caused by the Island flap. **g** and **h.** Periapical films after secondary alveolar cranial bone graft. No left lateral incisor is present, but good cleft space closure is evident.

(continued)

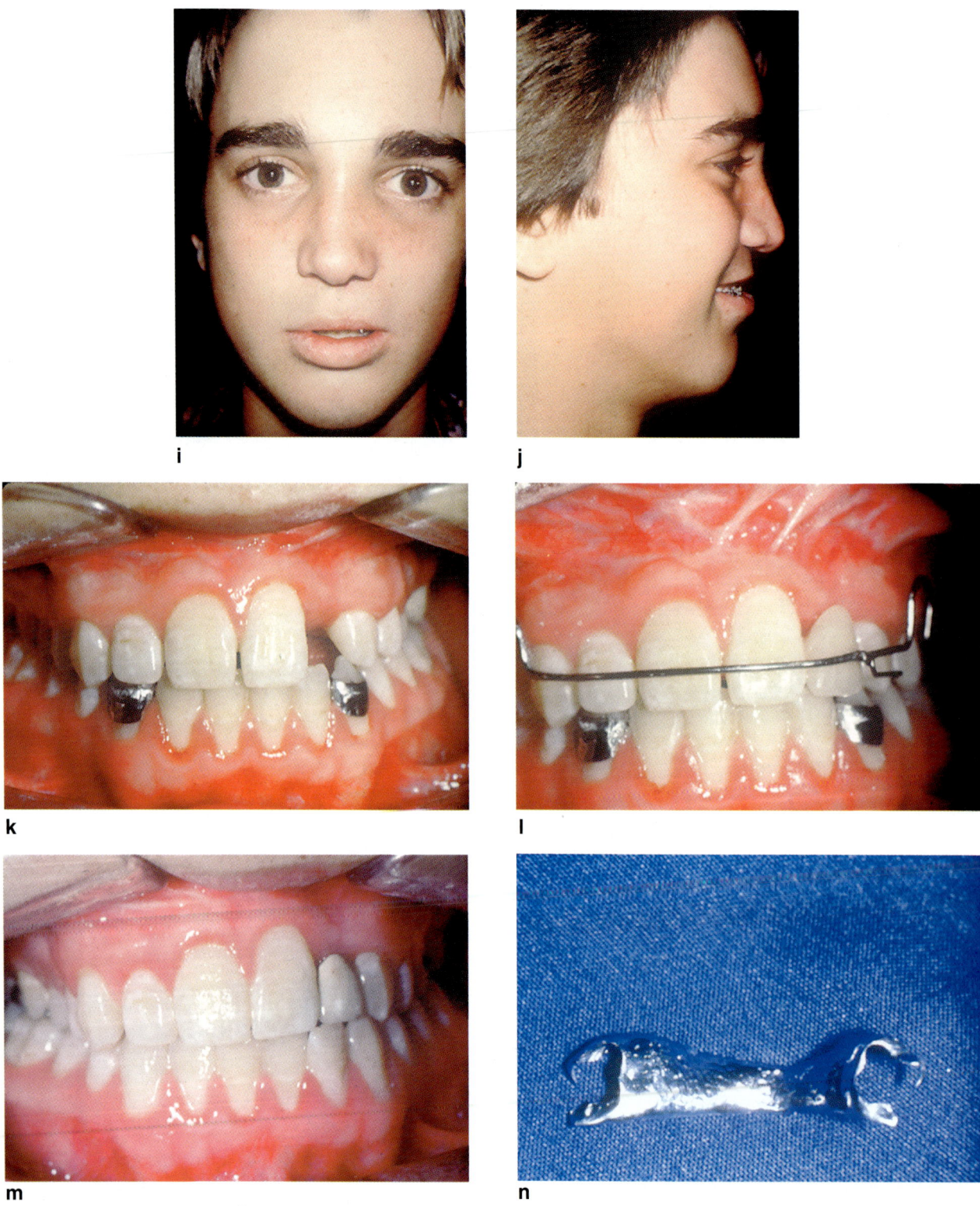

Fig 13–20. (continued)
i. and **j.** Facial photographs at 17 years of age showing good skeletal and soft tissue proportions. **k.** Ideal Class I (neutroocclusion). **l.** and **m.** 17 years of age wearing a Maryland fixed bridge to replace the missing lateral incisor. This is only a temporary solution until placement of a dental implant or a sturdier fixed bridge. **n.** A cast gold transpalatal removable brace is used to maintain the corrected arch form. Palatal collapse is predictable in the presence of transpalatal scar tissue. Thus, good occlusion requires some form of permanent arch retention.

SERIAL CASTS

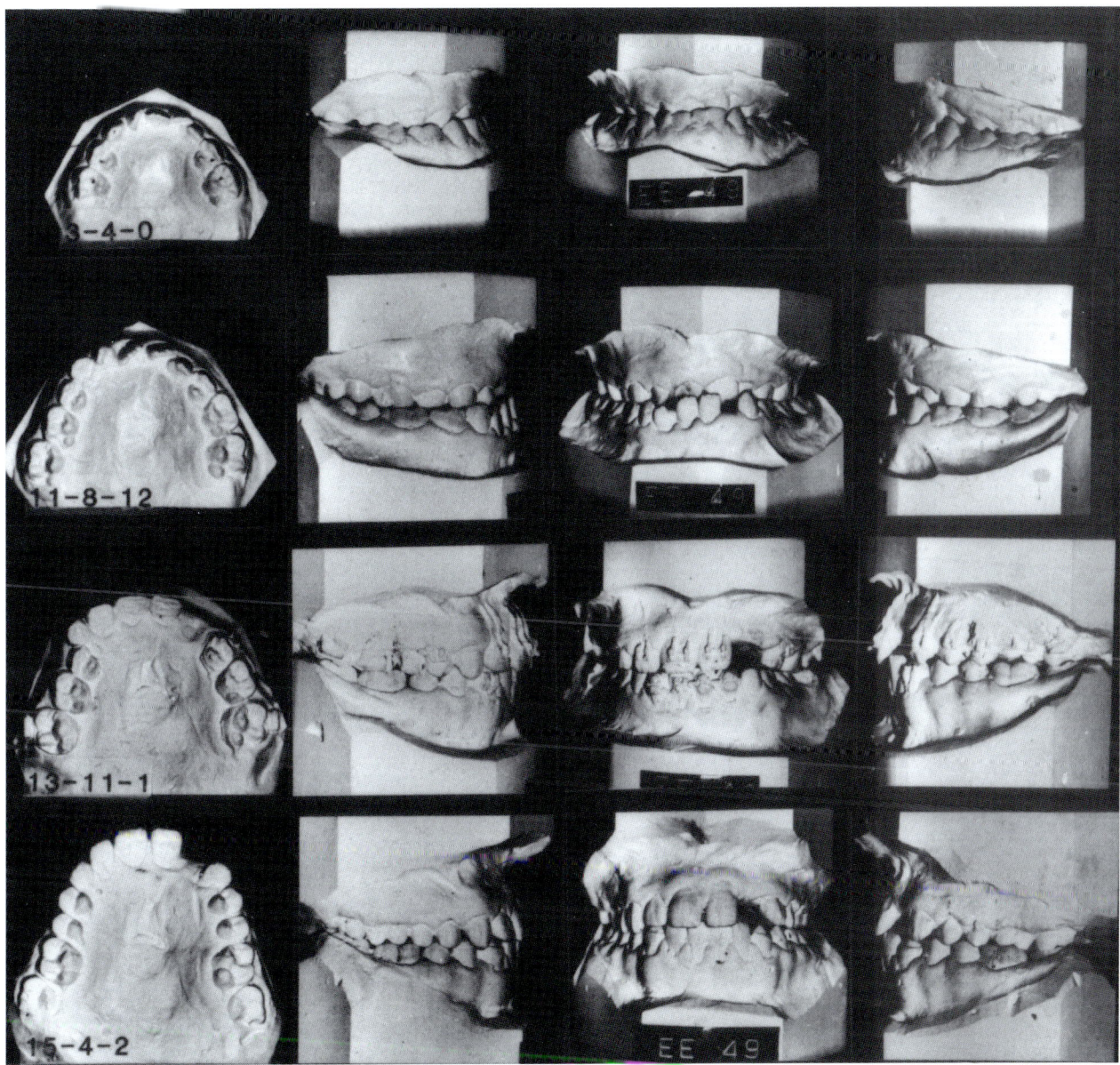

Fig 13–21. Serial casts of Case AB. 3-4-0. After Island flap hard and soft palate closure at 16 months of age resulting in bilateral buccal and anterior crossbites. **11-8-12.** Occlusion just prior to orthodontic treatment. **13-11-1.** After protraction mechanics using a Delaire style facial mask. **15-4-2.** Occlusion after orthodontics.

Comments: Because maxillary deficiency is almost always present "A" point (subnasal) in the premaxillary area needs to be brought forward by using labile root torque on a rectangular arch

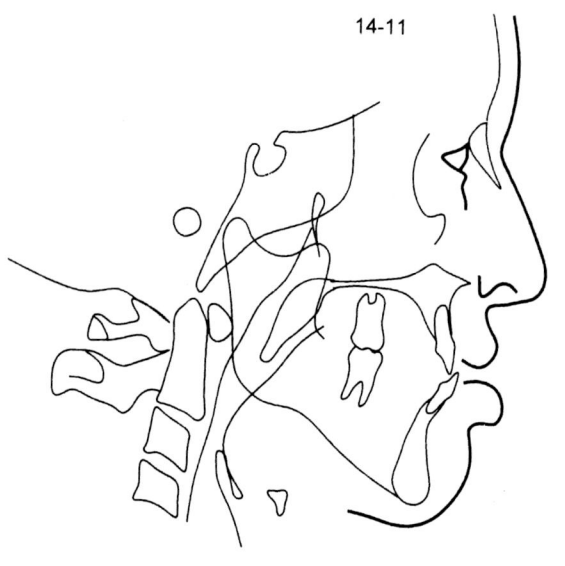
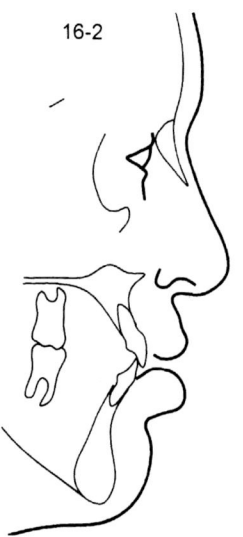

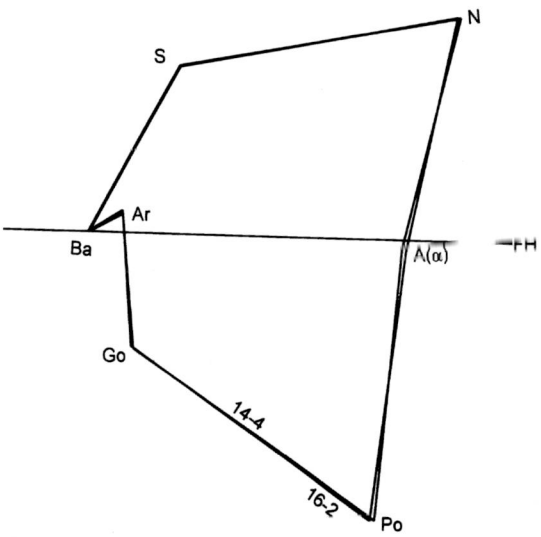

Fig 13-22. Case AB. a. Cephalometric tracings at 14-11 and 16-2. **b.** Superimposed polygons using Basion Horizontal method. A slight change in midfacial protrusion is noted after protraction forces were used to correct the midfacial retrusion and anterior crossbite. In this case the changes in the maxillary incisor axial inclination aided anterior crossbite correction more than maxillary protraction.

REFERENCES

1. Pruzansky S. Factors determining arch form in clefts of the lip and palate. *Am J Orthod.* 1955;41:827.
2. Subtelny JD. Width of the nasopharynx and related anatomic structures in normal and unoperated cleft palate children. *Am J Orthod.* 1955;41:889–909.
3. Aduss H, Pruzansky S. The nasal cavity in complete unilateral cleft lip and palate. *Arch Otolaryng.* 1967;85:53–61.
4. Bergland O. Treatment of cleft palate malocclusion in the mixed and permanent dentition. *Fortschr Kiefer Gesichtschir.* 1973;16/17:571–574.
5. Bergland O, Sidhu SS. Occlusal changes from the deciduous to the early mixed dentition in unilateral complete clefts. *Cleft Palate J.* 1974;11:317–326.
6. Berkowitz S. Timing cleft palate closure-age should not be the sole determinant. In: Cohen MM Jr, Rollnick BR, eds. *J Craniofac Gen and Devel Biol.* 1985;1(Suppl):69–83.
7. Latham RA. Orthopaedic advancement of the cleft maxillary segment: a preliminary report. *Cleft Palate J.* 1980;17:227.
8. McNeil CK. Orthodontic procedures in the treatment of congenital cleft palate. *Dent Rec.* 1950;70:126–132.
9. Semb G. A study of facial growth in patients with unilateral cleft lip and palate treated by the Oslo CLP team. *Cleft Palate Craniofac J.* 1991;28:1–47
10. Ross RB. Treatment variables affecting facial growth in complete unilateral cleft lip and palate. *Cleft Palate J.* 1987;24:

Part 1:	Treatment affecting growth.	5–23
Part 2:	Presurgical orthopedics.	24–32
Part 3:	Alveolus repair and bone grafting.	33–44
Part 4:	Repair of the cleft lip.	45–53
Part 5:	Timing of palate repair.	54–63
Part 6:	Techniques of palate repair.	64–70
Part 7:	An overview of treatment and facial growth.	71–77

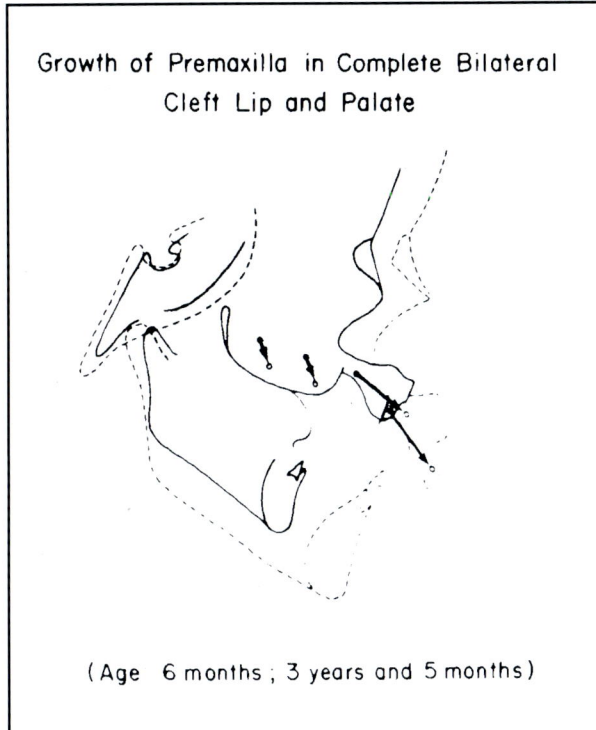

Fig 14–4. **To test growth at the premaxillar vomerine suture (PVS) in complete bilateral cleft of the lip and palate, two pairs of metal pellets were placed on either side of the PVS at 6 months of age.** At 3 years, 5 months of age, the distance between the anterior and posterior sets of pellets had increased with the growth at PVS. Note that there was no change in distance within each set of metal pellets. (Courtesy of Sam Pruzansky.)

midface with a Class 3 malocclusion. Semb[28] and Ross[29] established that, in the cleft population, both the maxilla and mandible—not solely the maxilla—are retropositioned within the face. If McNeil's[30] belief that the bilateral cleft palatal segments are left behind in their growth was accurate, a greater proportion of the cases must show a Class 3 malocclusion of one or both sides. As previously mentioned, Berkowitz's[31] mixed cross-sectional study of the occlusion in CBCLP determined that the maxillary complex was not positioned posteriorly relative to the mandible. Also, a buccal crossbite is not a predictable outcome, as McNeil had suggested. He therefore concluded that, although the midface and mandible are positioned posteriorly within the face, the maxilla is not retropositioned relative to the mandible and that McNeil's hypothesis that the maxilla in complete clefts of the lip and palate is retruded and needs to be brought forward was in error.

LONG-TERM RESULTS

Lateral Cephalometric Facial Growth Findings

Semb[25] conducted a serial lateral and frontal cephalometric study of 90 cases from the Oslo archives with bilateral cleft lip and palate. Since 1962 the treatment procedure has involved uniting the lip and closing the hard palate cleft space in two stages. No presurgical orthodontics were utilized because the surgeon and Bergland, an orthodontist and director of the program, believed that any bilateral cleft lip can be closed without presurgical palatal manipulation. In the period spanning 1950 to 1960, a von Langenbeck procedure was performed to close the hard-palate cleft between 3 and 4 years of age; after 1960, the timing of the closure was reduced to 18 months of age. Secondary alveolar bone grafting using cancellous iliac crest bone was performed prior to the eruption of the permanent canine teeth.

Twenty-five percent of the cases needed superior-based pharyngeal flaps, which were performed before the child started school. No orthodontics were utilized in the deciduous dentition. Protraction headgear was used in the mixed dentition in one third of the cases. Fixed retention was necessary in all cases. Semb's study showed that: (1) the maxilla progressively receded over time; (2) the mandible was retrusive with a steep mandibular plane with an increased gonial angle; (3) anterior lower-face height was elongated and posterior facial height reduced; (4) the facial growth pattern was notably different from the normal Bolton standards: (a) male and female facial growth patterns were similar except that the males' linear dimensions were larger; (b) the prominent premaxilla

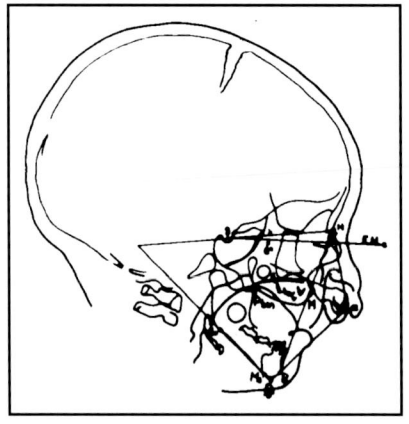
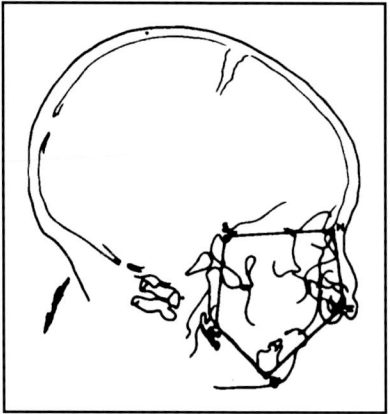
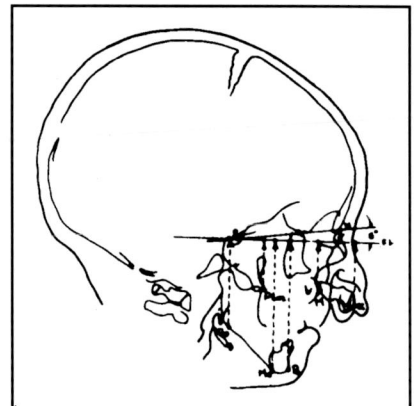

a

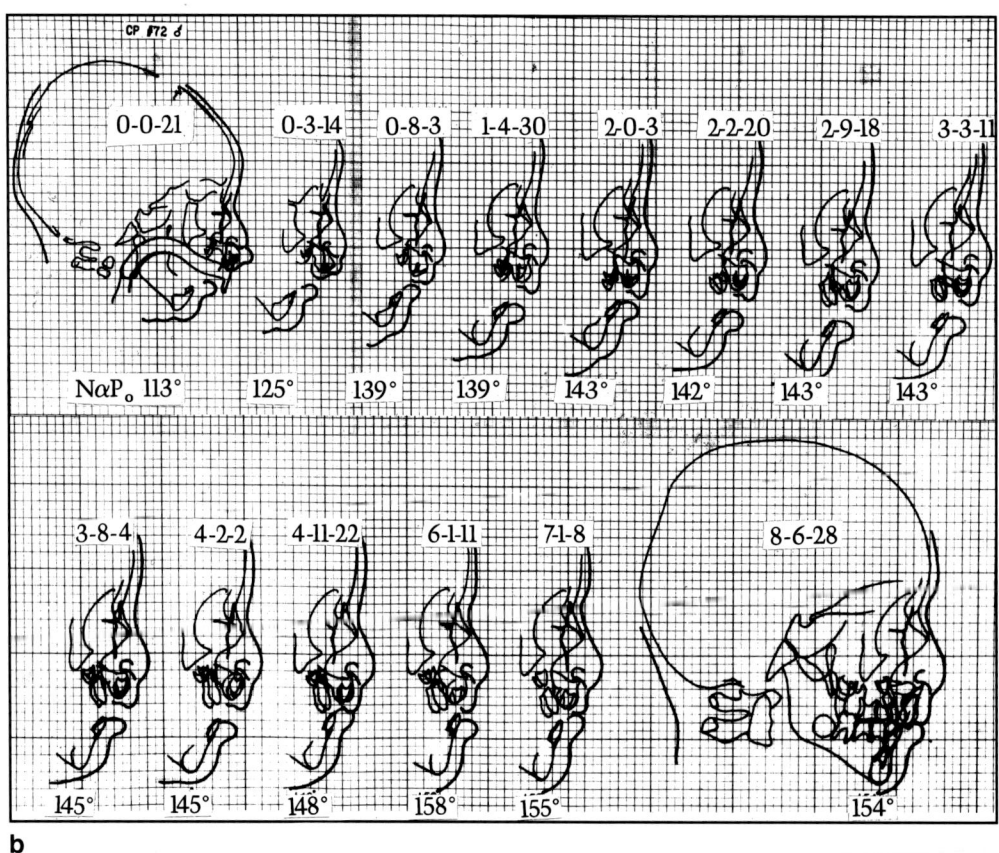

b

Fig 14–5. a. A method used to show serial changes in facial growth and development in CBCLP using Sella for registration while superimposing on the anterior cranial base. Facial angles and landmarks (*upper left*): Nasion (N), Pogonion (Po), Gonion (Go), Sella (S), Alpha (α) most anterior point on the premaxilla, Menton (Me), constructed Frankfort horizontal (FHc), Anterior point of the lateral palatal processes (M), Pterygomaxillary fissure (Ptm). Facial polygon (*upper middle*) drawn connecting landmarks S-N-α-Po-Me-Go-S. Landmark points (*upper right*) projected to a constructed Frankfort horizontal line which is drawn 6° from the anterior cranial base (SN) at S. **b.** An example of excellent facial growth. The cultural standard for a good aesthetic caucasian face is a "flat" face, having an angle of facial convexity of approximately 180°. Most newborn noncleft faces have a relatively acute facial profile associated with relative retrognathia which usually flattens with growth. Serial lateral cephalometric tracings showing changes in the angle of facial convexity (NαPo) from 113° to 154° in 8½ years.

(continued)

Fig 14–5. *(continued)*
c. Facial polygon of the case shown in b. Each polygon is super-imposed on SN and registered at Sella. The midfacial protrusion at (α) had not increased after 2 years, whereas both the anterior cranial base (N) and mandible had increased in size. The mandible grew forward and downward, flattening the facial profile. The timing of these growth changes is variable. **d.** Projection of landmark points to the constructed Frankfort horizontal line drawn 6° from SN at S. This growth projection system also shows that the midfacial protrusion did not increase after 2 years, whereas the forward projection of the mandibular body increased markedly until 8½ years of age. These are the main factors leading to the flattening of the facial profile. Good facial growth changes can occur early or late. (From Berkowitz S. *Growth of the Face with Bilateral Cleft Lip and Palate from 1 Month to 8 Years of Age.* Chicago, Ill: University of Illinois School of Dentistry; 1959. Thesis.)

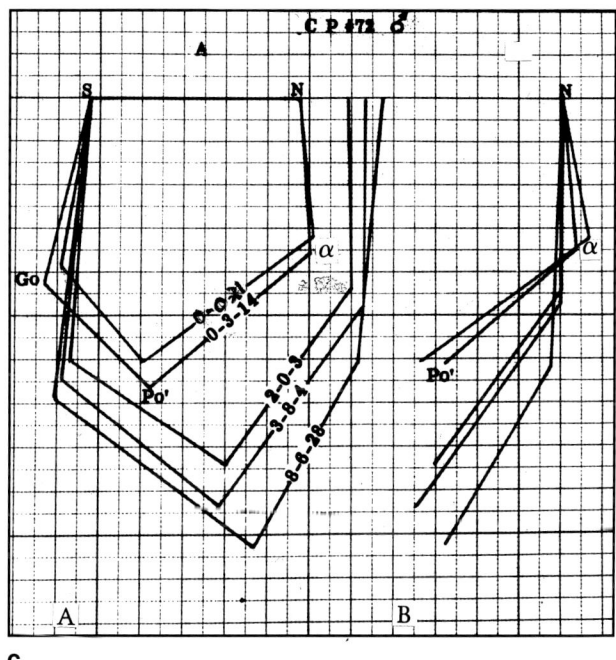

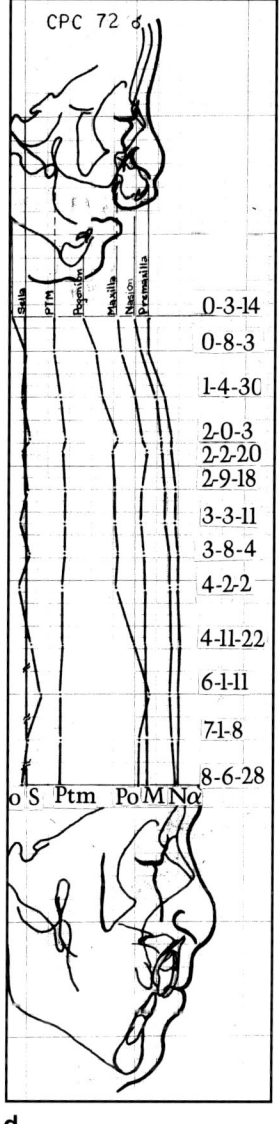

would gradually realign in the preschool years; and (c) surgical premaxillary setback was never required. Berkowitz's unpublished data are very similar.

Vargervik's[19] cross-sectional study of 51 males with BCLP treated with a variety of primary procedures (excluding premaxillary setback) showed cephalometric profile values similar to those reported by Hellquist et al,[32] Dahl,[33] Smahel,[34] Semb,[28] and Friede and Johanson.[35] The Oslo team's average for maxillary prominence and lower-face height were slightly more favorable. Narula and Ross,[36] reporting cross-sectional data on thirty 6-year-old subjects and mixed longitudinal data on 34 subjects with BCLP treated conventionally without surgical setback and vomer flap, concluded the maxillary length reached normal values at 16 years of age.

In the Swedish sample followed longitudinally by Hellquist et al,[32] similar facial convexity was also noted, although both the maxilla and mandible were reported to be slightly more prominent. The patients analyzed by Hellquist et al[30] had a two-stage lip closure, pushback palatoplasty, and, at an average age of 6, delayed periosteoplasty.

Friede and Johanson[35] reported facial growth in 13 Swedish children with bilateral clefts of the lip and palate (BCLP), five at age 7 and eight at age 10 years. The patients, who had had lip adhesion and vomer flap (without premaxillary setback) and velar closure with push back, also exhibited facial convexity similar to the Oslo sample.

Friede and Pruzansky's[4,5] cephalometric report of 27 North American children in three treatment

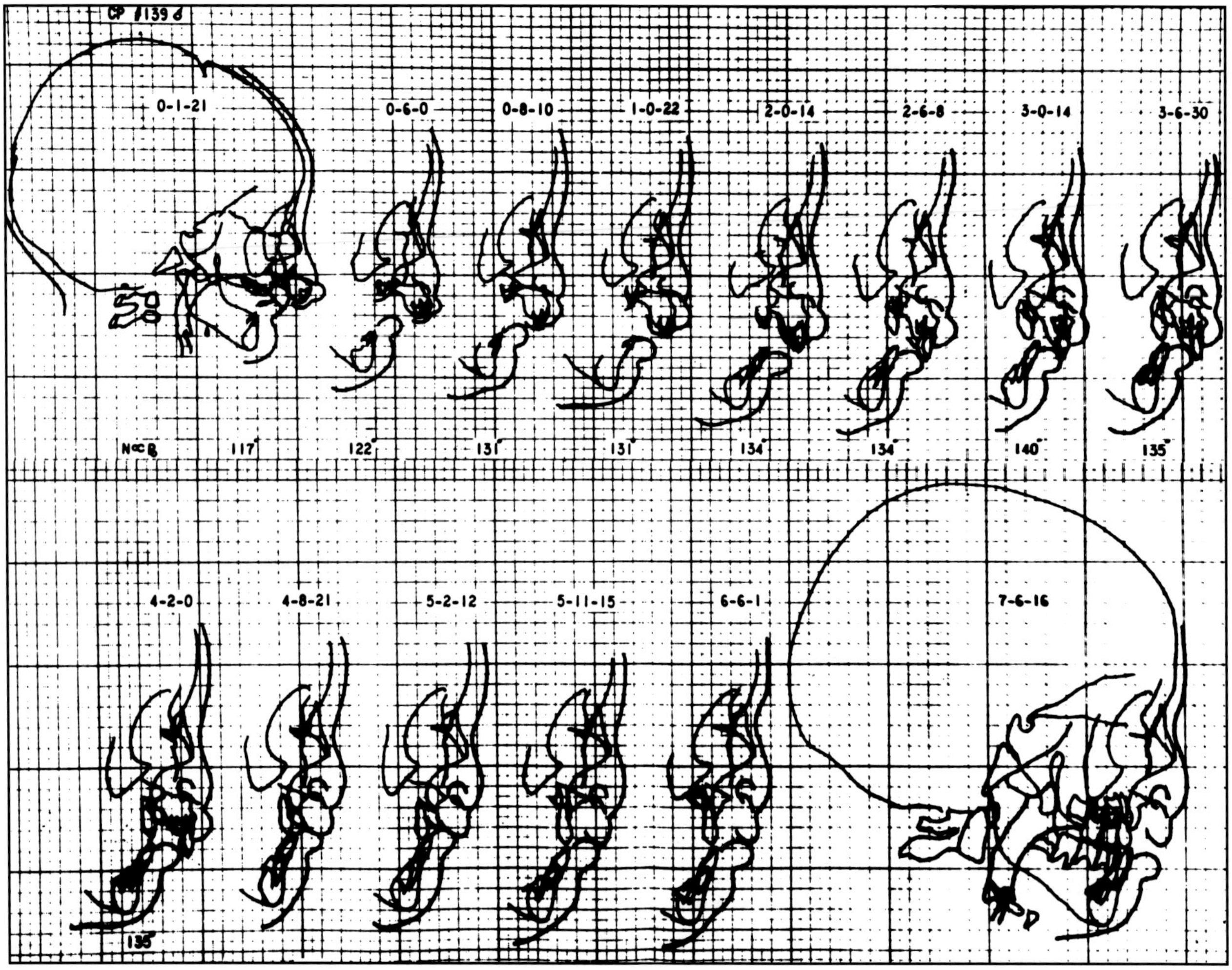

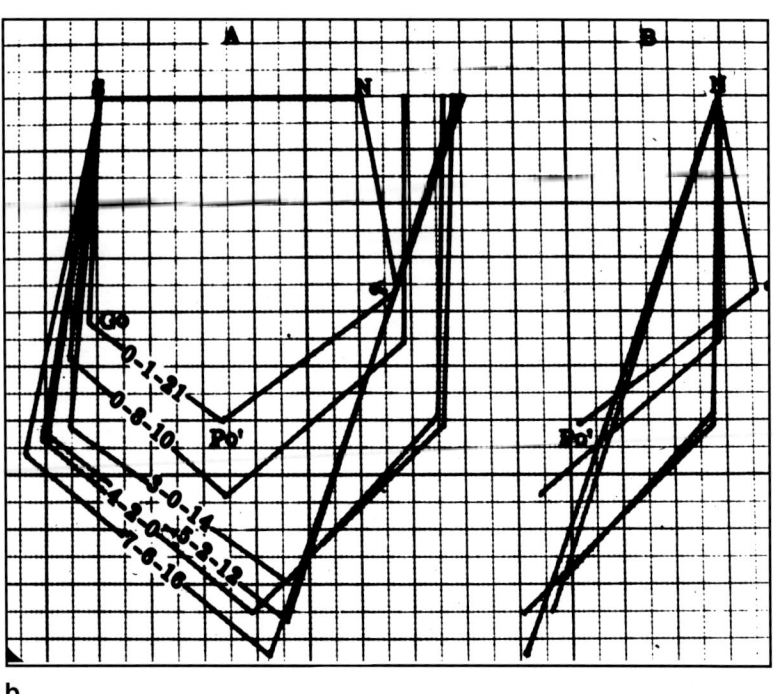

Fig 14-6. An example of "poor" facial growth changes. This evaluation is made when the acute facial profile seen at birth remains the same or worsens with time. **a.** Serial cephalometric tracings showing poor facial growth leading to premaxillary excision. The acute angle of facial convexity remained the same after 2 years. This treatment plan should be abandoned at any age even with severe midfacial protrusion. In similar growing faces, some clinicians believe premaxillary surgical setback is preferable for psychosocial reasons prior to starting elementary school. **b.** Superimposed polygons of case shown in **a** show a mandible that is growing vertically with very few horizontal growth increments. The premaxilla continued to grow forward although there was no forward growth between 3-0-14 and 4-2-0. Note the placement of the lower lip lingual to the premaxilla. The premaxilla was excised at 4-9.

COMPLETE BILATERAL CLEFT LIP AND PALATE

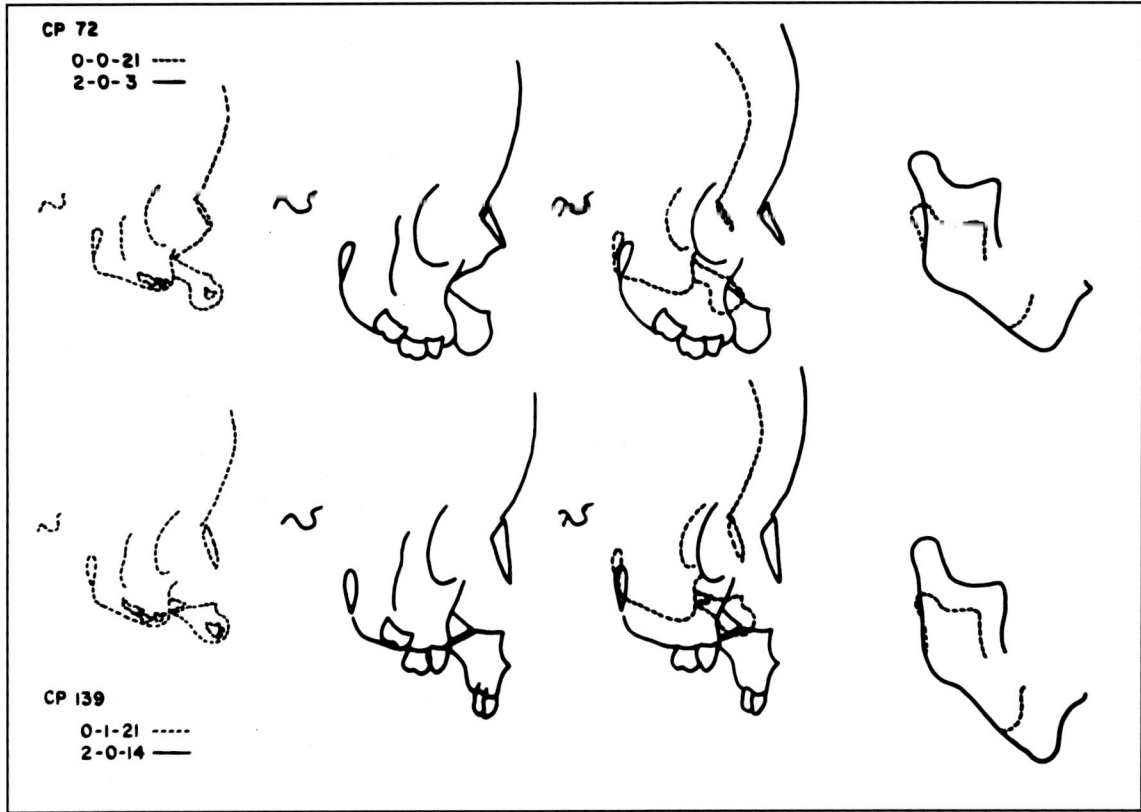

Fig 14–7. The first 2 years of maxillary and mandibular tracings of the cases with **good** (see Fig 14–5) and **bad** (see Fig 14–6) facial growth are compared to show the reasons for these evaluations. **CP-72:** Good facial growth. In this case, the degree of premaxillary protrusion relative to the lateral palatal segments (the anterior cleft space) was markedly reduced with growth. Premaxillary protrusion relative to the anterior cranial base was reduced as well. **CP-139:** Poor facial growth. The degree of premaxillary protrusion relative to the lateral palatal segments remained the same, while the premaxillary protrusion relative to the anterior cranial base increased.

Comments: Although mandibular growth in the two cases was similar in degree, the superimposed polygons show that the vertical direction of growth of the "bad" grower's mandible and not its size was the determining factor for the changes in the angle of facial convexity (NaPo). Tension at PVS created by the lower lip positioned lingual to the premaxilla increased premaxillary growth.

groups who were followed to 17 years of age do, however, show some differences in comparison with the Oslo sample. Six subjects treated by early premaxillary setback and seven treated by late setback (3 to 8 years of age) had profile values similar to those reported by the Oslo group. However, 14 subjects with no premaxillary setback had average values significantly more convex than those reported for the Oslo and other samples. None of the North American subjects had had vomer flaps, and it is implied that a more convex facial profile will be obtained if vomerplasty is excluded from primary surgery.

THE VOMER FLAP: GOOD OR BAD?

Semb's[28] report on the longitudinal data of the Oslo group is critical of those who condemn the vomer flap. She states that the possible growth-retarding effect of a vomer flap has been discussed by several authors (Pruzansky and Aduss,[37] Steinhardt,[38] Blocksma et al,[39] Friede and Morgan,[16] Friede and Johanson,[35] Delaire and Precious,[40,41] Friede and Pruzansky,[4] Friede et al,[42] Molsted,[43] Enmark et al[44]). Friede and

Pruzansky[4] observed more favorable growth in patients treated without a vomer flap; however, this is not a uniform finding in the comparative studies. Clinical centers not using a vomer flap have shown results similar to those where a vomer flap has been utilized. The extent to which the observation of a growth-retarding effect of a vomer flap can be generalized remains in some doubt, and may reflect other variations in sample composition or surgery.

The effects of a vomer flap on facial growth have also been considered by the Oslo CLP team (Bergland and Sidhu[43]) which reported the flap to be clinically insignificant. Only one patient in their sample of 90 cases exhibited any degree of maxillary retrusion where surgical maxillary advancement was judged necessary.

In the opinion of the Oslo team, a vomer flap provides the particular advantages of early separation of the nasal and oral cavities without artificial obturators, a low prevalence of symptomatic fistulae, an acceptable arch form, and a good foundation for mixed dentition alveolar bone grafting (Bergland et al[46]).

Berkowitz's unpublished finding of serial complete bilateral cleft lip show results similar to those of the Oslo group. He believes that the negative effect of a vomer flap on midfacial growth and arch form, as described by Prysdo et al,[45] has not been conclusively proven. Patients who have needed LeFort I advancement of only the lateral palatal segments have had very large anterior cleft spaces in the permanent dentition even after the posterior hard palate had been surgically closed at 18 to 24 months of age with a vomer flap. The premaxillae in these cases were in good overbite-overjet relationships prior to moving the palatal segments into a Class 2 relationship.

MANAGEMENT OF THE PROTRUDING PREMAXILLA

Bilateral complete cleft lip and palate remains the most difficult type of cleft to habilitate. Maxillary hypoplasia, the medial positioning of the maxillary buccal segments with subsequent buccal crossbite, and the persistence of premaxillary protrusion with resulting distortion of the facial profile are major concerns.

The immediate preschool age period is an important milestone in appraising the goals of the child's habilitation program and determining his or her readiness for entry into the education and social environment that will affect the youngster's important formative years in society. However, due to the nature of the facial deformity seen in BCLP, often with a protruding premaxilla, one must also look beyond this stage and consider the face at the adolescent period.

The severity of premaxillary protrusion in BCLP and the face in which it exists are highly variable. Each case requires individualized management. Although some patients have a favorable premaxillary position, in others the premaxilla will present serious problems in orthodontic and/or surgical management.

The surgeon is confronted with the following options when faced with a protruding premaxilla:

1. Uniting the lip over the protruding premaxilla and considering later surgical setback and other surgical options.
2. External elastics attached to a head bonnet or elastic tape to the checks.
3. Early surgical premaxillary setback.
4. Complete removal (excision of the premaxilla).
5. Early mechanical retrusion prior to lip surgery or presurgical orthopedic treatment (PSOT) without retraction and with or without primary bone grafting.

1. Uniting the Lip (Figs 14–8 through 14–13)

In all complete clefts of the lip and palate at birth, the wide dislocation of the lateral palatal segments coupled with the protruding premaxilla can be gradually overcome by following a treatment protocol that allows the palatal segments to move into proper orientation by the application of the physiological forces of a united lip without the need for presurgical orthopedic treatment.

Lip adhesion is followed by definitive lip surgery and observation of facial and palatal changes (Fig 14–8). If necessary, later surgical premaxillary setback, or surgically moving the lateral palatal segments forward to close a very large persistent anterior cleft space, can be considered.

Clinicians who favor this procedure believe the degree of midfacial protrusion will decrease with facial growth under the influence of the midfacial growth-restraining forces of the united lip (Berkowitz,[7] Wolfe and Berkowitz,[48] Pruzansky,[13,14] Friede and Pruzansky,[4] Mazaheri et al,[49] Bishara and Olin,[50] Aduss et al,[51] Vargervik[19]).

Findings by Bishara and Olin[50] and Aduss et al[51] support the conclusions drawn from earlier facial growth studies by Berkowitz,[7] Friede and Pruzansky,[4] Handelman and Pruzansky,[12] and Vargervik[19] that the protruding premaxilla tends to be molded back by lip pressure and can sometimes be aligned within the lateral palatal segments without resorting to neonatal maxillary orthopedics.

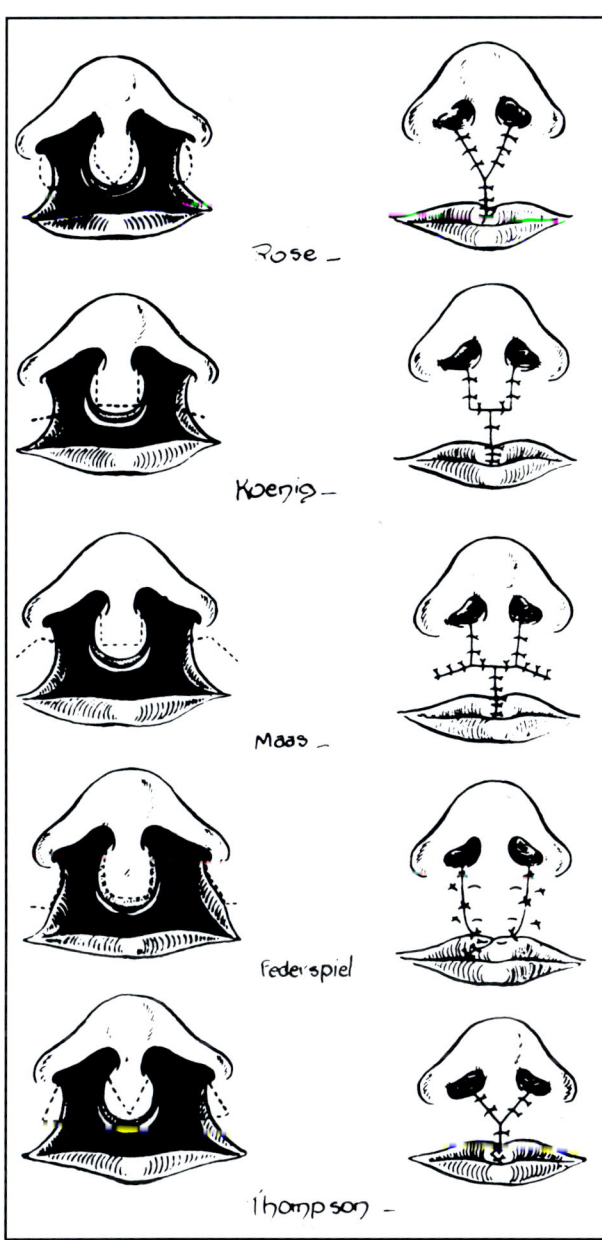

Fig 14-8. Various surgical techniques used to unite the lip in BCLP. Experience has shown that the best results are obtained when the prolabium is used to construct the entire midportion of the lip. (From, Millard DR Jr. Cleft Craft, Boston, Mass: Little, Brown and Co; 1980;3.)

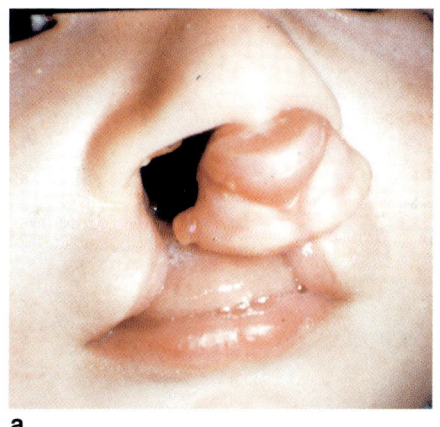

a

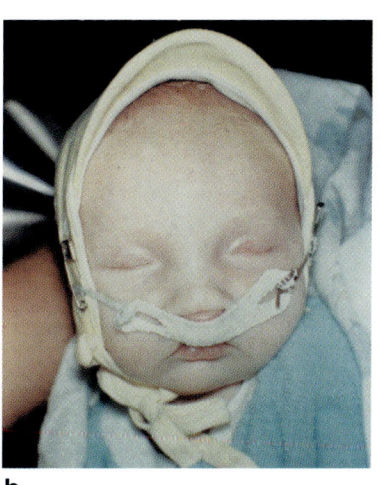

b

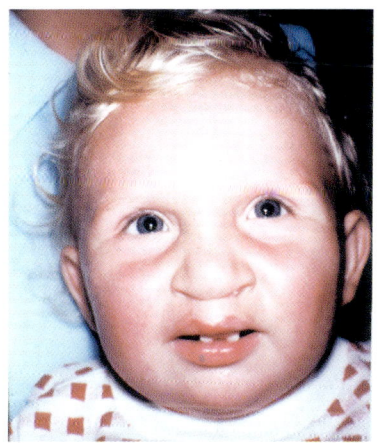

c

Fig 14-9. A head bonnet with an elastic strap (external facial traction) placed against premaxilla is an efficient and painless procedure to ventroflex the premaxilla prior to lip surgery. a. At birth. **b.** With head bonnet in place. **c.** After lip repair. The head bonnet aids the surgeon in reducing tension at the lip suture site. The force generated at PVS is less than that created by using mechanical premaxillary retraction (see Chapter 9).

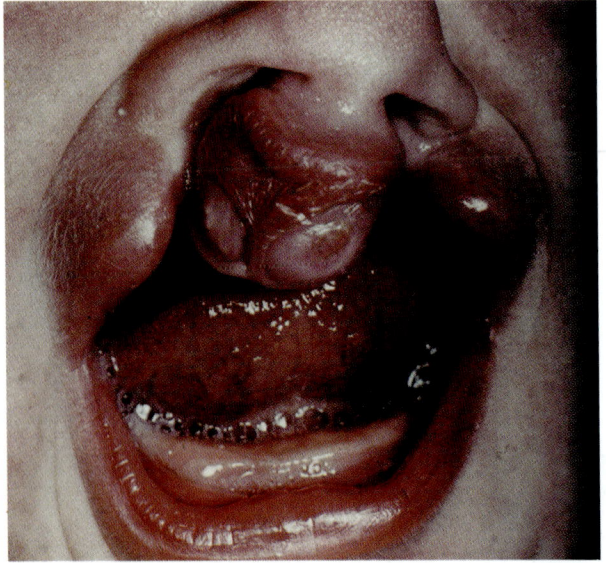
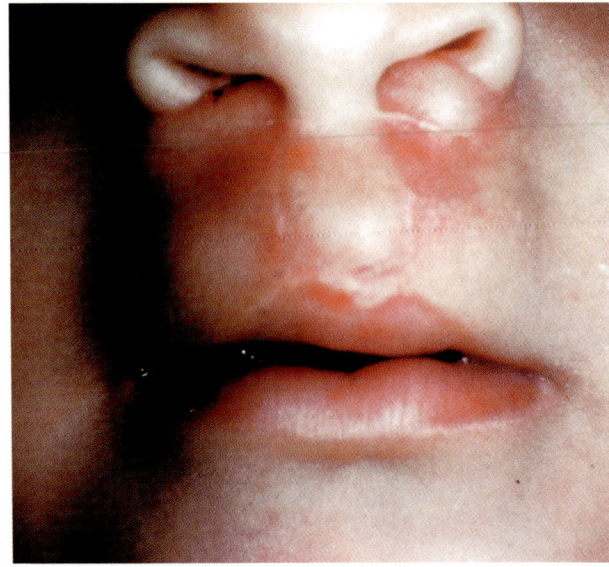

Fig 14–10. **Use of the prolabium for the center portion of the lip.** IBCLP. **a, b,** and **c.** Facial photographs at 20 days, 3 months, and 18 months. The banked fork flap (Millard): the tissue in the nostril is used to lengthen the columella at a later date. The procedure avoids going back to a good lip for tissue to reconstruct the columella.

The use of lip adhesion within the first 3 months followed by a definitive lip revision, usually within the first 6 months of age, permits the surgeon to perform surgery in stages and reduce strain at the lip suture when the definitive lip surgery is performed (Fig 14–12). Surgeons who favor this procedure are willing to postpone obtaining a maximum early aesthetic result for what they believe will offer superior long-term benefits. The most severe, unaesthetic premaxillary overbite at the deciduous and mixed (transitional) dentition, even with a buccal crossbite, will not interfere with dental function or swallowing or have long-term deleterious effects on speech and midfacial growth.

Various types of lip surgery (Fig 14–8) have the same effect of reducing premaxillary protrusion, resulting in premaxillary ventroflexion with the fulcrum at premaxillary vomerine suture (PVS). In complete bilateral clefts of the lip and palate, although there is always some strain at the lip suture site, there is no need, in most instances, to be concerned about the sutures parting. The increased

CASE REPORT: ONE-STAGE LIP CLOSURE PLACING THE PROLABIUM TO THE VERMILION

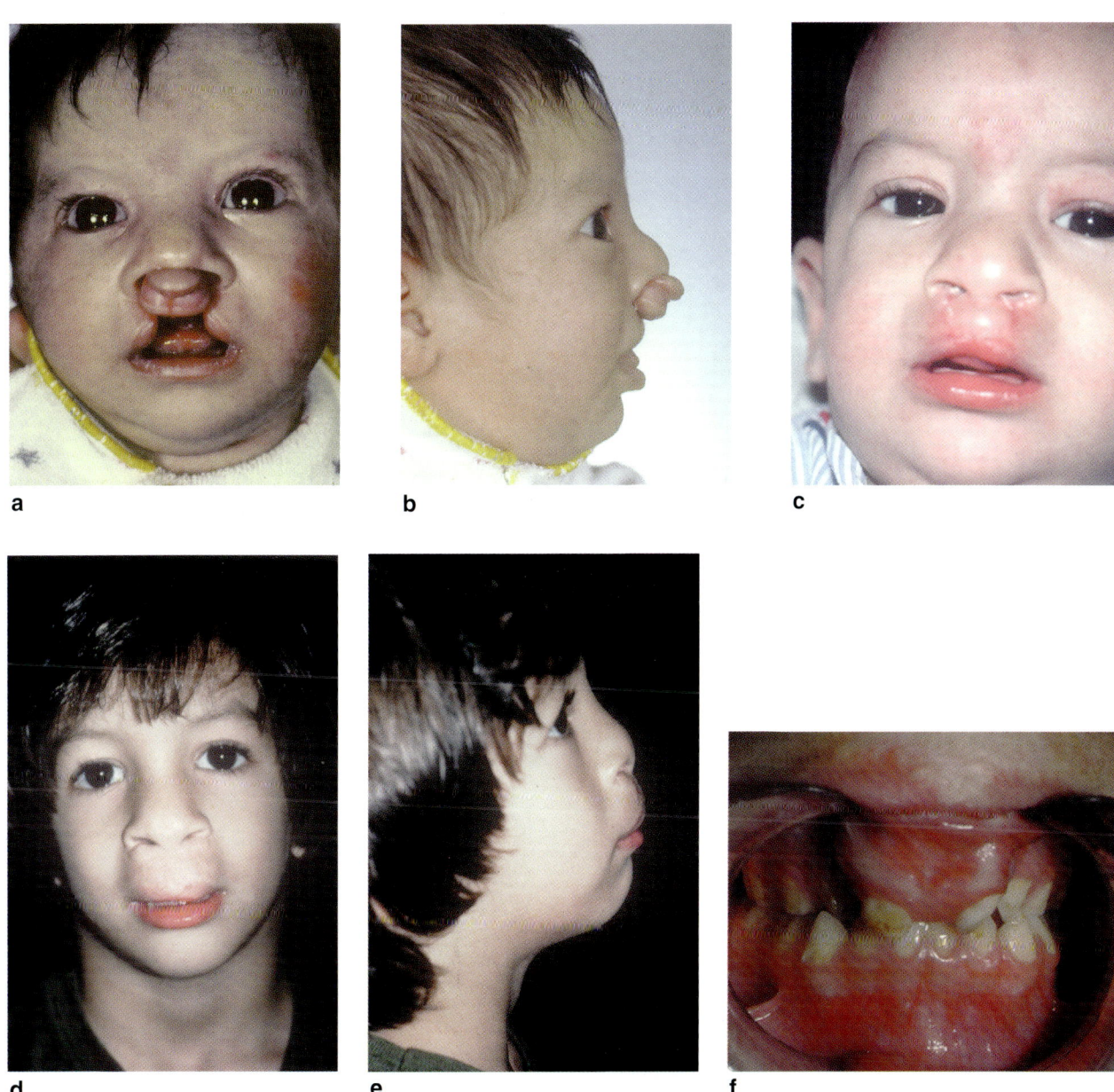

Fig 14–11. a-f. Millard's surgical lip procedure uses the prolabium to construct the entire midportion of the lip over the protruding premaxilla.

pressure of the united lip has an effect on the premaxillary vomerine suture with subsequent reduction in forward midfacial growth.

Serial facial photographs indicate that surgical procedures that use the entire prolabium for the central portion of the lip produce the best aesthetic results. A long, tight lip is the predictable result when the lateral lip elements are brought together beneath the prolabium (see Fig 14–10, a and b).

2. External Elastics Attached to a Head Bonnet or Elastic Tape Strapped to the Cheeks
(Fig 14-9)

These force delivery systems will reduce premaxillary protrusion prior to lip surgery, and only need to be utilized for approximately 1 or 2 weeks. Elastic forces exert the same backward pressure against the protruding premaxilla as a lip adhesion, resulting in premaxil-

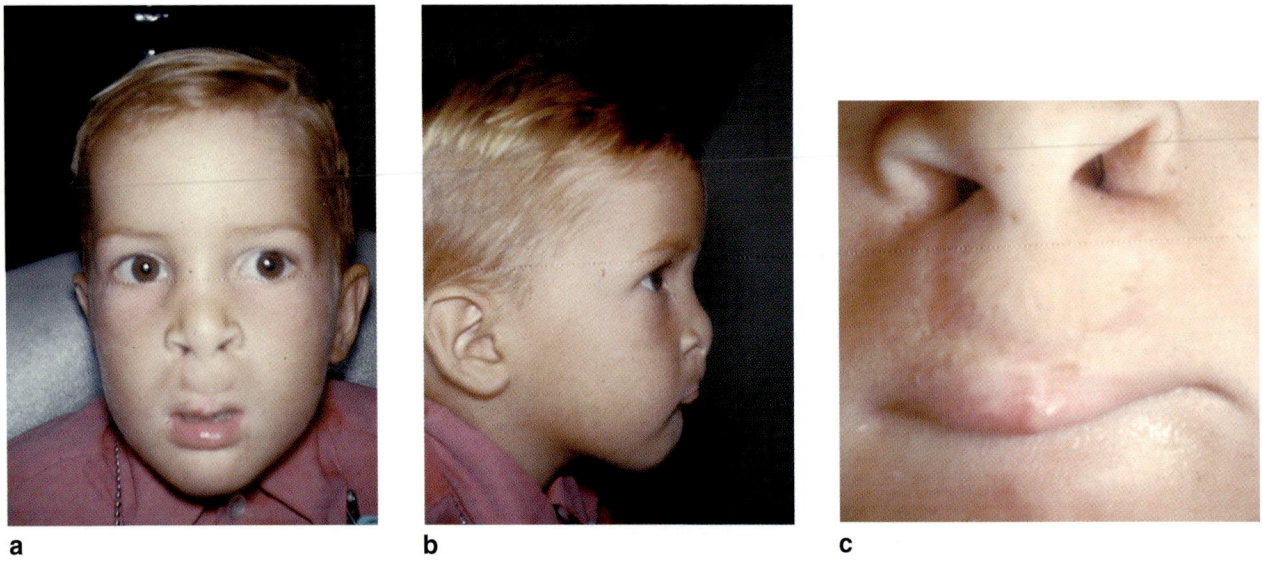

Fig 14–12. a-c. The lateral lip elements were brought below the prolabium creating a long tight lip.

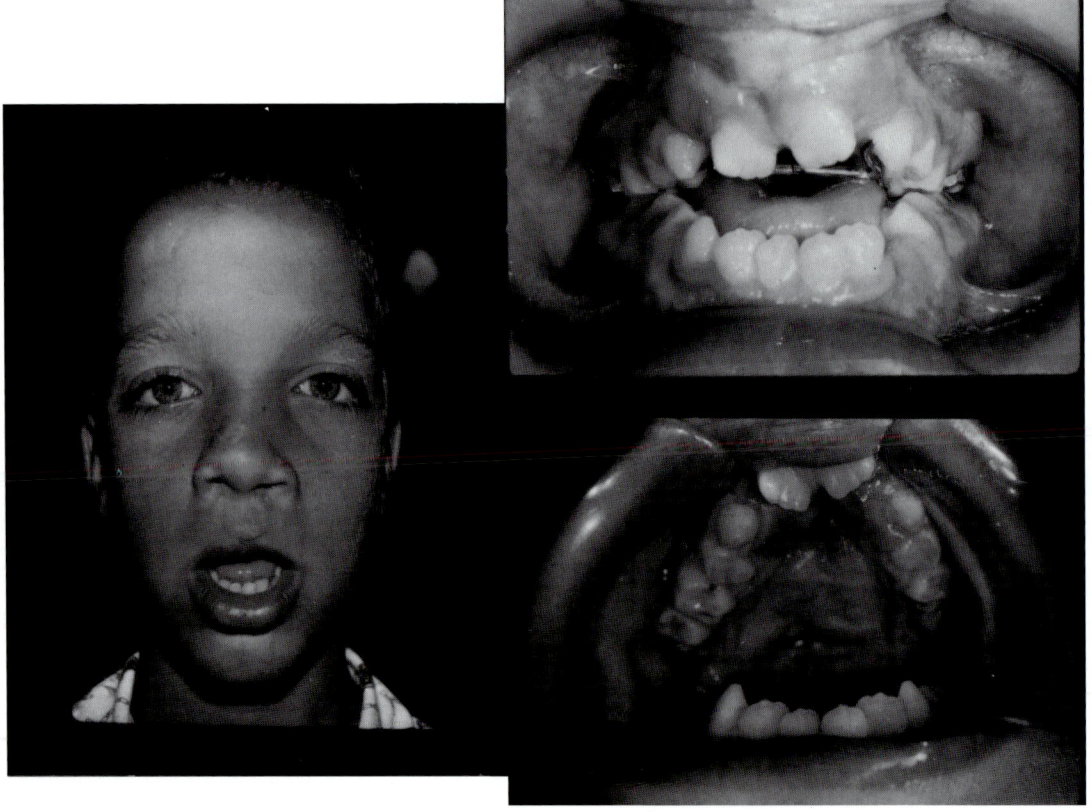

Fig 14–13. Early premaxillary surgical setback and palatal cleft closure at 7 months of age. The lateral lip elements were brought together below the prolabium. Results at 7 years of age: (1) long tight upper lip, (2) anterior open bite due to failure of the premaxilla to descend with the palate, and (3) the surgery (push back) used to close the palatal cleft at 7 months obliterated the vault space interfering with tongue posture. The tongue is, therefore, being carried forward with the tongue tip protruding, preventing the incisors from reaching the occlusal plane.

lary ventroflexion with the fulcrum at PVS. There are no valid reasons to object to the use of external facial traction forces for 1 to 2 weeks prior to lip surgery. This procedure, like lip adhesion, aids the surgeon in uniting the lips by reducing tension at the surgical site at the time when definite lip surgery is performed.

PROFILE CHANGES

Hanada and Krogman,[52] Berkowitz,[7] Bishara and Olin,[50] Boyne,[53] Vargervik,[19] Handelman and Pruzansky,[12] Friede,[9] Semb,[28] and Narula and Ross[38] all have performed longitudinal studies of the changing soft-tissue profile of bilateral cleft lip and/or palate (BCL/P) and reported that, with the slow resolution of the protruding premaxilla with growth, the profile became more harmonious in appearance. In the Oslo study of BCLP, Semb[25] concluded that early dentofacial orthopedics were not a necessary precursor to lip and palate closure in order to attain long-term positive profile changes.

Serial profile analyses reported in Berkowitz's earlier studies and the serial studies presented in this text demonstrate that, during the first 2 years following surgery, the united lip exerts a posteriorly directed pressure force on the protruding premaxilla. He speculates that this force is exerted through the nasal septum to the premaxillary vomerine suture, gradually retarding the forward and vertical growth of the nasal septum with the attached premaxilla. The growth of the lateral palatal segments does not appear to be affected by this force. Inhibition of midfacial growth coupled with forward, and vertical growth of the upper face and mandible is responsible for the eventual flattening of the facial profile (Figs 14–5, 14–14).

Protrusion of the midface is only slightly reduced due to the reduction-remodeling of the labile surface of the premaxilla associated with the eruption of the permanent incisors. Facial growth data suggest that the tendency toward mandibular prognathism can be considered advantageous, insofar as it masks the relative protrusion of the premaxilla. Comparison of the profile changes in children whose lips were united at 6 years with infants whose lips were united soon after birth showed less premaxillary protrusion for children whose lips were repaired in infancy. This suggests that the beneficial effect of lip repair is long-acting in that it continues to exert a restraint on the growth of the premaxillary-vomerine complex long after the lip is repaired (Friede and Pruzansky,[4] Berkowitz,[7] Vargervik[19]).

After the lip is united, there are no documented long-term benefits to using intraoral neonatal maxillary orthopedics to control the premaxilla's position relative to the lateral palatal segments (i.e., to inhibit the palatal segments from spontaneously moving together), nor is it important that the premaxilla be accommodated within the arch at this time. There is no evidence that overlapping palatal segments suffer growth inhibition. In most cases, proper premaxillary alignment within the lateral palatal segments can be easily achieved with orthodontics in the mixed dentition without resorting to neonatal maxillary orthopedics. The following cases show that orthodontics in the permanent dentition, in the absence of growth-inhibiting palatal surgery and with a good facial growth pattern, eventually will lead to excellent facial aesthetics and dental function. Any resulting buccal crossbite can be easily corrected at 4 or 5 years of age, when the child is manageable in a dental chair, using fixed tooth-borne or even removable arch expansion appliances. The author strongly favors the use of fixed appliances for arch expansion and retention.

Why Some Premaxillae Continue to Project Following Lip Repair and Others Do Not

A number of variables in treatment planning are beyond the control of the surgeon, for example, the patient's facial growth pattern and the amount of palatal osteogenic deficiency. The integrated growth of the entire face is important in endeavoring to resolve the profile deformity. When the end result is unfavorable—that is, the facial profile remains highly convex—the premaxilla and the body of the maxilla have grown forward with limited forward mandibular projection.

Facial growth studies by Handelman and Pruzansky[12] and by Berkowitz (presented in this chapter) have shown that, in highly convex facial profiles with a moderately protrusive premaxilla and a recessive mandible, the lip musculature usually is hypertonic and positioned over the incisor teeth, resulting in severe premaxillary ventroflexion. In mesognathic faces with isotonic or hypotonic lip musculature and a severely projecting premaxilla, the lower lip may be positioned lingual to the premaxilla and between the upper and lower incisors, creating an anterior component of force at the premaxillary vomerine suture (PVS). This may cause additional bony growth at the suture leading to greater premaxillary protrusion with a normal maxillary incisal axial inclination. The lower incisors may be tipped lingually.

Dental Occlusion

Analyses of the dental occlusion of many patients with complete bilateral clefts of the lip and palate at

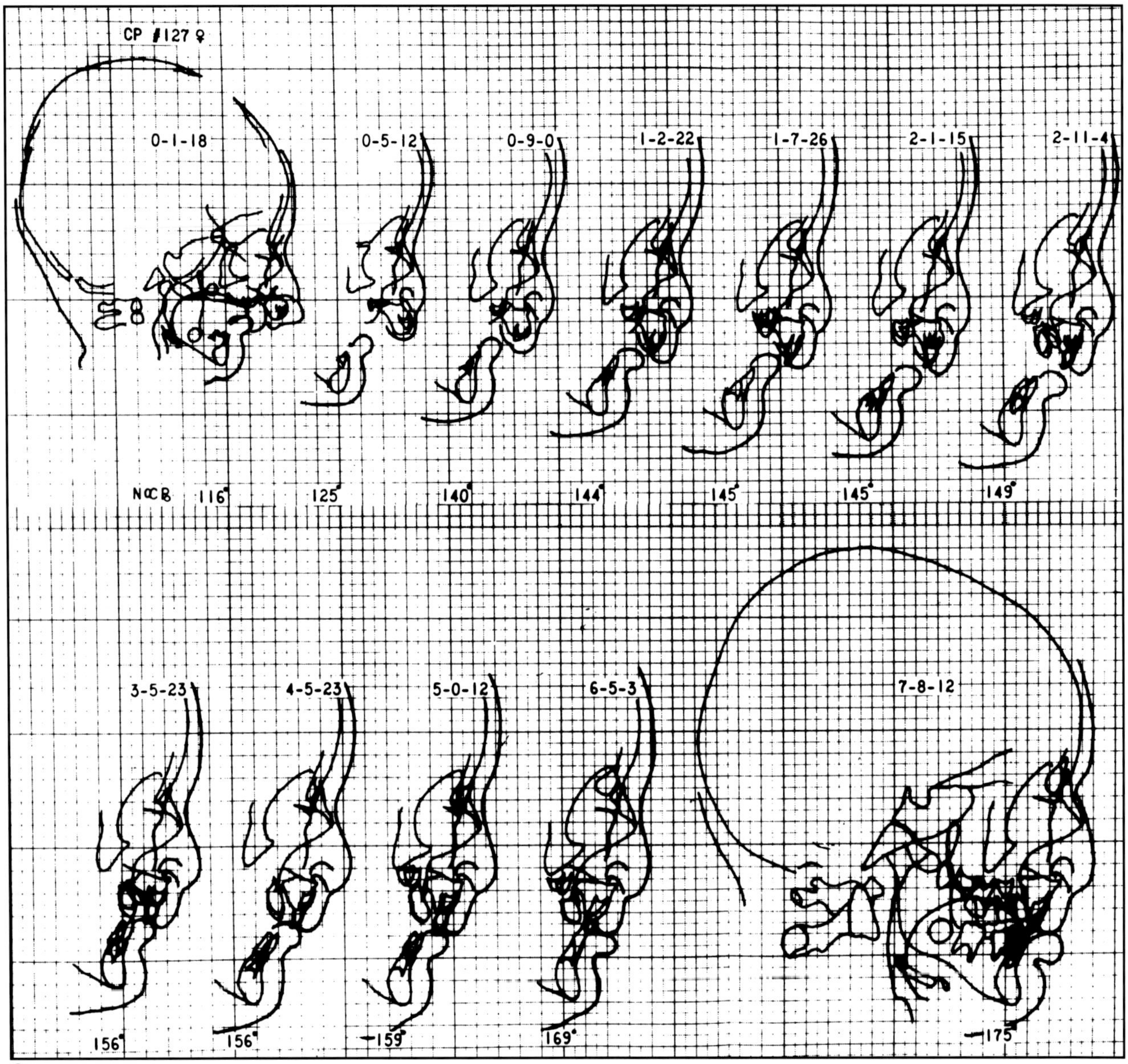

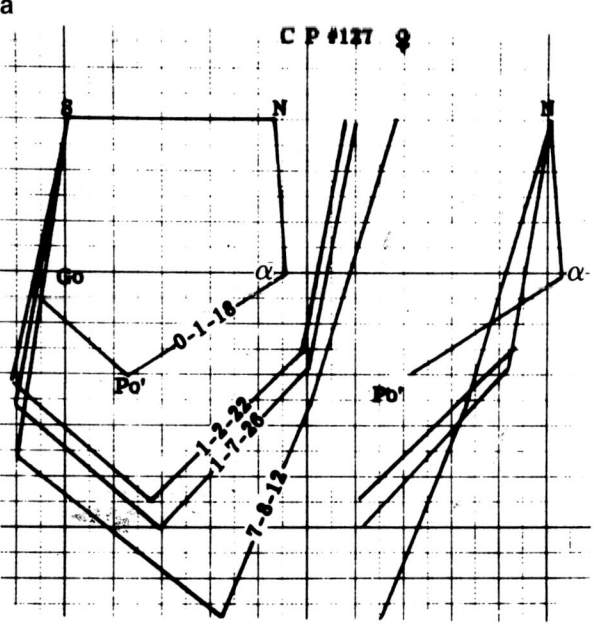

Fig 14–14. Good facial growth pattern with hypertonic lip musculature. a. Lateral cephalometric tracing shows a gradual increase in the angle of facial convexity (NαPo) from 116° to 169° with the greatest change (159° to 169°) occurring between 5 years and 6 years, 5 months of age. At 5 years the axial inclination of the anterior teeth is vertical with an appreciable incisor overjet. However, at 6 years, 5 months the premaxilla is palatally inclined, placing the upper and lower incisors in a tip-to-tip relationship. This usually occurs with a relatively retrognathic mandible when the lower lip also overlaps the upper incisors, increasing the muscle pressure against the premaxilla. If the lower lip is positioned between the upper and lower incisors, the premaxilla with its incisors will flare. **b.** Superimposed polygons show a very small mandible with a protruding premaxilla at 0-1-18. There is a marked anterior growth of the anterior cranial base (N) and, together with the mandible's vertical and horizontal growth changes, a reduction in the angle of facial convexity. Note that there is very little change in premaxillary protrusion within the face between ages 1-2-22 and 7-8-12.

6 years of age rarely show retruded maxillary shelves (i.e., a Class 3 relationship) (Berkowitz[7]). The buccal teeth are most often in a Class 1 or 2 relationship. A Class 3 relationship exists only if the maxilla is retrusive due to severely retarded growth caused by traumatic surgery and/or the phenotype of the patient. The mandible is rarely prognathic at this age. In many cases, due to osteogenic deficiency and severe dental crowding in the maxillary arch, some teeth will need to be extracted. This may or may not have to be done in the mandibular arch. There is conclusive evidence to suggest that the palatal shelves are deficient in mass, but there is no evidence they have lost their growth impetus from having been detached from the growing nasal septum.

Until proven otherwise, the surgeon should have confidence that the severe facial convexity seen at birth can diminish with time as the united lip restrains the forward development of the midface while the mandible increases in size and is positioned more downward and forward relative to the growing anterior cranial base.

CONSERVATIVE SURGICAL AND ORTHODONTIC TREATMENT SEQUENCE

Cleft lip and cleft palate defects offer a degree of habilitation that is not available for many equally serious congenital or acquired handicaps. Achieving this potential requires careful planning and skillful execution of treatment that respects individual growth patterns. (Table 14-1) The following cases were selected to show various treatment procedures, some of which were unsuccessful but nevertheless have teaching value because they reflect physiological principles.

After Birth

In general, no presurgical orthopedics should be provided in clefts of the lip and palate. In complete bilateral cases only, an external facial elastic may be utilized to ventroflex the protruding premaxilla to reduce tension at the surgical site when utilizing lip adhesion. External traction is usually not necessary in incomplete clefts of the lip and palate.

The Forked Flap (Fig 14-15)

All of the bilateral cases were treated with some form of Millard's Forked Flap.[68] It was designed to lengthen the columella as a primary or secondary procedure. Advantages include:

- Release of depressed nasal tip
- Lengthen the short columnella
- Reduce an unattractive wide prolabium
- Revision of bilateral lip scars
- Reduction of flaring alar base

Millard[68(p260)] suggests that the primary forked flap procedure is not appropriate for all bilateral cleft cases. Whether to use the procedure depends on: (1) The position of the premaxilla. The procedure should not be used when the premaxilla protrudes severely. (2) The size of the prolabium. The width of the prolabium determines whether the flap is possible, and the vertical length indicates the amount of columella lengthening available. (3) Columella length. This discrepancy must be measured not only in actual length in millimeters of the columella but an estimation of the patient's desired final length must also be made.

There are occasions where the forked flaps from the prolabium are banked with a subalar incision, whisker fashion. The alar base is not advanced medially in an attempt to leave a subalar gap in which to store the forks. Millard delays shifting of the banked forked flap into the columella for several years (from 6 months to 6 years).

In the Deciduous Dentition (3 to 6 Years of Age)

The purpose of treatment at this age is to realign the palatal segments in order to obtain a more normal contour to the alveolar ridge, reshape the palatal vault, and provide a more symmetrical foundation for the support of the lips and nose. These changes are possible because orthodontic treatment in cleft palate allows for the movement of palatal segments in addition to altering the position of the teeth within the bone. Because the roof of the mouth is also the floor of the nose, realignment of the palatal processes not only produces desirable alteration in the contour of the palate, but also induces similar changes within the floor of the nose.

Most clinicians agree that nontraumatic conservative surgery will not solve all problems for all complete bilateral cleft lip and palate cases. Although buccal crossbites can be corrected in the deciduous dentition, they advocate orthodontic/orthopedic repositioning of the premaxilla at a later age (in the mixed dentition prior to or after secondary alveolar bone grafting) when the facial growth pattern leaves no alternative and dictates that it is the procedure of choice. Some orthodontists prefer to do this in the permanent dentition.

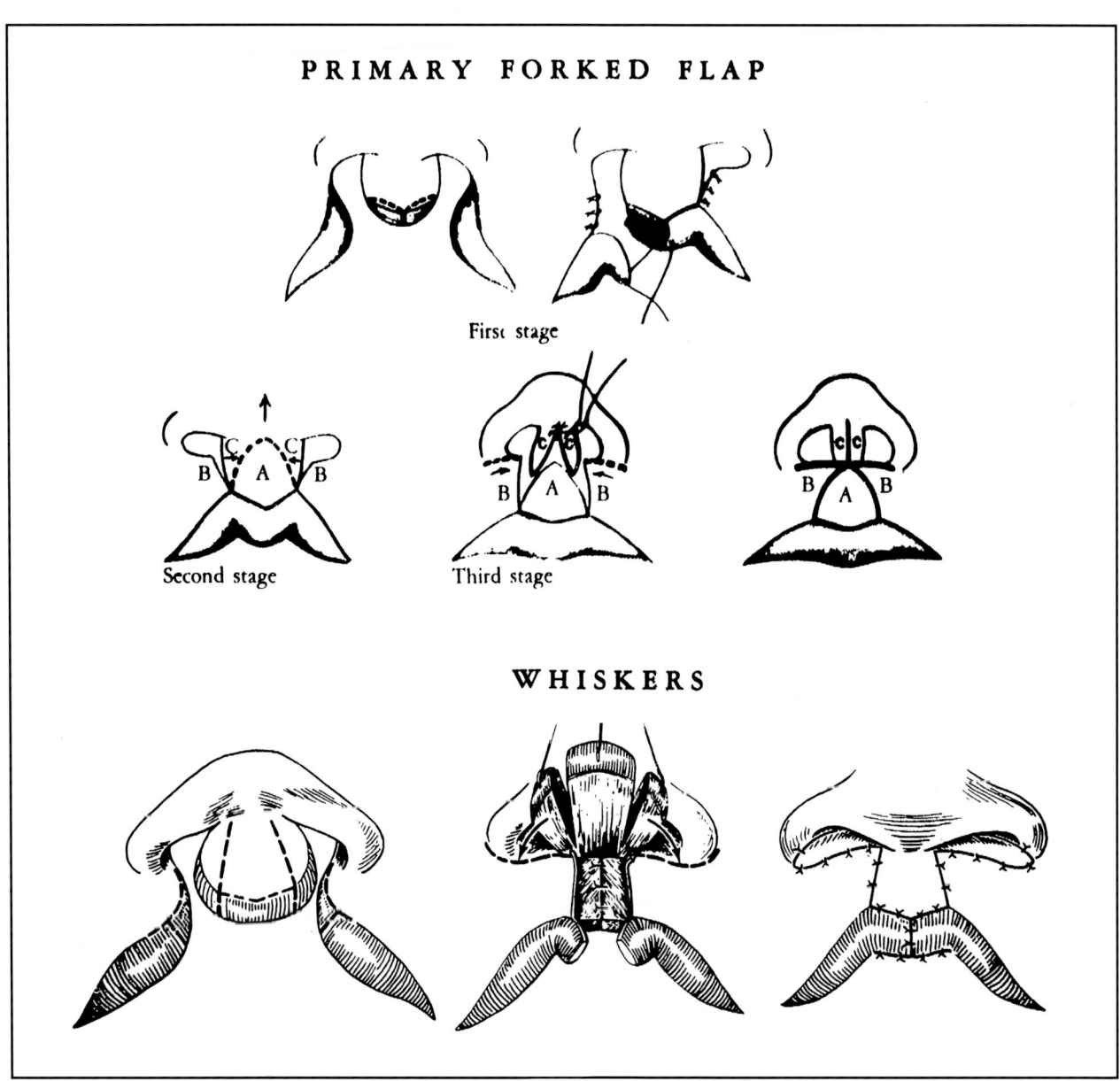

Fig 14–15. In 1956–1957 Millard designed a secondary forked flap for columella lengthening. He believed at times it is best to take a little tissue from the prolabium and the lip and store it in the area for later use in reconstructuring the columella. The forked flap was originally designed as a secondary procedure; however, it can be used as a primary procedure when the columella is extremely short and the prolabium is of reasonable size. **Top:** In the primary forked flap, the fork flap is elevated and advanced into the columella with release of the nasal tip. **Bottom:** The whisker fork flap involves joining the lip muscle and banking the fork. The alar bases are joined together in the midline and the forks partially tubed on themselves and led into the transverse incisions between the lip and alar bases, whisker fashion. This surgery is delayed several years. Millard likes this procedure best of all.

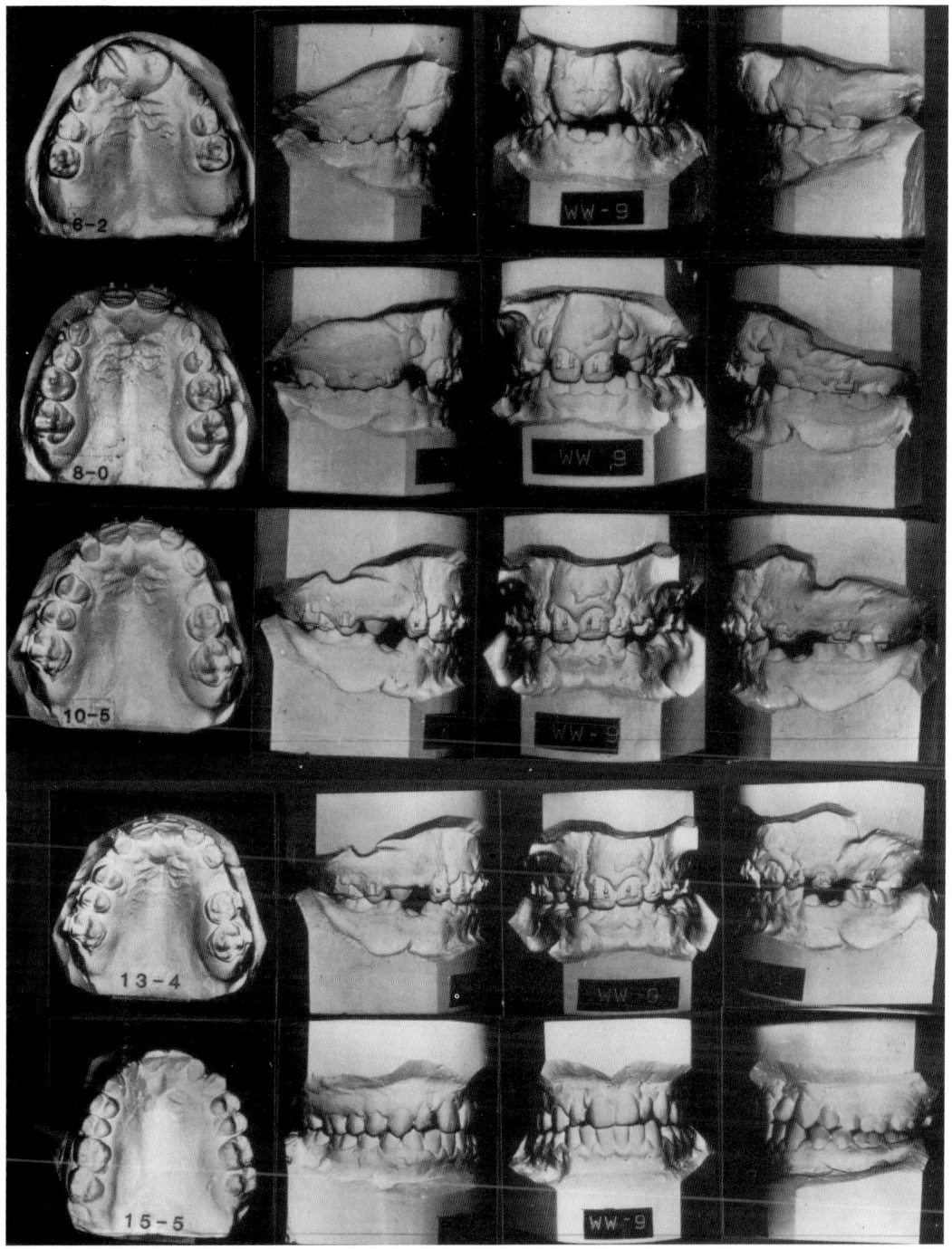

Fig 14–17. *(continued)*
6-2. The central incisors in the area of the cleft are frequently found to be rotated. **8-0.** Six months after a secondary alveolar cranial bone graft. The right and left lateral incisors have erupted through the graft. **10-5.** The lateral incisors are aligned with the central incisors. **15-5.** Excellent occlusion after orthodontia. A removable maxillary retainer is being used to maintain the arch form.

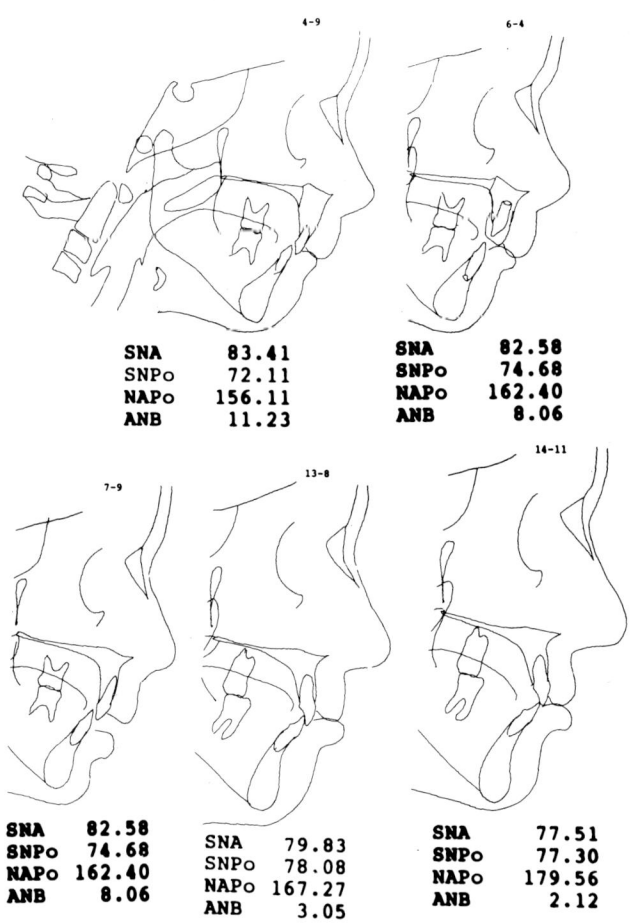

a

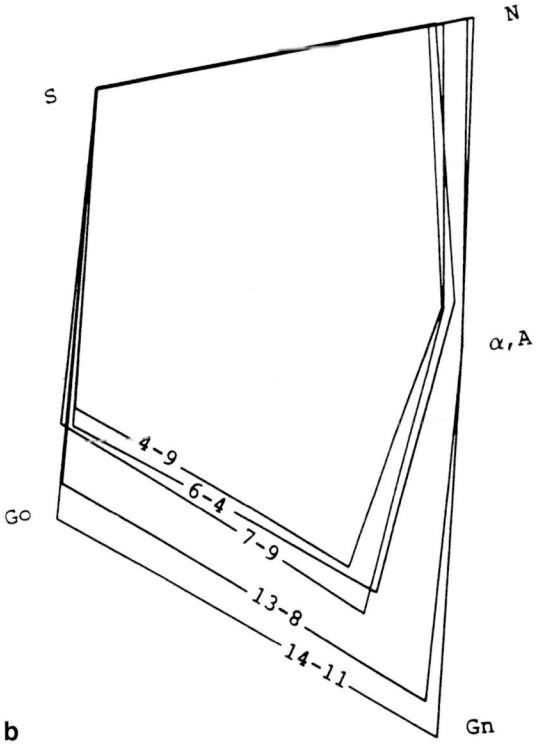

b

Fig 14–18. Case TM (WW-9). This series depicts an excellent facial growth pattern. a. Computerized tracings of facial skeletal and soft tissue profile changes. At 14-11, the profile measurements are well within the normal range. **b.** Facial polygons superimposed on the SN line and registered at S demonstrate that the excellent facial growth pattern reflects some anterior cranial base growth, very little forward growth of the midface, and excellent mandibular growth in a downward and forward direction. Note that the midface was still protrusive at 7-9, but after the mandibular pubertal growth spurt (13-8), the facial profile flattened markedly.

CASE REPORT: EXTREMELY SMALL PROTRUDING PREMAXILLA WITH NO TOOTH BUDS. CONSERVATIVE TREATMENT SUCCESSFUL AFTER UNSUCCESSFUL PSOT

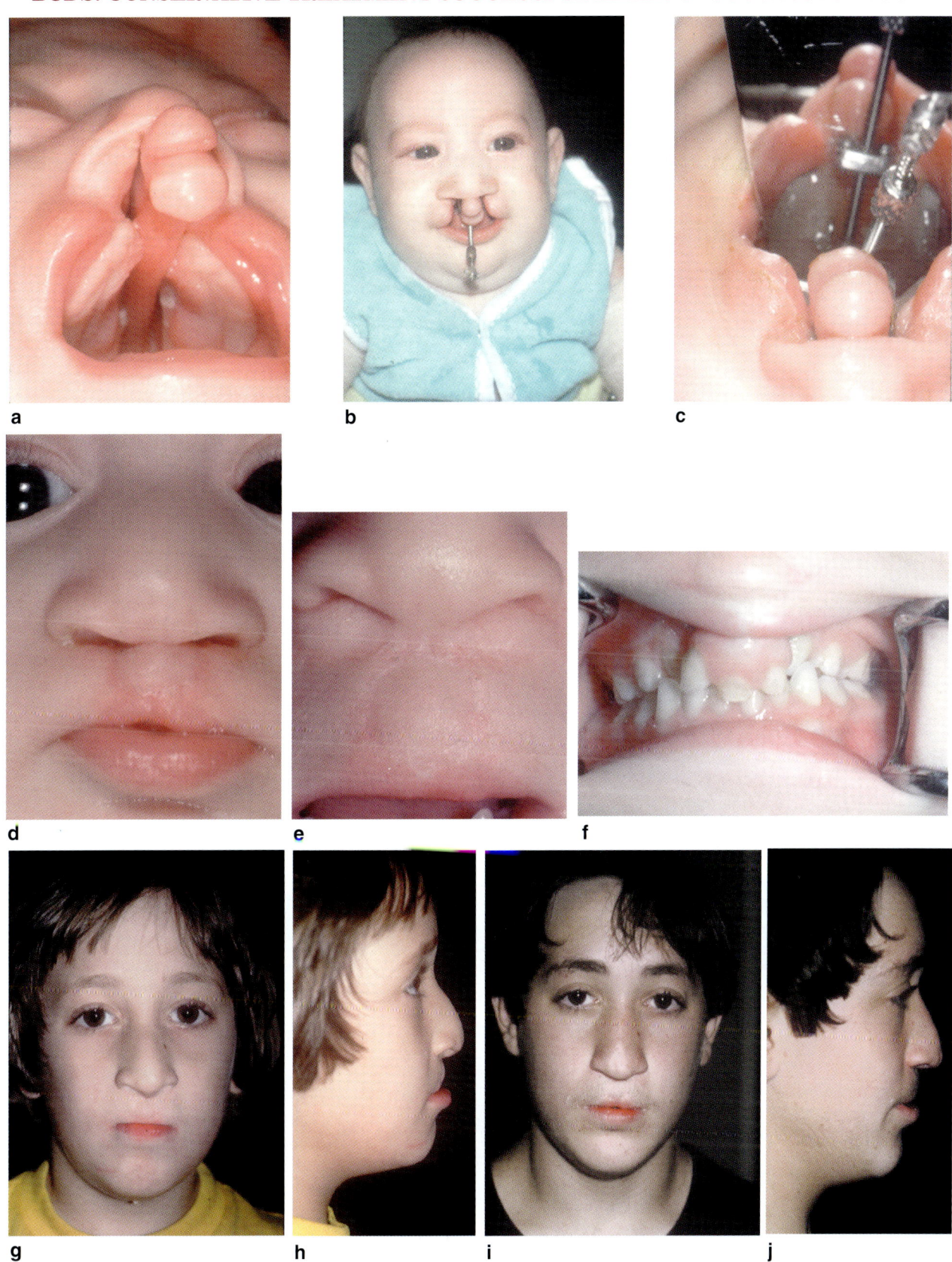

(continued)

Fig 14–19. *(continued)*

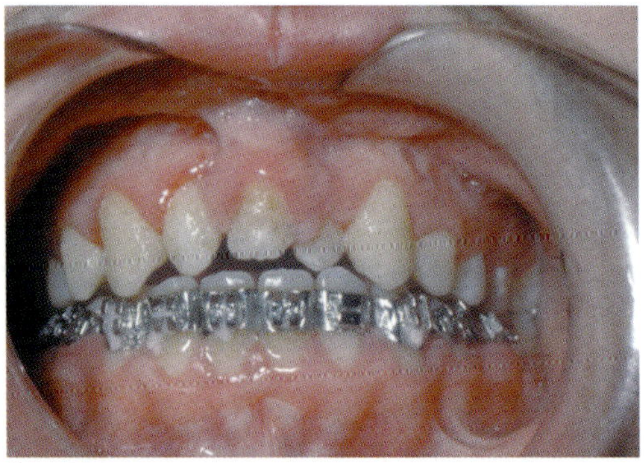

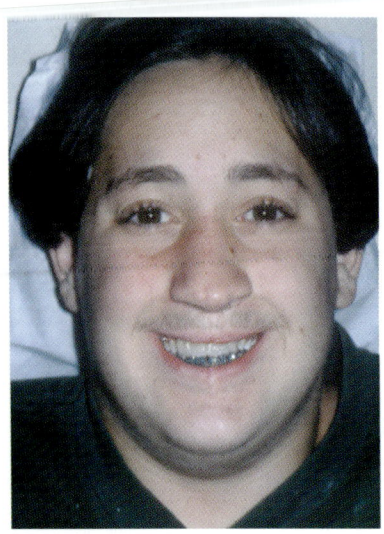

Fig 14–19. Case DK (AI-31) demonstrates unsuccessful use of Latham's presurgical premaxillary mechanical retraction procedure in a CBCLP, which then required the use of external facial elastics prior to lip surgery. **a.** At birth, note the very small protruding premaxilla. **b.** Facial photograph with Millard-Latham (M-L) mechanical premaxillary retraction appliance in place. **c.** Intraoral view of M-L appliance in place. The appliance was not able to retract the premaxilla due to its small size and was discarded. **d.** After wearing a head bonnet with an elastic strap for 2 weeks, the lip was united over the premaxilla. At 2 months the nasal tip is severely depressed. **e.** At 3 years of age, the banked tissue of the "forked flap" waiting to be placed in the columella. **f.** 5 years of age. Note excellent occlusion. Radiographs showed that there were no permanent incisors in the premaxilla. **g** and **h.** At 8 years of age, the nasal tip has been elevated, but there is poor upper lip support due to the now retruded premaxilla. Lower right and left first bicuspids were extracted at 13 years to reduce the anterior crossbite. **i, j,** and **k.** At 15 years of age, the mandible is growing forward at a more rapid rate and degree than the maxilla. The earlier buccal and anterior crosbites were corrected and two lateral incisors from the lateral palatal segments were brought into position, improving facial aesthetics. **l-q.** the maxillary anterior deciduous teeth were extracted and an anterior bridge fabricated to improve dental function and aesthetics.

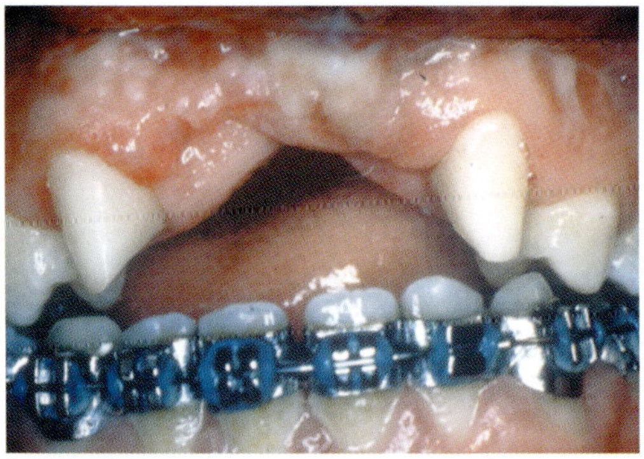

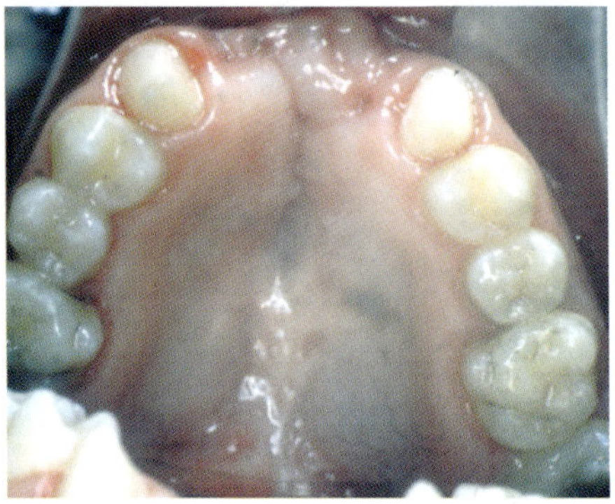

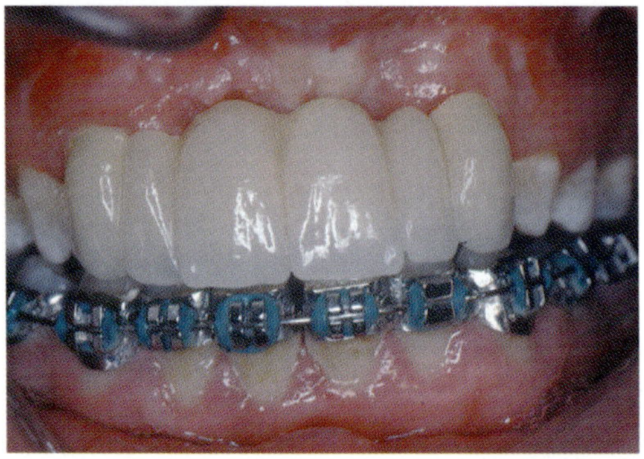

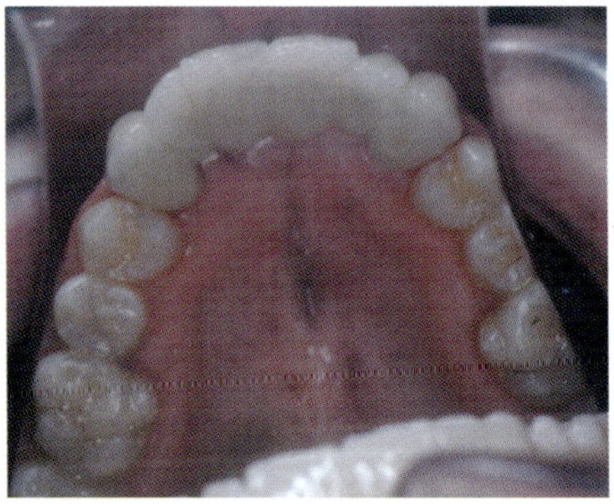

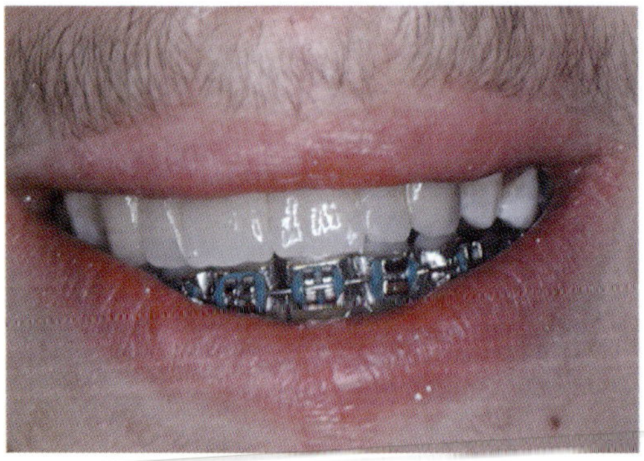

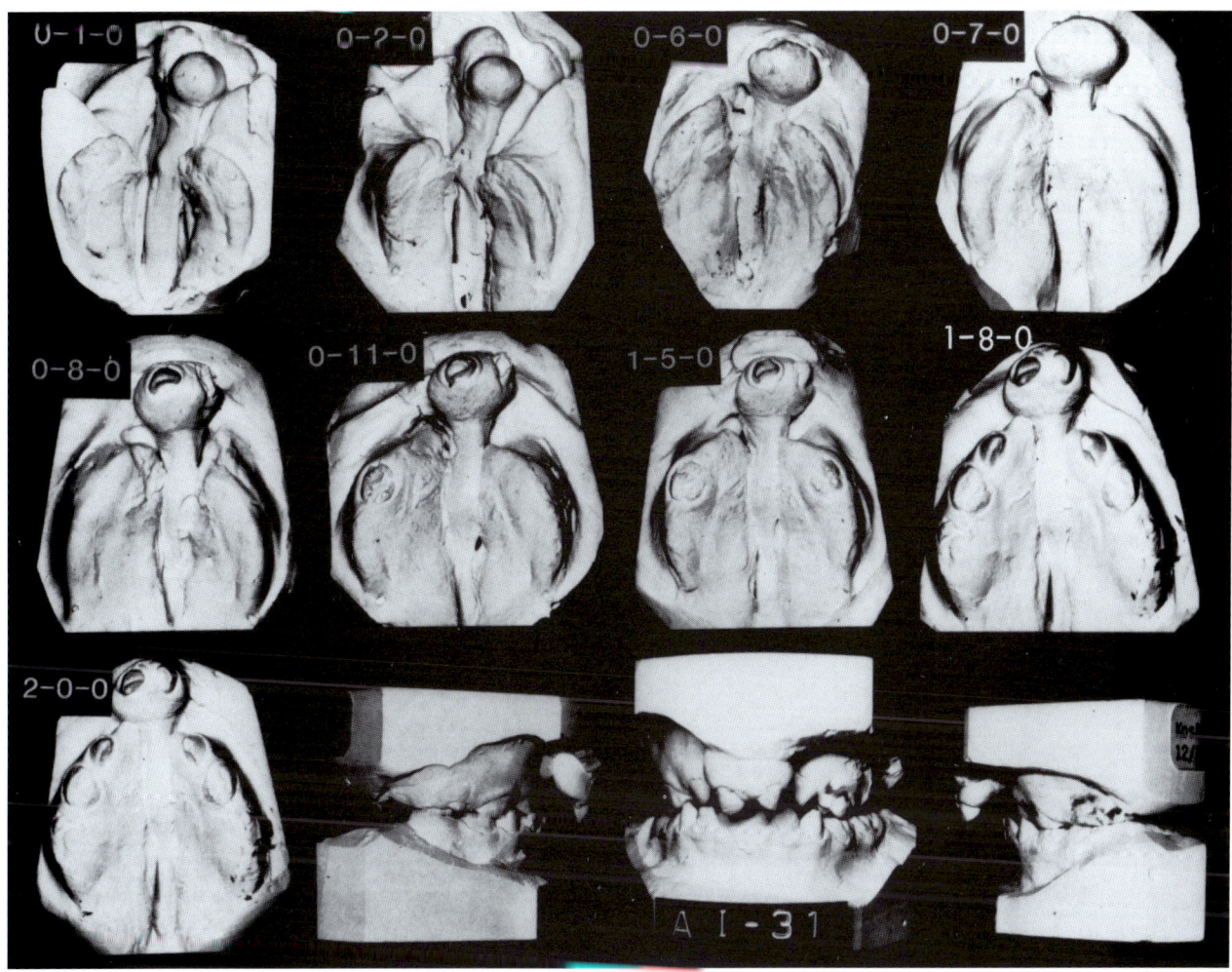

Fig 14–20. Case DK (AI-21). a. Serial dental casts. 1-1-0 and **0-2-0.** Note the severely protruding and small premaxilla. **0-2-0. 0-6-0.** The premaxilla ventroflexed under the influence of extraoral elastics attached to a head bonnet. **0-7-0.** Marked increase in palatal size coupled with a big reduction in the anterior cleft space. **2-0-0.** Class 2 occlusion with a severe overjet of the premaxilla with its anterior teeth. **3-6.** Note there is only a small overjet and overbite with a mesioangular rotation of the lateral segments placing the cuspids into crossbite. **4-4.** The premaxilla is forward of the lateral palatal segments, but the dental overbite/overjet is normal. This occlusal relationship remained for the next 5 years. The anterior cleft space is left open waiting for additional palatal growth. The anterior palatal cleft did not pose a speech or feeding problem and would allow for palatal expansion. **9-8.** The remaining deciduous central incisor is now in an anterior crossbite associated with the lack of midfacial development. **12-4.** The lower anterior teeth were unsuccessfully advanced to reduce the arch crowding. The excessive flaring necessitated extraction of the lower first bicuspids. This was followed by retraction of the incisor teeth and space closure with reduction of the severe anterior crossbite. **15-8.** Right and left deciduous lateral incisors are brought into position; however, an anterior arch discrepancy still remains. Because of the poor root development of the deciduous lateral incisors, they later were extracted and replaced with an anterior fixed bridge. *(continued)*

Fig 14–20. *(continued)*

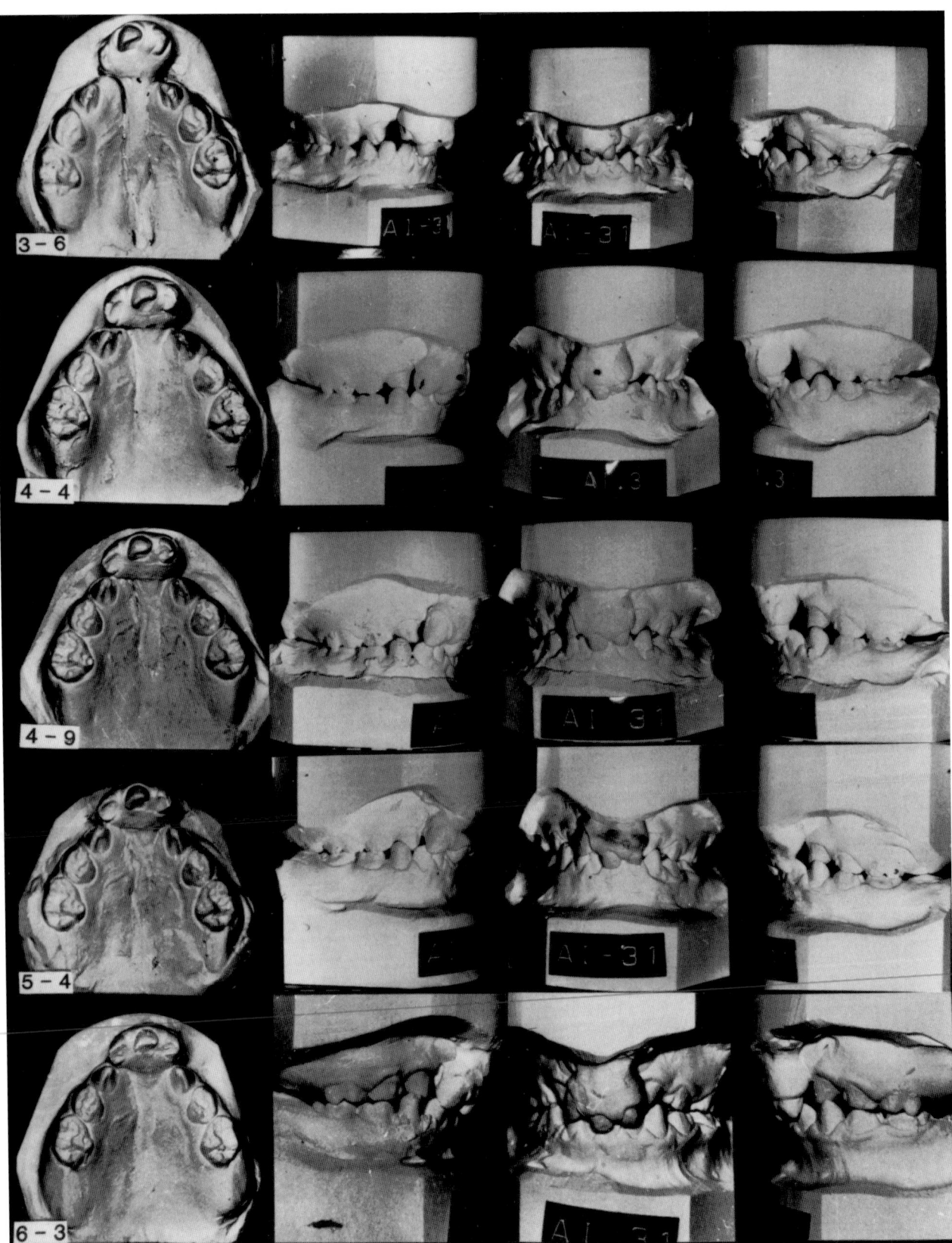

284

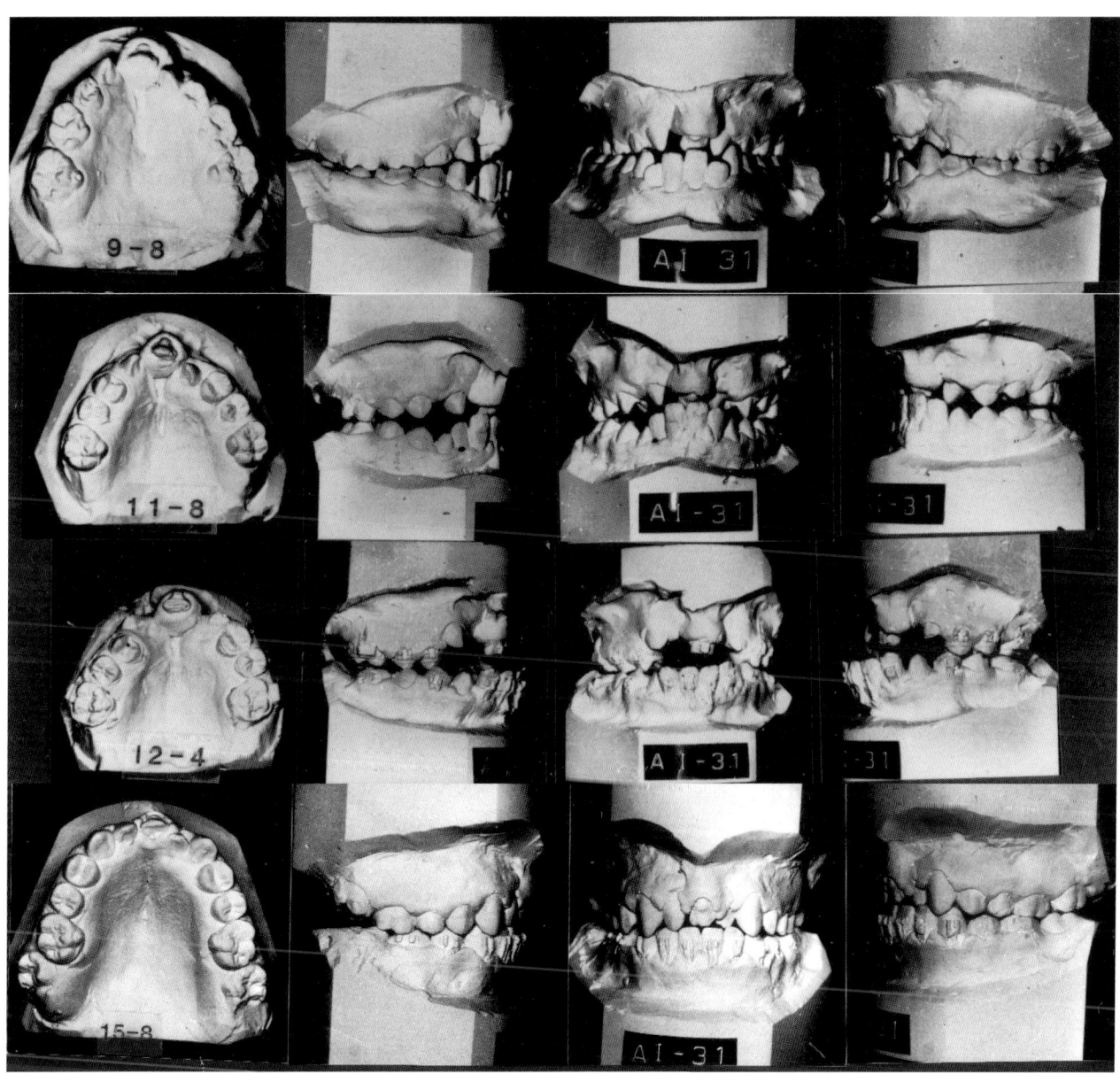

285

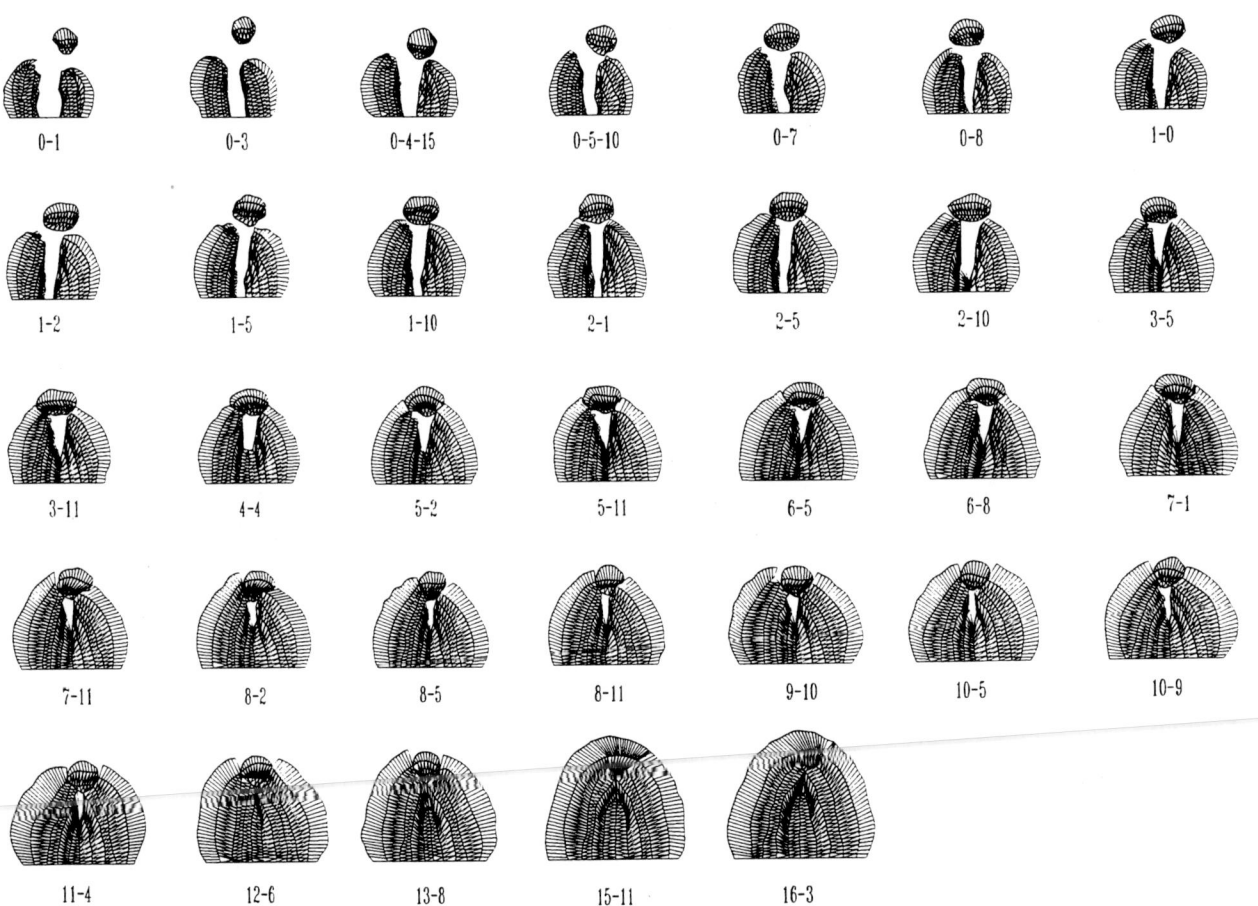

Fig 14–21. Case DK (AI-31). Computerized drawings of palatal casts using an electromechanical digitizer (see Chap 16). Each cast size is drawn to scale. The premaxilla is gradually "absorbed" by the lateral palatal segments after the initial ventroflexion. The ratio of palatal size to cleft size increases with growth. The anterior cleft space is left open until a secondary alveolar bone graft is placed.

TABLE 14–2. Surface Area of CBCLP. Case DK (AI-31).

Age	Skeletal Area				Cleft Space			Total
	Premax	RLS	LLS	Tot	Ant	Post	Tot	SA + CS
0-1	55.6	314.1	254.2	623.9	102.9	138.8	341.7	965.6
0-3	79.2	366.6	317.5	763.3	150.5	191.8	342.4	1105.7
0-4-15	86.1	362.4	300.8	749.3	56.1	259.3	315.4	1064.7
0-5-10	99.5	356.2	322.5	778.2	70.3	175.2	245.5	1023.7
0-7	111.7	361.9	321.3	794.9	45.2	168.0	213.2	1008.1
0-8	106.8	376.0	351.0	833.8	85.6	149.1	234.7	1068.5
1-0	100.3	428.1	327.2	855.6	55.6	198.8	249.4	1105.0
1-2	132.8	432.6	389.3	954.7	55.7	189.8	245.5	1200.2
1-5	127.6	507.3	418.1	1053.0	51.2	180.8	232.0	1285.0
1-10	132.6	493.4	421.1	1047.1	39.4	194.9	234.3	1281.4
2-1	117.8	492.6	473.0	1083.4	32.3	168.8	201.1	1284.5
2-5	116.7	503.0	456.0	1075.7	16.1	177.3	193.4	1269.1
2-10	133.6	556.3	449.3	1139.2	17.8	191.2	209.0	1348.2
3-5	102.2	451.8	434.3	988.3	11.2	97.7	108.9	1097.2
3-11	110.7	506.1	427.6	1044.4		94.4	94.4	1138.8
4-4	112.1	501.9	438.5	1052.5		95.4	95.4	1147.9
5-2	115.3	547.0	481.3	1143.6		97.2	97.2	1240.8
5-11	112.2	541.5	514.0	1167.7		82.5	82.5	1250.2
6-5	106.9	646.8	547.5	1301.2		85.7	85.7	1386.9
6-8	102.2	635.8	552.1	1290.1		97.8	97.8	1387.9
7-1	102.1	638.8	591.7	1332.6		67.8	67.8	1400.4
7-11	107.1	667.2	592.4	1366.7		53.3	53.3	1420.0
8-2	104.8	650.9	624.4	1380.1		40.6	40.6	1420.7
8-5	72.5	647.0	597.4	1316.9		40.5	40.5	1357.3
8-11	68.9	704.2	638.8	1411.9		41.6	41.6	1453.5
9-10	81.7	770.5	708.4	1560.6		42.8	42.8	1603.4
10-5#	64.5	726.4	702.4	1493.3		44.9	44.9	1538.2
10-9	86.5	745.0	704.0	1535.5		55.6	55.6	1591.1
11-4	109.9	782.8	804.1	1696.8		32.2	32.2	1729.0
12-6	103.7	799.8	895.7	1799.2				1799.2
13-8	81.1	895.4	914.3	1890.8				1890.8
15-11	83.8	1060.6	1037.2	2181.6				2181.6
16-3	75.4	1086.4	1069.3	2231.1				2231.1

Note: Premax = Premaxilla; RLS = Right Lateral Segment; LLS = Left Lateral Segment; Tot = Total Surface Area; Ant = Anterior Cleft Space; Post = Posterior Cleft Space; Tot = Ant + Post; SA + CS = Bony Surface Area + Cleft Space Area; #: changing teeth

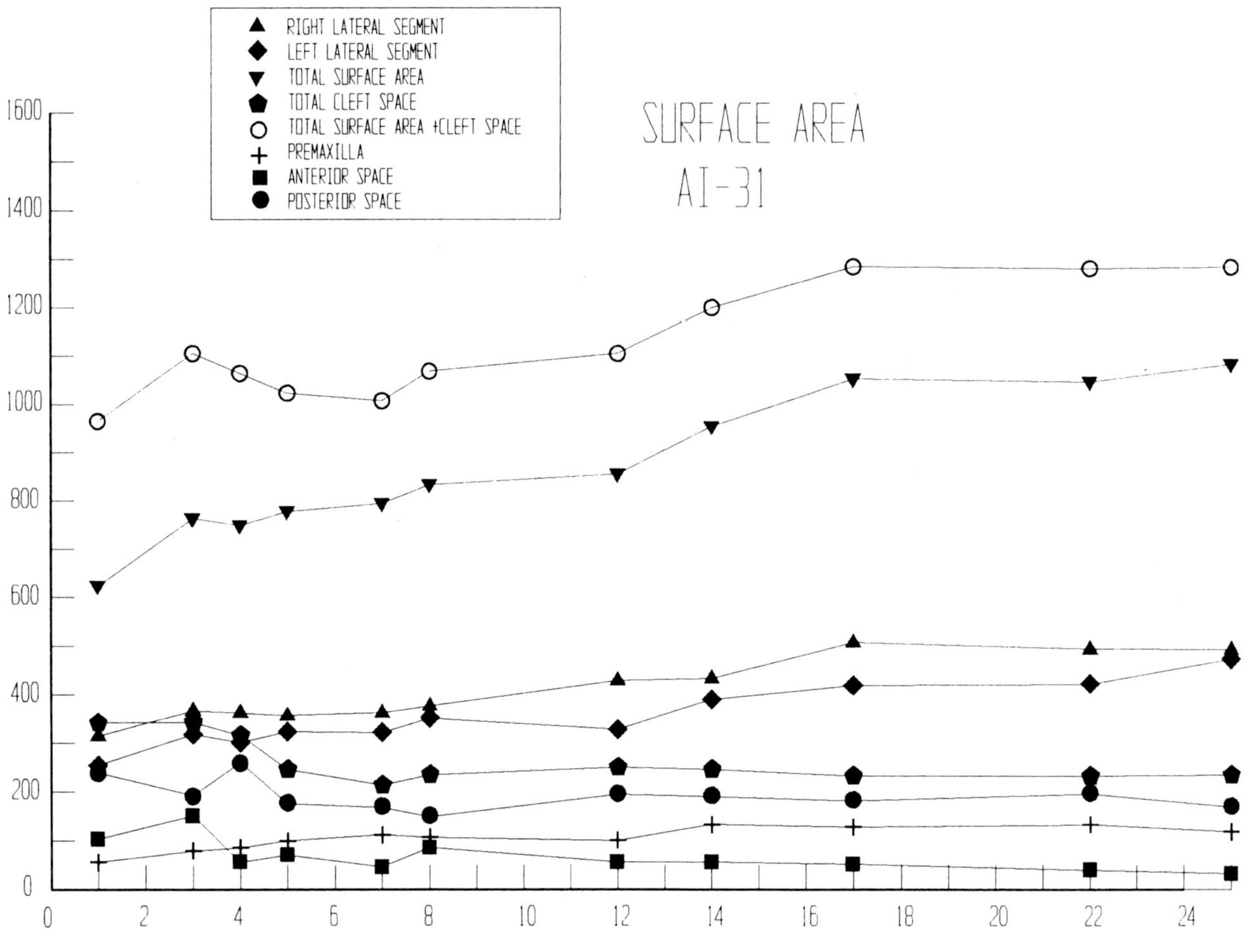

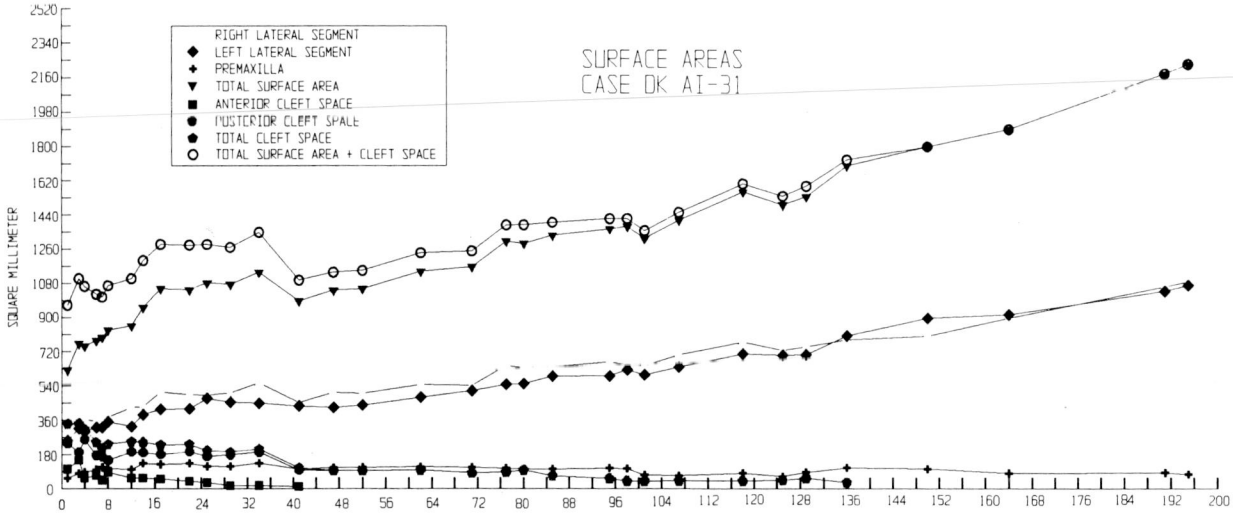

Fig 14-22. Case DK (AI-31). Premaxillary ventroflexion with medial movement of the lateral palatal segments caused a great reduction in the anterior and posterior cleft spaces by 5 months of age. Thereafter, for the next 19 months, the anterior cleft space gradually reduced, while the posterior cleft space showed some increase due to the increase in palatal length. Both lateral palatal segments showed a similar, gradually increasing growth rate.

Fig 14-23. Case DK (AI-31). After the initial change in cleft size brought on by medial movement of the lateral palatal segments and ventroflexion of the premaxilla, the greatest acceleration of cleft space closure occurred between 2-10 and 3-5. The premaxilla reached its largest size by 3 years, which is associated with eruption of the teeth. Palatal growth acceleration occurred between 1 to 3 months and 12 to 14 months and then gradually tapered off. The palatal segments had increased 37% in size by 1 year and 74% by 2 years. Palatal growth at its medial borders still occurs even though the total cleft space is increasing in size due to the increase in palatal length.

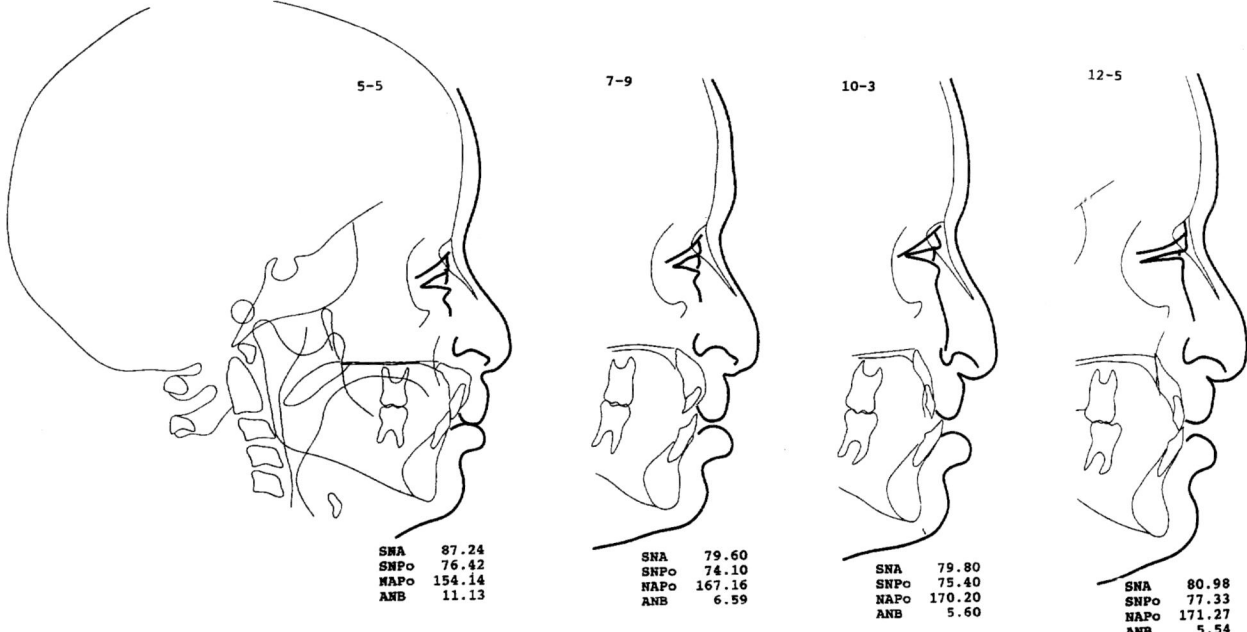

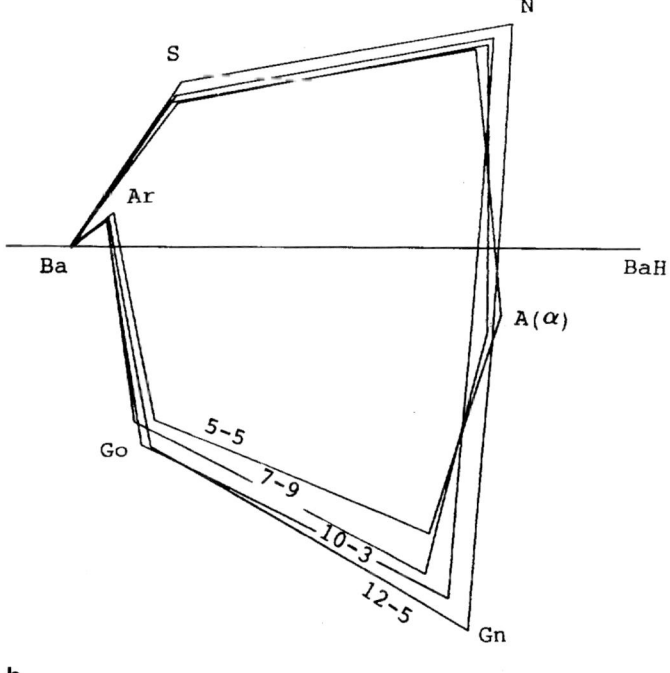

Fig 14–24. Case DK (AI-31). a. Serial lateral cephaloradiographic tracings show changes in the skeletal and soft tissue profile. The upper lip gradually became recessive, reflecting the lack of midfacial growth. **b.** Superimposed Basion Horizontal facial polygons of Coben. The midfacial protrusion seen at 12 years, 5 months is no different to that seen at 5 years, 5 months of age. At 10 years of age, the midface was more recessive, but with the application of premaxilla advancement orthodontics for 2 years, it was positioned more anteriorly. The lower jaw showed progressive downward and forward growth. As in all faces that grow well, this growth pattern was mainly responsible for the flattening of the facial profile.

CASE REPORT: EXCELLENT FACIAL AND PALATAL GROWTH IN CBCLP

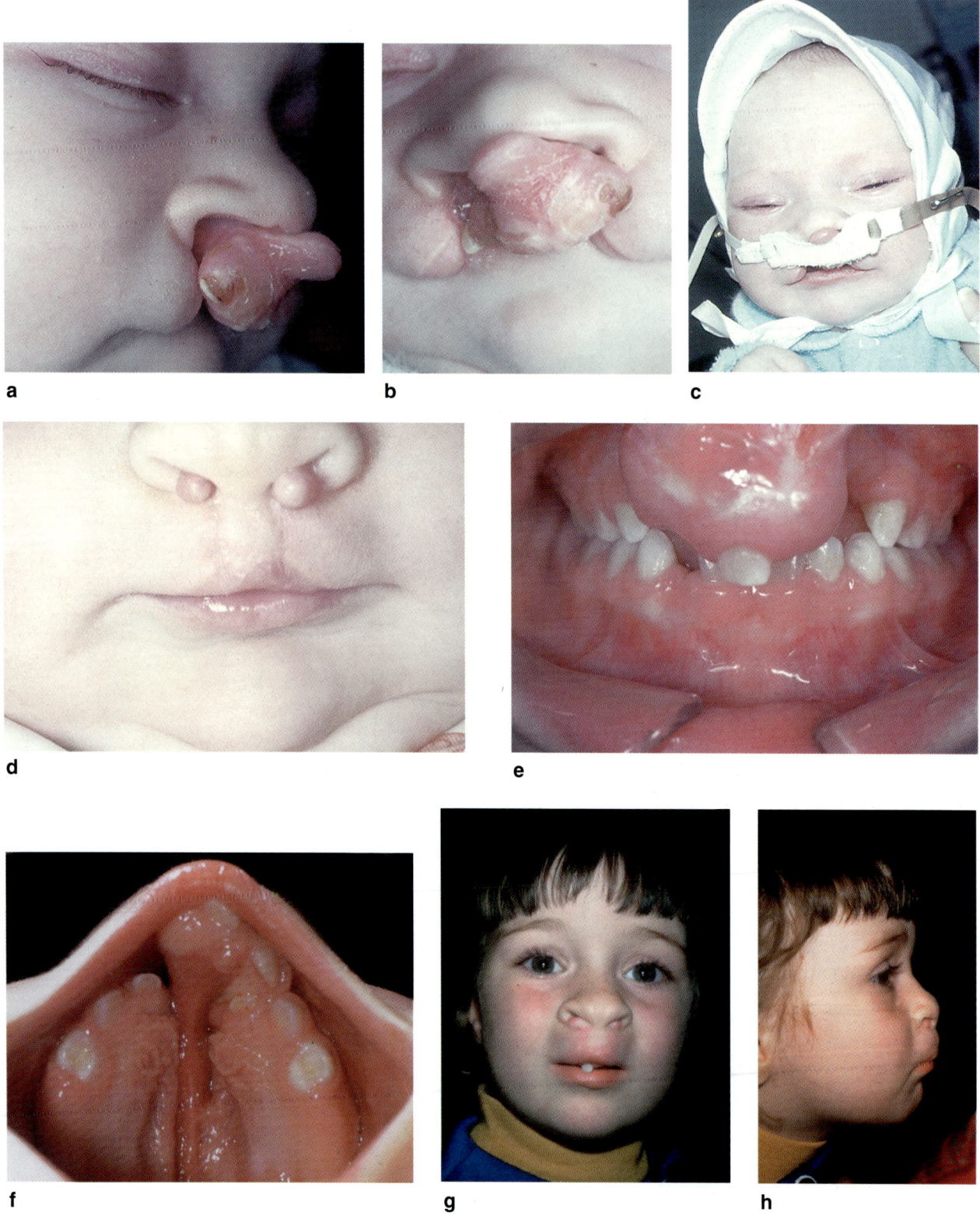

Fig 14–25. Case PM (KK-22). Serial photographs demonstrate excellent facial and palatal growth in CBCLP. Time is an ally! No presurgical orthopedics other than the use of external elastics off a head bonnet for 10 days prior to lip surgery were used. The palatal cleft was closed at 8 years of age using a modified von Langenbeck procedure. Secondary alveolar cranial bone grafting was done at 8 years of age. **a** and **b**. At birth, an extremely protrusive premaxilla. **c**. Head bonnet with elastic over the premaxilla. *(continued)*

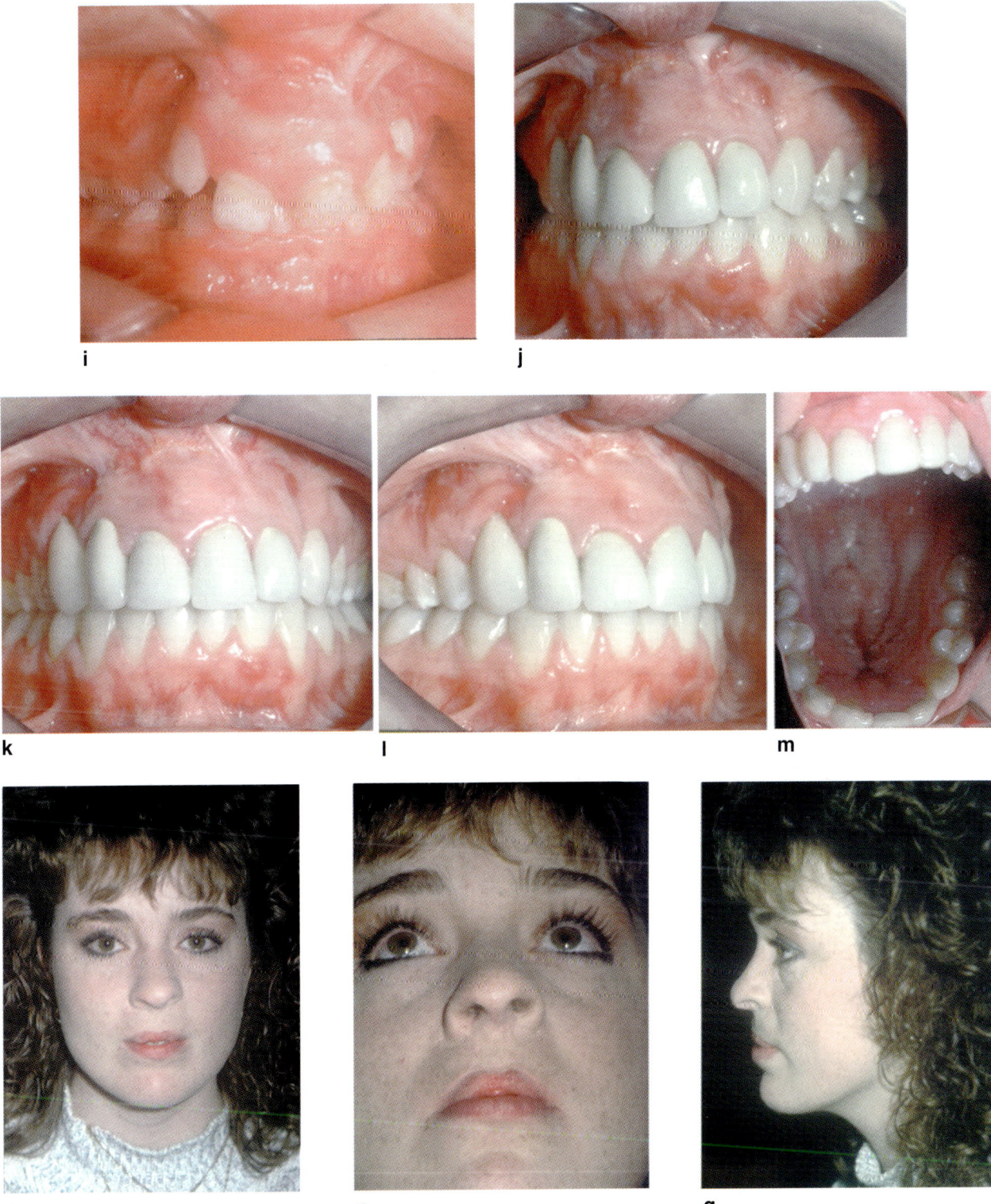

Fig 14–25. *(continued)*
d. The lip cleft was closed using Millard's forked flap procedure. The tissue in the nostril is used to reconstruct the columella at a later date so that the surgeon need not go back to the lip for tissue. **e.** Occlusal view at 5 years of age. Note that the premaxilla is still protrusive. **f.** Palatal view. The lip is being pushed forward by the protruding premaxilla. The palatal cleft was closed 4 months later. **g** and **h.** The face at 5 years showing upper lip protrusion. **i.** The premaxilla is still protrusive at 11 years of age. **j, k,** and **l.** At 20 years of age the occlusion is ideal. Minor imperfections in the anterior teeth were corrected by the use of composite material. **m.** Ideal arch form with a normal palatal vault space. **n.** Good alveolar bone support to the lateral incisors. **o, p,** and **q.** Facial photographs at 20 years of age showing a harmonious and pleasing soft tissue profile.

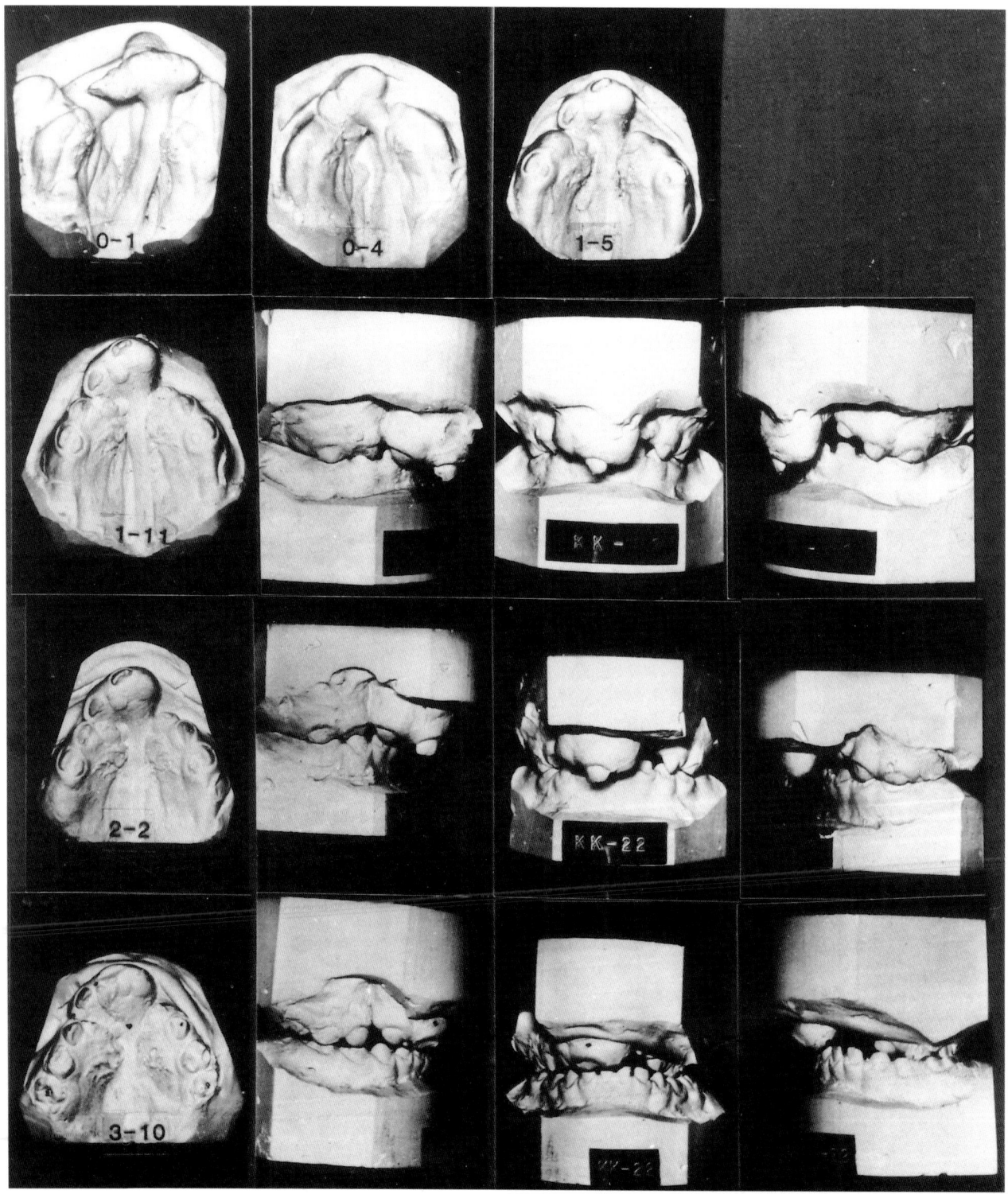

Fig 14–26. Case PM (KK-22). Serial casts: 0-1. At birth the septum is deviated to the left, and the right palatal segment is laterally displaced. **0-4.** With an external elastic and lip surgery, the premaxilla flexes ventrally and medially, making conact with both palatal segments. The remaining casts show excellent buccal occlusion in Class 2 relationship with a severe anterior overbite and overjet. By **8-3** the anterior overjet is markedly reduced by growth. **13-11.** Conventional orthodontics was eventually used to reduce the Class 2 occlusion and align the anterior teeth into an ideal overbite-overjet relationship.

(continued)

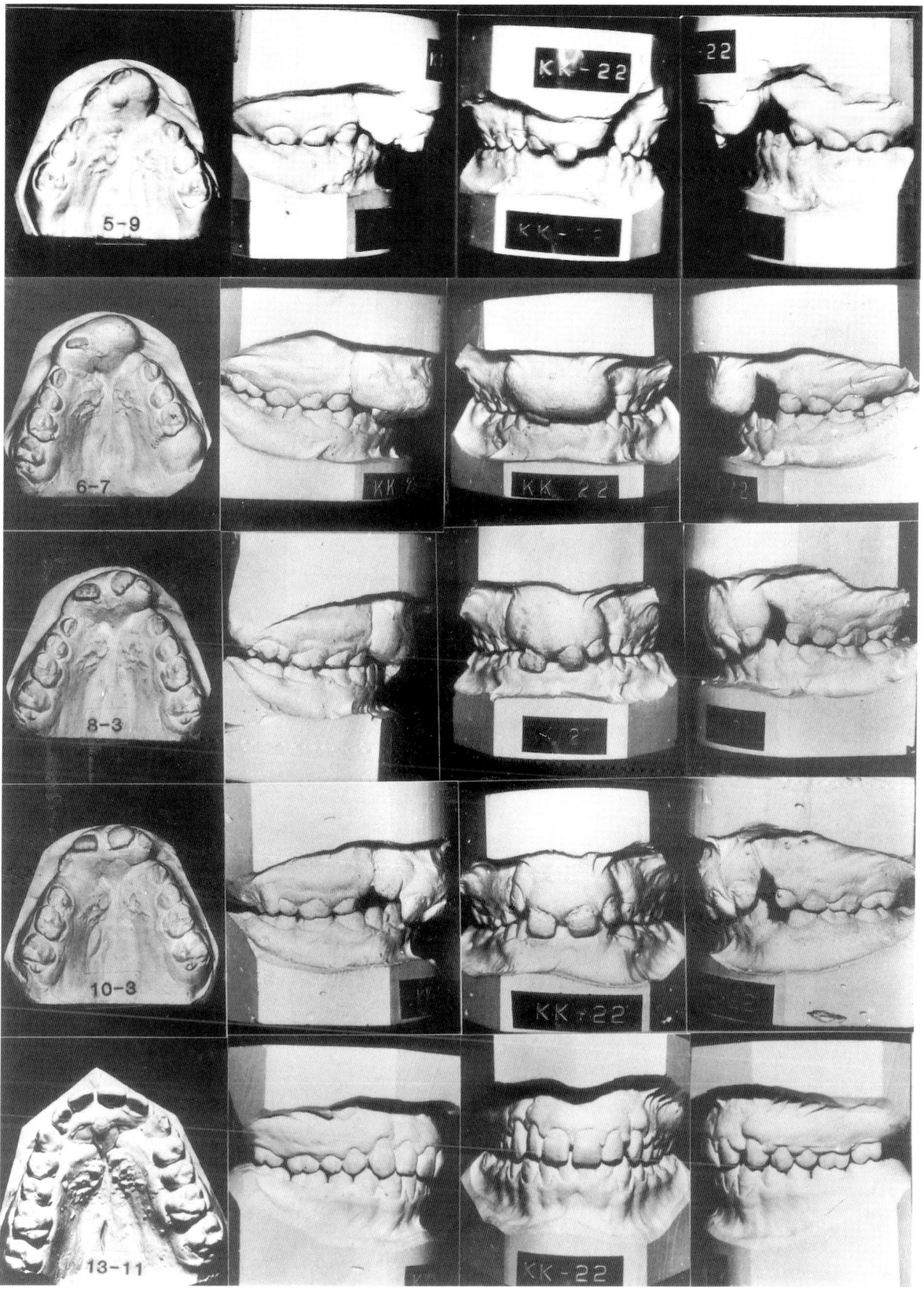

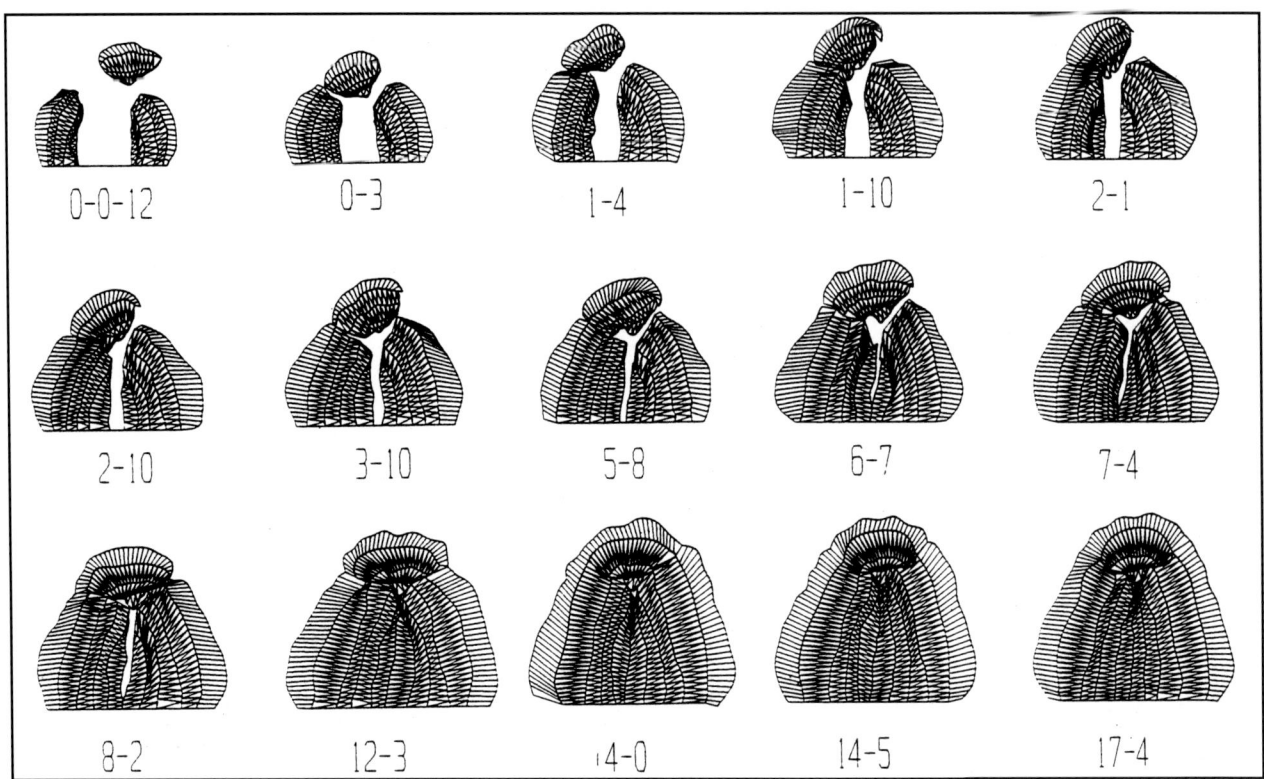

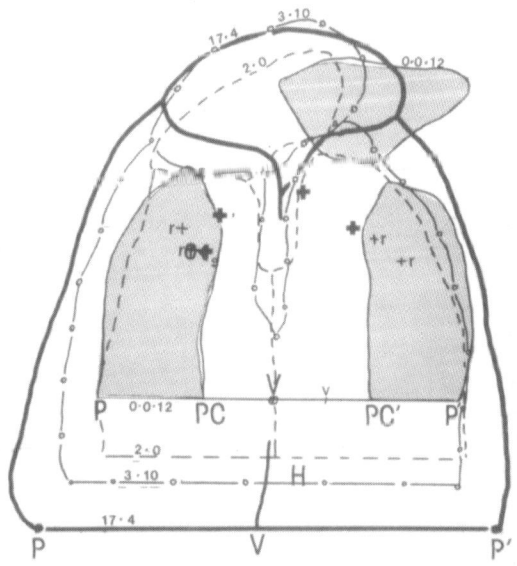

Fig 14–27. Case PM (KK 29) a. Computer-generated outlines of the serial casts were performed using an electromechanical digitizer. All casts are drawn to scale. The casts range from 12 days to 17 years, 4 months of age. This series demonstrates the spontaneous closure of the anterior and posterior cleft spaces after "molding action" brought on by uniting the lip and then by gradual palatal growth at the border of the cleft space. The premaxilla was initially aligned forward of the lateral palatal segments but was satisfactorily incorporated within the arch at a later age. **b.** Palatal outlines were superimposed using the rugae for registration. This series shows that the premaxilla's position within the maxillary complex at 17 years of age is similar to that seen at birth. Excellent growth occurs in all dimensions and is similar to the growth pattern seen in noncleft palates. Increased posterior palatal growth is necessary to accommodate the developing molars. Alveolar bone growth with tooth eruption increases midfacial height.

TABLE 14–3. Surface Area of CBCLP. Case PM (KK-22). The palatal surface area increased by 40% after 1 year, 4 months and by 76% at 2 years, 1 month. By 8 years, 2 months, the palatal surface area had increased two and a half times when the cleft space was closed.

Age	Skeletal Area				Cleft Space			Total
	Premax	RLS	LLS	Tot	Ant	Post	Tot	SA + CS
0-0-12	145.5	335.5	282.7	763.7	127.4	417.0	544.4	1308.1
0-3	150.2	397.4	377.6	925.2	65.4	331.5	396.9	1322.1
1-4	154.0	469.5	464.3	1087.8	36.8	265.5	302.3	1390.1
1-10	211.8	502.6	506.2	1220.6	70.4	216.3	286.7	1507.3
2-1	217.6	589.0	549.5	1356.1	79.8	195.3	275.1	1631.2
2-10	220.7	603.9	551.3	1375.9	95.8	193.2	289.0	1664.9
3-10	271.6	660.4	616.5	1548.5	122.6	206.3	328.9	1877.4
5-8	273.3	673.0	675.9	1622.2	123.6	201.2	324.8	1947.0
6-7	273.6	811.0	820.5	1905.1	115.0	206.5	321.5	2226.6
7-4	277.3	813.0	839.5	1929.8	106.7	185.2	291.9	2221.7
8-2	306.5	844.6	890.8	2041.9	101.1	155.4	256.5	2298.4
12-3	346.8	1087.1	1116.1	2550.0				2550.0
14-0	348.7	1161.8	1226.4	2736.9				2736.9
14-5	351.1	1198.8	1237.0	2786.9				2786.9
17-4	353.5	1211.0	1246.3	2840.8				2840.8

Note: Premax = Premaxilla; RLD = Right Lateral Segment; LLS = Left Lateral Segment; Tot = Total Surface Area; Ant = Anterior Cleft Space; Post = Posterior Cleft Space; Tot = Ant + Post; SA + CS = Bony Surface Area + Cleft Space Area

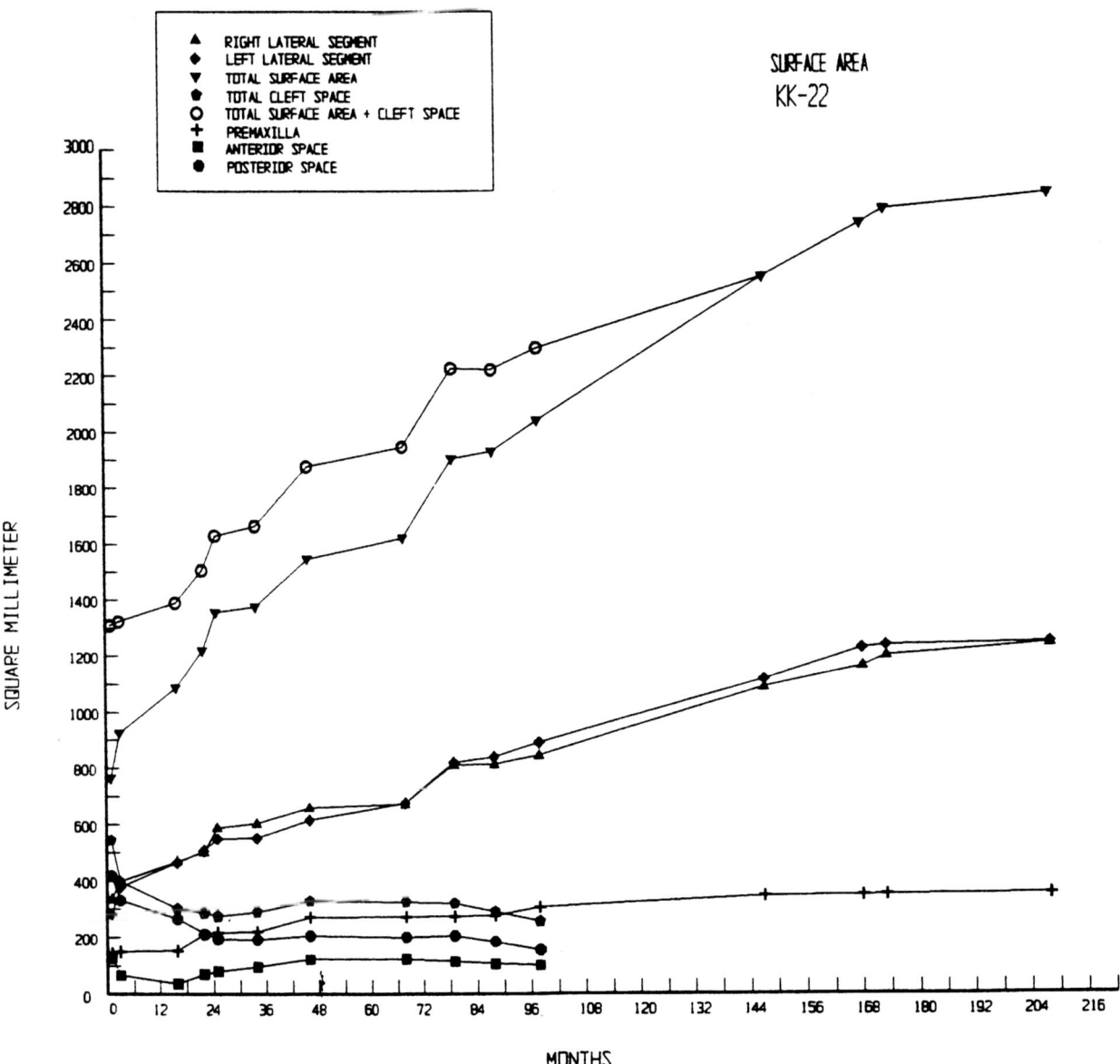

Fig 14-28. Case PM (KK-22) Time sequence analysis of serial palatal growth shows that both palatal segments are growing at the same rate and to the same degree. The premaxilla is also increasing in size with tooth eruption but at a lesser rate. The greatest palatal growth acceleration occurs the first 2 years and then tapers off. The anterior cleft space is initially reduced as a result of premaxillary ventroflexion, but thereafter it remains the same dimensions until the palatal cleft is closed. The posterior cleft space initially is reduced with palatal medial movement. The resulting posterior cleft space remains approximately the same size for the next 8 years. It must be remembered that the cleft length is increasing while the cleft width is decreasing. The net cleft area is gradually reducing with growth. All fistulae are closed by 148 months.

CASE REPORT: SEVERE PREMAXILLARY PROTRUSION IN IBCLP

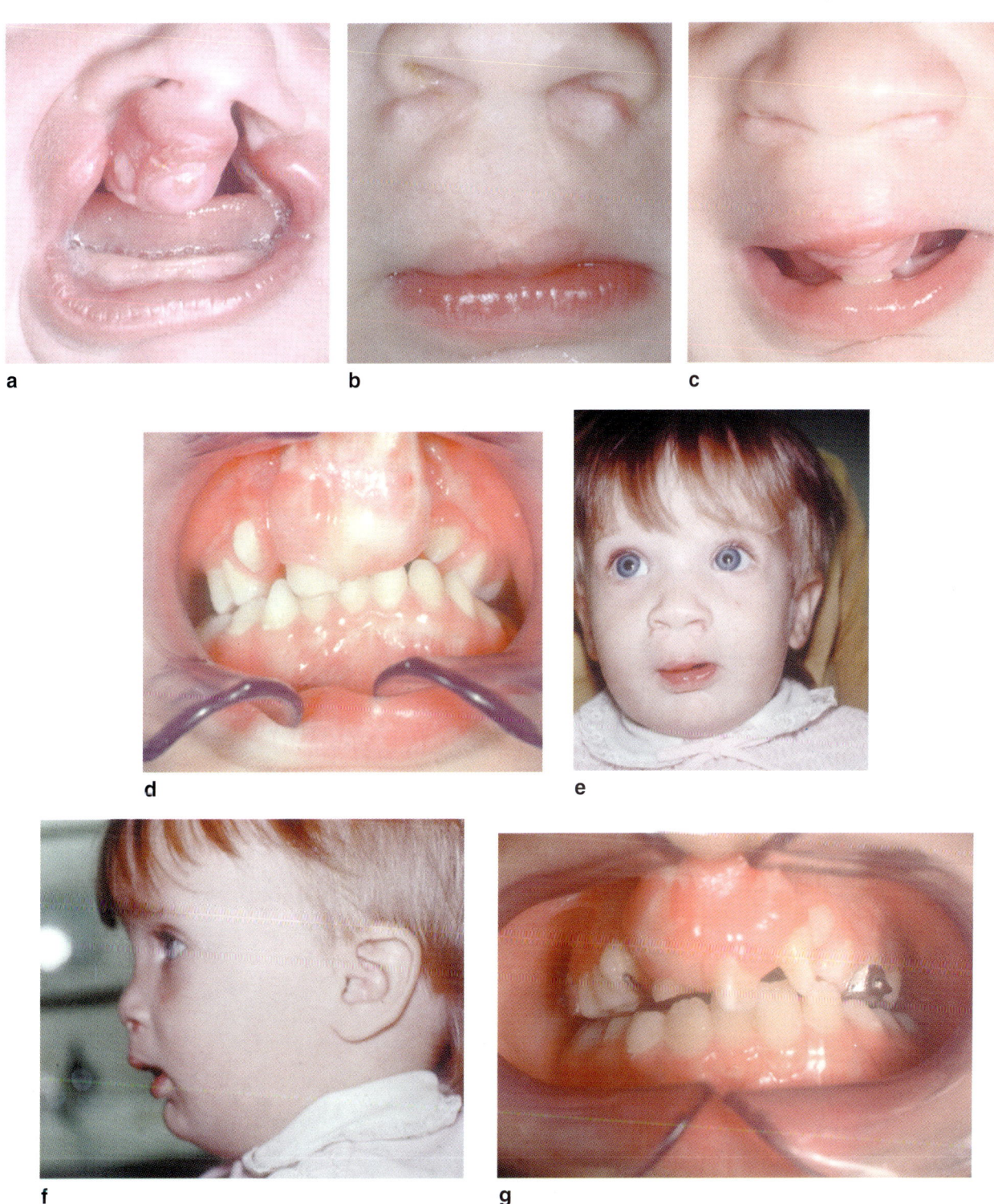

Fig 14–33. Case ML (KK-56) demonstrates severe premaxillary protrusion at birth in IBCLP. "Whisker" forked flap was performed at 2 months, definitive lip surgery at 6 months, and palatal cleft closure at 18 months. Secondary alveolar cranial bone grafting was placed at 8 years, 3 months. Maxillary surgery with chin augmentation was performed at 15 years, 7 months. **a-g.** Facial and intraoral photographs show progressive facial and occlusal changes. **h, i,** and **j.** Facial photographs at 8 years of age. **k.** After Lefort I advancement, the lateral incisor pontics were attached to the arch wire for aesthetics. **l** and **m.** Occlusal photograhs showing missing incisor spaces. **n, o,** and **p.** Intraoral photographs showing retainer with lateral incisor pontics in place. **q, r,** and **s.** Facial photographs at 17 years of age.

(continued)

Fig 14–33. *(continued)*

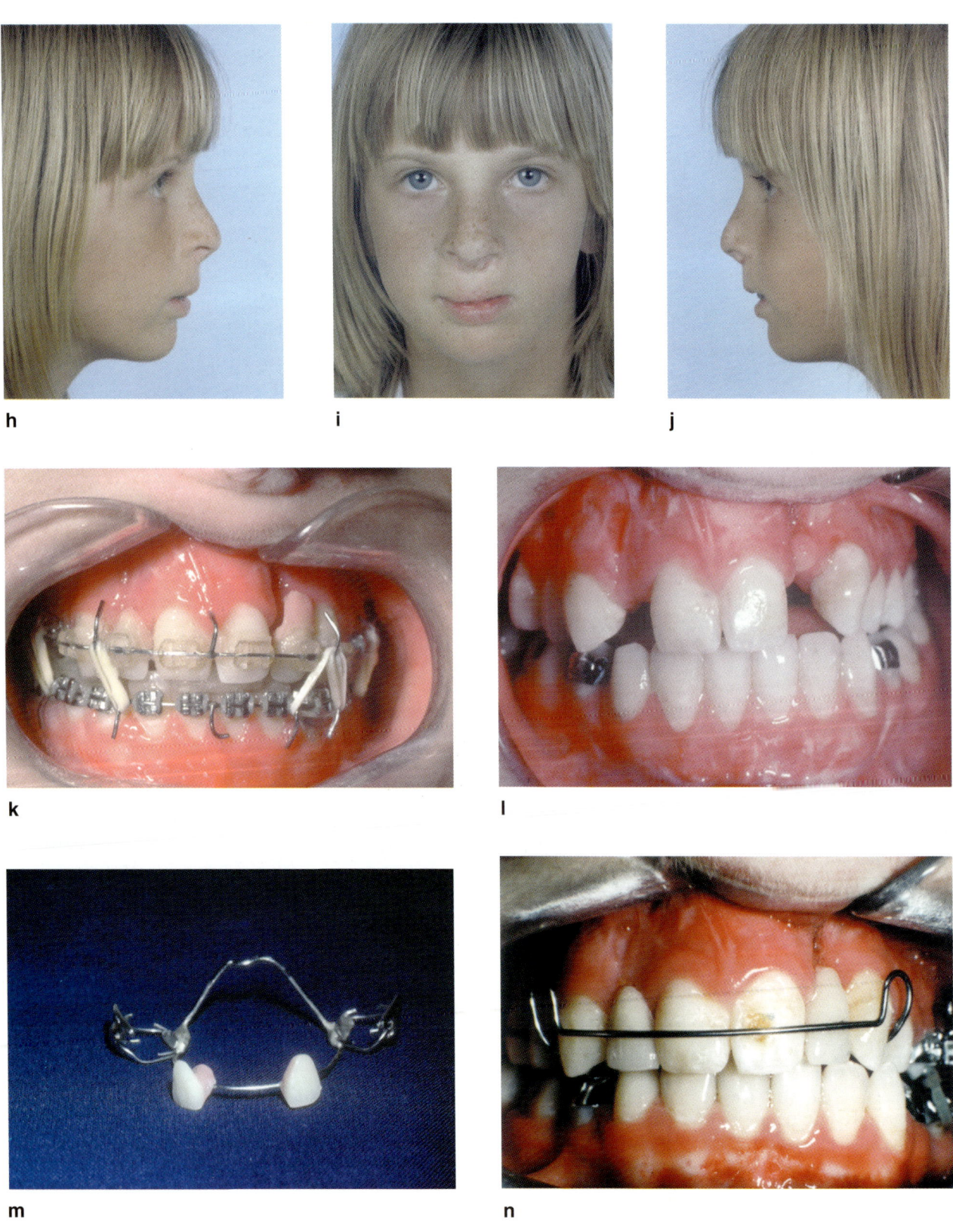

Fig 14–32. *(continued)*

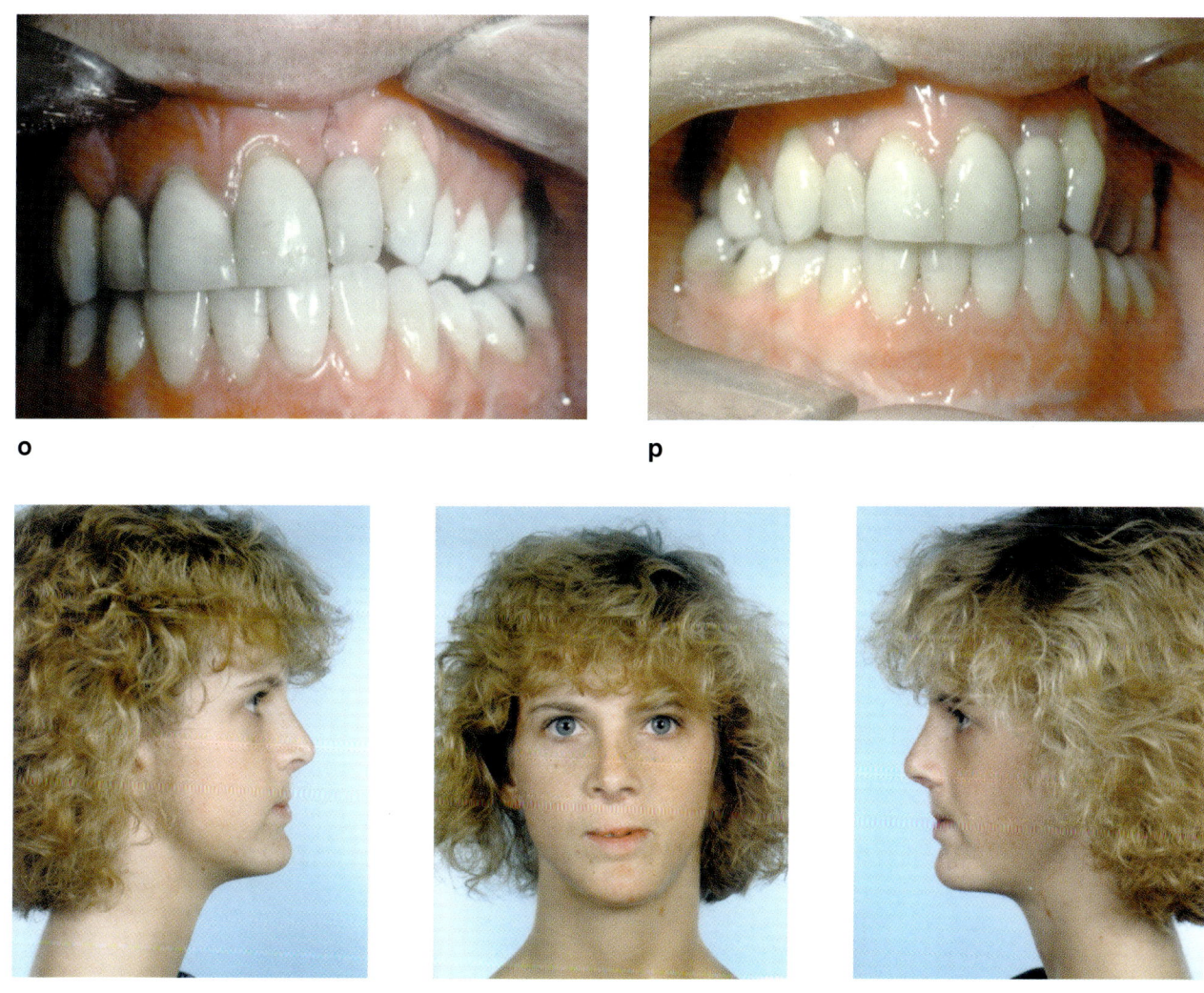

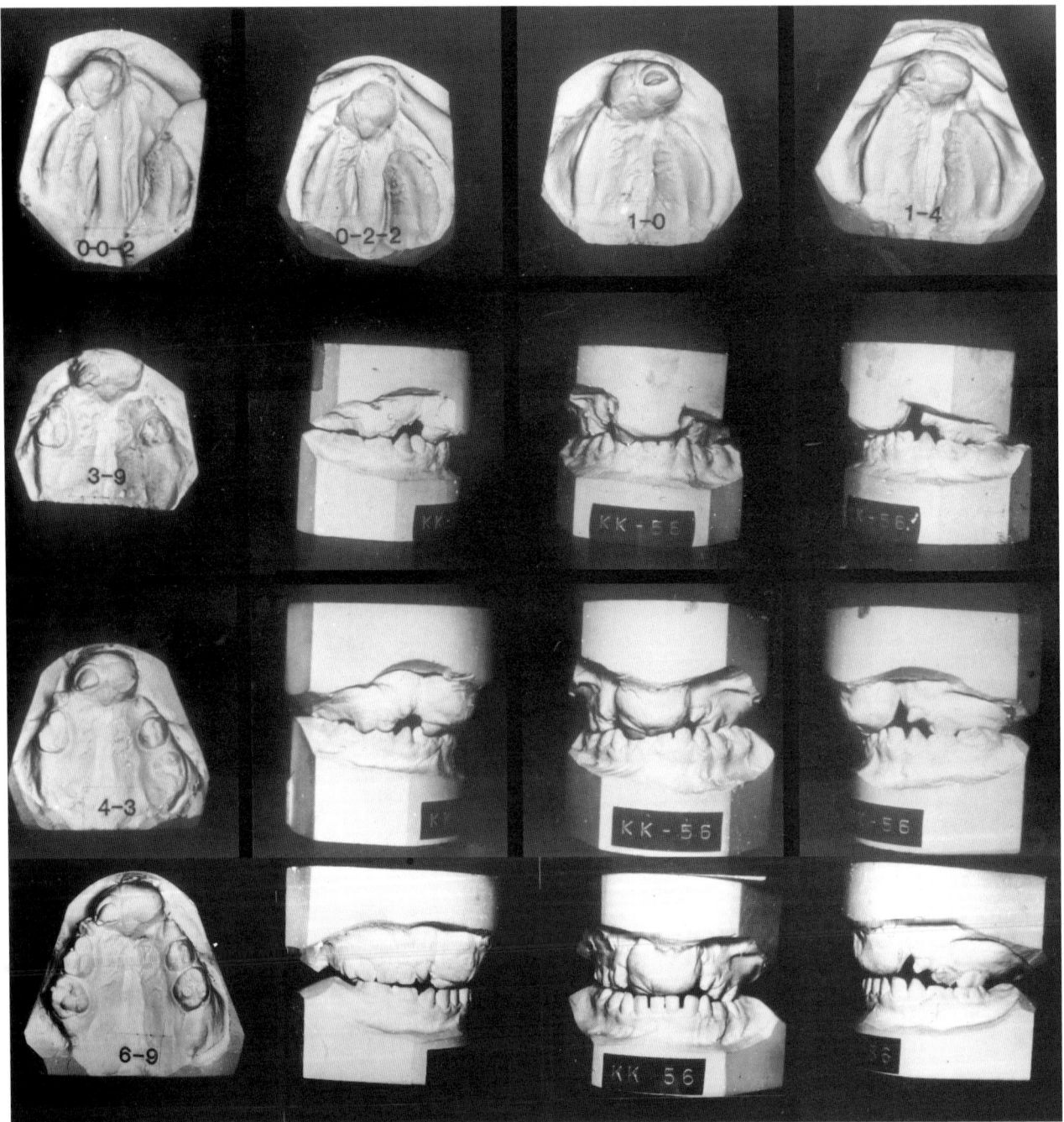

Fig 14–34. Case ML (KK-56). Serial casts from 0-0-2 to 4-3: With the establishment of an intact lip musculature, the premaxilla and lateral palatal segments molded into a good arch form. The premaxilla, although latero- and ventroflexed, still caused the upper lip to be pushed forward. The left buccal crossbite was corrected by 8 years of age and a fixed palatal retainer placed. **15-7.** Orthodontic treatment was designed not to correct the slight Class 2 occlusion of the left segment. **15-9.** After Lefort I osteotomy and final teeth alignment. Because the premaxilla was positioned slightly to the right and could not be centered orthodontically, it was decided to leave the left occlusion in Class 2 and the right occlusion in Class 1, thereby equalizing the space for the lateral incisors. **17-0.** A cuspid-to-cuspid fixed bridge replaced the missing lateral incisors and stabilized the relationship of all segments.

(continued)

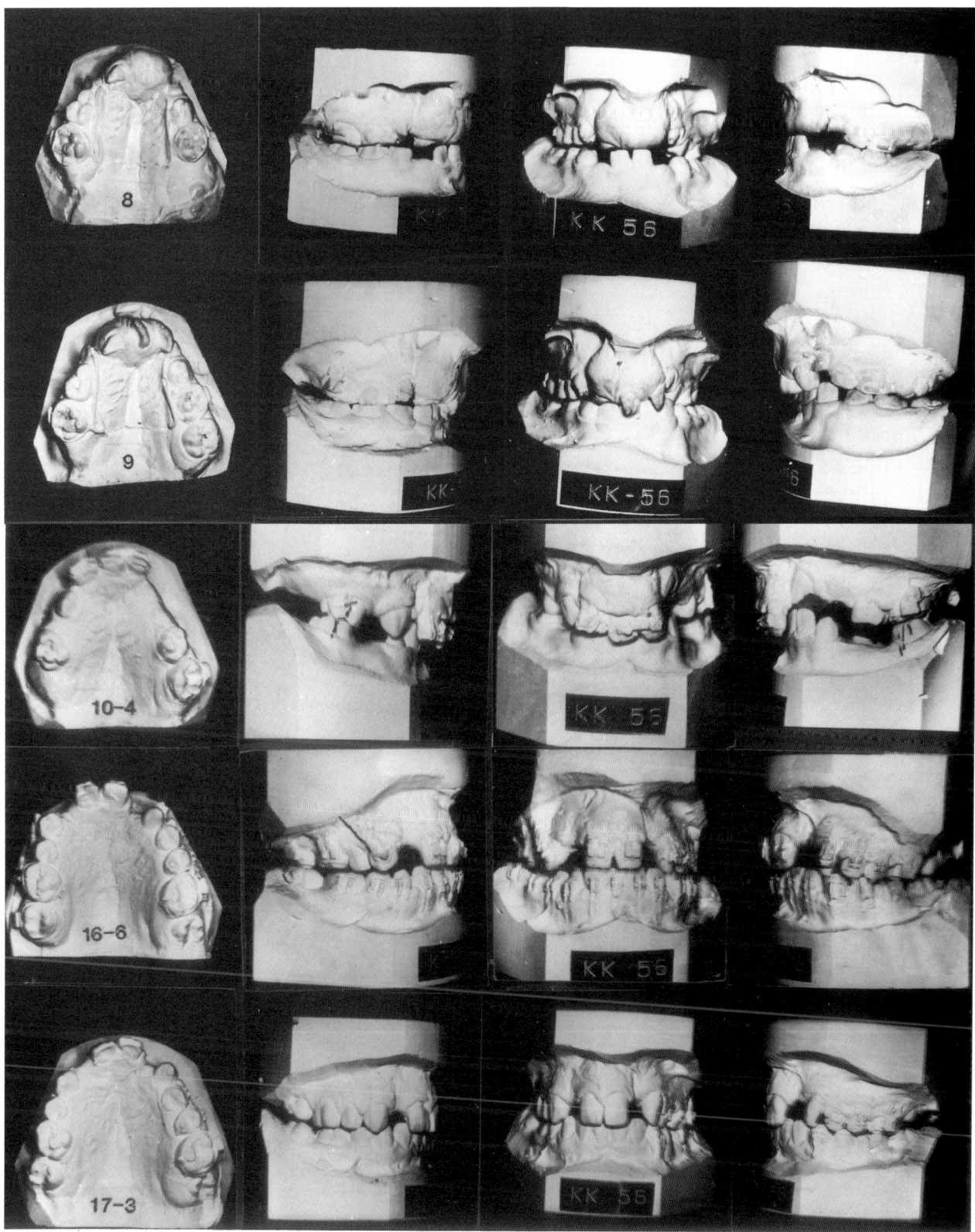

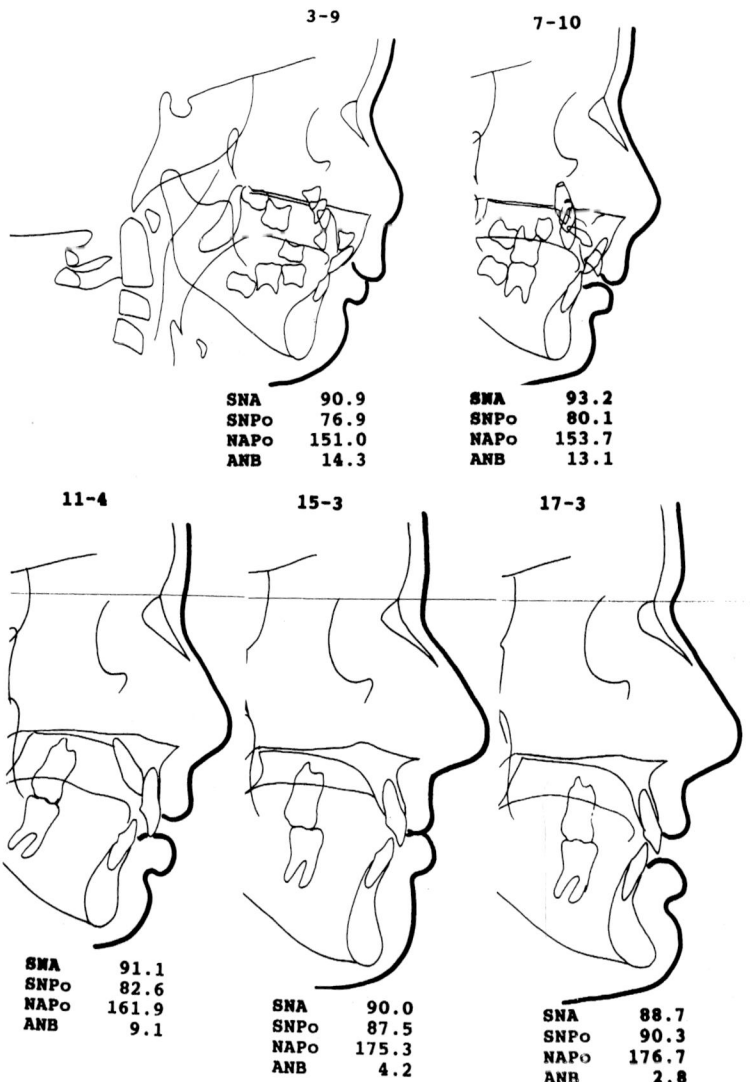

Fig 14-35. Case ML (KK-56). Serial cephalometric tracings showing well proportioned facial growth with a flattening of the facial profile. The protrusive premaxilla was present at 7-10. Orthodontia at 11 years of age improved the axial inclination of the maxillary incisors. The profile at 15-3 is more attactive than that at 17-3 as a result of the chin augmentation at 15-7. The chin point is too protrusive, resulting in a prominent sublabial fold.

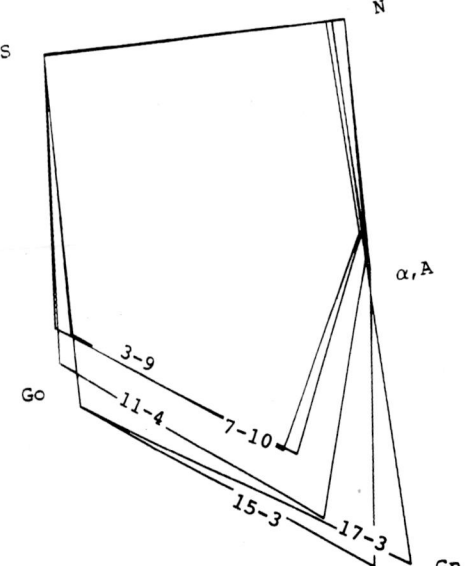

Fig 14-36. Case ML (KK-56). Superimposed polygons show an excellent facial growth pattern flattened the profile by 15-3. Midfacial osteotomy corrected the maxillary asymmetry. A chin augmentation was performed at 15-7 years which created a too prominent chin. The mandible continued to grow until 17-3 years of age, creating a slightly concave skeletal profile. The patient is considering having the chin prominence reduced.
Comment: Rarely should a chin augmentation be performed with a LeFort I advancement to avoid creating a "dished in" face if the midfacial advancement relapses. Note the small forward growth increments at the anterior cranial base and midface. The midfacial changes did show good vertical growth to maintain normal facial proportions.

CASE REPORT: CLOSURE OF A LARGE ANTERIOR CLEFT SPACE BY MOVING THE LATERAL PALATAL SEGMENT FORWARD

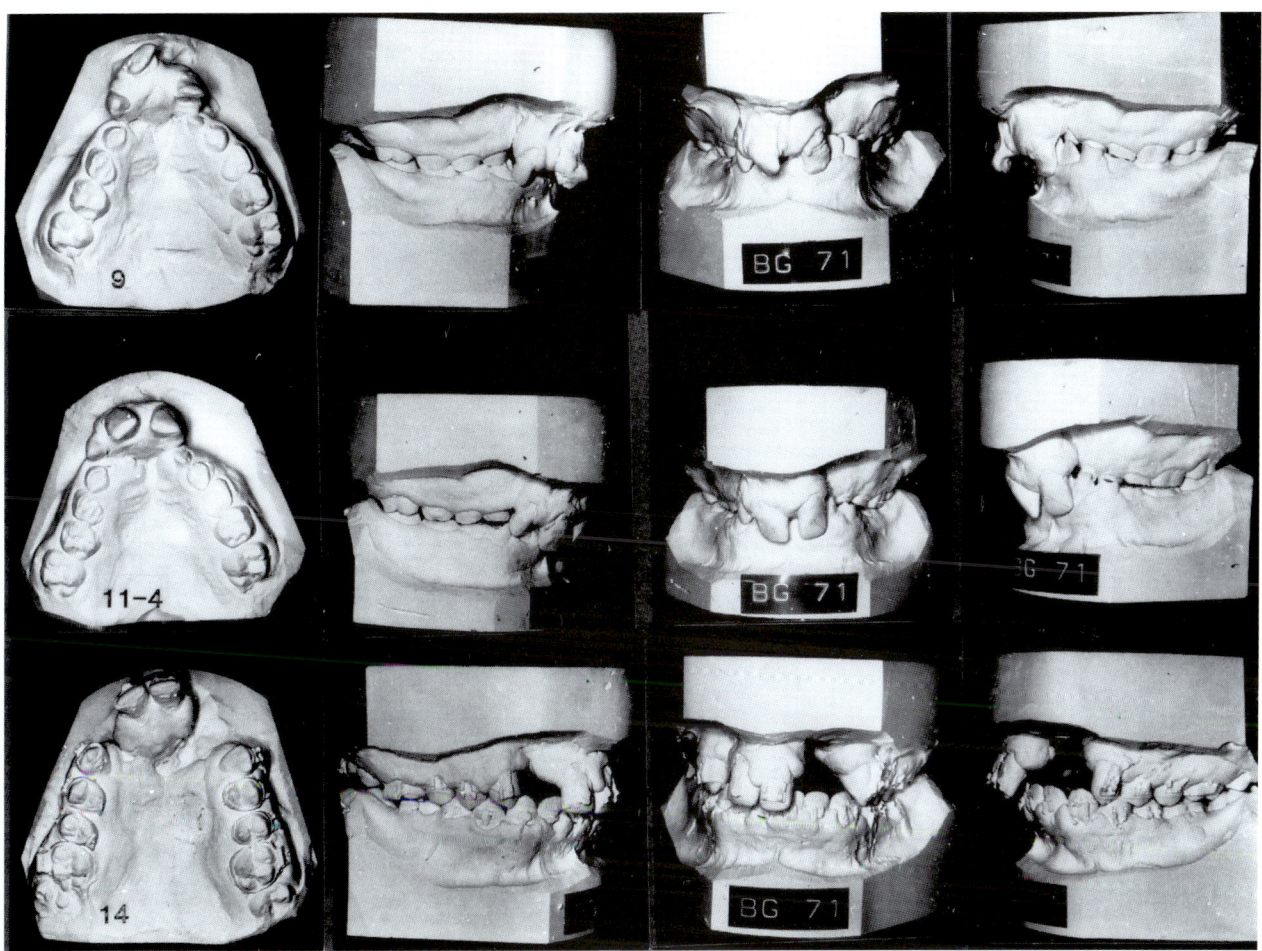

Fig 14–37. Case CW (BG-71). Serial casts demonstrate forward advancement of the buccal segments to reduce a very large anterior cleft space. There are instances when a marked osteogenic deficiency exists in both lateral incisor areas where the premaxilla is in a slight overjet-overbite relationship and the buccal segments in good Class 1 relationship. In these cases, there may be insufficient contiguous soft tissue to close the anterior cleft space when performing a secondary alveolar bone graft and create a normal site for tooth replacement. The treatment of choice is to advance both buccal segments simultaneously placing secondary alveolar bone grafts, yet leaving space for the lateral incisors. After surgery the cuspids were to return to their original Class 1 position. It was believed that with premaxillary setback alone there would be inadequate soft tissue to obtain adequate cleft closure.

(continued)

Fig 14–37. *(continued)*

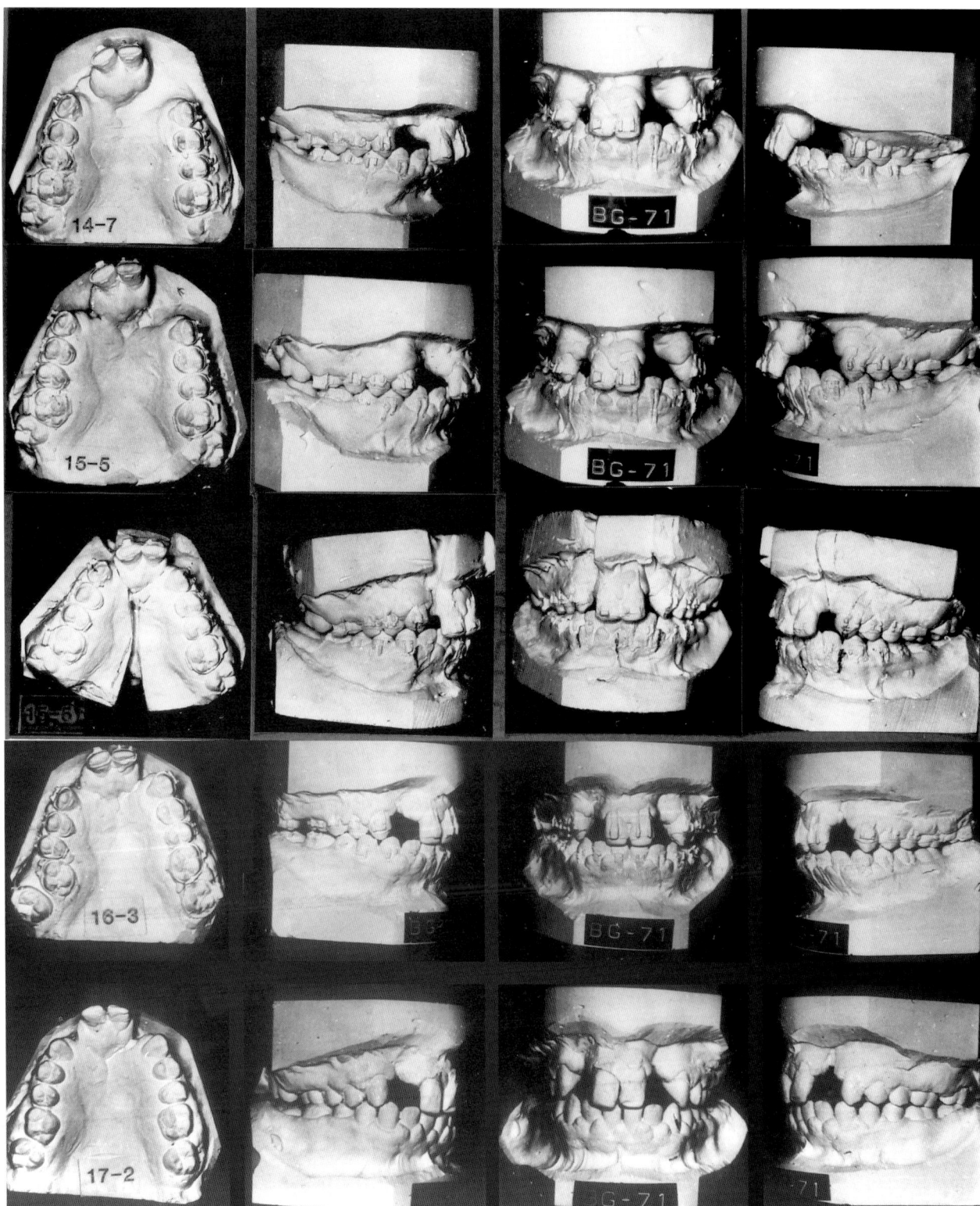

Fig 14–37. *(continued)*
15-5. Good premaxillary relationship with a large anterior cleft space. Class 1 posterior occlusion. Sectioned plaster casts with the posterior segments placed in Class 2 relationship. **16-3.** and **17-2.** Both buccal segments relapsed into Class 1. The main objective of closing the anterior cleft spaces was achieved. It might have been better to perform a secondary alveolar bone graft at 9 years of age, when all the palatal segments made contact, and then expanded the arch. Final casts show good Class 1 occlusion with a satisfactory overjet-overbite relationship. The anterior cleft space was closed. However, the alveolar bone graft did not take.

CASE REPORT: SEVERE MAXILLARY RETRUSION IN CBCLP IN ADOLESCENCE

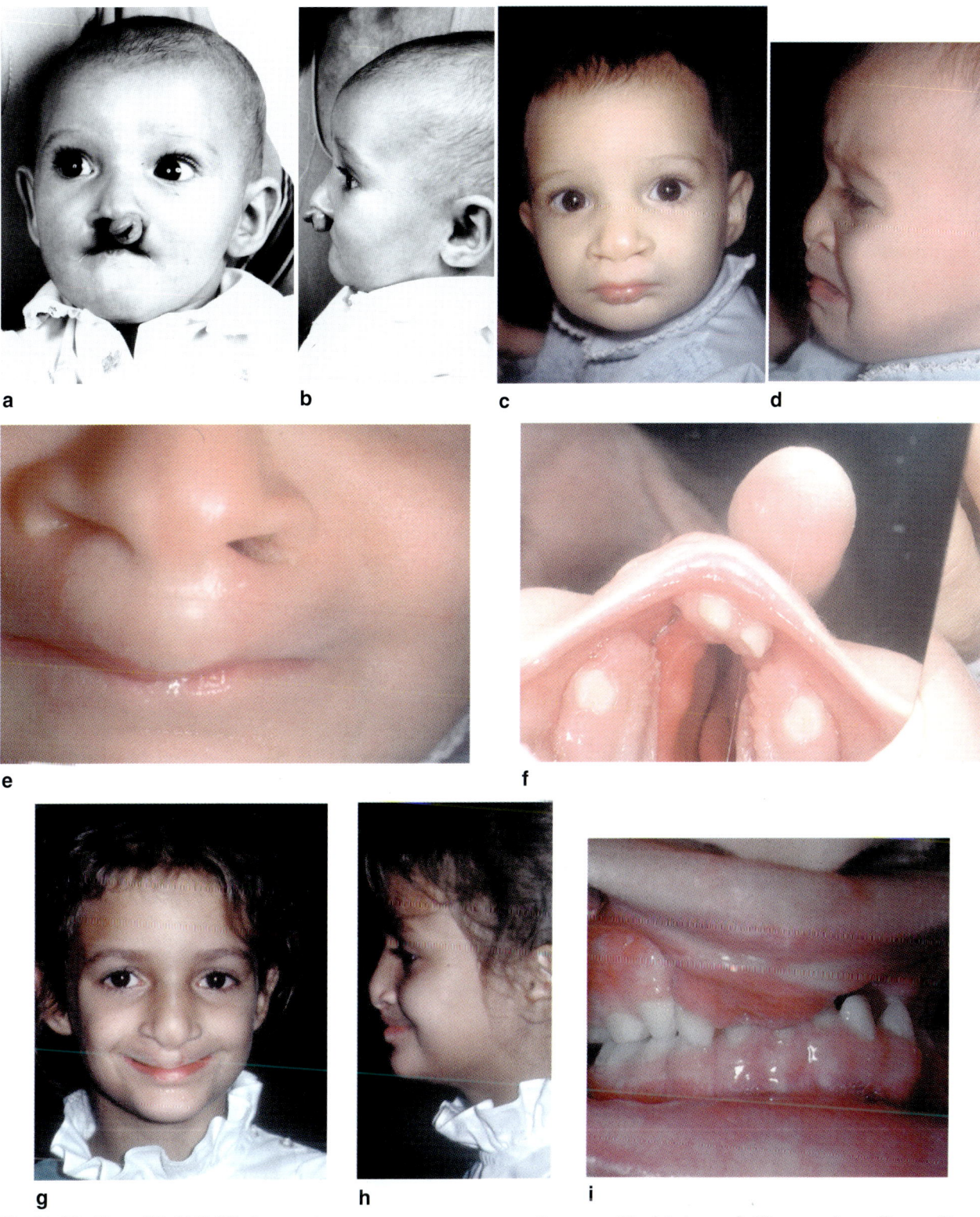

Fig 14–38. Case CS (AF-48) demonstrates severe premaxillary protrusion in a child with CBCLP at birth, resulting in maxillary retrusion in adolescence with the eventual loss of the premaxillary incisors. Lip adhesion was performed at 3 months with forked flap and posterior palate cleft closure at 3 years. No secondary alveolar bone grafts were utilized between 8–10 years of age. Premaxillary surgical advancement at 15 years to correct its retrusion. The premaxillary incisors were extracted due to severe periodontal bone loss, and the oronasal opening was closed at 16 years of age. **a** and **b**. Newborn. **c-i**. Even with premaxillary ventroflexion, the upper lip was still pushed forward.

(continued)

Fig 14–38. (continued)

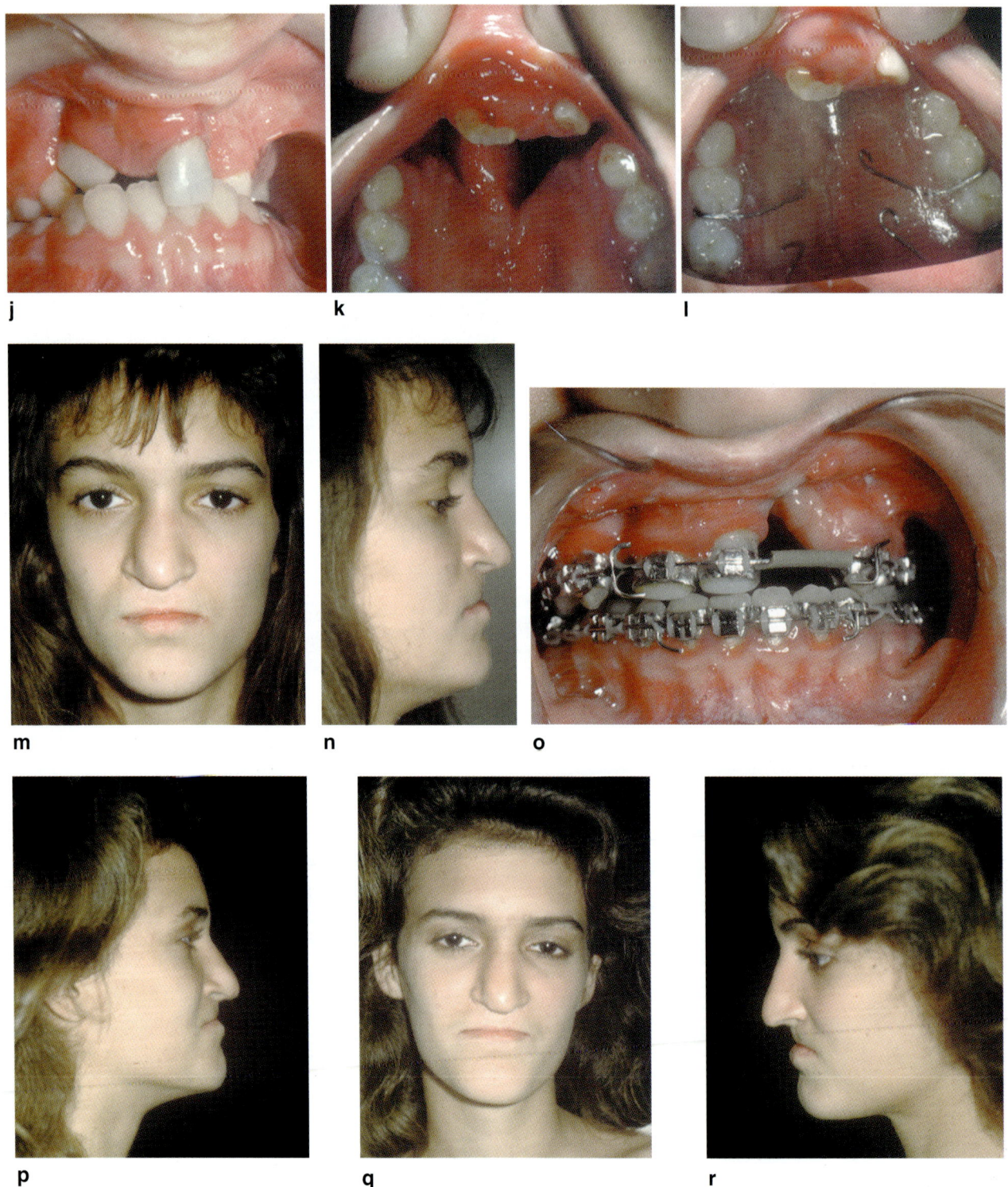

i-l. A plastic obturator was utilized at 6 years of age to close the very large anterior cleft space to aid speech development and feeding. **m-o.** At 14 years, a retrusive looking midface with an extremely tight upper lip and depressed nasal tip masked a good premaxillary overjet.

p-u. At 15 years following an unsuccessful attempt to surgically center the premaxilla and close the anterior cleft space. The maxillary incisor roots began to show severe external root absorption. A very large anterior cleft space remains.

(continued)

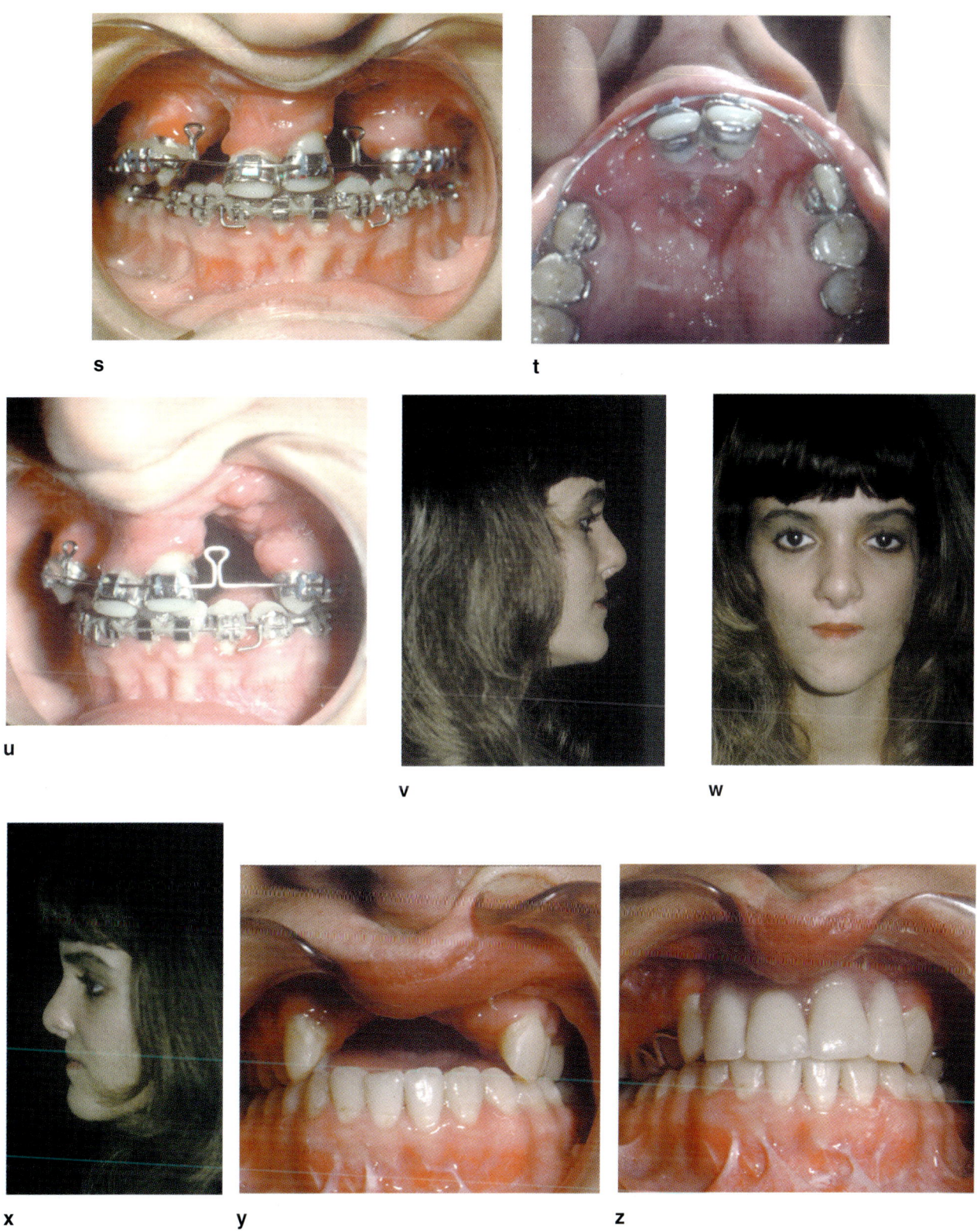

v-y. After lip and nose revision, the anterior teeth were extracted and the oronasal opening closed with adjoining soft tissue. **z.** A removable maxillary prosthesis replaced missing teeth and bumpered the upper lip.

Comments: It would have been better treatment to have surgically advanced both palatal segments to close the very large anterior cleft space. The root absorption was secondary to traumatic orthodontics utilized to maintain the incisor overjet.

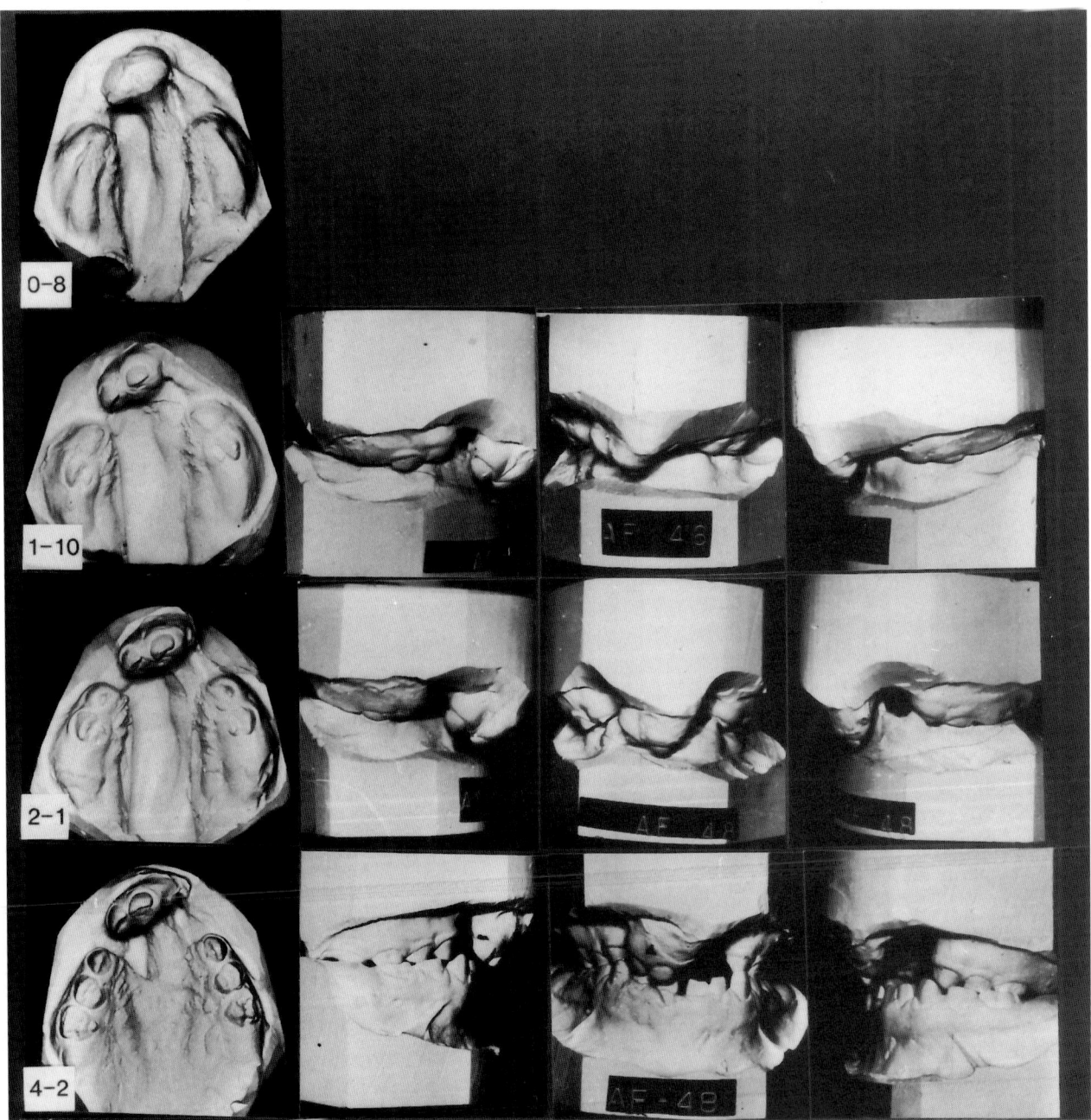

Fig 14–39. Case CS (AF-48). Serial casts show that the extreme premaxillary protrusion with large anterior cleft space at birth is still present at **6-1** years of age. **11-6.** With increased facial growth, the increasing tonicity of the buccal muscle forces collapsed the maxillary arch placing the posterior teeth in crossbite. The premaxilla is now upright and in an acceptable overbite-overjet relationship. **12-3.** Maxillary expansion has been initiated. The maxillary central incisors are in tip-to-tip relationship. **14.** Continued orthodontic treatment to advance the premaxilla and position the incisor teeth in proper overjet-overbite relationship.

(continued)

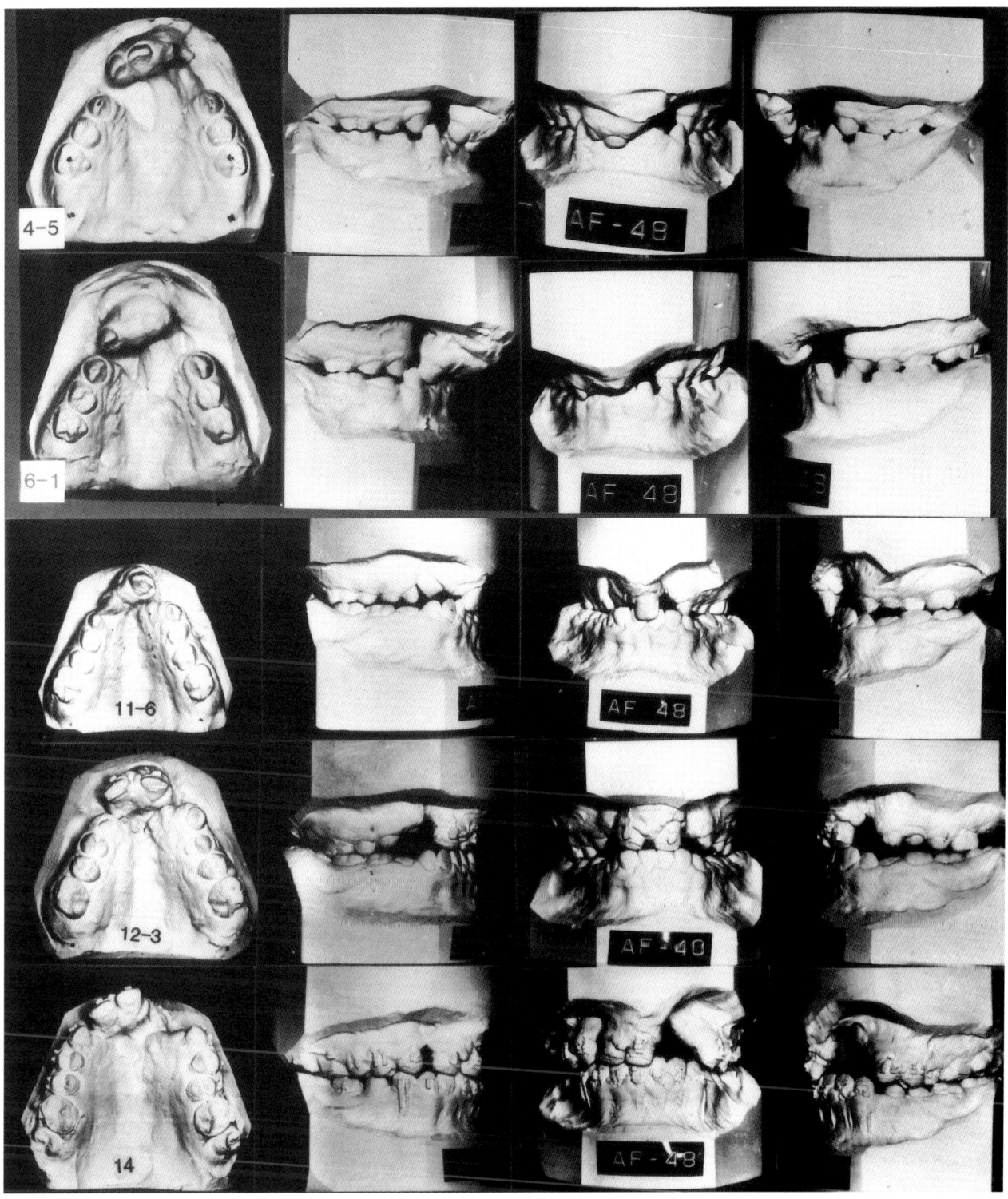

15-2, 16, and **16-6.** Premaxillary repositioning with soft tissue closure of the anterior cleft space was unsuccessful. As a result of the premaxillary central incisors showing external root absorption and loss of periodontal support, they were extracted and the oronasal opening closed with adjacent soft tissue. A removable maxillary prosthesis replaces the missing teeth and bumpers the upper lip.

Comment: As already suggested, the treatment of choice is to reposition the lateral palatal segments anteriorly while leaving the premaxilla as is.

(continued)

Fig 14–39. (continued)

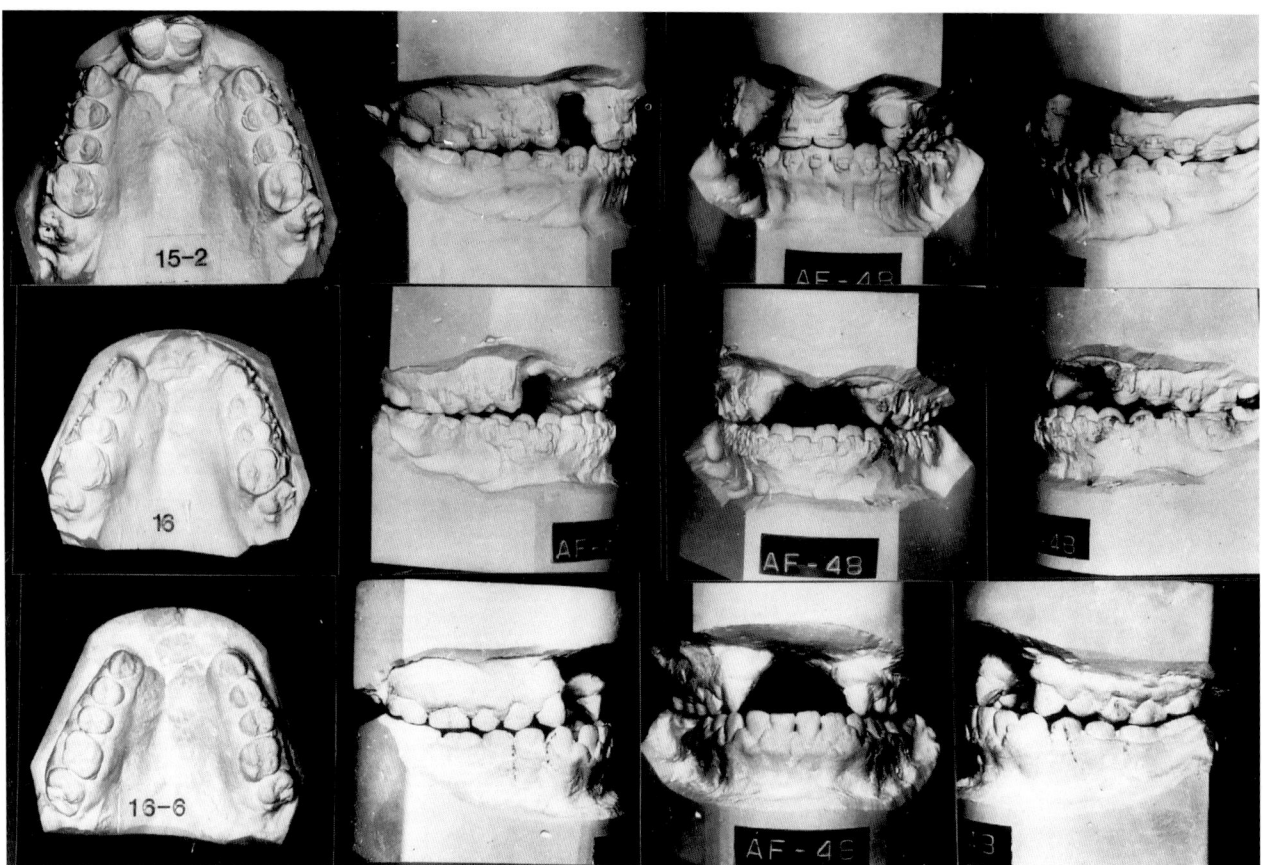

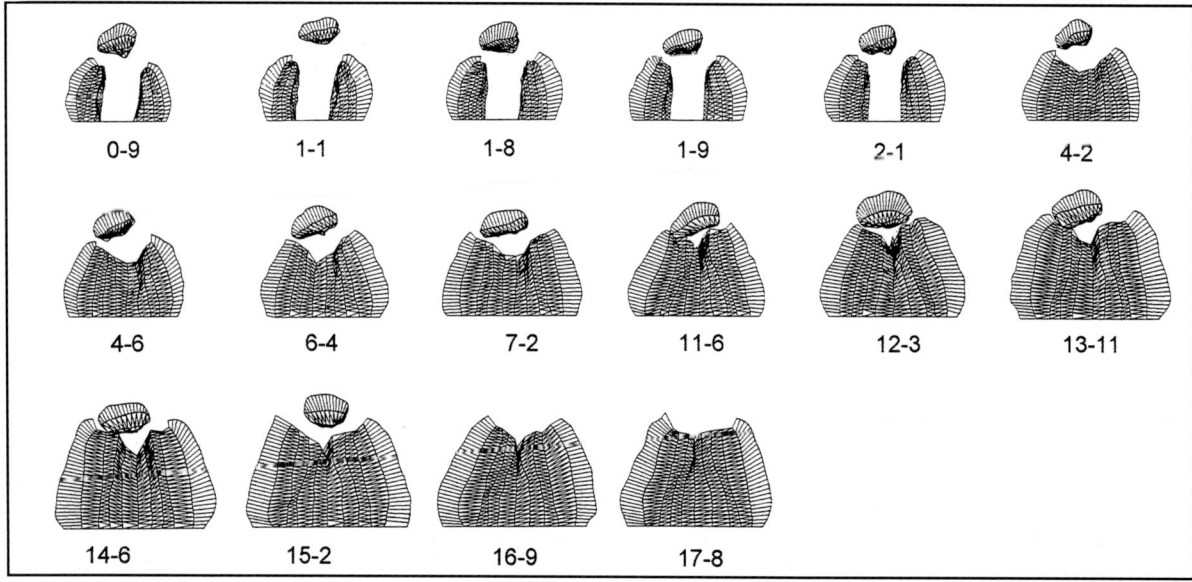

Fig 14–40. Case CS (AF-48). Computerized tracings of serial casts drawn to scale. This shows the lack of palatal growth and reduction in cleft space over 2 year prior to surgical closure of the palatal cleft. The anterior cleft space remains large up to 15-2 years. **16-9** and **17-8**: The premaxillary incisors were extracted.

Comment: This case clearly demonstrates the severe degree of osteogenic deficiency that can exist in bilateral clefts of the lip and palate. The once protruding premaxilla can become retrusive with growth (time) and may eventually need to be brought forward. Although palatal growth does occur, it may not be sufficient to appreciably reduce the posterior cleft space.

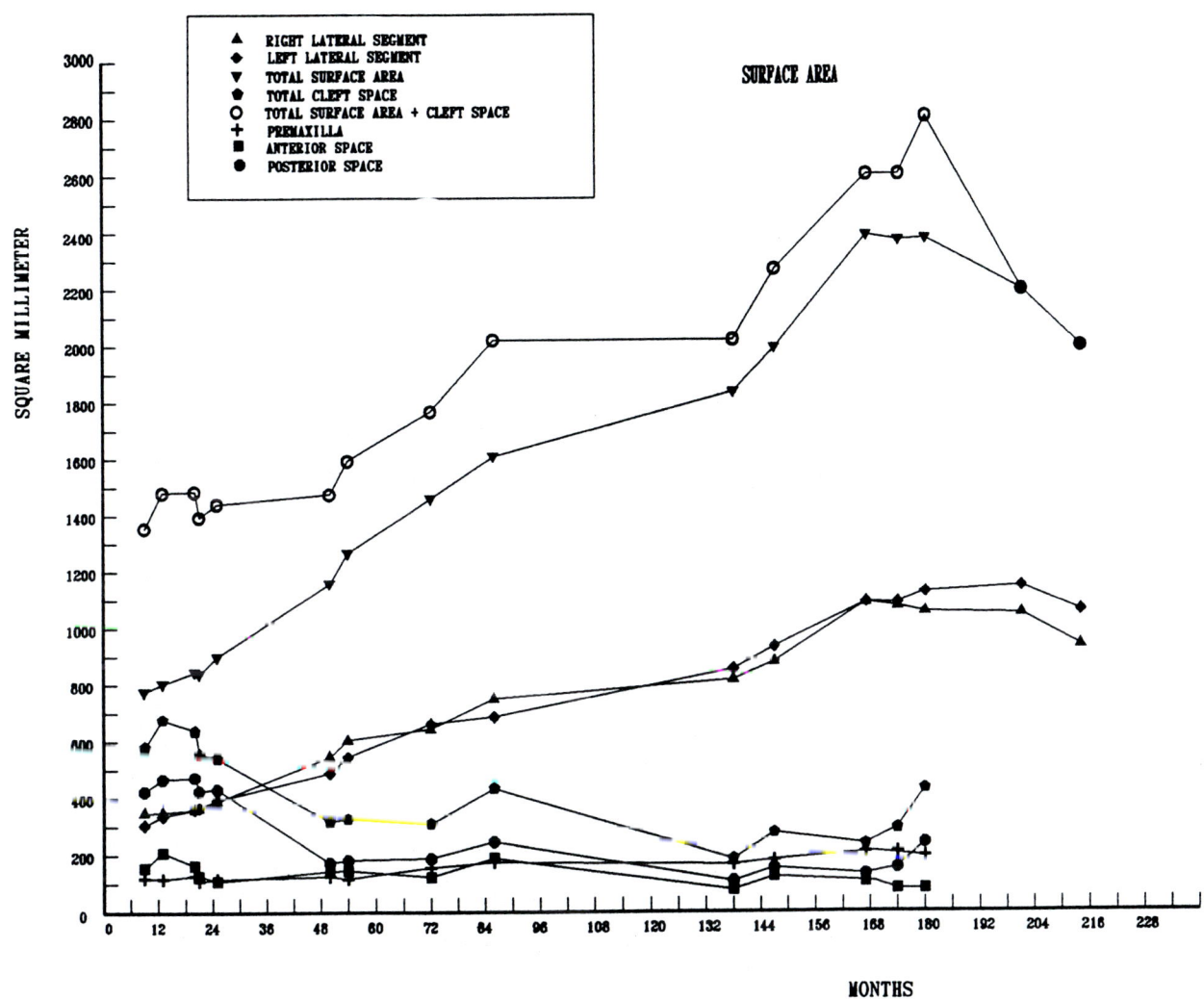

Fig 14–41. Case CS (AF-48). The palatal segments show a very gradual growth acceleration curve, while the posterior cleft space gradually reduces in size.

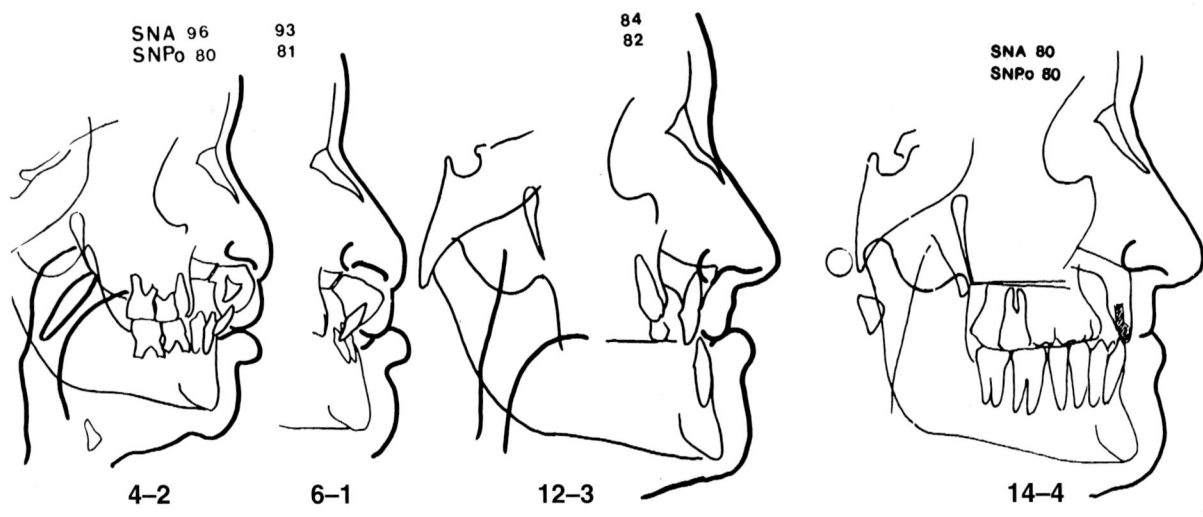

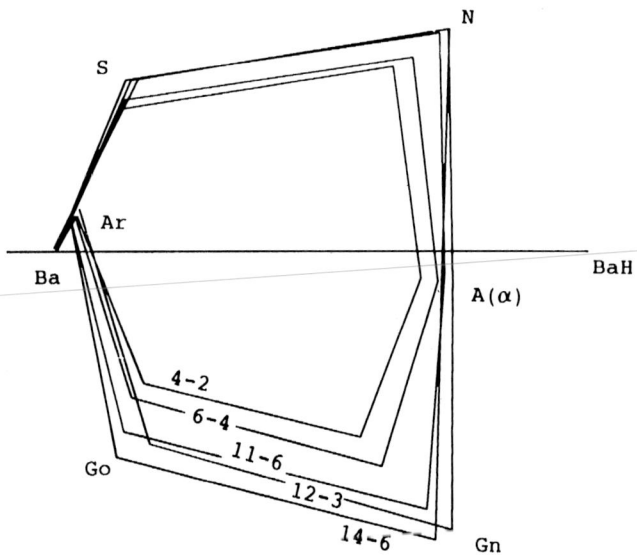

Fig 14–42. Case CS (AF-48). a. Serial cephalometric tracings. This analysis show a protrusive midface at 4-2 becoming recessive at 14-4. **b. Serial facial polygons superimposed according to Basion Horizontal method (Coben).** The midface advanced only slightly after 6-4, while the mandible showed progressive downward and forward growth until 14-6 flattening the facial profile.

Comments: This case clearly shows (1) that, even with a severely protruding premaxilla at birth, the premaxillary incisors can be in anterior crossbite after the pubertal growth spurt; (2) traumatic orthodontic advancement of the premaxillary incisors can lead to external root absorption and loss of alveolar support; and (3) surgical advancement of one or both lateral palatal segments, placing the cuspids in the lateral incisor spaces, with secondary alveolar bone grafting is the treatment of choice in cases when the premaxilla is in good overjet-overbite relationship and a large anterior cleft space exists. Only in very rare instances should the premaxilla be surgically set back to the lateral palatal segments. (4) Premaxillary surgical setback is contraindicated prior to the postpubertal facial growth spurt.

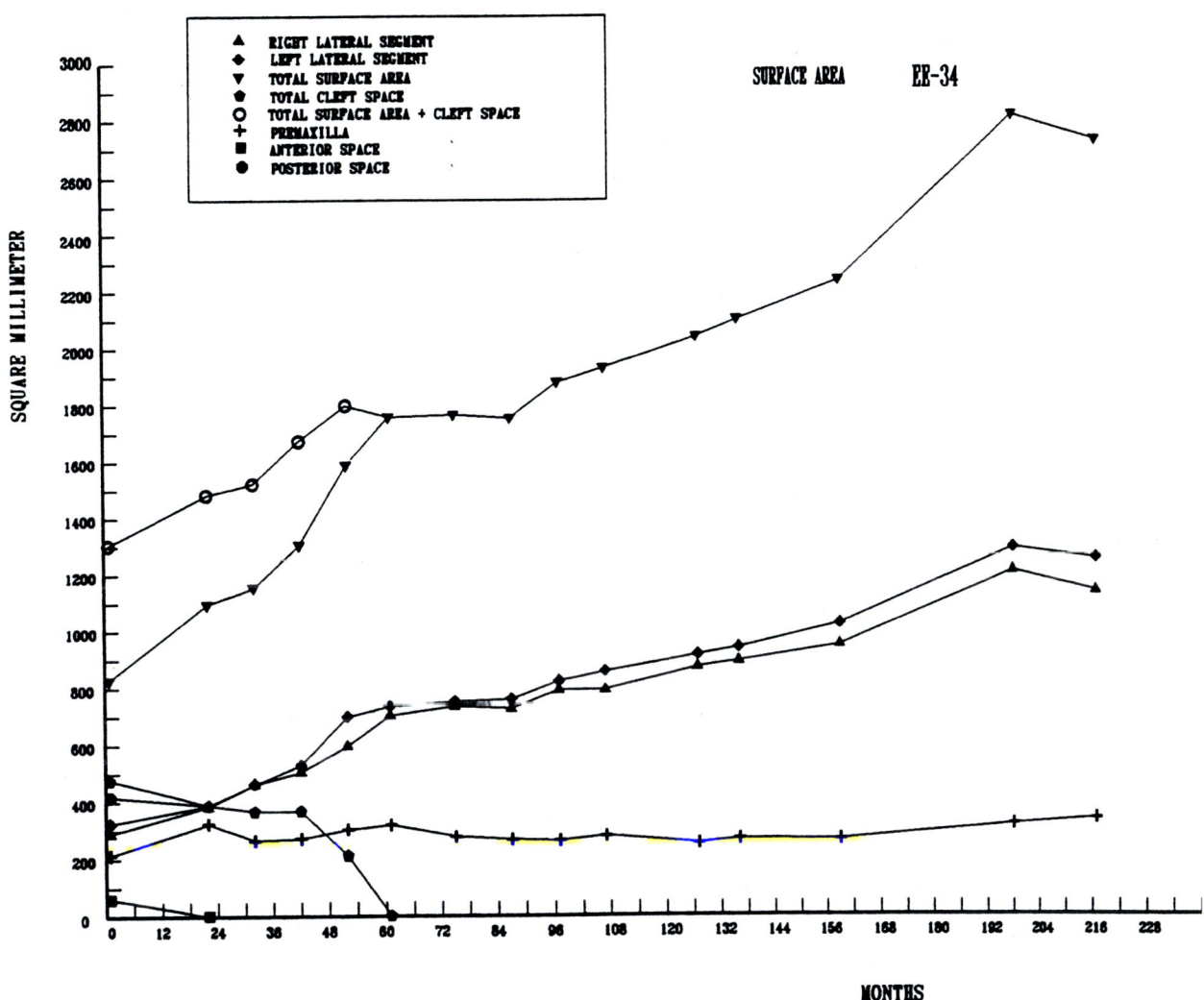

Fig 14-52. Case EE-34. Very gradual growth acceleration curve while the pasterior cleft space closed very rapidly between 42 and 52 months of age. The premaxilla's growth was negligible.

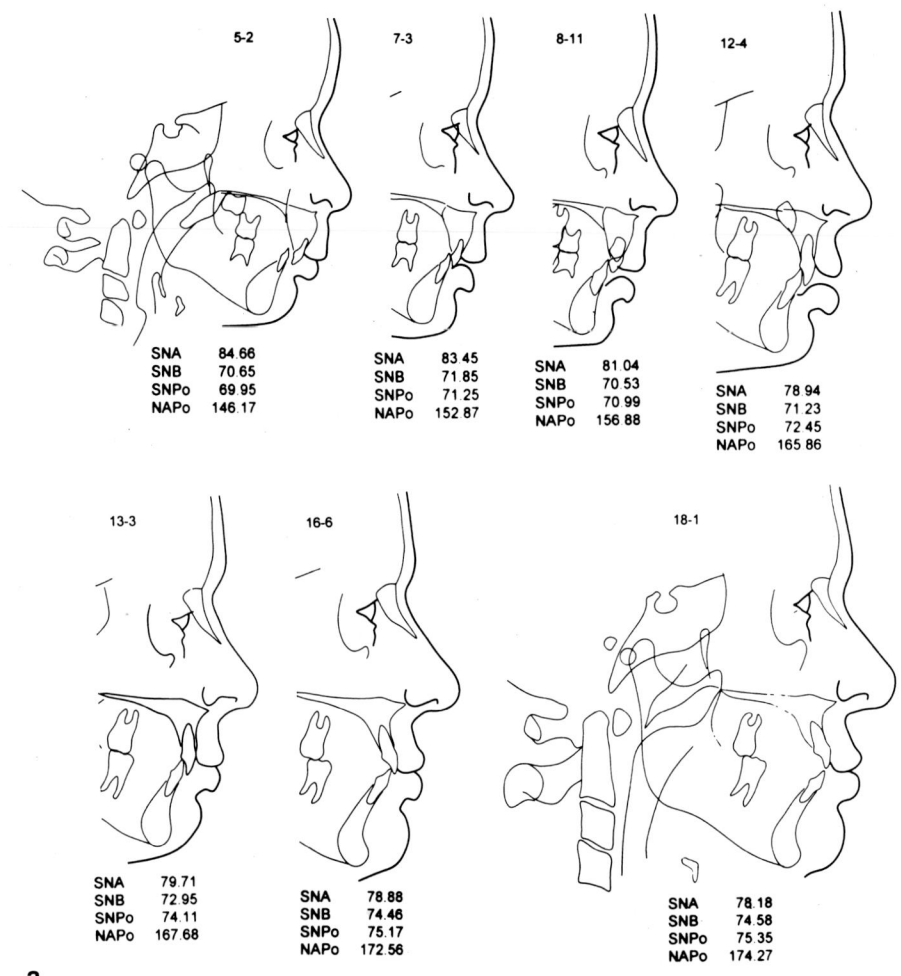

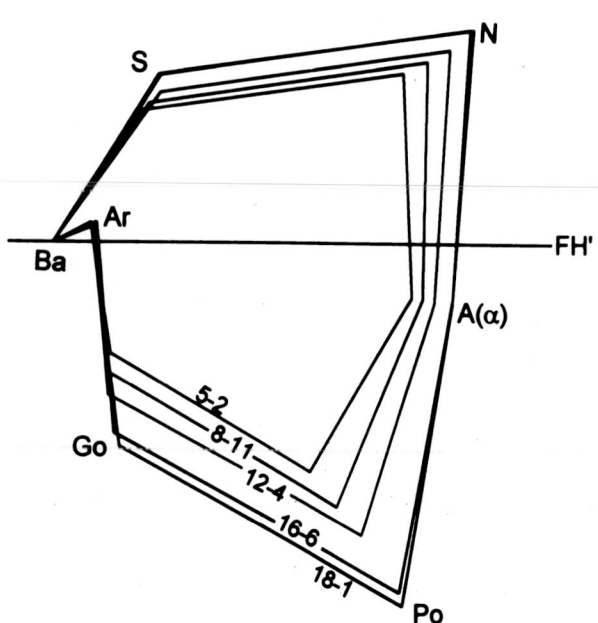

Fig 14–53. Case ES (EE-34). a. Serial cephalometric tracings show ideal facial measurements evolving. A superior-based pharyngeal flap is outlined in 18-1. **b.** Serial polygons superimposed according to the Basin Horizontal method (Coben). This series demonstrates an ideal facial growth pattern and reflects the use of physiological maxillary surgery:

1. The anterior cranial base shows good growth increments
2. Midfacial growth increments are continuous and only slightly less than those seen at N (Nasion).
3. Mandibular growth shows more forward than downward changes which is condusive to the flattening of the facial profile.

Comment: Taken together, all of these growth changes are conducive to the flattening of the facial profile. Such extensive midfacial growth is usually not seen in BCLP cases with such a large cleft space relative to the palate's surface area that have had the palatal cleft closed earlier than 43 months of age. We speculate that this finding strongly suggests that: (1) delaying palatal surgery to 3 years of age may be more conducive to good midfacial growth in some cases than early (before 1 year) palatal closure. However, we believe that it is not necessary to postpone palatal closure to after 5 years of age in all cases. (2) Hypotonic lip pressure has not exerted sufficient pressure through the premaxilla to the premaxillary vomerine suture to reduce its growth before 16–6. However, between 16–6 and 18–1 midfacial growth has ceased.

15

Summary of Treatment Concepts

Samuel Pruzansky once said that craniofacial surgery is "an experiment on nature's experiment." This statement is certainly true. All facial skeletal surgery—in growing or nongrowing patients—can be regarded as an investigation of craniofacial growth, form, and function.

Because facial skeletal surgery in growing children often affects craniofacial growth as well as function, informed decisions should be made concerning which structures need to be repositioned and reformed. Based on these decisions, a treatment plan is then formulated, and a working hypothesis for successful treatment is established. Three points need to be made at this juncture. First, remembering the value of failures as learning opportunities, clinicians cannot afford to forget failures; rather they must thoroughly analyze them so they are not repeated. Second, clinical investigators must be able to explain why some surgical procedures are successful and others fail. Third, clinicians must be able to fit the proper procedure to each individual problem and be willing to work with the consequences of their choices.

Not all clefts of the lip and/or palate within the same cleft type are alike.

1. The collected serial casts and cephalometric radiographs, beginning with those of the unoperated infant and continuing through adolescence presented in this book, provide a view of the wide spectrum of variations encountered within each cleft type in its untreated state and a record of the changes that occurred thereafter resulting from natural growth or specific therapeutic procedures. Clinical experience points out one critically important, fundamental fact: All clefts cannot be lumped together as a single phenomenon. Within each type of cleft there are great individual differences in the geometry and extent of the cleft defect and these differences are clinically signficant.

In a state-of-the-art monograph in 1972, Spriestersbach and co-workers[1(p115)] wrote: "Perhaps the greatest drawback to genetical and epidemiological research on clefts of the lip and palate has been the unfortunate tendency to lump them together." Twenty years prior to that report, the first line in the first paper to emerge from Pruzansky's[2(p509)] research stated: "Not all congenital clefts of the lip and palate are alike." This statement was to become the *leitmotif* of his subsequent research. He took great care to demarcate samples, according to varying cleft types, in his designs for epidemiological, morphological, functional, and genetic research.

2. Current methods of treatment, which favor staged treatment (i.e., closing the lip at birth and the palate at a later age, in one or two stages), offer a more encouraging prognosis than those which prevailed 50 years ago.

3. The age of the patient and the type of surgery applied are two variables in determining the effect of surgery on facial growth. Quantitative and qualitative characteristics of the cleft defect, plus the general health and genotype (facial growth pattern) of the individual patient, are additional determining factors. Under certain conditions, surgical repair of the palate is feasible quite early; in others, optimal conditions for repair will not become evident until a later age.

4. The natural history of children with clefts and those with specific syndromes demonstrates that some improve over time, some grow worse, and others remain unchanged in spite of the surgical effort.

5. Presurgical orthopedics, except for the use of a facial elastic to ventroflex the premaxilla to aid the surgeon prior to uniting the lip, have no long-term utility, and primary bone grafting has a deleterious effect on palatal and facial growth.

6. A critical review of the literature on the clinical management of cleft lip and cleft palate, together with an evaluation of the cumulative data from longitudinal palatal growth studies, has led most orthodontists to the following hypothesis: Conservative lip and palatal surgery facilitates rather than inhibits growth in both the maxillo-facial skeletal complex and the soft tissue of the labio-facial complex. In cleft palate cases, operative intervention, which minimally involves bone growth potential, will guide maxillo-facial growth in the individual in such a way that postoperative "catch-up" growth of the palate will result in acceptably normal development.

7. Within defined limits of mechanical and professional capability, the morphological and spatial relationships of the cleft palatal segments and facial growth patterns are the major determinants of the ultimate occlusion and arch form (not size). These variables, unique for each patient, could well be more indicative of the final treatment outcome than differences in the treatments employed by surgeons.

8. At the time the palatal cleft is closed, the relationship of the size and shape of the cleft space to the amount of available soft (mucoperiosteal) tissue surrounding the cleft, and the geometric relationship of the palatal processes to each other, are basic to determining the influence that scarring will have on the palatal arch form and the ability of the palate to develop normally.

9. Most skeletal malformations in cleft patients are the result of surgical procedures that have caused some growth retardation or to osteogenic deficiencies that lead to maxillary hypoplasia. All maxillary discrepancies are three-dimensional.

10. The concept that an increase in the amount of palatal scarring, beyond some critical threshold level, can reduce the palatal growth increments and cause palatal deformation appears to be valid, because the same surgical procedures, performed by the same surgeon on the same type of cleft, often lead to different palatal relationships. The reason for the different outcomes may, therefore, be due to variations in the palatal deformity at the time of surgery (i.e., the relative size of the cleft space to the size of the palatal segments which need to contribute soft tissue for cleft closure). The larger the cleft space relative to the amount of available tissue, the larger the area of denuded bone that must be left when the undermined palatal mucoperiosteum is moved medially to close the cleft space. The denuded bone heals by epithelialization, becoming a scar. The greater the scarring the more growth retardation and palatal deformation.

11. Although the tongue has been found to occupy the cleft space and be carried high into the nose at birth, no studies have shown that abnormal tongue habits negatively affect speech development. It appears that, with the closure of the palatal cleft between 18 and 30 months, and without the use of an obturator, children usually develop good speech if the velopharyngeal closure mechanism is functionally adequate.

12. There is no documented evidence that the cleft condition interferes with body growth or that, in most instances, the palatal defect cannot be effectively treated without feeding appliances. However, obturators may be useful in some neurological disturbances when palatal closure needs to be delayed beyond 3 years of age and parents complain of feeding problems. Most pediatricians and nurses recommend the use of a soft plastic feeding bag (e.g., Playtex Nurser) or a soft plastic bottle (e.g., Mead-Johnson's nurser) with a cross-cut, normal-sized nipple. The use of a Lamb's and Ross Laboratory nipples is strongly discouraged because of their abnormal shape and nipple length.

13. A child with a Pierre Robin sequence should never be given an obturator because the child's oral volume is already too small and an appliance will further compromise tongue positioning. Because the infant has a micrognathic mandible, the tongue must be carried high into the palatal cleft space during this critical early adjustment period. If an obturator or early palatal surgery is utilized for these children, it can force the tongue downward and backward, possibly closing off the airway space and interfering with breathing.

14. The use of a head bonnet with a facial elastic band or the use of elastic taped to the cheeks across the lips to reduce palatal distortion are acceptable methods to help the surgeon reduce tension at the surgical site. Such innocuous external facial forces will help bring the distorted lip and skeletal segments into a more normal relationship. This mode of treatment is acceptable to most parents and clinicians.

15. There is no proof that neonatal maxillary orthopedic appliances will stimulate palatal growth or reduce middle ear infections (Berkowitz[3]), nor has it ever been shown that these orthopedic procedures will prevent the need for future orthodontia and improve speech development. An obturator will be of some help if the cleft space remains open after 3 years of age and neurological problems interfere with feeding.

16. In many cases, protraction orthopedic forces can protrude the maxillary complex sufficiently to negate the need for surgical advancement. These forces are most efficient when applied before or during the pubertal growth spurt. After puberty, the effects change from orthopedic (bone) to orthodontic (dental) movements. The use of palatal expansion forces prior to the application of protraction devices can increase the potential for orthopedic movement of the maxilla.

Once midfacial recessiveness occurs at an early age, for example after premaxillary orthopedic retraction, it will not show increased growth acceleration to spontaneously improve midfacial skeletal and dental relationships.

REFERENCES

1. Spriestersbach DC, Dickson DR, Fraser FC, Horowitz SL, McWilliams BK, Paradise JL, Randall P. Clinical research in cleft lip and cleft palate: The state of the art. *Cleft Palate J.* 1973;10:113–165.
2. Pruzansky S. Not all dwarfed mandibles are alike. Proceedings of 1st Conference on Clinical Delineation of Birth Defects. Part 2, Malformation Syndromes, In: Bergsma, D, ed. *Birth Defects*. Original Article Series, The National Foundation, NY. February 1969: Vol 2:120–129.
3. Berkowitz S. Section III. Orofacial growth and dentistry: state of the art report on neonatal maxillary orthopedics which appeared in the *Cleft Palate J.* 1977;14:288–301.

emanating from the many and widely separated cleft lip and palate treatment centers, are usually anecdotal and understandably supportive of the clinics' own treatment concepts. Although the protocols may differ significantly, the authors tend to be satisfied with their own patients' facial, dental, and speech outcomes, all of which encourages few if any innovations in treatment approaches.

Certain questions inevitably arise: Do several different surgical procedures yield universally acceptable results which allow for normal palatal development? Are the outcome reports self-serving or can there indeed be a variety of effective surgical procedures? In cases of undeniable failure, what were the errors, if any, in diagnosis and treatment planning? In assessing failures, most surgeons focus solely on the surgical skills and/or surgical protocols involved, but this leaves other possible explanations still unexplored. In recent years, it has been suggested that variations in the physical characteristics of the deformity—the geometric relationship of the palatal segments to each other at birth and the size of the cleft space relative to the amount of available soft tissue used to close the cleft spaces—may have an impact on treatment outcomes (Stockli,[26] Berkowitz et al[17]). They have highlighted the importance of three-dimensional measurements and have urged that the arch form and the size of the cleft space at the time of surgery be taken into consideration in the treatment of infants with complete clefts of the lip and palate.

Lack of appreciation for the importance of the geometric relationships of the cleft palatal segments to each other has been the result, in great part, of the dearth of longitudinal records, such as serial palate casts and lateral cephaloradiographs, and an accurate palatal cast-measuring device for quantification and computer analysis of the palate's changing geometric form. Just as the microscope uncovered critical differences in tissue pathology, a three-dimensional measuring instrument could reveal palatal geometric information that has heretofore gone unnoticed, and the importance of which has not been appreciated. Fortunately, such a measuring instrument and a significant number of dental casts are now available.

STUDIES USING THREE-DIMENSIONAL TECHNIQUES

Berkowitz[27] initiated a study to determine the feasibility of using stereophotogrammetry to graphically describe the changing configuration of cleft palates. Data from the study supported the clinical impressions that palatal molding action with palatal growth, which occurred at the palate's medial border, effectively diminished the width of the cleft space. A second study (Berkowitz et al[17]) was undertaken to further improve the stereometric technology in order to permit the investigation of a larger number of casts. A profile study of nine complete unilateral cleft lip and palate casts demonstrated that the widths of the vault space varied greatly between cases. This was followed by another investigation using an "Optical Profilometer" (Berkowitz et al[28]) designed and built by National Aeronautics and Space Administration (NASA) for Berkowitz under a technology utilization transfer grant. This led to the use of an electromechanical digitizer as the instrument of choice for analytical studies of serial casts designed to describe the changing geometry and size of the palatal vault and the geometrical and size relationship between the greater and lesser palatal segments in complete unilateral cleft lip (CUCLP) and palate and the lateral palatal segments and premaxilla in complete bilateral clefts of the lip and palate (CBCLP) (Figs 16-1, 16-2, and 16-3).

Serial three-dimensional palatal growth studies to date have led Berkowitz to believe that size and geometric relationship of the palatal segments relative to the size of cleft space prior to surgery, coupled with the surgical procedure utilized, may influence the palate's subsequent arch form and size (Fig 16-4). If it does, the surgical skill or technique is not solely responsible for the different outcomes. This might explain why different surgical procedures can be equally successful and, conversely, why the same surgical procedure can cause a different result especially if extensive scarring has been produced (Figs 16-5 and 16-6, Table 16-1).

The following three-dimensional palatal growth studies were recently completed. These studies can be considered forerunners of multicenter efforts still to come which will reflect on the physiological attributes of the various surgical and orthopedic treatment procedures.

Study 1: Analysis of Longitudinal Growth of CUCLP and CBCLP

Subjects from Berkowitz's longitudinal facial-palatal growth records who did not have neonatal maxillary orthopedics were the subjects. Pre- and postsurgical casts are shown in Fig 6-7.

Eleven children with unilateral clefts and 14 children with bilateral clefts were measured for palate

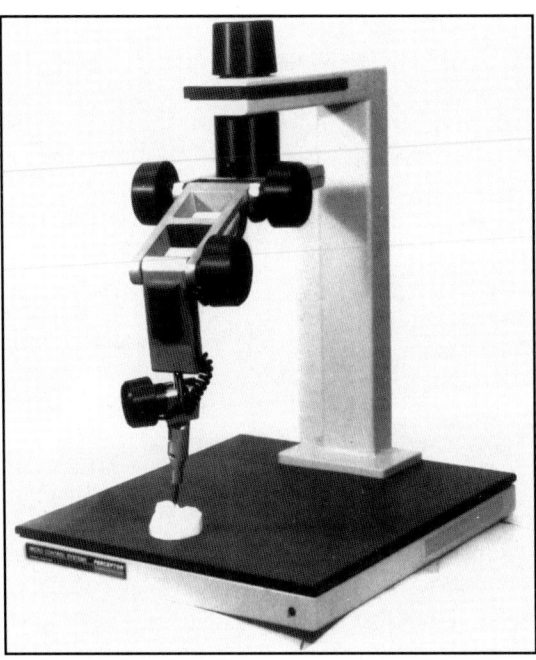

Fig 16–1. An electromechanical digitizer used to extrapolate x, y, and z coordinates from a plaster palatal cast.

area in mm² over a period of 5 years. For the unilateral cleft group, the measurements were made at approximately 6, 12, 24, 30, and 60 months. Each child in both groups was surgically treated to close the cleft area at approximately 24–36 months.

Statistical Methods

For each child, the monthly growth rate (in mm²/month) from 6 through 24 months was estimated by linear regression. In the unilateral cleft group, the monthly growth rate after surgical intervention was estimated by the change in palate area from 36 to 60 months. This rate was estimated in the bilateral cleft group after surgical intervention over the period of 30 to 60 months. Mean growth rates before and after surgical repair were compared within each group by the paired Student's t-test. Pre- and postsurgical differences in mean growth rates between the two cleft types was compared using the two-sample Student's t-test. In addition, growth rates and the change in growth rate before and after intervention were correlated with the estimated size of the closure at surgery.

Results (Fig 16–8)

Individual monthly growth rates and group means are shown in Table 16–1. The growth rates of the two groups before surgery (Unilateral = 12.9 mm²/month, Bilateral = 15.7, mm²/month) are not significantly different. However, after surgery, the growth rate of the Bilateral group (3.9 mm²/month) is statistically smaller ($p = .013$) than that of the Unilateral group (8.7 mm²/month). Comparing pre- and postsurgery growth rates, the change in growth rate for the Unilateral group (Mean = 4.3, SE = 3.3) was not significantly different from zero, whereas the change of growth rate in the Bilateral group (Mean = 11.9, SE = 2.3) was significantly different from zero.

The estimated size of the "gap" to be surgically repaired was 80.5 mm² in the Unilateral group and 112.5 mm² in the Bilateral group. These cleft sizes are not significantly different; however, this may be due to the small sample size. In a larger sample size, this difference in cleft space size probably would be significant. For all subjects combined, the remaining gap at surgery was significantly negatively correlated with the presurgical growth rate ($r = 0.52$, $p = 0.034$, one-tailed). For the Unilateral group alone, this cor-

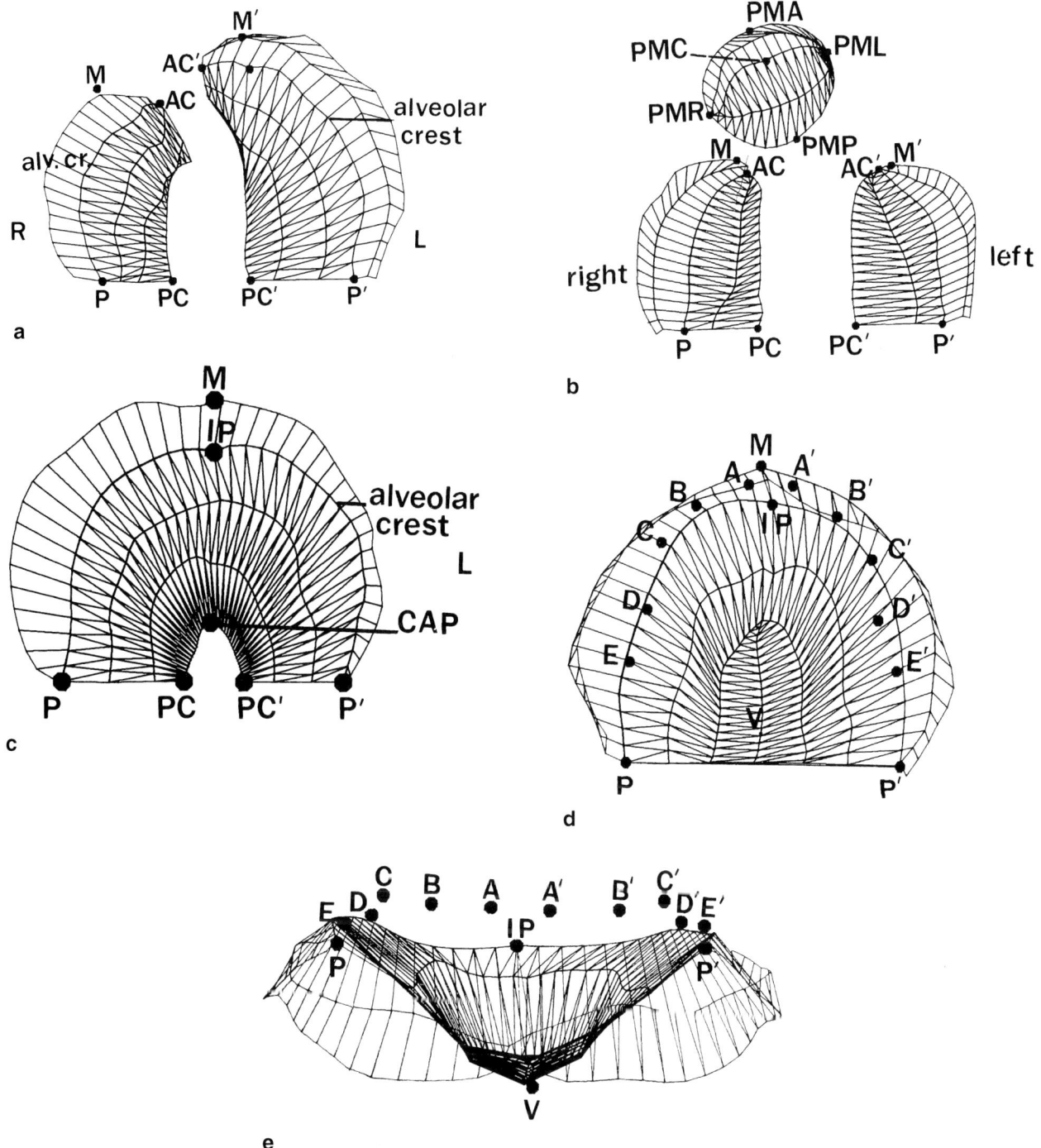

Fig 16-2. Computer-generated images of various cleft palate types. **a.** Complete unilateral cleft lip and palate. **b.** Complete bilateral cleft lip and palate. **c.** Isolated cleft palate. **d.** Normal palate: occlusal view. **e.** Normal palate: postero-anterior view. (P: Postgingivale comparable to PTM [pterygomaxillary fissure on a lateral cephalograph]. It is the posterior border of the hard palate; PC: Landmark on the P-P line at the cleft; AC: Anterior point of the alveolar ridge at the cleft; M: The most anterior point of the palatal segment IP: Incisal papilla point; V: Highest vault point; A: Deciduous central incisor, B: Deciduous lateral incisor. C: Deciduous cuspid, D: Deciduous first molar; E: Deciduous second molar)

Palatal Surface Area

Before cleft closure: Bounded laterally by P to AC, P to Pc and PC' to P', P' to Ac'

After cleft closure: Includes cleft space bounded by AC to AC' and PC to PC'.

Cleft Space Area: Anterior limit AC-AC and posterior boundary PC to PC'.

In Bilateral Clefts:

Anterior Cleft Space: Bounded anteriorly by the premaxilla's outer point of the alveolar crest RPM or LPM to AC and posteriorly by line AC to AC'.

Posterior Cleft Space: Bounded by AC to AC, AC to PC, and PC to PC'.

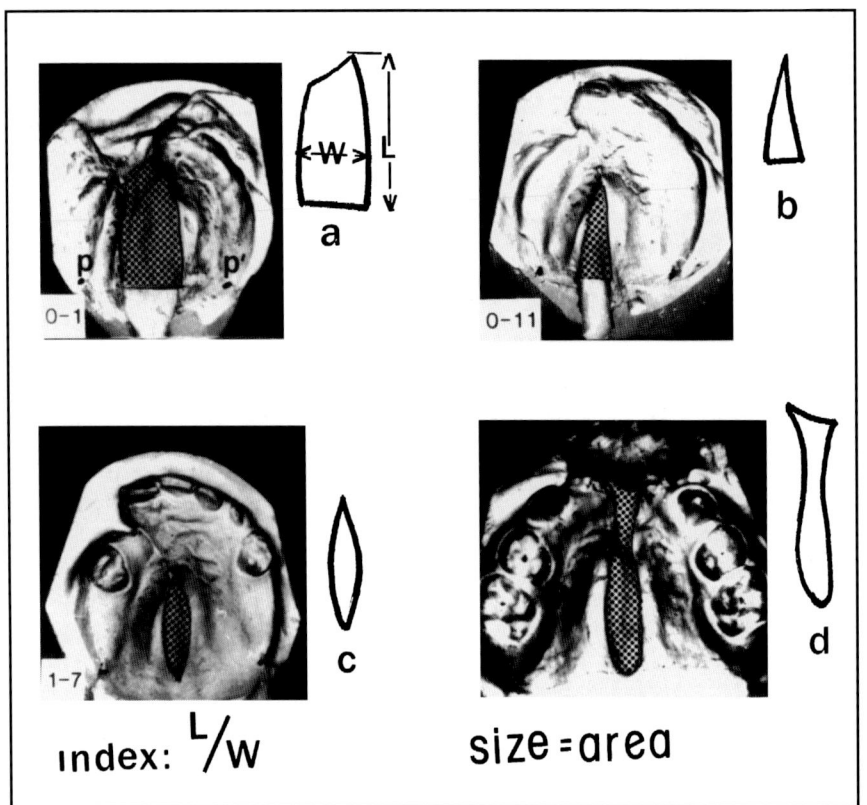
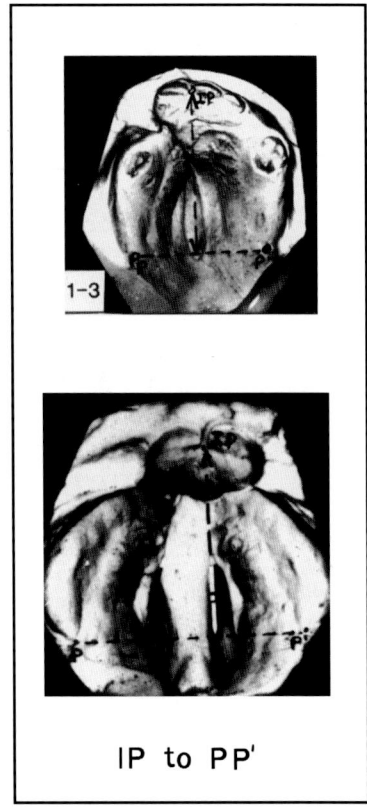
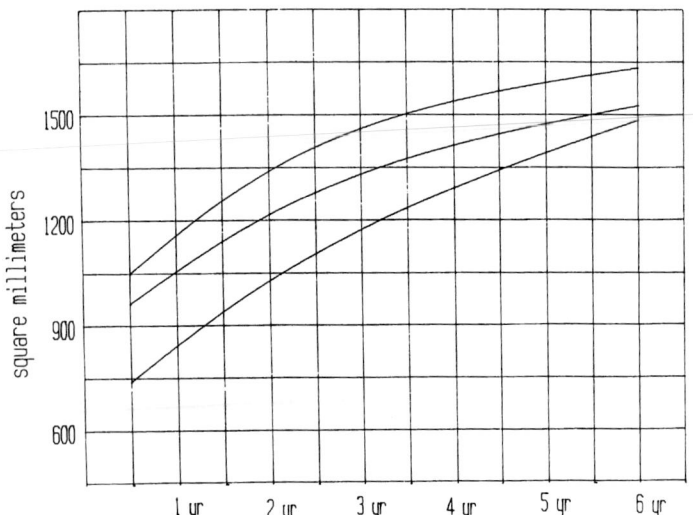

TOTAL PALATAL SURFACE AREA +/−1 STANDARD DEVIATION

TIME SEQUENCE ANALYSIS OF PALATAL GROWTH IN A NON − CLEFT LIP AND PALATE   10 cases

Fig 16-3. a. Size and shape of the cleft space. **b.** Antero-posterior lengths measured from incisal papilla point (IP) to line P-P1. **c.** Time sequence analysis of palatal growth in 10 noncleft lip and palate cases. Total palatal surface area +/− 1 standard deviation.

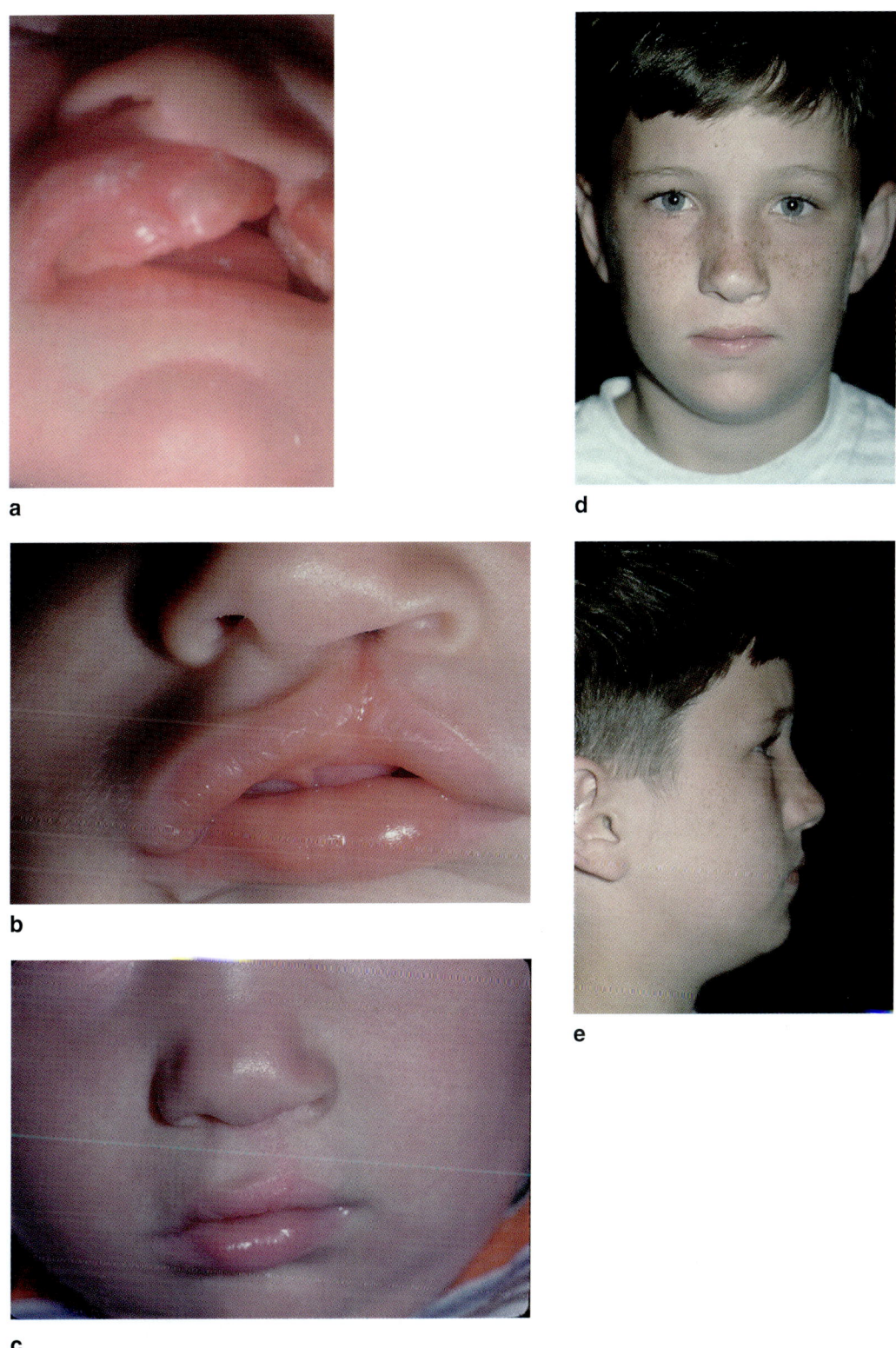

Fig 16–4. **Case JH (AQ-74). Excellent occlusion in CUCLP following lip and palate surgery.** Lip adhesion was performed at 2 months and definitive lip surgery at 7 months. Palate cleft closure at 19 months using a modified von Langebeck procedure. **a**, **b**, **c**, **d**, and **e**. Facial photographs show excellent lip, nose and facial changes following surgery.

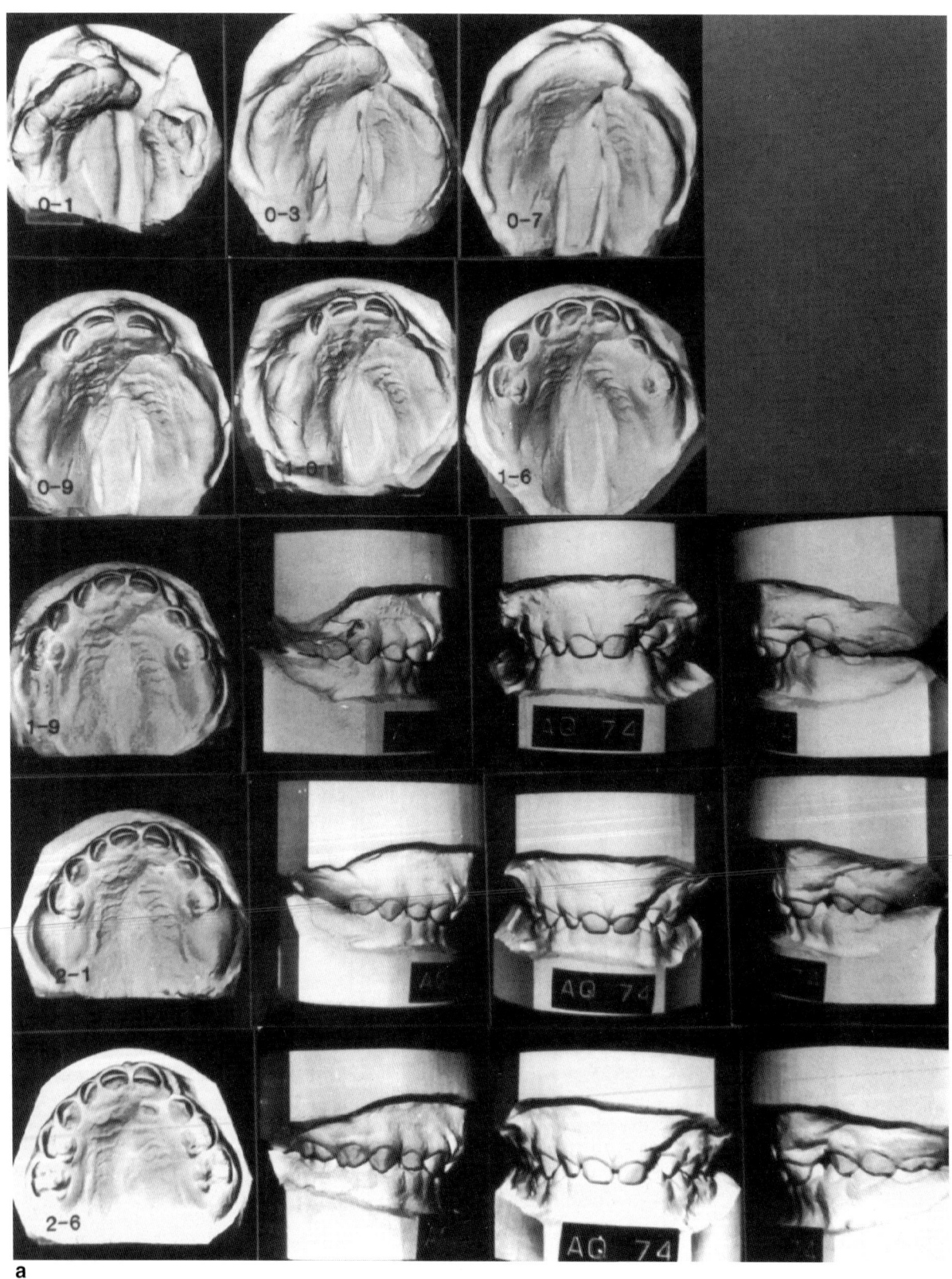

Fig 16–5. a. Serial dental casts for Case JH (AQ-74) show: **0-1.** Separated palatal segments soon after birth. **0-3.** Palatal segments move together forming a butt joint relationship. **0-7, 0-9, 1-6,** and **1-9.** What appears to be a "collapsed" state is

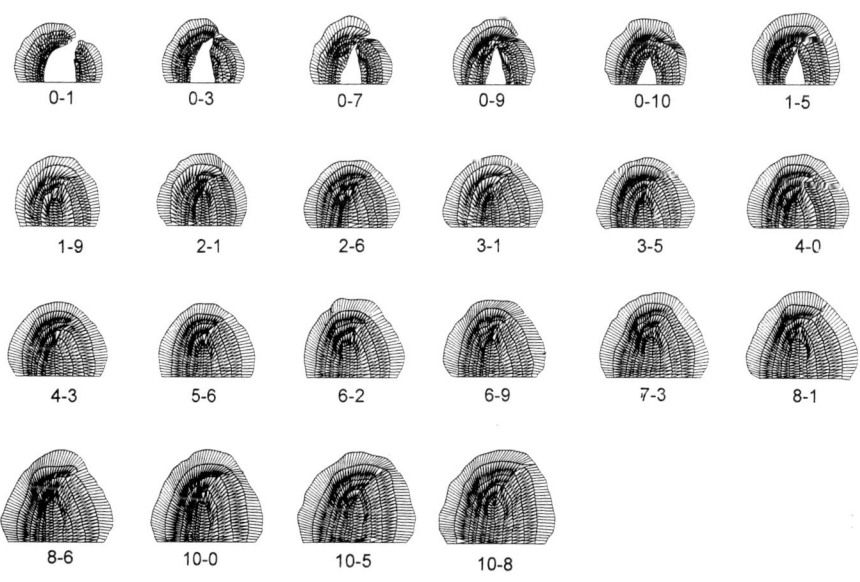

not so. **2-1** and **2-6**. The buccal teeth are in an ideal occlusal relationship. **10-0**, **10-5**, and **10-8**. Palatal growth maintains the excellent palatal arch relationship. The central incisors were brought together at 8 years of age prior to secondary alveolar bone grafts. **b.** Computer-generated images of serial casts drawn to scale. This series demonstrates the decrease in cleft spaces associated with an increase in palatal size.

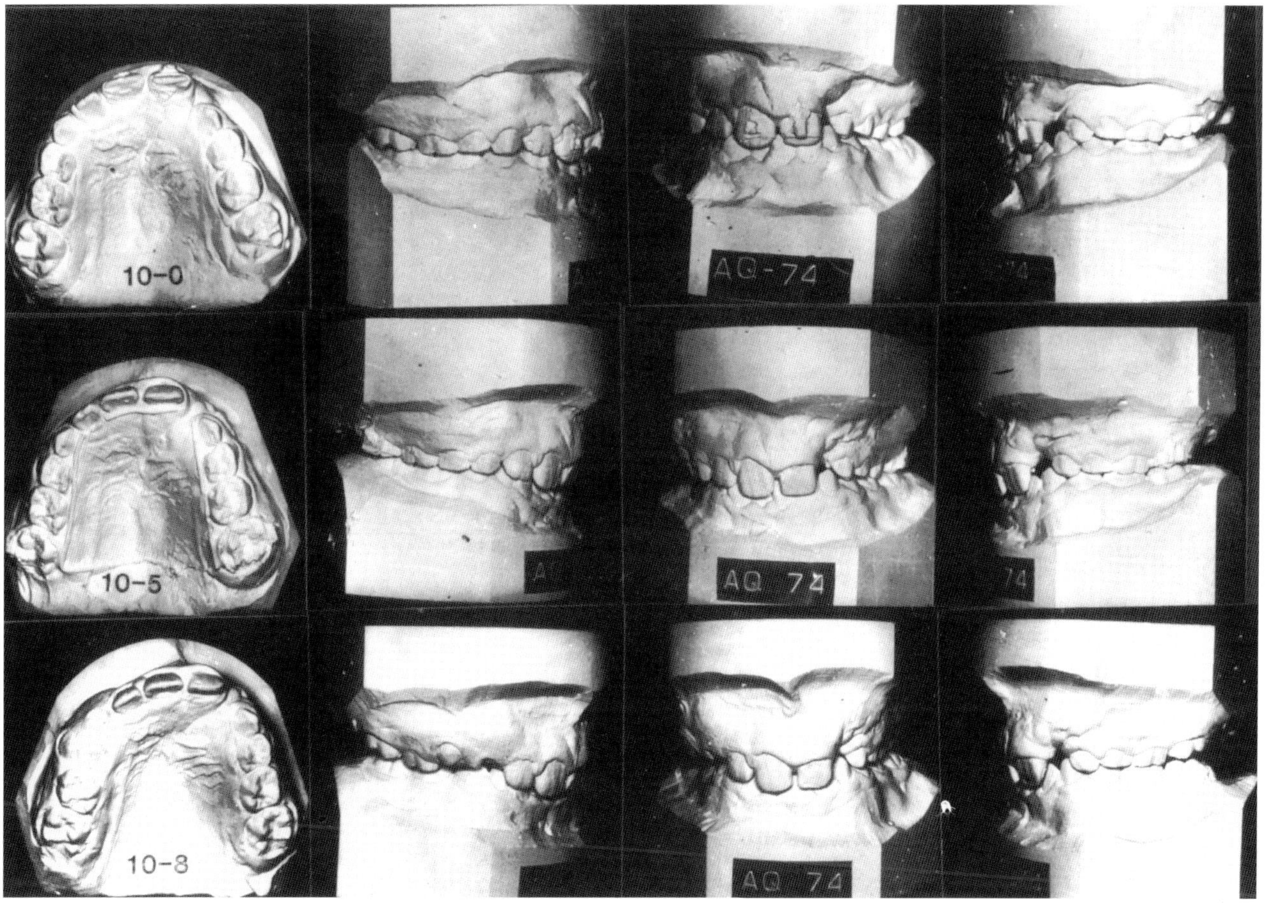

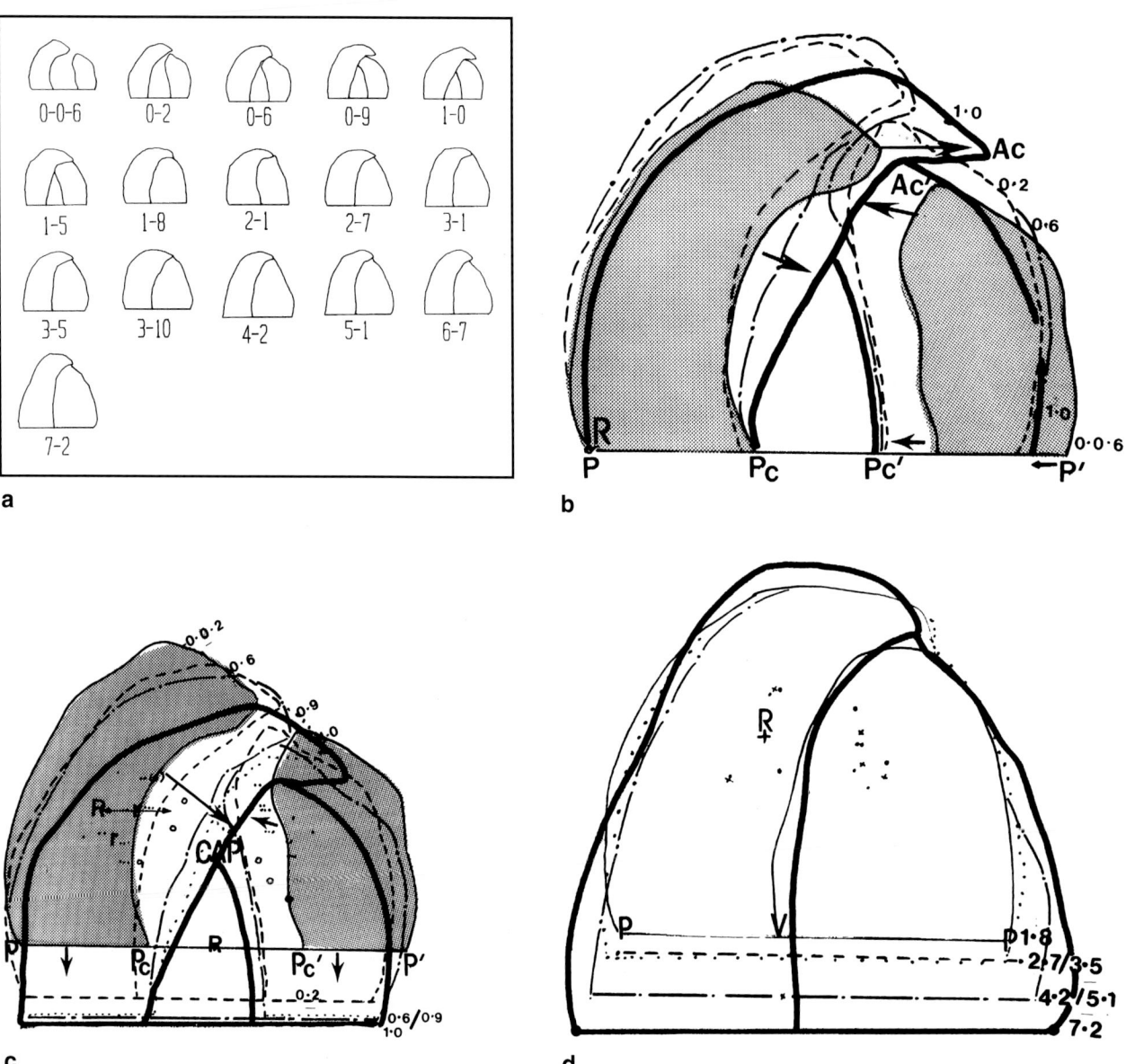

Fig 16–6. a. Computer-created serial casts drawn to scale from birth to 7 years and 2 months. **b.** Outline tracings at 6 days, 2 months, and 1 year of age superimposed on the baseline P-P1 and registered at midpoint of the line. This illustration shows the medial movement and changes in size of the palatal segments. **c.** The same palatal segments are superimposed on the palatal rugae to show the amount and direction of palatal growth and movement brought on by uniting the lip. From 2 days to 1 year of age. **d.** Outline of palatal segments from 1 year and 8 months of age to 7 years and 2 months. This illustration shows that most of the palatal growth occurs posteriorly with a slight increase in width with little anterior bony apposition.

TABLE 16–1. Surface area changes over time for Case. PM. KK-22.

Age	Skeletal Area				Cleft Space		Total	Total
	Premaxilla	RLS	LLS	Total	Antereior	Posterior	Total	SA + CS
0-0-12	145.5	335.5	282.7	763.7	127.4	417.0	544.4	1308.1
0-3	150.2	397.4	377.6	925.2	65.4	331.5	396.9	1322.1
1-4	154.0	469.5	464.3	1087.8	36.8	265.5	302.3	1390.1
1-10	211.8	502.6	506.2	1220.6	70.4	216.3	286.7	1507.3
2-1	217.6	589.0	549.5	1356.1	79.8	195.3	275.1	1631.2
2-10	220.7	603.9	551.3	1375.9	95.8	193.2	289.0	1664.9
3-10	271.6	660.4	616.5	1548.5	122.6	206.3	328.9	1877.4
5-8	273.3	673.0	675.9	1622.2	123.6	201.2	324.8	1947.0
6-7	273.6	811.0	820.5	1905.1	115.0	206.5	321.5	2226.6
7-4	277.3	813.0	839.5	1929.8	106.7	185.2	291.9	2221.7
8-2	306.5	844.6	890.8	2041.9	101.1	155.4	256.5	2298.4
12-3	346.8	1087.1	1116.1	2550.0				2550.0
14-0	348.7	1161.8	1226.4	2736.9				2736.9
14-5	351.1	1198.8	1237.0	2786.9				2786.9
17-4	353.5	1241.0	1246.3	2840.8				2840.8

Note: RLS = Right Lateral Segment
LLS = Left Lateral Segment
Total = Total Surface Area
SA + CS = Bony Surface Area + Cleft Space Area

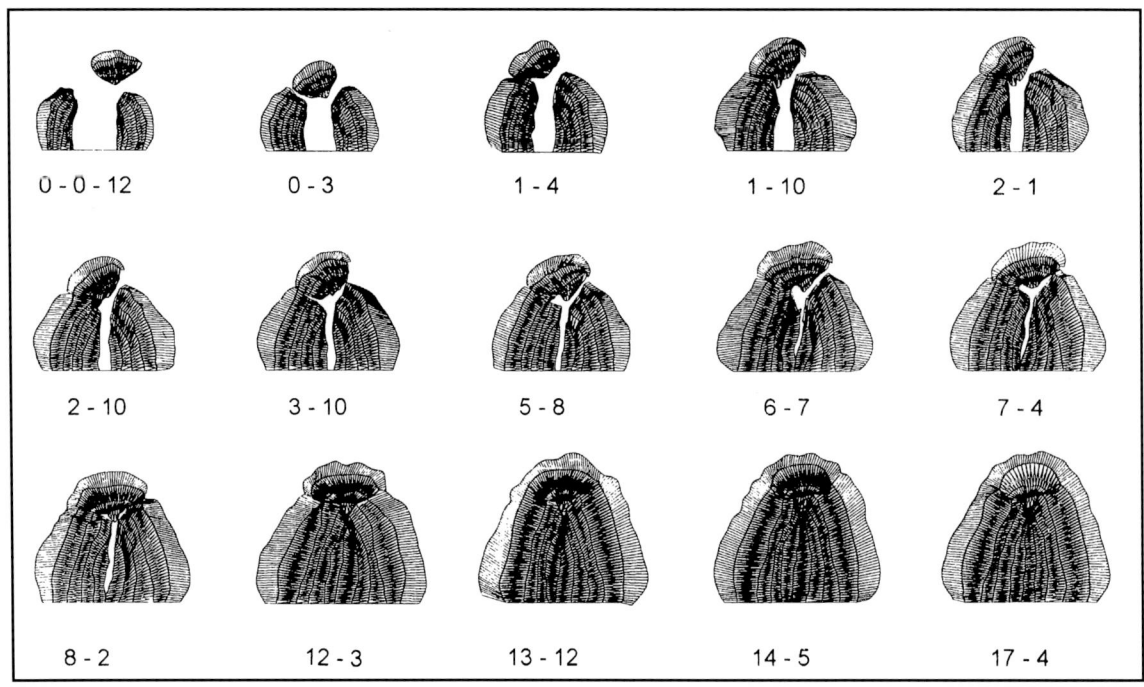

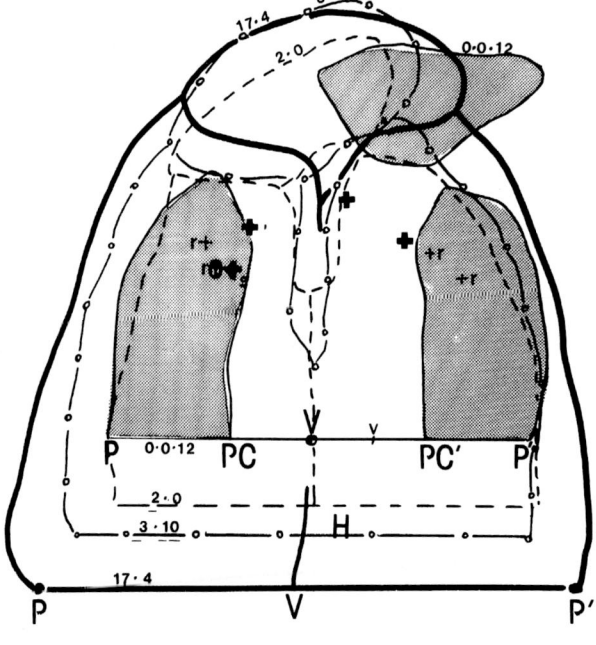

Fig 16–7. Case PM (K-22). a. Computer-drawn serial casts of a complete bilateral cleft lip and palate drawn to scale showing quantitative and geometric palatal changes as a result of growth and treatment. No presurgical orthopedics. **b.** Serial casts superimposed on the base line P to P, registered at V (the point where the vomer meets the base line). This shows changes in palatal size and palatal relationships. **c.** Serial casts from 12 days to 17 years and 4 months.

These casts were superimposed on the rugae points with the PP' line parallel. Most of the palatal growth occurred posteriorly with only a slight increase in midfacial protrusion when compared to the initial premaxillary protrusion. The width increased in proportion to length. **d.** Time sequence analysis of palatal growth in a complete bilateral cleft of the lip and palate. By 6 years the palatal growth (including cleft space) more than doubled.

(continued)

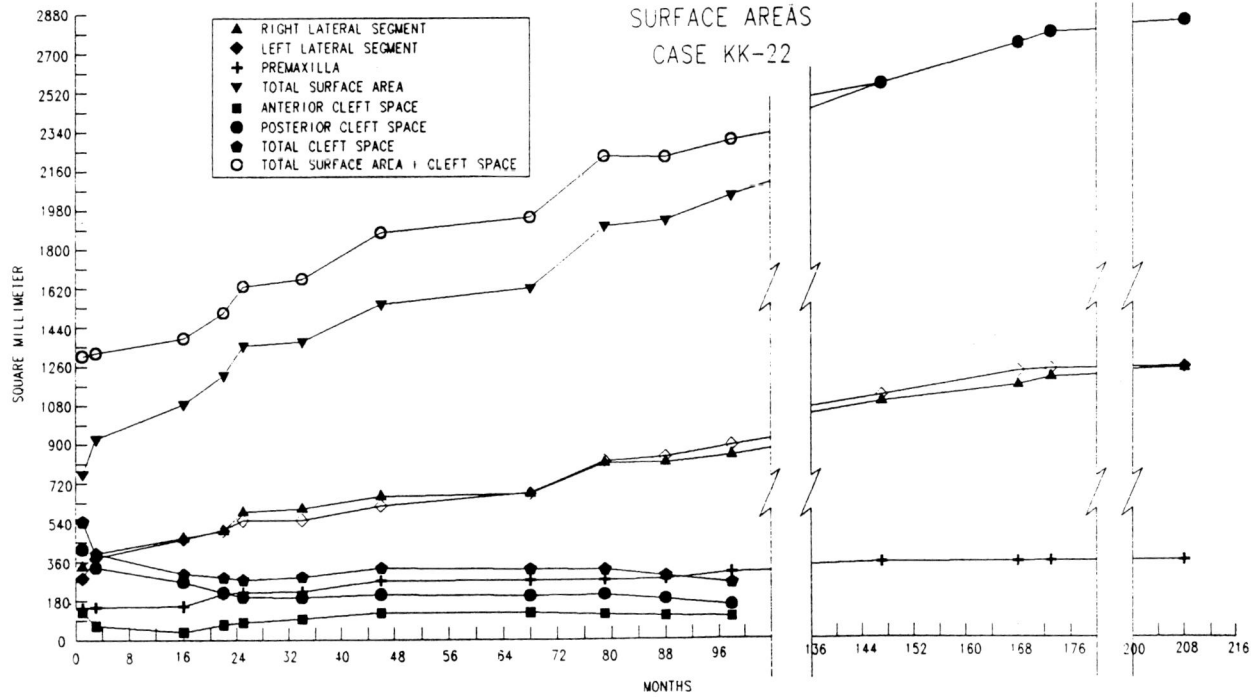

d

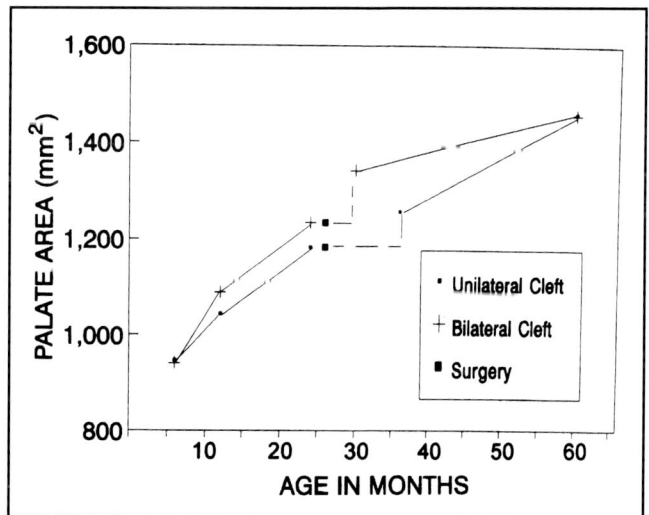

Fig 16-8. Graph showing growth changes in surface area of 14 CBCLP and CUCLP prior to and after palatal cleft closure surgery. The palatal growth acceleration in the CBCLP was greater the first year then similar in both cleft types up to 25 months, just prior to palatal surgery. At the time of surgery the cleft space in the CBCLP series was greater than in the CUCLP series. After surgery the palatal growth acceleration curve of the CBCLP series decreased while that of the CUCLP series increased. A modified von Langenbeck procedure to close the cleft space was used in both cleft types. The sample of cases is being increased to determine the influence of cleft size on future palatal growth and development.

relation was not significant ($r = 0.31$, $p = 0.175$, one-tailed), while it was significant for the Bilateral group ($r = 0.52$, $p = 0.029$, one-tailed).

Discussion

These findings indicate that the two cleft groups had similar growth rates prior to surgery but dissimilar cleft gap sizes at the time of surgery. Following surgery, the unilateral group showed a greater, but not statistically significant, difference in growth rate. We suspect that, if the sample size is increased, the difference in growth acceleration would be significant. The bilateral cleft group showed a statistically smaller cleft space than that of the unilateral group. Both groups started out with approximately the same mean palate surface area. Before palatal surgery, both groups had similar growth rates with the bilateral group slowing in growth after surgery. The negative correlation of the estimated cleft space at surgery with the presurgery growth rate is a measure of the validity of the measurements. To more closely analyze the patterns of growth before and after surgery, data points spaced more closely in time, especially just before and just after surgery, are planned. These data show that growth patterns can be measured and analyzed.

Study 2: Quantitative Study of a Case with CBCLP Treated With Presurgical Orthopedics
(Fig 16-9)

This study was undertaken to graphically demonstrate the geometric changes that occurred to a palate with a CBCLP that had undergone presurgical orthopedic treatment by Kuijpers-Jagtman at Nijmegan Cleft Palate Center in The Netherlands. Besides the changes in palatal surface area and cleft space, all

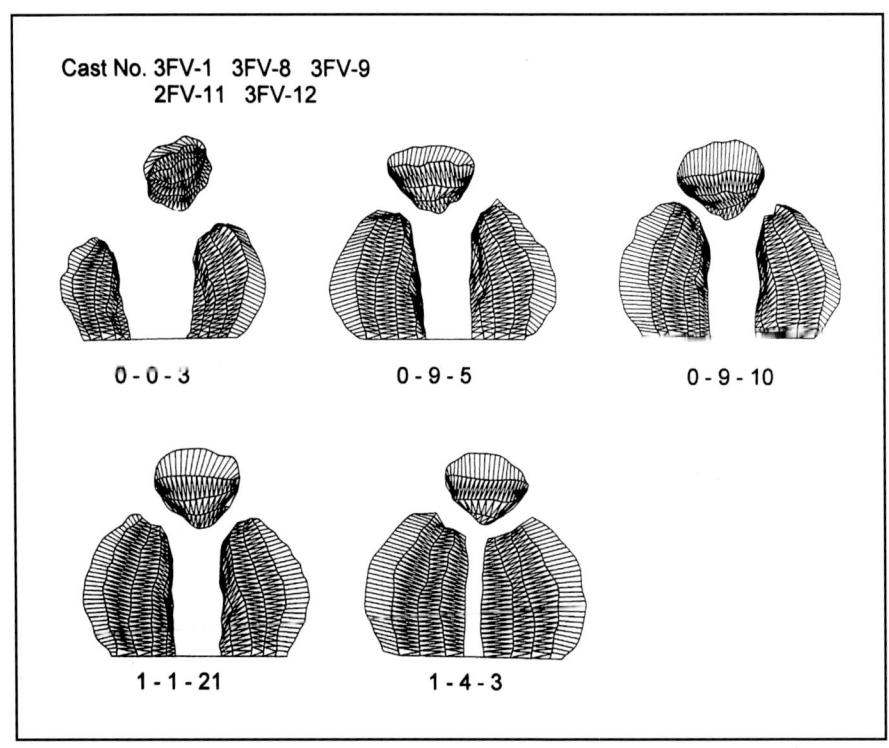

Fig 16–9. a. Computerized drawings of serial casts of a CBCLP in which presurgical orthopedics were applied by A.M. Kuypers-Jagtman (KU Nijmegen). This procedure is utilized to aid lip closure. All casts are drawn to scale and aligned on P-P' line. **b.** Superimposition of the outlines of the casts taken at 3 days, 1 year, and 4 months using the palatal rugae points shows that the projecting premaxilla's geometric rela-

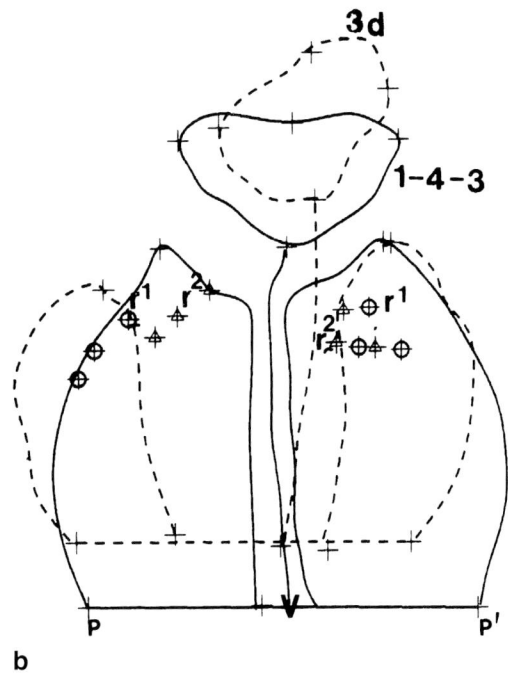

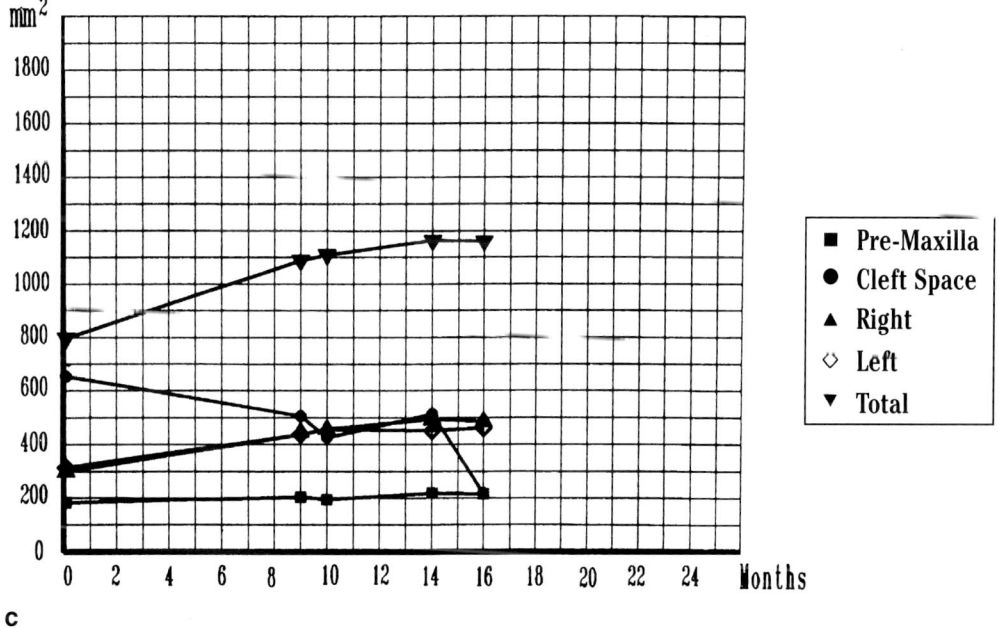

tionship within the maxilla remains the same while the lateral palatal segments increase in size mainly by growth at the medial and posterior borders. **c.** Premaxillary and lateral palatal segment growth shows a gradual acceleration of the lateral segment's growth while the premaxilla does not show an increase in size. Palatal growth acceleration is less in this case than that shown in Figure 16-6 for a series of CBCLP cases that did not undergo PSOT. This difference does not imply that PSOT has caused diminished palatal growth, but taken on an individual basis reflects only normal variation in growth acceleration curves.

other dimensions can be quantified and compared with CUCLP and CBCLP cases that were treated differently at this and other institutions. A prospective clinical trials study is now under way. One of the goals of this research is to verify whether presurgical orthopedic treatment enhances palatal growth.

REFERENCES

1. Hughes PCR. Morphometric studies of catch-up-growth in the rat. In: Dixon AD, Sarnat BG, eds. *Factors and Mechanisms Influencing Bone Growth.* New York: Alan R. Liss; 1982:433–446.
2. Wilson PN, Osbourn DF. Compensatory growth after undernutrition in mammals and birds. *Biol Rev.* 1960;35:324–363.
3. Feinstein AR. The architecture of clinical research (continued). clinical biostatics IV. *Clin Pharmacol Ther.* 1970;2:595–610.
4. Berkowitz S. Timing cleft palate closure-age should not be the sole determinant.In: Cohen MM Jr, Rollnick BR, eds. Samuel Pruzansky Fetschrift. *J Craniofac Genet Devel Biol.* 1985;1(Suppl):69–83
5. Pruzansky S. Description classification and analysis of unoperated clefts of the lip and palate. *Am J Orthod.* 1953;39:590.
6. Slavkin HC. *Congenital Malformations of the Craniofacial Complex. Developmental Cranio-facial, Biology.* Philadelphia. Lea and Febiger 1979:281–295.
7. Ross RB, Johnston MC. *Cleft Lip With or Without Cleft Palate—Embryogenesis, Epidiemiology and Etiology, Cleft Lip and Palate.* Baltimore, Md: Williams and Wilkins; 1972:17–40.
8. Subtelny JD. Orthodontic principles in treatment of cleft lip and palate. In: Bardach J, Morris HL, eds. *Multidisciplinary Management of Cleft Lip and Palate.* Philadelphia, Pa: WB Saunders; 1990:615–641.
9. Slaughter WB, Pruzansky S, Harris HL. Cleft lip and cleft palate, surgical considerations. *Pediatr Clin North Am.* 1956;3:1029–1047.
10. Pruzansky S. Factors determining arch form in clefts of the lip and palate. *Am J Orthod.* 1955;41(11):827–851.
11. Pruzansky S. The foundations of the cleft palate center and training program at the University of Illinois. *Angle Orthod.* 1957;27:69–82.
12. Pruzansky S, Lis EF. Cephalometric roentgenography of infants: sedation, instrumentation and research. *Am J Orthod.* 1958;44(3):159–186.
13. Pruzansky S, Aduss H. Arch form and the deciduous occlusion in complete unilateral clefts. *Cleft Palate J.* 1964;1:411–418.
14. Pruzansky S, Aduss H, Berkowitz S, Ohyama K. Monitoring growth of the infant with cleft lip and palate. *Trans Eur Orthod Soc.* 1973:538–546.
15. Lis E, Pruzansky S, Koepp-Baker H, Kobes H. S Wilson, eds. Cleft lip and cleft palate: perspectives in Management. *Pediatr Clef North Am.* 1956;3:995–1028.
16. Krogman WM, Mazaheri M, Harding RL. A longitudinal study of craniofacial growth in children with clefts as compared to normal, birth to six years. *Cleft Palate J.* 1979;12–59.
17. Berkowitz S, Kricher J, Pruzansky S. Quantitative analysis of cleft palate casts. *Cleft Palate J.* 1974;11:134–161.
18. Mapes AH, Mazaheri M, Harding RL, Meier JA, Carter HE. A longitudinal analysis of the maxillary growth increments of cleft lip and palate patients (CLP). *Cleft Palate J.* 1974;11:450–462.
19. Ashley-Montague MF. The form and dimensions of the palate in the newborn. *Inst J Orthod.* 1934;20:694–704.
20. Sillman JH. Dimensional changes of the dental arches. Longitudinal study from birth to 25 years. *Am J Orthod.* 1964;50:824–842.
21. Richardson AS. Dental development during the first two years of life. *J Can Dent Assoc.* 1967;33:418–429.
22. Brash JL. The genesis and growth of deformed jaws and palates. *Dent Board UK.* 1924:67.
23. Huddart AG. Maxillary arch dimensions in cleft palate cases. In: Cole RM, ed. *Early Treatment of Cleft Lip and Palate, Proceedings of Second International Symposium.* Chicago, Ill: Northwestern University Cleft Lip and Palate Institute; 1970:46–54.
24. Huddart AG, Huddart AM. An investigation to relate the overall size of the maxillary arch and area of palatal mucosa in cleft lip and palate cases at birth to the overall size of the upper dental arch at 5 years of age. In: Cohen MM Jr, Rollnich BR, eds. Samuel Pruzansky Fetschrift. *J Craniofac Genet Devel Biol.* 1985; 1(Suppl):89–95.
25. Mazaheri M, Harding RL, Cooper JA, Meier JA, Jones, TS. Changes in arch form and dimensions of cleft patients. *Am J Orthod.* 1971;60:19–31.
26. Stockli PW. Application of quantitative method of arch form evaluation in complete unilateral cleft lip and palate. *Cleft Palate J.* 1971;8:322–341.
27. Berkowitz S. Stereophotogrammetric analysis of casts of normal and abnormal palates. *Am J Orthod.* 1971;60:1–17.
28. Berkowitz S, Gonzalez G, Nghiem-phu L. An optical profilometer—a new instrument for the three dimensional measurement of cleft palate casts. *Cleft Palate J.* 1982;19(2):129–138.
29. Ross RB. Treatment variables affecting facial growth in complete unilateral cleft lip and palate. *Cleft Palate J.* 1987;24:5–77.

Index

A

Adolescents, 5, 276
    premaxillary protrusion, 266
    profile changes, 280
Advancement, maxillary. *See* Maxillary advancement
Agenesis, premaxillary. *See* Binder's syndrome
        (premaxillary agenesis)
American Academy of Cleft Palate Prosthesis, 1
American Cleft Palate-Craniofacial Association, 4
    address, 4
    multidisciplinary team management, 1–2
American Cleft Palate Educational Foundation
    Parent-Patient Liaison Committee, 4
Apert syndrome (acrocephalosyndactly Type I) syndrome, 209
Audiologist, 1, 2

B

Binder's syndrome (premaxillary agenesis), 57

C

Casts, serial
    overview, 7–9
Cephaloradiographs
    Basion Horizontal
        Coben superimposition, 8, 156, 163, 171, 235, 243, 250, 254, 316, 332, 349
    bilateral cleft lip and palate (BCLP), 323
    complete bilateral cleft lip and palate (CBCLP)
        Millard-Latham procedure, 160
    complete unilateral cleft lip and palate (CUCLP)
        presurgical orthopedic treatment (PSOT), 156
    convexity, angle of facial, 271
    facial
        angles, overview, 8
        changes, 98–99, 262–264
        growth, 262
        landmarks to Frankfurt horizontal line, overview, 8
        midfacial
            growth retardation, 88
        polygons, 137
    overview, 8
    facial growth, 271
    facial growth findings, long-term, 261–265
    incomplete bilateral cleft lip and palate (IBCLP), 132
    measurement standardization, 7
    midfacial
        protrusion reduction, 149
    Millard-Latham procedure, 132
    neonatal maxillary orthopedics, 10, 126
    overview, 7–9
    Passavant's pad, 210
    pharyngeal space, 207–208
    pharyngeal space, skeletal structures surrounding, 195–196
    presurgical orthopedic treatment (PSOT), 132
    procedures, 7–9
    protrusive midface, 316
    push-back procedures, 89, 90
    roentgenography, 213
    speech, 189–190
    superimposition examples, 9, 10
    unilateral cleft lip and palate (UCLP), 126
Cinefluoroscopy, 190
Clefts. *See also* Congenital palatal insufficiency (CPI);
        Embryopathogy; individual conditions
    alveolus, 219, 221, 257. *See also* lip under Clefts
    bilateral
        secondary alveolar bone graft (SABG), 106
    bilateral cleft lip and palate (BCLP), 16, 89
        cephaloradiographic serial study, 98–99
        columella repair, 339, 352
        convexity, facial, 263
        lip pits, 42
        malocclusion, 321–323
        mandibular development, 19
        neonatal maxillary, 121, 123–125
        neonatal maxillary orthopedics, 138
        palatal expansion appliance, 299
        premaxillary setback, 263, 266
        profile changes, 272
        protraction headgear, 99, 266
        variations, 36

Clefts *(continued)*
  categories, 30–38
  cervical spine, 212, 213–216
  cleft lip and palate (CLP)
    mandibular development, 19
    nasal cavity, 212
    overview, 32, 34
    palatal growth, 361–362
  combined
    classification, 34
  complete bilateral cleft lip and palate (CBCLP), 257–352
    abberant muscle forces, 30
    classification, 34, 36
    closure, two-stage, 260
    dentition, 47–48
    facial growth, 99
      serial changes, 262–265
    geometry, maxillary to mandibular arches, 18
    Kernahan-Rosenstein procedure, 117
    Latham-Millard presurgical orthopedics, 133–134
    Le Fort I maxillary advancement (osteotomy), 175
    lip musculature hypertonic, 271, 272
    metallic implants, surgical, 259
    Millard-Latham procedure, 127, 139–141, 145–146, 157–160
    muscle forces, aberrant, 31
    "nasal septum growth" thesis, 259
    neonatal maxillary orthopedics, 117, 118, 133–134
    occlusion, 272–273
    orthopedic appliances. *See also* Orthopedics, neonatal maxillary
      presurgical, 120–121
      presurgical (Latham), 131
    orthopedic protraction, 172
    palatal growth, postsurgical, 80
    palatoplasty, 73
    premaxillary protrusion, 117, 257, 309–316
      real or apparent?, 257
    premaxillary retrusion, mechanical, 336–337
    premaxillary vomerine suture (PVS), 66, 257–261
    premaxilla size, 258
    presurgical orthopedic treatment (PSOT), 123–125, 374–376
    protraction, maxillary, 165–186
    pterygomaxillary fissure, 262
    serial casts, 372
    stereophotogrammetry, 363–375
    treatment sequence, 290–294
    treatment sequencing, 281–289
    ventroflexion, premaxillary, 55, 309
  complete unilateral cleft lip and palate (CUCLP), 63, 219, 222–223
    abberant muscle forces, 30
    case reports, 226–235, 238–243, 244–250, 251–254
    catch-up growth, 91–93
    cephaloradiographs, 156
    classification, 34
    crossbite, 98
    dentition, 45, 47–48
    facial growth, 99, 226–235, 238–243
    geometry, maxillary to mandibular arches, 18
    growth, surface area, 97
    Kernahan-Rosenstein procedure, 117
    lateral cephaloradiographs, 156
    lip adhesion, 69–70
    malocclusion, 98
    mandibular development, 19
    maxillary protraction, 251–254
    midfacial recessiveness, 251–254
    Millard-Latham procedure, 127, 139–141, 150, 153, 161
    multicenter study, 224
    neonatal maxillary
      orthopedics, 117, 128–130
        appliances, 118
      primary bone grafting, 126
    neonatal maxillary orthopedics, 223
    occlusion, 140–141
    occlusion, postsurgical, 367
    orthopedic appliances
      presurgical, 119
    orthopedic protraction, 168–171
    palatal growth, 233, 238–243
    palatoplasty, 74
    pre-/postsurgical, 54, 57
    presurgical orthopedic treatment (PSOT), 122, 130, 155–156, 266
      none, 59, 226
    protraction, maxillary, 165–186
    secondary alveolar bone graft (SABG), 226, 241
    serial casts, 154–156
    stereophotogrammetry, 363–375
    xerographic studies, 362
  and contiguous skeletal structures, 47
  effect on palatal arch form, 29–39
  feeding appliances, 358
  hemifacial microsomia, 23, 183
  incomplete bilateral cleft lip and palate (IBCLP), 67
    classification, 36
    facial/palatal growth good (study), 277
    Latham appliance, 131–132
    lip adhesion, 71
    midfacial growth good (case report), 324–332
    neonatal maxillary orthopedics, 131–132
    pre-postsurgical, 54
    prolabium, 268
  incomplete cleft lip
    pre-/postsurgical, 54
  incomplete unilateral cleft lip and palate (IUCLP), 34
    classification, 34
  individual differences, 357–358
  lip, 257
    adhesion, 59, 60–62, 67–68, 69–71, 244
    elastic traction, 55–56, 58
    overview, 31–32, 33, 219, 221
    pressure changes, 55
    surgery, 55–56, 67–68

morphogenesis, palatal, 52
muscle force
    aberrant, 30
    reversal, 55–56
nasal cavity, 212
nasopharyngeal growth, 209
and nasopharyngeal skeletal structures, 209
neonatal, 51–57. *See also* Embryopathology
orbicularis oris, 65
palatal. *See also* Palatal
    closure, 79–80
    combined, 34
    cross-bite, 45
    etiology, 361
    growth, 96, 97. *See also* Facial growth
    isolated
        overview, 35–38, 219, 220
        variations, 37
    mandibular development, 19–22
    primary, 34
    secondary, 34, 51, 53, 361
    surgery
        common procedures, 80
        overview, 68–76
skeletal malformation, 358
and skull base malformations, 209
soft palate, 219
submucous cleft palate
    summary, 38
unilateral cleft lip and palate (UCLP), 16, 81
    embryopathology, 53
    facial characteristics, 223, 224
    frequency, 45
    Le Fort I maxillary advancement (osteotomy), 181–182
    multicenter study, 224
    neonatal maxillary, 119–121
        primary bone grafting, 126
    neonatal maxillary orthopedics, 138
    speech, 78
    surgery and facial growth, 55
    variations, overview, 35
uvulae, 219
variations, individual, 357–358
vomer fracture, 55, 131
Clinic coordinator, 2
Complete bilateral cleft lip and palate (CBCLP). *See under* Clefts
Congenital palatal insufficiency (CPI)
    cervical spine anomalies, 213–217
    overview, 38–39
Craniofacial dysostoses. *See* Crouzon's disease (craniofacial dysostoses)
Craniofacial growth. *See* Facial growth
Crossbite. *See* Dentistry
Crouzon's disease (craniofacial dysostoses), 209
    mandibular development, 26
    surgery, 184–185

D

Dentistry, 1, 2. *See also* Orthodontics
    crossbite, 60–62, 82, 94–95, 98, 99, 139–141, 147–149, 158, 165, 168, 175, 226, 241, 246, 253, 272, 276, 277, 278, 320, 321, 325
    elastic traction, 55–56, 58
    incisor space, cleft lateral, 150–156
    occlusion
        buccal, 58
        Class 2, 241
        complete bilateral cleft lip and palate (CBCLP), 272–273
        effects, mechanical presurgical orthopedic forces, 139–142
        surgical timing, 78
        timing, 98
        and vomer flap, 98
    occlusion, postsurgical
        complete unilateral cleft lip and palate (CUCLP), 367
    open bite, 150, 336
    overbite/overjet, 58, 91, 93, 135–136, 155, 180, 266, 276, 278, 292, 312, 321, 325, 333, 344
    overjet, 58, 63, 91, 93
    prosthesis, 56, 236–237
    replacement, missing teeth, 236–237
    "round house" fixed bridge, 82–83, 84
    secondary alveolar bone graft (SABG), 105, 109, 110–112, 230, 241
    tooth eruption, maxillary fistula, 234
    transpalatal strut, 83, 84
Dysmorphologist, 1

E

Elastic traction, 55–56, 58
Embryopathology
    adequacy, parts, 53
    deficiency versus displacement, 53–55
    displacement versus deficiency, 53–55
    embryonal influences, aberrant, 79–80
    etiology
        failure to fuse, 51
        shelf forces decreased, 51
        shelves narrow, 53
        tongue resistance, 51
    fetal influences, aberrant, 79–80
    inadequacy, 53
    mesenchymal deficiency, 51, 53, 235, 243
    Mesodermal Migration theory, 51
    morphogenesis, 52
    overgrowth, 53
    palatal, 51–55
    palatal shelf movement, 53
    primary palate formation, 51, 52
    research, 361
    secondary palate clefts
        etiology, 51, 53

Embryopathology *(continued)*
  teeth, supranumerary, 53
  tongue movement, 53
  unilateral cleft lip and palate (UCLP), 53

F

Facial characteristics
  case reports, 225–254
  multicenter complete unilateral cleft lip and palate (CUCLP) study, 224–225
  neonatal maxillary orthopedics, 223
  Oslo study, 223
  unilateral cleft lip and palate (UCLP), 223, 224
Facial development
  premaxillary protrusion, 272–273, 274
Facial growth, 13–27, 98–99. *See also* Grafting; Mandibular development; Palatal
  anteroposterior, 65
  basion horizontal concept (Coben), 18–19, 88, 250, 254, 316, 332, 349
  bone growth stimulation, 16
  case reports, 238–243
  catch-up growth, 90–98. *See also* Surgery, catch-up growth
  changes
    bad, 264–265
    birth to age 17, 87
    good, 265
    serial study, 262–265
  cleft lip and palate (CLP), 361–362
  collapse prevention need, 16
  complete bilateral cleft lip and palate (CBCLP), 99
  complete unilateral cleft lip and palate (CUCLP), 99, 226–235, 244–250
  contractility, nonmuscular connective tissue cells, 76
  cranial growth and cleft maxilla position, 47–48
  findings, long term (cephalometric), 261–265
  functional matrix theory, 13–15
  genetic control theory, 13
  Matrix, Functional, 65
  maxillary
    advancement, 165–186. *See also* Maxillary advancement
    growth, 65, 68–69
      surgery, 76–79
    maldevelopment overview, 66–67
    speech production trade-off, 78
  maxillofacial development, 78, 118
  mesenchymal deficiency, 51, 53
  mesognathic, 272
  midfacial
    growth good (case report), 324–332
    growth retardation, 88
    protrusion, 257–261, 263
    recessiveness, 251–254
    retrusion, 165, 317–318. *See* Maxillary advancement
    and vomer flap, 266
  mucoperiosteum, palatal, 65
  muscle force
    balance, normal, 29
  muscle force reversal, 55–56
  nasal septum theory (cartilage-directed growth), 15–18
  nasomaxillary complex, 259
  Oslo study, 223
  palatal fusion graphic summary, 38
  palatal growth, 17–18
  poor (case report), 317–318
  postnatal craniofacial growth systems, 17
  premaxillary vomerine suture (PVS), 31, 65–66
  profile changes, 272–273, 280, 289, 305–306, 349
  pterygomaxillary fissure, 262
  pterygomaxillary suture, 65–66
  research, 361–362
  studies, longitudinal, 77, 98
  studies, serial, 76–77, 78, 90
  surgical influence, 65–66, 78
    timing, 78
  and surgical repair type, 224
  unilateral cleft lip and palate (UCLP), 55
  vertical, 65
Family. *See also* Support groups
  -centered approach, 2, 3
  choices, 2–3
  informed consent, 11–12
  and team responsibilities, 4–5
Feeding appliances, 358

G

Geneticist, 1, 2
Genetics, 37–38
  genetic control theory, 13
  lip pits, 41
Grafting. *See also* Surgery
  alloplastic materials, 112–113
  autogenous bone, 113
  bilateral, 112
  hydroxylapatite, 112–113
  Le Fort I maxillary advancement (osteotomy), 179
  and neonatal maxillary, 116–119
  primary, 103
  secondary alveolar bone graft (SABG), 103–113, 169, 226, 230, 234, 241, 244, 279, 286, 290, 308, 325, 327, 341
    adolescents, 276
    advantages, 103–104
    autograft versus allogenic graft or allioimplant, 104–105
    bilateral clefts, 106
    calvarial bone, 105–106
    cranial secondary alveolar bone graft (CSABG), 106–107, 109, 110–112
    dentistry, 105, 107
    kinds, 104
    long-term effects, 106–112
    sequencing, 275
    sources, fill material, 104–105
Growth, facial. *See* Facial growth

H

Hydroxylapatite, 112–113
Hygiene, 45–47
Hypoplasia
    maxillary, 358
    palatal, 60–62

L

Lip pits, 41–42
Lip surgery. *See* under Surgery

M

Management. *See also* Team management, multidisciplinary
    "Parameters for Evaluation and Treatment of Patients with Cleft Lip/Palate or Other Craniofacial Anomalies," 4
Mandibular development. *See also* Facial growth
    cleft palate, 19–22
    Crouzon's disease (craniofacial dysostoses), 26
    mandibulofacial dysostosis, 19–20, 26
    Pierre Robin sequence, 19, 20–22, 25
    postnatal growth patterns, 19–20
Maxillary advancement
    articulatory bones, maxilla, 166
    Crouzon's disease (craniofacial dysostoses), 184–185
    Le Fort I maxillary advancement (osteotomy), 172–180
        complete bilateral cleft lip and palate (CBCLP), 175–177
        and grafting, 179
        occlusal changes after, 176
        procedures illustrated, 173–174
        Schuchardt procedure, 179
        timing, 172, 178
        unilateral cleft lip and palate (UCLP), 180, 181–182
    orthopedic protraction
        arch retainer, palatal, 168
        case report, 251–254
        complete bilateral cleft lip and palate (CBCLP), 172
        complete unilateral cleft lip and palate (CUCLP), 168–171
        Delaire-style protraction facial mask, 165, 167, 172, 251–254
        force of, 165, 172
        labile-lingual appliances, 172
        quad helix expander, 168
        timing, 172, 178
    premaxillary advancement, 341–343
    protraction. *See* Maxillary advancement, orthopedic protraction
    relapse, postsurgical, 180
        causes, 180
        elastic tension, 180
        miniplates versus wire fixation, 180
    speech, 186
Micrognathia, mandibular
    isolated cleft palate, 37

Millard-Latham procedure. *See also* Surgery, orthopedics
    alveoloperiosteoplasty, 138–139
    alveolosteoplasty, 158
    benefits, 142
    bilateral cleft lip and palate (BCLP), 138
    cephaloradiographs, 132, 137
    complete bilateral cleft lip and palate (CBCLP), 131, 133–134, 139–141, 145–146, 157–160
    complete unilateral cleft lip and palate (CUCLP), 128–130, 131, 139–141, 150, 153, 161
    dental occlusion, 139–144
    disadvantages, 139, 161
    gingivoperiosteoplasty, 130
    incomplete bilateral cleft lip and palate (IBCLP), 131–132
    Latham orthopedic force system, 127
    length, orthopedic treatment, 139
    manipulation, segment, 127
    mucoperiosteal flap, 138
    premaxillary vomerine suture (PVS), 139, 161
    Principilization of Plastic Surgery, 127, 129, 138
    rationale, 138
    serial casts, 135–136, 159
    timing, 138
    unilateral cleft lip and palate (UCLP), 138
    von Langenbeck procedure, 127, 138
        modified, 158
Morphogenesis, palatal, 52
Multicenter complete unilateral cleft lip and palate (CUCLP) study, 224

N

Nasometer, 192–193
Nasopharyngeal port
    augmentation, posterior pharyngeal wall, 216
    cervical spine anomalies, 212, 213–216
    faucial arch, posterior, 208
    flaps, pharyngeal, 207–212
    growth, 208–209
        and clefts, 209
    muscle overview, 195–196
    nasal cavity, 212–213
    oropharynx, 208
    palatopharyngeal fold, 208
    pharynx, 195–196, 207–208
    skeletal architecture influence, 214–217
    speech, 209–212
        Passavant's pad, 210
    speech aid appliances, 212, 213, 214
    sphincteric pharyngoplasty of orticochea, 215–216
    swallowing, 209, 212
    velopharyngeal closure, 210–212
    velopharyngeal closure improvement, 207–216
    velum, 207–208
        elevation, 323
        speech, 211
        velar lengthening (push-back procedures), 212–215
        velar split, 210–211

Nasopharyngoscopy, video, 191–192
Neonatal maxillary orthopedics. *See under* Orthopedics
Neurologist, 2

O

Orthodontics, 76, 79, 82, 85, 231, 238, 292, 312, 325–326, 341, 346, 350. *See also* Dentistry
    adolescents, 276
    adult, 228
    arch retention, permanent, 252, 276
    assessment, 7
    dentition, permanent, 270, 271, 272, 274
    expansion appliances, 272
    fixed appliances, 272
    informed consent, 12
    maxillary retainer, 246
    neonatal maxillary
        complete bilateral cleft lip and palate (CBCLP), 145–146
        complete unilateral cleft lip and palate (CUCLP), 153
    open bite, 150
    orthognathic-orthodontic procedure, 333–335
    orthopedic plates, 79
    palatal expansion appliances, 299
    palatal retainer, fixed, 227
    premaxillary overjet/overbite correction (adult), 351
    premaxillary protrusion, 271, 272
    premaxillary setback, 336
    presurgical, 108, 261. *See also* Orthopedics, neonatal maxillary
    prosthesis, 56, 236–237
    protraction, 336
    protraction headgear, 99, 261, 266
    secondary alveolar bone graft (SABG), 105, 107, 110, 275
    timing, 275
    transpalatal removable metal strut, 83
    treatment
        success, 339–340
    treatment, length, 139
    treatment sequence, 273–353
Orthodontist, 2, 7, 78, 179
Orthopedics
    acrylic appliance, 117
    appliances, presurgical
        complete bilateral cleft lip and palate (CBCLP), 119–120
    dentofacial, early, 272
    extraoral facial strap, elastic, 117
    maxillary protraction, 165–186, 319, 358–359. *See* Maxillary advancement
        case report, 251–254
    neonatal maxillary, 59, 115–116, 122, 123–125, 130, 155–156, 157–160, 266, 359. *See also* Surgery, orthopedics
        active/passive appliances, 118
        alveoloperiosteoplasty, 138–139
        alveolar cleft space closure, 116–119
            Kernahan–Rosenstein procedure, 117
            results, long-term, 117–119
        alveoloperiosteoplasty, 138–139
            fixed mechanical palatal manipulation, 127–139
        alveolosteoplasty, 158
        complete bilateral cleft lip and palate (CBCLP), 117, 118, 121, 122–125, 157–160
            Latham-Millard procedure, 133–134
        complete unilateral cleft lip and palate (CUCLP), 117, 118, 119–121, 120, 122, 126, 223
            serial casts, 154–156
        compression procedure (steel-clamp-silver wire), 127, 138
        dental occlusion, 139–144
        facial characteristics, 223
        fixed mechanical palatal manipulation to alveoloperiosteoplasty, 127–139
        force system, Latham, 127
        gingivoperiosteoplasty, 130, 138
        infections, 358
        Latham appliance, 126–137, 145–146, 281–286
        Latham-Millard premaxillary retraction appliance, 131–132
        manipulation, segment, 127
        Millard-Latham procedure, 127–129, 131–133. *See also* main heading Latham-Millard procedure; main heading Millard-Latham procedure
        Netherlands approach, 119, 121
        "NORM" theory, 127
        obturators, 358
        Oslo study, facial characteristics, 223
        periosteoplasty, 126–127, 138
        pinned orthopedic appliance, presurgical (Latham), 128–130
        premaxillary protrusion, 272
        presurgical, 120–121
        presurgical palatal manipulation, 115–116
        primary bone grafting, 116–119
            critique, 118–119
            effect, long-term, 126
            Kernahan-Rosenstein procedure, 117
            results, long-term, 117–119
        Rosenstein appliance illustration, 116
        soft plus hard acrylic appliance, 119
        strappings, external elastic, 118
        unilateral cleft lip and palate (UCLP), 126
        utility, long-term, 126
        vomer fracture, 131–132
        von Langenbeck procedure, 127, 138
        wire wings, adjustable, 118
        Zurich concept, 119
obturators, 310, 358
and palatal growth, 98
periosteoplasty, 263
premaxillary chain retractor with maxillary expander (Latham), 131
presurgical, 79–80, 98–99, 104, 357–358. *See also* Orthopedics, neonatal maxillary

Orthopedics *(continued)*
  research, 360–361, 374–376
  presurgical orthopedic treatment (PSOT). *See* Orthopedics, neonatal maxillary
  secondary alveolar bone graft (SABG), 110, 226
Overbite. *See* Dentistry, overbite/overjet
Overjet. *See* Dentistry, overbite/overjet

P

Palatal. *See also* Clefts, palatal
  adequacy, 53
  arch form variations, 56
  distortion, 53
  distortion versus inadequacy, 53–55
  embryopathology, 51–55
  expansion appliances, 299
  growth, 96–97
    cleft lip and palate (CLP), 361–362
    complete unilateral cleft lip and palate (CUCLP), 233, 238–243, 244–250
    research, 361–362
    time sequence analysis, 366
    where occurs, 330
  hypoplasia, 60–62, 257
  inadequacy versus distortion, 53–55
  lengthening, 78, 89, 212–215
  manipulation, presurgical, 115–116. *See also* Orthopedics, neonatal maxillary
  mucoperiosteum, 65
  osteogenic deficiency, 272
  palatal lift appliance (PLA), 212, 215, 249
  surgery
    and deformation, 213
    overview, 68–76. *See also* Surgery
    types (primary), 72
Parent-Patient Liaison Committee, American Cleft Palate Educational Foundation, 4
Pediatrician, 1, 2, 358
  feeding appliances, 358
Pierre Robin sequence, 80
  glossoptosis, 21–22
  mandible recovery, 337
  mandibular development, 19, 20–22, 25
  obturators, 358
  tracheostomy, 21–22
Plastic surgeon, 1, 2, 7, 74, 80
Premaxillary agenesis. *See* Binder's syndrome (premaxillary agenesis)
Premaxillary protrusion, 117, 266
  convexity, angle of facial, 271
  head bonnet/elastic strap, presurgical, 266, 267, 269, 272, 275
  lip surgery, 266–269, 271, 272
  management, 266–272
  "nasal septum growth" thesis, 259
  neonatal maxillary orthopedics, 272
  premaxillary
    setback, 263, 266, 335–336
    vomerine suture (PVS), 257, 259

profile changes, 272–273, 280
prolabium procedure, 269, 270
real or apparent?, 257
retraction (mechanical), premaxillary, 259, 336–337
severe from birth, 300–306, 309–316
Premaxillary vomerine suture (PVS)
  complete bilateral cleft lip and palate (CBCLP), 66, 257–261
  facial growth, 31, 65–66
  growth testing, 261
  and lip repair, 272
  metallic implants, surgical, 259
  premaxillary retrusion, mechanical, 336–337
  premaxillary setback, 336
  profile changes, 272
  surgery, 65–66, 139
Presurgical orthopedic treatment (PSOT). *See* Orthopedics, neonatal maxillary
Prosthesis, dental, 56, 236–237

R

Referral, 1
Research
  cephaloradiographs, dentition, 7–9
  clinical trials, overview, 11–12
  early studies, 9
  embryopathology, 361
  facial growth, 76–77, 78, 90, 98
  informed consent, 11–12
  longitudinal, 7–12
  measurement standardization, 7
  measuring techniques, 362–363
  methods, 10–11
  morphologic growth changes, 7
  palatal growth, 361–362
  presurgical orthopedics, 360–361
  presurgical state, 360
  prospective studies, overview, 11
  randomized clinical trial (RCT) method, overview, 11
  retrospective studies, overview, 10–11
  roentgencephalometry, 12
  serial casts, dentition, 7–9
  stereophotogrammetry, 363–375
    need for, 362–363
  surgery, 363
  three-dimensional measuring techniques
    need for, 362–363
  three-dimensional technique studies, 363–375
Robin sequence. *See* Pierre Robin sequence
Roentgencephalometry, 12

S

Secondary alveolar bone graft (SABG). *See* under Grafting
  secondary alveolar bone graft (SABG). *See* under Surgery
Social Security act of 1935, Crippled Children's Programs (Part 2, Title V), 1

Social worker, 1, 2
Speech. *See also* Nasopharyngeal port
　aeromechanical measurement, 193
　appliances, 213, 214
　articulation
　　anterior, 212
　　errors, 211
　　skills, 78
　　tests, 189
　assessment, 189–193
　auditory training, 212
　cephaloradiographs, 189–190
　cinefluoroscopy, 190
　consonants, denasalized nasal, 211
　hypernasality, 211, 212
　intelligibility
　　scales, 189
　levator reconstruction, 78
　maxillary advancement, 186
　midface growth integrity, 78
　nasometer, 192–193
　nasopharyngeal port, 209–212
　　Passavant's pad, 210
　the oral-nasal acoustic ration (TONAR), 193
　palatal
　　efficiency rating computer instantaneously (PERCI), 193
　　lengthening, 78. *See also* Surgery, push-back
　lift appliance (PLA), 212, 215
　poor, 77
　production, 53, 74, 77–78, 99
　　maxillary growth trade-off, 78
　push-back procedure, 78
　　island flap, 78
　studies, 78–79
　surgery, 358
　　timing, 78
　therapy, 38
　treatment, 189–193
　ultrasound, 191
　unilateral cleft lip and palate (UCLP), 78
　unintelligible, 127
　velar muscles hypoplastic, 186
　velopharyngeal. *See also* Velopharyngeal
　　closure, 210–212
　　competency, 53, 78
　　incompetency, 214
　velum, 211
　videofluoroscopy, 190–191
　video nasopharyngoscopy, 191–192
　von Langenbeck procedure, 78
　　levator reconstruction (intravelor veloplasty), 78
　　mucoperiosteal flaps, pipedal advanced to midline, 78
　Warren and Dubois technique, 193
Speech-language pathologist, 1, 2, 74, 78–79, 190, 211, 212, 214
　isolatated cleft palate, 35
　submucous cleft palate, 38
Spine, cervical. *See* Cervical spine

Stereophotogrammetry, 363–375
Support groups, 3–4
　newsletter, national, 4
　Parent-Patient Liaison Committee, American Cleft Palate Educational Foundation, 4
Surgeon, neurosurgeon, 2
Surgeon, oral, 1
Surgeon, oral/maxillo-facial, 2
Surgeon, plastic, 1, 2, 74
　training, 7
Surgery. *See also* Facial growth; Grafting
　adolescents, 276
　alveoloperiosteoplasty, 138–139
　alveolosteoplasty, 158
　and apnea, sleep, 211
　assessment, 7
　asymmetry, facial, 183
　augmentation, posterior pharyngeal wall, 216
　bilateral cleft lip and palate (BCLP), 89
　　cephaloradiographic serial study, 98–99
　bonnet use (head), 266, 267, 269, 272, 275, 290–291, 324, 358
　catch-up growth, 90–98
　　defined, 90
　and catch-up growth, 359
　closure
　　maxillary fistula, 231
　　nasal mucosa, 72
　　oral mucosa, 72
　　oronasal fistula, 236–237
　　palate (summary), 79–80
　　pharyngeal flaps, 207–212, 261, 332
　　two-stage, 260
　collapse prevention priority, 99
　columella repair, 339, 352
　common approaches, 80
　complete bilateral cleft lip and palate (CBCLP), 55, 66, 73, 80
　　closure
　　　two-stage, 260
　　facial growth, 99
　　forked flap, primary (Millard), 273, 274, 275, 291
　　mucoperiosteal flaps, 131
　complete unilateral cleft lip and palate (CUCLP), 54, 57, 59, 63, 74, 85
　　catch-up growth, 91–93
　　crossbite, 98
　　facial growth, 99
　　malocclusion, 98
　　mucoperiosteal flaps, 131
　compression (wiring), 76
　contractility, nonmuscular connective tissue cells, 76
　Crouzon's disease (craniofacial dysostoses), 184–185
　delay (by age), 76–77
　embryonal influences, aberrant, 79–80
　embryopathology, 53–55
　　adequacy, parts, 53
　　distortion, palatal parts, 53, 54

and facial growth, 65–66, 224
fetal influences, aberrant, 79–80
flap
    Abbe (lip-switch), 352–353
    banked fork (Millard), 268
    forked, primary (Millard), 273, 274, 275, 291, 324
Furlow procedure, 79
gingivoperiosteoplasty, 130, 131, 138
grafting
    secondary alveolar bone graft (SABG), 244
hard palate delayed, 77
head bonnet use, 266, 267, 269, 272, 290–291, 324, 358
hemifacial microsomia, 183
history, 68, 72–76
incomplete bilateral cleft lip and palate (IBCLP), 67
    forked flap, primary (Millard), 324
    pre-/postsurgical, 54
island flap, 89
island flap procedure, 81
    Millard's, 80. *See also* under Surgery, push-back
Kirschner wire, 335, 340
Le Fort I maxillary advancement (osteotomy), 82, 84, 172–180, 300, 303, 336. *See also* under Maxillary advancement
    and grafting, 179
    occlusal changes after, 176
    procedures illustrated, 173–174
    Schuchardt procedure, 179
Le Fort I posterior-impaction, 317
Le Mesurier procedure. *See* Millard under Surgery
lip, 55–56, 56, 63, 99, 132, 150, 358
    adhesion, 59, 60–62, 67–68, 68, 69–71, 130, 158, 244, 263, 266, 268, 309
    complete unilateral cleft lip and palate (CUCLP), 266–269
    incomplete cleft, 54
    neonatal maxillary orthopedics, 272
    overview, 67–68
    premaxillary protrusion, 271, 272
    premaxillary retrusion, mechanical, 336–337
    and secondary alveolar grafting, 104
lip-switch (Abbe flap), 352–353
and Logan's bow, 225
maxillary growth, 65, 68–69, 76–79, 80
maxillary hypoplasia, 358
maxillary maldevelopment overview, 66–67
metallic implants, 259
Millard-Latham procedure, 127–139. *See also* main heading Millard-Latham procedure
Millard procedure, 223
Millard rotation, 91, 121, 226, 238
morphological variant importance, 77
mucoperiosteal flap, 78, 79, 138
mucoperiosteum, palatal, 65
muscle force reversal, 55–56
neonatal maxillary
    alveoloperiosteoplasty, 127
nonphysiological, 78
nontraumatic, 80

orbicularis oris, 65
orthodontics, 79–90. *See also* Orthodontics
    presurgical, 108, 261
orthognathic-orthodontic, 333–335
orthopedic plates, 79
orthopedics
    presurgical, 79–80, 98–99, 104, 357–358. *See also* Millard-Latham procedure; Orthopedics, neonatal maxillary
osteogenic deficiencies, 358
osteotomy. *See* Le Fort I maxillary advancement (osteotomy)
and outcome, 363
palatal, 358
    deformation, 213
    growth inhibiting, 272
    history, 68, 74, 76
    overview, 68–76
palatal deformation, 358
palatal growth, 80, 363
palatoplasty, 72–73, 74, 211, 213, 223, 263
periosteoplasty, 126–127, 135–136, 138, 263
physiological variant importance, 77
postponing correction (by age), 76–77
postsurgical occlusion, 367
premaxilla repositioning (adult), 350
premaxillary excision (complete removal), 336, 338–339
premaxillary protrusion, 259, 266
premaxillary setback, 263, 266, 335–336, 345
    premaxillary advancement, 341–343
premaxillary vomerine suture (PVS), 65–66, 139, 161
presurgical. *See also* Orthopedics, neonatal maxillary
    orthopedics, 360–361, 374–376
    presurgical orthopedic treatment (PSOT), 266. *See* Orthopedics, neonatal maxillary
prolabium, 268
    Millard, 269, 270
pterygomaxillary suture, 65–66
push-back, 78, 81, 89, 90, 270
    after Braithwaite, 75
    island flap, 78, 82, 85–86, 89. *See also* Surgery, island flap
    and palatoplasty, 213, 263
    retroposition, 74
push-back procedures, 74, 75, 212–215
randomization of surgical procedures, 11–12
research, 363
    presurgical orthopedics, 360–361
    presurgical state, 360
rotation advancement, 244
scarring, 65, 68, 78, 80, 83, 89, 90, 98, 215, 252, 329, 358
    with island flap procedure, 85–86
Schuchardt procedure, 179
secondary alveolar bone graft (SABG), 251, 275, 276, 279, 286, 308, 325, 327, 341
skeletal, 183
skeletal malformation, 358
speech, 358
sphincteric pharyngoplasty of orticochea, 215–216

Surgery *(continued)*
  staged surgical treatment, 68–69
  staphylorrhapy, 79
  surgical-orthopedic combined procedure. *See* Millard-Latham procedure
  Teflon implantation, 216
  timing, 74, 76–77, 79, 80, 98, 126, 224, 275
    catch-up growth, 90–98. *See also* Surgery, catch-up growth
    isolated cleft palate, 219, 220
    lip adhesion, 268
    maxillofacial development, 78
    Millard-Latham procedure, 138
    speech, 78, 211
  treatment sequence, 273–353
  unilateral cleft lip and palate (UCLP), 55, 81
    speech, 78
  Veau-Wardill-Kilner procedure, 74, 79, 213. *See also* Surgery, push-back
  ventroflexion, premaxillary, 268, 272, 309, 344–345
  vomer flap, 263
    complete unilateral cleft lip and palate (CUCLP), 98
    early, 98
    evaluation, 265–266
    and occlusion, 98
    two layer, palato-, 98
  vomer flaps, 79
  vomer fracture, 55, 131
  vomer resection
    premaxillary setback, 335–336
  von Langenbeck
    modified, 244
  von Langenbeck procedure, surgery, 78, 79, 80, 127, 138, 223, 278–279, 290
    levator reconstruction (intravelor veloplasty), 78
    modified, 158, 241, 324, 341
    mucoperiosteal flaps, pipedal advanced to midline, 78
    serial study, 98–99
    simple closure, 73, 74
  V-Y procedure. *See* Surgery, push-back
  Wardill-Kilner procedure. *See* Veau-Wardill-Kilner procedure under Surgery
Swallowing
  and nasopharyngeal port, 209, 212

T

Team management, multidisciplinary, 1–2. *See also* individual disciplines
  composition, 2–3
  coordinator, 2–3
  history, 1
  responsibilities, 4–5
Teeth, supranumerary, 53
Traction, elastic, 55–56, 58
Treacher Collins syndrome (mandibulofacial dysostosis), 24
Treatment. *See also* Orthodontics; Speech; Surgery
  sequence, 273–353
    adolescence, 276
    in deciduous dentition, 273
    in mixed dentition, 275
    summary, concepts, 357–359

U

Ultrasound, 191
Unilateral cleft lip and palate (UCLP). *See* under clefts
Uvulae clefts, 219

V

Velopharyngeal. *See also* Speech
  closure, 89, 207–216, 213, 214, 298, 358
    pharyngeal flaps, 207–212
    speech aid appliances, 212, 213, 214
  competency, 53, 78, 180, 356
  function. *See* Velopharyngeal, competency
  incompetence, 213
  incompetency, 214
  insufficiency, 223
  nomenclature standardization, 213
  taxonomy, 213
  valving, 213
Velum. *See* under Nasopharyngeal port; Speech
Videofluoroscopy, 190
  multi-view, 190–191
Video nasopharyngoscopy, 191–192
von Langenbeck. *See* under Surgery
V-Y procedure. *See* under Surgery

DATE DUE

DEMCO 38-297